# Teaching Students with Special Needs in Inclusive Settings

## THIRD EDITION

**TOM E. C. SMITH**
University of Arkansas at Little Rock

**EDWARD A. POLLOWAY**
Lynchburg College

**JAMES R. PATTON**
University of Texas

**CAROL A. DOWDY**
University of Alabama at Birmingham

**ALLYN AND BACON**
Boston   London   Toronto   Sydney   Tokyo   Singapore

SENIOR EDITOR: Virginia Lanigan
DEVELOPMENTAL EDITOR: Linda Bieze
PRODUCTION ADMINISTRATOR: Deborah Brown
EDITORIAL ASSISTANT: Jennifer Connors
PHOTO RESEARCHER: Sarah Evertson, Image Quest
COMPOSITION BUYER: Linda Cox
MANUFACTURING BUYER: Megan Cochran
MARKETING MANAGER: Brad Parkins
EDITORIAL-PRODUCTION SERVICE: P. M. Gordon Associates/Nancy Lombardi
TEXT DESIGNER AND COMPOSITOR: Karen Mason
COVER ADMINISTRATOR: Linda Knowles

Copyright © 2001, 1998, 1995 by Allyn & Bacon
A Pearson Education Company
160 Gould Street
Needham Heights, MA 02494

Internet: www.abacon.com

**Library of Congress Cataloging-in-Publication Data**

Teaching students with special needs in inclusive settings / Tom E.C. Smith ... [et al.].--
3rd ed.
    p. cm.
    Includes bibliographical references and index.
    ISBN 0-205-32147-X
    1. Inclusive education—United States.   2. Special education—United States.   3.
Handicapped children—Education—United States.   4. Classroom management—United
States.   I. Smith, Tom E. C.

LC1201.T43 2001
371.9'046—dc21

                                                        00-033156

Printed in the United States of America

10 9 8 7 6 5 4 3   VHP 04 03 02

*For*

*Debi, Jake, Alex, Suni*
*Carolyn and Lyndsay*
*Joy and Kimi*
*Jim, Cameron, and Meredith*

# Brief Contents

# Contents

# ◩ Special Features

# Preface

A great deal has happened in the special education world since the publication of the second edition of *Teaching Students with Special Needs in Inclusive Settings.* Of primary importance was the final passage of the 1997 reauthorization of the Individuals with Disabilities Education Act (IDEA) and the issuance of regulations for this new legislation. While much of IDEA has remained the same since the original law was passed as Public Law 94-142 in 1975, there are some significant modifications to the law, which are discussed in detail in Chapter 1.

As we noted in both the first and second editions of this book, our position on inclusion remains to focus on the child, not on the physical location. Rather than allowing a philosophy or specific service model to dictate services, we strongly encourage educators to develop programs for students with disabilities based on individual student needs, not the needs of a particular program model. In other words, while we strongly support serving students with disabilities with their nondisabled peers as much as possible, we are definitely not opposed to pulling them out of these classrooms in order to provide them with services that may be unavailable in general classroom settings. And, as students with disabilities get older, it is highly likely that their curricular needs will change, depending on the nature of their disabilities, and may be very different from the curricular needs for nondisabled students. In these cases, schools must provide an appropriate alternative curriculum in order to meet the needs of individual students. *Appropriateness* remains a word that has strong implications in special education. Indeed, *appropriateness* must drive educational efforts for students with disabilities over any other consideration.

## HIGHLIGHTS OF NEW AND UPDATED MATERIAL IN THE THIRD EDITION

▲ We have **updated all discussions of IDEA 1997** to reflect the reauthorizations and implementation guidelines of 1999, giving teachers the latest information about these important requirements.

▲ We have **enhanced discussions of collaboration** throughout the text and especially in Chapter 2, Designing Inclusive Classrooms: Effective Instruction and Collaboration, to guide classroom teachers in capitalizing on this positive instructional orientation.

▲ Special attention is given to **changes in the IEP process and statewide assessment issues.**

▲ We have defined **vocabulary terms** in marginal glosses to help readers grasp new concepts easily.

## GENERAL ORGANIZATION AND CONTENT OF THE THIRD EDITION

The third edition continues to offer extensive **practical suggestions** for classroom teachers, including attention to **cultural and linguistic diversity, fostering social acceptance,** and **consultation and collaboration.**

**Chapters 1** and **2** present **a sound rationale for inclusion** so that general education teachers not only learn how to meet student needs but also understand why they are asked to do so. **Chapter 3 focuses on the IEP process,** including referral, assessment, and development of individual programs for students.

Chapters 4–11 each focus on specific categories of disabilities and exceptionalities to help teachers identify students with special needs who are included in their general education classrooms. These same chapters also include practical strategies, adaptations, and interventions for teaching these students.

Chapters on **students with ADD/ADHD (Chapter 5) and students at risk for school failure (Chapter 12)** address needs beyond the clinical categories of special education.

**Chapters 14** and **15** provide strong coverage of **both elementary** and **secondary curriculum and instruction,** including **preschool** and **transition from high school,** to help teachers at all levels create inclusive classrooms.

## SPECIAL FEATURES AND PEDAGOGY IN THE THIRD EDITION

High-interest special features are integrated into each chapter to give specific, practical ideas that teachers can use:

- ◢ **Inclusion Strategies** provide practical ideas for implementing inclusion in the classroom.
- ◢ The new **Rights and Responsibilities** feature examines legal cases and issues to illustrate the many laws that affect students with disabilities and their teachers.
- ◢ **Technology Today** boxes feature practical information about the ever-changing technology available to the teachers and students in today's inclusive classrooms.
- ◢ **Diversity Forum** boxes provide in-depth information about how a teacher in an inclusive classroom can meet the needs of culturally diverse students.
- ◢ **Personal Spotlight** features in each chapter highlight teachers, parents of children with special needs, and individuals with special needs, bringing reality to text discussions and providing insight into the views of people most affected by the challenges of inclusion.
- ◢ **Margin Notes** throughout the book are organized around three themes: (1) **Teaching Tip** provides brief, specific suggestions related to corresponding content; (2) **Cross-Reference** provides additional information found in other chapters in the text; and (3) **Consider This** presents issues that call for problem-solving or creative thinking related to a difficult topic.

## SUPPLEMENTS FOR INSTRUCTORS AND STUDENTS

- ◢ **Instructor's Resource Manual with Test Bank and Masters**—Provides a chapter overview, teaching outline, focus questions, activities, teaching strategies, and discussion questions for each chapter, plus convenient transparency/handout masters. Contains more than 1,000 test items—true/false, multiple choice, and essay—which are also available as a Computerized Test Bank on disk for both PC and Macintosh.
- ◢ **Professionals in Action Videotape: Teaching Students with Special Needs**— Newly available, this *Professionals in Action* video is approximately two hours in length and consists of five 15–30 minute modules presenting viewpoints and approaches to teaching students with various disabilities, in general education classrooms, separate education settings, and various combinations of the two. Each module explores its topic via actual classroom footage, and interviews with general and special education teachers, parents, and students themselves. The five modules are:
  1. Working Together: The Individualized Education Program (IEP)
  2. Working Together: The Collaborative Process

3. Instruction and Behavior Management
4. Technology for Inclusion
5. Working with Parents and Families

◢ **The "Snapshots" Video Series for Special Education**—*Snapshots: Inclusion Video* (© 1995, 22 minutes in length) profiles three students of differing age levels and with various levels of disability in inclusive class settings. *Snapshots 2: Video for Special Education (categorical organization)* (© 1995, 20–25 minutes in length) is a set of six videotaped segments designed specifically for use in your college classroom. Each segment profiles three individuals, their families, teachers, and experiences. You'll find these programs to be of high interest to your students; instructors who have used the tapes in their courses have found that they help in disabusing students of stereotypical viewpoints, and put a "human face" on course material. The topics explored are:
1. traumatic brain injury
2. behavior disorders
3. learning disabilities
4. mental retardation
5. hearing impairment
6. visual impairment

◢ **The Allyn & Bacon Special Education Transparency Package**—The Transparency Package has been revised and expanded to include approximately 100 acetates, more than half of which are full color.

◢ **Allyn & Bacon's Digital Media Archive for Special Education**—Allyn and Bacon provides an array of media products to enliven your classroom presentations. The Digital Media Archive electronically provides charts, graphs, tables, and figures on one cross-platform CD-ROM. The Digital Media Archive goes one step further by including weblinks and video and audio clips, as well as electronic images.

◢ **Companion Website with Online Practice Tests**—The Companion Website for *Teaching Students with Special Needs in Inclusive Settings,* Third Edition [www.abacon.com/SPPD] features chapter outlines, activities, weblinks, and practice tests for students, plus numerous teaching resources for the instructor, including downloadable PowerPoint presentations to enhance your classroom lectures.

## ACKNOWLEDGMENTS

It seems that each new edition of a textbook requires at least as much work as previous editions. As a result, we would like to thank many individuals who provided support to us during our efforts with this third edition. First and foremost, we must mention the support provided by those significant individuals in our life, especially Debi, Carolyn, Joy, and Jim. Of equal importance are the children in our lives who seem to be the center of most of our everyday activities and who motivate us to try to make a difference in educational services for other children. Specifically, this includes Jake, Suni, Alex, Lyndsay, Kimi, Cameron, and Meredith.

As always, we would never have accomplished this task without the wonderful people at Allyn and Bacon. While Ray Short, our editor for the first two editions retired, we still want to thank him for his original and continued support, as well as people who have picked up his mantle and provided new support for this edition, namely Virginia Lanigan our editor, Linda Bieze our developmental editor, Deborah Brown, our production editor, and Jennifer Connors, editorial assistant. We would also like to acknowledge the very positive support received from Nancy Lombardi at

P.M. Gordon Associates, who copyedited the manuscript and worked with us during the production phase, and to Karen Mason, the designer and typesetter.

Finally, we want to thank individuals who reviewed the book and provided very useful feedback on the second edition. These included Ellen Brantlinger, Indiana University; Linda E. Denault, Worcester State College; Lou Gurecka, Clarion University; Sher L. Hamilton, Butler University; Jennifer Kilgo, University of Alabama at Birmingham; Merilee A. Rosberg, Mount Mercy College; Kathlene Shank, Eastern Illinois University; and Ruth Nash Thompson, Edinboro University of Pennsylvania.

Tom E. C. Smith
Edward A. Polloway
James R. Patton
Carol A. Dowdy

## ABOUT THE AUTHORS

**TOM E. C. SMITH** is Professor of Teacher Education at the University of Arkansas at Little Rock. He received his Ed.D. from Texas Tech University and has taught at the University of Arkansas, Fayetteville campus and the University of Alabama at Birmingham. He is the author of 18 textbooks and has published more than 50 articles in professional journals. He currently serves as the Executive Director of the Division on Mental Retardation and Developmental Disabilities of the Council for Exceptional Children and was appointed by President Clinton in 1994 to the President's Committee on Mental Retardation.

**EDWARD A. POLLOWAY** is Professor of Special Education at Lynchburg College in Virginia where he has taught since 1976. He also serves as Vice President for College and Community Administration. He received his Ed.D. from the University of Virginia. He has served on national boards of the Council for Exceptional Children and the Council for Learning Disabilities. Most recently, he was on the committee that revised the definition of mental retardation for the American Association on Mental Retardation. The author of 10 books and more than 80 articles in special education, his primary interests are in the areas of learning disabilities and mental retardation.

**JAMES R. PATTON** is the Executive Editor at Pro-Ed in Austin, Texas, and an Adjunct Associate Professor at the University of Texas at Austin. He received his Ed.D. from the University of Virginia. He has authored numerous textbooks, book chapters, and journal articles; his professional interests include life skills instruction, lifelong learning, science education, and transition. He has served on national boards of the Council for Exceptional Children, Council for Learning Disabilities, and the National Joint Committee on Learning Disabilities.

**CAROL A. DOWDY** is Professor of Special Education at the University of Alabama at Birmingham where she has taught since receiving her Ed.D. degree from the University of Alabama, Tuscaloosa. She has written seven books in special education and published more than 30 articles on learning disabilities. She has served on the national board of the Council for Learning Disabilities and the Professional Advisory Board for the Learning Disabilities Association of America, and has worked closely with the federal department of Vocational Rehabilitation to assist in their efforts to better serve adults with learning disabilities.

# Inclusive Education: An Introduction

*After reading this chapter, you should be able to:*

◢ Describe the evolution of services for students with special needs

◢ Describe different disabilities served in public schools

◢ State the differences among IDEA, Section 504, and the ADA

◢ Describe the advantages and disadvantages of different service delivery models for students with special needs

◢ Give an overview of legislation that has affected students with disabilities

◢ Discuss methods that enhance the inclusion of students with disabilities

◢ Discuss the role of school personnel in inclusion

Megan is 11 years old and has had many problems in school. In kindergarten, she already seemed to be behind her peers. She did not start with many of the readiness skills that other students had. In first grade, after Megan continued to fall behind, her teacher, Mrs. Bland, referred her for an evaluation. The evaluation revealed that Megan was eligible for special education, falling into the mild mental retardation range. An individualized education program (IEP) was developed, and she was placed in a resource room for half of the school day. Megan immediately began to do better. Her academic skills improved and her social skills progressed. She remained in this type of placement, roughly half-time in a general classroom and half-time in the resource room for the next two years. By the middle of the third grade, however, Megan's academic performance and behavior started to decline. For the first time she indicated that she did not like school and actually began to get sick in the mornings prior to school time. At her review in May, the school indicated that it was moving toward an inclusive service model where Megan would receive her special education services in the regular classroom beginning the next year. Megan's parents were apprehensive. They were concerned that her behavior problems would only increase and that she would fall farther and farther behind her peers. With the urging of school personnel, they finally agreed to try the new arrangement.

At the beginning of fourth grade, Megan seemed out of sorts in the classroom. Although she was provided supports by special education personnel, she had a very difficult time adjusting to the new classroom and all of her classmates. This began to change, however, by the middle of the year. With the cooperative learning activities that her teacher, Ms. Yates, implemented, she began to feel more comfortable in the classroom. She not only did better academically, but her social skills also improved. She actually enjoyed playing with some of her nondisabled peers, who also enjoyed her company. By the end of the fourth grade, Megan was included in all aspects of her class, not only the academic activities.

Now in the fifth grade, Megan is blossoming. She is doing better academically and has made many new friends. Her parents are amazed at her attitude toward school. Although there have been many accommodations and modifications, Megan acts and feels as if she is a regular member of the class.

## QUESTIONS TO CONSIDER

1. Why did Megan initially do better when she was placed in a special education classroom?
2. What factors are involved in making inclusion successful for students with disabilities and for nondisabled students?

The public education system in the United States is like no other in the world. Rather than catering strictly to the needs of certain groups of students, such as those who are wealthy, those with certain academic potential, or those from certain genders, the U.S. education system is for all children. It attempts to offer 13 years of free, equal educational opportunities to all children, including those with **disabilities** and others who have learning or behavior problems. Students do not have to pass certain tests to attend various schools, nor do their families need to pay for a comprehensive educational program. Students do not have to choose, early in their school years, the school track that they will follow.

The U.S. Constitution, which guarantees equal opportunities for all citizens, is the basis for the free public educational system. Since their beginning in the Common School Movement in the mid-1800s, public schools have evolved into a system that provides educational opportunities for all students. In the early 1900s, girls were the first class of citizens who secured public educational opportunities after first being denied them, followed by students from racial minorities in the 1950s, and finally by students with disabilities in the 1970s. Litigation and legislation played important roles as each group secured the right to participate in public educational programs (Lipsky & Gartner, 1996).

## HISTORY OF EDUCATION FOR STUDENTS WITH DISABILITIES

Prior to federal legislation passed in the mid-1970s, many schools simply told parents of students with disabilities that they did not have programs for their children. The only recourses available for most parents were private educational programs or programs specifically designed for "handicapped" students. In many cases, parents paid for these educational programs out of their own resources. And in many situations, students with disabilities stayed home.

In some schools, students with **physical disabilities** or **mental retardation** were provided with services, but these services were nearly always in self-contained, isolated classrooms. These students rarely interacted with nondisabled students, and their teachers did not routinely come into contact with other teachers in the school. In addition to isolating the students, the programs that did exist were also very small. Therefore, very few students were served.

In addition to these public school programs, some children received services in **residential programs.** Typically, children with mental retardation and with sensory deficits were placed in these settings. In 1965, approximately 100,000 children, from birth to 21 years old, lived in institutions for persons with mental retardation in the United States (White, Lakin, Bruininks, & Li, 1991). The first school for children with deafness in the United States was established in 1817 as the American Asylum for

*DISABILITIES* encompass a variety of specific conditions, including mental and physical impairments.

*PHYSICAL DISABILITIES* affect the body. Examples include cerebral palsy, spina bifida, and polio.

*MENTAL RETARDATION* is a condition characterized by a low IQ score (about 70 or below) and deficits in adaptive skills.

*RESIDENTIAL PROGRAMS* are programs provided in live-in settings.

the Education of the Deaf and Dumb (now the American School for the Deaf) (Moores, 1993); the first school for children with visual problems, the New England Asylum for the Blind, was begun in 1832. In 1963, nearly 50% of all legally blind children in the United States lived in residential schools for the blind. This percentage had dropped to 24% by 1978 (Kirchner, Peterson, & Suhr, 1985) and was reported as only 8.6% in 1995–1996 (U.S. Department of Education, 1998). These residential programs offered daily living supports as well as some education and training.

Since the mid-1970s, services to students with disabilities have changed dramatically. Not only are more appropriate services provided by schools, but they also are frequently provided in both **resource rooms** and general education classrooms by collaborating special education and classroom teachers. Many different developments brought about this change, including parental advocacy, legislation, and litigation. The federal government played a major part in the evolution of special education services. As early as 1986, Madeline Will, then Assistant Secretary for the Office of Special Education and Rehabilitation Services, noted that public schools should prepare all students to be independent, productive citizens of their community.

Services for students with disabilities evolved in three distinct phases: **relative isolation, integration** (or **mainstreaming**), and **inclusion.** In the relative isolation phase, students were either denied access to public schools or permitted to attend in isolated settings. In the integration phase, which began in the 1970s, students with disabilities were mainstreamed, or integrated, into general education programs when this was deemed appropriate. Finally, the inclusion phase, starting in the mid-1980s, emphasized that students with disabilities should be fully included in school programs and activities. This phase differed from the integration phase in a minor but very significant way.

While both integration and inclusion resulted in students with disabilities being in general classrooms, in the inclusion phase it was assumed that these students belonged in general classrooms, whereas in the integration phase they were considered to be special education students who were simply placed in the general classroom part of the time. The importance of empowerment and self-determination for students with disabilities has been a focus of inclusion efforts, to better prepare students for the highest degree of independence possible (Field, Hoffman, & Spezia, 1998; Polloway, Smith, Patton, & Smith, 1996). Figure 1.1 depicts the historical changes in the education of students with disabilities in public education.

Because all children are eligible for public education in the United States, teachers in today's public schools must provide instruction and other educational services that meet the needs of a very diverse student population. They must develop ways

**CONSIDER THIS**
Should all children, even those with very different learning needs, have access to free educational services in public schools? Why or why not? What about the extensive costs that may be incurred?

**RESOURCE ROOMS** are classrooms where students with special needs go for short periods of the day for specialized instruction.

**RELATIVE ISOLATION** means that students in special programs are not involved with nondisabled students much of the day.

**INTEGRATION** involves placing students with disabilities in general classrooms for at least part of the school day.

**MAINSTREAMING** is the term originally used by educators to describe placing students with disabilities in general classrooms for at least part of the school day.

**INCLUSION** describes the philosophy that all students, including those with special needs, belong with their nondisabled peers. This term has come to replace mainstreaming.

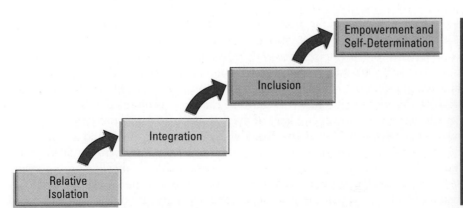

**FIGURE 1.1**

Historical Changes in Education for Students with Disabilities

From "Historic Changes in Mental Retardation and Developmental Disabilities" by E. A. Polloway, J. D. Smith, J. R. Patton, and T. E. C. Smith, 1996, *Education and Training in Mental Retardation and Developmental Disabilities, 31,* p. 9. Used by permission.

## INCLUSION STRATEGIES

One of the results of the inclusion movement has been a change in the way individuals with disabilities are labeled. "People first" language has become the appropriate nomenclature for individuals with disabilities. The following provides examples of using "people first" language:

| Say | Do Not Say |
| --- | --- |
| Person with a disability | The disabled person |
| Billy with mental retardation | Mentally retarded Billy |
| Children with autism | The autistic children |
| Classroom for students with mental retardation | The mentally retarded classroom |
| Students with visual impairments | The blind students |
| Bus for students with disabilities | The special education bus |
| Individuals with disabilities | Disabled individuals |
| Disability or disabled | Handicap or handicapped |
| The boy with cerebral palsy | The cerebral palsied boy |
| The girl with a hearing impairment | The deaf girl |
| Mary with a learning disability | The learning disabled girl |

to serve as many students as possible in general education environments (Smith & Smith, 1989). Traditionally, teacher education programs have focused on teaching students who do not have learning or behavior problems. However, today's teachers do not have the luxury of teaching only students who learn easily and behave in a manner the teachers deem appropriate based on their own standards. They must be prepared to deal effectively with all kinds of students. The nearby Inclusion Strategies feature shows a positive result of the inclusion movement—a change in the way individuals with disabilities are labeled.

## STUDENTS WITH SPECIAL NEEDS

**CONSIDER THIS**
What is a typical child? Is there such a thing as an average child or person? Can schools afford to look at each child as a unique learner?

**SECTION 504 OF THE REHABILITATION ACT**
is a civil rights act that protects individuals with disabilities from discrimination in entities that receive federal funding.

Many students do not fit the mold of the "typical" student. They include those with identified disabilities, those who are classified as gifted and talented, and those who are "at risk" for developing problems. It has been estimated that 11% of school-age children, or approximately 5.4 million students, are classified as disabled (U.S. Department of Education, 1999). Another 10% to 20% experience learning and behavior problems but not significantly enough to be classified as disabled under the federal special education law. However, many of these students are still considered to have a disability under **Section 504 of the Rehabilitation Act of 1973,** and are therefore eligible for certain services and protections (Smith & Patton, 1998). Still another group of students who require special attention are those at risk for developing problems. These students exhibit various characteristics that often result in school problems (Morgan, 1994a). Adding all these students together, plus gifted students and those who obviously need assistance, but do not fit into any distinct group, results in approximately half of all students in public schools. Although many of these students do not meet the specific classification criteria as "disabled" and are therefore not eligible for special education or 504 services, school personnel cannot afford to ignore the special problems of these students (Cosden, 1990; Greer, 1991; Hill, 1991; Morgan, 1994).

Diversity among students in public schools represents the norm rather than the exception (Johnson, Pugach, & Devlin, 1990). If public schools are to be effective, school personnel must address the needs of each of these groups. They must be able to identify these students and help develop and implement programs. A first step for classroom teachers is to understand the types of students they need to serve.

## Students with Disabilities

One of the largest and most visible groups of students with special needs in the public school system includes those formally classified as having disabilities as defined by the Individuals with Disabilities Education Act (IDEA). **Students with disabilities** are defined as those who exhibit one of several specific conditions that result in their need for special education and related services; the number of children served in each category are listed in Table 1.1.

Many different types of students are found in these 12 categories. For example, the broad area of **other health impairments** covers students with a variety of conditions, including hemophilia, diabetes, epilepsy, and sickle cell anemia. Even the category of

**STUDENTS WITH DISABILITIES** are those children served in public schools under IDEA.
**OTHER HEALTH IMPAIRED (OHI)** is the federal disability category that includes children with health problems that can result ineligibility for special education and related services.

| TABLE 1.1 | Disability of Students (Ages 6 through 21) Being Served in U.S. Public School Special Education Programs, 1997–1998 | |
| --- | --- | --- |
| **Disability** | **Number** | **Percent** |
| Specific learning disabilities | 2,748,497 | 51.1 |
| Speech or language impairments | 1,065,074 | 19.8 |
| Mental retardation | 602,111 | 11.2 |
| Emotional disturbances | 454,363 | 8.4 |
| Other health impairments | 190,935 | 3.5 |
| Multiple disabilities | 106,758 | 1.9 |
| Hearing impairments | 69,537 | 1.3 |
| Orthopedic impairments | 67,422 | 1.2 |
| Autism | 42,487 | 0.8 |
| Visual impairments | 26,015 | 0.5 |
| Traumatic brain injury | 11,895 | 0.2 |
| Deaf-blindness | 1,454 | 0.04 |
| Developmental delay | 1,935 | 0.06 |
| **All disabilities** | **5,388,483** | **100.0** |

From *21st Annual Report to Congress on the Implementation of IDEA,* 1999, Washington, DC: U.S. Department of Education.

# RIGHTS & RESPONSIBILITIES

## Comparison of IDEA, Section 504, and ADA

| Area | IDEA | 504 | ADA |
|---|---|---|---|
| **WHO IS COVERED?** | All children ages 3–22 who have one of the designated disability areas who need special education. | All individuals who have a disability as defined; no age restrictions. | Same as 504 |
| **WHO MUST COMPLY?** | All public schools in states that participate in IDEA. | An entity that receives federal funds of any kind or amount. | Any business, governmental agency, or public accommodation other than churches or private clubs. |
| **WHAT IS THE BASIC REQUIREMENT?** | Provide eligible children with a free appropriate public education. | Do not discriminate against any individual because of a disability. | Same as 504 |
| **DUE PROCESS REQUIREMENTS** | Provide notice and gain consent before taking specific actions with a child. | Provide notice. | Same as 504 |
| **SPECIFIC REQUIREMENTS** | IEP | Accommodation plan | Same as 504 |
| | Nondiscriminatory assessment | Same as IDEA | Same as IDEA |
| | Least restrictive environment | Same as IDEA | Same as IDEA |
| **DEFINITION OF FREE APPROPRIATE PUBLIC EDUCATION (FAPE)** | A student's individual program determined by an IEP. | An individual program designed to meet the disabled student's educational needs as well as the needs of nondisabled students are met. | Same as 504 |
| **TRANSITION REQUIREMENTS** | Begin transition planning at age 14. | No requirement | No requirement |
| **ASSESSMENT** | Nondiscriminatory comprehensive assessment before determining eligibility and developing an IEP; required every 3 years unless determined not needed. | Nondiscriminatory preplacement assessment before determining eligibility for 504 services and protections; required before any significant change of placement. | Same as 504 |

| Area | IDEA | 504 | ADA |
|------|------|-----|-----|
| COMPLAINTS | Administrative appeals process must be available and mediation must be offered. Attorney's fees may be required if parents prevail. | Administrative appeals must be offered; parents may go straight to federal court or file complaint with the Office of Civil Rights. | Same as 504; may file complaint with Department of Justice. |
| DESIGNATED COORDINATOR | No requirement | At least one person in each district must be designated in writing as the district 504 coordinator. | Same as 504 (ADA coordinator) |
| SELF-STUDY | No requirement | Each district must form a committee and do a self-study to determine any areas where physical or program discrimination occurs. A plan to correct deficiencies must be developed. | Same as 504. Only areas added since 504 self-study must be reviewed. |
| MONITORING AGENCY | U.S. Department of Education—Office of Special Education | Office of Civil Rights | Department of Justice |

learning disabilities comprises an extremely heterogeneous group of students. The fact that disability categories are composed of different types of students makes drawing simple conclusions about them impossible.

Students who need special assistance do not all fit neatly into disability categories defined by IDEA. Other federal statutes, namely Section 504 of the Rehabilitation Act, and the **Americans with Disabilities Act (ADA),** use a very different definition of disability, employing a functional, not a categorical, model. Under Section 504 and the ADA, a person is considered to have a disability if that individual (1) has a physical or mental impairment that substantially limits one or more of the person's major life activities; (2) has a record of such an impairment, or (3) is regarded as having such an impairment. The acts do not provide an exhaustive list of such impairments but require the functional criterion of "substantial limitation" to be the qualifying element (Smith & Patton, 1998).

The *AMERICANS WITH DISABILITIES ACT* is a federal law, passed in 1990, that protects all Americans with disabilities from discrimination.

The Rights and Responsibilities feature compares the elements of IDEA, Section 504, and the ADA. Although school personnel must adhere to the requirements and criteria established by the U.S. Department of Education, they must also remember that many students who are ineligible for classification as disabled still need assistance if they are to succeed in educational programs.

Most students with disabilities experience mild disabilities and are included in general education classrooms for at least a portion of each school day. A smaller number of students, with more severe disabilities, are more typically educated in segregated special education environments (McLeskey, Henry, & Hodges, 1999). However, even some students with more severe disabilities are included in general education classrooms part of the time (Hobbs & Westling, 1998; Thousand & Villa, 1990; York & Vandercook, 1991). Most classroom teachers will be directly involved in educating students with disabilities. This means that collaboration among parents, special education teachers, and general classroom teachers is critical in order for students with disabilities to receive an appropriate education (Wood, 1998). The following section provides a brief overview of each of the major disability categories recognized in most school districts.

**MENTAL RETARDATION**    The disability category that has been recognized for the longest time in most school districts is mental retardation. Students with mental retardation are usually identified through intelligence tests and measures of adaptive behavior, which indicate a person's ability to perform functional activities expected of age and cultural norms. By definition, individuals with mental retardation score less than 70–75 on individual intelligence tests and have concurrent deficits in adaptive behavior (American Association on Mental Retardation, 1992). Their general characteristics include problems in learning, memory, problem solving, and social skills (Beirne-Smith, Patton, & Ittenbach, 1994; Buck & Smith, in press).

**LEARNING DISABILITIES**    The learning disabilities category accounts for more than 50% of all students served in special education. This category is beset with problems of definition and programming, but continues to include more children than all other special education categories combined (Smith, Dowdy, Polloway, & Blalock, 1997). In general, students with learning disabilities do not achieve commensurate with their abilities. Although the cause of learning disabilities is unclear, the controversial assumption is that a neurological dysfunction causes the learning disability (Hynd, Marshall, & Gonzalez, 1991).

**EMOTIONAL DISTURBANCE**    Students with emotional disturbance, or who have emotional and behavior problems, exhibit inappropriate behaviors or emotions that result in disruptions for themselves or others in their environment. Whereas the federal government uses the term *emotional disturbance,* specifically eliminating from the category children and youth who are socially maladjusted, other groups prefer the terms *emotional and behavior disorders* or *behavior disorders.* Mental health professionals use still other terms, such as *conduct disorder* and *depression.* In addition to terminology, professionals serving children with these problems also differ on definitions of the problems and the types of services they provide (Kauffman & Wong, 1991).

**DEAF/HEARING IMPAIRMENTS**    Students with hearing impairment include those whose permanent or fluctuating impairments in hearing adversely affect their educational performance. Those considered deaf have impairments that result in difficulties in processing linguistic information through hearing, with or without amplification (Final Regulations, IDEA, 1999).

**VISUAL IMPAIRMENTS** These are students whose educational performance is adversely affected because of impairments in vision, even with correction. The category includes both students who are partially sighted and those who are blind (Final Regulations, IDEA, 1999).

**ORTHOPEDIC IMPAIRMENTS** Many students experience problems related to their physical abilities. Cerebral palsy, spina bifida, amputations, and muscular dystrophy are a few examples. For these students, physical access to educational facilities and accommodating problems with writing and manipulation are important concerns.

**OTHER HEALTH IMPAIRMENTS** Students are classified as having other health impairments when they have limited strength, vitality, or alertness due to chronic or acute health problems. Examples include asthma, diabetes, epilepsy, hemophilia, and leukemia. Attention deficit disorder (ADD) or attention deficit hyperactivity disorder (ADHD) may be included in this category (Final Regulations, IDEA, 1999).

**AUTISM** In the 1990 reauthorization of Public Law [PL] 94-142, Congress added autism as a separate disability category. Autism is a lifelong disability that primarily affects communication and social interactions. Children with autism typically relate to people, objects, and events in abnormal ways; they insist on structured environments and display many self-stimulating behaviors (National Information Center for Children and Youth with Handicaps, 1990).

**TRAUMATIC BRAIN INJURY** In addition to autism, Congress added traumatic brain injury (TBI) as a separate disability category in 1990. TBI was defined by Savage (1988) as an insult to the brain that often results in impaired cognitive, physical, or emotional functioning. Prior to the addition of TBI as a separate disability category under IDEA, children with this condition were typically served under the disability category that related to their functional limitations (e.g., mental retardation for cognitive deficits or learning disabilities for erratic academic performance).

**SPEECH OR LANGUAGE IMPAIRMENTS** For some children, speech difficulties are a serious problem. When the impairment results in a need for special education and related services, children are considered eligible for services under IDEA. Most of these children need speech therapy. Teachers need to work closely with speech and language specialists when dealing with this group of students.

## Students Classified as Gifted and Talented

Some students differ from their peers by having above-average intelligence and learning abilities. These students, classified as **gifted and talented,** were traditionally defined and identified using intelligence quotient test scores (IQ scores). IQ scores of 120 or higher were the primary criteria for identifying gifted and talented students. Current criteria are much broader. Although no single definition is accepted by all groups, most focus on students who are capable of making significant contributions to society in a variety of areas, including academic endeavors and creative, mechanical, motor, or fine arts skills.

*GIFTED AND TALENTED (GT)* describes children who excel in academic subjects as well as students who excel in other areas, such as the arts.

## Students Eligible for Section 504 and the ADA

As previously noted, many students not eligible for IDEA services may have disabilities that are covered under Section 504, because the definition of disability in Section 504 and the ADA is broader than the definition used in IDEA. Eligibility for Section 504 and the ADA is based on a student having a physical or mental impairment that results in a substantial limitation in one or more major life activities. Examples of major life activities include breathing, walking, seeing, hearing, and learning. Schools are required to refer students who are thought to be eligible for services and protections under Section 504 and the ADA for evaluation. If students are determined eligible, schools must provide reasonable accommodations for them in academic and non-academic areas (Smith & Patton, 1998).

## Students at Risk for School Problems

Some students who do not fit into a specific disability category and do not have an above-average capacity to achieve also present problems for the educational system. These students, classified as being **at risk,** manifest characteristics that could easily lead to learning and behavior problems (Cosden, 1990; Greer, 1991; Heward & Orlansky, 1992; Johnson, Pugach, & Devlin, 1990). Students considered at risk include the following:

*AT RISK* is used to describe children who are more likely than others to experience learning and behavior problems because of environmental factors.

**CONSIDER THIS**
Should students who are considered at risk for developing learning and behavior problems be provided special services?

◢  Potential dropouts
◢  Drug and alcohol abusers
◢  Students from minority cultures
◢  Students from low-income homes
◢  Teenagers who become pregnant
◢  Students who speak English as a second language
◢  Students who are in trouble with the legal system

*all controversial* (handwritten annotation)

*T̶eenage girls who have babies are at risk for dropping out of school.*

These students may present unique problems for teachers who attempt to meet their educational needs in general education classrooms. Since students in the at risk group are not eligible for special education services, classroom teachers bear the primary responsibility for their educational programs, which need to be modified to meet these students' needs.

## CURRENT SERVICES FOR STUDENTS WITH SPECIAL NEEDS

Most students with special needs receive a portion of their education from classroom teachers in general education classrooms. For students who are gifted or at risk, this is routine. Students in these two groups have always remained in general education classes for most of their instruction. Similarly, students who are eligible for Section 504 and the ADA are served in general classrooms because they are not eligible for IDEA services. However, students with disabilities historically have been served in segregated special education classrooms; they rarely interacted with nondisabled students and classroom teachers.

Since the mid-1980s, however, students with disabilities have been served more and more in general classrooms with their nondisabled peers. In fact, "one of the most significant changes that has occurred in public education in the United States over the past 15 years has been the movement toward inclusion—that is, educating students with disabilities for increasingly more of the school day in general education classrooms" (McLeskey, Henry, & Hodges, 1998, p. 4). This expansion of inclusion entails more than merely physically locating students with special needs in classrooms with their chronological age peers; it requires that they be included in all aspects of the classroom and their educational needs met through services provided within the general education classroom. The nearby Personal Spotlight highlights a school principal's experiences in moving from segregated to inclusive classrooms.

### Actions Leading to Inclusion of Students with Disabilities

During the years 1950 to 1970, the self-contained classroom became the primary setting for serving students with disabilities. This service model greatly limited the interaction of students with disabilities with general education teachers and students, thus isolating them. This segregated service approach gave way to mainstreaming students with disabilities into general education classrooms, either full-time or for part of each school day. The process of mainstreaming did not just happen but came about as a result of several factors. These included the civil rights movement, federal and state legislation, litigation, and actions by advocacy groups.

**THE CIVIL RIGHTS MOVEMENT** Prior to the 1950s, many students from minority racial groups were educated in "separate but equal" schools. Most towns had separate schools for African American children and separate schools for white children. Often, Mexican American and Asian children were educated in the "white" schools. The civil rights movement to eliminate discrimination based on racial differences emerged as a social force in the 1950s. It culminated in the 1960s with the dismantling of the system of school segregation on the basis of race. State and federal court cases and legislation mandated equal access to all schools by children from all backgrounds.

**CONSIDER THIS**

How available do you think services for students with disabilities would be today were it not for the civil rights movement of the 1960s? Would services be better or worse for these students?

## *personal* SPOTLIGHT

### School Principal

Lillie Carter is the principal of a K–6 elementary school in Little Rock, Arkansas, that serves almost 400 students. She has been an educator for more than 20 years and has been a principal since the late 1980s. Lillie has had the opportunity to see special education services move from being very limited to the current situation in which the provision of an appropriate education for students with disabilities is a legal requirement and an educational priority.

**LILLIE CARTER**
*Principal, Pulaski Heights Elementary School, Little Rock, AR*

Lillie views the evolution of special education services very positively. She notes that not too many years ago, students who needed special help could not get it simply because there were no resources. When special classes began to be developed, Lillie believed that they were a positive step

forward. However, she considers the current inclusion movement to be the best way of serving all children with special needs.

Lillie loves her job. She believes that she is in a position to serve all of the students who attend "her" school. Since the school is in the inner city, its students are very diverse. Lillie thinks that one of the reasons that the school can meet the needs of all of its students is its policy of inclusion. She views inclusion as a way that all students, not just those who meet specific eligibility criteria, can benefit. She says that her teachers have responded positively to the inclusion movement for the most part. Those who initially expressed concerns usually changed their minds about inclusion after they had a chance to serve children with special needs in the classroom, with appropriate support services.

Lillie notes that some disadvantages are associated with inclusion. They include scheduling students in appropriate classrooms and arranging the necessary supports for both students and teachers. However, despite these disadvantages, Lillie is a strong supporter of inclusion. In her own words, "Inclusion is a way that all of my teachers can serve all of my students best. It makes us all equal in the eyes of the school."

Parents of students with disabilities soon realized that they could emulate the successful actions of civil rights groups and gain better services for their children. Using legislation, litigation, and advocacy, they sought to gain equal opportunities for their children, who had been denied access to public education solely on the basis of having a disability.

**LEGISLATION**   Probably the factor most responsible for the inclusion of students with disabilities was legislation, which was often enacted in response to litigation. Parents of students with disabilities noted that the civil rights legislation passed in the 1960s helped break down racial segregation barriers in schools. Therefore, they advocated for legislation that would have the same result for their children. In advocating for appropriate legislation, parents also noted that funds needed to be provided and teachers appropriately trained to meet the needs of students with disabilities.

The most important legislation to help students with disabilities access general education programs was Public Law (PL) 94-142, which was passed in 1975 and implemented in 1978. However, prior to its passage, several other legislative acts helped pave the way. These included (Smith, Price, & Marsh, 1986):

1. *PL 83-531* (1954): Provided funds for research in mental retardation. This was the first federal legislation related to mental retardation.

2. *PL 89-10* (1964): Provided funds for educating disadvantaged students. Students with disabilities were often included in these programs.
3. *PL 89-313* (1965): Provided funds for children in hospitals and institutions. It still provides funding for children educated in these settings.
4. *PL 91-230* (1969): Consolidated federal programs for students with disabilities; recognized learning disabilities as a disability. It sparked the rapid expansion of services for students classified as having a learning disability.
5. *PL 92-424* (1972): Required that 10% of Head Start funds go to children with disabilities. Thus, many children with disabilities were included in Head Start programs.
6. *Section 504 of the Rehabilitation Act of 1973:* A civil rights statute for persons with disabilities. It applied to organizations that received federal funds and prohibited discrimination based on the presence of a disability.
7. *PL 93-380* (1973): Forerunner of PL 94-142; required services for students with disabilities. Many of the provisions of PL 93-380 were later incorporated in PL 94-142.

**Public Law 94-142,** the Education for All Handicapped Children Act (EHA), literally opened the doors of public schools and general education classrooms to students with disabilities. In fact, the basic intent of PL 94-142 was to provide equal educational opportunity for students with disabilities (Berres & Knoblock, 1987). Under PL 94-142, schools are required to seek out and implement appropriate educational services for all students with disabilities, regardless of the severity, to provide appropriate, individualized services to students with disabilities, and to actively involve parents in the educational process. For general education teachers, the most important part of the legislation is the requirement that students with disabilities be educated with their nondisabled peers as much as possible.

Since its original passage in 1975, PL 94-142 has been reauthorized by Congress several times. While each reauthorization has made changes in the original law, the basic requirements have remained relatively intact. The 1986 reauthorization mandated services for children ages 3–5 with disabilities. In the 1990 reauthorization, the legislation was renamed the **Individuals with Disabilities Education Act (IDEA),** and the word *handicap* was replaced throughout with the word *disability.* In addition, two new separate categories of disabilities were added—autism and TBI—and schools were required to develop transition planning for students when they turned 16 years old. The most recent reauthorization of the act was in 1997. Table 1.2 summarizes some of the key components of the legislation, including the most recent reauthorization. The following paragraphs describe some of the most important elements found in IDEA.

*Child Find.* IDEA requires schools to seek out students with disabilities. In order to meet this mandate, schools have conducted a number of activities, including the dissemination of "child find" posters, commercial and public television announcements, newspaper articles, and other widespread public relations campaigns. The 1997 reauthorization requires schools to identify highly mobile children, such as homeless children and migrant children, who may qualify.

*Nondiscriminatory Assessment.* Before students can be classified as disabled and determined to be eligible for special education services, they must receive a comprehensive evaluation. The evaluation must not discriminate against students from

**PUBLIC LAW 94-142** is the federal law passed in 1975 mandating appropriate educational programs for students with disabilities.

**INDIVIDUALS WITH DISABILITIES EDUCATION ACT (IDEA)** is the 1990 and 1997 reauthorization of Public Law 94-142. It requires states and local schools to provide an appropriate educational program for students with disabilities.

| TABLE 1.2 | Key Components of the Individuals with Disabilities Education Act (IDEA) (1997) |
|---|---|
| **Provisions** | **Description** |
| Least restrictive environment | Children are educated with nondisabled children as much as possible. |
| Individualized education program | All children served in special education must have an individualized education program (IEP). |
| Due-process rights | Children and their parents must be involved in decisions about special education. |
| Due-process hearing | Parents and schools can request an impartial hearing if there is a conflict over special education services. |
| Nondiscriminatory assessment | Students must be given a comprehensive assessment that is nondiscriminatory in nature. |
| Related services | Schools must provide related services, such as physical therapy, counseling, and transportation, if needed. |
| Free appropriate public education | The primary requirement of IDEA is the provision of a free appropriate public education to all school-age children with disabilities. |
| Mediation | Parents have a right, if they choose, to have a qualified mediator attempt to resolve differences with the school. Using mediation should not deny or delay a parent's request for a due-process hearing. |
| Transfer of Rights | When the student reaches the age of majority, as defined by the state, the school shall notify both the parents and the student and transfer all rights of the parents to the child. |
| Discipline | A child with a disability cannot be expelled or suspended for 10 or more cumulative days in a school year without a manifest determination as to whether the child's disability is related to the inappropriate behavior. |
| State Assessments | Children with disabilities must be included in district-wide and state-wide assessment programs with appropriate accommodations. Alternative assessment programs must be developed for children who cannot participate in district-wide or state-wide assessment programs. |
| Transition | Transition planning and programming must begin when students with disabilities reach age 14. |

**NONDISCRIMINATORY ASSESSMENT** means testing children in a way that does not discriminate against them because of race, socioeconomic, or language factors.

minority cultural groups. The Diversity Forum feature describes ways to be sensitive to cultural diversity when assessing a student. The requirement for **nondiscriminatory assessment** resulted from evidence that certain norm-referenced standardized tests are inherently discriminatory toward students from minority racial and disadvantaged socioeconomic groups. Teachers and other school personnel must be extremely cautious when interpreting standardized test scores for their students. The scores may not reflect an accurate estimate of the student's abilities.

An **INDIVIDUALIZED EDUCATION PROGRAM** is required for all children with disabilities served under IDEA.

*Individualized Education Program (IEP).* A key requirement of IDEA is that all students with disabilities have an **individualized education program (IEP).** The IEP, based on information collected during the comprehensive assessment, is developed by a group of individuals knowledgeable about the student. At a minimum, this group must include the following.

1. The parents of the child
2. At least one regular education teacher of the child (if the child is, or may be, participating in the regular education environment)
3. At least one special education teacher of the child, or if appropriate, at least one special education provider of the child
4. A representative of the public agency who
   (a) Is qualified to provide, or supervise the provision of, specially designed instruction to meet the unique needs of children with disabilities;
   (b) Is knowledgeable about the general curriculum and about the availability of resources of the public agency
5. An individual who can interpret the instructional implications of evaluation results
6. At the discretion of the parent or the agency, other individuals who have knowledge or special expertise regarding the child, including related services personnel as appropriate
7. If appropriate, the child (Final Regulations, IDEA, 1999, 300.344)

For students who have transition plans, additional individuals should attend the IEP/transition planning meeting. The parent's participation is critical, although schools may proceed to develop and implement an IEP if a parent simply does not wish to meet with the team. However, parents are uniquely qualified to provide important information during the development of an appropriate program for their child.

# DIVERSITY FORUM

## Diversity-Sensitive Assessment

In the data-gathering and assessment phase of the intervention process, there are several ways to gather more accurate information and to make the experience more sensitive to and appropriate for families from diverse cultures:

▲ When selecting commercially available assessment instruments, choose only those that are appropriate for the language and culture of the child and family.

▲ If the family is limited- or non-English proficient, work with a trained interpreter who can interpret language as well as *cultural cues* . . . . Remember that what is not said can be as meaningful in some cases as what is said.

▲ Arrange the assessment at a time that allows the people important to the family to be present. For example, although the father may not have any direct caregiving responsibilities for the child, it may be important for him to be present during an assessment. In fact, it may be the father, or another family member such as the grandmother, who holds the decision-making powers in the family with respect to the child's education or treatment.

▲ Conduct the assessment where the family can be most comfortable. Although the home is typically the preferred place, if the family is not comfortable with outsiders visiting, use the program site or another neutral place.

▲ Gather only the data necessary to begin to work with the child and family. Limit the numbers of forms, questionnaires, and other types of paperwork.

▲ Include as few assessors as possible. Additional observations or information can be obtained at another time.

▲ Gather information in those areas in which the family has expressed concern. Tending to the family's issues first is a sign of respect for *all* families.

▲ Explain every step of the assessment and its purpose to the family. Explanations may need to occur several times and be made in several different ways.

From *Developing Cross-Cultural Competence* (p. 354) by E. W. Lynch and M. J. Hansen, 1992, Baltimore, MD: Brookes. Used by permission.

**CONSIDER THIS**
Should students without disabilities have an IEP? What would be the advantages, disadvantages, and impact of such a requirement?

**LEAST RESTRICTIVE ENVIRONMENT (LRE)**
refers to the legal requirement to educate students with disabilities with their nondisabled peers.

*Least Restrictive Environment.*    IDEA also requires that a student's education take place in the **least restrictive environment.** The law further states that special classes, separate schooling, or other removal of students with disabilities from general educational settings should happen only when they cannot succeed in general education classrooms, even with supplementary aids and services. "In the 1997 Amendments to the IDEA, for the first time supplementary aids and services were expressly defined as 'aids, services, and other supports that are provided in regular education classes or other education-related settings to enable children with disabilities to be educated with nondisabled children to the maximum extent appropriate'" (Etscheidt & Bartlett, 1999, p. 164). This adds emphasis and clarification to the purpose of supplementary aids and services. The least restrictive environment requirement obviously results in the inclusion of many students with disabilities in general education classrooms. Exactly how much each student is included depends on the student's IEP. Some students are able to benefit from full-time inclusion, whereas others may require only minimal placement in general education classrooms. IDEA requires that schools provide a continuum of placement options for students, with the IEP determining the most appropriate placement.

For the majority of students with disabilities and other special needs, placement in general education classrooms for at least a portion of each school day is the appropriate option. Students with more severe disabilities may be less likely to benefit from inclusion and will generally spend less time with their nondisabled peers.

**CONSIDER THIS**
Why should students with severe disabilities not be served in institutional or other segregated services? Are there some children who you think should be placed in these types of settings? Why or why not?

The implementation of the least restrictive environment concept means that all classroom teachers will become involved with students with special needs. General education teachers and special education teachers must share in the responsibility for educating students with disabilities. This requires close communication among all teachers involved with specific students (Cramer, 1998; Walther-Thomas et al., 2000).

**DUE-PROCESS SAFE-GUARDS** are the legal rights that children with disabilities and their parents have regarding educational programs.

*Due-Process Safeguards.*    Providing **due-process safeguards** to students with disabilities and their parents is another requirement of IDEA. Prior to this legislation, school personnel often made unilateral decisions about a student's education, including placement and specific components of the educational program; parents had little input and little recourse if they disagreed with the school. Due-process safeguards make parents and schools equal partners in the educational process. Parents must be notified and give their consent before schools can take certain actions with their child.

When the school and parents do not agree on the educational program, either party can request a due-process hearing. In this administrative appeals process, parents and schools present evidence and testimony to an impartial hearing officer who decides on the appropriateness of an educational program. The decision of the hearing officer is final and must be implemented unless it is appealed to state or federal court. Table 1.3 provides a brief description of the due-process safeguards provided by IDEA.

**LITIGATION**    In addition to legislation, litigation has played a major role in the development of current services to students with disabilities. Beginning with the *Brown* v. *Board of Education* case and continuing for the next several decades, litigation helped "radicalize" the way students with disabilities are served in public schools (Prasse, 1986). Important litigation has focused on numerous issues, including (1) the right to education for students with disabilities, (2) nonbiased assessment for students, (3) procedural safeguards for students with disabilities, (4) the right to an extended school year at public expense for some students, (5) related services for students,

| TABLE 1.3 | Due-Process Requirements of IDEA | |
|---|---|---|
| **Requirement** | **Explanation** | **Reference** |
| Opportunity to examine records | Parents have a right to inspect and review all educational records. | 300.501 |
| Independent evaluation | Parents have a right to obtain an independent evaluation of their child at their expense or the school's expense. The school pays only if it agrees to the evaluation or if it is required by a hearing officer. | 300.502 |
| Prior notice; parental consent | Schools must provide written notice to parents before the school initiates or changes the identification, evaluation, or placement of a child. Consent must be obtained before conducting the evaluation and before initial placement. | 300.503 300.505 |
| Contents of notice | Parental notice must provide a description of the proposed actions in the written native language of the home. If the communication is not written, oral notification must be given. The notice must be understandable to the parents. | 300.504 |
| Impartial due-process hearing | A parent or school may initiate a due-process hearing if there is a dispute over the identification, evaluation, or placement of the child. | 300.507 |

From *Final Regulations, IDEA 1999,* Washington, DC: U.S. Government Printing Office.

(6) the right to be educated in general education classrooms, and (7) the interpretation by the U.S. Supreme Court of the intent of Congress in PL 94-142 (Smith, 1990; Turnbull, 1998). Several landmark court cases from the 1970s, 1980s, and 1990s helped shape current special education services.

*Brown* v. *Board of Education (1954).* As previously noted, the civil rights movement in the 1950s and 1960s served as a blueprint for parents who advocated for equal opportunities for their children with disabilities. The landmark civil rights court case, *Brown* v. *Board of Education,* initiated the dismantling of racially segregated public education. As a result, it provided a legal precedent for dismantling segregated public education based on disabilities. The *Brown* case, therefore, even though it did not focus on students with disabilities, was a very important case for special education (Turnbull, 1993).

*PARC* v. *Pennsylvania (1971).* In the early 1970s, the Pennsylvania Association for Retarded Citizens (PARC) represented a group of parents of students with mental retardation and filed suit against the state of Pennsylvania because children with mental retardation were denied access to public education. The case resulted in a consent decree in which the state agreed to provide educational programs for students with mental retardation. Additionally, the state agreed to seek out these students and provide educational programs in general education environments whenever possible (Smith, 1990; Turnbull, 1998).

**CONSIDER THIS**

How are students with disabilities similar to students from racial minorities? Are similar educational services being offered to both groups of students?

**CONSIDER THIS**

How can schools deal with the financial impact of special services for students with disabilities? Is there a limit to how much should be spent on a single child?

*Mills* v. *District of Columbia (1974).*   About the same time as the *PARC* case, a group of parents in Washington, D.C., filed suit against the public school system, requesting that access to public schools be provided for their children with mental retardation. The court ruled in favor of the parents, expanding the ruling to include all students with disabilities. Furthermore, the *Mills* court refused to allow schools to claim fiscal inability as an excuse for not providing appropriate services to this group of students (Podemski et al., 1995). This ruling has been used as precedent in cases where limited financial resources were the stated reason for inappropriate services.

*Rowley* v. *Henry Hudson School District (1984).*   In 1984, the U.S. Supreme Court ruled on its first case related to PL 94-142. The Henry Hudson School District in New York had provided the services of a sign language interpreter for a student for one school year, but refused to provide the service in a subsequent year because the student was doing well. The due-process hearing officer, federal district court, and federal appellate court ruled in favor of the parents, requiring the school to provide the interpreter. These rulings stated that the sign language interpreter was needed to maximize the student's educational achievement. However, the U.S. Supreme Court reversed all previous rulings and stated that a sign language interpreter was not required. In making the ruling, the Court for the first time interpreted the congressional intent of PL 94-142. It stated that Congress never intended for schools to "maximize" the educational progress of students with disabilities, but simply to make available to these students an appropriate educational program (Turnbull, 1998).

**CONSIDER THIS**

What is the difference between a *best* or *maximal* educational program and one that meets the minimum requirements for a child? How do these terms apply to nondisabled children's educational programs in public schools?

Although many advocates of students with disabilities were upset by the ruling, after further consideration, most agreed with the fairness of the decision. In reality, the public education system in the United States does not promise to maximize the achievement ability of most students. What it does provide is a sound, free education for all students. Therefore, schools are required to make a free appropriate education accessible to students with special needs—not the best program, but one that meets the unique needs of each student.

*Oberti* v. *Clementon School District (1992).*   The parents of Rafael Oberti appealed a due-process hearing officer's ruling that their son, who had Down syndrome and an IQ of 59, should be placed in a classroom for students with mild mental retardation until he was ready for inclusion in a general education setting. The parents appealed this decision to federal district court. The court, and a subsequent federal appeals court, ruled in favor of the parents, noting that the burden of proof for removing a student from general education settings rested with the school. Further, the ruling stated that a school district must first consider placing students in general education classrooms, with the use of supplementary aids and services, including classroom assistants, before exploring other, more restrictive alternatives. This case is noteworthy for its support of inclusion.

*Sacramento City Unified School District* v. *Holland (1994).*   In another case related to inclusion, the parents of Rachel Holland, a student with moderate mental retardation, appealed the school district's placement, which consisted of half-time in a special education class and half-time in non-academic general education settings, such as music class. The case, which began in 1990 with a due-process hearing and culminated in the U.S. Court of Appeals for the Ninth Circuit, finally resulted in a decision strongly supportive of inclusion. The court ruled that full-time placement of Rachel in a general education setting, with support services, was appropriate (Victory in landmark "full inclusion" case, 1994).

*D.B.* v. *Ocean Township Board of Education (1997).* In this case, the U.S. District Court for the state of New Jersey ruled on a parental request that their daughter be placed in a residential program. The 16-year-old student had an IQ of 36 and was classified as having moderate mental retardation. The school district proposed placement in a self-contained special education program with speech therapy and other related services. A hearing was called at the request of the parents, and the hearing officer ruled that the appropriate placement was the residential program. However, this ruling was reversed when the school district appealed the decision to the district court. In its ruling, the court noted that IDEA only requires schools to provide access to an appropriate education and that the residential placement did not satisfy the least restrictive environment component of IDEA.

*Cedar Rapids Community School District* v. *Garrett F (1999).* This U.S. Supreme Court case dealt with the provision of medical services to a student who had sustained severe injuries in a motorcycle accident when he was four years old. As a result of the accident, the child needed physical care during the school day. The school district refused to provide this care because it believed the services to be medical and therefore not required by IDEA. In its ruling, Court adopted a position that services provided by a physician were medical, and were not required by IDEA, but that services provided by a nurse or another qualified person other than a physician were not considered medical services and were therefore required. This case is very important because it means that schools have to provide medical services for students served under IDEA, as long as those services are not provided by a physician.

> *[handwritten note]* → doesn't require phycian, school MUST Provide service!

**PARENTAL ADVOCACY** The third primary force that facilitated the inclusion of students with disabilities in general classrooms was parental advocacy. Parents not only encouraged schools to integrate students with disabilities, but they were also directly involved with the legislation and litigation that broke down barriers for these students. Without them, Congress would not have passed PL 94-142. Also, parental advocacy was directly responsible for litigation that forced many schools to include students with disabilities in general education classrooms. The result was a powerful coalition that targeted discriminatory practices that excluded students with disabilities from public education.

Parents have unified their efforts and maximized their influence by forming advocacy groups. The power of such organizations frequently results in changes in educational systems. The **Arc** (formerly the Association for Retarded Citizens), formed in 1950 as the National Association of Retarded Children, played a major role in getting local school districts, state education agencies, and the federal government to require the inclusion of students with disabilities in general education classrooms. Following the lead of the Arc, other groups, such as the Association for Children with Learning Disabilities (ACLD) (now the Learning Disabilities Association), continued to pressure schools to provide appropriate educational services in the least restrictive setting.

**ARC** is a parent advocacy group for individuals with mental retardation.

## WHERE SHOULD STUDENTS WITH DISABILITIES BE EDUCATED?

The setting in which students with disabilities should receive educational and related services is a much discussed, much debated topic. In fact, as early as 1989, Jenkins and Heinen wrote that the issue has "received more attention, undergone more modifications, and generated even more controversy than have decisions about how or what these students are taught" (p. 516). The setting affects those who provide these services and the collaboration required to provide them (Smith, Finn, & Dowdy, 1993).

Approximately 70% of all students with disabilities are included for a substantial portion of each school day in general education classrooms and taught by general education classroom teachers (U.S. Department of Education, 1998). They spend at least a portion of each school day with their age-appropriate peers. Despite these numbers, there are still many students with disabilities who receive most or all of their education in separate, special education settings.

While still raging, the debate about where students should be educated has shifted in favor of more inclusion, which can be implemented in many different ways. Students can be placed in general education classrooms for a majority of the school day and "pulled out" periodically and provided instruction in resource settings by special education teachers. Or they can be placed full-time in general education classrooms; this is commonly referred to as **full inclusion.** In this latter model, special education teachers may go into general education classrooms and work with students who are experiencing difficulties or work directly with classroom teachers to develop and implement methods and materials that will meet the needs of many students. Schools use the model that best suits their needs. Full inclusion is uncommon; most proponents of inclusion believe that pulling students out briefly for specific services is appropriate.

*FULL INCLUSION* means that all students with disabilities are in general education classes all day.

*Children with disabilities were often educated in isolated, self-contained classes between 1950 and 1970.*

The specific placement of students with disabilities falls along a continuum of options. This **continuum-of-services model** provides a range of options, from placement in institutions to full-time placement in general education classrooms (Deno, 1970). The 1997 reauthorization of IDEA requires schools to have a continuum of alternative placements available "to meet the needs of children with disabilities for special education and related services" (IDEA Final Regulations, 1999, 300.551). This includes instruction in regular classes, special classes, special schools, home instruction, and instruction in hospitals and institutions.

The **CONTINUUM-OF-SERVICES MODEL** provides placement and programming options for students with disabilities along a range from least to most restrictiveness.

## The Special Education Classroom Approach

Traditionally, students with disabilities received their educational programs in specialized classrooms, typically called **self-contained classrooms.** Serving students with disabilities in special programs was based on the presumption that general educators did not have the skills necessary to meet the needs of all students representing different learning needs (Shanker, 1994–1995). The result was the removal of students from the general education environment and an education provided by specialists.

*SELF-CONTAINED CLASSROOMS* provide a special education environment where students with disabilities are segregated from their nondisabled peers for most or all of the school day.

In the special education classroom approach, students receive the majority of their educational program from a special education teacher specifically trained to serve the population of students with mental retardation, learning disabilities, or some other specific disability.

Self-contained special education classes were the preferred and dominant service model between 1950 and 1970 (Idol, 1983; Podemski et al., 1995; Smith, 1990; Smith et al., 1986). Special education teachers were trained to teach students with disabilities, but usually only students with one kind of disability, in all subject areas. However, the primary focus was on a functional curriculum. Students placed in self-contained special education classrooms rarely interacted with their nondisabled peers, often even eating lunch alone. Likewise, the special education teacher interacted very little with nondisabled students or classroom teachers.

Many general education teachers liked the self-contained special class model because they did not have to deal with students who differed from their view of "typical" children. The role of classroom teachers in the self-contained model was extremely limited. They might have indirect contact with students with disabilities but rarely had to instruct them. The primary role of general education teachers in the self-contained model was to refer students to the special education program. This primarily occurred in lower elementary grades, where the majority of students with disabilities are identified.

*CONSIDER THIS*
Think about services for students with disabilities when you were in school. Did you have much contact and interaction with students with disabilities? Why or why not?

During the late 1960s and early 1970s, parents and professionals began questioning the efficacy of the self-contained model (Smith et al., 1986). Indeed, Dunn's 1968 article concluded that segregated classes did not result in improved academic performance for students with mental retardation. With the passage of PL 94-142 and the requirement to serve students with disabilities in the least restrictive environment, the special class model was doomed as the preferred service model (Blackman, 1989). In the 1995–1996 school year, only 21.6% of all students with disabilities were served in separate classes, compared to nearly 100% of students with disabilities prior to passage of PL 94-142 (U.S. Department of Education, 1998). The movement away from special class programs has not been without dissent. Advocates for special classes have noted several problems with inclusion. Arguing against including all students with disabilities in general education classes, Fuchs and Fuchs (1994–1995) note that separate settings have several advantages.

◢   Education is provided by well-trained special educators.
◢   Education is selected from a variety of instructional methods, curriculums, and motivational strategies.
◢   The system monitors student growth and progress.

**NORMALIZATION**

means making life as normal as possible for individuals with disabilities.

Regardless of these advantages, the self-contained model has had many critics. The movement away from self-contained classrooms was sparked by several factors, including the growing philosophy of **normalization.** Normalization can be defined as "the creation of as normal as possible a learning and social environment for the exceptional child and adult" (Kirk & Gallagher, 1989, p. 14). Special classes, which segregate students with disabilities from their nondisabled age peers, cannot be considered a "normal" school placement. One way to implement the philosophy was through inclusion, which resulted in the widespread reduction of special classes.

One final reason for the demise of the self-contained special class model was a growing awareness of the diversity of students with disabilities. Although the special class was the predominant model, the majority of students with disabilities served in special education were those with mild mental retardation. As exceptional populations, such as students with learning disabilities, emotional problems, and those at risk for school failure, were recognized, the number of students needing special education grew significantly. The feasibility of serving all of these students in isolated special classes became less attractive. Including these students in general classrooms would be beneficial to all of them (Wang, Reynolds, & Walberg, 1994–1995).

## The Resource Room Model

**CONSIDER THIS**
Public Law 94-142 (IDEA) greatly changed services for students with disabilities. Was this good or bad? Why or why not?

The passage of PL 94-142 in 1975 resulted in significant changes in the way students with special needs were served. The least restrictive environment mandate requires schools to place students with disabilities with their nondisabled peers as much as possible. Regulations implementing the law required schools to ensure "that to the maximum extent appropriate, children with disabilities, including children in public or private institutions or other care facilities, are educated with children who are not disabled" (*Federal Register,* 1993, August 23, p. 42497). Further, "special classes, separate schooling, or other removal of children with disabilities from the general educational environment occurs only when the nature or severity of the disability is such that education in regular classes with the use of supplementary aids and services cannot be achieved satisfactorily" (p. 42497). These definitions did not change in the 1997 reauthorization.

The primary service delivery option used for most students with disabilities (except for those with speech impairments) became the resource room (U.S. Department of Education, 1995). The resource room is a special education classroom. However, unlike the self-contained special class, students go to the resource room only for special instruction. Students who use resource rooms spend part of each school day with their nondisabled, chronological age peers and attend resource rooms for special assistance in deficit areas (Smith et al., 1993).

**CONSIDER THIS**
What problems are created by students coming and going from general education classrooms? How can teachers deal with some of these problems?

Prior to the passage of PL 94-142, the resource room model was used in some school districts but was not widespread. As a result of PL 94-142, the resource room became the leading placement option for students with disabilities. The *20th Annual Report to Congress* shows that 28.7% of all students with disabilities received special education services in resource rooms during the 1995–1996 school year (U.S. Department of Education, 1998).

**ADVANTAGES OF THE RESOURCE ROOM MODEL**   Several obvious advantages make the resource room model preferable to the self-contained special class. Most important, students with disabilities have an opportunity to interact with their chronological age peers (York, Vandercook, MacDonald, Heise-Neff, & Caughey, 1992). In the special class model, students are isolated from these peers. This is noteworthy because students have a tendency to model other students. Therefore, students who interact only with other students who are disabled may not have access to nondisabled role models. This can result in inappropriate behaviors and poor study habits, rather than desirable behaviors. Opportunities for social interactions are enhanced in the resource room model.

The integration of students with disabilities through the resource room model, which became very popular during the early 1980s, can also have a positive impact on nondisabled students. Students in general education classrooms develop a more positive opinion of students with disabilities placed in their classes than they do of students with disabilities who are placed in full-time special classes (Staub & Peck, 1994–1995; York et al., 1992). In a study that investigated the outcomes of integrating students with severe disabilities in general education classes in a middle school, nearly 90% of the nondisabled students thought that the integration should be continued in the future (York et al., 1992).

Another important advantage of the resource room model is that students with disabilities are able to receive instruction from several teachers. In self-contained special class settings, only special education teachers provide instruction. Students miss the advantage of working with different teachers with diverse expertise. Although this may not have a negative effect at the elementary school level, where the majority of instruction focuses on basic skill development, as students get older and are enrolled in content classes, they need the opportunity to be taught by teachers who are experts in particular content areas.

In the resource room, students with disabilities receive intensive instruction in areas in which they are having difficulties, and yet they remain in general education classrooms for socialization activities and instruction in specific subject areas. The resource room enables students to receive instruction in basic skills areas twice: in the general education room with their chronological age peers and in the resource room in a one-on-one or small group setting (Rich & Ross, 1989).

*CROSS-REFERENCE*
Chapter 2 focuses extensively on creating environments for successfully including students in general education classrooms.

**DISADVANTAGES OF THE RESOURCE ROOM MODEL**   Despite the numerous advantages of the resource room model, this approach does not offer the ultimate answer to the complex question of how to place all students with disabilities in appropriate educational settings (Rich & Ross, 1991). Identifying students as needing special education and requiring them to leave the general education classroom, even for only part of the day, can be detrimental. Guterman (1995) found this concern to be one "unifying element" among students interviewed about their special education placement. Dunn's article in 1968 questioned the efficacy of serving students with disabilities in separate classes. His article, along with others, helped move the field from segregated to integrated services. Research currently being reported is similarly questioning the efficacy of resource room services. While there are many advantages to serving students with disabilities in resource rooms, some professionals question the benefit from such services over more fully integrated services. Waldron and McLeskey (1998) found that students with learning disabilities educated in general education classes made more progress in reading than their peers who were in noninclusive settings. In math, the percentage of students with disabilities who made progress comparable to their nondisabled peers was about the same when served in inclusive or noninclusive settings. Another study investigating the differences between instruction in general and special education classrooms for students with severe disabilities found that students in the inclusive classroom received significantly more instruction time than those in special education classrooms (Helmsetter, Curry, Brennan, & Sampson-Saul, 1998). So, while these studies do not conclude that resource rooms are harmful, they do question the benefit of placing some students with disabilities in segregated settings.

*CROSS-REFERENCE*
Read Chapter 6 on Serious Emotional Disturbance to see how modeling appropriate behaviors can impact students with this type of disability.

**ROLE OF SPECIAL EDUCATION PERSONNEL**   In the resource room model, a key role of special education personnel is to collaborate with classroom teachers to deliver appropriate programs to students with disabilities. Resource room teachers cannot simply focus on their students only when they are in the special education classroom. Close collaboration between the resource room teacher and the classroom teacher must occur to ensure that students receiving instruction in the special education room and general education classroom are not becoming confused by contradictory methods, assignments, curricula, and so on. The special education teacher should take the lead in opening up lines of communication and facilitating collaborative efforts.

**ROLE OF CLASSROOM TEACHERS**   Unlike the special class model, the resource room model requires that classroom teachers play numerous roles related to students with disabilities. One primary role is referral. The majority of students with mild disabilities and other special needs are referred for services by classroom teachers. Students with mild mental retardation, learning disabilities, and mild behavior problems are often placed in lower elementary classrooms before their problems become apparent enough to warrant a referral. Also, students with visual and hearing losses and physical or health problems may also be placed in lower elementary grades because the problems are not easily recognized or have not yet resulted in significant learning or behavior difficulties. General education teachers are often the first to recognize that a student is experiencing problems that could require special education services.

Classroom teachers also play the important role of implementing interventions that can ameliorate problems and thereby prevent unnecessary referrals. This means that fewer students will be labeled with a disability and served in special education programs. Many states and local school districts actually require classroom teachers to implement and document intervention strategies attempted prior to a formal referral (Smith et al., 1997). These strategies will be discussed extensively in Chapter 3.

## Inclusive Education Programs

Just as full-time special class placement of students with disabilities received criticism in the early 1970s, resource room programs began to be criticized in the 1980s. Madeline Will, formerly assistant secretary of the U.S. Department of Education, helped formulate the criticism of the resource room model and spur the movement toward inclusion. In 1986 she stated, "Although well-intentioned, this so-called 'pull-out' approach to the educational difficulties of students with learning problems has failed in many instances to meet the educational needs of these students and has created, however unwittingly, barriers to their successful education" (p. 412).

Since the mid-1980s there has been a call for dismantling the dual education system (general and special) in favor of a unified system that attempts to meet the needs of all students. Rather than spend a great deal of time and effort identifying students with special problems and determining if they are eligible for special education services, proponents of a single educational system suggest that efforts be expended on providing appropriate services to all students. In the early 1980s, this model was advocated for students classified as gifted and talented by Renzulli and Reis (1985). Their model, called schoolwide enrichment, offered gifted programming services to all students without their having to meet restrictive eligibility criteria.

The model for more fully including students with special needs in general education programs was originally called the **Regular Education Initiative (REI).** More recently, the term *inclusion* has been used to identify this program model. Inclusion has been defined in many different ways. Unfortunately, the term *full inclusion* was originally used, suggesting that all students with disabilities, regardless of the severity of the disability, be included full-time in general education classes (Fuchs & Fuchs, 1994–1995). This approach was advocated by several professional and advocacy groups, most notably **The Association for the Severely Handicapped (TASH)** and the Arc. Their encouragement of full-time general education classroom placement for all students resulted in a great deal of criticism and skepticism.

Currently, the terms *inclusion* and *responsible inclusion* are used to identify the movement to provide services to students with disabilities in general education settings. It is acknowledged that within the context of inclusion, some services to students may be necessary outside the general education classroom. Proponents suggest that all students with disabilities *belong* with their nondisabled peers. Smith (1995) states that inclusion means "(1) that every child should be included in a regular classroom to the optimum extent appropriate to the needs of that child while preserving the placements and services that special education can provide; (2) that the education of children with disabilities is viewed by all educators as a shared responsibility and privilege; (3) that there is a commitment to include students with disabilities in every facet of school; (4) that every child must have a place and be welcome in a regular classroom." (p. 1). Rogers (1993) notes that supporters of inclusion use the term "to refer to the commitment to educate each child, to the maximum extent appropriate, in the school and classroom he or she would otherwise attend" (p. 1). When support services are required, these services should be provided in the general education classroom setting as much as possible. In an inclusive model, students attend the schools and classes they would if they did not have disabilities (*Winners all: A call for inclusive schools,* 1992).

The concept of inclusion has a values orientation, "based on the premise that all individuals with disabilities have a right to be included in naturally occurring settings and activities with their neighborhood peers, siblings, and friends" (Erwin, 1993, p. 1). Inclusion, therefore, means more than simply placing students with disabilities in general education classrooms. It means giving students the opportunity to participate as members in all school activities and affirming their right to such opportunity.

As early as 1984, Stainback and Stainback suggested the following reasons to support inclusion:

1. *"Special" and "regular" students:* The current dual system of general and special education assumes that there are two distinct types of children, special and regular. In reality, all students display a variety of characteristics along a continuum; there simply is no way to divide all students into two groups. All students exhibit strengths and weaknesses that make them unique.
2. *Individualized services:* There is no single group of children who can benefit from individualized educational programming. The dual system of special and general

**CONSIDER THIS**
Why are some people opposed to merging special education and general education into one system?

**REGULAR EDUCATION INITIATIVE (REI)** was the name of the movement in the 1980s to place students with disabilities in education classes for the entire school day.

**THE ASSOCIATION FOR THE SEVERELY HANDICAPPED (TASH)** is an advocacy group for individuals with severe disabilities.

**CONSIDER THIS**
How can terms such as mainstreaming, inclusion, and full inclusion complicate services for students with disabilities? What could be done to clarify terminology?

*There are numerous advantages to including students with disabilities in general classrooms.*

education adopts the notion that students with disabilities require individual education, whereas other students do not. In fact, some research suggests that students with diverse characteristics do not benefit from different instructional techniques. If future research concludes that individualized instruction does indeed result in improved education, then all students should be afforded the opportunity.

3. *Instructional methods:*   Contrary to many beliefs, there are not special teaching methods that are effective only with students who have disabilities. Good, basic instructional programs can be effective for all students.

4. *Classification:*   A dual system of education, general and special, requires extensive, time-consuming, and costly efforts to determine which system students fit into and, in the case of those students determined to be eligible for special education, which disability category they fit into. Unfortunately, classification often is unreliable, results in stigma, and does not lead to better educational programming.

5. *Competition and duplication:*   Perpetuating the general and special systems has resulted in competition between professionals as well as duplication of effort. If the educational system is to improve, all educators must work together, sharing expertise, effective methods, and educational goals.

6. *Eligibility by category:*   The dual system results in extensive effort being spent on determining who is eligible for special services. The programs for students are often based not on their specific needs, but on which category they are placed in. Placements and even curricular options are often restricted on the basis of clinical classification. For example, students classified as having mental retardation may be placed in work–study programs without having the opportunity to participate in regular vocational education.

**CONSIDER THIS**
How can serving students based on their individual needs benefit all students, not just those fitting into certain disability categories? Do the benefits outweigh the disadvantages?

7. *"Deviant" label:* A major negative result of the dual system is the requirement to place "deviant" labels on students. In order to determine that a student is eligible for the special system, a clinical label must be attached to him or her. Few, if any, would argue that clinical labels result in positive reactions. The routine reaction to the labels "mental retardation," "emotionally disturbed," and even "learning disabled" is an assumption that the student is not capable of functioning as well as other students.

Although proponents of inclusion have articulated numerous reasons to support the model, many oppose its implementation (Fuchs & Fuchs, 1994–1995). Al Shanker, past president of the American Federation of Teachers, noted that "we need to discard the ideology that inclusion in a regular classroom is the only appropriate placement for a disabled child and get back to the idea of a 'continuum of placements,' based on the nature and severity of the handicap" (1994–1995, p. 20). Several professional and advocacy groups also support the continued use of a continuum of placement options. These include the Council for Exceptional Children (CEC), American Council on the Blind, Commission on the Education of the Deaf, and the Council for Children with Behavior Disorders. It also should be noted that the U.S. Department of Education does not mandate inclusion. Rather, the most recent reauthorization of IDEA in 1997 requires that schools provide a continuum of alternative placement options for students (Final Regulations, IDEA, 1999).

**ADVANTAGES OF INCLUSION** Numerous studies have documented some of the advantages of inclusion. The National Center on Educational Restructuring and Inclusion (NCERI) conducted a study of inclusion in school districts implementing the model. The study identified 891 schools in 267 districts implementing an inclusive educational model. All 50 states were involved in the study. Their findings included the following:

*CONSIDER THIS*
How can some of the problems caused by inclusion be addressed in order to facilitate success in school for all students?

1. The number of school districts reporting inclusive education programs has increased significantly since 1994.
2. Outcomes for students in inclusive education programs, both general and special education, are positive.
3. Teachers participating in inclusive education programs report positive professional outcomes for themselves.
4. Students with a wider range of disabilities are in inclusive education programs.
5. School restructuring efforts are having an impact on inclusive education programs, and vice versa. (*National study on inclusion*, 1995, p. 1).

Several studies have concluded that inclusion results in specific benefits for both students with disabilities and those without disabilities. These include developing a better understanding and acceptance of other students (Giangreco, Dennis, Cloninger, Edelman, & Schattman, 1993; Peck, Carlson, & Helmstetter, 1992).

Further studies indicate that students with disabilities do as well or better academically in general classrooms as they do in special education classrooms (Waldron & McLeskey, 1998); that students with disabilities have more instructional time in general classrooms than in special education classrooms (Helmstetter, et al., 1998); and that teachers generally support serving students with disabilities in general education classes (Hobbs & Westling, 1998). The Inclusion Strategies feature summarizes other empirical studies supporting inclusion.

Although not mandatory, parental and teacher support for inclusion is very important. Hobbs and Westling (1998) note that many parents have mixed views.

# INCLUSION STRATEGIES

## Empirical Support for Inclusion

As inclusion has increased, several studies have offered some empirical support for the practice. Here are some examples:

▲ Brinker (1985) found that children with severe disabilities had more episodes of social engagements when in more inclusive environments. In integrated settings, most of their interactions were with nondisabled children as opposed to other children with disabilities. They socially approached nondisabled children more often and were more often approached by nondisabled peers rather than peers with disabilities. This finding suggests that inclusive environments are more likely to promote social interactions than are environments that include only children with disabilities.

▲ Evans, Salisbury, Palombaro, Berryman, and Hollowood (1992) reported that some children with severe disabilities, although not all, were considered to be very popular by their peers and that the degree of their disability was not related to their popularity. They found high levels of interactions between peers with and without disabilities, but also found that these decreased somewhat during the year.

▲ Hunt, Farron-Davis, Beckstead, Curtis, and Goetz (1994) found that children with disabilities in inclusive settings fared better than students in separate special classes in several areas. Students with milder disabilities had more instructional objectives devoted to academic skills, had more interaction time with students without disabilities, and spent more of their time grouped with other students and less time

alone when compared to similar students in special classes. Students with more severe disabilities in inclusive settings had more appropriate IEP objectives, had more active levels of engagement, and worked more on academic skills than their counterparts in special classes.

Other studies have shown that inclusive education does not appear to have a detrimental effect on students without disabilities and often may have positive effects.

▲ Sharpe, York, and Knight (1994) found that elementary-school-age children's academic grades, test scores, and ratings of social behavior did not decrease as a result of being in classrooms with children with disabilities.

▲ In a study of middle school students, Peck, Donaldson, and Pezzoli (1990) reported that many nondisabled peers experienced personal satisfaction as a result of their opportunities to interact with peers with severe disabilities. Areas of benefit include self-concept, social cognition, reduced fear of differences, tolerance of others, development of personal principles, and experiencing nondemanding friendships.

▲ In a survey of more than 1,000 middle and high school students, Hendrickson, Shokoohi-Yekta, Hamre-Nietupski, and Gable (1996) found that many of these students (38%) were friends with students with severe disabilities and that most others thought such friendships were possible and beneficial to students both with and without disabilities. Nevertheless, the students felt that it would not be easy to form friendships with students with severe disabilities.

From "Promoting Successful Inclusion" by T. Hobbs and D. L. Westling, 1998, *Teaching Exceptional Children, 31,* p. 13. Used by permission.

While they believe that inclusion has some obvious benefits for their children, they also worry about their children being in integrated placements.

Teachers, for the most part, have expressed support for inclusion. After reviewing several studies, Scruggs and Mastropieri (1996) noted that most teachers support inclusion, are willing to teach students in their classrooms (although they are fewer than those who support the concept), and believe that inclusion results in positive benefits for students with disabilities and does not harm other students or the instructional process. Hobbs and Westling (1998) note that the success of inclusion is related to many different factors, "perhaps the most important being teachers' preparation, attitudes, and opportunity for collaboration" (p. 13).

**DISADVANTAGES OF INCLUSION**   Just as there are many supporters of inclusion and reasons for its implementation, there are also professionals and parents who decry the movement. Among the reasons they oppose inclusion are the following:

1. General educators have not been involved sufficiently and are therefore not likely to support the model.
2. General educators as well as special educators do not have the collaboration skills necessary to make inclusion successful.
3. There are limited empirical data to support the model. Therefore, full implementation should be put on hold until sound research supports the effort.
4. Full inclusion of students with disabilities into general education classrooms may take away from students without disabilities and lessen their quality of education.
5. Current funding, teacher training, and teacher certification are based on separate educational systems.
6. Some students with disabilities do better when served in special education classes by special education teachers.

Although some of these criticisms may have merit, others have been discounted. For example, research indicates that the education of nondisabled students is not negatively affected by inclusion (*National study on inclusion*, 1995). Therefore, though the movement has its critics, research on inclusion provides support for its continuation.

**ROLE OF SPECIAL EDUCATION PERSONNEL**   In the inclusion model, special education personnel become much more integral to the broad educational efforts of the school. In the dual system, special education teachers provide instructional programming only to students identified as disabled and determined eligible for special education programs under state and federal guidelines. In inclusive schools, these teachers work with a variety of students, including those having difficulties but not identified specifically as having a disability. The special education teacher works much more closely with classroom teachers in the inclusion model.

**ROLE OF CLASSROOM TEACHERS**   The role of classroom teachers also changes dramatically. Their former role had been primarily identification and referral, and possibly to provide some instructional services to students with disabilities, but in the inclusive school, they become fully responsible for all students, including those with identified disabilities. Special education support personnel are available to collaborate on educational programs for all students, but the primary responsibility is assumed by the classroom teacher.

**CONSIDER THIS**
How would you feel if you were a classroom teacher who was suddenly asked to teach a student with a disability and you did not have any skills in special education?

# CLASSROOM TEACHERS AND STUDENTS WITH DISABILITIES

Teachers must develop strategies to facilitate the successful inclusion of students with disabilities in general education classrooms. Neither classroom teachers nor special education teachers want students with disabilities simply "dumped" into general education classes (Banks, 1992), and the successful inclusion of students does not normally happen without assistance. School personnel must work on effective, cooperative methods to provide appropriate programs to all students.

■ *FIGURE* **1.2**  Comfort Level of Implementing Various Strategies

| | Curriculum-Based Assessment — | Cooperative Learning — | Self-Management — | Classwide Peer Tutoring — | Strategy Instruction — | Direct Instruction — | Goal Setting — |
|---|---|---|---|---|---|---|---|
| 6. Extremely Comfortable → | | | | | | | |
| 5. Moderately Comfortable → | | ♦ | | | | | |
| 4. Comfortable → | | | | | | ♦ | |
| 3. Slightly Comfortable → | | | ♦ | ♦ | ♦ | | ♦ |
| 2. Moderately Uncomfortable → | ♦ | | | | | | |
| 1. Extremely Uncomfortable → | | | | | | | |

KEY: —— Effective Practices Known
♦ Comfort Level with Effective Practices

From "Inclusive Practices of Classroom Teachers" by M. E. King-Sears and C. S. Cummings, 1996, *Remedial and Special Education, 17*, p. 218. Used by permission.

***CURRICULUM-BASED ASSESSMENT*** is assessment of the student based on what is being taught in the curriculum.

***COOPERATIVE LEARNING*** uses teams of children to teach each other and work together on various learning activities.

***SELF-MANAGEMENT*** allows students to manage their own behavior or learning needs.

***PEER TUTORING*** is students helping each other in learning situations.

***STRATEGY INSTRUCTION*** is teaching students the skills that they need to succeed in academic and social situations.

***DIRECT INSTRUCTION*** is the instructional approach in which students are taught specific skills and content.

***GOAL SETTING*** focuses on setting specific goals for students in learning activities.

Two methods are generally used to implement inclusion: facilitating the acceptance of the students with disabilities and providing services to support their academic success. Chapter 2 provides extensive information on creating classroom environments to enhance acceptance and provide academic supports; later chapters provide specific, practical suggestions for providing academic supports.

King-Sears and Cummings (1996) note seven different practices that teachers can use to help students succeed in inclusive settings. These include (1) **curriculum-based assessment,** (2) **cooperative learning,** (3) **self-management,** (4) **peer tutoring,** (5) **strategy instruction,** (6) **direct instruction,** and (7) **goal setting.** Figure 1.2 depicts the comfort of teachers in using these seven different methods. Clearly, some practices are only moderately or slightly comfortable, suggesting that in order for inclusion to be successful, teacher training and preparation need to be modified.

Classroom teachers play a vital role in the education of students with disabilities. As noted by Hobbs and Westling (1998), teachers possibly play the most important role in the success of inclusion. Classroom teachers must be able to perform many different functions, such as the following:

▲ Acting as a team member on assessment and IEP committees
▲ Advocating for children with disabilities when they are in general education classrooms and in special programs
▲ Counseling and interacting with parents of students with disabilities
▲ Individualizing instruction for students with disabilities
▲ Understanding and abiding by due-process procedures required by federal and state regulations
▲ Being innovative in providing equal educational opportunities for all students, including those with disabilities

# TECHNOLOGY TODAY

## Technology-Based Applications That Can Assist Individuals with Mild Disabilities

| Student Characteristics | Technologies and Applications |
| --- | --- |
| Deficits in basic academic subjects and skills | Drill-and-practice software, integrated learning systems, hypermedia |
| Need for repeated practice and review | Drill-and-practice software, integrated learning systems, teacher tool software, hypermedia |
| Memory deficits | Personal productivity tools |
| Short attention span | Gamelike software activities, simulations, instruction supported or delivered by videodiscs |
| Inefficient learning strategies | Problem-solving software, personal productivity tools |
| Lack of background knowledge | Content-area software, videodisc macrocontexts, hypermedia |
| Lack of higher-order skills | Writing tools, simulation and problem-solving software, instruction supported and delivered by videodiscs, content-area software, electronic networks, personal productivity tools |
| Motivational deficits | All technology-based applications |

From "Computers and Individuals with Mild Disabilities" by C. M. Okolo. In *Computers and Exceptional Individuals,* edited by J. D. Lindsey, 1993, p. 113. Austin, TX: Pro-Ed. Used by permission.

Sharing responsibility among classroom teachers, special education teachers, and other specialists, such as reading teachers, is the key to providing effective educational programs for all students.

In general, the classroom teacher controls the educational programs for all students in the classroom, including students with disabilities, students at risk for developing problems, and those classified as gifted and talented. The attitude of the teacher toward students and the general climate the teacher establishes in the classroom have a major impact on the success of all students, particularly those with disabilities.

Classroom teachers need to be able to use a variety of techniques when meeting the needs of students included in their classes. Technology can be a great asset. The nearby Technology Today feature provides examples of technology-based applications.

The primary function of teachers, both general education and special education teachers, is to teach. Good teaching has been described in many different ways. Researchers have attempted to define good teaching based on student outcomes, parental opinions, peers, supervisor ratings, and self-evaluations. One way to gauge good teaching is to ask those who are taught. A 15-year-old student with learning disabilities was asked just this question and provided 20 good teaching tips. Although the student was describing good teaching qualities for special education teachers, the same suggestions relate to classroom teachers who are dealing with students with disabilities (Gallegos & Gallegos, 1990).

**CONSIDER THIS**
What tips would you give teachers to enhance the inclusion of students with special needs in general education classrooms?

1. Teachers should be more understanding.
2. Teachers should be more involved with the students.
3. I feel that some teachers will not pay attention.
4. I think that teachers should look at the students a little better than what they do.
5. Teachers should put students where they belong and where they can handle it at that level.
6. My math teacher watches me constantly.
7. I think that the teacher should be helpful in and out of the classroom.
8. Some teachers like my math teacher don't give students a chance to talk about what they need.
9. I don't think that teachers should do things that bother or disturb and also do things that make us uncomfortable.
10. Don't believe every test score that you see.
11. Students shouldn't have to answer every single question after a chapter.
12. Teachers should be patient with the students.
13. The teachers shouldn't pick a teacher's pet.
14. The teachers should come well dressed to school instead of old clothing.
15. Teachers shouldn't give students homework that they can't finish in a classroom.
16. The teachers should be more appreciative to students when they do a good job. They need that kind of help.
17. The teachers should let students do what they want to do. Like get a drink and use the pot.
18. Teachers shouldn't touch opposite sex students. That makes students feel uncomfortable.
19. I don't like some teachers that hit students.
20. Some students should be rewarded for the good they do. (p. 15)

# Summary

## Students with Special Needs

▲ The public school system in the United States attempts to provide 13 years of equal educational opportunity to all its citizens.

▲ Today's student population is very diverse and includes students with a variety of disabilities.

▲ During the 1950s and 1960s, students from minority cultures won the right to equal educational opportunities.

▲ Many students in today's schools have specific special needs.

▲ A sizable percentage of students are at risk for developing problems, present learning or behavior problems, or may be classified as having a disability.

▲ The largest group of students with special needs in the public school system consists of those formally classified as having disabilities.

▲ Although there are 12 recognized categories of disabilities in schools, many students do not fit neatly into a specific category.

▲ Mental retardation, learning disabilities, and emotional and behavior disorders make up the majority of student disabilities.

▲ Students who are at risk for developing problems, and those considered gifted and talented, also require special attention from school personnel.

## Current Services for Students with Special Needs

▲ Services for students with disabilities have evolved significantly over the past 20 years.

▲ Services for students with disabilities focus on inclusion—including students in general education classroom situations as much as possible.

▲ The civil rights movement, legislation, litigation, and parental advocacy all helped shape the service system for students with disabilities.

▲ Public Law 94-142, now the IDEA, provides the framework for services to students with disabilities in school settings.

▲ IDEA requires that students with disabilities be educated in the least restrictive environment, using an IEP.

### Where Should Students with Special Needs Be Educated?

▲ About 70% of all students with disabilities spend a substantial portion of each school day in general education classrooms.

▲ The preferred service model for students with disabilities between 1950 and 1970 was segregated classroom settings.

▲ In the self-contained model, special education teachers were trained to teach specific types of students, primarily based on clinical labels.

▲ Classroom teachers had a very limited role in special education in the self-contained classroom model.

▲ Many parents advocated for more inclusion of their students than was possible in the self-contained model.

▲ The least restrictive environment mandate of PL 94-142 was the impetus for the development of the resource room model.

### Classroom Teachers and Students with Disabilities

▲ General education teachers play a very critical role in providing services to students with disabilities.

▲ The attitudes of classroom teachers are extremely important in the quality of services rendered to students with disabilities.

# urther Readings

*Annual report to Congress on the implementation of the Individuals with Disabilities Education Act.* (1999).

Erwin, E. J. (1993). The philosophy and status of inclusion. *The Lighthouse,* 1–4.

Juul, K. D. (1978). European approaches and innovations in serving the handicapped. *Exceptional Children, 44,* 322–330.

Smith, T. E. C (1990). *Introduction to education* (2nd ed.). St. Paul, MN: West Publishing.

Special edition. (1994, December and 1995, January). *Educational Leadership.*

Stainback, S., & Stainback, W. (1987). Integration versus cooperation: A commentary. *Exceptional Children, 54,* 66–68.

Turnbull, H. R. (1998). *Free appropriate public education: The law and children with disabilities* (4th ed.). Denver, CO: Love Publishing.

Wang, M. C., & Birch, J. W. (1984). Effective special education in regular classes. *Exceptional Children, 52,* 33–40.

Will, M. C. (1986). Educating students with learning problems—a shared responsibility. *Exceptional Children, 52,* 411–415.

*Winners all: A call for inclusive schools.* (1992). Alexandria, VA: The National Association of State Boards of Education.

# 2

# Designing Inclusive Classrooms: Effective Instruction and Collaboration

*After reading this chapter, you should be able to:*

◢ Discuss the concept of diversity

◢ Explain different perceptions among teachers, students, and parents regarding inclusion

◢ Delineate critical dimensions of inclusive classrooms

◢ Describe the role of classroom management, curricular options, and accommodative practices in inclusive classrooms

◢ Discuss the range of personnel supports in inclusive classrooms

◢ Create and maintain successful inclusive classrooms

◢ Describe different methods of maintaining inclusive programs after they are initiated

◢ Describe the consultation/collaboration and co-teaching strategies used in inclusive classrooms.

There are 2 third-grade classrooms at the Walker Elementary School. The school has an inclusive service model for students with disabilities, and both third grades include students with disabilities. Both classroom teachers may use similar support services. But the classroom environments vary greatly as does the success of the students with disabilities.

Before being assigned to a third-grade classroom 2 years ago, Ms. Johnson was a special education teacher. She taught students with learning disabilities and mild mental retardation in a resource room. When the school moved to an inclusive education model, she asked for a general classroom since she was also certified as an elementary teacher. Ms. Johnson's philosophy is that all students belong and all are capable of success. She uses many cooperative learning activities, arranges social activities among all of her students, and welcomes support services from special education personnel. The students with disabilities in her classroom appear to be doing very well.

Across the hall is Ms. Baker's third grade. Ms. Baker has taught for 25 years and uses "tried and true" methods. Her students sit in neat rows, and she expects their work to be neat and on time. Ms. Baker has never been sure about the inclusive education model and does not understand why special education teachers do not teach their students in the special education room since this method worked well for many years. She does not welcome so-called specialists coming into her class, giving her advice about how to teach, after her long teaching career. The students with disabilities in her classroom are falling behind. Many also have behavior problems. Some of these students need extra time, and with the distractions that some of their behaviors cause, Ms. Baker wants to return to the old special education resource room model.

## QUESTIONS TO CONSIDER

1. What are some basic differences between Ms. Johnson's and Ms. Baker's approaches to teaching children?
2. How can inclusion work when general classroom teachers are resistant?
3. How would Ms. Johnson feel if the principal began placing all of the students with disabilities in her classroom to avoid placing them with Ms. Baker?

*I*ncluding students with special needs in general education classrooms continues to receive significant attention on a philosophical level. However, less discussion has focused on specific ways to accomplish this task successfully. Addressing the needs of a wide range of students is a daunting challenge for general educators in schools today. This chapter discusses some of the key features of sound inclusive settings. It also addresses how to create and maintain these settings and the collaborative relationships that help them function well.

The critical issue underlying successful inclusion is the acceptance of diversity. Unfortunately, this is not likely to happen easily and without major changes in the way many schools operate. The complexity of the challenge is explained by Ferguson (1995):

**CONSIDER THIS**
What does the term diversity include? Is our society becoming more or less diverse?

> The real challenge is a lot harder and more complicated than we thought. Neither special or general education alone has either the capacity or the vision to challenge and change the deep-rooted assumptions that separate and track children and youths according to presumptions about ability, achievement, and eventual social contribution. Meaningful change will require nothing less than a joint effort to reinvent schools to be more accommodating to all dimensions of human diversity. (p. 285)

Although Ferguson's admonition is accurate and perhaps overwhelming, positive steps toward successful inclusion can be taken on a classroom-by-classroom and school-by-school basis. It is important to remember that one teacher can have a dramatic effect on the lives of students who are different and who have learning challenges.

The discussion of inclusion and how to make it work has focused mostly on students with disabilities. However, both gifted students and at risk students often face the same obstacles to acceptance and the same problems gaining access to appropriate programming. Consequently, all of the ideas in this chapter apply to gifted students and at risk students as well as those with other special needs.

**CROSS-REFERENCE**
Refer to Chapters 11 and 12 on gifted students and at risk students to determine how inclusion applies to these groups of students.

Developing effective inclusive classrooms has relevance for students' immediate needs as well as their long-term needs. In the short term, students need to learn in settings along with their peers (that is, inclusive schooling). In the long term, we want these students, as adults, to live, work, and play along with their peers in their home communities (that is, inclusive living). Without the opportunity to grow and learn with nondisabled peers throughout their lives, individuals with disabilities will not be able to accomplish these goals.

While the merits of inclusion have been debated, the reality is that the movement has taken hold. A comparison of national placement figures from the 1987–1988 and 1995–1996 school years shows an increase from 28.88% to 45.95% in the number of students with disabilities educated in general education classrooms, at least part of the day. This represents a 60% increase in the number of students with disabilities served in these settings (U.S. Department of Education, 1990, 1998).

## PERCEPTIONS OF INCLUSION

A significant amount of discussion has surrounded the movement toward inclusion. On the philosophical level, only a few arguments have been levied against this movement. It is, however, primarily on the implementation level that concerns have arisen. Studies focusing on attitudes toward inclusion have involved two primary groups: general education teachers and parents. Highlights of the attitudes of these two groups are presented briefly in this section.

Scruggs and Mastropieri (1996) studied teacher perceptions of mainstreaming and inclusion by analyzing research that had been conducted on this topic between 1958 and 1995. Their results reflect many current issues related to responsibly including students with special needs in general education settings. Overall, they found that nearly two-thirds of general education classroom teachers support, for the most part, the concept of inclusion (Hobbs & Westling, 1998). However, when asked whether they were willing to teach students with disabilities in their own classes, many teachers expressed concerns or a lack of willingness to do so. This response was affected by the type of disability and the perceived impact on the teacher. A relatively low percentage of teachers (33% or less) felt that they had sufficient time, expertise, training, and resources (material support and support personnel) to enable them to work successfully with students with special needs (Scruggs & Mastropieri, 1996). These findings coincide with Roach's (1995) comment: "Teachers' fears seem to arise not so much from concerns about the philosophy of inclusion as from concerns and doubts about teachers' own teaching abilities as they relate to specific students" (p. 298).

Parents' attitudes about inclusion vary greatly. For parents of students with disabilities, the reaction to the inclusion movement is mixed, ranging from complete support of the idea (i.e., as propounded by the Arc) to skepticism, especially concerning the concept of full inclusion. This latter orientation is reflected in the position statements of various parent organizations, most notably the Learning Disabilities Association of America. A national survey of parents (Elam & Rose, 1995) found that they supported federal funding for services to students with disabilities. However, only about one-fourth of these parents thought that students with learning problems should be included in the same classes with nondisabled students.

This attitudinal research provides a glimpse of the task faced by professionals who support teaching students with special needs in inclusive settings. First, accurate information about inclusion, in general, and individuals who need to be included, must be distributed to teachers, parents, and the general public. Yet the greatest challenge will be changing an educational system that presents great barriers to inclusion since teachers' perceptions, attitudes, and opportunities for collaboration are directly related to the success of inclusion. There is reason to believe that these changes can occur (Hobbs & Westling, 1998).

**CONSIDER THIS**
What factors would make teachers who support inclusion more willing to accept students with disabilities into their classrooms?

**CONSIDER THIS**
Often parents of students with mental retardation are more supportive of inclusion than parents of students with less severe disabilities. Why do you think this is the case?

## CRITICAL DIMENSIONS OF INCLUSIVE CLASSROOMS

The concept of inclusion purports that students with special needs can be active, valued, fully participating members of a school community in which diversity is viewed as the norm and high-quality education is provided through a combination of meaningful curriculum, effective teaching, and necessary supports (Ferguson, 1995). Anything less is unacceptable. Inclusion is distinctly different from the notion of

**FIGURE** **2.1** Structure and Philosophy: Differences between Traditional and Inclusive Models

| Traditional Models | Inclusive Educational Models |
|---|---|
| 1. Some students do not "fit" in general education classes. | 1. All students "fit" in general education classrooms. |
| 2. The teacher is the instructional leader. | 2. Collaborative teams share leadership responsibilities. |
| 3. Students learn from teachers and teachers solve the problems. | 3. Students and teachers learn from each other and solve problems together. |
| 4. Students are purposely grouped by similar ability. | 4. Students are purposely grouped by differing abilities. |
| 5. Instruction is geared toward middle-achieving students. | 5. Instruction is geared to match students at all levels of achievement. |
| 6. Grade-level placement is considered synonymous with curricular content. | 6. Grade-level placement and individual curricular content are independent of each other. |
| 7. Instruction is often passive, competitive, didactic, and/or teacher-directed. | 7. Instruction is active, creative, and collaborative among members of the classroom. |
| 8. Most instructional supports are provided outside the classroom. | 8. Most instructional supports are provided within the classroom. |
| 9. Students who do not "fit in" are excluded from general classes and/or activities. | 9. Activities are designed to include students though participation levels may vary. |
| 10. The classroom teacher assumes ownership for the education of general education students, and special education staff assume ownership for the education of students with special needs. | 10. The classroom teacher, special educators, related service staff, and families assume shared ownership for educating all students. |
| 11. Students are evaluated by common standards. | 11. Students are evaluated by individually appropriate standards. |
| 12. Students' success is achieved by meeting common standards. | 12. The system of education is considered successful when it strives to meet each student's needs. Students' success is achieved when both individual and group goals are met. |

Adapted from "Problem-Solving Methods to Facilitate Inclusive Education" by M. F. Giangreco, C. J. Cloninger, R. E. Dennis, and S. W. Edelman, 1994, in *Creativity and Collaborative Learning: A Practical Guide to Empowering Students and Teachers* edited by J. S. Thousand, R. A. Villa, and A. I. Nevin, Baltimore: Paul H. Brookes Publishing. Used by permission.

integration or mainstreaming, in which students with special needs are educated in physical proximity to their age peers, yet without significant attention paid to the qualitative features of this arrangement. Both integration and mainstreaming begin with the notion that students with disabilities belong in special classes and should be *integrated* as much as possible in general classrooms. Inclusion, on the other hand, assumes that all students *belong* in the general education classroom and should be pulled out only when appropriate services cannot be provided in the inclusive setting. While seemingly a simple difference, these two approaches vary significantly. Several key structural and philosophical differences distinguish the inclusive model and more traditional special education models. Figure 2.1 depicts some of these differences.

Five essential features characterize successful inclusion of students with special needs (Webber, 1997). They are (1) a sense of community and social acceptance, (2) an appreciation of student diversity, (3) attention to curricular needs, (4) effective management and instruction, and (5) personnel support and collaboration. When in place, they make the general education classroom the best possible placement option. Each of these five critical dimensions is discussed in the following sections of this chapter.

**TEACHING TIP**

Teachers can create opportunities for students with disabilities to be full members of their classrooms with such methods as peer support systems.

## Sense of Community and Social Acceptance

In desirable inclusive settings, every student is valued and nurtured. Such settings promote an environment in which all members are seen as equal, all have the opportunity to contribute, and all contributions are respected. Deno, Foegen, Robinson, and Espin (1996) describe the ideal school settings as "caring and nurturant places with a strong sense of community where all children and youth belong, where diversity is valued, and where the needs of all students are addressed" (p. 350).

*If students with special needs are to enjoy a sense of acceptance in general classrooms, teachers must play a critical role.*

**CONSIDER THIS**
How are the attitudes of administrators linked to the attitudes of teachers regarding inclusion? Is this linkage important or not?

Students with special needs are truly included in their classroom communities only when they are appreciated by their teachers and socially accepted by their classmates. An understanding teacher more effectively meets students' instructional and curricular needs, and social acceptance among classmates contributes to students' self-perception of value. Both of these goals are equally critical to creating effective inclusive settings and responsible learning environments. It is imperative that we address the need for acceptance, belonging, and friendship (Schaffner & Buswell, 1996); Lang and Berberich (1995) suggest that inclusive classrooms should be characterized as settings where basic human needs are met. Figure 2.2 highlights critical needs that should be prominent in an inclusive classroom community.

Teachers play a very critical role in creating a positive classroom environment. Three qualities are essential to establishing a successful inclusive setting: teacher attitude, teacher expectations, and teacher competence (Schulz & Carpenter, 1995).

Teachers must have a positive attitude about students with special needs being in their classrooms. If they are not supportive of their inclusion, other students will detect this attitude and be less likely to accept the students. Teachers also have to expect students with special needs to perform at a high level. Students often achieve at a level that is expected of them; if teachers expect less they get less. Finally, teachers need to have the skills necessary to meet the instructional needs of students with special needs. Teaching all students the same way will not be effective for many students with special needs. In addition to these three qualities, teachers also must prepare students to interact with others whose physical characteristics, behaviors, or learning-related needs require special consideration. (Specific techniques for doing this are presented later in the chapter.) Students must acquire 2 areas of competence to function well in inclusive settings (Schulz & Carpenter, 1995):

**CONSIDER THIS**
How likely is it that students with special needs will be successfully included if teachers leave peer acceptance of these students to chance? Why?

1. *Knowledge:*   Accurate information about specific differences that students possess and the effects that these differences will have on their classmates
2. *Peer interactions:*   Development of various informal peer interactions, which lead to peer support and bona fide friendships

Though 100% success cannot be guaranteed in making inclusion work in every classroom, well-prepared students and capable, optimistic teachers can set the stage for a positive educational experience for each person in the class.

*FIGURE **2.2***

The Basic Needs of Children in a Learning Environment

*From All Children Are Special: Creating an Inclusive Classroom (p. 73), by G. Lang and C. Berberich, 1995, York, ME: Stenhouse Publishers. Used by permission.*

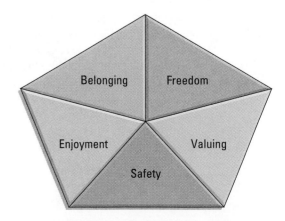

## Appreciation of Student Diversity

To maximize learning, a teacher needs to understand each individual in the classroom as well as possible. In addition to recognizing and responding to each student's educational needs, teachers must be sensitive to the cultural, community, and family values that can have an impact on a student's educational experience. For instance, the nature of teacher-student interactions may be directly affected by certain cultural factors, or the type of home-school contact will be dictated by how the family wants to interact with the school.

Different types of diversity exist within classroom settings. It is important to recognize and celebrate each one. Schwartz and Karge (1996) have identified the following types of differences: racial and ethnic diversity; gender and sexual orientation; religious diversity; physical, learning, and intellectual differences; linguistic differences; and behavior and personality diversity. Although the following chapters focus on areas of exceptionality, and to a lesser extent cultural diversity, teachers should consider the much broader range of individual variance.

Diversity is enriching. All students can flourish in an atmosphere in which diversity is recognized, opportunities exist to better understand its various forms, and differences are appreciated. Clearly, a classroom setting that champions differences provides a welcoming environment for students whose learning, physical, emotional, and social needs vary from those of their classmates. All students benefit from being in an inclusive classroom. Students learn tolerance and the ability to accept differences in each other, as well as having opportunities to benefit from cooperative learning and other alternative instructional strategies.

**CONSIDER THIS**
Describe the ways in which today's school population can be diverse. What kinds of actions can school personnel take to show sensitivity to this diversity?

## Attention to Curricular Needs

Many discussions of inclusion lose track of an important consideration: what the student needs to learn. If the individual curricular needs of a student are not being met, the educational placement must be re-examined. A student's learning and life needs should drive programmatic efforts and decisions (Smith & Hilton, 1994). Good teachers vary their curricula to meet the needs of the students (Walther-Thomas, Korinek, McLaughlin, & Williams, 2000). While some students with disabilities included in general classrooms may be able to deal effectively with the curricula, many need substantial modifications (Van Laarhoven, Coutinho, Van Laarhoven-Myers, & Repp, 1999). Fortunately, curricular needs can usually be addressed within the context of the general educational classroom.

**CONSIDER THIS**
Can you imagine a situation in which a student with special needs cannot be taught in a general education classroom? What would be an appropriate action if this were the case?

Curricular concerns include 2 issues: (1) content that is meaningful to students in a current and future sense, and (2) approaches and materials that work best for them. Dealing with the first issue helps ensure that what students need to learn (i.e., knowledge and skills acquisition) is provided within the inclusive setting. The second issue involves choosing how to teach relevant content. Scruggs and Mastropieri (1994) found that the provision of appropriate curriculum appeared to be meaningfully associated with success in general education classes. Teachers can modify the academic level of the content and focus more on functional objectives, reduce the content to a manageable amount, and change how students are asked to demonstrate mastery of the content.

## Effective Management and Instruction

Another essential component of successful inclusive settings is a set of classroom practices conducive to learning for students with a range of needs. These practices include four elements: successful classroom management, effective instructional techniques, appropriate accommodative practices, and instructional flexibility.

***CROSS-REFERENCE***
For more information on
appropriate classroom
management techniques
for inclusive settings, see
Chapter 13.

**SUCCESSFUL CLASSROOM MANAGEMENT**   Classrooms that encourage learning are characterized by sound organizational and management systems. Classroom management—including physical, procedural, instructional, and behavior management—sets the stage for the smooth delivery of instruction. This topic is so important that an entire chapter is dedicated to a more in-depth discussion.

**EFFECTIVE INSTRUCTIONAL TECHNIQUES**   An impressive body of literature validates the effectiveness of certain instructional practices (Brody & Good, 1986; Rosenshine & Stevens, 1986). Mastropieri and Scruggs (1993) have summarized key elements of effective instructional practice: daily review, specific techniques for presenting new information (see Figure 2.3), guided practice, independent practice, and formative evaluation. These concepts are addressed throughout this book as they apply to children with various special needs. Chapters 14 and 15 specifically address instructional concerns in elementary and secondary classes, respectively.

*FIGURE* **2.3**   How to Present New Information: "SCREAM"

**S** TRUCTURE
Provide overview and review new information as you proceed. Follow your objective carefully and be sure students understand the sequence and purpose of your presentation.

**C** LARITY
Avoid unnecessary digressions. Use clearly stated examples. Provide instances and non-instances of new concepts. Use simple, direct, clear language. Avoid vague references (e.g., *"a thing like this," "and so on," "you know"*).

**R** EDUNDANCY
Students usually need to hear, see, and/or experience new concepts several times before they understand them well. Repetition allows new vocabulary or terminology to become more familiar, reinforces new learning as it proceeds, and allows students to practice and test their understanding by predicting what you will say when you are reinforcing previously mentioned concepts.

**E** NTHUSIASM
Students pay more attention, show more interest, apply themselves better, and learn more when the teacher is enthusiastic. The heightened stimulus arouses their curiosity more, and they will begin to model your attitude toward the subject.

**A** PPROPRIATE PACE
Monitor students' understanding so that you proceed neither too swiftly nor too slowly through the content. If you move too slowly, you will bore them. Move too fast, and you will lose them.

**M** AXIMIZE ENGAGEMENT
Students learn best when they are directly engaged with the teacher, rather than passively listening. Ask lots of questions directly related to the lesson you are teaching. Ask direct questions about your presentation (e.g., *"What did we say was the major difference between monerans and protists?"*); ask application questions to test comprehension (e.g., *"Give me an example of an insulator that you can see in the classroom"*); and prompt reasoning to promote active thinking (e.g., *"We said that some dinosaurs had twenty rows of teeth. What might that tell us about those dinosaurs?"*). When students answer questions, acknowledge the correctness of response or quality of the thought, give corrective feedback on any part of the response that needs correction, and ask the question again later. Use student responses to guide your instructional delivery.

Adapted from *A Practical Guide for Teaching Science to Students with Special Needs in Inclusive Settings* (p. 14), by M. A. Mastropieri and T. E. Scruggs, 1993, Austin, TX: Pro-Ed.

**APPROPRIATE ACCOMMODATIVE PRACTICES** Some students will require special adaptations to the physical environment, the curriculum, the way instruction is provided, or the assignments given to them. Scruggs and Mastropieri (1994) note that instructional supports are a key variable in classrooms where inclusion is successful. Chapters 4–10 provide examples of disability-specific accommodations that might be needed.

The concept of supports within classrooms is a particularly critical one and refashions inclusion as "supported education" (Snell & Drake, 1994). They include accommodations and modifications to enhance learning and acceptance in the general education curriculum. Accommodations consist of changes in the manner in which students are taught, including changes in instruction, assignments and homework, and testing. Modifications, on the other hand, generally refer to changes in policies that may affect students with disabilities. Altering the school curriculum or attendance policy would be an example of a modification. Whenever possible, accommodative supports should be designed so that they benefit not only students with special needs, but also other students in the class as well (Stainback, Stainback, & Wehman, 1997). The idea has merit for three primary reasons. First, it provides support to other students who will find the accommodations helpful. Second, this approach can minimize overt attention to the fact that a certain student needs special adaptations. Third, it enhances the likelihood of treatment acceptance, that is, the likelihood that teachers will see the specific strategy as feasible, desirable, helpful, and fair.

One support that can have a significant impact on the success of inclusion efforts is the use of assistive technology. Ranging from low-tech (e.g., optical devices) to high-tech (e.g., computer-based augmentative communication systems) applications, assistive technology can allow students with specific disabilities to participate more fully in ongoing classroom activities. Moreover, as Woronov (1996) acknowledges, nondisabled students can benefit from assistive technology as well. The nearby Technology Today feature lists special education web sites that can support inclusion.

*CONSIDER THIS*
How can appropriate accommodative practices benefit all students, including those without special needs?

**INSTRUCTIONAL FLEXIBILITY** The ability to respond to unexpected and changing situations to support students with special needs is a key characteristic of responsible inclusive settings. As Schaffner and Buswell (1996) note, classroom teachers need to develop the capabilities that families have acquired to react successfully and spontaneously to challenges that arise on a day-to-day basis. Teachers must be flexible; they must be able to handle behavior problems, provide extra support during instruction, modify assessment techniques, and orchestrate social interactions.

## Personnel Support and Collaboration

Some students with special needs require personnel supports to allow them to benefit from placement in inclusive settings, in addition to the instructional supports noted earlier (accommodative practices and assistive technology). Special education teachers, **paraeducators** (teacher aides), and other related service professionals such as speech and language pathologists, occupational and physical therapists, and audiologists are typically involved in providing support to students with disabilities. They also assist general education teachers in inclusive settings through a variety of models, including collaboration–consultation, peer support systems, teacher assistance teams, and co-teaching. Table 2.1 summarizes these approaches. Equally important is administrative support for inclusion, as reflected by attitudes, policies, and practices at the district and individual school level (Podemski et al., 1995; Scruggs & Mastropieri, 1994).

*PARAEDUCATORS* are teacher aides and other support staff who assist educators.

### Web Resources on Inclusion and Disability

| Inclusion | Disability Resources |
|---|---|
| http://www.ici.coled.umn.edu/ici | http://www.iser.com |
| http://www.asri.edu/cfsp/brochure/abtcons.htm | http://www.ed.gov/offices/OSERS/OSEP/index.html |
| http://www.tash.org | http://www.schwablearning.org |
| http://interwork.sdsu.edu | http://www.mankato.msus.edu/dept/comdis/ |
| http://www.nyise.org/college.htm | kuster2/welcome.html |
| http://www.ldonline.org | http://www.ldonline.org |
| | http://www.downsyndrome.com |
| | http://www.iltech.org |
| | http://www.sau.edu/cwis/internet/wild/disabled/ |
| | disindex.htm |
| | http://www.hsdc.org |
| | http://www.ncld.org |

From *Quick Guide to the Internet for Special Education 2000 Edition* (p. 13) by M. Male and D. Gotthoffer, 2000, Boston: Allyn and Bacon.

---

| TABLE 2.1 | Types of Collaborative Efforts |
|---|---|

| Approach | Nature of Contact with Student | Description |
|---|---|---|
| **COLLABORATION–CONSULTATION** | indirect | General education teacher requests the services of the special education teacher (i.e., consultant) to help generate ideas for addressing an ongoing situation. The approach is interactive. |
| **PEER SUPPORT SYSTEMS** | indirect | Two general education teachers work together to identify effective solutions to classroom situations. The approach emphasizes the balance of the relationship. |
| **TEACHER ASSISTANCE TEAMS** | indirect | Teams provide support to general education teachers. Made up of core members plus the teacher seeking assistance, it emphasizes analyzing the problem situation and developing potential solutions. |
| **CO-TEACHING** | direct | General and special education teachers work together in providing direct service to students. Employing joint planning and teaching, the approach emphasizes the joint responsibilities of instruction. |

From *Cooperative Teaching: Rebuilding the Schoolhouse for All Students* (p. 74) by J. Bauwens and J. J. Hourcade, 1995, Austin, TX: Pro-Ed. Used by permission.

COLLABORATION–CONSULTATION  **Collaboration–consultation** is a model that emphasizes a close working relationship between general and special educators. "Effective collaboration consists of designing and using a sequence of goal-oriented activities that result in improved working relationships between professional colleagues. The responsibility for collaborating can either be the sole responsibility of one individual who seeks to improve a professional relationship, or a joint commitment of two or more people who wish to improve their working relationship" (Cramer, 1998, p. 3).

There are several benefits of collaboration (Mundschenk & Foley, 1997):

1. Collaboration facilitates the ongoing planning, evaluation, and modification necessary to ensure the success of included placements.
2. Collaboration enables general education classrooms to meet the needs of students with and without disabilities in new and exciting ways.
3. Collaboration can provide the personal and professional support of highly skilled colleagues.
4. Collaboration can result in personal and professional growth for all participants.
5. Collaboration helps teachers identify ways to access the skills, knowledge, and expertise of other teachers (p. 58).

Through collaborating with each other, general education and special education teachers can bring more ideas and experiences to help students achieve success. Through consultation, teachers can assist each other in utilizing skills that also result in positive outcomes for students.

PEER SUPPORT SYSTEMS  **Peer support systems** are one of the best means of providing support to students with disabilities in general education classrooms because students rely on the natural support of other students. Students can supply social supports or instructional supports. These student supports "fit well with the current movement to individualize instruction and to support and meet the needs of all students" (Van Laarhoven et al., 1999, p. 172). Peer support for instruction can be provided in several different ways such as partner learning, peer tutoring, and cooperative learning (Walther-Thomas et al., 2000). Table 2.2 summarizes each of these peer support models. When implementing any peer support system, school personnel must always remember that, while these approaches may work extremely well in some situations, the peers providing the support are also students. As such, they may provide a great deal of help, but providing the necessary support to enable students to be successful remains a professional responsibility.

TEACHER ASSISTANCE TEAMS  Another model to provide support to students in general education classrooms is the use of **teacher assistance teams.** Teacher assistance teams can be defined as "school-based, problem-solving teams designed to enable all teachers to meet the needs of their students demonstrating difficulties" (Walther-Thomas et al., 2000, p. 140). These teams are comprised of teachers and other instructional support personnel, either elected or voluntary; they provide a forum where problems are raised and discussed, and solutions are developed. The use of teacher assistance teams enables educators to bring a diverse set of skills and experience to bear on specific problems.

While the specific composition of teacher assistance teams should not be prescribed, members of these teams should have experience and knowledge that would be helpful in solving specific student problems. Members of the team should also not

*COLLABORATION–CONSULTATION* is a support model where special education professionals work with general education teachers in a consulting role.

*TEACHING TIP*
Teachers who use the collaboration–consultation model should spend time together socially in order to better understand each other.

*PEER SUPPORT SYSTEM* is a support model where students with disabilities in the general education classroom are supplied with social or instructional support by their nondisabled peers.

*TEACHING TIP*
When selecting students to be part of a peer support system, teachers must consider the student's maturity level as well as his or her ability level.

*TEACHER-ASSISTANCE TEAM* is a support model comprised of teachers and instructional support personnel where solutions are developed for specific problems of students demonstrating difficulties.

| **TABLE 2.2** | **Description of Various Peer Support Systems** |
|---|---|

**PARTNER LEARNING**

- Students work in pairs to practice skills
- Examples include peer modeling and paired reading
- Behaviors include completing various academic tasks, following routines, or engaging in social activities

**PEER TUTORING**

- More structured and ongoing than partner learning
- Offers an alternative to one-on-one instruction
- Enhances social skills
- Provides opportunities for correction and feedback
- Can be beneficial for both tutors and tutees
- Best results when tutoring sessions are regularly scheduled

**COOPERATIVE LEARNING**

- Utilizes peer discussion groups and projects
- Promotes improved academic achievement and classroom climate
- Enhances interactions among diverse students
- Facilitates social skill development
- More structured cooperative activities are recommended for less experienced learners
- Requires carefully planned and monitored learning experiences

From *Collaboration for Inclusive Education* (p. 11) by C. Walther-Thomas, L. Korinek, V. L. McLaughlin, & B. T. Williams, 2000, Boston: Allyn and Bacon. Used by permission.

be over committed and be willing to serve (McCullough, 1992). Forcing teachers to serve on assistance teams leads to problems. Since administrative support is important for the success of teams, it is recommended that administrators either participate as team members or designate a team member to represent the administration.

**CO-TEACHING** is a model where a special education teacher and a general classroom teacher share teaching responsibilities in one classroom.

**TEACHING TIP**
Teachers who use the co-teaching model should determine which team members have expertise in specific areas and take advantage of those skills.

**CO-TEACHING**    A further model to provide support for students in general education classrooms is **co-teaching.** Co-teaching is an arrangement of two or more teachers or other school staff who collectively assume the responsibilities for the same group of students on a regular basis (Thousand & Villa, 1990). This model "provides students with an educational environment that lends itself to an increased potential for individualized instruction to meet the needs of all students" (Van Laarhoven, 1999, p. 170). Co-teaching usually occurs at set times, such as during second period every day, or certain days of each week. When students with disabilities are included in general education classrooms, the special education teacher, who becomes a co-teacher, is usually present (Friend & Bursuck, 1999). Co-teachers perform many tasks jointly, including planning and teaching, developing instructional accommodations, monitoring and evaluating students, and communicating student progress (Walther-Thomas et al., 2000).

*P*araeducators can provide direct services to some students with special needs in general classrooms.

Co-teaching can take the form of interactive teaching, station teaching, parallel teaching, and alternative teaching (Walther-Thomas et al., 2000). Figure 2.4 summarizes the advantages and disadvantages of these variations.

One of the obvious difficulties in implementing the co-teaching model is insuring the compatibility of the individuals working together. Co-teaching requires individuals who are willing to give up some control and accept positive, constructive criticism from colleagues. Common characteristics of successful co-teachers include (Walther-Thomas et al., 2000):

- professional competence
- personal confidence
- respect of colleagues
- professional enthusiasm
- respect for colleagues' skills and contributions
- good communication and problem-solving skills
- personal interest in professional growth
- flexibility and openness to new ideas
- effective organizational skills
- previous experience teaming with others
- willingness to invest extra time in the process as needed
- commitment to planning weekly with partner
- voluntary participation in co-teaching

Co-teaching works extremely well when the co-teachers are committed to the success of students and find a common ground for working together. Since it requires the development of a unique relationship, it will not work in all situations.

The use of paraeducators to provide direct support to students with significant learning problems is occurring more commonly (Pickett & Gerlach, 1997). If their knowledge of working with students with disabilities is minimal, paraeducators must be trained and supervised carefully if they are to provide critical assistance to

FIGURE *2.4*

Variations of Co-Teaching: Advantages and Disadvantages

| Variation | Advantages | Disadvantages |
|---|---|---|
| **Interactive Teaching**<br><br>(Whole group)<br>Partners alternate roles presenting new concepts, reviewing, demonstrating, role playing, and monitoring. | ▲ Provides systematic observation/data collection<br>▲ Promotes role/content sharing<br>▲ Facilitates individual assistance<br>▲ Models appropriate academic, social, and help-seeking behaviors<br>▲ Teaches question asking<br>▲ Provides clarification (e.g., concepts, rules, vocabulary) | ▲ May be job sharing, not learning enriching<br>▲ Requires considerable planning<br>▲ Requires modeling and role-playing skills<br>▲ Becomes easy to "typecast" specialist with this role |
| **Station Teaching**<br><br>(Small group)<br>Students in groups of three or more rotate to various teacher-led and independent work stations where new instruction, review, and/or practice is provided. Students may work at all stations during the rotation. | ▲ Provides active learning format<br>▲ Increases small-group attention<br>▲ Encourages cooperation and independence<br>▲ Allows strategic grouping<br>▲ Increases response rate | ▲ Requires considerable planning and preparation<br>▲ Increases noise level<br>▲ Requires group and independent work skills<br>▲ Is difficult to monitor |
| **Parallel Teaching**<br><br>(Small group)<br>Students are divided into mixed-ability groups, then each partner teaches a group. The same material is presented in each group. | ▲ Provides effective review format<br>▲ Encourages student responses<br>▲ Reduces pupil–teacher ratio for group instruction/review | ▲ Not easy to achieve equal depth of content coverage<br>▲ May be difficult to coordinate<br>▲ Requires monitoring of partner pacing<br>▲ Increases noise level<br>▲ Encourages some teacher–student competition |
| **Alternative Teaching**<br><br>(Big group; small group)<br>One partner teaches an enrichment lesson or reteaches a concept for the benefit of a small group, while the other partner teaches and/or monitors the remaining members of the class. | ▲ Facilitates enrichment opportunities<br>▲ Offers absent students "catch up" time<br>▲ Keeps individuals and class on pace<br>▲ Offers time to develop missing skills | ▲ May be easy to select the same low-achieving students for help<br>▲ Creates segregated learning environments<br>▲ Is difficult to coordinate<br>▲ May single out students |

From *Collaboration for Inclusive Education* (p. 190) by C. Walther-Thomas, L. Korinek, V. L. McLaughlin, and B. T. Williams, 2000, Boston: Allyn and Bacon. Used by permission.

students in inclusive classrooms. The practice could have great potential as long as proper safeguards ensure that paraeducators implement support services effectively.

Establishing a circle of friends for students can assist the development of a peer support network. This is particularly important for students who are different and who are new to a classroom situation. As Pearpoint, Forest, and O'Brien (1996) assert:

> In the absence of a natural circle of friends, educators can facilitate a circle process, which can be used to enlist the involvement and commitment of peers around an individual student. For a student who is not well connected or does not have an extensive network of friends, a circle of friends process can be useful. (p. 74)

The use of a circle of friends is further discussed in Chapter 7.

The five critical dimensions we have discussed are essential to making inclusive settings effective. Appropriate programming for students with disabilities should always be based on an "individual student's needs as determined by an interdisciplinary team and represented by the student's IEP" (Smith & Hilton, 1994, p. 8). Just as important, however, is the need to evaluate those instructional settings on the basis of the five critical dimensions.

## CREATING AND MAINTAINING INCLUSIVE CLASSROOMS

This section presents practical ways to establish responsible inclusive classrooms and to ensure that they continue to provide appropriate educational programs to students. Specific ideas for preparing staff and students who do not have special needs as well as mechanisms for developing collaborative relationships are discussed.

### Preparing Staff for Inclusion

A comprehensive program for preparing a school setting for inclusion must consider the involvement of all staff members. As Roach (1995) points out, "Successful planning models ensure that *all* teachers, paraprofessionals, and related service personnel are included in the process" (p. 298). Although many preservice training programs acquaint teachers-in-training with working with students with diverse needs, the nature of this preparation varies greatly. Moreover, many teachers who are already in the field have not been exposed to information important for implementing good inclusive practices. This fact is supported by the data discussed earlier in this chapter.

The primary goals of all preservice and in-service training of general education teachers include creating positive attitudes about working with students with diverse needs and allaying apprehensions and concerns teachers might have about their competence to address the needs of these students. These goals are achieved by 3 major training-related activities: (1) opportunities to see good examples of inclusion, (2) provision of information about inclusion, student diversity, and inclusion-related practices, together with the development of skills that a teacher needs to feel comfortable and competent when working with students with special needs, and (3) time to plan with team members.

**EXPOSURE TO GOOD INCLUSIVE CLASSROOMS**   Nothing is more encouraging and motivating than to see wonderful examples of what one wants to achieve. It is essential that teachers have opportunities to visit schools or classrooms that

**CONSIDER THIS**
How could the use of paraprofessionals be a detriment to the successful inclusion of students with special needs in a general education classroom?

**CONSIDER THIS**
Why is preparing school staff for inclusion important? How could a prepared staff make a difference in the success of inclusion?

**CONSIDER THIS**
If examples of good inclusion classrooms are unavailable in a school district, how can teachers in that district be exposed to such examples?

demonstrate the 5 critical dimensions of inclusion discussed earlier in this chapter. It is one thing to talk about these practices, and yet another thing to see them being implemented. A number of projects throughout the country have developed model inclusion classrooms. These settings can serve as demonstration sites that teachers can observe and imitate.

**INFORMATION AND SKILLS NEEDED**    Teachers regularly express a desire to know more about the inclusion process, the needs of students with learning-related challenges, and ways to address these needs. Teachers must find practical ways of matching individual needs with sound instructional practices. For teachers to become comfortable in making and implementing such decisions, they must have sufficient training in management techniques, instructional strategies, and curriculum adaptation tactics.

Teachers can also benefit from instruction in topics such as social skills, self-determination, learning strategies, and study skills. From time to time, updates and new ideas in these important areas can be offered to teaching staff to spark strategies and deepen knowledge. In turn, teachers can enhance the social acceptance of students with special needs by instructing their classes in social skills, such as how to make and keep friends.

Other skills are also needed in most inclusive arrangements. First and foremost are skills in collaboration. General education teachers will need to work collaboratively with other professionals within the school setting, especially special education staff, and with parents or other individuals who are responsible for students at home.

Collaboration can be viewed as "an ongoing style of professional interaction in which people voluntarily engage in shared program planning, implementation, evaluation, and overall program accountability" (Bauwens & Hourcade, 1995, pp. 6–7). Each person involved needs skills in collaborating with others, whether professional or home-school collaboration is the focus. Inclusive settings require that professionals working both within the school and with the family develop relationships that facilitate communication and cooperation. For these relationships to be productive, new skills may need to be learned by all parties.

**PLANNING TIME**    Planning is essential when teams are used to provide instruction and support to students with disabilities in general education classrooms. This is the case whether the primary model used is teacher assistance teams, collaboration-consultation, or co-teaching.

**CONSIDER THIS**

How can administrators make time available for teams of teachers to plan? Why is it important for administrators to support this planning effort?

Making planning time available for school staff requires the support of school administrators. If school administrators support inclusion, they generally find a way to arrange for planning opportunities for professionals and paraprofessionals. On the other hand, if they are not supportive of inclusion or do not see the need for planning time, then they are less likely to make the time available.

Making time for teachers and other staff members to plan for specific students can be accomplished in several ways. Arranging for team members to have the same planning periods, having split schedules for teachers, utilizing roving aides to cover classes, and providing financial incentives are only a few methods for finding planning time. Regardless of how it is accomplished, the fact remains that without time to plan, many attempts to provide supports for students with disabilities in general education classes will be unsuccessful.

## Preparing Students for Inclusion

Like those for staff, the goals for preparing students for inclusion focus on developing positive attitudes and allaying concerns. Ultimately, we want students to understand the needs of others who are different and to welcome them into the classroom community as valued members. Many nondisabled students have not been involved with students with special needs. As a result, the movement to inclusive schools often results in their being unprepared for dealing with such diverse classrooms. While nondisabled students are generally supportive of inclusion, they need to be prepared for the changes that accompany this educational model. Awareness programs, class discussions, simulations, guest speakers, and social interactions can pave the way for inclusion.

**AWARENESS PROGRAMS** Over the years, an assortment of formal programs has emerged to help change the attitudes of nondisabled students toward their classmates who have special needs. Tovey (1995) describes three programs that promote this type of awareness: Friends Who Care, New Friends, and Kids on the Block. These programs are highlighted in Table 2.3.

**DISCUSSIONS** In-class discussion is a good way to address topics related to students with special needs. Topics for discussion can be found in a variety of sources, including books and films about disabilities or famous people with special needs who have been successful in a variety of fields. Guest speakers can also be effective. Schulz and Carpenter (1995) warn, however, that "caution must be taken to ensure that the discussions are based on accurate information, avoiding the possibility that uninformed biases would form the core of the exchanges" (p. 400).

*TEACHING TIP*
When attempting to prepare students for the inclusion of students with special needs, teachers should use a variety of techniques and not rely on only one method.

| TABLE 2.3 | **Disability Awareness Programs** |
|---|---|
| **Program** | **Description** |
| **FRIENDS WHO CARE** (National Easter Seals Society) | ■ Elementary level curriculum.<br>■ Information about major types of disabilities.<br>■ Hands-on activities.<br>■ Recommends inviting guest speakers.<br>■ Package contains teacher's guide, videotape, worksheet activities, guest speaker guidelines, posters, etiquette bookmarks, and attitude survey. |
| **NEW FRIENDS** (Chapel Hill Training Outreach Project) | ■ Goal—to promote awareness and understanding of disabilities.<br>■ Parents and children make dolls out of cloth patterns—the dolls are used for instructional purposes. |
| **KIDS ON THE BLOCK** | ■ Lifesize puppets include disabled and nondisabled.<br>■ Skits are scripted—puppeteers follow the scripts.<br>■ Presents various situations in which certain information is discussed.<br>■ Audience is given an opportunity to ask the puppets questions after the skit is over.<br>■ Uses volunteers as puppeteers. |

From "Awareness Programs Help Change Students' Attitudes toward Their Disabled Peers" by R. Tovey, 1995, *Harvard Educational Letter, 11*(6), pp. 7–8. Used by permission.

# INCLUSION STRATEGIES

## Books That Focus on Disabilities

Arnold Katrin. *Anna Joins In,* Abingdon Press, 1982
    The story of Anna, who in spite of sickness was a happy little girl. Shows how one can live with a chronic illness. Children with cystic fibrosis can identify with Anna's experiences. Also helps healthy children gain more understanding of the lives of children with disabilities.

Begna, Barbara; Jensen, Shirlee. *I Can't Always Hear You,* Raintree Publishers, 1980
    The story of Kim, who is hearing impaired. Tells about her first days at her new school and how she overcomes being different by discovering that everyone is unique in one way or another.

Benham, Helen. *Scholastic Feeling Free: Feeling Free,* Scholastic Magazines, 1978
    *Feeling Free* helps find answers to questions like: What is Braille? What is it like to be deaf? in a wheelchair? etc.

Berry, Joy Wilt. *What to Do When Your Mom or Dad Says . . . Get Good Grades!!!* Living Skills Press, 1981
    This book helps equip students with skills to get the most out of tests.

Berry, Joy. *Every Kid's Guide to Being Special,* Children's Press, 1987
    This book teaches children that being different and unique is O.K., and this is what makes everyone a special person.

Berry, Joy. *Good Answers to Tough Questions About Physical Disabilities,* Children's Press, 1990
    This book helps children learn what a disability is, how people with physical disabilities function, how people feel about people with disabilities, etc.

Berry, Joy. *Overcoming Prejudice and Discrimination,* Children's Press, 1987
    Children are taught what opinions, prejudice, and discrimination are.

Blos, Joan W. *Old Henry,* William Morrow, 1987
    The author writes wisely and with humor about different kinds of people learning to get along.

Brighton, Catherine. *My Hands, My World,* Macmillan, 1984
    This book tells the story of Maria, who is blind. It takes you through a quiet day with the young blind girl. The whole feeling is dreamlike, yet sensitive and strong, taking readers into a very special world of feeling.

Cairo, Shelley. *Our Brother Has Down's Syndrome,* Annick Press, 1988
    This book is about a boy named Jai who has Down syndrome. It talks about his special needs and his similarities to "normal" kids.

Dekay, James T. *Left-Handed Kids: Why Are They So Different?* M. Evans, 1989
    A book about left-handedness that's sure to bring a smile to lefties everywhere.

Edwards, Jean and Dawson. *My Friend David,* David Communications, 1983
    This book is divided into two parts. The first part tells the story of a friendship between two people, one of whom has Down syndrome. The second part of the book is a resource guide about Down syndrome for parents and professionals.

Emmert, Michelle. *I'm the Big Sister Now,* Whitman, 1989
    Amy Emmert, the older sister of the author, was born severely disabled with cerebral palsy. In this book, Michelle tells her sister Amy's story.

Fisher, Gary; Cummings, Rhoda. *The Survival Guide for Kids with L.D.,* Free Spirit Publishing, 1990
    For kids who have learning differences. In this book you will find 10 ways to get along better in school, tips for making and keeping friends, 8 ways to get along better at home, what happens when you grow up, how YOU can be a winner, and much more.

Frandsen, Karen. *Michael's New Haircut,* Children's Press, 1986
    The real experiences of the author's two children and her students are the basis of this book.

Friedberg, Joan; Mullins, June; Suklennik, Adelaide. *Accept Me as I Am,* R. R. Bowker, 1985
    A resourceful guide to meet the needs of special groups, ranging from people with disabilities and elderly to the gifted. Materials are extremely helpful in reaching out to extraordinary people.

Gailbraith, Judy. *The Gifted Kids Survival Guide: For Ages 10 and Under,* Free Spirit Publishing, 1984
    This book is to help answer the questions of gifted children. It will help them understand why they think and learn the way they do.

▼

Giff, Patricia Reilly. *Watch Out, Ronald Morgan!,* Viking Penguin, 1985
Ronald Morgan gets new glasses, but continues to fumble. Then he realizes he needs to watch out for himself and straightens out.

Golant, Mitch; Drane, Bob. *It's O.K. to Be Different,* RGA Publishing Group, 1988
The purpose of this book is to help children deal with characteristics that make them different or special, and then to accept their own differences.

Hasler, Eveline. *Martin Is Our Friend,* Abington, 1981
Martin realizes that he is different from other children, as they often make fun of him. However, he has a friend, Aurora, a reddish brown horse he loves to ride. When Aurora breaks out of the corral and Martin rescues her, the other children begin to respect and understand him.

Hausherr, Rosemarie. *Children and the AIDS Virus,* Clarion Books, 1989
This book will help young readers deal with their fear of AIDS. It will also inspire children to treat those who have AIDS with compassion and concern.

Hazen, Barbara Shock. *Why Are People Different?* Western Publishing, 1985
This book teaches children about the feelings of prejudice.

Janover, Caroline. *Josh, A Boy with Dyslexia,* Waterfront Books, 1988
*Josh* is a gripping story for children and expresses beautifully what self-esteem can mean to a child with dyslexia. Includes information on the characteristics of dyslexia and a list of organizations that deal with learning disabilities.

Kamien, Janet. *What If You Couldn't . . . ?* Charles Scribner's Sons, 1979
A book about disabilities that asks the reader to imagine that he or she is the person with the disability, and then introduces experiments that help to understand how it feels to have that disability. Also explained is how to make use of various supports and aids to help the person with disabilities.

Konczal, Dee; Pesetski, Loretta. *We All Come in Different Packages,* The Learning Works, 1983
This book contains individual and group activities to help children recognize the similarities and differences between themselves and people who are blind, communicatively disabled, crippled, deaf, learning disabled, or retarded.

Kuklin, Susan. *Thinking Big,* Lothrop, Lee & Shepard, 1986
*Thinking Big* tells it like it really is for both the young dwarf and the parents of a dwarf. The book makes it clear that being small is no great disaster and that little people of all ages can and do enjoy normal lives.

Langoulant, Allan. *Everybody's Different,* Lothian Publishing, 1990
*Everybody's Different* will entertain, educate, and amuse. Through wonderful colors and rich details, we understand how different we all are: different faces, hairstyles, dress, lifestyles, languages, and pastimes.

Lasker, Joe. *He's My Brother,* Whitman, 1980.
A young boy describes the experiences of his slow learning brother at school and at home.

Lasker, Joe. *Nick Joins In,* Whitman, 1980
Shows that disabled children can be educated alongside nondisabled children.

Lawrence, Jim. *The Ugly Duckling,* Modern Publishing, 1987
Reveals that beauty, or acceptable looks, is in the eyes of the beholder.

Levi, Dorothy Hoffman. *A Very Special Friend,* Kendall Green, 1989
In search of a friend her own age, 6-year-old Frannie meets Laura, who is deaf, and learns sign language from her.

Litchfield, Ada B. *A Button in Her Ear,* Whitman, 1976
The story of Angela, whose parents discover her hearing problem when her responses don't make sense. Her parents and teachers reinforce Angela's healthy attitude toward using a hearing aid. Discussion on communication and the process of determining hearing loss.

Lobato, Debra J. *Brothers, Sisters, and Special Needs,* Brookes, 1990
Stories of siblings of children with disabilities and how they cope.

McConnell, Nancy P. *Different and Alike,* Current, 1982
This book explores differences such as being deaf, blind, mentally or physically disabled, and the ways in which we are all alike or different.

McDonnell, Janet; Ziegler, Sandra. *What's So Special About Me? I'm One of a Kind,* Children's Press, 1988
A girl nicknamed Anna Banana rejoices in all the ways she is special.

▼

Meyer, Donald J.; Vadasy, Patricia F.; Fewell, Rebecca R. *Living with a Brother or Sister with Special Needs,* University of Washington Press, 1985
This book gives siblings simple, clear explanations about the causes and nature of disabilities and support for their feelings about their sibling with special needs.

Nystrom, Carolyn. *The Trouble with Josh,* Lion Publishing, 1989
This book describes the life of a young boy who is hyperactive and has difficulty learning. His story helps us to understand the needs of children like Josh, and their families.

Perska, Robert. *Circles of Friends,* Abingdon Press, 1988
A warm, sensitive collection offering true stories and issues to ponder, concerning friendships between people with disabilities and people without disabilities. Shows how friendships cut across age groups, generations, and races.

Peterson, Jeanne Whitehouse. *I Have a Sister, My Sister Is Deaf,* Harper & Row, 1977
An excellent vehicle for explaining the world of the totally deaf to children ages 4 to 8. Discusses the life of a very special sister who likes to do things that others like to do, such as jumping, climbing, and playing the piano.

Picotti; Hoyt; Varley; La Monica. *My Full Life,* Epilepsy Assoc. of Western Washington, 1986
The purpose of this book is to encourage your child to participate in self-expression through the completion of this book.

Pirner, Connie White. *Even Little Kids Get Diabetes,* Whitman, 1991
A young girl who has had diabetes since she was 2 years old describes her adjustments to the disease.

Powell, Thoma H.; Ogle, Peggy Ahrenhold. *Brothers and Sisters—A Special Part of Exceptional Families,* Brookes, 1985
A one-of-a-kind book offering advice to parents and professionals on techniques and services that can help non-handicapped siblings better understand their unique feelings and circumstances.

Quinn, Patricia O., M.D.; Stern, Judith M. *Putting on the Brakes,* Random House, 1991
Young people's guide to understanding attention deficit/hyperactivity disorder (ADHD).

Quinsey, Mary Beth. *Why Does That Man Have Such a Big Nose?* Parenting Press, 1986
This book shows a positive attitude toward differences in people and how they look. Different does not have to mean bad, wrong, or scary, but can be a recognition of everyone's uniqueness.

Rabe, Tish Sommers. *Elmo Gets Homesick,* Sesame Street/Golden Press, 1990
This book helps children to understand and overcome the anxiety of being homesick.

Rogers, Fred. *If We're All the Same,* Random House, 1987
This book helps children appreciate themselves for who they are and teaches them to enjoy the fact that they are both different and unique.

Rosenberg, Maxine B. *Living in Two Worlds,* Lothrop, Lee & Shepard Books, 1986
Just under 2 percent of all children born in the U.S. are of mixed racial and ethnic heritage. Here, as the children themselves speak about who they are and how they feel about themselves, it becomes clear that the special challenges they experience go hand in hand with the special benefits of belonging to more that one culture.

Rosenberg, Maxine B. *Making a New Home in America,* Lothrop, Lee & Shepard Books, 1986
This book explores the feelings of four young newcomers to the United States.

Rosenberg, Maxine. *My Friend Leslie,* Lothrop, Lee & Shepard Books, 1983
This book presents a multi-handicapped kindergarten child, who is well accepted by her classmates, in various settings within the school.

Sanford, Doris. *Don't Look at Me,* Multnomah Press, 1986
This book is to help children who don't feel good enough about themselves to take on a new perspective and to help them like themselves.

Sanford, Doris. *I Can Say No,* Multnomah Press, 1987
A breakdown in communication between family members leads to the discovery that David's older brother is using drugs. Lists guidelines for parents to help a child stay off drugs.

From *Books That Focus on Disabilities* (pp. 9–13), by Pacific Training Associates, 1992, Tacoma, WA: Author. Used by permission.

Imaginative literature offers many examples of characters with special needs. A great source of information is children's literature. A number of books have been written about disabilities or conditions that might directly relate to students who are about to be included in a general education class. The preceding Inclusion Strategies feature (pp. 52–54) lists several titles.

For secondary level students, films can stimulate discussion about people with special needs. A listing of such films can be found in Table 2.4. However, a note of caution is warranted, as this table includes some films containing characterizations that are "disablist" (an updated term for "handicapist"). This means making generalizations about individuals with disabilities that relate to their inability to do things that nondisabled persons can do.

Salend (1994) recommends the development of lessons about successful individuals with disabilities, focusing on their achievements and the ways they were able to deal with the challenges their disabilities have presented. Teachers can generally find successful individuals with disabilities in their own communities. These persons, plus famous people with disabilities, such as Tom Cruise (learning disabilities) and Christopher Reeve (physical disabilities), can be the focus of lessons that can help nondisabled students understand the capabilities of individuals with disabilities.

Guest speakers with disabilities provide positive role models for students with disabilities, give all students exposure to individuals who are different in some way, and generate meaningful class discussion. However, the choice of guest speakers must match the intended purposes of the teacher. For example, securing a guest speaker who is in a wheelchair and who has a negative attitude about his or her condition may not serve a positive purpose for the class. Advance planning and communication ensures

*Teachers often need to work together to solve some of the problems created by inclusion.*

| TABLE 2.4 | | Motion Pictures with Characters Who Are Disabled or Gifted | |
|---|---|---|---|
| **Title** | **Identifier** | **Title** | **Identifier** |
| **KEY** | | King of Hearts | BD |
| Behavior Disorder | BD | La Strada | MR |
| Gifted | G | Last Picture Show, The | MR |
| Hearing Impairment | HI | Little Man Tate | G |
| Learning Disability | LD | Lorenzo's Oil | PHI |
| Mental Retardation | MR | Man Without a Face, The | PHI |
| Physical or Health Impairment | PHI | MASH | VI, PHI (H) |
| Traumatic Brain Injury | TBI | Miracle Worker, The | VI, PHI (H) |
| Visual Impairment | VI | Moby Dick | PHI |
| | | My Left Foot | PHI |
| Awakenings | BD | Of Mice and Men | MR |
| Bedlam | MR | One Flew Over the Cuckoo's Nest | BD |
| Being There | MR | Ordinary People | BD |
| Benny and Joon | BD | Other Side of the Mountain, The | PHI |
| Best Boy | MR | Patch of Blue, A | VI |
| Bill | MR | Philadelphia | PHI |
| Blackboard Jungle | At Risk | Places in the Heart | VI |
| Born on the Fourth of July | PHI | Rain Man | Autism |
| Butterflies Are Free | VI | Regarding Henry | TBI |
| Camille Claudel | BD | Rudy | LD |
| Charley | MR | Scent of a Woman | VI |
| Children of a Lesser God | PHI (H) | See No Evil, Hear No Evil | VI |
| Coming Home | PHI | Sneakers | VI |
| Deliverance | MR | Stand and Deliver | At Risk |
| Dr. Strangelove | PHI | Sting, The | PHI |
| Dream Team | BD | Sybil | BD |
| Edward Scissorhands | PHI | Tim | MR |
| Elephant Man, The | PHI | Tin Man | PHI (H) |
| Fisher King, The | BD | To Kill a Mockingbird | MR |
| Forrest Gump | MR | To Sir with Love | At Risk |
| Gaby: A True Story | PHI (P) | Wait Until Dark | VI |
| Hand That Rocks the Cradle, The | MR | Whatever Happened to Baby Jane? | PHI |
| Heart Is a Lonely Hunter, The | PHI (H) | What's Eating Gilbert Grape? | PHI |
| I Never Promised You a Rose Garden | BD | Young Frankenstein | PHI |
| If You Could See What I Hear | VI | Zelly and Me | BD |

that maximum benefit is achieved from this type of experience and avoids inappropriate presentations. Guest speakers who are comfortable and effective when talking with students usually can be identified through local agencies and organizations.

**SIMULATIONS**   Simulating a specific condition, to give students the opportunity to feel what it might be like to have the condition, is a common practice. For example, visual impairment is often simulated by blindfolding sighted students and having them perform activities that they typically use their vision to perform. In another simulation, students can use a wheelchair for a period of time to experience this type of mobility.

Although simulations can be effective in engendering positive attitudes toward individuals with special needs, this technique should be used with caution. Bittner (cited in Tovey, 1995) warns that "it is impossible to pretend to have a disability. An able-bodied kid sitting in a wheelchair knows he can get up and walk away" (p. 8). Some simulation activities seem to be amusing, rather than meaningful, to students. Therefore, teachers must use caution when simulations are conducted to ensure that they serve their intended purpose.

**CONSIDER THIS**
How could having a guest speaker with a disability backfire on a teacher's effort to prepare the class for the inclusion of students with special needs?

## Maintaining Effective Inclusive Classrooms

Setting up a responsible inclusive classroom does not guarantee that it will remain effective over time. Constant vigilance concerning the critical dimensions of inclusive settings and ongoing reevaluation of standard operating procedures can ensure continued success. Blenk (1995) describes an effective process for ongoing evaluation:

**CONSIDER THIS**
Why is ongoing monitoring of the effectiveness of an inclusion program necessary? Why not evaluate effectiveness only every 5 years?

> On a daily basis, teaching colleagues should be observing inclusive procedures and educational techniques. These observations need to be shared among the teacher group to decide whether the practice achieved its intended outcomes, and if not, what changes could occur. Individual staff conferences and meetings, even if they are only two minutes long, need to happen on an ongoing basis to maintain communication in the teaching staff and to share experiences and impressions, sometimes *at that moment!* (p. 71)

A related method of dealing with ongoing issues is the use of problem-solving sessions (Roach, 1995). With this strategy, teachers meet and work together to find ways to handle specific inclusion-related situations that have become problematic. In addition to identifying resources that might be helpful, the teachers also generate new strategies to try out.

Maintaining flexibility contributes to long-term success; rigid procedures cannot adequately address the unpredictable situations that arise as challenges to management and instruction. The nearby Personal Spotlight highlights one student's successful inclusion in a general education setting. Unforeseen problems will inevitably surface as a result of including students with special needs in general education classrooms. The more pliant a school can be in dealing with new challenges, the more likely it is that responsible inclusion will continue.

## *personal* SPOTLIGHT

### Mother

Connie Fails had two children before she and her husband, Leslie, decided to adopt Kate from Thailand. Kate was 5-1/2 years old when they got her. They knew when they adopted her that she did not have any arms. Although Kate's disability is visually obvious and can be very restrictive, she has made the adjustment to a new culture and to a world of nondisabled people very successfully. Kate is currently in the third grade. She has been included in general classrooms since being enrolled in public school in kindergarten.

**CONNIE FAILS**
*Little Rock, Arkansas*

There have been some "ups and downs," Connie says, but the overall experience has been very positive. Connie has made a point to treat Kate as she treats her other children. She says: "We do not make any adaptations for Kate that are not necessary. Rather, we let her try to achieve success, in whatever she does, without any special supports."

Connie says that Kate came to her family with a great deal of self-esteem and a lack of self-consciousness. And, although she is very aware of her disability, she does just about anything she wants to do. For the past three years, she has played in a summer softball league. She holds the bat with her neck and actually hits the ball fairly often. She may not hit it hard, Connie says, but "Kate feels as good about a little hit as the other girls feel about a big hit."

While many of Kate's public school experiences have been successful, there have been some negative things. It was almost two years after Kate began going to a particular school that Connie learned that Kate could not get a drink out of the water fountain. Also, the outside door to the school was so heavy that Kate could not open it by herself. A door was installed after her first year at the school that she can open without any difficulty. Still, Connie feels that these small accommodations seemed to take longer than they should have.

Overall, Connie is very positive about Kate's experiences in schools. An important factor in Kate's success was the selection of a particular school. She believes that parents of students with disabilities must consider which school will meet their child's needs best. These criteria include variables such as the physical accessibility of the school, as well as the attitudes of the school staff.

## PLANNING FOR SUCCESSFUL INCLUSION ONE STUDENT AT A TIME

Regardless of how much time and effort have been expended to create an environment that is conducive for students with disabilities to achieve success in general education classrooms, the fact remains that planning must be accomplished for students on an individual basis. Students with disabilities cannot simply be placed in a school, regardless of the supports provided or teaching methods used and be expected to succeed. School personnel must develop a planning model that provides opportunities for school staff to develop supportive, individualized inclusive environments for each student.

Van Laarhoven et al. (1999) provide a planning model for determining the support needed for each student prior to implementing inclusion. The model, depicted in Figure 2.5, includes both a list of possible environments for a student and steps to ensure an inclusive environment that is geared to each student. When determining the least restrictive environment for an individual student during the IEP process,

*FIGURE* **2.5**

Steps in the Development of a Plan to Support Successful Inclusion of Students with Disabilities

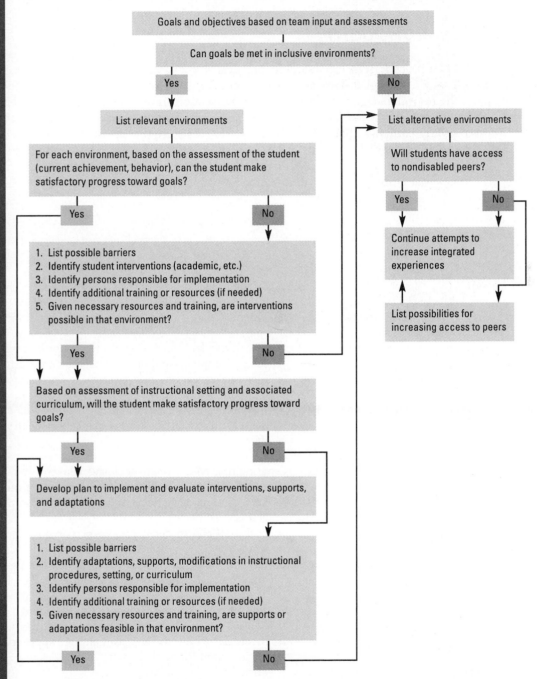

From "Assessment and Adaptation of the Student, Instructional Setting, and Curriculum to Support Successful Integration" by T. Van Laarhoven, M. Coutinho, T. Van Laarhoven-Myers, and A. C. Repp (p. 163), in *Inclusion: The Integration of Students with Disabilities,* edited by M. J. Coutinho and A. C. Repp, 1999, Belmont, CA: Wadsworth Publishing. Used by permission.

school personnel should be sure that each student's unique characteristics have been considered in the planning process.

## FINAL THOUGHT

The concept of inclusion and its practical applications keeps evolving as just one of the changing dynamics in the schools today. According to Ferguson (1995), "The new challenge of inclusion is to create schools in which our day-to-day efforts no longer assume that a particular text, activity, or teaching mode will 'work' to support any particular student's learning" (p. 287). Because the inclusive classroom contains many students with diverse needs, teachers must be equipped to address an array of challenges. To do so effectively, teachers need to create classroom communities that embrace diversity and that are responsive to individual needs.

 **Summary**

### Perceptions of Inclusion

◢ Inclusion of students with special needs in general education classes has received more attention on a philosophical level than on a practical level.

◢ The critical issue of successful inclusion is the acceptance of diversity.

◢ Effective inclusive settings have an impact on the student's immediate as well as long-range needs.

◢ On a philosophical level, there are few arguments against inclusion.

◢ Although many teachers support the concept of inclusion, a large percentage are uncomfortable about teaching students with special needs in their own classrooms.

◢ The opinions of parents regarding inclusion vary greatly.

### Critical Dimensions of Inclusive Classrooms

◢ Five essential features must be in place to ensure maximum success of inclusion, including creating a sense of community and social acceptance, appreciating student diversity, attending to curricular needs, effectively managing and instructing of students, and offering access to adequate personnel supports.

◢ The concept of inclusion affirms that students with special needs can be active, valued, and fully participating members of the school community.

◢ Students with special needs will be truly included in their classrooms only when they are appreciated by their teachers and socially accepted by their classmates.

◢ Teachers play a critical role in the success of inclusion.

◢ The curricular needs of students cannot be lost in the philosophical and political debate on inclusion.

◢ Effective classroom management is an important component in a successful inclusive classroom.

◢ Accommodative practices that are good for students with special needs are usually good for all students.

### Creating and Maintaining Inclusive Classrooms

◢ Appropriately trained personnel, in adequate numbers, is a major factor in successful inclusion programs.

◢ Both staff and students must be prepared for inclusion.

◢ Once inclusion is initiated, its effectiveness must be monitored to ensure its ongoing success.

### Planning for Successful Inclusion One Student at a Time

◢ In order to be effective, planning an appropriate environment for students with disabilities must be carried out one student at a time.

◢ School personnel must develop supports that provide each student with the least restrictive environments possible that still meet the individual needs of each student.

# urther Readings

Cramer, S. (1998). *Collaboration: A successful strategy for special education.* Boston: Allyn & Bacon.

Deno, S. L., Foegen, A., Robinson, S., & Espin, C. (1996). Commentary: Facing the realities of inclusion for students with mild disabilities. *Journal of Special Education, 30,* 345–357.

Fox, T., & Williams, W. (1991). *Implementing best practices for all students in their local school.* Burlington, VT: University of Vermont.

National Association of State Boards of Education. (1992). *Winners all: A call for inclusive schools.* (chapter 5) Alexandria, VA: Author.

Schwartz, S. E., & Karge, B. D. (1996). *Human diversity: A guide for understanding* (2nd ed.). New York: McGraw-Hill.

# Chapter 3

# Identifying and Programming for Student Needs

*After reading this chapter, you should be able to:*

◢ Describe steps in the special education process, including due-process procedures

◢ Identify the rights and responsibilities of students with disabilities and their parents in the special education process

◢ List prereferral intervention strategies that have been successful in the general education classroom

◢ Discuss the uses of assessment throughout the special education process

◢ List the major components of an IEP

◢ Describe the role of the general education teacher during assessment and in the development of an IEP

ast year was my first year to teach! I was so happy to be assigned a fourth-grade class of 25 students. My class had children from several cultures; I met with parents and planned activities to expose the class to the rich differences. The special education teachers contacted me about the needs of several children who were in my class for some or all of a day.

My lack of experience was balanced by my eagerness and enthusiasm. Each day I spent several hours planning exciting learning experiences. I was so caught up in the process of teaching that it took me a couple of months to realize that one of my students was floundering, despite my efforts. Angelina was new to our school so I could not consult with other teachers to gain insight. She was a puzzle. Some days were better than others. She had difficulty following directions, seldom finished her work or handed in homework; her desk and papers were a mess, and she spent too much time looking for pencils and supplies needed to complete an activity. She read slowly and laboriously and had problems decoding and predicting unknown words. I tried to talk to her but she had little to say. She was a loner with only one or two friends with whom she seemed comfortable.

The school had a child study team that met weekly to discuss children like Angelina who were experiencing problems. I didn't like admitting that I needed help, but I was glad that the resource was available. I let Angelina's parents know I was concerned about her progress and was seeking help within the school. I filled out the required form requesting a brief summary of the problems and attached examples of Angelina's work.

The child study team meeting, held at 7:00 A.M., gave us uninterrupted time. The team was composed of an experienced teacher from each grade, the assistant principal, the counselor, and a special education teacher. Other teachers were there to discuss children having difficulties in their classrooms. When Angelina's case was discussed, I came up with some strategies, and the team agreed they would be appropriate. I guess I just needed the peer support to give me ideas and confidence to help Angelina. Thanks to intervention strategies developed by this team, Angelina finished fourth grade. I never had to refer her for additional testing. Both she and her parents were pleased. I think she will be successful in fifth grade, I'm glad the child study team is in place so that Angelina and others like her will have help if problems arise.

## QUESTIONS TO CONSIDER

1. What suggestions can you make to help Angelina?
2. How would you feel about making accommodations to keep Angelina in a general education classroom?
3. Do you think treating Angelina differently was fair to the other students?

*I*n the preceding vignette, a concerned teacher identified Angelina's needs and reached out for resources that would help keep her successfully learning in the general education classroom. As described in the nearby Personal Spotlight, Lauren's needs were met through a combination of special education and general education services. This chapter focuses on identifying the needs of students like Angelina and Lauren, and programming for those needs in an inclusive classroom, whenever possible.

For a student who needs to be evaluated to determine if he or she is eligible for special educational services, a comprehensive process is in place in every school system throughout the country. This process is governed by the Education for All Handicapped Children Act (PL 94-142) and its successor, the Individuals with Disabilities Education Act (IDEA; PL 101-476) (1990, 1997), as well as by regulations in each state. This chapter reviews key steps in the process: *prereferral, child study, referral, assessment,* and the development and implementation of *individualized education programs (IEPs).*

## *personal* SPOTLIGHT

### Mother and Daughter Team

**SUSAN AND LAUREN PARRISH**

After Lauren suffered a stroke as a complication of open heart surgery at 8 months, her parents were given an uncertain prognosis for her recovery. As developmental milestones began to emerge slowly, it was evident that Lauren had cognitive and physical disabilities, as well as speech and language deficits. During her earlier years, she received physical and speech therapy in her home with visiting specialists. When it was time to enroll in the public schools her parents and teacher decided to begin her education in a self-contained class with other children with severe disabilities. There Lauren received intense remediation by a physical therapist and a speech therapist. She also learned many self-help skills such as potty training and self-feeding. Lauren met many of her learning goals through the help of an intense program implemented by the special education teacher. It was soon evident that Lauren would benefit from an experience in an inclusive classroom. She joined a class of students in kindergarten and made tremendous improvements.

At first it was considered a challenge for Lauren to use her walker daily on the long walk required to get to the general education kindergarten class. Soon, this strengthened her legs, and her walking skills were greatly improved. Three years later, she threw away her walker! The increased verbal interactions with her peers greatly enhanced her language and speech abilities. She had always been able to listen and understand most of what was said to her, but now others were able to understand what she wanted to say. Lauren continues to work hard and is making progress both socially and academically. However, her mother says that every year she goes to the IEP team hoping that these same services will be available for her in the next grade. She doesn't know what the future holds for Lauren, but because of the great improvements that have been made during her three years of inclusion, the future looks bright. Susan believes that it took a team approach and experience in both a self-contained and inclusive setting to increase Lauren's chances for a productive future.

Let us begin by placing these procedures in a broad context. All educational procedures must be consistent with the due-process clause under the Constitution, which ensures that no person will be deprived of legal rights or privileges without appropriate established procedures being followed. The implications of the due-process clause have resulted in regulations in IDEA (1997) that give parents and students with disabilities significant rights throughout the special education process. These are listed in the nearby Rights and Responsibilities feature. While these basic rights are guaranteed nationwide, procedures guiding the special education process may vary from state to state. Figure 3.1 contains an example of how the special education process is carried out in one state. The flowchart in Figure 3.1 shows the procedures put in place after screening and efforts to modify the general education classroom were ineffective. A referral to evaluate the eligibility for special education services has been made resulting in these steps.

The key players in the process include special and general education teachers, administrative staff, ancillary personnel (e.g., school psychologists, speech–language therapists, school social workers), parents, and the student. Even though teamwork is required by IDEA (1997), involving many people should not be simply an issue of compliance or happenstance. Many people should have a vested interest in the educational program for a student, and consideration of a student's needs is best accomplished by

**CROSS-REFERENCE**
Refer to Chapter 1 for a comprehensive summary of the provisions of IDEA.

# RIGHTS & RESPONSIBILITIES

According to the 1999 Rules and Regulations for Parent Participation under IDEA (1997), school personnel must

- Make reasonable efforts to ensure parental participation in group discussions relating to the educational placement of their child.
- Notify parents of meetings early enough to ensure they will have an opportunity to attend and use conference or individual calls if they cannot attend.
- Inform parents of the purpose, time, location, and who will attend a meeting.
- Notify parents that they, or school personnel, may invite individuals with special knowledge or expertise to IEP meetings.
- Schedule the meetings at a mutually agreed upon time and place.
- Provide written notification (in the parent or guardian's native language) before any changes are initiated or refused in the identification, evaluation, educational placement, or provision of a free, appropriate public education.
- Obtain written consent from parents before the initial evaluation, initial provisions of special education and related services, or before con-

ducting a new test as part of a reevaluation. Parents have a right to question any educational decision through due-process procedures.

- Inform parents that they have the right to an independent educational evaluation that may be provided at public expense, if the evaluation provided by the education agency is determined to be inappropriate.
- Inform parents of requirements for membership on the IEP Committee including an invitation to the student to attend beginning at age 14 or younger if appropriate.
- Use interpreters or take other action to ensure that the parents understand the proceedings of the IEP meetings.
- Notify parents of the need to develop a statement regarding transition services at age 14.
- Inform parents of requirement to consider transition services needed for students by age 16.
- Consider the student's strengths and the parental concerns in all decisions.
- Provide the parents with a copy of the IEP at no cost.
- Help parents acquire skills necessary to support implementation of their child's IFSP or IEP.
- Inform parents of their right to ask for revisions to the IEP or invoke due-process procedures if they are not satisfied.
- Allow parents to review all records and request amendments if deemed appropriate.

■ *FIGURE* **3.1**    Special Education Process

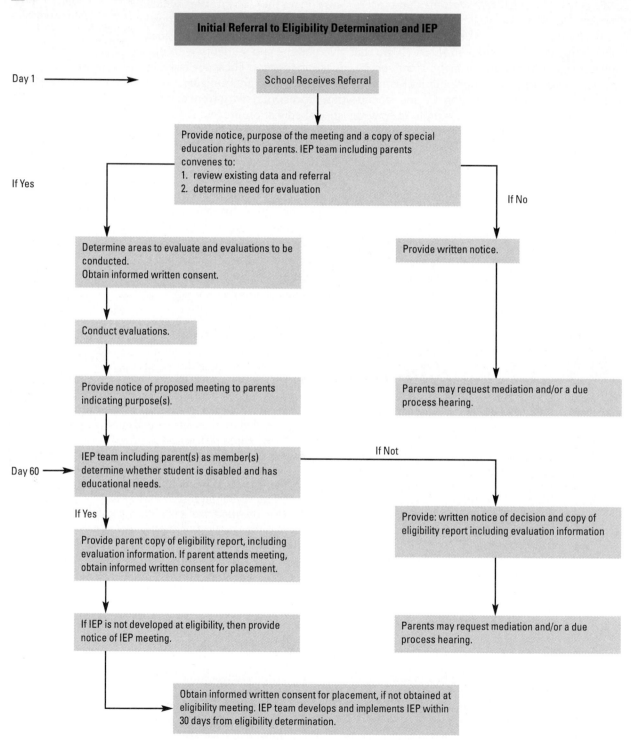

**Initial Referral to Eligibility Determination and IEP**

Day 1 ⟶

School Receives Referral

Provide notice, purpose of the meeting and a copy of special education rights to parents. IEP team including parents convenes to:
1. review existing data and referral
2. determine need for evaluation

If Yes

If No

Determine areas to evaluate and evaluations to be conducted.
Obtain informed written consent.

Provide written notice.

Conduct evaluations.

Provide notice of proposed meeting to parents indicating purpose(s).

Parents may request mediation and/or a due process hearing.

Day 60 ⟶

IEP team including parent(s) as member(s) determine whether student is disabled and has educational needs.

If Not

If Yes

Provide parent copy of eligibility report, including evaluation information. If parent attends meeting, obtain informed written consent for placement.

Provide: written notice of decision and copy of eligibility report including evaluation information

If IEP is not developed at eligibility, then provide notice of IEP meeting.

Parents may request mediation and/or a due process hearing.

Obtain informed written consent for placement, if not obtained at eligibility meeting. IEP team develops and implements IEP within 30 days from eligibility determination.

a team approach. Thus, decisions are made by a team representing various disciplines and relationships with the student. Teams are charged with making decisions concerning eligibility for special services, design of the IEP, evaluation of annual progress made on implementation of the IEP, and reevaluation of eligibility.

## PREREFERRAL CHILD STUDY AND REFERRAL PROCESS

**M**ost schools have also developed and implemented techniques to study and intervene in the general education classroom before referring a student for formal evaluation. The **prereferral child study** and the **referral process** involve contacts and collaboration between general and special education teachers. The purpose of the collaboration is the development of **prereferral interventions** (i.e., interventions to be attempted in the general education classroom prior to formal referral for evaluation for special education).

The prereferral child study and referral process ordinarily begin with concerns voiced by a classroom teacher about the performance or progress of a student. Other sources could be parents, end-of-year reviews of student progress, or an external service provider. At this juncture a group of on-site personnel review available information and attempt to generate suggestions to address the student's difficulties. Depending upon geographical area, this team may be referred to as a screening committee, a **child study committee,** or a teacher assistance team (Walther-Thomas, Korinek, McCoughlin, & Williams, 2000).

Initially, the team attempts to assist the teacher in targeting the most significant problems in the classroom and to identify strategies to address those concerns, such as alternative teaching methods, modifications of task requirements, or behavioral interventions. Figure 3.2 displays a child study team referral made by a second-grade teacher for one of her students. Table 3.1 contains a form that can be used by the child study team to document the action of the committee. For Robert, whose challenges were identified in Figure 3.2, the team recommended getting help from a paraprofessional and a peer, giving him a daily outline, using a tape recorder, using a behavior chart with self-checking, home-school notes, and videotaping behaviors to show him.

The prereferral intervention techniques are generally implemented for at least one grading period, typically 6–9 weeks; however, the teacher and the team may be flexible and specify a different time period, according to the needs of the individual student. At the end of the agreed-upon period, the team evaluates the success of the prereferral intervention to determine if a referral for comprehensive special education evaluation is warranted. However, the purpose of child study or teacher assistance teams is to review concerns and design prereferral interventions rather than to pass cases on for comprehensive special education evaluation. This process appears to be both *effective* in helping teachers and students and *efficient* in generally forwarding referrals of only those students needing specialized services (Safran & Safran, 1996).

Unfortunately, prereferral intervention does not work for all students. Figure 3.3 shows a referral form completed for a student who was brought before the child study team. Notice the documentation of the prereferral interventions that were implemented for Frank and the additional information that will be included for consideration. As noted earlier (see Figure 3.1), the referral is submitted to the designated school official who provides written notice to the parents, documenting the time, purpose of the meeting, and the parents' rights in the special education process. The IEP team, including the parents and the student when appropriate, convenes to review the

---

**PREREFERRAL CHILD STUDY** identifies special abilities and disabilities of a student in the general education classroom and implements intervention strategies to enhance success and possibly negate the need for a special education referral.

**REFERRAL PROCESS** identifies and refers a child for special education services who might be eligible under IDEA.

**PREREFERRAL INTERVENTIONS** are strategies for modifying the curriculum, teacher instructions, or student activities that are implemented prior to considering a referral to determine if the student is eligible for special education.

**CHILD STUDY COMMITTEE** is a school-based team designed to assist teachers in problem solving to identify techniques to meet the needs of at risk students in a general education class.

**CONSIDER THIS**
Estimate the lapsed time from a teacher's initial concern about a student to implementation of special education services. Is this time frame reasonable from the perspective of the student? the parent? the teacher?

**FIGURE 3.2**

Request for
Assistance
Completed for
Robert

*From Collaboration for Inclusive Education: Developing Successful Programs (p. 152) by C. Walther-Thomas, L. Korinek, V. McLaughlin, & B. T. Williams, 2000, Boston: Allyn and Bacon.*

---

**Request for Assistance**

Date: 1/7

Student's name:   Robert E.

Age:  8 yrs. 2 mos.

Teacher's name:   Sally Sparks

Grade:  2

Team Contact:
(Assigned by Team Leader)

1. What specific student behaviors are interfering with classroom success?

   Doesn't complete assignments or work independently; off-task and

   inattentive; disrupts other students; difficulty following directions

2. Describe the student's individual strengths and interests:

   Reads on 3rd-grade level

   Draws well

   Likes adult attention

3. What *exactly* does the student need to *do* to be more successful in your classroom?

   Attempt and complete assignments on his level

   Follow classroom directions

   Stop disrupting others during seatwork

4. What strategies or interventions have your tried thus far?

   Frequent reminders and warnings

   Stay in from recess when he doesn't finish work

   Drawing when he gets his work done (but he seldom hears this)

5. Provide any background information and/or available assessment data directly relevant to this request.

   Informal Reading Inventory scores = 3.2 level

   on grade level in math (2nd grade)

| TABLE 3.1 | Format for Child Study Team Meetings |
| --- | --- |
| **Agenda** | **Action Plan** |
| 1. Introduce participants | Persons in attendance: |
| 2. Review request for assistance | Intervention goal: |
| 3. Brainstorm interventions | List of ideas generated on reverse side or attachment: |
| 4. Select intervention(s) | Teacher's chosen intervention(s): |
| 5. Identify support needs | Materials and/or collaborative assistance needed: |
| 6. Plan evaluation | Criterion for success and how it will be measured: |
| 7. Schedule follow-up | Date set to review progress: |

Adapted from *Collaboration for Inclusive Education: Developing Successful Programs* (p. 153) by C. Walther-Thomas, L. Korinek, V. McLaughlin, and B. T. Williams, 2000. Boston: Allyn and Bacon.

existing data and to determine if the referral will be accepted for a formal evaluation to decide eligibility for special education services.

Figure 3.4 reviews the steps from prereferral to the writing of the IEP; it includes specific steps for teachers to take before a referral and the information needed to make a referral. The most common reasons for referrals reported by Lloyd, Kauffman, Landrun, and Roe (1991) were primarily reading and attention problems. Some students also exhibited difficulties with writing, math, language, and sensory skills and showed aggressive or immature behavior.

The evaluation process and assessment battery must be comprehensive and flexible enough to address the difficulties of any child referred across all ages, grades, and cultures. Because the vast majority of students who are disabled are referred during

**TEACHING TIP**
Be very specific when describing a student's problem in the classroom. The descriptions provided for Robert's problems are much more helpful than writing, "Robert is having problems in reading" or "Robert is performing below grade level."

## STEPS LEADING TO THE IEP

1. A teacher notices that a student is having serious academic or behavioral difficulty.
2. The teacher consults the student's parents and tries the instructional or behavior management strategies she or he believes will resolve the problem.
3. If the problem is not resolved the teacher asks for the help of the child study (or teacher assistance) team.
4. With the help of the team, the teacher implements and documents the results of strategies designed to resolve the problem.
5. If the problem is not resolved after reasonable implementation of the team's suggestions, the teacher makes a referral for evaluation.*
6. The student is evaluated in all areas of known or suspected disability, including medical, psychological, social, and educational evaluations.
7. With the results of the evaluation components in hand, the IEP Committee determines whether the student is eligible for special education.
8. If the student is found eligible, then an IEP must be written.

## WHAT SHOULD I DO BEFORE MAKING A REFERRAL?

☑ Hold at least one conference to discuss your concerns with the parents (or make extensive and documented efforts to communicate with the parents).

☑ Check all available school records, and interview other professionals involved with the student to make sure you understand the student's history and efforts to help that have already been made.

☑ Ask the child study team—or the principal, the school psychologist, and at least one other teacher who knows the student—to help you devise strategies to solve the problem.

☑ Implement and document the results of the academic and behavior management strategies you have tried.

## WHAT INFORMATION SHOULD I BE ABLE TO PROVIDE AT THE TIME OF REFERRAL?

☑ A statement of exactly what you are concerned about

☑ An explanation of why you are concerned

☑ Detailed records from your observations of the problem, including samples of academic work

☑ Records documenting the strategies you have used to try to resolve the problem and the outcomes of those strategies

* Note: Referrals may also be made by parents or administrators who believe the student may have a disability.

Adapted from *Introduction to Learning Disabilities* (p. 121) by D. P. Hallahan, J. M. Kauffman, and J. W. Lloyd, 1999, Boston: Allyn and Bacon.

the elementary years, the process is often less visible at the secondary level. However, since the demands of the middle school and high school settings are more complex, it is critical that child study and referral continue at these levels as well. Thus, the special education process, including referral and assessment, may begin at any age.

**ASSESSMENT** is the process of collecting information about a student to evaluate strengths and needs to help make educational decisions in each phase of the special education process.

## ASSESSMENT

**Assessment** is the process of gathering relevant information to use in making decisions about students (Salvia & Ysseldyke, 1998). It is a dynamic, continuous process

*Members of a child study team may help develop prereferral interventions for students having problems.*

that guides and directs decisions about students with suspected or known disabilities. Assessment is so integral to the special education process that much of what educators do is mandated by law. However, across the states there is still variability as to the types of procedures used, the specific approaches to assessment, and the criteria used to determine student eligibility. The following section provides a brief overview of the purpose of assessment during each phase of the special education process, approaches recommended to gather information, and the legal mandates regarding assessment. A discussion of possible bias in assessment and the role of the general education teacher is also included.

## Purpose of Assessment throughout the Special Education Process

Assessment is critical in each of the four major phases of the special education process, as shown in Table 3.2. During the **screening** phase, including the steps of prereferral and referral discussed previously, the concerns the teachers and parents expressed are the result of their informal "assessment" of the student's lack of progress. Their concern comes from their observations and interactions with the student in the natural environment. When parents and teachers get concerned, they may consult others who have worked with the child or review previous records or current work. At this point these students are at risk for failure, and the first level of assessment for special education services has begun.

If a referral is made and the IEP team accepts the referral, the **identification** and **eligibility** phase of assessment begins. During this phase the child is formally evaluated to determine if he or she has a disability and is eligible for special education services. The student's intellectual ability, strengths, and limitations are evaluated individually by trained professionals. These results are studied by the IEP team along with the information gathered during the screening, prereferral, and referral phases. If the student is determined to be eligible, assessment data is needed for **program planning.** Existing data is studied further and new data may be collected to help the IEP team select goals and objectives or benchmarks, as well as identify the most effective methods of instruction to include in the IEP. After the IEP has been implemented, assessment is conducted to **monitor** and **evaluate** the student's progress. The student is assessed annually to evaluate the outcome of the IEP and provide a measure of accountability. In addition, the student's eligibility or need for services is reconsidered by the IEP team every 3 years and additional assessments may be required to

*SCREENING* is the phase of assessment where parents and teachers express their concerns about a student's lack of progress and where the student is observed to determine the possibility of disabilities.

*IDENTIFICATION* involves a formal evaluation of the student.

*ELIGIBILITY* is determined through assessment to determine if a student meets the requirements for special education services.

*PROGRAM PLANNING* is the process by which the school staff establishes goals for the student and identifies the most effective methods for instruction.

*MONITORING* allows the teacher to observe the student's progress over a period of time.

*EVALUATION* establishes the outcome of the IEP and provides a measure of accountability.

| TABLE 3.2 | Assessment Decisions throughout the Special Education Process | | |
| --- | --- | --- | --- |
| **Type of Assessment** | **Type of Information Gathered** | **Decision(s) Usually Made** | **When Information Is Usually Gathered** |
| Screening, Prereferral, Referral | Observation to determine possible disability or developmental delay; screening for vision, hearing, health, or physical concerns; review of existing records or products. | Whether or not a student should be referred for additional assessment. | Prior to formal assessment for eligibility. |
| Identification, Eligibility | Evidence of disability or developmental delay, extent of the disability, and need for special education services. Standardized, norm-referenced, comparative information generally used. | Whether or not a student is eligible for a program or services as specified in the state's criteria for eligibility. | Prior to entry into a program. Decision reviewed at least every 3 years. |
| Program Planning | Evidence of the student's skills and behaviors; family preferences and priorities for the student; settings in which the student spends time and the demands of those settings. Primarily interviews and informal measures used. | What type of activities, materials, and equipment to use with the individual student. What adult and peer interactions may work best with the student and what accommodations, modifications, or support services are needed. | Intensively at the beginning of a program year; during the first several weeks a student is in a program; during and immediately after any major changes in a student's life. This is an ongoing process. |
| Progress Monitoring and Evaluation | Evidence of the student's skills and behaviors in comparison to those skills at the beginning of the student's entry into the program; family satisfaction and indication of whether or not their priorities have been met; student's ability to be successful in the setting(s) in which he or she spends time. | To determine the effectiveness of programming for an individual student or group of students; to determine the change in a student's skill and behaviors; to determine family satisfaction; to evaluate a program's overall effectiveness. | Periodically, as needed to determine whether or not intervention is effective; at the end of a program year or cycle; when dictated by administrative policy and funding sources. |

Adapted from *Young Children with Special Needs* (p. 89) by R. Gargiulo and J. Kilgo, 2000, Albany, NY: Delmar Publishers/An International Thomson Publishing Company.

make decisions at that time. The results of each phase of this assessment determine which of several approaches to assessment are used.

## Approaches to Assessment

Salvia and Ysseldyke (1998) identified 4 approaches used to gather information on students: (1) observation (2) recollection (via interview or rating scale), (3) record or portfolio review, and (4) testing. Data collected through naturalistic **observation** can be highly accurate and provide detailed, relevant information on how the student performs in the natural environment. The observer may be systematically looking for one or more specific behaviors, such as inattention or inappropriate comments. In this approach, the frequency, duration, and intensity of the behavior(s) are usually recorded for study. The student's behavior can then be compared to normal standards of his or her peers or to the individual's previous behavior. Another method of collecting observational data is more anecdotal, in which case the observer records *any* behavior that seems significant. This type of data may be more subjective than the systematic recordings and harder to validate. Observational data may also be collected using audiotape or videotape.

In data collection involving **recollection,** individuals familiar with the student are asked to recall events and interpret the behaviors. The most commonly used are interviews or ratings scales that can be obtained from the students through a self-report or from peers, family members, teachers, counselors, or others. Through interviews, parents' concerns and preferences can be determined. Since interviews are generally held in person, reactions to questions can be observed and, when appropriate, questions can be explored more thoroughly. **Ratings scales** offer a structured method of data collection involving asking the rater to respond to a statement by indicating the degree to which an item describes an individual. Figure 3.5 demonstrates an excerpt of a rating scale used to identify strengths or limitations that might be considered in planning instruction or developing needed accommodations. When using rating scale data, care should be taken to confirm the rater's ability to understand the scale and determine the possibility of bias in reporting.

Another important component of assessment is record or **portfolio review.** Existing information such as school cumulative records, databases, anecdotal records, nonschool records, or student products (often found in a student's portfolio) should be reviewed carefully for insight into the student's needs and strengths. Usually a school will consider the same kinds of records for each child being considered to maintain consistency.

The most common method of gathering information on students is through **testing.** Testing, formal or informal, is the process of presenting challenges or problems to students and measuring the student's competency, attitude, or behavior by evaluating his or her responses (Ysseldyke & Olsen, 1999).

**Formal assessment** instruments are generally available commercially. They typically contain detailed guidelines for administration, scoring, and interpretation as well as statistical data regarding **validity,** reliability, and **standardization procedures.** They are most often **norm-referenced**—that is, the tests provide quantitative information comparing the performance of an individual student to others in his or her norm group (determined, for example, by age, grade, or gender). Test results are usually reported in the form of test quotients, percentiles, and age or grade equivalents. These tools are most useful early in an assessment procedure, when relatively little is known of a student's strengths and weaknesses, and thus they may help identify areas in which informal assessment can begin. The ability to compare the student to his or her age and grade peers is also an advantage in making eligibility and placement decisions and fulfilling related administrative requirements.

Table 3.3 demonstrates various types of scores obtained through standardized testing and the range of scores that may suggest a mild, moderate, or severe deficit.

Professionals can make better informed decisions about the use of formal instruments if they study the instrument and become familiar with its features, benefits,

**OBSERVATION** is the systematic process of gathering information by looking at students in their environment.

**RECOLLECTION** allows individuals familiar with the student to recall events and interpret the behavior of the student.

**RATING SCALES** offer a structured method of date collection involving asking the rater to respond to a statement by indicating the degree to which an item describes an individual.

**PORTFOLIO REVIEW** is a systematic collection of students' work and records of their behavior that can be used as evidence to monitor the growth of their skills, knowledge, behaviors, or attitudes.

**TESTING** is the component of the assessment process where specific questions are asked and a response is recorded and evaluated.

**FORMAL ASSESSMENT** uses standardized tests and guidelines to obtain quantitative information comparing the performance of a student to others in the same norm group.

**VALIDITY** is the truth or acceptability of data.

**STANDARDIZATION PROCEDURES** help the teacher to ensure that test results will be accurate and acceptable.

**NORM-REFERENCED** tests provide quantitative information comparing the performance of an individual student to others in his or her norm group.

FIGURE **3.5** Excerpt from a Rating Scale

FIGURE **3.5** Excerpt from a Rating Scale

**Strengths and Limitations Inventory: School Version**

Directions: This checklist may be completed during an interview or given to parents, teachers, or other professionals to complete. Informants should check each item according to the frequency of the behavior. Specific examples or comments should be provided when possible. Any characteristic seldom or never observed <u>may be</u> considered a strength or ability. Characteristics observed often or very often may pose functional limitations in an academic or vocational setting.

NAME: _____ DATE: _____

COMPLETED BY: _____ RELATIONSHIP TO INDIVIDUAL: _____

| Please check each item based on your personal interview, knowledge, and/or observation | No Opportunity to Observe | Never | Sometimes | Often | Very Often | Specific comments, observations, and examples should be provided whenever possible. |
|---|---|---|---|---|---|---|
| **I. ATTENTION/IMPULSIVITY/HYPERACTIVITY** | | | | | | |
| 1. Exhibits excessive nonpurposeful movement (can't sit still, stay in seat). | | | | | | |
| 2. Is easily distracted by auditory stimuli. | | | | | | |
| 3. Is easily distracted by visual stimuli. | | | | | | |
| 4. Does not stay on task for appropriate periods of time. | | | | | | |
| 5. Has difficulty completing assignments. | | | | | | |
| 6. Verbally or physically interrupts conversations or activities. | | | | | | |
| 7. Loses place when reading orally. | | | | | | |
| 8. Sits and does nothing (daydreams). | | | | | | |
| 9. Rushes through work with little regard for detail (careless). | | | | | | |
| 10. Does not pay attention to most important stimuli. | | | | | | |
| 11. Shifts from one uncompleted activity to another. | | | | | | |
| 12. Does not appear to listen to what is being said. | | | | | | |
| 13. Talks beyond appropriate limits. | | | | | | |
| 14. Loses items needed for activities or tasks (paper, pencil, assignments). | | | | | | |
| 15. Has difficulty working/playing quietly. | | | | | | |
| **II. REASONING/PROCESSING** | | | | | | |
| 16. Makes poor decisions. | | | | | | |
| 17. Makes frequent errors. | | | | | | |
| 18. Has trouble using previously learned information in a new situation. | | | | | | |
| 19. Has delayed verbal responses. | | | | | | |
| 20. Takes longer to do a task than peers. | | | | | | |

Adapted from *Attention-Deficit/Hyperactivity Disorder in the Classroom* (pp. 48–49) by C. Dowdy, J. Patton, T. E. C. Smith, and E. A. Polloway, 1998, Austin, TX: Pro-Ed.

| TABLE 3.3 | | Relation of Various Standard Scores to Percentile Rank and to Each Other | | | | |
|---|---|---|---|---|---|---|
| | **STANDARD SCORES** | | | | | |
| **PERCENTILE RANK** | **Quotients** | **NCE Scores** | **T-scores** | **Z-scores** | **Stanines** | **DEFICIT** |
| 99 | 150 | 99 | 83 | +3.33 | 9 | |
| 99 | 145 | 99 | 80 | +3.00 | 9 | |
| 99 | 140 | 99 | 77 | +2.67 | 9 | |
| 99 | 135 | 99 | 73 | +2.33 | 9 | |
| 98 | 130 | 92 | 70 | +2.00 | 9 | |
| 95 | 125 | 85 | 67 | +1.67 | 8 | |
| 91 | 120 | 78 | 63 | +1.34 | 8 | none |
| 84 | 115 | 71 | 60 | +1.00 | 7 | |
| 75 | 110 | 64 | 57 | +0.67 | 6 | |
| 63 | 105 | 57 | 53 | +0.33 | 6 | |
| 50 | 100 | 50 | 50 | +0.00 | 5 | |
| 37 | 95 | 43 | 47 | −0.33 | 4 | |
| 25 | 90 | 36 | 43 | −0.67 | 4 | |
| 16 | 85 | 29 | 40 | −1.00 | 3 | mild |
| 9 | 80 | 22 | 37 | −1.34 | 2 | |
| 5 | 75 | 15 | 33 | −1.67 | 2 | moderate |
| 2 | 70 | 8 | 30 | −2.00 | 1 | |
| 1 | 65 | 1 | 27 | −2.33 | 1 | |
| 1 | 60 | 1 | 23 | −2.67 | 1 | severe |
| 1 | 55 | 1 | 20 | −3.00 | 1 | |

From "The Role of Standardized Tests in Planning Academic Instruction" (p. 377) by D. D. Hammill and B. R. Bryant, in *Handbook on the Assessment of Learning Disabilities,* edited by H. L. Swanson, 1991, Austin, TX: Pro-Ed. Copyright 1991 by Pro-Ed, Inc. Used by permission.

and possible liabilities. One way to do this is to consult one or more of the excellent resources on tests. Two particularly apt sources are the *Tenth Mental Measurements Yearbook* (Conoley & Kramer, 1989) and *Tests in Print* (1989). Both are periodically revised and updated.

Although formal testing provides quantitative and sometimes qualitative data based on student performance, tests can only obtain a measure of a student's best performance in a contrived situation; they cannot broadly represent a student's typical performance under natural conditions. When considered in isolation, the results of formal tests can also result in lost data that can lead to poor decisions in placement and instructional planning. Rigid administration and interpretation of test results can obscure, rather than reveal, a student's strengths and weaknesses, as shown in Figure 3.6. It has become increasingly apparent that traditional, formal approaches must be replaced or used in combination with assessment techniques that more accurately represent a student's typical skills.

**CONSIDER THIS**
Test scores often confuse and concern parents. The information in Table 3.3 will help parents interpret scores more accurately. Notice that the 50th percentile rank is in the nondeficit range. A score indicating a mild disability begins with a score of 16th percentile, and a moderate deficit begins with a score of 5th percentile.

*FIGURE* **3.6**

Illustration of Useful Information Lost during Standardized Testing

From *Improving Educational Outcomes for Children with Disabilities: Principles for Assessment, Program Planning, and Evaluation* (pp. 16–17) by M. Kozloff, 1994, Baltimore, MD: Brookes. Used by permission.

The author notes that:
There are many competent ways to respond to "What is this?" Indra said what potatoes are for and what the duck was doing. Ms. Adams scores Indra's answers incorrect because the test Ms. Adams is using narrowly defines as correct those answers with object-naming function. Thus, Ms. Adams underestimates the size of Indra's object-naming repertoire and does not notice the other functions of Indra's vocabulary.

**Informal tests and measurements** are usually more loosely structured than formal instruments and are more closely tied to teaching. Such tools are typically devised by teachers to determine what skills or knowledge a child possesses. Their key advantage is the direct application of assessment data to instructional programs. By incorporating informal tests and measurements and by monitoring students' responses each day, teachers can achieve a more accurate assessment of growth in learning or behavioral change. Following is a brief discussion of general types of informal assessment procedures.

**Criterion-referenced testing (CRT)** compares a student's performance with a criterion of mastery for a specific task, disregarding his or her relative standing in a group. This form of informal assessment can be especially useful when documentation of progress is needed for accountability because the acquisition of skills can be clearly demonstrated. As Taylor (2000) stresses, CRTs are quite popular because they focus attention on specific skills in the curriculum, provide measures of progress toward mastery, and assist teachers in designing instructional strategies. Traditionally, most criterion-referenced tests have been produced by teachers, but publishers have begun to produce assessment tools of this type.

One important and popular form of criterion-referenced assessment is **curriculum-based assessment,** which, unlike norm-referenced tools, uses the actual curriculum as the standard and thus provides a basis for evaluating and modifying the curriculum for an individual student (McLoughlin & Lewis, 1999). This type of assessment can have a role in many important tasks: identification, eligibility, instructional grouping, program planning, progress monitoring, and program evaluation. Curriculum-based assessment can focus attention on changes in academic behavior within the context of the curriculum being used, thus enhancing the relationship between assessment and teaching (Deno & Fuchs, 1987).

There are several types of curriculum-based assessment, most are informal procedures but some are formal and have been standardized. **Alternative assessment**

*TEACHING TIP*
When the results of standardized tests differ significantly from your observations and experiences with a student, consult the examiner. Additional assessment may be necessary.

*INFORMAL TESTS AND MEASUREMENTS* are usually more loosely structured than formal assessments and are more closely tied to teaching.

*CRITERION REFERENCED TESTING (CRT)* assesses whether or not a student has mastered a targeted skill.

*CURRICULUM-BASED ASSESSMENT* is a method of measuring the degree to which students have learned the material taught in their classroom.

procedures have emerged as the dissatisfaction with group administered standardized tests has increased. Two terms commonly used to describe these procedures are **authentic assessment** and portfolio assessment. These assessment methods use similar techniques such as requiring students to construct, produce, perform, or demonstrate a task. These types of student responses are considered alternatives to typical testing responses, such as selecting from multiple choice items, a technique commonly used on standardized, formal tests. An example of an authentic assessment would be assigning a student the task of asking an individual they do not know for help. The individual being asked would be trained to evaluate the quality of the interaction and recommend the supports or accommodations that a student might need to improve the interaction (Ysseldyke & Olsen, 1999). Portfolio assessment has been described in the previous section on assessment approaches.

**Ecological assessment** is another approach used with many types of informal assessment. As educational assessment has increasingly begun to reflect a trend toward appreciating the ecology of the student, data obtained are now more frequently analyzed in relation to the child's functioning in his or her various environments. Although a full discussion of ecological assessment is beyond the scope of this chapter, the following information highlights some basic considerations, and the nearby Inclusion Strategies feature provides an example of a classroom ecological inventory.

The focus of ecological assessment is to place the evaluation process within the context of the student's environment. Its central element is *functionality*—how well the student operates in the current environment or the one into which he or she will be moving. This focus shifts a program's emphasis from correcting deficits toward determining how to build on strengths and interests. This type of assessment is particularly useful in early childhood.

An emphasis on ecological assessment necessarily broadens the assessment process. Additionally, it offers professionals a way of validating findings. The following questions can help teachers better understand the student and why he or she is having difficulty succeeding in school. Answers should help educators develop a positive learning environment and identify specific strategies to reduce negative influences on learning:

- ◢ In what physical environment does the student learn best?
- ◢ What is useful, debilitating, or neutral about the way the student approaches the task?
- ◢ Can the student hold multiple pieces of information in his or her memory and then act on them?
- ◢ How does increasing or slowing the speed of instruction affect the accuracy of the student's work?
- ◢ What processing mechanisms are being used in any given task?
- ◢ How does this student interact with a certain teaching style?
- ◢ With which professional has the student been most successful? What characteristics of the person seem to contribute to the student's success?
- ◢ What is encouraging to the student? What is discouraging?
- ◢ How does manipulating the mode of teaching (e.g., visual or auditory presentation) affect the student's performance? (Waterman, 1994, pp. 9–10)

## Legal Requirements for Assessment

PL 94-142, the first major law dealing with special education policy, contains many of the assessment mandates that still exist today. The final regulations for the IDEA

**ALTERNATIVE ASSESSMENTS** are techniques that provide alternatives to the traditional, standardized tests and directly examine student performance.

**AUTHENTIC ASSESSMENT** uses real life activities. For example, instead of completing a worksheet on punctuation, a student would correctly punctuate while writing a letter.

**ECOLOGICAL ASSESSMENT** evaluates individuals in the context of their environment.

**TEACHING TIP**
When entering a new school system, ask the principal or lead teachers to describe the assessment instruments typically used. If curriculum-based assessment has not been developed, organize a grade level team to begin this important process.

**CROSS-REFERENCE**
For more information on designing effective classrooms, see Chapter 13.

# INCLUSION STRATEGIES

## Classroom Ecological Inventory

Special Education Teacher _____     Grade _____ Date _____

General Education Teacher _____     Number of Students in General Class _____

Student _____

### PART 1: CLASSROOM OBSERVATION

**Physical Environment**

*Directions: Please circle or provide the appropriate answer.*

1. Is there an area for small groups?                                          Yes          No
2. Are partitions used in the room?                                            Yes          No
3. Is there a computer in the classroom?                                       Yes          No
4. Where is the student's desk located? (for example, front of room, back, middle, away from other
   students, etc.) _____

**Teacher/Student Behavior**

*Directions for #1–#4: Please circle the appropriate answer.*

1. How much movement or activity is tolerated by the teacher?    Much     Average     Little     Unclear
2. How much talking among students is tolerated?                 Much     Average     Little     Unclear
3. Does the teacher use praise?                                  Much     Average     Little     Unclear
4. Was subject taught to the entire group or to small groups?             Entire      Small

*Directions for #5–#7: Please provide an appropriate answer.*

5. During the observation, where did the teacher spend most of the time? (for example, at the board, at teacher's
   desk, at student's desk) _____

6. What teaching methods did you observe while in the classroom? (for example, teacher modeled the lesson, asked
   students to work at board, helped small groups, helped individual students) _____
   _____

7. How did the teacher interact with students who appeared to be low achieving or slower than their classmates?
   (for example, helped them individually, talked to them in the large group) _____
   _____

**Posted Classroom Rules**

If classroom rules are posted, what are they?

| **Special Education** | **General Education** |
|---|---|
| _____ | _____ |
| _____ | _____ |
| _____ | _____ |

Is there any other pertinent information you observed about this classroom that would be helpful in reintegrating
the student? (for example, crowded classroom)

_____

_____

▼

▼

## PART 2: TEACHER INTERVIEW

| | Special Ed | General Ed |
|---|---|---|
| **Classroom Rules** | | |

**Classroom Rules**

1. During class are there important rules? (Yes or No)  _____  _____
2. If yes, how are they communicated? (for example, written or oral)  _____  _____
3. If class rules are *not* posted, what are they?  _____  _____

_____  _____

_____  _____

4. If a rule is broken, what happens? What is the typical consequence?  _____  _____
5. Who enforces the rules? (teacher, aide, students)  _____  _____

**Teacher Behavior**

1. a.  Is homework assigned? (Yes or No)  _____  _____
   b.  If so, indicate approximate amount (minutes) of homework, and  _____  _____
   c.  the frequency with which it is given.  _____  _____

*Directions for #2–#4: Using a 3-point scale (1 = Often, 2 = Sometimes, 3 = Never), rate each item according to frequency of occurrence in class. Place an asterisk (\*) in the right-hand margin to indicate important differences between the special and regular education classrooms.*

| | Special Ed | General Ed | | | Special Ed | General Ed |
|---|---|---|---|---|---|---|
| 2. Assignments in Class | | | | 4. Academic/Social Rewards | | |
| a. Students are given assignments: | | | | a. Classroom rewards or reinforcement include: | | |
| • that are the same for all | \_\_\_\_ | \_\_\_\_ | | • material rewards (example, stars) | \_\_\_\_ | \_\_\_\_ |
| • that differ in amount or type | \_\_\_\_ | \_\_\_\_ | | b. Classroom punishment includes: | | |
| • to complete in school at a specified time | \_\_\_\_ | \_\_\_\_ | | • time out | \_\_\_\_ | \_\_\_\_ |
| • that, if unfinished in school, are assigned as homework | \_\_\_\_ | \_\_\_\_ | | • loss of activity-related privileges (example, loss of free time) | \_\_\_\_ | \_\_\_\_ |
| b. Evaluation of assignment: | | | | • teacher ignoring | \_\_\_\_ | \_\_\_\_ |
| • teacher evaluation | \_\_\_\_ | \_\_\_\_ | | • reprimands | \_\_\_\_ | \_\_\_\_ |
| • student self-evaluation | \_\_\_\_ | \_\_\_\_ | | • poorer grade, loss of star, etc. | \_\_\_\_ | \_\_\_\_ |
| • peer evaluation | \_\_\_\_ | \_\_\_\_ | | • extra work | \_\_\_\_ | \_\_\_\_ |
| 3. Tests | | | | • staying after school | \_\_\_\_ | \_\_\_\_ |
| a. Tests are | | | | • physical punishment (example, paddling) | \_\_\_\_ | \_\_\_\_ |
| • presented orally | \_\_\_\_ | \_\_\_\_ | | | | |
| • copied from board | \_\_\_\_ | \_\_\_\_ | | 5. To what extent do each of the following contribute to an overall grade? *Estimate the percentage for each so that the total sums to 100%.* | | |
| • timed | \_\_\_\_ | \_\_\_\_ | | | | |
| • based on study guides given to students prior to test | \_\_\_\_ | \_\_\_\_ | | • homework | \_\_\_\_ | \_\_\_\_ |
| • administered by resource teacher | \_\_\_\_ | \_\_\_\_ | | • daily work | \_\_\_\_ | \_\_\_\_ |
| b. Grades are: | | | | • tests | \_\_\_\_ | \_\_\_\_ |
| • percentages (example, 75%) | \_\_\_\_ | \_\_\_\_ | | • class participation | \_\_\_\_ | \_\_\_\_ |
| • letter grades (example, B+) | \_\_\_\_ | \_\_\_\_ | | | | |
| • both | \_\_\_\_ | \_\_\_\_ | | | | |

6. Please list skills that have been taught since the beginning of the school year (general education teacher only):

| Skill | Will Reteach Later? (Yes or No) |
|---|---|
| _____ | _____ |

From "Classroom Ecological Inventory" by D. Fuchs, P. Fernstrom, S. Scott, L. Fuchs, and L. Vandermeer, 1994, *Teaching Exceptional Children, 26*, pp. 14–15.

Amendments of 1997 continue to address and refine the assessment process. The law specifically addresses the concept of nondiscriminatory evaluations. Only tests that are not racially or culturally biased can be used to determine a disability and the extent of special education and related services that the student needs. If possible, the tests are to be administered in the student's native language or with other means of communication. Those professionals using assessment procedures on a student with limited English proficiency have to ensure that they are measuring the disability and the need for special education, not the student's English language skills. Eligibility also cannot be determined if the deficits are found to be a reflection of a lack of instruction in reading or math.

Any assessment measures must be validated for the specific purpose for which they are used and administered by an individual trained to give the test. No single procedure or test can be the sole criterion for determining eligibility for special education. The student must be assessed in all areas of suspected disability. These areas might include health, vision, hearing, social and emotional status, intelligence, academic performance, communication status, and motor abilities. The variety of assessment tools and strategies used must provide relevant, functional information to directly assist in determining the needs of the student. Information provided by parents must also be considered. Finally, the information must address how to enable the student to participate and progress in the general education curriculum (or for a preschool student, to participate in appropriate activities).

Significant trends in the area of assessment include a focus on the informal assessment procedures that produce more relevant, functional information, as described in the previous section. This type of assessment offers information helpful in eligibility determination as well as IEP development. The increase of the importance of parental input is apparent in the IDEA Amendments of 1997, as is the focus on increasing the student's chances for successful participation in the general education classroom. This includes participation in state or district-wide assessments given to all students. The increased emphasis on participation in the general education cur-

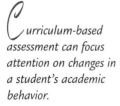

*Curriculum-based assessment can focus attention on changes in a student's academic behavior.*

| TABLE 3.4 | Assessment Accommodations |

| Setting | Timing | Scheduling |
|---|---|---|
| ■ Individual<br>■ Small group<br>■ Study carrell<br>■ Separate location<br>■ Special lighting<br>■ Adaptive or special furniture<br>■ Special acoustics<br>■ Minimal distractions environment | ■ Extended time<br>■ Flexible schedule<br>■ Frequent breaks during testing<br>■ Frequent breaks on one subtest but not another | ■ Specific time of day<br>■ Subtests in different order<br>■ Frequent breaks during testing<br>■ Frequent breaks on one subtest but not another |

| Presentation | Response | Other |
|---|---|---|
| ■ Audiotape<br>■ Braille edition<br>■ Large print<br>■ Audio amplification devices, hearing aids<br>■ Noise buffers<br>■ Prompts on tape<br>■ Increased space between items<br>■ Fewer items per page<br>■ Simplify language in directions<br>■ Highlight verbs in instructions by underlining<br>■ One complete sentence per line in reading passages<br>■ Key words or phrases in directions highlighted<br>■ Sign directions to student<br>■ Read directions to student<br>■ Re-read directions for each page of questions<br>■ Multiple choice questions followed by answer down side with bubbles to right<br>■ Clarify directions<br>■ Cues (arrows, stop signs) on answer form<br>■ Provide additional examples<br>■ Visual magnification devices<br>■ Templates to reduce visible print<br>■ Eliminate items that cannot be revised and estimate score | ■ Mark in response booklet<br>■ Use brailler<br>■ Tape record for later verbatim translation<br>■ Use of scribe<br>■ Word processor<br>■ Communication device<br>■ Copying assistance between drafts<br>■ Adaptive or special furniture<br>■ Dark or heavy raised lines<br>■ Pencil grips<br>■ Large diameter pencil<br>■ Calculator<br>■ Abacus<br>■ Arithmetic tables<br>■ Spelling dictionary<br>■ Spell checker<br>■ Special acoustics<br>■ Paper secured to work area with tape/magnets | ■ Special test preparation<br>■ On-task/focusing prompts<br>■ Others that do not fit into other categories |

Adapted from *Testing Students with Disabilities: Practical Strategies for Complying with State and District Standards,* by M. L. Thurlow, J. E. Elliott, and J. E. Ysseldyke, 1998, Thousand Oaks, CA: Corwin Press.

riculum is not useful without a measure of the student's progress in the curriculum. The IEP team may decide that the student with a disability should not participate in the traditional testing program without accommodations. Table 3.4 provides an array of accommodations that may be adopted by the IEP team for a student. The team also may decide that participation in standardized testing is not appropriate even with accommodations. In this case, the team must identify an alternate assessment procedure that allows the student to demonstrate what he or she has learned. Alternate assessment activities may encompass a variety of activities, including authentic assessment or portfolio assessment (Yell & Shriner, 1997).

### Issues of Bias in Assessment

By the year 2010 in the United States, the number of students from diverse cultures is expected to increase by 37%, rising to approximately 24 million students. This will present one of the greatest challenges for special educators—accurately assessing culturally and linguistically diverse students for disabilities (CEC, 1997).

The importance of ensuring fair and equitable assessment procedures clearly was emphasized in IDEA. This basic assumption of the law stated that assessment procedures must be established to make sure

> that testing and evaluation materials and procedures utilized for the purposes of evaluation and placement of handicapped children will be selected and administered so as not to be racially or culturally discriminatory. Such material or procedures shall be provided and administered in the child's native language or mode of communication, unless it is clearly not feasible to do so, and no single procedure shall be the sole criterion for determining an appropriate educational program for a child.

As Waterman (1994) notes, this regulation within IDEA stemmed directly from court cases that served as legal precursors to this federal legislation. For example, these cases related to the use of IQ in the placement of minority children into classes for students with mental retardation (e.g., *Larry P.* v. *Riles,* 1972; *Diana* v. *State Board of Education,* 1970) and "tracking systems" in the public schools (e.g., *Hobson* v. *Hansen,* 1967). The decision in *Hobson* v. *Hansen* stipulated that tests standardized on a white middle-class population were used to effectively classify students by socioeconomic status rather than by ability. As Wallace et al. (1992) stresses,

> it is clear that bias in the evaluation of students, particularly those from a minority background, can and will significantly affect the educational opportunities afforded these youngsters. To minimize the effects of bias in the evaluation, it is absolutely essential that every [professional] . . . be aware of the various ways in which bias is exhibited and take steps to minimize its effects when making educational decisions. (p. 473)

In addition to racial or cultural bias in assessment, a separate concern is the accurate assessment of individuals who experience sensory or motor disabilities. For example, individuals who have hearing impairments may require a nonverbal test, whereas persons who have visual impairments require measures that do not rely on object manipulation and do not include cards or pictures (Hoy & Gregg, 1994). An individual with a severe motor impairment may have limited voluntary responses and may need to respond via an eye scan or blink. Other students may have limited receptive or expressive language capabilities. Students who have multiple disabilities compound the difficulties of administering the assessment task. Browder and Snell (1988) note that some individuals simply lack "test behaviors." For example, they may refuse to stay seated for an assessment session or may exhibit interfering self-stimulatory behavior (e.g., hand flapping, rocking). Such disabilities or behaviors may cause the test to measure problems rather than assess functioning. Considered collectively, these problems can make traditional testing procedures ineffective, resulting in discriminatory practices despite the best intentions of the tester (Luckasson et al., 1992). Implementation of accommodations appropriate for the needs of each student with a disability greatly reduces this type of test bias. Refer back to Table 3.4 for a list of commonly used accommodations.

## Role of the Classroom Teacher in Assessment

The preceding discussion has outlined the assessment process related to special education. Although much of this information is critical to all professionals involved in evaluating students with disabilities, this question remains: Which concerns specifically apply to the classroom teacher? The following list suggests ways in which the general education professional can take an active role in the assessment process.

1. Ask questions about the assessment process. Special education teachers and school psychologists should be committed to clarifying the nature of the assessments used and the interpretation of the results.
2. Seek help as needed in conveying information to parents. Special education teachers may offer the support you need during a conference.
3. Provide input. Formal test data should not be allowed to contradict observations in the classroom about a student's ability, achievement, and learning patterns. A valid diagnostic picture should bring together multiple sources of data.
4. Observe assessment procedures. If time and facilities are available (e.g., a one-way mirror), observing the testing process can be educational and can enhance your ability to take part in decision making.
5. Consider issues of possible bias. Since formal assessments are often administered by an individual relatively unknown to the child (e.g., a psychologist), inadvertent bias factors between examiner and examinee may be more likely to creep into the results. Work with other staff to ensure an unbiased process.
6. Avoid viewing assessment as a means of confirming a set of observations or conclusions about a student's difficulties. Assessment is exploratory and may not lead to expected results. Too often, after a student is not judged eligible for special services, various parties feel resentment toward the assessment process. However, the key commitment should be to elicit useful information to help the student, not to arrive at a foregone eligibility decision that may please the student, parent, or teacher.

> **CONSIDER THIS**
> Do you feel that the role of the classroom teacher in the assessment process is realistic? In what areas do you feel comfortable participating? In what areas are you uncomfortable?

# INDIVIDUALIZED EDUCATION PROGRAMS

The results of a comprehensive disability assessment can also be translated into educational plans. The individualized education program (IEP) is an annual description of services planned for students with disabilities and is a requirement under IDEA. This requirement places the focus of intervention on individual needs. The IEP is developed by a team composed of teachers, a school administrator, the parents, and, when appropriate, the student. After analyzing relevant diagnostic data, the multidisciplinary team writes an IEP reflecting the student's educational needs.

## Federal Regulations for IEPs

IDEA and the final regulations (Federal Register, 1999) for the IDEA Amendments of 1997 specify content for IEPs in general, content for transition services for students beginning no later than age 14, and special requirements for plans for children birth to 3. The law also requires that a student be notified of the transfer of his or her rights at least one year prior to reaching the **age of majority** specified by law in his or her state. For example, in Alabama the age of majority is 19 so by age 18 the student must sign the IEP verifying that this right has been explained. After this birthday, students can make decisions regarding school, independent living, and work. In extreme cases, when students are judged incapable of making their own decisions and protecting their own rights, the courts will award guardianship to parents or another advocate.

The general requirements of an IEP for students between ages 3 to 21 include:

*AGE OF MAJORITY* varies by state and is the age at which an individual assumes control of his or her own decisions regarding school, independent living, and work.

◢ A statement of present levels of performance and how the disability affects the student's progress in the general education curriculum (or appropriate activities for preschoolers).

◢ Measurable annual goals including short-term benchmarks or objectives enabling the student to be involved in and progress in the regular curriculum (as appropriate) and meet the annual goals.

◢ Special education and related services for the student and supplemental aids.

◢ Program modifications or supports for school personnel to help the student be involved in and progress in both the curriculum and extra curricular and non-academic activities.

◢ An explanation of the extent, if any, that the student will not participate in regular education classes.

◢ Modifications to be used in state- or district-wide assessment of student achievement or an explanation of how the student is to be assessed if different from nondisabled peers.

◢ Projected dates for beginning of services and the frequency, location, and duration of services and modifications.

◢ How progress toward annual goals and modifications is to be measured.

◢ How parents will be regularly informed, at least as often as parents of non-disabled students, of progress toward the annual goals and whether progress will enable the student to meet goals by year end.

◢ For students age 14 or younger, if appropriate, a statement of transition needs that focuses on the student's course of study (e.g., advanced classes or a vocational program).

◢ Beginning at age 16 or younger, if appropriate, in addition to the preceding information, a statement of interagency responsibilities or linkages if needed.

Other special considerations include:

*CONSIDER THIS* Some individuals are negative about the use and value of IEPs. Do you see a purpose in their development? How would you improve the process?

◢ For students whose behavior impedes their learning or that of others, behavior strategy supports and interventions, when appropriate.

◢ For limited English proficient students, language needs as they relate to the IEP.

◢ For a child who is blind or visually impaired, Braille instruction, unless the IEP team determines that use of Braille is not appropriate.

◢ For hearing impaired students, language and communication needs, opportunities for communication with peers and teachers in the student's language and communication mode, including direct instruction in the mode.

◢ Assistive technology devices and services for eligible students.

*Parental involvement in the development of the individualized education program is both a legal requirement as well as an important aspect in the design of appropriate school programs.*

The written plan for children ages birth to 3 and their families, referred to as the Individualized Family Service Plan (IFSP), serves as a guide for available early intervention services. The basic philosophy underlying the IFSP is that infants and toddlers with known or suspected disabilities are uniquely dependent on their families and can best be understood within the context of their families. Thus, the intent of the IFSP is to focus on the family unit and to support the natural caregiving role of families. Many of the components of the IFSP are the same as those of the IEP; however, there are several important differences. For example, the goals in the plan are referred to as outcome statements, which reflect changes that families want to see for their child and for themselves. The outcome statements on the IFSP are family-centered rather than child-centered as they are on the IEP. In addition, a service coordinator must be identified for each family who is responsible for the implementation of the IFSP and coordination with other agencies and persons. Finally, a transition plan must be included to support the child and family when moving to the next stage of services at age 3.

## Components of an IEP

Major components in the IEP are present levels of performance, annual instructional goals, and short-term objectives or benchmarks. *Level of performance* provides a summary of assessment data on a student's current functioning, which serves as the basis for establishing annual goals. Therefore, the information should include data for each priority area in which instructional support is needed. Depending on the individual student, consideration might be given to reading, math, and other academic skills; written and oral communication skills; vocational talents and needs; social skills; behavioral patterns; self-help skills; or motor skills.

Performance levels can be provided in various forms, such as formal and informal assessment data, behavioral descriptions, and specific abilities delineated by checklists or skill sequences. Functional summary statements of an individual's strengths and weaknesses draw on information from a variety of sources rather than relying on a single one. Test scores in math, for example, might be combined with a description of how the child performed on a curriculum-based measure such as a computational checklist. In general, the phrasing used to define levels of performance should be positive and describe things the child *can do.* For example, the same information is conveyed by the two following statements, but the former demonstrates the more positive approach: "The student can identify 50% of times tables facts" versus "The student does not know half of the facts." Appropriately written performance levels provide a broad range of data in order to help generate relevant and appropriate annual goals.

**ANNUAL GOALS** are academic, social, and behavioral goals selected by the IEP team.

The second, and central, IEP instructional component is **annual goals.** Each student's goals should be individually determined to address unique needs and abilities. Since it is obviously impossible to predict the precise amount of progress a student will make in a year, goals should be reasonable projections of what the student will accomplish. To develop realistic expectations, teachers can consider a number of variables, including the chronological age of the child, the expected rate of learning, and past and current learning profiles.

Annual goals should be measurable, positive, student-oriented, and relevant (Polloway & Patton, 1997). *Measurable* goals provide a basis for evaluation. Statements should use terms that denote action and can therefore be operationally defined (e.g., *pronounce, write*), rather than vague, general language that confounds evaluation and observer agreement (e.g., *know, understand*). *Positive* goals provide an appropriate direction for instruction. Avoiding negative goals creates an atmosphere that is helpful in communicating with parents as well as in charting student progress. Goals should also be *oriented to the student.* Developing students' skills is the intent, and the

# TECHNOLOGY TODAY

## Suggested Internet Goals across the Grades

**Grades 1–2 Internet Skills**
- To recognize a web site
- To work in a web site using links
- To use the Netscape menu for "back, forward, home"

**Grades 3–4 Internet Skills**
- To recognize what makes up a URL (web site address)
- To access a web site by using its URL
- To perform a simple search using Yahooligans! or other kid-safe search engines
- To send and receive e-mail

**Grades 5–8 Internet Skills**
- To conduct research using a variety of search engines

- To become familiar with and apply proper netiquette
- To bookmark sites and create bookmark files
- To print from the Internet
- To cut and paste from the net into documents
- To judge the validity of information
- To understand how information is processed on the Internet

**Grades 9–12 Internet Skills**
- To create a home page and web site
- To use features of e-mail (i.e., flagging, filing, attachments)
- To do extensive research
- To set preferences
http://www.onlineschoolyard.com

From "Learning at CyberCamp" by C. Goldstein, 1998, *Teaching Exceptional Children,* 30(5), p. 16. Used by permission.

only measure of effectiveness should be what is learned, rather than what is taught. Finally, goals must be *relevant* to the individual's actual needs in terms of remediation and other desirable skills. The nearby Technology Today feature provides a suggestion of Internet goals that would be beneficial for students at various grade levels.

Annual goals should subsequently be broken down into *short-term objectives*, given in a logical and sequential series to provide a general plan for instruction.

Short-term objectives can be derived only after annual goals are written. They should be based on a task analysis process; skill sequences and checklists can be used to divide an annual goal into components that can be shaped into precise objectives. Each broad goal will generate a cluster of objectives. The four criteria applied to annual goals are also appropriate to short-term objectives. Since objectives are narrower in focus, an objective's measurability should be enhanced with a criterion for mastery. For example, a math short-term objective might read, given 20 multiplication facts using numbers 1–5, John will give correct answers for 90%. These benchmarks should be obtained from the general education curriculum being used by the student's nondisabled peers. A portion of an IEP containing annual goals, short-term objectives, and method of evaluation is presented in Table 3.5.

## Role of the Classroom Teacher in the IEP

Although IEPs are supposed to be jointly developed by all those involved in the student's educational program, in practice the task has often largely fallen to special education teachers. Some abuses of the system have been common. Instances in which general education classroom teachers ask if they were "allowed to see the IEP" and

| TABLE 3.5 | Examples of Lark's IEP Goals and Objectives |
|---|---|

**Goal 2: Lark will follow school and team rules.**

| Objectives | Criteria | Evaluation Procedures |
|---|---|---|
| ■ Lark will wear appropriate clothing to school<br>■ Lark will use appropriate language on the bus and at school<br><br>■ Lark will talk respectfully to teachers and other school personnel | ■ 0 occurrences per week of being sent home for dress code violations<br>■ 0 occurrences per week of inappropriate language<br><br>■ 0 referrals for inappropriate language per week | ■ Teacher observation using school dress code requirements<br>■ Number of referrals to office or disciplinary actions for inappropriate language<br>■ Number of referrals to office or disciplinary actions for inappropriate language |

**Goal 4: Lark will develop effective organizational and study skills.**

| Objectives | Criteria | Evaluation Procedures |
|---|---|---|
| ■ Lark will record all class assignments in a daily planner<br>■ Lark will complete and submit assignments<br>■ Lark will attend and participate in the student homework support group | ■ 90%<br><br>■ 4 of 5 days (80%) with 80% accuracy<br>■ 6 of 8 times/month (75%) | ■ Daily checks by teacher and grandmother<br>■ Daily records in teacher grade books<br>■ Student self-evaluation and peer evaluations of participation |

Adapted from *Collaboration for Inclusive Education: Developing Successful Programs* (p. 226) by C. Walther-Thomas, L. Korinek, V. McLaughlin, & B. T. Williams, 2000, Boston: Allyn and Bacon.

**TEACHING TIP**
As a general education teacher, you should be invited to participate in the IEP meeting of any child in your class. If you were not present, ask the special education teacher to give you a copy of the child's strengths, weaknesses, and goals to incorporate into your daily planning.

**TEACHING TIP**
The IEP is a plan, not a contract. If teachers are making a good faith effort to implement the IEP, they cannot be held responsible for lack of progress. Ongoing communication with the IEP team is critical, and a revision of the IEP may be necessary.

of parents being asked to copy over the IEP in their handwriting so they "would be involved in its 'writing'" (Turnbull & Turnbull, 1986) have been too frequent.

The 1999 final regulations for the IDEA Amendments of 1997 state that the extent of involvement of the regular education teacher in the developing, reviewing, and revising of IEPs will be determined on a case by case basis. However, as a member of the IEP team, the general education teacher must, to an appropriate extent, participate in the development, review, and revision of the student's IEP. This includes assisting in developing positive behavioral intervention and strategies (discussed further in Chapter 6), determining supplemental aids and services needed, and identifying program modifications.

Ideally, the classroom teacher would be very involved in the IEP meeting. If this does not occur, a different means of teacher input should be developed (e.g., a pre-IEP informal meeting); otherwise the document may not reflect the student's needs in the inclusive classroom. Furthermore, a copy of the IEP itself should be readily available as a reference tool throughout the year. In particular, the teacher should keep the goals and benchmarks at hand so that the IEP can influence instructional programs.

An IEP's annual goals and short-term objectives ultimately should be reflected in instructional plans in the classroom; however, short-term objectives are not intended to be used as weekly plans, let alone daily plans. Teachers should refer to the document periodically to ensure that instruction is consistent with the long-term needs of the student. When significant variance is noted, it may become the basis for a correction in instruction or perhaps a rationale for a change in the goals or objectives of the IEP.

In concluding their discussion on IEPs, Epstein et al. (1992) indicate that teachers must not lose sight of the spirit of individualization that should guide the IEP process. Teachers need to view the documents not just as a process of legal compliance but rather as a tool for meeting students' individual needs. Unless guided by the rationale and spirit that informed the original development of the IEP concept, the process can degenerate into a mere bookkeeping activity. Instead, well thought-out IEPs should

# DIVERSITY FORUM

## Involving Parents with Limited English Skills

1. Have letters, notices, progress reports, school handbooks, and information packets translated into the languages of families of all students.

2. Have individuals available to answer the school telephone who speak the languages of parents.

3. Have newsletters or key newsletter articles translated.

4. Record phone messages in other languages so non-English speaking parents can also keep track of their children's coursework and school events.

5. Use school newsletters to announce cultural and other events sponsored by other language groups represented in the school.

6. Integrate bilingual and multicultural materials in school displays, publications, libraries, and classrooms.

7. Use paid or volunteer interpreters to promote communication with limited English parents.

8. Hire bilingual parent coordinators or find volunteers to meet with parents in their homes and at parent centers, churches, and other gathering places to talk about school-related issues.

9. Recruit, train, and hire bilingual parents to be paraprofessionals in the schools.

10. Make special efforts to welcome parents with limited English skills who visit the school.

From "Strategies for Working with Culturally, Linguistically, and Ethnically Diverse Populations," 1999, *LDA Newsbriefs,* March/April, p. 11. Used by permission.

form the foundation for individually designed educational programs for students with disabilities. The teacher should maintain efforts to include parents in the implementation and evaluation of the IEP. This takes extra effort, especially if the parents have limited English skills, but the effect on outcomes is significant. The nearby Diversity Forum provides ideas for ways to include those parents with limited English skills.

# Summary

## Prereferral Child Study and Referral Process

▲ All procedures associated with special education programs must be consistent with due-process requirements.

▲ Each state provides time lines that govern the referral/assessment/IEP process.

▲ Prereferral intervention is a process of assisting students in the general education classroom prior to referral for full assessment.

▲ Child study or teacher assistance committees are responsible for helping teachers modify instruction for a student experiencing learning difficulties.

▲ Well-trained child study teams can assist teachers and limit referrals.

## Assessment

▲ Assessment includes testing but also a broader range of methods that help define a student's strengths and problems leading to the development of educational interventions.

▲ Formal assessment is based on the administration of commercial instruments, typically for survey or diagnostic purposes.

▲ Informal assessment includes a variety of tools that can enhance a teacher's knowledge of students' learning needs.

▲ Curriculum-based measures are tied to the class curriculum and assess a student within this context.

▲ Ecological assessment places the evaluative data within the context of a student's environment.

▲ Authentic and portfolio assessment documents a student's ability to construct, perform, produce, or demonstrate a task.

▲ The control of bias in assessment is not only essential to accurate and fair evaluation, but also a legal requirement.

▲ Classroom teachers may not administer the formal assessments but nevertheless are important members of any assessment process and should be informed about the assessment process and the IEP.

## Individualized Education Programs

▲ The final regulations of the IDEA Amendments of 1997 contain very specific mandates for assessment, developing the IEP or IFSP, and ensuring parental involvement throughout the special education process.

# Further Readings

Conoley, J..C., & Kramer, J. J. (1992). *Eleventh mental measurements yearbook.* Lincoln, NE: Buros Institute.

Conoley, J. C., & Kramer, J. J. (1989). *Tests in print.* Lincoln, NE: Buros Institute.

Ysseldyke, J. E., Christenson, S., & Kovaleski, J. F. (1994). Identifying students instructional needs in the context of classroom and home environments. *Teaching Exceptional Students, 26*(3), 37–41.

Following are publications from the National Information Center on Handicapped Children and Youth (NICHCY). To request material write NICHCY, PO Box 1492, Washington, DC 20013.

*Education of children & youth with special needs: What do the laws say?* (#ND 15)

*Assessing children for the presence of a disability* (Vol. IV, No. 1, 1994)

*Individualized education plans* (LG 2)

*Bibliography on assessing children for the presence of a disability: Schools* (B1)

*Bibliography on assessing children for the presence of a disability: Families* (B2)

# Chapter 4

# Teaching Students with Learning Disabilities

*After reading this chapter, you should be able to:*

◢ Identify the characteristics of a learning disability (LD)

◢ Discuss the impact of cultural diversity on identification and intervention for LD

◢ Describe the criteria for eligibility for LD services

◢ Compare the traditional approaches to intervention for individuals with LD at the preschool, elementary, and secondary levels

◢ Describe the challenges faced by adults with LD

◢ Make modifications in teaching methods and classroom management to address academic, social, emotional, and cognitive differences

◢ Prepare children in a general education classroom to accept a student with an LD

Alonzo was 6 years old when he eagerly started first grade. Problems began to emerge as the reading program expanded from picture books with lots of repetition to books containing unknown words. Alonzo had difficulty using context clues, and he had limited phonemic awareness in decoding a new word. His first report card showed "needs improvement" in reading, listening, and following directions. The bright spot in Alonzo's first-grade achievement was his above-average functioning in math, his ability to pay attention, and good social skills. Alonzo was promoted to second grade. Over the summer, his family moved to another state.

Alonzo adjusted to the new school and worked well for the first 9 weeks of review, and then began to have trouble finishing his work. He became frustrated with written assignments and often complained of stomachaches, asking to stay home from school. His teachers felt that he was still adjusting to a new school.

By the middle of the year, his parents, teacher, and child study team agreed that accommodations were needed. The special education teacher put together material to review skills and phonemic elements Alonzo had not mastered. His parents agreed to work on this material at home. He also worked with a fifth-grade peer helper who read with him one-on-one three days a week. The classroom teacher agreed to restate oral instructions, to continue working on phonics, and to encourage Alonzo to predict unknown words based on meaning and evaluate whether the word he guessed fit with the rest of the words in the sentence.

After 6 weeks the child study team still felt that Alonzo was struggling too much so they recommended a special education referral. His tests showed average intelligence and deficits in reading skills, writing, and listening. It was determined that Alonzo had a learning disability, making him eligible for special education services. Although signs of learning disabilities were present, the school proceeded slowly in identifying him as a child with a learning disability. (As seen in Chapter 1, school personnel and parents want to avoid labeling because it can be detrimental to children.)

Alonzo attended a resource class in third grade. Through these services, his reading of multisyllable words greatly improved as did his writing and listening skills. By fourth grade, he remained in the general education classroom full time, needing only periodic work with the learning disabilities teacher.

## QUESTIONS TO CONSIDER

1. What alerted Alonzo's teacher to a possible learning disability?
2. How might his move have been a factor in his school performance?
3. What would have happened to Alonzo if he had not received special education services in third grade?

*J*ust as it is difficult to distinguish children with **learning disabilities (LD)** from their peers by looks, you cannot distinguish adults with learning disabilities from other adults. You may be surprised to find that many important and famous people have achieved significant accomplishments in spite of experiencing a severe learning disability. Adults with learning disabilities can be found in all professions. They may be teachers, lawyers, doctors, blue-collar workers, or politicians! Read the vignettes that follow, and see whether you can identify the names of the individuals with learning disabilities:

During his childhood, this young man was an outstanding athlete, achieving great success and satisfaction from sports. Unfortunately, he struggled in the class-room. He tried very hard, but he always seemed to fail academically. His biggest fear was being asked to stand up and read in front of his classmates. He was frequently teased about his class performance, and he described his school days as sheer torture. His only feelings of success were experienced on the playing field.

When he graduated from high school, he didn't consider going to college because he "wasn't a terrific student, and never got into books all that much." Even though he was an outstanding high school pole vaulter, he did not get a single scholarship during his senior year. He had already gone to work with his father when he was offered a $500 football scholarship from Graceland College. He didn't accept that offer; instead he trained in track and field. Several years later, he won a gold medal in the Olympics in the grueling decathlon event! In case you haven't guessed, this story is about Bruce Jenner.

This individual was still illiterate at age 12, but he could memorize anything! Spelling was always impossible for him, and as he said, he "had trouble with the A, B, and that other letter." He also was a failure at math. He finally made it through high school, but he failed his first year at West Point. He did graduate, with the help of tutors, one year late. His special talent was in military strategy, and, during World War II, he became one of the United States' most famous generals. Of course, this story is about George Patton.

Other famous people with learning disabilities include Leonardo da Vinci, Tom Cruise, Cher, Nelson Rockefeller, Winston Churchill, Woodrow Wilson, F. W. Wool-worth, Walt Disney, Ernest Hemingway, Albert Einstein, George Bernard Shaw, and Thomas Edison (Harwell, 1989; Silver, 1995). Like these and others, individuals with learning disabilities are often misunderstood and teased early in life for their inade-quacies in the classroom. To be successful in life, they had to be creative and persis-tent. Adults with learning disabilities succeed by sheer determination in overcoming their limitations and focusing on their talents.

Perhaps the most difficult aspect of understanding and teaching students with learning disabilities is the fact that the disability is hidden. When students with obvi-ously normal intelligence fail to finish their work, interrupt inappropriately, never seem to follow directions, and turn in sloppy, poorly organized assignments, it is nat-ural to blame poor motivation, lack of effort—even an undesirable family life.

However, the lack of accomplishment and success in the classroom does have a cause; the students are not demonstrating these behaviors to upset or irritate their teachers. A learning disability is a cognitive disability; it is a disorder of thinking and reasoning. Because the dysfunction is presumed to be in the central nervous system, the presence of the disability is not visible (Harwell, 1989).

The individuals with learning disabilities described earlier have experienced the frustration of living with a disability that is not easily identified. Children with learning disabilities look like the other students in their grade. They can perform like the other students in some areas, but not in others. Like Alonzo in the first vignette, a child may have good social skills and make good grades in math, but fail in reading. Another child may be able to read and write at grade level but fail in math and get in trouble for misconduct. Students with learning disabilities also may perform inconsistently. They may know spelling words on Thursday and fail the test on Friday.

In this chapter you will study the patterns of strengths and weakness of children, youth, and adults who experience unexplained underachievement. Professionals from many fields have joined the search for a definition and causes of these disabilities, as well as methods to identify affected children and to successfully accommodate or remedy the disability. The answers are still evolving, but much progress has been made in this exciting field.

## BASIC CONCEPTS ABOUT LEARNING DISABILITIES

### Learning Disabilities Defined

The initial studies of children later described as having learning disabilities were done by physicians interested in brain injury in children. Over the years, more than 90 terms were introduced into the literature to describe these children (Deiner, 1993). The most common include *minimal brain dysfunction (MBD), brain damage, central process dysfunction,* and *language delay.* To add to the confusion, separate definitions were also offered to explain each term. The term *specific learning disabilities* was first adopted publicly in 1963 at a meeting of parents and professionals. Kirk (1962) developed the generic term *learning disabilities* in an effort to unite the field, which was torn between individuals promoting different theories regarding underachievement. The term was received favorably because it did not have the negative connotations of the other terms and did describe the primary characteristic of the children.

In 1968 a committee appointed by the U.S. Office of Education (USOE) developed a definition of learning disabilities that has been modified only slightly over the years. This definition, retained in IDEA (1997), states:

> "Specific learning disability" means a disorder in one or more of the basic psychological processes involved in understanding or in using language, spoken or written, which may manifest itself in an imperfect ability to listen, think, speak, read, write, spell or to do mathematical calculations. The term includes such conditions as perceptual handicaps, brain injury, minimal brain dysfunction, dyslexia, and developmental aphasia. The term does not include children who have learning problems which are primarily the result of visual, hearing, or motor handicaps, of mental retardation, or emotional disturbance, or of environmental, cultural, or economic disadvantage. (USOE, 1977, p. 65083)

Although according to Mercer, Jordan, Allsopp, and Mercer (1996), this definition is used by a majority of states, it has been criticized over the years for including concepts that are unclear or difficult to use to identify children with a learning disability (Hammill, Leigh, McNutt, & Larsen, 1981). The concept of deficits in "psychological processes" is the most nebulous and has been interpreted in several ways, including perceptual-motor deficits, deficits in the process of taking in information, difficulty in making sense of information and expressing knowledge effectively, and deficits in cognitive processes such as attention, memory, and metacognition (the way one thinks about and controls his or her cognitive processing, e.g., self-monitoring, predicting, and planning). When the U.S. Office of Education (1977) published the criteria for identifying students with learning disabilities, the processing component was not included in the requirements, and the language and academic problems were described within the context of a **discrepancy factor.** These criteria will be described later in the chapter.

A more straightforward definition is offered by Harwell (1989), who identifies an individual with a learning disability as one who

**DISCREPANCY FACTOR** in learning disabilities refers to children with levels of academic and/or language achievement that are unexpectedly low, given their overall ability or level of intelligence. This discrepancy concept is used widely but it has been criticized. Can you consider its pros and cons?

1. can see.
2. can hear.
3. has general intelligence in the near-average, average, or above-average range.
4. has educational difficulties that do not stem from inadequate educational experience or cultural factors.
5. does not acquire and use information efficiently because of an impairment in perception, conceptualization, language, memory, attention, or motor control.

## Prevalence and Causes of Learning Disabilities

In today's schools, there are by far more students with learning disabilities than with any other disability. A report from the U.S. Department of Education (1997) shows that in the 1995–1996 school year, 2,597,231 (51.2%) of the students with disabilities between ages 6 and 21 were learning disabled. The report also shows that approximately four boys are identified to every girl.

Experts generally agree that learning is hindered in children with learning disabilities because of neurological abnormalities causing a problem in how the brain processes information (Hallahan & Kauffman, 1999). In a pamphlet for parents, the American Academy of Pediatrics (1988) describes the problem as

> similar to a distorted television picture caused by technical problems at the station. There is nothing wrong with the TV camera at the station or the TV set at home. Yet, the picture is not clear. Something in the internal workings of the TV station prevents it from presenting a good picture. There may be nothing wrong with the way the children take in information. Their senses of sight and sound are fine. The problem occurs after the eyes or ears have done their job. (p. 7)

Why this happens generally remains unknown. The literature suggests several causes, primarily hereditary factors and trauma experienced before birth, during birth, and after birth.

1. *Genetic factors:* Some studies have cited the large number of relatives with learning problems in children identified with learning disabilities. Chromosomal abnormalities and structural brain differences have also been linked to learning disabilities. Research in this area continues to show promise.

2. *Causes occurring before birth:* Learning problems have been linked to injuries to the embryo or fetus caused by the birth mother's use of alcohol, cigarettes, or other drugs, such as cocaine and prescription and nonprescription drugs. Through the mother, the fetus is exposed to the toxins, causing malformations of the developing brain and central nervous system. Although significant amounts of overexposure to these drugs may cause serious problems, such as mental retardation, no safe levels have been identified.

3. *Causes occurring during birth process:* These traumas may include prolonged labor, anoxia, prematurity, and injury from medical instruments such as forceps. Although not all children with a traumatic birth are found to have learning problems later, a significant number of children with learning problems do have a history of complications during this period.

4. *Causes occurring after birth:* High fever, encephalitis, meningitis, stroke, diabetes, and pediatric AIDS have been linked to LD. Malnutrition, poor postnatal health care, and lead ingestion can also lead to neurological dysfunction (Hallahan, Kauffman, & Lloyd, 1999).

> **TEACHING TIP**
> Often parents will ask teachers what causes a learning disability. To respond, you might discuss some of the possible causes and suggest that the specific cause is seldom identifiable for individual children. Reassure parents that pinpointing the cause is not important in planning and implementing effective intervention strategies.

Advances in neurological research and use of computerized neurological techniques such as computerized axial tomography (CAT) scan and positron emission tomography (PET) scan have made professionals more inclined to believe in a neurological explanation of learning disabilities. Widespread use of these tests to identify a learning disability has not been forthcoming for several reasons: such procedures are expensive, are invasive, and the documented presence of a neurological dysfunction does not affect how the child is taught (Hallahan, Kauffman, & Lloyd, 1999). However, this research is important to advance knowledge of this type of disability.

## Characteristics of Students with Learning Disabilities

Learning disabilities are primarily described as deficits in academic achievement (reading, writing, and mathematics) and/or language (listening or speaking). However, children with learning disabilities may have significant problems in other areas, such as social interactions and emotional maturity, attention and hyperactivity, memory, cognition, metacognition, motor skills, and perceptual abilities. Since learning disabilities are presumed to be a central nervous system dysfunction, characteristics may be manifested throughout the lifespan, preschool through adult (Mercer, 1997).

The most common characteristics of students with LD are described briefly in the following sections, concentrating on the challenges they may create in a classroom. Students with learning disabilities are a heterogeneous group. A single student will not have deficits in all areas. Also, any area could be a strength for a student with learning disabilities, and the student might exceed the abilities of his or her peers in that area. An understanding of characteristics of children with learning problems is important in developing prereferral interventions, in making appropriate referrals, and in identifying effective accommodations and intervention strategies. Figure 4.1 displays the possible strengths and weaknesses of children with learning disabilities.

**ACADEMIC DEFICITS** During the elementary years a discrepancy between ability and achievement begins to emerge in students with learning disabilities. Often puzzling to teachers, these students seem to have strengths similar to their peers in several areas, but their rate of learning in other areas is unexpectedly slower. The vignette that began this chapter profiles a typical child with learning disabilities: above-average ability in math; average ability in language, attention, and social skills; and severe deficits in reading, written expression, and listening.

*FIGURE 4.1*

Areas of Possible
Strengths and Deficits of
Students with Learning
Disabilities

**Academics:**
Reading
Math
Writing

**Attention and Hyperactivity**

**Language:**
Speaking
Listening

**Cognition**

**Learning Disabilities**

**Memory**

**Metacognition**

**Social–Emotional Maturity**

**Perception**

**Motor Skills and Coordination**

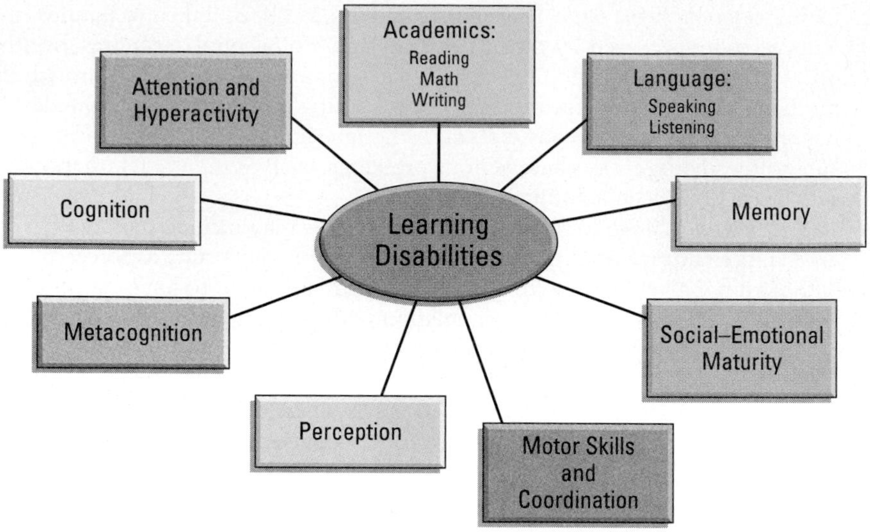

The academic problems that identify a learning disability fall into the areas of reading, math, and written expression. The most prevalent type of academic difficulty for students with learning disabilities is reading. One study found that approximately 80% of the children identified as learning disabled have primary deficits in the area of reading and related language functions (Moats & Lyon, 1993). Problems may be noted in *basic reading skills* and *reading comprehension.* Children with learning disabilities may struggle with oral reading tasks. They may read in a strained voice with poor phrasing, ignore punctuation, and grope for words like a much younger child. Oral reading problems cause tremendous embarrassment to these children. Carnine, Silbert, and Kameenui (1990) confirm that a student's self-image and feelings of confidence are greatly affected by reading experience. Deficits in reading skills can also lead to acting out behavior and poor motivation.

Some children with learning disabilities may be able to say the words correctly but not remember what they have read. Comprehension problems may include one or more of the following: (1) identifying the main idea, (2) recalling basic facts and events in a sequence, and (3) making inferences or evaluating what has been read (Mercer, 1997).

Another major academic problem area is mathematics. Students with learning disabilities may have problems in *math calculations* or *math reasoning* (USOE, 1977). These conceptual and skill areas include deficits in the four operations, the concept of zero, regrouping, place value, basic math concepts (e.g., one-to-one correspondence, sets), and solving math problems (Smith, Polloway, Dowdy, & Blalock, 1997). Children may have *abilities* in calculation but have *disabilities* in math reasoning; they may make many errors in calculations but be able to perform calculations to solve a math word problem. Often the rate of response interferes with success in math; for example, a child may be able to perform the skill, but unable to complete the number of problems required during the time allowed.

Learning disabilities in the area of *written expression* are beginning to receive more recognition as a potentially serious problem. The three main areas of concern are handwriting, spelling, and written expression, including mechanics and creativity. The impact of written language problems increases with a student's age because so many school assignments require a written product.

*During grades 2 through 6, academic problems begin to become very obvious.*

**LANGUAGE DEFICITS**  Language deficits are found in the areas of *oral expression* and *listening comprehension.* Since these two areas control our ability to communicate with others, a deficit can have a major impact on quality of life—including life in a general education classroom. Studies have found that more than 60% of students with learning disabilities have some type of language disorder (Bryan, Bay, Lopez-Reyna, & Donahue, 1991). Common oral language problems include difficulty in retrieving words; children often use a less appropriate word because the right word will not come to them (Mathinos, 1991). The response rate and sentence articulation of children with learning disabilities may be slower than that of their nondisabled peers (Ackerman, Dykman, & Gardner, 1990). If ample time is not allowed for a response, the student's behavior may be misinterpreted as failure to understand or refusal to participate. Children with learning disabilities tend to use simpler, less mature language and confuse sequences in retelling a story. These deficits in expressive language suggest possible difficulties in receptive language or listening as well (Smith, 1994). Listening problems also can be easily misinterpreted. A child with a disability in listening demonstrates that disability in a negative way, for example, by failing to follow directions or by appearing oppositional or unmotivated. A teacher's careful observation and assessment of a student's language ability is important for ensuring the student's success.

A new area of concern and research for children with language-learning disabilities is the area of **pragmatics,** or use of language in social communication situations. Children with these disabilities are sometimes unsuccessful in fully participating in conversation. They may need extra time to process incoming information, or they may not understand the meaning of the words or word sequences. They may miss nonverbal language cues. They may not understand jokes; they may laugh inappropriately or at the wrong times. Group work is often difficult, as is giving or following directions. Language disabilities can contribute significantly to difficulties in other social situations as well (Lapadat, 1991).

*PRAGMATICS* is the study of how effectively individuals use language in social situations.

**SOCIAL–EMOTIONAL PROBLEMS**  The literature suggests that to be socially accepted, students should be cooperative, share, offer pleasant greetings, have positive interactions

**CROSS-REFERENCE**
Often students with learning disabilities who have social-emotional difficulties will present challenges in behavior management in the classroom. Refer to Chapter 13 for more information in this area.

with peers, ask for and give information, and make conversation (Gresham, 1982). Some children with learning disabilities have a real strength in the area of social skills. However, several characteristics of learning disabilities, like those noted concerning language, can create difficulties in social and emotional life.

A study by Kavale and Forness (1996) shows that a perception of low academic achievement was directly related to reduced acceptance, less interaction, greater rejection, and lower social status among peers. Often positive interactions and exchange of information do not occur between children with learning disabilities and their peers or teachers. Because of behavior and language differences, children with learning disabilities need more guidance and structure. Over time, this can create feelings of overdependency, and eventually *learned helplessness* can occur. Social deficits have even been known to lead to school failure (Bryan, 1999).

Years of failure can create other concerns. Wright-Strawderman and Watson (1992) found that 36% of a sample of students with learning disabilities indicated depression. Other researchers have reported psychological problems including feelings of incompetence, inadequacy, frustration, and anger (Ness & Price, 1990). Research by Kavale and Forness (1996) demonstrated that 75% of students with learning disabilities were significantly different from their nondisabled peers on most measures of social competence.

By adolescence, a student's combined cognitive and language deficits can interfere significantly with deciding how to act in the new social situations brought about by increased independence. When interacting with normal adolescents who have advanced language skills, students with disabilities may experience greater failure in communication and may suffer more rejection (Polloway & Smith, 1992). The negative self-image of teenagers with learning disabilities is evident in Geisthardt and Munsch's (1996) study, which found that adolescents with learning disabilities were more likely to report that they had failed a class and less likely to report that they had been selected for a school activity than their nondisabled peers. They were also less likely to call on peers for support when dealing with a personal or academic problem.

In summary, Gorman (1999) proposes that learning disabilities may result in or increase emotional distress. Emotional issues may mask or exacerbate a child's LD. However, she also notes that positive emotional health can enhance the performance of students with learning disabilities. By being sensitive to emotional issues, you can take care to include students with learning disabilities in supportive situations and provide reinforcement for specific successes. General praise statements such as "Good work!" or "You are really smart!" will not have much impact because they are not believable to the students. Commenting on or rewarding specific accomplishments will be more effective. Additional examples of appropriate interventions in this area for inclusive classrooms are discussed later in this chapter and in future chapters.

**CROSS-REFERENCE**
Many students with learning disabilities have attention deficit/hyperactivity disorders. This topic is covered more extensively in Chapter 5.

**ATTENTION DEFICITS AND HYPERACTIVITY**    Attention is a critical skill in learning. Conte (1991) suggests that to be effective learners, children must be able to initiate attention, direct their attention appropriately, sustain their attention according to the task demands, and shift attention when appropriate. Deficits in these areas can have an impact on all aspects of success in school. When children are "not paying attention," they cannot respond appropriately to questions, follow directions, or take notes during a lecture. The excess movement of a hyperactive student can draw sharp criticism when it negatively affects the learning environment. Social problems occur when the student interrupts others and does not listen to his or her peers. Students with attention problems often have trouble finishing assignments or rush

One impo[...]
ing learning di[...]
Use of these ac[...]
work rate are [...]
incorrectly. Ex[...]
Rights and Res[...]

### CULTURA[...]

Since learning [...]
and the numbe[...]
ing steadily, in[...]
ward, 1994). A[...]
apply to the pe[...]
a learning disa[...]
program plann[...]

Accurately [...]
no small chall[...]
related to div[...]
Teachers some[...]
view special e[...]
gelman, & Jin[...]
assessment an[...]
found that too[...]
achievement t[...]
difference. Th[...]
ineffective in [...]
ond language.[...]
of a learning [...]
quately respor[...]
impact of lan[...]
Forum. Respo[...]
on the test!

### STRATEG[...]
### FOR STUL[...]

**O**ver the [...]
  have bec[...]
tory and visua[...]
academic area[...]
Larsen (1974)[...]
basic academi[...]
instruction w[...]
guage, social-[...]
attention. Ma[...]
improving the[...]

through their work with little regard for detail. Estimates of the number of students with learning disabilities that have attention problems range from 41% to 80% (DeLong, 1995). Attention deficits are covered more thoroughly in Chapter 5.

**MEMORY DEFICITS**   Several studies have suggested that students with learning disabilities have more deficits in memory than students without learning disabilities (Beale & Tippett, 1992). Students with memory deficits have trouble retaining learned information. They may have difficulty in repeating information recently read or heard, following multiple directions, or performing tasks in the correct sequence. Teachers and parents may also report that the memory skills are inconsistent—for example, such a student may know the multiplication facts on Thursday and fail the test on Friday!

**COGNITION DEFICITS**   Cognition refers to the ability to reason or think (Hallahan, Kauffman, & Lloyd, 1996). Students with problems in this area may make poor decisions or frequent errors. They may have trouble getting started on a task, have delayed verbal responses, require more supervision, or have trouble adjusting to change. Understanding social expectations may be difficult. They may require concrete demonstrations. They often have trouble using previously learned information in a new situation.

**METACOGNITION DEFICITS**   Hallahan et al. (1999) refer to **metacognition** as "thinking about thinking." Metacognitive deficits include the inability to control and direct one's own attention and mental processes (Wong, 1991). Students with problems in this area might have difficulty focusing on listening, purposefully remembering important information, connecting that information to prior knowledge, making sense out of the new information, and using what they know to solve a problem. They often lack strategies for planning and organizing, setting priorities, and solving problems. An important component of metacognition is the ability to regulate one's own behavior when one perceives that one is acting inappropriately or making mistakes.

*METACOGNITION* is the ability to think about thinking.

**PERCEPTUAL DIFFERENCES**   Perceptual disorders affect the ability to recognize stimuli being received through sight, hearing, or touch and to discriminate between and interpret the sensations appropriately. A child with a learning disability might not have any problems in these areas, or he or she might have deficits in any or all of them. Research has shown that visual perception is more important at very young ages but is not a major requirement for higher level academics (Smith, 1994). Identification of deficits and training in the perceptual processes was emphasized in the early 1970s; however, it is no longer a prominent consideration in the education of children with learning disabilities.

**MOTOR SKILL AND COORDINATION PROBLEMS**   This area has also been deemphasized in the identification of an intervention for children with learning disabilities because it is not directly related to academics. However, it is common for children with learning disabilities to display problems in gross motor areas; they often cannot throw and catch a ball or may have a clumsy gait. Common fine motor deficits include difficulties with using scissors, buttoning clothing, and handwriting. Individuals with learning disabilities may also have a slow reaction time. Consideration of motor skills and coordination is important in the selection of a postsecondary educational program and ultimately in the identification of a career.

## *DIVERSITY FORUM*    Impact of Language/Vocabulary Differences on Listening and Reading Comprehension

Given this passage:

Before the flangbong, the smarmly gribbles were very murggy. So, they went to the libenstar and libensed their smarmly zwibucks. Then the gribbles went to their yibode counsiber's nebber and libensed themselves. Once they were all flarkly and foebush, the gribbles borrowed their counsiber's marbork and went happily to the flangbong.

See if you can answer these questions.

1. Who was very murggy?
2. What did the gribbles do to their zwibucks? When did they do it?
3. What did the gribbles do to themselves? Where did they do it?
4. Whose marbork did the gribbles borrow?
5. Why do you think the gribbles wanted to be flarkly and foebush?

From *Introduction to Learning Disabilities* (p. 296), by D. D. Hallahan, J. M. Kauffman, and J. W. Lloyd, 1999, Boston: Allyn and Bacon. Used by permission.

disabilities. Other nontraditional approaches have been proposed and some even have a large following, though they may not be supported by research. Teachers need to be well informed on all approaches so that they can provide objective information to parents who seek to understand and address their child's difficulties. The following section discusses the accepted traditional approaches for each age level and a brief overview of some of the nontraditional approaches.

### Traditional Approaches

In a review of various treatment approaches, Lloyd (1988) concludes that no single approach to learning disabilities can be cited as the best. He does suggest that the most effective ones are structured and goal-oriented, provide multiple opportunities for practice, include a strategy, foster independence, and are comprehensive and detailed. Many of the following approaches adhere to these principles. They all can

**Examples**

**Flexible Time**

Extended time

Alternating le
test sections (
and longer)

More frequen

Extended test
over several d

From "The IDI
Teacher Traine
Publishing Co.

*M*ost children with learning disabilities are identified during the first and second grades.

be implemented in a general education classroom and may benefit many nondisabled students as well. The strategies are discussed according to age levels—preschool, elementary, secondary, and adult. The largest section concerns the elementary school student; however, many elementary-level techniques are equally effective at the secondary level.

**PRESCHOOL SERVICES**   In addition to the controversy surrounding assessment and identification of learning disabilities in preschool children, much has been written for and against the educational effectiveness and cost-effectiveness of early intervention programs for these children. Bender (1995) summarizes research in this area by stating that early intervention for some preschool children with learning disabilities—particularly those from low socioeconomic minority groups—is effective.

Mercer (1997) provides an overview of the curriculum models primarily used in preschool programs for children with learning disabilities. These include developmental, cognitive, and behavioral models. The **developmental model** stresses provision of an enriched environment. The child is provided numerous experiences and opportunities for learning. Development is stimulated through language and storytelling, field trips, and creative opportunities.

The **cognitive model** (or constructionist model) is based on Piaget's work. Stimulating the child's cognitive or thinking abilities is the primary focus. Activities are designed to improve memory, discrimination, language, concept formation, self-evaluation, problem solving, and comprehension. This new area of research is experiencing great success.

Concepts learned by direct instruction and the theory of reinforcement form the basis for the **behavioral model.** Measurable goals are set for each student, behaviors are observed, and desirable behavior is reinforced. Direct instruction is provided to accomplish goals, and progress is charted to provide data that determine the next instructional task.

Mercer (1997) recommends a program that combines features from each approach. He suggests some structure, availability of free-choice activities, direct instruction in targeted areas, daily charting and feedback, developmental activities, and spontaneous learning experiences. These methods allow individual needs to be met in an inclusive setting without stigmatizing the children. Since children at this age are more likely to be falsely identified as learning disabled because of a maturational lag or lack of educational opportunities, it is particularly important to teach them in inclusive settings if at all possible. When a new student with learning disabilities is included in a general education preschool classroom, teachers can facilitate the transition by communicating frequently with parents before, during, and after the child's exit from one place and entrance into the new setting. Parents can provide information on their child's communication skills, strengths, and preferences. The following list is adapted from Hadden and Fowler (1997) and shows questions that teachers can ask to encourage parents to share their child's uniqueness.

1. How does your child communicate?
2. What things are the most difficult for your child to learn?
3. What types of things does your child enjoy learning?
4. What are your child's favorite toys and activities?
5. How does your child get along with other children?
6. What types of rewards work best for your child (e.g., hugs praise, stickers)?
7. What types of discipline work best with your child?

*DEVELOPMENTAL MODEL* is an intervention strategy based on providing multiple activities that stimulate language, academic, and motor development. *COGNITIVE MODEL* is an intervention approach that focuses on teaching students how to deal with their own problems through reasoning and problem solving. *BEHAVIORAL MODEL* is an intervention approach in which measurable goals are identified, direct instruction is provided, and desirable behavior is reinforced.

8. What kind of support or help, if any, does your child need during routines such as eating, dressing, toileting, and napping?
9. What was your child working on in the last program that you would like to see continued in the new program?
10. What other goals would you like to see for your child in the new program?
11. What do you see as your child's strengths?
12. What other information would you like to share about your child? (pp. 36–39).

**CONSIDER THIS**
According to Lyon's study, intervention in reading skills in grades 1–3 is critical. Should all students who are behind their peers in reading ability be helped during these years? What are possible positive and negative outcomes of providing a special education program for all of these children who are at risk for later failure?

**ELEMENTARY SERVICES**   By fifth grade, 76% of the children with learning disabilities have been identified; more children are identified during the first and second grades than at any other time (McLesky, 1992). The importance of intervention during the early elementary years is validated by a study cited by Lyon (1995), suggesting that 74% of the children with a reading disability in the third grade remained disabled in the ninth grade. As discussed in the section on characteristics, many of these deficits remain a problem throughout an individual's life. The intervention begun during elementary years may be equally important at the secondary level and for some adults. Intervention is important in academic and language deficits, social–emotional problems, and cognitive and metacognitive deficits.

Children with learning disabilities may have academic and language deficits in any or all of the following areas:

▲ Basic reading skills
▲ Reading comprehension
▲ Math calculation
▲ Math reasoning
▲ Written expression
▲ Oral expression
▲ Listening

Since these areas are usually the focus of an elementary curriculum, they can very often be addressed in the general education classroom. Both general and special education teachers have been trained to provide instruction in these areas, so collaborative teaching is possible. Because of the uneven skill development in children with learning disabilities, individualized assessment is often required to identify areas that specifically need to be addressed. Informal methods, such as the curriculum-based assessment discussed in Chapter 3, are usually effective for planning instruction. This assessment should include an evaluation of the student's strengths, which may indicate the most effective method for instruction.

*WHOLE LANGUAGE METHOD* is a reading approach that focuses on using writing, oral language, and literature to develop reading and comprehension skills.
*PHONOLOGIC AWARENESS* is an individual's ability to see the relationship between sounds and words.
*SEQUENTIAL PHONICS PROGRAMS* teach phonetic sounds and rules in order to enable students to decode phonetically regular and irregular words.

Because student strengths and weaknesses are so diverse, a single method of teaching may not meet the needs of all students with learning disabilities. For example, in the area of reading instruction, the general education teacher may use a reading approach based on reading literature for meaning; development in areas such as phonics will occur naturally as the reader becomes more efficient. In this method, often referred to as the **whole language method,** the teacher might note difficulty with a phonetic principle during oral reading and subsequently develop a mini-lesson using text to teach the skill. Unfortunately, many children with learning disabilities do not readily acquire the alphabet code because of limitations in processing the sounds of letters. Their reading disability may be the result of a deficit in **phonologic awareness** (Fletcher, Shaywitz, & Shankweiler, 1994). These students need a more highly structured **sequential phonics program** that teaches the application of phonologic rules to print (Duane & Gray, 1991; Lyon, 1991; Rooney, 1995). One strength of the whole language method is its focus on the comprehension of authentic reading material; the teacher using the phonics method must purposely develop those important comprehension skills. These two reading methods are discussed further in Chapter 14.

Another way to facilitate success for students with learning disabilities in inclusive settings is teaching a **strategy** to apply during the process of learning new information or skills. A strategy is defined by Deshler and Lenz (1989) as an individual's approach to a task. It includes how "a person thinks and acts when planning, executing, and evaluating performance on a task and its subsequent outcomes" (p. 203). Students with learning disabilities may not automatically develop strategies for learning, or the ones they develop may be inefficient. The phases of one effective strategy to increase reading comprehension are highlighted in the nearby Inclusion Strategies feature. Additional strategies are discussed in Chapter 15.

**STRATEGY** is a specific technique focused on more efficiently learning and/or performing a task.

Written language is often difficult to master for children and adults with learning disabilities. Unfortunately, making too many accommodations in this area may result in underdeveloped skills. For example, if a student is always allowed to use another

---

## INCLUSION STRATEGIES

### Reading Comprehension Strategies for the General Education Classroom

**BRAINSTORMING:** Have students think about what they already know on the topic from prior lessons, reading, movies, and so forth.

**PREVIEW:** Have students work in small groups to preview assigned text. Give them 2 minutes to search for clues about key ideas, characters, settings, etc. Give students 6 minutes to discuss their predictions and develop their "preview."

**CLICK:** After reading a designated portion of text, have students write down words they "click" on. These are words or information that they know about and that can extend information in text.

**CLUNK:** When students "clunk," they come to words or information they don't recognize or understand and need to know to learn new information. These words/ideas are written down to explore for them through a "de-clunking" strategy. Strategies for solving "clunks" are included in Table 4.1.

| TABLE 4.1 | Strategies for Solving Clunks |
|---|---|
| **CLUNK CARD #1:** | Re-read the sentence with the clunk and the sentences before or after the clunk, looking for clues. |
| **CLUNK CARD #2:** | Re-read the sentence without the word. Think about what would make sense. |
| **CLUNK CARD #3:** | Look for a prefix or suffix in the word that might help. |
| **CLUNK CARD #4:** | Break the word apart and look for smaller words. |

From "Teaching Reading Comprehension Skills to Students with Learning Disabilities in the General Education Classroom (Part II)" by S. Vaughn and J. Kingner, 1999, *Learning Disabilities, 9*(2), pp. 8–9. Used by permission.

**TEACHING TIP**
Many students with learning disabilities will resist the challenge to write because of prior negative feedback. Try giving them multiple opportunities without grading, and then grade only one to two skills at a time. For example, one week you might grade punctuation and the next, spelling. You can also give one grade for content and another for mechanics, and then average the two scores for the final grade.

student's notes or allowed to take tests orally in place of written exams, the short-term benefits may be helpful, but instruction and experience in note taking and writing essay answers must be continued if growth is to occur in these areas. A study by Palinscar and Klenk (1992) suggests that special education teachers frequently limit students' writing tasks to copying words and filling out worksheets, so it is important in inclusive classrooms that students be exposed to a variety of writing opportunities. Students with LD must be given specific instruction in the fundamental aspects of writing if they are to be competent in this area (Graham & Harris, 1997).

Improvement in oral language may be stimulated by promoting a better self-concept and enriching the language environment. These and other techniques are discussed by Candler and Hildreth (1990). They suggest that a poor self-concept can be addressed through encouraging more successful communication experiences and having the student self-evaluate the successes. Relaxation therapy may be needed to open students to more communication opportunities. The classroom can also be designed with areas where students are encouraged to talk. Cooperative learning activities also promote increased verbal interactions. Providing opportunities for students to share their experiences and expertise is also a nonthreatening way to promote use of oral language. Listening and praise help reinforce talking.

Poor listening skills also limit individuals with learning disabilities, influencing both success in the classroom and in social interactions. In Heaton and O'Shea's (1995) effective strategy, which can be modified for use with all age groups, students follow these steps:

**L**   **L**ook at the teacher.
**I**   **I**gnore the student next to you.
**S**   **S**tay in your place.
**T**   **T**ry to visualize and understand the story.
**E**   **E**njoy the story.
**N**   **N**ice job! You're a good listener.

**TEACHING TIP**
The amount of software available for supporting instruction can be overwhelming, and costly mistakes can be made when ordering a program based on a catalog description alone. Organize a plan for the teachers in your school to share the names of effective software. Preview a copy before ordering, whenever possible.

Computers and other technology can assist in teaching individuals with learning disabilities in inclusive classrooms. Olsen and Platt (1996) describe the following advantages of technology:

◢ It is self-pacing and individualized.
◢ It provides immediate feedback.
◢ It has consistent correction procedures.
◢ It provides repetition without pressure.
◢ It confirms correct responses immediately.
◢ It maintains a high frequency of student response.
◢ It builds in repeated validation of academic success.
◢ It is an activity respected by peers.
◢ It is motivating.
◢ It encourages increased time on task.
◢ It minimizes the effects of the disability.

The computer can be used effectively for curriculum support in math, writing, language arts, social studies, science, and other areas. Various types of software provide instructional alternatives such as tutoring, drill and practice, simulation, and games. With so many choices available, teachers should carefully evaluate each program for ease of use and appropriateness for exceptional students.

Intervention related to social interactions and emotional maturity is critical for many students with learning disabilities. The inclusion movement provides opportunities for interactions; the question is how to best prepare both the children with disabilities and nondisabled children for positive interactions. Changing a student's self-image, social ability, and social standing is difficult. Until recently, the research and literature on learning disabilities focused primarily on the efficacy of treatments for the most obvious characteristic—academic deficits. The importance of social skills is just now being recognized and given the attention it deserves.

Intervention in the area of social standing and interaction can take two courses: changing the child or changing the environment. Optimally, both receive attention. Good teaching techniques can lead to academic achievement and eventually to higher self-esteem. Teachers can create a positive learning environment, incorporate praise and encouragement for specific accomplishments, set goals, and be very explicit about expectations for academic work and behavior in the class. They can also monitor progress closely and provide frequent feedback (Mercer, 1997).

Students should be asked higher level questions that require problem solving and reasoning. Opportunities need to be provided for students to generalize learned information across settings. The most effective learning environment is supportive but encourages independence. Students should be given responsibilities. They should be reinforced for making positive comments about themselves and about other students (Mercer, 1997). Figure 4.3 provides innovative examples of ways of meeting the social and emotional needs of several students.

The overall goal of social programs is to teach socially appropriate behavior and social skills that are self-generated and self-monitored. The cognitive problems of students with learning disabilities often make this type of decision making very difficult. FAST is an example of a strategy that can be effectively applied to the social skills training curriculum. It aids in interpersonal problem solving by developing questioning and monitoring skills, brainstorming solutions, and developing and implementing a plan to solve the problem. The steps are displayed in Figure 4.4.

Intervention in cognitive and metacognitive skills has only recently received support from learning disabilities professionals. Powerful techniques are being studied to improve learning. Some of the ideas are relatively simple and require only common sense. First, and most important, is being sure a child is paying attention to the stimulus being presented. This might be done by dimming the lights, calling for attention, or establishing eye contact. Without attention, learning will not take place.

Lerner (1993) suggests that teachers present new information in well-organized, meaningful chunks. As new information is presented to be memorized, it should be linked to previously learned, meaningful information. For example, to teach subtraction, the teacher would demonstrate the relationship to addition. Students should also be encouraged to rehearse new information and be given many opportunities for practice. These and other effective learning strategies are presented in Figure 4.5 in this chapter and throughout the text.

**SECONDARY SERVICES**    Academic and language deficits, social and emotional problems, and differences in cognitive and metacognitive functioning continue to plague many adolescents with learning disabilities. With the focus on content classes in middle and high school, **remediation** of basic skills often is minimal. This can be problematic for students having difficulty passing the high school graduation exam required in many states for a regular diploma. Students who continue to benefit from remediation should be provided these opportunities.

*CONSIDER THIS*
Describe some situations you have observed in which a child displayed inappropriate social skills or responses in the classroom. How could the FAST strategy have been used to prevent recurring problems?

*REMEDIATION* is individualized or group instruction to improve the basic skills of reading, writing, and/or math.

FIGURE *4.3*

Profiles of Students and Related Interventions for Selected Social, Emotional, and Behavioral Characteristics

**SOCIAL SKILLS DEFICITS**

Nobody seems to like Barry. He often is called rude or inconsiderate. For example, he may relate the details of a neighborhood rumor even though the face of one of his classmates is red with embarrassment, or he thoughtlessly may interrupt a serious conversation between two adults. He cannot tell when his listeners have lost interest. To help Barry identify critical social and nonverbal cues, his teacher involves him in role-playing games such as Charades and a social skills curriculum.

**POOR SELF-CONCEPT**

Melanie, a secondary school student, has faced repeated failure and frustration throughout her school years. She has few friends and seldom initiates social interactions or takes part in school activities. When given an academic task, Melanie frequently responds, "That's too hard for me. I can't do it." Melanie's English teacher, who has taken an individual interest in her, has minimized her anxiety about failure through the use of support and success techniques. The teacher is helping Melanie attribute her failures to insufficient effort and praises her for effort regardless of the accuracy of her responses. She also uses Melanie as a peer tutor to enhance her feelings of self-worth.

**DEPENDENCY**

As a young child, Brad was very dependent on his mother. She gave him excessive attention and assistance. Now, he frequently turns to his teacher with requests such as "Help me" or "Show me how." Brad's teacher is trying to provide him with appropriate academic tasks and success experiences and is reinforcing him for effort. Brad also works independently with self-correcting materials and computer software programs that provide him with immediate feedback without the teacher being present.

**LONELINESS**

Tessa usually works, plays, and eats alone. She sits quietly at her desk, staring into space, rather than working or participating in discussions. She seldom willingly joins group activities or even initiates a conversation. She does not share and frequently makes negative comments that reduce the likelihood of further interaction (e.g., "You sure are dumb. Don't you know how to do anything right?"). Tessa's teacher is providing her with much support and praise and gradually is encouraging various interpersonal relationships. Peer teaching and instructional games in which Tessa is paired with a competent, accepting student are providing Tessa with appropriate peer contact. The teacher systematically reinforces any group participation or positive social interaction.

**DISRUPTIVE BEHAVIOR**

Larry is often out of his seat or yelling across the room. He starts fights over minor incidents, such as tripping or butting in line. Larry's teacher is using social skills training and behavior modification techniques to reduce his disruptive behavior. She reinforces and praises him for appropriate behavior and ignores him as much as possible when he is being disruptive. When she must reprimand him, she does so quietly so that others cannot hear.

**HYPERACTIVITY**

Richard's mother describes her son as having been in a state of perpetual motion since he was very young. It seems impossible for him to sit still for even a few minutes. At mealtime, he quickly stuffs his food in his mouth and is then once again on the go. In the classroom Richard is easily excitable and constantly in motion. For example, he frequently is out of his seat, shuffling papers, moving his feet or legs, or tapping his pencil on his desk. Richard's activity level causes him to have frequent accidents (e.g., while riding his bicycle), and he sometimes unintentionally hurts a classmate when playing too rough on the playground. Richard takes Ritalin every morning under his doctor's prescription, and his classroom teacher structures Richard's daily work schedule according to his attention span, reinforces him when he is less active, and frequently allows him to perform tasks that permit him to move about the room.

*FIGURE* **4.3**   (continued)

▼

| **DISTRACTIBILITY** | According to her teacher, Amy is highly distractible and has a short attention span. She can work on an assignment for a short time, but she is diverted quickly by any noise or motion in the room. She stares out the window or daydreams and her assignments go uncompleted. Her teacher uses a carrel to isolate Amy from potentially distracting auditory and visual stimuli. She also encourages Amy to use verbal mediation (i.e., quietly talking to herself about what she is doing) while performing a task and gives her praise for on-task behavior. |
|---|---|
| **IMPULSIVITY** | Jane's impulsivity is evident in class. She is usually the first person to complete and hand in a worksheet, always without checking the accuracy of her responses. Jane's grades in math especially have been affected by her tendency to respond impulsively, even though she usually can correct a wrong response when given the opportunity. She talks out of turn and without thinking says things that may hurt someone's feelings. Jane's teacher is encouraging her to pause before acting or speaking. In math her teacher has Jane estimate the answers and check her work. Also, through contingency contracts Jane is reinforced according to an accuracy criterion (percent correct) for each task. |

From *Students with Learning Disabilities* (5th ed.) (p. 625), by C. Mercer, 1997, Upper Saddle River, NJ: Merrill.

However, the accommodations described in the next section and the learning strategies described in the previous section can also be used with secondary students to facilitate basic skill acquisition and to make learning and performance more effective and efficient (Deshler, Ellis, & Lenz, 1996). For example, instead of trying to bring basic skills to a level high enough to read a chapter in a content area textbook written on grade level, a teacher might assist students in comprehension by reading the heading and one or two sentences in each paragraph in a chapter. Figure 4.6 shows how the PASS method can be used as a reading comprehension strategy.

*FIGURE* **4.4**   Strategies for Developing Interpersonal Problem Solving

**FAST Strategy**

| *F*REEZE AND THINK | What is the problem? Can I state the problem in behavioral terms? |
|---|---|
| *A*LTERNATIVES | What could I do to solve the problem? List possible alternatives. |
| *S*OLUTION | Which alternatives will solve the problem in the long run? Which are safe and fair? Select the best long-term alternative. |
| *T*RY IT | How can I implement the solution? Did it work? If this particular solution fails to solve the problem, return to the second step and pick another alternative that might solve the problem. |

From "FAST Social Skills with a SLAM and a Rap," by R. McIntosh, S. Vaughn, and D. Bennerson (1995), *Teaching Exceptional Children,* *28*(1), 37–41. Used by permission.

*FIGURE* **4.5**   Learning Strategies

### SELF-QUESTIONING

Students quietly ask themselves questions about the material. This process is also referred to as verbal mediation. The internal language, or covert speech, helps organize material and behavior. Camp and Bash (1981) suggest the following types of questions:

What is the problem? (or) What am I supposed to do?

What is my plan? (or) How can I do it?

Am I using my plan?

How did I do?

### VERBAL REHEARSAL AND REVIEW

Students practice and review what they have learned. This self-rehearsal helps students remember. People forget when the brain trace, which is a physical record of memory, fades away. Recitation and review of material to be learned help the student remember.

Students observe the instructor's modeling of verbalization of a problem.

Students instruct themselves by verbalizing aloud or in a whisper.

Students verbalize silently.

### ORGANIZATION

To aid in recall, students figure out the main idea of the lesson and the supporting facts. The organization of the material has a great deal to do with how fast we can learn it and how well we can remember it. Already-existing memory units are called chunks, and through *chunking*, new material is reorganized into already-existing memory units. The more students can relate to what they already know, the better they will remember the new material.

### USING PRIOR KNOWLEDGE

New material is linked to already-existing memory units. The more students can relate what they are learning to what they already know, the better they will remember.

### MEMORY STRATEGIES

If new material is anchored to old knowledge, students are more likely to remember it. For example, one student remembered the word *look* because it had two eyes in the middle. Some pupils can alphabetize only if they sing the "ABC" song. Some adults can remember people's names by using a mnemonic device that associates the name with a particular attribute of that individual, for example "blond Bill" or "green-sweater Gertrude."

### PREDICTING AND MONITORING

Students guess about what they will learn in the lesson and then check on whether their guesses were correct.

### ADVANCE ORGANIZERS

This technique establishes a mindset for the learner, relating new material to previously learned material. Students are told in advance about what they are going to learn. This sets the stage for learning and improves comprehension and the ability to recall what has been learned.

### COGNITIVE BEHAVIOR MODIFICATION

This behavioral approach teaches students self-instruction, self-monitoring, and self-evaluation techniques (Meichenbaum, 1977). There are several steps:

The teacher models a behavior while giving an explanation.

The student performs the task while the teacher describes it.

The student talks the task through out loud.

The student whispers it to himself or herself.

The student performs the task with nonverbal self-cues.

### MODELING

The teacher provides an example of appropriate cognitive behavior and problem-solving strategies. The teacher can talk through the cognitive processes being used.

### SELF-MONITORING

Students learn to monitor their own mistakes. They learn to check their own responses and become conscious of errors or answers that do not make sense. To reach this stage requires active involvement in the learning process to recognize incongruities.

From *Learning Disabilities: Theories, Diagnosis, and Teaching Strategie*s (6th ed.) (pp. 207–208), by J. W. Lerner, 1993, Boston: Houghton Mifflin. Used by permission.

**REVIEW, REVIEW, AND PREDICT**

> Preview by reading the heading and one or two sentences.
>
> Review what you know already about this topic.
>
> Predict what you think the text will be about.

 **SK AND ANSWER QUESTIONS**

**Content-Focused Questions**

> Who? What? When? Where? Why? How?
>
> How does this relate to what I already know?

**Monitoring Questions**

> Is my prediction correct?
>
> How is this different from what I thought it was going to be about?
>
> Does this make sense?

**Problem-Solving Questions**

> Is it important that it make sense?
>
> Do I need to reread part of it?
>
> Can I visualize the information?
>
> Do I need to read it more slowly?
>
> Does it have too many unknown words?
>
> Do I need to pay more attention?
>
> Should I get help?

 **UMMARIZE**

> Say what the short passage was about.

 **YNTHESIZE**

> Say how the short passage fits in with the whole passage.
>
> Say how what you learned fits with what you knew.

*FIGURE* **4.6**

PASS Reading Comprehension Strategy

From *Teaching Strategies and Methods* (2nd ed.) (p. 29), by D. Deshler, E. S. Ellis, and B. K. Lenz, 1996, Denver, CO: Love Publishing. Reprinted by permission.

*TEACHING TIP*
When teaching the PASS strategy to students, model use of the strategy as you "think aloud" while applying the strategy to a chapter they have to read. This demonstration will make the process more concrete for students.

The teacher can also make an impact on student learning and performance by accounting for individual differences when developing and implementing lesson plans. Many students fail, not because of an inability to perform but because they don't understand directions, cannot remember all of the information, or cannot process verbal information fast enough. Most adults and older children automatically lower the language they use when speaking to younger children or individuals with obvious disabilities. Unfortunately this is not typically done for school-age children and adults with LD—even though they may have language-based learning disabilities. Johnson

(1999) suggests the following strategies to meet the needs of students with language difficulties in an inclusive classroom setting:

◢ Be conscious of the level of language used, including rate of presentation, complexity of vocabulary, and sentence structure.

◢ Prepare a list of relevant terms prior to instruction; pretest students to determine their level of understanding.

◢ Adjust the level of language until students have basic concepts.

◢ Use demonstrations as needed.

◢ Repeat instructions individually to students if necessary.

◢ Select a method of testing knowledge to match the student's best method of communication. For example, a student may be able to select the correct answer from options given but not be able to answer open-ended questions.

◢ Provide feedback that is clear and specific. Give positive reinforcement to help develop self-esteem.

As noted earlier in the chapter, a major problem for secondary students with learning disabilities is low self-concept and social and emotional problems that often stem from years of school failure. To help ameliorate unhappiness, school environments must be structured to create successful experiences. One method involves **self-determination,** or making students more active participants in designing their educational experiences and monitoring their own success. Students should be active in IEP meetings. This is particularly important when a student is deciding whether to continue postsecondary education or to obtain employment after high school (Lovitt, Cushing, & Stump, 1994).

While giving students more power and responsibility for determining their life outcome is very important at the secondary level, it is also important to maintain communication and involvement with parents (Jayanthi, Bursuck, Epstein, & Polloway,

*SELF-DETERMINATION* is a philosophy supporting the right of individuals with disabilities to be in charge of their own lives.

*A*dolescents should be active participants in meetings concerning them.

1999). Parents can promote responsibility in their children by setting clear expectations and consequences in regard to homework. Teachers can help by

▲ Giving parents and students information on course assignments for the semester, available accommodations, and policies.
▲ Providing progress reports, including descriptive comments on the quality of homework.
▲ Putting assignment calendars on brightly colored paper to prevent misplacement.
▲ Collaborating with other teachers to prevent homework overloads.
▲ Communicating with parents regarding the amount of time students spend completing homework and adjusting workload correspondingly.
▲ Understanding that homework may be a low priority in some families where other stressors such as family illness or school attendance may be a priority.

Motivation is also a key ingredient to successful high school programming. Fulk and Montgomery-Grymes (1994) suggest the following techniques for increasing motivation:

▲ Involve students in decision making.
  1. Provide a menu from which students can select assignments to demonstrate knowledge.
  2. Allow flexible due dates.
  3. Involve students in scoring and evaluating their own work.
  4. Vary the length of assignments for differing student abilities.
  5. Set goals with the students.
▲ Create and maintain interest.
  1. Challenge each student at the optimal level.
  2. Show enthusiasm as you introduce lessons.
  3. Give clear, simple directions.
  4. Set specific expectations.
  5. Explain the relevance of each lesson.
  6. Vary your teaching style.
▲ Address affective variables.
  1. Maintain a positive classroom environment.
  2. Give frequent feedback on performance.
  3. Acknowledge all levels of achievement.

High school students with learning disabilities especially need to acquire transition skills (e.g., abilities that will help students be successful after high school in employment and independent living). For students in inclusive settings, teachers can find ways to integrate transition topics into the regular curriculum. For example, when an English teacher assigns letter writing or term papers, students might focus their work on exploring different career opportunities. Math teachers can bring in income tax and budget forms to connect them to a variety of math skills. When planning any lesson, ask yourself, "Is there any way I can make this meaningful to their lives after high school?" See Table 4.2 for more ideas.

**ADULT SERVICES**  The instruction provided in high school classes can have a powerful impact on the outcome for adults with learning disabilities. The life skills applications of various school activities and lessons are described in Chapter 15. Relevant lessons in the general education curriculum can help adults be more successful in

| TABLE 4.2 | Examples of Study Skill Functions in and out of the Classroom |
|---|---|

| Study Skill | School Examples | Life Skills Applications |
|---|---|---|
| READING RATE | Reviewing an assigned reading for a test<br>Looking for an explanation of a concept discussed in class | Reviewing an automobile insurance policy<br>Reading the newspaper |
| LISTENING | Understanding instructions about a field trip<br>Attending to morning announcements | Understanding how a newly purchased appliance works<br>Comprehending a radio traffic report |
| NOTE TAKING/ OUTLINING | Capturing information given by a teacher on how to dissect a frog<br>Framing the structure of a paper | Writing directions to a party<br>Planning a summer vacation |
| REPORT WRITING | Developing a book report<br>Completing a science project on a specific marine organism | Completing the personal goals section on a job application<br>Writing a complaint letter |
| ORAL PRESENTATIONS | Delivering a personal opinion on a current issue for a social studies class<br>Describing the results of a lab experiment | Describing car problems to a mechanic<br>Asking a supervisor/boss for time off work |
| GRAPHIC AIDS | Setting up the equipment of a chemistry experiment based on a diagram<br>Locating the most densely populated regions of the world on a map | Utilizing the weather map in the newspaper<br>Deciphering the store map in a mall |
| TEST TAKING | Developing tactics for retrieving information for a closed-book test<br>Comparing notes with textbook content | Preparing for a driver's license renewal test<br>Participating in television self-tests |
| LIBRARY USAGE | Using picture files<br>Searching a computerized catalog | Obtaining travel resources (books, videos)<br>Viewing current periodicals |
| REFERENCE MATERIALS | Accessing CD-ROM encyclopedias<br>Using a thesaurus to write a paper | Using the yellow pages to locate a repair service<br>Ordering from a mail-order catalog |
| TIME MANAGEMENT | Allocating a set time for homework<br>Organizing a file system for writing a paper | Maintaining a daily "to do" list<br>Keeping organized records for tax purposes |
| SELF-MANAGEMENT | Ensuring that homework is signed by parents<br>Rewarding oneself for controlling temper | Regulating a daily exercise program<br>Evaluating the quality of a home repair |

From *Teaching Students with Learning Problems to Use Study Skills: A Teacher's Guide* (p. 7), by J. J. Hoover and J. R. Patton, 1995, Austin, TX: Pro-Ed. Reprinted by permission.

many aspects of independent living. Individuals with learning disabilities are often deficient in choosing and carrying out strategies, and they do not automatically generalize previously learned information to new challenges. Other cognitive difficulties include organizing thoughts and ideas, integrating and remembering information from a variety of sources, and solving problems (Ryan & Price, 1992). Intervention in these areas must often be implemented for adults if the high school curriculum is not based on future needs and challenges (Dowdy & Smith, 1991).

An important study by Gerber and Reiff (1998) identified important characteristics of highly successful adults with learning disabilities. Development of many of these factors can be encouraged by teachers and other individuals; however, some factors seem to be innate personality traits of the individuals themselves. One of the strongest predictors for success was the desire and willingness to persist and work extremely hard. Identifying appropriate goals and working to meet them was also important. The successful adults developed a plan and then worked hard to accomplish their goals.

They also were able to reframe their feelings about having a learning disability, gradually identifying and accepting their own strengths and weaknesses. Once the weaknesses were identified, they took creative action to build strategies, techniques, and accommodations to offset the impact of the disability. The study also showed that it was important to find a "goodness of fit": choosing goals that would be possible to attain. Finally, successful adults were willing to seek help from supportive people, such as spouse or an individual at an agency. As one highly successful adult with learning disabilities said, "You must learn where your strengths are and how you can use them and where your weaknesses are and how to avoid them or compensate. I have learned to accept who I am, what I can do, what I cannot do, who I should not try to be, and who I should try to be" (Ginsberg, Gerber, & Reiff, 1994, p. 210).

Unfortunately, many adults leave high school without the skills and confidence necessary to find employment to help them realize their maximum potential and to live independently. According to Michaels (1994), problems in work settings can include the following:

- ◢ Following instructions
- ◢ Getting started on tasks
- ◢ Maintaining attention to task
- ◢ Organizing and budgeting time
- ◢ Completing tasks
- ◢ Checking for errors
- ◢ Requesting support when appropriate
- ◢ Using self-advocacy skills to obtain resources
- ◢ Having difficulty with interpersonal skills

These skills can be taught and should be addressed in a secondary curriculum. For adults with learning disabilities who still need support, a variety of agencies are available to address needs such as improving literacy skills, obtaining a high school equivalency certificate (called a GED), and meeting goals in areas such as financial aid for further education, employment, and independent living. Figure 4.7 lists examples of these important resources (excerpted from *LDA Newsbriefs*, 1996).

The primary adult agency that offers treatment and intervention to promote employment for adults with learning disabilities is the Rehabilitation Services Administration. An office of this vocational rehabilitation agency is located in every state. Vocational evaluators are trained to identify each individual's strengths and the characteristics that will limit employment. Counselors provide a variety of employment-related services to those who are eligible (Dowdy, 1996). Other agencies are explored in a text on adult agencies by Cozzins, Dowdy, & Smith (1999).

**TEACHING TIP**

Ask students with disabilities to call the agencies listed in Figure 4.7 to identify services available in your local area. Have them research others and then create a resource directory. They might organize each entry by referral process, range of services, or cost.

*FIGURE* **4.7** Adult Agencies

| | |
|---|---|
| **GED HOTLINE (1-800-626-9433)** | General Education Development (GED) Hotline has a 24-hour operator service that provides information on local GED classes and testing services. *They have an accommodations guide for people taking the GED who have a learning disability.* |
| **NATIONAL LITERACY HOTLINE (1-800-228-8813)** | Literacy Hotline has a 24-hour bilingual (Spanish/English) operator service that provides information on literacy/education classes, GED testing services, volunteer opportunities, and a *learning disabilities brochure.* |
| **HEATH RESOURCE CENTER (1-800-544-3284)** | National Clearinghouse on Postsecondary Education for Individuals with Disabilities (HEATH Resource Center) has information specialists available 9:00 A.M.–5 P.M. ET (Monday–Friday) who provide resource papers, directories, information on national organizations, and a *resource directory for people with learning disabilities.* |
| **JOB ACCOMMODATION NETWORK (1-800-526-7324)** | Job Accommodation Network (JAN) has a free consulting service 8:00 A.M.–8:00 P.M. ET (Monday–Thursday) and 8:00 A.M.–5:00 P.M. ET (Friday) that provides information on equipment, methods, and modifications for persons with disabilities to improve their work environment. All information is specific to the disability, *including learning disabilities.* |
| **LEARNING RESOURCES NETWORK (1-800-678-5376)** | Learning Resources Network (LERN) has an operator service 8:00 A.M.–5:00 P.M. ET (Monday–Friday) that provides information to practitioners of adult continuing education. They also give consulting information, take orders for publications, and provide phone numbers of associations and organizations that deal with learning disabilities. |

From "Toll Free Access to Adult Services," *LDA Newsbriefs*, 1996, *31*, 22–24. Used by permission.

## Controversial Approaches

Some interventions, often presented to the public through television or newsstand magazines, are controversial and have not been validated as effective for students with learning disabilities. Educators may be asked for an opinion on these therapies by parents who are attempting to find solutions to their children's frustrating problems. A brief overview of these nontraditional approaches follows. More extensive reviews are provided by Rooney (1991) and Silver (1995).

*TINTED GLASSES* are used to reduce eye sensitivity and enhance reading ability. So far studies do not support the use of this therapy.
*ORTHOMOLECULAR THERAPY* uses large doses of vitamins and minerals to improve learning. Studies do not support the use of this therapy.

One controversial therapy involves the prescription of **tinted glasses** as a cure for dyslexia. In this approach, light sensitivity, said to interfere with learning, is treated by identifying a colored lens to reduce sensitivity. Rooney (1991) notes that the studies that support this treatment do not meet acceptable scientific standards and should be viewed with caution.

An older treatment theory is **orthomolecular therapy,** involving vitamins, minerals, and diet. Proponents of this treatment claim that large doses of vitamins and minerals straighten out the biochemistry of the brain to reduce hyperactivity and to increase learning. Hair analysis and blood studies are used to determine the doses needed.

Feingold's diet is another dietary treatment frequently cited. Feingold (1975) proposes that negative behaviors such as hyperactivity and limited learning are due to the body's reaction to unnatural substances such as food colorings, preservatives, and artificial dyes. His patients are asked to keep a comprehensive diary of their diet and to avoid harmful chemical substances. Other diets focus on avoiding sugar and caffeine.

Another proponent of orthomolecular therapy suggests that negative behaviors result from allergies to food and environmental substances (Silver, 1995). The research on the efficacy of these diet-related interventions usually consists of clinical studies without control groups. When control groups are used, the diets do not substantiate the claims made for them. Only a small percentage of children benefit from them.

**Vision therapy** or training is another controversial treatment for individuals with a learning disability. It is based on the theory that learning disabilities are the result of visual defects that occur when the eyes do not work together and that these deficits can be cured by visual training. This widespread practice has been supported primarily by groups of optometrists. The American Academy of Ophthalmology (1984) has issued a statement clearly stating that "no credible evidence exists to show that visual training, muscle exercises, perceptual, or hand/eye coordination exercises significantly affect a child's Specific Learning Disabilities" (p. 3).

Silver (1995) reviewed another controversial therapy involving the use of **vestibular dysfunction** medication to cure dyslexia. He notes that the relationship between dyslexia, the vestibular system, and the medication was not supported by research. Silver also warns that physicians often do not diagnose dyslexia consistently and are prescribing doses of medication that are not recommended by pharmaceutical companies.

Silver is also concerned about the widespread use of other medications such as Ritalin for learning and attention problems. He warns that prescriptions are often given based on the recommendations of parents or teachers alone, without a comprehensive evaluation. Rooney (1991) states that the actual effectiveness of the medication is less an issue than the concerns that (1) the medication is prescribed without a thorough evaluation, (2) educational and behavioral treatments are not implemented in conjunction with the medication, and (3) there is insufficient monitoring of the effects of the medication. Monitoring these effects is a very important part of the role of classroom teachers. Use of medication is discussed further in Chapter 5.

*CONSIDER THIS*
Many parents are drawn to nontraditional approaches to treating learning disabilities because they promise a quick cure. How will you respond when a parent asks your opinion of the value of one of these approaches for his or her child?

*VISION THERAPY* uses exercises for eye muscles and eye-hand coordination to improve reading. Studies do not support the use of this therapy.

*VESTIBULAR DYSFUNCTION* is an inner ear problem that causes bodily equilibrium to be off balance.

## CLASSROOM ACCOMMODATIONS FOR STUDENTS WITH LEARNING DISABILITIES

When you are developing classroom accommodations, remember the wide range of behaviors identified earlier that might characterize individuals with learning disabilities. The heterogeneity in this population is sometimes baffling. No child with a learning disability is going to be exactly like any other, so teachers must provide a wide range of accommodations to meet individual needs. In the following sections, accommodations are discussed for each of the areas described earlier: academic and language deficits, social–emotional problems, and other differences such as attention, memory, cognition, metacognition, perception, and motor skills.

### Academic and Language Deficits

Recall that students with learning disabilities may manifest deficits in the academic areas of reading skill, reading comprehension, math calculation, math applications, listening, speaking, and written language. Chapters 14 and 15 provide extensive modifications for students with learning disabilities at the elementary and secondary levels. Some general guidelines proposed by Chalmers (1991) include these:

◢ Preteach vocabulary and assess the prior knowledge of students before you introduce new concepts.

◢ Establish a purpose for reading that gives students a specific goal for comprehension.

◢ Provide multiple opportunities to learn content: cooperative learning activities, study guides, choral responses, and hands-on participation.

◢ Provide oral and written directions that are clear and simple.

◢ Have students rephrase directions to make sure they understand them.

◢ Reduce time pressure by adjusting requirements: give more time to complete a challenging project or shorten the assignment. Ask students to work every other problem or every third problem so they won't be overwhelmed.

◢ Provide frequent feedback, and gradually allow students to evaluate their own work.

◢ Have students use an assignment notebook to record important information and daily assignments.

◢ Provide options for students to demonstrate their knowledge or skill (e.g., videotape presentation, artwork, oral or written report).

◢ Use demonstrations and manipulatives frequently to make learning more concrete.

◢ Modify textbooks as shown in Figure 4.8.

◢ Avoid crowding too much material on a single page of a worksheet.

◢ Provide a listening guide or a partial outline to assist students in note taking.

◢ Use a buddy system for studying or for note taking. Allow a good note taker to work with the student with the learning disability, sharing notes duplicated on carbon paper or NCR paper.

◢ Allow students to tape-record lectures if necessary.

◢ Reduce the homework load, or allow the parent to write the student's dictated answers.

*FIGURE **4.8***

Guidelines for Adapting Content Area Textbooks

Adapted from "Guidelines for Adapting Content Area Textbooks: Keeping Teachers and Students Content," by J. S. Schumm and K. Strickler, 1991, *Intervention in School and Clinic, 27*(2), pp. 79–84.

Determine "goodness of fit" by comparing the readability level of the text and the student's reading ability. If accommodations are needed, consider the following:

1. **SUBSTITUTE TEXTBOOK READING BY**
   ■ supplying an audiotape of the text.
   ■ pairing students to learn text material together.
   ■ substituting the text with direct experiences or videos.
   ■ holding tutorial sessions to teach content to a small group.

2. **SIMPLIFY TEXT BY**
   ■ developing abridged versions (volunteers may be helpful).
   ■ developing chapter outlines or summaries.
   ■ finding a text with similar content written at a lower level.

3. **HIGHLIGHT KEY CONCEPTS BY**
   ■ establishing the purpose for reading.
   ■ overviewing the assignment before reading.
   ■ reviewing charts, graphs, vocabulary, and key concepts before reading.
   ■ reducing amount of work by targeting the most important information or slowing down pace of assignments.

For students with learning difficulties in writing, a word processor can be invaluable. It allows students to see their work in a more legible format and simplifies proofreading and revising. The spell checker and grammar checker of many word processing programs can encourage success in writing, and a talking word processor may provide valuable assistance for students who also have difficulty in reading. The following list describes recommended programs (Pracek, 1996; MacArthur, 1998).

**TEACHING TIP**
Each word processing program has unique features. Try to have several programs available so students can experiment and find the one that works best for them.

▲ *Dr. Peet's TalkWriter* is a talking program that includes letter recognition and simple word processing. Available from Hartley (1-800-247-1380), it uses the Echo Speech synthesizer and works on Apple computers.
▲ *Primary Editor Plus* is a talking word processing program that includes a spell checker and a feature that allows children to draw pictures using the mouse or keyboard. It is available from IBM Eduquest (1-800-426-4338).
▲ *Telepathic 2.0* is a word prediction program based on spelling and word frequency. It works on DOS and Windows (1-800-828-2600).
▲ *FrEdWriter* is a public domain word processing program that may be copied freely. A Spanish version is also available. It works on an Apple computer.
▲ *Word Processing for Kids* is a public domain program that runs on MS-DOS. It was designed to teach word processing to students.

These and other types of technology can be critically important in facilitating success in inclusive settings for students with LD. More examples of effective technology to address the areas of reading and math are found in the nearby Technology Today feature.

Students and adults with LDs in the area of reading are also eligible to apply for services from Reading for the Blind & **Dyslexic.** A catalog of services and application forms are available by calling (800) 221-4792. The forms require verification of the disability by a professional in disability services. This agency will provide a cassette tape of *any* book requested. The tapes are available at no cost; however, there may be a one-time charge for the special equipment needed to play the tapes.

*DYSLEXIC* is a medical term to describe an individual with severe reading difficulties.

## Social–Emotional Problems

As discussed earlier, the social and emotional problems of individuals with learning disabilities may be closely tied to academic failure. Many of the academic accommodations already described will encourage success in the classroom, which ultimately leads to a better self-concept, increased emotional stability, and greater confidence in approaching new academic tasks. A student who has deficits in social skills may need previously described training. However, some accommodations may still be needed even when the training begins to show results. All students need to work in an isolated setting in the classroom during particularly challenging times. Distractions caused by peers may interfere with meeting academic challenges successfully. However, if teachers make the student with learning disabilities sit in a segregated portion of the room all the time, it sends a bad message to others. Including students with disabilities in group activities such as cooperative learning provides them with models of appropriate interactions and social skills. Identify the students in the classroom who seem to work best with individuals with a learning disability, and give them opportunities to interact. When conflicts arise, provide good modeling for the student by verbalizing the bad choices that were made and the good choices that could have been made.

## Assistive Technology for Deficits of Students with Learning Disabilities

| Area of Deficit | Description of Technology |
| --- | --- |
| READING | Audio recording reads textbook material and answers to chapter or workbook questions |
| | Software (e.g., Inspiration) enables readers to comprehend narrative story or expository writing elements through graphic depiction |
| | Audio recording presents definitions of words (e.g., Franklin Speaking Language Master) |
| | Text is scanned into computer so it can be read by speech synthesis (e.g., JAWS) |
| WRITTEN EXPRESSION | Piece of plastic that is attached where the pencil is grasped |
| | Software for outlining and organizing writing |
| | Standard tape recorder for dictation of written products |
| | Software that assists with sentence structure and syntax (e.g., Co:Writer) |
| | Voice recognition enabling dictation of written content (e.g., Dragon Dictate, Kurzweil Voice) |
| MATHEMATICS | Devices for checking answers; talking calculators (Radio Shack Talking Calculator Model Ec-208); large keyed calculators |
| | Specially designed clocks that tell time verbally |
| | Various devices for monitoring time |

Adapted from "Using Technology Adaptations to Include Students with Learning Disabilities in Cooperative Learning Activities" by D. P. Bryant and B. R. Bryant (1998), *Journal of Learning Disabilities, 31*(1), p. 54.

Because these individuals may have difficulty responding appropriately to verbal and nonverbal cues, teachers should avoid sarcasm and use simple concrete language when giving directions and when teaching. If the student has difficulty accepting new tasks without complaint, consider providing a written assignment that the student can refer to for direction. When a student frequently upsets or irritates others in the classroom, you might agree on a contract to reduce the inappropriate behavior and reinforce positive peer interaction. Periodically review the rules for the classroom, and keep them posted as a quick reference. To assist students who have difficulty making and keeping friends, you can subtly point out the strengths of the individual with the learning disability to encourage the other students to want to be his or her friend. Allowing the student to demonstrate his or her expertise in an area or to share a hobby may stimulate conversations that can eventually lead to friendships.

Because many of these students cannot predict the consequences of negative behavior, teachers need to explain the consequences of rule breaking and other inappropriate behavior. Though you can implement many behavior management techniques to reinforce positive behavior, it is important to train the student in methods of self-monitoring and self-regulation. The ultimate goal is for the student to be able to identify socially inappropriate behavior and get back on track.

## Cognitive Differences

Cognitive problems described earlier include deficits in attention, perception, motor abilities, problem solving, and metacognition. Accommodations for individuals exhibiting problems in attention will be described more fully in Chapter 5. Accommodations can also help individuals with difficulties or preferences in the area of perception. For some students, presenting information visually through the overhead projector, reading material, videos, and graphics will be most effective. Other individuals will respond better by hearing the information. Teachers can accommodate these individual differences by identifying the preferred style of learning and either providing instruction and directions in the preferred style or teaching in a multisensory fashion that stimulates both auditory and visual perception. Combining seeing, saying, writing, and doing provides multiple opportunities for presenting new information. It also helps children remember important information.

Difficulties in the area of motor abilities might be manifested as poor handwriting skills or difficulty with other fine motor activities. Accommodations might include overlooking the difficulties in handwriting and providing a grade based not on the appearance of the handwriting but on the content of the material. You might allow these students to provide other evidence of their learning, such as oral reports or special projects. Let them select physical fitness activities that focus on their areas of strength, rather than their deficits.

Students with difficulties in problem solving require careful direction and programming. Their deficits in reasoning skills make them especially prone to academic failures. The instructional strategies described earlier will remedy problems in this area; also frequent modeling of problem-solving strategies will strengthen developing skills.

Students with problems in the area of metacognition need to keep an assignment notebook or a monthly calendar to project the time needed to complete tasks or to prepare for tests. Students should be taught to organize their notebooks and their desks so that materials can be retrieved efficiently. If students have difficulty following or developing a plan, assist them in setting long-range goals and breaking down those goals into realistic steps. Prompt them with questions such as "What do you need to be able to do this?" Help students set clear time frames in which to accomplish each step. Assist them in prioritizing activities and assignments, and provide them with models that they can refer to often.

Encourage students to ask for help when needed and to use self-checking methods to evaluate their work on an ongoing basis. Reinforce all signs of appropriate self-monitoring and self-regulation in the classroom. These behaviors will facilitate success after high school.

Accommodations for attention deficits and hyperactivity are addressed in Chapter 5. Other teaching tips for general educators are offered in Chapters 13, 14, and 15. They focus on behavior management and accommodations for elementary and secondary classrooms. The following list of recommended guidelines for teaching children and adolescents with learning disabilities has been compiled from work by Mercer (1997), Deiner (1993), and Bender (1995).

# Chapter 5

# Teaching Students with Attention Deficit/ Hyperactivity Disorder

*After reading this chapter, you should be able to:*

▲ Discuss the legal basis for services to students with attention deficit/hyperactivity disorder (ADHD)

▲ Describe the characteristics and identification process for students with ADHD, including the impact of cultural diversity

▲ Discuss educational, technological, and medical intervention

▲ Design strategies to enhance instruction and classroom accommodations

▲ Develop methods for promoting a sense of community and social acceptance

Jenny is 20 years old and is a successful student at a four-year college. For many years Jenny and her parents did not think she would be able to attend college. She was raised in a rural part of Alabama; her parents had not gone to college, but they had high hopes for their child, who was obviously very bright. However, when Jenny entered school, she was soon labeled a failure. She did not seem to listen to the teacher, she didn't follow instructions, she would leave unfinished work and begin a new project, she seldom had appropriate school supplies, and she rarely turned in homework. Her mother said she knew Jenny did her homework because she helped her, and she also purchased the necessary school supplies. She couldn't understand what was going on between home and school.

The teachers called Jenny's mom frequently to complain that Jenny wasn't trying and to urge her to get Jenny to straighten up! Her mother tried to get help at school, but Jenny didn't qualify for special education services. She did not have any mental retardation or serious emotional disturbance, and her academic skills were not low enough to qualify her for a learning disabilities class. Jenny's mother tried to help with lessons, but by high school, the demands were beyond the abilities of the family members, and school had become so painful for Jenny that she started skipping classes. She was befriended by a group of students who were also skipping school, but they were into drugs. Jenny was really heading for trouble when her mother heard of services for adolescents and adults available through a state agency, Vocational Rehabilitation (VR).

Through VR, Jenny was diagnosed as having an attention deficit/hyperactivity disorder (ADHD). She elected to leave school and obtain her GED. She learned that colleges had special services for students with ADHD, so she applied and was admitted. At the university, she takes her tests in a distraction-free environment and is allowed to use 2 1/2 times the normal testing period. Another student takes notes for Jenny in classes, and a tutor is available if she has special problems in class. It looks as if Jenny will finish college and lead a productive life. She is still very bitter about her treatment in school. She says that if she is a success in life, it will be in spite of her school experiences—not because of them! She attributes her current success to the effort and support of her mom.

## QUESTIONS TO CONSIDER

1. How could Jenny's teacher or counselor have made a difference in her school years?
2. Can you describe the law that would have given Jenny the right to special accommodations in the general education classroom?
3. How could Jenny's school years have been more positive?

A ttention deficit/hyperactivity disorder (ADHD) is a complex condition that has been a major concern in public education for several years. It is a complicated but intriguing condition and a real challenge for classroom teachers. This condition remains controversial because professional perspectives and personal opinions vary regarding the nature of ADHD and effective intervention techniques. In the past few years awareness of this disability has significantly increased, along with successful intervention plans for students who struggle with it.

The legal basis for services and protection against discrimination for ADHD comes from IDEA and Section 504 of the Rehabilitation Act of 1973 (PL 93-112). When IDEA was reauthorized in 1990, a big debate took place as to whether to add ADHD as a separate handicapping condition. Some people were very disappointed when that did not happen. However, in 1991 the U.S. Department of Education did issue a policy memorandum indicating that students with attention deficit disorder (the department's term) who need special education or related services can qualify for those services under existing categories.

The category of other health impaired (OHI) was recommended as the appropriate classification for students whose primary disability is ADHD. This category includes "any chronic and acute condition that results in limited alertness and adversely affects educational performance" (U.S. Department of Education, 1991).

The final regulations for implementation of the 1999 amendments to IDEA actually amended the definition of OHI to add attention deficit disorder (ADD) and ADHD to the list of conditions that could render a child eligible under OHI. The definition provides the explanation that a child with ADD or ADHD has a heightened awareness or sensitivity to environmental stimuli, and this results in a limited alertness to the educational environment (U.S. Department of Education, 1999). In other words, the child is so busy paying attention to everything going on around him or her that attention is directed away from the important educational stimuli, and school performance is negatively affected.

Before the 1999 U.S. Department of Education regulations were published, many professionals assumed that students with ADHD were being served under the category of learning disability. However, in a school-based study of students with ADHD, Reid, Maag, Vasa, & Wright (1994) found that nearly 52% were identified with behavior disorders, 29% were identified with learning disabilities, and 9% were identified with mental retardation. Studies have shown that only 50% of students with ADHD were qualifying for special education services. This underserved group of students quickly came to the attention of school professionals. It is now recognized that a sizable number of students with ADHD are floundering in school and not qualifying for special services that would encourage academic success. In an effort to find a basis for services for this population, the U.S. Department of Education determined that Section 504 applies to these individuals and serves as a legal mandate to provide assessment and services. To date, the category of OHI has not been widely used to serve students with ADHD (Reid et al., 1994); Section 504 has been and may continue to be the primary legal basis for services to this population.

Section 504 is not a special education law but a civil rights law. It mandates special education opportunities and related aids and services to meet individual educational needs for persons with disabilities as adequately as the needs of those who are not disabled. Section 504 provides protection for a larger group of individuals with disabilities and differs in some respects from IDEA. It protects any individual with a disability, defined as "any physical or mental impairment that substantially limits one or more major life activities." Since learning is one of the stated life activities, it was determined that this law does apply to schools. If a school has reason to believe that any student has a disability as defined under Section 504, the school must evaluate the student. If the student is determined to be disabled under the law, the school must develop and implement a plan for the delivery of services that are needed (Council of Administrators of Special Education, 1992).

**CROSS-REFERENCE**
Section 504 of the Rehabilitation Act of 1973 and IDEA are introduced in Chapter 1. Compare the provisions of these important legislative acts.

If a student with ADHD does not qualify for services under IDEA, services might be made available under Section 504. Although its required services and procedures are not as specific as those found in IDEA, Section 504 does provide an avenue for accommodating the needs of students with ADHD in the schools. Figure 5.1 provides a flowchart demonstrating how both IDEA and Section 504 work together to provide appropriate services to students with ADHD.

Teachers must understand ADHD in order to recognize the characteristics of ADHD and, most important, to implement effective intervention strategies and accommodations to facilitate success for these children in their classrooms.

## BASIC CONCEPTS ABOUT ATTENTION DEFICIT/HYPERACTIVITY DISORDER

Attention deficit/hyperactivity disorder is an invisible, hidden disability in that no unique physical characteristics and no definitive psychological or physiological tests differentiate these children from others. However, ADHD is not hard to spot in the classroom.

> Just look with your eyes and listen with your ears as you walk through the places where children are—particularly those places where children are expected to behave in a quiet, orderly, productive fashion. In such places, children with ADHD will identify themselves quite readily. They will be doing or not doing something which frequently results in their receiving a barrage of comments and criticisms such as, "Why don't you ever listen?" "Think before you act." "Pay attention." (Fowler, 1992, p. 3)

Unfortunately, the disabling behaviors associated with ADHD may be misunderstood and misinterpreted as a sign of being lazy, unorganized, and even disrespectful. The condition can be recognized only through specific behavioral manifestations that may occur during the learning process. As a **developmental disability**, ADHD becomes apparent before the age of 7; however, in as many as two-thirds of the cases, it continues to cause problems in adulthood. During the school years ADHD may have an impact on success in both academic and nonacademic areas. It occurs across all cultural, racial, and socioeconomic groups. It can affect children and adults with all levels of intelligence (Fowler, 1992).

**DEVELOPMENTAL DISABILITY** is a disability appearing before the age of 7 that has a direct impact on a person's mental or physical development.

**FIGURE 5.1**

IDEA/504 Flowchart

From *Student Access: A Resource Guide for Educators: Section 504 of the Rehabilitation Act of 1973* (p. 25), by the Council for Administrators of Special Education, 1992, Reston, VA: Author. Used by permission.

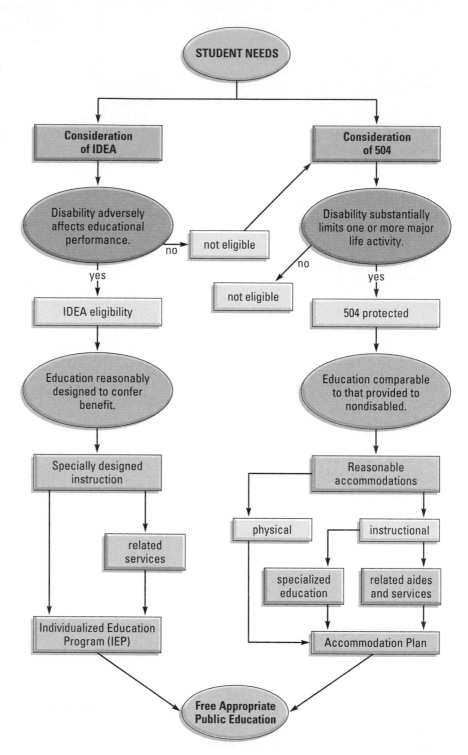

## Attention Deficit/Hyperactivity Disorder Defined

Although a variety of terms have been used over the years to describe this disorder, currently the term *attention deficit/hyperactivity disorder* is most common. The terminology stems from the **Diagnostic and Statistical Manual of Mental Disorders** (4th ed.; *DSM-IV;* American Psychiatric Association, 1994). On a global level, the **International Classification of Diseases** (10th ed.; *ICD-10,* 1992) is used to describe these children. This classification system uses the term *hyperkinetic disorders* to describe conditions related to problems in attention and hyperactivity.

ADHD primarily refers to deficits in attention and behaviors characterized by impulsivity and hyperactivity. The *DSM-IV* classifies ADHD as a disruptive disorder expressed in persistent patterns of inappropriate degrees of attention or hyperactivity–impulsivity. A distinction must be made between ADHD and other disorders such as conduct disorder (e.g., physical fighting) and oppositional defiant disorder (e.g., recurrent patterns of disobedience). The *DSM-IV* has been widely adopted as a guide to the diagnosis of ADHD. According to this document, ADHD encompasses four types of disabilities. The diagnostic criteria for ADHD are presented in Figure 5.2. The identification of the specific type of ADHD depends on the number of symptoms in Sections 1 and 2 that can be ascribed to the child. For example, a combination of attention deficit and hyperactivity is designated if six or more symptoms are identified from each section. A diagnosis of attention deficit/hyperactivity with predominant problems with attention is indicated if six or more symptoms are identified from Section 1 only. A third type of attention deficit/hyperactivity disorder has a predominant number of hyperactivity–impulsivity behaviors. Last, a category called "attention deficit/hyperactivity disorder not otherwise specified" is typically used for students who do not meet the criteria for ADHD but have significant symptoms related to the condition.

**THE DIAGNOSTIC AND STATISTICAL MANUAL OF MENTAL DISORDERS** (4th ed.) is the diagnostic guide and classification system for mental disorders published by the American Psychiatric Association.

**INTERNATIONAL CLASSIFICATION OF DISEASES** (10th ed.) is a published system used internationally for classifying physical and mental disorders.

*There are many different theories regarding the cause of ADHD.*

*FIGURE* **5.2**    Criteria for Attention Deficit/Hyperactivity Disorder

A.  Either (1) or (2):

(1) **Inattention:** At least six of the following symptoms of inattention have persisted for at least 6 months to a degree that is maladaptive and inconsistent with developmental level:

(a) Often fails to give close attention to details or makes careless mistakes in schoolwork, work, or other activities

(b) Often has difficulty sustaining attention in tasks or play activities

(c) Often does not seem to listen to what is being said to him or her

(d) Often does not follow through on instructions and fails to finish schoolwork, chores, or duties in the workplace (not due to oppositional behavior or failure to understand instructions)

(e) Often has difficulties organizing tasks and activities

(f) Often avoids and strongly dislikes tasks that require sustained mental effort (such as schoolwork and homework)

(g) Often loses things necessary for tasks and activities (e.g., school assignments, pencils, books, tools, or toys)

(h) Often is easily distracted by extraneous stimuli

(i) Often is forgetful in daily activities

(2) **Hyperactivity–impulsivity:** At least six of the following symptoms of hyperactivity-impulsivity have persisted for at least six months to a degree that is maladaptive and inconsistent with developmental level:

**Hyperactivity:**

(a) Often fidgets with hands or feet or squirms in seat

(b) Often leaves seat in classroom or in other situations in which remaining in seat is expected

(c) Often runs about or climbs excessively in situations where it is inappropriate (in adolescents and adults, may be limited to subjective feelings of restlessness)

(d) Often has difficulty playing or engaging in leisure activities quietly

(e) Always is "on the go" or acts as if "driven by a motor"

(f) Often talks excessively

**Impulsivity:**

(g) Often bursts out answers to questions before the questions have been completed

(h) Often has difficulty waiting in lines or awaiting turn in games or group situations

(i) Often interrupts or intrudes on others (e.g., butts into others' conversations or games)

B.  Some symptoms that caused impairment were present before age 7.

C.  Some symptoms that cause impairment are present in two or more settings (e.g., at school, work, and at home).

D.  There must be clear evidence of clinically significant impairment in social, academic, or occupational functioning.

E.  Does not occur exclusively during the course of a pervasive developmental disorder, schizophrenia or other psychotic disorder, and is not better accounted for by mood disorder, anxiety disorder, dissociative disorder, or a personality disorder.

From *Diagnostic and Statistical Manual of Mental Disorders* (4th ed.) (pp. 83–85) by the American Psychiatric Association, 1993, Washington, DC: Author. Used by permission.

Identification of the characteristics associated with ADHD is critical in the diagnosis. The teacher often brings the ADHD-like behaviors to the attention of the parents. When parents initiate contact with the school to find help, as Jenny's parents did, they will be served best by teachers who are already well-informed about this condition and the special education assessment process.

## Prevalence and Causes of Attention Deficit/Hyperactivity Disorder

**CONSIDER THIS**
Review the characteristics and criteria in Figure 5.2. Can you think of examples of situations in which these characteristics might be observed in a school setting? at home? at work?

ADHD is more common than any other child psychiatric disorder (Nolan, Volpe, Gadow, & Sprafkin, 1999). Estimates of the prevalence of attention deficit/hyperactivity disorder in school-age children range from a conservative figure of less than 2% to a more liberal figure of 30%; however, 3%–5% is most probable (American Psychiatric Association, 1994). The extreme differences found in prevalence figures reflect the lack of agreement on a definition and the difficulty and variance in identification procedures. Regardless of the exact prevalence figure, a substantial number of students with this condition attend general education classrooms. Hyperactivity and impulsivity are most likely to be observed in preschool and elementary children; inattention is more common in adolescents. While boys are overrepresented in each subtype (Nolan et al., 1999), there is some concern that girls and children from minority families are at risk for not being identified to receive services (Bussing, Zima, Perwien, Belin, & Widawski, 1998).

Several theories have been developed to explain the primary causes of ADHD. Most professionals agree that ADHD is a neurologically based condition. The causes might be

▲ neuroanatomical—related to brain structure.
▲ neurochemical—related to a chemical imbalance in the brain or a deficiency in chemicals that regulate behavior.
▲ neurophysiological—related to brain function.
▲ some combination of these causes.

Some data suggest that genetics plays a significant role in ADHD. Studies have shown that parents and siblings of children with this disorder have higher rates of ADHD than expected in the general population. This suggests a familial association with various features of ADHD. It is possible for neurological conditions to be transmitted genetically, predisposing an individual to hyperactivity or attention problems. Little or no evidence points to physical environment, social factors, diet, or poor parental management as causes of ADHD (Barkley, 1991).

For most students, the precise cause of the problem may never be understood. Riccio, Hynd, Cohen, and Gonzales (1994) report that neurological evidence that precisely explains ADHD is not yet available. Although many parents want to understand why their children have a developmental disability such as ADHD, its cause is really not relevant to educational strategies or medical treatment. These can succeed without pinpointing the root of the problem.

## Characteristics of Students with Attention Deficit/Hyperactivity Disorder

The characteristics of ADHD manifest themselves in many different ways in the classroom. Recognizing them and identifying accommodations or strategies to lessen the impact in the classroom constitute a significant challenge for teachers. The

**CONSIDER THIS**
Refer to the opening vignette in this chapter. Identify Jenny's characteristics that would lead a teacher or parent to suspect ADHD.

characteristics listed in the *DSM-IV* criteria highlight the observable behaviors. Barkley (1991) groups these characteristics into the following five features:

1. *Limited sustained attention or persistence of attention to tasks:* Particularly during tedious, long-term tasks, the students become rapidly bored and frequently shift from one uncompleted activity to another. They may lose concentration during long work periods and fail to complete routine work unless closely supervised.

2. *Reduced impulse control or limited delay of gratification:* This is often observed in an individual's difficulty in waiting for his or her turn while talking to others or playing. Students may not stop and think before acting or speaking. They may have difficulty working toward long-term goals and long-term rewards, preferring to work on shorter tasks that promise immediate reinforcement.

3. *Excessive task-irrelevant activity or activity poorly regulated to match situational demands:* Individuals with ADHD are often extremely fidgety and restless. Their movement seems excessive and often not directly related to the task—for example, tapping pencils, rocking, or shifting positions frequently. They also have trouble sitting still and inhibiting their movements when the situation demands it.

4. *Deficient rule following:* Individuals with ADHD frequently have difficulty following through on assignments and instructions. The problem is not due to inability to comprehend the instructions, memory impairment, or defiance. The instructions simply do not regulate behavior or stimulate the desired response.

5. *Greater than normal variability during task performance:* Individuals with ADHD demonstrate considerable variation in the accuracy, quality, and speed in which they perform their assigned tasks. Their relatively high performance on some occasions, coupled with low levels of accuracy on other occasions, can be baffling. Low levels of performance often occur with repetitive or tedious tasks.

**TEACHING TIP**
As another technique for recording a student's behavior, observe a child for 3–5 minutes every hour during a school day, and document whether the child is on or off task. Record what the child is supposed to be doing, what he or she is actually doing, and the consequences of that behavior (e.g., praise, ignoring). Figure the percentage of on- and off-task behavior.

Barkley (1991) points out that many of these characteristics are prevalent in normal individuals, particularly young children; however, the behaviors occur to a far greater degree and at a higher frequency in individuals with ADHD. Figure 5.3 cites specific behaviors from the previous categories that are reported during preschool and later periods by parents and teachers, showing how the behaviors can be manifested in different environments.

The characteristics of ADHD may also be present in adulthood. For some individuals the condition continues to cause problems and limitations in the world of work, as well as in other life activities. Barkley (1991) reports that between 35% and 65% of individuals with ADHD will have trouble with tendencies toward aggressiveness, inappropriate conduct, and violation of social norms or legal mandates during adolescence. As many as 25% may be antisocial as adults.

Goldstein and Goldstein (1990) suggest that the characteristics of ADHD affect ultimate success of many aspects of adult adjustment: intelligence, socioeconomic status, socialization, activity level, ability to delay rewards, limiting aggression, and family mental health. For some adults the effects of ADHD linger, but change somewhat—for example, hyperactivity may evolve into a general feeling of restlessness. Other symptoms may also be felt or observed to a lesser degree. In any case, ADHD can have significant effects on adult outcomes. Teachers who can identify and plan meaningful interventions for students with ADHD can have a powerful impact on their success during the school years as well as their quality of life as adults.

**FIGURE 5.3**   Characteristics of Children with ADHD during Preschool and School-Age Periods as Reported by Parents and Teachers

PRESCHOOL AGE

**Parents' Reports**

excessive busyness

accidents related to independence

resistance to routines, e.g., brushing teeth, getting dressed

shifts frequently across play activities

talks too much

easily upset or frustrated

disruptiveness

noncompliance

aggressive in play

**Teachers' Reports**

more activity

more talking

less time spent on any single activity

noncompliance

SCHOOL AGE

**Parents' Reports**

fidgeting, talking especially during homework

greater dependence on adults

noisiness

interrupting

bossiness

less sharing; rough play

poor peer relations

immature social interactions; few friends

self-centered

easily bored

**Teachers' Reports**

fidgeting

out of seat

requiring more supervision

more talking

interrupting

off task, especially visual off task (looks about)

bossiness

erratic productivity

intrudes on others' activities

poor persistence of effort

From the *Ch.A.D.D. Manual* (pp. 11–12) by Mary Fowler, 1992, Fairfax, VA: CASET Association. Used by permission.

## Identification, Assessment, and Eligibility

For years the assessment and diagnosis of attention deficit/hyperactivity disorder were considered the responsibility of psychologists, psychiatrists, and physicians. However, the mandates of Section 504 of PL 93-112 as interpreted by the assistant secretary for civil rights (Cantu, 1993) charged public education personnel with responsibility for this assessment. If a school district suspects that a child has a disability that substantially limits a major life activity such as learning, the district is required to provide an assessment. If the disability is confirmed, the school district must then provide services. Since ADHD is often covered under Section 504, a child suspected of having it may be eligible both for assessment and services.

## RIGHTS & RESPONSIBILITIES
### Parent Rights under Section 504

Section 504 of the Rehabilitation Act provides services for students identified as having a disability that substantially limits a major life activity. As parents, you have the following rights:

1. The right to be informed of your rights under Section 504 of the Rehabilitation Act.
2. The right for your child to have equal opportunities to participate in academic, nonacademic, and extra-curricular activities in your school.
3. The right to be notified about referral, evaluation, and programs for your child.
4. The right for your child to be evaluated fairly.
5. The right, if eligible for services under 504, for your child to receive accommodations, modifications, and related services that will meet his/her needs as well as the needs of nondisabled students are met.

6. The right for your child to be educated with nondisabled peers as much as possible.
7. The right to an impartial hearing if you disagree with the school regarding your child's educational program.
8. The right to review and obtain copies of your child's school records.
9. The right to request attorney fees related to securing your rights under Section 504.
10. The right to request changes in the educational program of your child.

Signed:       Parent(s): _____       Date: _____
School Representative: _____       Date: _____

From "Section 504 and Public Schools: A Practical Guide" (p. 73) by T. E. C. Smith and J. R. Patton, 1998, Austin, TX: Pro-Ed. Adapted by permission.

Because teachers are often the first to suspect the presence of ADHD, they should be familiar with its specific behaviors and the commonly used assessment techniques. Although the formal assessment for ADHD must be performed by specially trained school personnel, teachers participate on the interdisciplinary team that reviews the assessment data to determine if the attention problems do limit learning and to plan the individualized program, if appropriate. Teachers may also be called on to complete informal assessment instruments that, with other data, will help in determining the presence of ADHD.

Atkins and Pelham (1991) support the participation of teachers as an important source of information in ADHD assessment. They note that teachers spend a significant amount of time with students in a variety of academic and social tasks, are considered more objective than parents, and have a better sense of normal behaviors for the comparison group. Their research has demonstrated that teachers can differentiate well between students with and without symptoms of ADHD.

Burnley (1993) proposes a four-part plan that could be implemented to structure the interdisciplinary assessment process for schools. This plan is similar to that used by school personnel as they determine eligibility for services under IDEA. A modified version of Burnley's process is described in the following sections. It is important to note that parents have rights guaranteed throughout this process. These rights are listed in a communication to parents found in the nearby Rights and Responsibilities feature.

### STEPS IN THE ASSESSMENT PROCESS

*Step 1: Preliminary Assessment and Initial Child Study Meeting.* Initially, a teacher who has been trained in identifying the symptoms of attention deficit/hyperactivity

| Teacher: _____ | School: _____ | |
| Child: _____ | Grade: _____  Age: _____ | |

| Class Activity | Child's Behavior | Date/Time |
| --- | --- | --- |
| | | |
| | | |
| | | |
| | | |

disorder according to the school's criteria may begin to observe that a particular student manifests these behaviors in the classroom to a greater degree than his or her peers do. At this point, the teacher should begin to keep a log to document the child's ADHD-like behaviors, noting the times at which behaviors appear to be more intense, more frequent, or of a longer duration. Figure 5.4 provides a simple format for this observational log.

If the teacher's anecdotal records confirm the continuing presence of these behaviors, the referral process should be initiated and the observational log turned in as documentation. At that point a less biased observer should come into the classroom to provide comparative information (Schaughency & Rothlind, 1991). Schaughency and Rothlind (1991) caution that this form of data collection is costly in terms of professional time; however, if the observation period is not long enough, behavior that occurs infrequently may be missed. The assessment team should realize that direct observation is just one source of information to be considered in the identification process.

As soon as the school suspects that a child is experiencing attention problems, the parents should be notified and invited to meet with the child study team. Often the parents, the teacher, the principal, and the school counselor will come together for the initial meeting. During this meeting parents should be asked to respond to the observations of the school personnel and describe their own experiences with attention problems outside of the school setting. If the team agrees that additional testing is needed, a trained individual should step in to direct the assessment process. This person must understand the impact of ADHD on the family; the bias that might occur during the assessment process because of cultural, socioeconomic, language, and ethnic factors; and other conditions that may mimic ADHD and prevent an accurate diagnosis.

*Step 2: Formal Assessment Process: Follow-Up Meeting of the Child Study Team.* Although schools are not required to use a specific set of criteria to identify attention deficit/hyperactivity disorder, the *DSM-IV* criteria described earlier are highly recommended (McBurnett, Lahey, & Pfiffner, 1993). The following questions, recommended by Schaughency and Rothlind (1991), need to be addressed during the formal assessment process:

1. Is there an alternative educational diagnosis or medical condition that accounts for the attention difficulties?

2. Are the behaviors demonstrated by the child developmentally appropriate? (For example, children with mental retardation may be diagnosed correctly as having ADHD, but only if their attention problems are significantly different from those of the children at comparable developmental levels.)
3. Does the child meet the *DSM-IV* criteria?
4. Do the ADHD-like behaviors affect the child's functioning in several settings, such as home, school, and other social situations?

A variety of methods and assessment procedures will be needed to answer these questions. The school system will most likely interview parents and teachers, obtain a developmental history, evaluate intellectual and academic performance, administer rating scales to multiple informants, and document the impact of the behavior through direct observation.

Atkins and Pelham (1991) suggest the following as the most typical components of a comprehensive assessment battery for identifying ADHD-like behaviors:

▲ Observation
▲ Interviews with the child, parents, and teachers
▲ Review of intellectual and academic achievement testing
▲ Review of school records
▲ Rating scales completed by the teachers, parents, and possibly peers
▲ Medical examination (in some cases)

After the necessary observations have been made, the interview process can begin. According to Woodrich (1994), an interview with parents might include the following topics:

▲ The student's health, psychiatric, and developmental history
▲ Family history
▲ Details of referral concern
▲ The student's behavior at home
▲ School history and previous testing
▲ Interpersonal and social development

Woodrich (1994) recommends that the following areas be addressed during the teacher interview:

▲ Class work habits and productivity
▲ Skill levels in academic subjects
▲ Length of time attention can be sustained for novel tasks and for monotonous tasks
▲ Degree of activity during class and on the playground
▲ Class structure and standards for self-control
▲ Degree of compliance with class rules
▲ Manifestation of more serious conduct problems
▲ Onset, frequency, and duration of inappropriate behavior in the antecedent events
▲ Peer acceptance and social skills
▲ Previous intervention techniques and special services now considered appropriate

An interview with the child is appropriate in many cases, to determine the child's perception of the reports by the teacher, attitude toward school and family, and perception of relationships with peers. Although the child's responses will be slanted by personal feelings, it still is an important source of information.

The assessment of achievement and intelligence is not required in the identification of ADHD. However, the results of achievement and intelligence tests might suggest that the child can qualify for services under IDEA (1997) in categories of learning disabilities or mental retardation. Also, knowing the levels of intelligence and achievement will help eventually in developing an intervention plan.

Rating scales that measure the presence of ADHD symptoms are widely used to quantify the severity of the behaviors. They offer a way to objectively measure the extent of the problem. Rating scales should be completed by several informants who know the child in a variety of settings. The results should be compared to responses from interviews and the results of observations. Some rating scales are limited to an assessment of the primary symptoms contained in the *DSM-IV* criteria; other assessment instruments are multidimensional and might address emotional–social status, communication, memory, reasoning and problem solving, and cognitive skills such as planning and self-evaluation. Figure 5.5 contains an excerpt from the "Strengths and Limitations Inventory: School Version" (Dowdy, Patton, Smith, & Polloway, 1998).

A medical examination is not required in the diagnosis of ADHD; however, because symptoms of certain medical conditions may mimic those of ADHD, a medical exam should be considered. Schools may hesitate to recommend it because, according to federal law, any medical examination required to assist the team in making a school-related decision is considered a "related service," and the school must provide it at no cost to the parents (Worthington, Patterson, Elliott, & Linkous, 1993). No specific laboratory tests have been developed to diagnose ADHD (American Psychiatric Association, 1994). However, a physician might identify sleep apnea, anemia, hyperthyroidism, or side effects from medication as the primary cause of problem behaviors.

When the child study team reconvenes to review all of the data, the following *DSM-IV* (1994) criteria should be considered:

◢ Six or more of the 9 characteristics of inattention and/or 6 or more of the 9 symptoms of hyperactivity–impulsivity should be demonstrated as present for longer than six months.

◢ The behaviors observed should be considered maladaptive and developmentally inconsistent.

◢ The symptoms should have been observed since or before age 7.

◢ The limitations that stem from the characteristics should be observed in two or more settings (e.g., home, school, work).

◢ The characteristics are not considered solely the result of schizophrenia, pervasive developmental disorder, or other psychiatric disorder, and they are not better attributed to the presence of another mental disorder such as anxiety disorder or mood disorder.

The child study team should look for consistency across reports from the assessment instruments and the informants to validate the existence of ADHD. If it is confirmed, the team must determine if it has caused an adverse effect on school performance and if a special educational plan is needed. Montague, McKinney, and Hocutt (1994) cite the following questions developed by the Professional Group on Attention and Related Disorders (PGARD) to guide the team in determining educational needs:

1. Do the ADHD symptoms negatively affect learning to the extent that there is a discrepancy between the child's productivity with respect to listening, following directions, planning, organizing, or completing academic tasks requiring reading, math, writing, or spelling skills?

**CONSIDER THIS**

If your school has a policy stipulating that teachers should not recommend services that the school system might have to pay for (e.g., a medical exam), how will you proceed when you feel a child is in need of such services? What are your options?

FIGURE **5.5**    Sample Test Items from "Strength and Limitations Inventory: School Version"

| | Never Observed | Sometimes Observed | Often Observed | Very Often Observed |
|---|---|---|---|---|
| **ATTENTION/IMPULSIVITY/HYPERACTIVITY** | | | | |
| Exhibits excessive nonpurposeful movement (can't sit still, stay in seat). | | | | |
| Does not stay on task for appropriate periods of time. | | | | |
| Verbally or physically interrupts conversations or activities. | | | | |
| Does not pay attention to most important stimuli. | | | | |
| **REASONING/PROCESSING** | | | | |
| Makes poor decisions. | | | | |
| Makes frequent errors. | | | | |
| Has difficulty getting started. | | | | |
| **MEMORY** | | | | |
| Has difficulty repeating information recently heard. | | | | |
| Has difficulty following multiple directions. | | | | |
| Memory deficits impact daily activities. | | | | |
| **EXECUTIVE FUNCTION** | | | | |
| Has difficulty planning/organizing activities. | | | | |
| Has difficulty attending to several stimuli at once. | | | | |
| Has difficulty monitoring own performance throughout activity (self-monitoring). | | | | |
| Has difficulty independently adjusting behavior (self-regulation). | | | | |
| **INTERPERSONAL SKILLS** | | | | |
| Has difficulty accepting constructive criticism. | | | | |
| Exhibits signs of poor self-confidence. | | | | |
| **EMOTIONAL MATURITY** | | | | |
| Inappropriate emotion for situation. | | | | |
| Displays temper outbursts. | | | | |
| Does not follow classroom or workplace "rules." | | | | |

From *Attention Deficit/Hyperactivity Disorder in the Classroom: A Practical Guide for Teachers,* by C. A. Dowdy, J. R. Patton, T. E. C. Smith, and E. A. Polloway, 1998, Austin, TX: Pro-Ed. Reprinted by permission.

**2.** Are inattentive behaviors the result of cultural or language differences, socio-economic disadvantage, or lack of exposure to education?

**3.** Are the inattentive behaviors evidence of stressful family functioning (e.g., death or divorce), frustration related to having unattainable educational goals, abuse, or physical or emotional disorders (e.g., epilepsy or depression)?

If question 1 is answered positively and questions 2 and 3 are answered negatively, the team can conclude that an educational need exists that requires special services. At that point, a planning meeting should address the educational program.

*Step 3: Collaborative Meeting for Strategy Development.*    This meeting might be very emotional and overwhelming for parents, or it might generate relief and hope that the services can truly assist the child. The team must be sensitive to the feelings of the parents and take adequate time to describe the results of the testing. If the parents are emotionally upset, it may help to wait a week before developing the intervention plan for school services.

*Step 4: Follow-Up and Progress Review.*    After the educational plan has been developed, the parents and school personnel should monitor the child's progress closely to ensure success. Adjustments may be needed occasionally to maintain progress. For example, a reinforcement for good behavior may eventually lose its novelty and need to be changed. The ultimate goal is to remove accommodations and support as the child becomes capable of self-regulating his or her behavior. As the setting and school personnel change each year, reevaluating the need for special services will yield benefits. As the student becomes more efficient in learning and demonstrates better social skills under one plan, a new, less restrictive plan must be designed to complement this growth.

## Cultural and Linguistic Diversity

When ADHD coexists with cultural and linguistic diversity, it presents a special set of challenges to the educator. Failure to address the special needs of these children can be detrimental to their academic success. Issues related to assessment and cultural diversity have been discussed previously; the same concerns exist in the identification and treatment of students with ADHD. To address the needs of multicultural students with ADHD, teachers must become familiar with their unique values, views, customs, interests, and behaviors and their relation to instructional strategies (Wright, 1995). *DSM-IV* (American Psychiatric Association, 1994) simply states that service-eligible behaviors cannot be the result of cultural differences.

Barkley (1990) raises the issue that the chaotic home environment of many minority populations existing below the poverty level exacerbates the problems of children with ADHD. When teachers use carefully organized and structured instruction, these students benefit. Wright (1995) suggests that, first and foremost, teachers should treat students with respect, attempt to establish good rapport with them, and only then impose instructional demands. Streeter and Grant (1993) encourage teachers to make educational experiences more meaningful to students by developing activities and homework that acknowledge cultural differences and build on the specific experiences of the student. Teachers can integrate personal and community experiences into teaching an academic concept to help make it relevant. Additional suggestions for helping at risk students are located in the nearby Diversity Forum.

**TEACHING TIP**
Begin a parent conference by talking about the strengths of the student! Give parents time to respond to the limitations observed in the school setting by having them report examples of behavior from home and other environments.

**CONSIDER THIS**
Complete an in-depth study of the characteristics or educational needs of a particular culture. Share your findings with other groups in the class.

*DIVERSITY FORUM*   **Practical Suggestions for Helping**
**At Risk Learners**

◢ Guide students to learn how they learn best.
◢ Understand that inattention, disorganization, and inability to complete work are signs of the disability—not disrespect or laziness!
◢ Model the desired results or behavior. A child may need a picture of his or her room clean before he or she can clean the room.

◢ Don't just tell students to study, to memorize, to review—give them strategies.
◢ If a student has trouble sitting still, find him or her a place to move about while he or she does the work.
◢ Praise students often telling them what they did and why it was good.

Adapted from "At Risk Students: No Instant Solution" by S. M. Glazer, 1998, *Teaching Pre-K–8, 28*(7), pp. 84–86. Used by permission.

## EDUCATIONAL INTERVENTION

General and special education teachers need to work closely with parents, physicians, and support personnel to develop and maintain successful educational intervention. For many students, accommodations in general education classes are enough to improve learning; however, other students may need special education support services and placement. Medication may also be indicated to enhance learning for students with ADHD. The following sections will discuss these issues.

### Continuum-of-Placement Options

Under Section 504, a local education agency must provide a free appropriate public education to each qualified child with a disability. The U.S. Department of Education suggests that the placement of choice for children with ADHD should be the general education classroom, with appropriate adaptations and interventions.

Although students with ADHD may be found in a variety of special education settings, Reid et al. (1994) found that the majority of students classified as special education students spent most or all of the school day in general education classes. Since the general education teacher is responsible for the learning experience most of the time, it is imperative that these teachers understand the condition and have strategies for dealing with it in their classrooms. Special educators must be knowledgeable in order to collaborate effectively with general educators to develop educational plans that might modify curriculum, instruction, and environment. Both special education and general education teachers also need to be effective managers of behavior and skillful in teaching students how to regulate their own behavior.

### Developing Educational Plans

If a local education agency decides that a child has a disability under Section 504, the school must determine the child's educational needs for regular and special education or related aids and services. Although this law does not mandate a written individualized education program (IEP), implementation of a written individualized education plan is recommended (U.S. Department of Education, 1991). Most school systems have opted to develop written plans; they are generally referred to as student accommodation plans, individual accommodation plans, or 504 plans.

It is recommended that this plan be developed by a committee that includes parents, professionals, and, as often as possible, the student. The areas identified as caus-

ing significant limitations in learning should be the target of the intervention plan. The committee should determine the least amount of accommodation needed to stimulate success in learning and social development. If medication therapy is being used, the plan should also indicate the school's role in administering the medication and special precautions or considerations regarding side effects (Katsiyannis, Landrum, & Vinton, 1997). When a conservative intervention plan has been developed and implemented, additional goals and interventions can be added as needed.

Each local education agency must have an identified 504 coordinator or officer responsible for maintaining a fair and responsive evaluation process and plan for developing accommodations plans. They monitor students' needs and communicate with parents and teachers as necessary.

Figure 5.6 presents an example of an educational accommodation plan developed by Conderman and Katsiyannis (1995) for a fictional third-grade student. Notice that an intervention plan was identified for three areas of concern. In each area, the person responsible for implementing the strategy was also noted. Although it is much simpler than an IEP, it serves to document legally the plan agreed upon by the team members.

## The Role of Medication

Since many students with ADHD will be prescribed medication by their physicians, teachers need to understand the types of medications used, commonly prescribed dosages, intended effects, and potential side effects. Medication therapy can be defined as treatment by chemical substances that prevent or reduce inappropriate behaviors, thus promoting academic and social gains for children with learning and behavior problems (Dowdy et al., 1998). Although medication therapy has been used to treat children with ADHD since the 1940s, it is still not exactly understood why or how some chemicals affect attention, learning, and hyperactivity. Studies have shown that different outcomes occur for different children. In 70% to 80% of the cases, children with ADHD respond in a positive manner to psychostimulant medication (Fowler, 1992; Spencer, Biederman, Wilens, Harding, O'Donnell, & Griffin, 1996). The desired outcomes include increased attention, more on-task behavior, completion of assigned tasks, improved social relations with peers and teachers, increased appropriate behaviors, and reduction

**TEACHING TIP**
When you are employed in a new school district, meet the special education and 504 coordinators to obtain an overview of policies and procedures for assessment and delivery.

**CONSIDER THIS**
Adolescents often refuse to take medication prescribed for ADHD. What do you think happens during this developmental period that might account for this behavior?

FIGURE **5.6**   Example of a General Education Accommodation Plan

FIGURE **5.6**   Example of a General Education Accommodation Plan

### General Education Accommodation Plan

Name: Joshua Green      School/Grade: Platte Valley Elementary, 3rd

Date: 6/5/95      Teacher: Myrna Mae (lead teacher)

Participants in Development of Accommodation Plan

Mr. and Mrs. Walter Green    Julie Hartson      Myrna Mae, Teacher      Arlo Wachal, Teacher
parent(s)/guardian(s)      principal      teacher(s)

Joel Schaeffer, Counselor    Violette Schelldorf, Nurse

Building Person responsible for monitoring plan: Joel Schaeffer, Counselor      Follow-up Date: 6/5/96

Currently on Medication _x_ Yes ___ No   Physician: Eveard Ewing, M.D.   Type: Ritalin   Dosage: 15 mg twice daily

| Area of Concern | Intervention of Teaching Strategies | Person Responsible for Accommodation |
|---|---|---|
| 1. Assignment Completion | 1. Daily assignment sheet sent home with Josh<br>2. Contract system initiated for assignment completion in math and social studies | Myrna Mae<br>Parents will initial daily, and Josh will return the form<br>Myrna Mae, Arlo Wachal |
| 2. Behavior/Distractibility | 1. Preferential seating-study carrel or near teacher, as needed<br>2. Daily behavior card sent home with Josh | Myrna Mae, Arlo Wachal<br><br>Parents will initial daily; and Josh will return the form |
| 3. Consistency of Medication | 1. Medication to be administered in private by school nurse daily at noon | Violette Schelldorf |

Comments:

   Josh will remain in the general education classroom with the accommodations noted above.

*Mr. & Mrs. Walter Green*

Parental Authorization for 504 Plan

| I agree with the accommodations described in this 504 plan. | I do not agree with the accommodations described in this 504 plan. I understand I have the right to appeal. |
|---|---|

From "Section 504 Accommodation Plans," by G. Conderman and A. Katsiyannis, 1995, *Intervention in School and Clinic, 31*(1), p. 44. Used by permission.

of inappropriate, disruptive behaviors such as talking out loud, getting out of seat, and breaking rules. These changes frequently lead to improved academic and social achievement as well as increased self-esteem.

For some children, the desired effects do not occur. In these situations the medication has no negative effect, but simply does not lead to the hoped for results. However, parents and teachers often give up too soon, prematurely concluding that the medication did not help. It is important to contact the physician when no effect is noticed, because the dosage may need to be adjusted or a different type of medication is needed.

Another possible response to medication is side effects. Side effects are changes that are not desired. Figure 5.7 lists the most common side effects of the medications used for ADHD. This checklist may be used by parents and teachers when communicating with physicians. Teachers should constantly be on the lookout for signs of side effects and report any concerns to parents or the child's physician.

The most commonly prescribed medications for ADHD are **psychostimulants** such as Dexedrine (dextroamphetamine), Ritalin (methylphenidate), and Cylert (pemo-

**PSYCHOSTIMULANTS** are medications that stimulate the inhibitory system of the brain and result in an increase in attention and ability to focus.

---

### Side Effects Checklist: Stimulants

Child _____  Date Checked _____
Person Completing Form: _____  Relationship to Child _____

#### I. SIDE EFFECTS

Directions: Please check any of the behaviors which this child exhibits while receiving his or her stimulant medication. If a child exhibits one or more of the behaviors below, please rate the extent to which you perceive the behavior to be a problem using the scale below (1=Mild to 7=Severe).

| | Mild | | | | | | Severe |
|---|---|---|---|---|---|---|---|
| 1. Loss of appetite | 1 | 2 | 3 | 4 | 5 | 6 | 7 |
| 2. Stomachaches | 1 | 2 | 3 | 4 | 5 | 6 | 7 |
| 3. Headaches | 1 | 2 | 3 | 4 | 5 | 6 | 7 |
| 4. Tics (vocal or motor) | 1 | 2 | 3 | 4 | 5 | 6 | 7 |
| 5. Extreme mood changes | 1 | 2 | 3 | 4 | 5 | 6 | 7 |
| 6. Cognitively sluggish/disoriented | 1 | 2 | 3 | 4 | 5 | 6 | 7 |
| 7. Excessive irritability | 1 | 2 | 3 | 4 | 5 | 6 | 7 |
| 8. Excessive nervousness | 1 | 2 | 3 | 4 | 5 | 6 | 7 |
| 9. Decreased social interactions | 1 | 2 | 3 | 4 | 5 | 6 | 7 |
| 10. Unusual or bizarre behavior | 1 | 2 | 3 | 4 | 5 | 6 | 7 |
| 11. Excessive activity level | 1 | 2 | 3 | 4 | 5 | 6 | 7 |
| 12. Light picking of fingertips | 1 | 2 | 3 | 4 | 5 | 6 | 7 |
| 13. Lip licking | 1 | 2 | 3 | 4 | 5 | 6 | 7 |

#### II. PSYCHOSOCIAL CONCERNS

Please address any concerns you have about this child's adjustment to medication (e.g., physical, social, emotional changes; attitudes toward the medication, etc.).

#### III. OTHER CONCERNS

If you have any other concerns about this child's medication (e.g., administration problems, dosage concerns), please comment below.

#### IV. PARENT CONCERNS (FOR PARENTS ONLY)

Using the same scale above, please check any behaviors which this child exhibits while at home.

| | Mild | | | | | | Severe |
|---|---|---|---|---|---|---|---|
| 1. Insomnia; sleeplessness | 1 | 2 | 3 | 4 | 5 | 6 | 7 |
| 2. Possible rebound effects (excessive hyperactivity, impulsivity, inattention) | 1 | 2 | 3 | 4 | 5 | 6 | 7 |

**FIGURE 5.7**
Stimulant Side Effects Checklist

From *ADHD Project Facilitate: An In-Service Education Program for Educators and Parents* (p. 55) by R. Elliott, L. A. Worthington, and D. Patterson, Tuscaloosa, AL: University of Alabama. Used by permission.

---

line). Studies have shown that 84%–93% of medical professionals prescribing medicine for children with ADHD select methylphenidate (Forness, Sweeney, & Toy, 1996). This medication is considered a "mild central nervous system stimulant, available as tablets of 5, 10, and 20 mg for oral administration" (*Physician's Desk Reference*, 1994, p. 835). A typical dosage of Ritalin for an initial trial is 5 mg, two to three times daily. Students who are described as anxious or tense, have tics, or have a family history or diagnosis of **Tourette's syndrome** are generally not given Ritalin (*Physician's Desk Reference*, 1999). The specific dose of medicine must be determined individually for each child. Generally, greater side effects come from higher dosages, but some students may need

**TOURETTE'S SYNDROME** is a disorder that results in body tics and vocalizations that are inappropriate, such as shouting profanity.

FIGURE **5.9**

Sample of Contingency Contract

From *Attention Deficit Disorder in the Classroom: A Practical Guide for Teachers* (p. 90) by C. A. Dowdy, J. R. Patton, T. E. C. Smith, and E. Polloway, 1998, Austin, TX: Pro-Ed.

**Contract**

This agreement is between _____ and _____.
                                    (student)                        (teacher)

The contract begins on _____ and continues until

_____. The terms of this contract include the following:

The student will:

_____
_____
_____
_____

When these things are completed, the teacher will:

_____
_____
_____
_____

Student's Signature: _____ Date_____
Teacher's Signature: _____ Date_____

Another behavior management technique is cuing or signaling ADHD students when they are on the verge of inappropriate behavior. First, student and teacher sit down privately and discuss the inappropriate behavior that has been creating problems in the classroom. The teacher offers to provide a cue when the behavior begins to be noticed. Teachers and students can have fun working together on the signal, which might involve flipping the light switch, tapping the desk lightly, or simple eye contact (Wood, 1984). These cuing techniques help establish a collegial relationship between the teacher and the student that says, "We are working on this together; we have a problem, but we also have a plan."

## Making Instructional Accommodations

Barkley (1990) says "Knowing what to do is a strategy problem. Doing what you know is a motivational problem." His research suggests that ADHD may be caused by neurological differences in the motivational center of the brain; however, children with ADHD are often misunderstood and labeled lazy or unmotivated, as if they are choosing not to perform at their maximum potential. Teacher comments such as, "I know you can do this work, because you did it yesterday" or "You can do better; you just aren't trying" probably suggest a lack of understanding of the inconsistent performance characteristic of this disability (Flick, 1998). Instead, teachers need to find ways to cope with the frustration and stress sometimes involved in working with these students, while modifying their teaching style, their curriculum, and possibly their expectations in order to engineer academic success for these students.

MODIFYING TEACHER BEHAVIOR   Since students with ADHD are not easily stimulated, they need novelty and excitement in their learning environment. Although structure and consistency are extremely important, students need challenging, novel

*Cuing or signaling students is one method that teachers can use to help get their attention.*

activities to keep them focused and learning. Fowler (1992) reports that the incidence of inappropriate behavior increases during nonstimulating, repetitive activities. She suggests that teachers vary activities, allow and encourage movement that is purposeful and not disruptive, give frequent breaks, and even let students stand as they listen, take notes, or perform other academic tasks. Here are some recommendations from Yehle and Wambold (1998) for enhancing large group instruction:

◢ Begin with an attention grabber (e.g., joke, question of the day).
◢ Distribute an outline of your lecture to assist with note taking; provide copies of overheads.
◢ Pace the lesson, giving more time for difficult concepts.
◢ Use visual aids such as a graphic organizer as often as possible.
◢ Clap, alter you tone of voice, or use different colored chalk to draw attention to important material.
◢ Repeat important information several times during the lecture; ask students to repeat in unison.
◢ Ask frequent questions of individual students by name throughout the presentation.
◢ Walk around the room monitoring and checking work frequently.
◢ Try to turn a lesson into a game format (e.g., the Jeopardy game show) for a fun review.
◢ Stay close to students and use frequent eye contact.
◢ Close each lesson with a review, set the stage for the next lesson, and give reminders about homework.

Templeton (1995) suggests that teachers speak clearly and loudly enough for students to hear, but not too fast. She points out that enthusiasm and humor will help engage students and excite those who might become easily bored and distracted. She

**CONSIDER THIS**
If you are currently teaching, complete the *Time-on-Task Self-Assessment*; if not, rewrite the questions and use them as an observation tool to evaluate a teacher who is willing to be observed. Analyze the results and identify changes that are indicated to improve learning in the classroom.

also recommends helping students see the value in what they learn and the importance of the material. During a long lecture period, teachers might list main ideas or important questions on the chalkboard or by using the overhead projector, to help students focus on the most important information. When a student's attention does wander, a small, unobtrusive signal such as a gentle pat on the student's shoulder can cue the student to return to the task. To perk up tiring students, teachers can try a quick game of Simon Says or assigning purposeful physical activities such as taking a note to the office, feeding the animals in the classroom, or returning books to the library. Prater (1992) provides a self-assessment for teachers to determine if they are doing everything they can to increase each student's attention to task during instructional time. This strategy for improving instruction for all students is included in the nearby Inclusion Strategies feature.

**MODIFYING THE CURRICULUM**   Although students with ADHD are typically taught in the general education classroom, using the regular curriculum, they need a curriculum adapted to focusing on "doing" and one that avoids long periods of sitting and listening. These adaptations can benefit all students. For example, experience-based learning, in which students might develop their own projects, perform experiments, or take field trips, can help all students grow as active learners. Cronin (1993) suggests that teachers modify curriculum by using activities that closely resemble challenges and experiences in the real world. Resources can be found in story problems included in traditional textbooks, curriculum-based experiments and projects, or extended activities such as writing letters to environmental groups to obtain more information than is offered in a textbook.

Describing a related curriculum model, Stephien and Gallagher (1993) suggest that problem-based learning provides authentic experiences in the classroom. In this model, students are asked to solve an "ill-structured problem" before they receive any instruction. Teachers act as coaches and tutors, questioning the student's hypotheses and conclusions and sharing their own thoughts when needed during "time out" discussions. Students act as doctors, historians, or scientists, or assume other roles of individuals who have a real stake in solving the proposed problem. When students "take ownership" of the problem, motivation soars. Teachers can model problem-solving strategies by thinking out loud and questioning their own conclusions and recommendations. This model, a modification of cooperative learning groups (Jones & Jones, 1995) described earlier in the text, increases self-directed learning and improves motivation. The nearby Technology Today feature describes how technology can be used to complement a variety of learning techniques commonly used in a general education classroom.

Teachers are also encouraged to use frequent reinforcement and vary their assessment techniques. Oral examinations, portfolio assessment, and informal measures are alternative assessment methods that provide a different perspective on what students know. Raza (1997) suggests that these techniques let students know that their teachers are not as concerned with how they perform on tests as they are with what the students have learned.

## Developing Student-Regulated Strategies

The previous sections on classroom environment and instructional accommodations focused on activities that the teacher directs and implements to increase the success of children with ADHD. This section describes student-regulated strategies. Dowdy et al. (1998) define *student-regulated strategies* as interventions, initially taught by the

## INCLUSION STRATEGIES

### Time-on-Task Self-Assessment for Teachers

Read the following statements and rate yourself according to the following scale:

| N | R | S | U | A |
|---|---|---|---|---|
| **never** | **rarely** | **sometimes** | **usually** | **always** |

**DURING GROUP INSTRUCTION:**

1. Students are attending to me before I start the lesson. _____
2. Students use choral group responses to answer questions. _____
3. Individual students answer questions or orally read when called in a random order. _____
4. I ask a question, then call on a student to answer. _____
5. Students answer correctly most of the questions I ask. _____
6. I have all my materials and supplies ready before class begins. _____
7. If possible, I write all the necessary material on the board, an overhead, or poster before instructing. _____
8. I use some type of signal with group responses. _____
9. Students are involved in reading directions, practice items, or the answers. _____
10. Students are involved in housekeeping procedures such as passing out papers. _____

**DURING SEATWORK:**

11. I move around the classroom checking students' work. _____
12. I can make eye contact with all of my students. _____
13. I allow students to work together and to talk about their seatwork. _____
14. Immediately after instruction my students can work on their seatwork without any questions. _____
15. Students need not wait for my assistance if they have questions about their seatwork. _____
16. I spend little time answering questions about what the students are to do next. _____
17. Most of my students finish their work about the same time. _____

**DURING INSTRUCTION OR SEATWORK:**

18. I spend little time reprimanding students for misbehavior. _____
19. My students are not restless. _____
20. My students follow a routine for transition times (i.e., getting materials ready, collecting papers, lining up for lunch). _____
21. My students respond quickly during transition times. _____
22. I have well-defined rules for appropriate behavior in my classroom. _____
23. I consistently provide appropriate consequences for students who are and remain on-task. _____
24. I teach my students self-management procedures (e.g., self-monitoring, self-instruction). _____

From "Increasing Time-on-Task in the Classroom" by M. A. Prater, 1992, *Intervention in School and Clinic, 28*(1), pp. 22–27.

# *T*ECHNOLOGY *T*ODAY

## Guidelines for Using the Computer to Support Major Instructional Principles

| Principle | Summary | Guidelines |
|---|---|---|
| DIRECT INSTRUCTION | If teachers describe objectives and demonstrate exact steps, students can master specific skills more efficiently | 1. Use programs that specify exact steps and teach them clearly and specifically.<br>2. Show the relationship of computer programs to steps in the direct teaching process. |
| MASTERY LEARNING | Given enough time, nearly all learners can master objectives. | 1. Use programs that provide extra help and practice toward reaching objectives.<br>2. Use programs to stimulate and enrich students who reach objectives early.<br>3. Use record-keeping programs to keep track of student performance. |
| OVERLEARNING AND AUTOMATICITY | To become automatic, skills must be practiced and reinforced beyond the point of initial mastery. | 1. Use computer programs to provide self-paced individualized practice.<br>2. Use computer programs that provide gamelike practice for skills that require much repeated practice.<br>3. Use computer programs that provide varied approaches to practicing the same activity. |
| MEMORIZATION SKILLS | Recall of factual information is a useful skill that enhances learning at all levels. | 1. Use computer programs to provide repeated practice and facilitate memorization.<br>2. Use programs designed to develop memory skills. |
| PEER TUTORING | Both tutor and pupil can benefit from properly structured peer tutoring. | 1. Have students work in groups at computers.<br>2. Use programs that are structured to help tutors provide instruction, prompts, and feedback.<br>3. Teach students to give feedback, prompts, and instruction at computers. |
| COOPERATIVE LEARNING | Helping one another is often more productive than competing for score rewards. | 1. Have students work in groups at computers.<br>2. Use programs that promote cooperation.<br>3. Provide guidelines for cooperative roles at computers. |
| MONITORING STUDENT PROGRESS | Close monitoring of student progress enables students, teachers, and parents to identify strengths and weaknesses of learners. | 1. Use programs that have management systems to monitor student progress.<br>2. Use record-keeping programs.<br>3. Use computers to communicate feedback. |
| STUDENT MISCONCEPTIONS | Identifying misconceptions helps develop an understanding of topics. | 1. Use programs to diagnose misconceptions.<br>2. Use programs to teach correct understanding of misunderstood concepts. |
| PREREQUISITE KNOWLEDGE AND SKILLS | Knowledge is usually hierarchical; lower-level skills must be learned before higher-level skills can be mastered. | 1. Use programs to assess prerequisite knowledge and skills.<br>2. Use programs to teach prerequisite skills. |

From "Principles behind Computerized Instruction for Students with Exceptionalities" (p. 39) by E. Vockell and T. Mihail, 1993, *Teaching Exceptional Children* (Spring).

teacher, that the student will eventually implement independently. These interventions developed from the study of cognitive behavior modification, an exciting new field combining behavioral strategies with cognitive intervention techniques.

Fiore, Becker, and Nerro (1993) note that these cognitive approaches directly address core problems of children with ADHD, including impulse control, higher-order problem solving, and self-regulation. Because this is a new field, teachers are encouraged to validate their effectiveness in their classrooms (DuPaul & Eckert, 1998). Fiore et al. (1993) argue that teachers should try implementing these approaches, bearing in mind that they do need further study.

The benefits of implementing self-regulation strategies for children with ADHD include the following:

▲ Modifying impulsive responses
▲ Increasing selective attention and focus
▲ Providing verbal mediators to facilitate academic and social problem-solving challenges (e.g., self-talk to calm down during an argument)
▲ Teaching self-instructional statements to assist students in "talking through" problems and tasks
▲ Providing strategies that may develop prosocial behaviors and lead to improved peer relations (Rooney, 1993)

The following discussion addresses four types of student-regulated strategies: study and organizational tactics, self-management, learning strategies, and social skills.

**STUDY AND ORGANIZATIONAL TACTICS**    Students with ADHD have difficulty organizing their work and developing effective study skills in general education classrooms. To help them with organization, teachers may designate space for students to keep materials, establish the routine of students writing down their assignments daily in an assignment notebook, and/or provide notebooks in different colors for each subject (Yehle & Wambold, 1998).

Hoover and Patton (1995) suggest teaching 11 study skills: increasing and/or adjusting reading rate according to the purpose for reading, listening, note taking, writing reports, giving oral presentations, using graphic aids, taking tests, using the library, using reference material, time management, and self-management. Students should practice planning as an organizational strategy. Before giving an assignment such as a term paper, deciding how to break the task into small parts and how to complete each part should be practiced. Students should also practice estimating how much time is needed for various activities so they can establish appropriate and realistic goals. Outlining skills can also help with organization and planning. Students may want to use a word processor to order their ideas and to help organize their work.

**SELF-MANAGEMENT**    The primary goal of programs that teach self-management or self-control is to "make children more consciously aware of their own thinking processes and task approach strategies, and to give them responsibility for their own reinforcement" (Reeve, 1990, p. 76). Here are some advantages of teaching self-control:

▲ It saves the teacher's time by decreasing the demand for direct instruction.
▲ It increases the effectiveness of an intervention.
▲ It increases the maintenance of skills over time.
▲ It increases a student's ability to use the skill in a variety of settings. (Lloyd, Landrum, & Hallahan, 1991, p. 201)

*TEACHING TIP*

Practice what you teach! Identify an activity or task that you need to accomplish by a date in the future (e.g., develop a unit on ecology). Break down the steps to completion, including target dates. Model your planning skills by "thinking out loud" for your students. This will make the concept of planning and organizing more concrete for them.

FIGURE **5.10**    Self-Management Planning Form

Student _____Geoff_____    Teacher _____Mr. Sherman_____

School _____Lane Middle School_____    Date _____10-31-92_____

**STEP 1: SELECT A TARGET BEHAVIOR**

(a) Identify the target behavior.
*Geoff talks without raising his hand and does not wait to be recognized by the teacher during structured class time. Geoff talks to himself and to peers in a voice loud enough to be heard by the teacher standing 2 feet or more away from Geoff.*

(b) Identify the replacement behavior.
*During structured class times, Geoff will raise his hand without talking and wait to be recognized by the teacher before talking.*

**STEP 2: DEFINE THE TARGET BEHAVIOR**

Write a clear description of the behavior (include conditions under which it is acceptable and unacceptable).
*Given a structured class setting with teacher-directed instructional activity, Geoff will raise his hand and wait to be called on before talking 9 out of 10 times. Geoff may talk without raising his hand during unstructured, non-instructional times and during class discussion.*

**STEP 3: DESIGN THE DATA-RECORDING PROCEDURES**

(a) Identify the type of data to be recorded.
*Geoff will make a plus mark (+) on his data sheet if he raises his hand and waits to be called on before talking during each 5-minute interval for 9 intervals. If he talks without raising his hand, Geoff will mark a minus (−).*

(b) Identify when the data will be recorded.
*Geoff will self-record his third-period English class.*

(c) Describe the data recording form.
*Geoff will use 5 × 8 index cards with 5 rows of 9 squares each, one row for each day of the week. At the end of each row will be a box marked "Total" in which Geoff will record the total number of pluses earned that day.*

▼

Polloway and Patton (1997) cite four types of self-regulation. In *self-assessment,* the individual determines the need for change and also monitors personal behavior. In *self-monitoring,* the student attends to specific aspects of his or her own behavior. While learning to self-monitor, a student can be given a periodic beep or other cue to signal that it is time for him or her to evaluate "on" or "off" task behavior. In *self-instruction,* the student cues himself or herself to inhibit inappropriate behaviors or to express appropriate ones. In *self-reinforcement,* the student administers self-selected reinforcement for an appropriate behavior that has been previously specified. Figure 5.10 demonstrates a self-management planning form that was completed to help a middle school student control his talking out in class. Other behaviors commonly targeted for self-regulation include completing assignments (productivity), appropriate classroom behavior (such as staying in one's seat), accuracy of work (such as percent correct), and staying on task (Johnson & Johnson, 1998).

**LEARNING STRATEGIES**    Deshler and Lenz (1989) define a learning strategy as an individual approach to a task. It includes how an individual thinks and acts when

FIGURE **5.10**    *(continued)*

### STEP 4: TEACH THE STUDENT TO USE THE RECORDING FORM
Briefly describe the instruction and practice.
*The teacher will review the data recording form with Geoff, showing him where and how to self-record. The teacher will role play with Geoff the use of a timer and will model examples and nonexamples of appropriate hand raising.*

### STEP 5: CHOOSE A STRATEGY FOR ENSURING ACCURACY
*Geoff will match his self-recording form with the teacher's record at the end of each English period.*

### STEP 6: ESTABLISH GOAL AND CONTINGENCIES
(a) Determine how the student will be involved in setting the goal.
*Geoff will meet with the teacher and discuss his goal and then share the goal with his parents.*

(b) Determine whether or not the goal will be made public.
*No*

(c) Determine the reinforcement for meeting the goal.
*Each day that Geoff meets his performance goal, the teacher will buy Geoff a soda from the soda machine.*

### STEP 7: REVIEW GOAL AND STUDENT PERFORMANCE
(a) Determine how often the student and teacher will review performance.
*Geoff and the teacher will meet one time per week before school to review the progress and make new goals.*

(b) Identify when and how the plan will be modified if the goal is met or is not met.
*If Geoff has not met his performance goal for 3 consecutive days, the teacher will schedule an extra meeting with Geoff. If Geoff meets his goal for 3 consecutive days, the teacher and Geoff will modify his goal at their next meeting.*

### STEP 8: PLAN FOR REDUCING SELF-RECORDING PROCEDURES
*Geoff will match with teacher's record daily, then 3 days per week, and eventually 1 day per week (picked randomly).*

### STEP 9: PLAN FOR GENERALIZATION AND MAINTENANCE
*Geoff will self-record initially in English only. When he can successfully self-record, accurately match the teacher's record, and has met his performance goal in English for 2 weeks, he will begin self-recording in math and then social studies. When Geoff has met his performance goal for 3 weeks, self-recording will be eliminated and Geoff will earn the reinforcer for maintaining his performance goals.*

From "Self-Management: Education's Ultimate Goal," by J. Carter, 1993, *Teaching Exceptional Children, 25*(3), pp. 28–32.

planning, executing, or evaluating performance. The learning strategies approach combines what is going on in an individual's head (cognition) with what a person actually does (behavior) to guide the performance and evaluation of a specific task. All individuals use strategies; however, not all strategies are effective.

The learning strategies method of instructions was described in Chapter 4 as an effective method for improving academic performance for students with learning disabilities. This type of intervention is also particularly beneficial for students with ADHD (DuPaul & Eckert, 1998). Edmunds and his colleagues (1999) developed a method to "encourage" students to create their own strategies or cues to address a task that was difficult for them. One student who felt he needed to be a more "active listener" during lectures described a strategy to improve his history notes. His "cues" are found in Figure 5.11.

**SOCIAL SKILLS**   Because students with attention deficit/hyperactivity disorder often do not exhibit good problem-solving skills and are not able to predict the consequences of

*FIGURE* **5.11**

Taking Notes in
History Class

From "Cognitive Credit
Cards: Acquiring Learning
Strategies" (p. 71) by A. L.
Edmunds, 1999, *Teaching
Exceptional Children*,
March/April. Used with
permission.

### Taking Notes in History Class

▲ What did I read/study/write about last
night?

▲ How was it related to what we did *last*
class?

▲ What do I predict the topic will be about
today?

▲ What is the introduction of today's topic?

▲ Why is the topic important to what I
already know?

▲ How many major/minor points *will* the
teacher make?

▲ How many major/minor points *did* the
teacher make?

▲ What kind of questions could be asked
on a test?

▲ Do I have any concerns that need to be
cleared up?

▲ Do I need to talk to the teacher?

their inappropriate behavior, specific and direct instruction in social skills may be necessary. Although it is better for students to be able to assess their own inappropriate behavior and adjust it to acceptable standards, many students may need social skills training first. Landau, Milich, and Diener (1998) recommended that training be done throughout the year in groups of 4–8, with classmates in groups of the same gender. The sessions should include practice, modeling, and reinforcement of appropriate behavior during real-life peer problem situations. Including appropriate, well-liked children in each group can promote desirable modeling and encourage important new friendships.

## Promoting a Sense of Community and Social Acceptance

The Professional Group for Attention and Related Disorders (PGARD) proposes that most children with ADHD can be served in the general education program by trained teachers providing appropriate instruction and modifications. The two critical features for successful inclusion of students with ADHD are the skills and behaviors of the teachers and the understanding and acceptance by the general education peers.

**COMMUNITY-BUILDING SKILLS FOR TEACHERS**   One of the most important aspects of promoting success for children with ADHD is the teacher. Fowler (1992) suggests that success for children with ADHD might vary from year to year, class to class, teacher to teacher. She reports that the most commonly cited reason for a positive or negative school experience is the teacher. She cites the following 17 characteristics of teachers as likely indicators of positive learning outcomes for students with ADHD:

*CONSIDER THIS*

Use the characteristics of
an effective teacher as a
tool for self-assessment.
Identify your strengths
and determine goals for
improving your teaching
skills.

1. Positive academic expectations
2. Frequent review of student work
3. Clarity of teaching (e.g., explicit directions, rules)
4. Flexibility
5. Fairness
6. Active interaction with the students

7. Responsiveness
8. Warmth
9. Patience
10. Humor
11. Structured and predictable approach
12. Consistency
13. Firmness
14. Positive attitude toward inclusion
15. Knowledge of and willingness to work with students with exceptional needs
16. Knowledge of different types of effective interventions
17. Willingness to work collaboratively with other teachers (e.g., sharing information, requesting assistance as needed, participating in conferences involving students)

**RESOURCES FOR DEVELOPING AWARENESS IN PEERS**   Teachers with these traits will provide a positive role model for general education students in how to understand and accept children with ADHD. Teachers should confer with parents and the child with ADHD to obtain advice on explaining ADHD to other students in the classroom. The child with ADHD may wish to be present during the explanation or even to participate in informing his or her classmates. The following books and publications may help introduce this topic to students with ADHD and their peers.

*Jumping Johnny Get Back to Work—A Child's Guide to ADHD/Hyperactivity*
    Michael Gordon, Ph.D., Author
    Connecticut Association for
        Children with LD
    18 Marshall Street
    South Norwalk, CT 06854
    (203) 838-5010

*Shelley, the Hyperactive Turtle*
    Deborah Moss, Author
    Woodbine House
    5616 Fishers Lane
    Rockville, MD 20852
    (800) 843-7323

*Sometimes I Drive My Mom Crazy, but I Know She's Crazy about Me!*
    Childworks
    Center for Applied Psychology, Inc.
    P.O. 61586
    King of Prussia, PA 19406
    (800) 962-1141

*You Mean I'm Not Lazy, Stupid, or Crazy?*
    Peggy Ramundo and Kate Kelly,
        Authors
    Tyrell & Jerem Press
    P.O. Box 20089
    Cincinnati, OH 45220
    (800) 622-6611

*Otto Learns about His Medicine*
    Michael Gaivin, M.D., Author
    Childworks
    Center for Applied Psychology, Inc.
    P.O. 61586
    King of Prussia, PA 19406
    (800) 962-1141

*Eagle Eyes: A Child's View of Attention Deficit Disorder*
    Jeanne Gehret, M.A., Author
    Childworks
    Center for Applied Psychology, Inc.
    P.O. 61586
    King of Prussia, PA 19406
    (800) 962-1141

*Feelings about Friends*
    Linda Schwartz, Author
    The Learning Works
    P.O. Box 6187
    Santa Barbara, CA 93160
    (800) 235-5767

*Brakes: The Interactive Newsletter for Kids with ADHD*
    Magination Press
    19 Union Square West
    New York, NY 10003
    (800) 825-3089

## Collaborating with Parents of Students with Attention Deficit/Hyperactivity Disorder

Teachers can often promote success for students with ADHD by working closely with parents to practice and reinforce desirable academic and social behavior. Flick (1998) suggests the following parent-centered activities.

◢ Practice and reinforce school behaviors such as following directions, completing homework, getting along with siblings and friends, and obeying rules.

◢ Post and review home and school rules frequently.

◢ Use the same signal used by the teacher to cue the child when inappropriate behaviors are observed; examples include the commonly used finger placed over lips or a more personal or "secret cue" developed in collaboration among the child, parents, and the teacher.

◢ Develop a home-school reporting system that communicates positive behaviors and problem areas between parents and teachers.

 **ummary**

### Basic Concepts about Attention Deficit/Hyperactivity Disorder

◢ ADHD is a complex condition that offers a real challenge to classroom teachers.

◢ The legal basis for service delivery and protection for students with ADHD comes from IDEA and Section 504 of the Rehabilitation Act of 1973.

◢ Under IDEA, students with ADHD may be served through the category of "other health impaired"; children with ADHD as a secondary disability may be primarily diagnosed as behaviorally disordered, learning disabled, or mentally retarded.

◢ ADHD is a hidden disability with no unique physical characteristics to differentiate children who have it from others in the classroom.

◢ The diagnosis of ADHD is primarily based on the criteria in the *Diagnostic and Statistical Manual of Mental Disorders (DSM-IV).*

◢ Many theories exist to explain the cause of ADHD; however, ADHD is considered primarily a neurologically based condition.

◢ ADHD manifests itself across the lifespan; characteristics include limited sustained attention, reduced impulse control, excessive task-irrelevant activity, deficient rule following, and greater than normal variability during task performance.

◢ The process for determining eligibility for services based on ADHD includes a preliminary assessment, an initial meeting of the child study team, a formal assessment and follow-up meeting of the child study team, a collaborative meeting to develop an intervention plan, and follow-up and progress reviews.

◢ Cultural and linguistic diversity complicates issues related to assessment and treatment for children with ADHD.

### Educational Intervention

◢ A continuum of placement options is available to students with ADHD, and the selected placement is based on their individual needs and abilities.

◢ The majority of students with ADHD spend all or most of the school day in general education classes.

◢ An individual accommodation plan is written collaboratively with parents, professionals, and when possible, the student, to identify interventions that will create success in the general education classroom.

◢ Medication is frequently used to enhance the educational experience of students with ADHD.

◢ The most commonly prescribed medication is a psychostimulant such as Dexedrine, Ritalin, and Cylert.

◢ Both positive outcomes and negative side effects should be monitored for individual children taking medication for ADHD.

### Strategies for Instruction and Classroom Accommodations for Students with Attention Deficit/Hyperactivity Disorder

◢ Classroom accommodations include environmental management techniques, instructional accommodations, and student-regulated strategies.

◢ Techniques used to manage the classroom environment include strategies for group management, physical arrangement of the room, and individual behavior management techniques.

◢ Through instructional accommodations, teachers modify their behavior to include novel and stimulating activity, to provide structure and consistency, to allow physical movement as frequently as possible, to include cooperative learning activities, and to give both spoken and written direction.

◢ The curriculum for students with ADHD should be stimulating and include experience-based learning as well as problem-solving activities.

◢ Student-regulated strategies include study and organizational tactics, self-management techniques, learning strategies, and social skills training.

◢ Effective teachers for students with ADHD provide positive classroom environments, frequently review student work, and are flexible, fair, responsive, warm, patient, consistent, firm, and humorous. They develop a knowledge of the strengths and needs of their students with ADHD and are knowledgeable about different intervention strategies. They are also willing to work collaboratively with other teachers, parents, and professionals.

# ◢*urther Readings*

American Psychiatric Association. (1994). *Diagnostic and statistical manual of mental disorders* (4th ed.). Washington, D.C.: Author

Conderman, G., & Katsiannis, A. (1995). Section 504 accommodation plans. *Intervention in School and Clinic, 31*(1), 42–45.

Deshler, D., Ellis, E., & Lenz, B. K. (1996*). Teaching adolescents with learning disabilities: Strategies and methods* (2nd ed.). Denver: Love Publishing.

Fuchs, D., Fernstrom, P., Scott, S., Fuchs, L., & Vandermeer, L. (1994). Classroom ecological inventory. *Teaching Exceptional Children, 26*(3), 14–15.

Janover, C. (1997). *Zipper: The kid with ADHD.* Bethesda, MD: Woodbine House Publisher.

McBurnett, K., Lakey, B., & Pfiffer, L. (1993). Diagnosis of attention-deficit disorders, in DSM-IV: Scientific basis and implications for education. *Exceptional Children, 60*(2), 108–117.

Smith, T. E. C., & Patton, J. R. (1998). *Section 504 and public schools.* Austin, TX: Pro-Ed.

# Teaching Students with Emotional and Behavioral Disorders

*After reading this chapter, you should be able to:*

◢ Define emotional and behavioral disorders

◢ Describe the characteristics of children and youth with emotional and behavioral disorders (E/BD)

◢ Understand the nature of E/BD

◢ Discuss ways to identify and evaluate students with E/BD

◢ Identify effective interventions for students with E/BD

◢ Discuss the role of teachers in meeting the needs of students with E/BD in general education classrooms

*F*rank is a 6-year-old kindergartner who always seems to be in trouble. On the very first day of school, he stole some crayons from one of his new classmates. When confronted with the fact that the crayons in his desk belonged to another student, Frank adamantly denied stealing them. Frank's behavior became more difficult over the first six months of the school year. Ms. Walters, Frank's kindergarten teacher, uses a classroom management system that rewards students with checkmarks for appropriate behaviors. Students can redeem their checkmarks at the end of the week for various toys. Frank has never earned enough checkmarks to get a toy. Now he openly states that he doesn't care if he ever receives any checkmarks.

Frank's primary behavioral difficulty is his inability to leave his classmates alone. He is constantly pinching, pulling hair, or taking things from other students. Ms. Walters has placed Frank's chair separate from those of the other students in an attempt to prevent him from bothering them. Still, he gets out of his chair and manages to create disturbances regularly. Ms. Walters has sent Frank to the principal's office on numerous occasions. Each time he returns, his behavior improves, but only for about half of the day. Then he returns to his previous behavioral patterns. Frank's schoolwork has begun to suffer as a result of his behavior problems. While many of his classmates are beginning to read and can write their names, Frank still has difficulties associating sounds with letters and can print his name only in a very rudimentary form.

Ms. Walters has had four parent conferences about Frank. On each occasion, only Frank's mother came to the school. She indicates to Ms. Walters that she does not know what to do with Frank. There is no father figure in the home, and Frank has already gotten to the point where spankings don't seem to work. Ms. Walters and Frank's mother are both concerned that Frank's behavior will continue to get worse unless some solution is found. They are currently discussing whether to retain him in kindergarten for the next school year.

## QUESTIONS TO CONSIDER

1. Why did the behavior management system used by Ms. Walters not work with Frank?
2. What are some strategies that Ms. Walters can use that might result in an improvement in Frank's behavior?
3. Would retention be likely to benefit Frank? Why or why not?
4. How would it help or hurt Frank if he were labeled as E/BD?

*A*lthough most children and youth are disruptive from time to time, the majority do not display negative behaviors sufficient to create serious problems in school. Most comply with classroom and school rules without needing extensive interventions. However, some students' behaviors and emotions result in significant problems for themselves, their peers, and their teachers. This may be due to the way school personnel deal with various student behaviors. The behavior may continue even after several interventions have been tried. Students with significant school problems, such as Frank in the preceding vignette, may require identification and intervention. At a minimum, they require that classroom teachers try different methods in an effort to enhance the student's school success and reduce the problem behavior.

Although emotional and behavioral problems may result in serious and life-threatening actions (e.g., violence, attempted suicide), they have long been associated with acting out and disruptive behaviors in classrooms—in general, discipline problems. The primary problem faced by most teachers when dealing with students with emotional and behavior problems is classroom discipline.

Behavior problems clearly are a major concern for professional educators. For example, in a survey of general education classroom teachers, the behavior of students was cited as a primary reason for their deciding to leave the teaching profession (Smith, 1990). Teachers noted that they spent too much time on student behavior problems and not enough on instruction. In a national study by Knitzer, Steinberg, and Fleisch (1990), it was found that 80% of all students identified as having emotional and behavior problems are educated in regular schools. Nearly 50% of these students spend some or all of their school day in general education classrooms with general education classroom teachers, not special education teachers. The general public shares educators' concern about behavior problems. A Phi Delta Kappa/Gallup survey of attitudes toward public schools reveals that 15% of respondents ranked behavior problems and discipline as the number two problem in public schools, second only to drugs, which ranked first, with 16% (Elam, Rose, & Gallup, 1996).

**CONSIDER THIS**
What kinds of children do you think of when you hear the term *emotionally disturbed*? Can this term have an impact on teachers' expectations of children?

**SERIOUS EMOTIONAL DISTURBANCE** is the disability category in IDEA that includes children with emotional problems.

**EMOTIONAL AND BEHAVIORAL DISORDER (E/BD)** is the term preferred by some professional groups to refer to children with emotional problems.

Students who experience emotional and behavioral disorders receive a variety of labels. The federal government historically has identified this group as **seriously emotionally disturbed (SED)** within the Individuals with Disabilities Education Act. Whereas SED is the category used in most states, others classify this group of children as having behavioral disorders. The *Council for Children with Behavior Disorders (CCBD)* of the *Council for Exceptional Children* refers to the group as **emotionally and behaviorally disordered (E/BD)** because it believes the term better describes the students served in special education programs. *E/BD* is the term that will be used throughout this chapter.

## BASIC CONCEPTS ABOUT EMOTIONAL AND BEHAVIORAL DISORDERS

*T*his section provides basic information about emotional disturbance and behavioral disorders. Understanding children with these problems will aid teachers and other educators in developing appropriate intervention programs. Figure 6.1 illustrates a personal perspective on intervention programs.

*FIGURE* **6.1**    A Parent's Perspective on E/BD: Patti Childress (Lynchburg, VA)

From:        **pchildress [mailto: patti@inmind.com]**

Sent:        **Tuesday, June 6, 2000 11:42 PM**

TO:          **Polloway, Edward 'Ed'**

Subject:     **Re: Concerns**


Dr. Polloway:

Thanks for trying to help and please keep thinking about resources that can assist me as both a teacher and a parent.

It bothers me tremendously when I see children with E/BD often getting a "raw deal." People seem to think that it is fine for these children to have a disorder and maybe/maybe not receive special services, but heaven forbid if they can't control themselves or if they do something that appears to be a bit irrational. At times I feel like I am jumping in front of a firing squad to protect that [ child whom some seem to see as that] "bad kid that shouldn't be in school anyway." I would like to work with a group that supports parents, provides understanding and advocacy regarding disorders, and seeks support and additional resources for help, etc. What is available in this field? Much is needed.

I have always had a huge heart for "the kid who is a little bit or a long way out there" even before I became a parent of a child with a mood disorder.

From an educational perspective, I know that these children can be very difficult in a group; however, they seem to function much better when they feel in control, are able to make choices, and are spoken to in a calm tone.

From a parent's perspective, I am an educated individual with a traditional home make-up: dad, mom, daughter, and son. . . and I know the difficulties of saying, "Yeah, we've got a very bright child with mood problems." We've been through every medication from ritalin to cylert and clonodone. The next stop would be lithium, weekly counseling, and psychiatric treatment to regulate the medications. I want teachers to understand that getting "meds" is not an easy task or a quick fix. It has taken us over a year of trying various medications until we have, hopefully, found the right combination for now. It requires the constant efforts of counselor, doctor, parents, and teachers working together and exchanging information.

Children without support have got to have advocates to help them get help. These children are very fragile and need to be treated as such. My heart goes out to such a child and the family that simply does not understand why their child is not like everybody else's. Int the school environment, even when I listen to special education teachers, I do not find the same level of empathy and understanding for children with E/BD as for those with LD.

## Emotional and Behavioral Disorders Defined

For students with emotional and behavioral disorders to be identified accurately and appropriately placed in educational programs, a critical prerequisite is the need for an acceptable definition of this condition. The challenges in developing an acceptable definition of emotional/behavioral disorders have been frequently stated. Kaufmann (1995) indicated that the definitional problem has been made more difficult by the different conceptual models that have been used in the field (e.g., psychodynamic, biological, sociological, behavioral, ecological, educational), the different purposes for definition (e.g., educational, legal, mental health), the difficulties in measuring both emotions and behavior, the range and variability of normal and deviant behavior, the complex relationships of emotional and behavioral disorders to other exceptionalities, and the transient nature of many emotional/behavioral problems. Although no single definition is accepted by all parties, the one currently used by the federal government for its category *seriously emotionally disturbed (SED)* has been adopted in most state departments of education; it is as follows:

**CONSIDER THIS**
What impact can a definition that is vague, like the federal definition of SED, have on identification of and services to children?

(i) The term means a condition exhibiting one or more of the following characteristics over a long period of time and to a marked extent, which adversely affects educational performance:
   (A) An inability to learn which cannot be explained by intellectual, sensory, or health factors;
   (B) An inability to build or maintain satisfactory relationships with peers and teachers;
   (C) Inappropriate types of behavior or feelings under normal circumstances;
   (D) A general pervasive mood of unhappiness or depression; or
   (E) A tendency to develop physical symptoms or fears associated with personal or school problems.
(ii) The term includes children who are schizophrenic. The term does not include children who are socially maladjusted unless it is determined that they are seriously emotionally disturbed. (*Federal Register,* p. 42478)

Although this definition is used by most states and local education agencies (Skiba, Grizzle, & Minke, 1994), it leaves a lot to be desired. The definition is vague and may leave the reader wondering just what a child with serious emotional disturbance is like. When this definition is interpreted broadly, many more children are served than when the definition is interpreted narrowly. As evidenced by the underserved nature of this disability category, most states and local school districts seem to interpret the definition narrowly and serve far fewer children in the category than prevalence estimates project as needing services.

**THE DIAGNOSTIC AND STATISTICAL MANUAL (DSM-IV)** is used by medical and psychological professionals to provide diagnostic criteria for psychological disorders.

Creating another problem, most agencies other than schools that provide services to children and adolescents with emotional problems use the definition and classification system found in the ***Diagnostic and Statistical Manual of Mental Disorders (DSM–IV).*** This manual, published by the American Psychiatric Association (1994), uses a definition and classification system totally different from the one used in public schools. This only adds to confusion and results in fragmented services; some children are considered disabled according to one system but not disabled according to the other.

**CONSIDER THIS**
Do some children reflect several of these different categories? If so, what is the purpose of placing them in the specific subcategory of E/BD?

## Classification of Emotional and Behavioral Disorders

Children who experience emotional and behavioral disorders make up a very heterogeneous population. Professionals have subcategorized the group into smaller,

| TABLE 6.1 | Major Components of the *DSM-IV* Classification System |
|---|---|
| Disorders usually first evident in infancy, childhood, or adolescence | Somatoform disorders |
| Organic mental syndromes and disorders | Dissociative disorders |
| Psychoactive substance use disorders | Sexual disorders |
| Schizophrenia | Sleep disorders |
| Delusional disorders | Factitious disorders |
| Psychotic disorders not elsewhere classified | Impulse control disorders not elsewhere classified |
| Mood disorders | Adjustment disorders |
| Anxiety disorders | Psychological factors affecting physical condition |
|  | Personality disorders |

From *Diagnostic and Statistical Manual of Mental Disorders* (4th ed.), by the American Psychiatric Association, 1994, Washington, DC: Author.

more homogeneous subgroups so that these students can be studied, understood, and better served (Wicks-Nelson & Israel, 1991). Several different classification systems are used to group individuals with emotional and behavioral disorders.

One classification system focuses on the clinical elements found in the field of emotional and behavior problems. This system is detailed in the *DSM-IV* (American Psychiatric Association, 1994), a manual widely used by medical and psychological professionals, though far less frequently used by educators. It categorizes emotional and behavioral problems according to several different clinical subtypes, such as developmental disorders, organic mental disorders, and schizophrenia. Educators need to be aware of the *DSM-IV* classification system, because of the occasional need to interact with professionals from the field of mental health. Table 6.1 lists the major types of disorders according to this system.

The classification schemes used by teachers and other educators are usually associated with functional behaviors and related interventions. For example, one classification system used in schools was developed by Quay and Peterson (1987). They described six major subgroups of children with emotional and behavior disorders:

1. Individuals are classified as having a **conduct disorder** if they seek attention, are disruptive, and act out. This category includes behaving aggressively toward others.
2. Students who exhibit **socialized aggression** are likely to join a "subcultural group," a group of peers who are openly disrespectful to their peers, teachers, and parents. Delinquency, truancy, and other "gang" behaviors are common among this group.
3. Individuals with **attention problems–immaturity** can be characterized as having attention deficits, being easily distractible, and having poor concentration. Many students in this group are impulsive and may act without thinking about the consequences.
4. Students classified in the **anxiety/withdrawal group** are self-conscious, reticent, and unsure of themselves. Their self-concepts are generally very low, causing them to simply "retreat" from immediate activities. They are also anxious and frequently depressed.
5. The subgroup of students who display **psychotic behavior** may hallucinate, deal in a fantasy world, talk in gibberish, and exhibit other bizarre behavior.
6. Students with **motor excess** are hyperactive. They have difficulties sitting still, listening to other individuals, and keeping their attention focused. These students are often hypertalkative.

**CONDUCT DISORDERS** are attention-seeking, acting out, and disruptive behaviors.

**SOCIALIZED AGGRESSIVE** is the classification used for students who join gangs and other groups that display aggressive behaviors.

**ATTENTION PROBLEMS–IMMATURITY** describes students who are easily distracted and have poor concentration.

**ANXIETY/WITHDRAWAL** is the classification used for students who are self-conscious, reticent, and unsure of themselves.

**PSYCHOTIC BEHAVIORS** are behaviors such as hallucinating that suggest severe emotional problems.

**MOTOR EXCESS** describes children who are hyperactive or have increased levels of motor activity.

**CROSS-REFERENCE**
For more information on autism, read Chapter 9.

At one time, children with *autism* were included in the federal definition of serious emotional disturbance. Since these children frequently displayed behaviors that were considered extremely atypical, it was thought that they were experiencing emotional problems. However, over the past decade, professionals and advocates have come to acknowledge that autism is not an emotional problem but has an organic base. The result has been the removal of autism from the SED category. In the 1990 amendments to PL 94-142, autism was made a separate disability category. Autism is discussed in Chapter 9.

Classification becomes less important when school personnel utilize a functional assessment/intervention model. This approach, which will be described in more detail later, emphasizes finding out which environmental stimuli result in inappropriate behaviors. Once these stimuli are identified and altered, the inappropriate behaviors may decrease or disappear (Foster-Johnson & Dunlap, 1993). In such instances, the process of classifying a student's problem becomes less relevant to the design of educational programs.

## Prevalence and Causes of Emotional and Behavioral Disorders

Compared to children classified as having learning disabilities and mental retardation, the category of E/BD represents a much smaller number of children. The *20th Report to Congress on the Implementation of the Individuals with Disabilities Education Act* noted that 0.92% of the school population were served as EB/D during the 1996–1997 school year (U.S. Department of Education, 1998).

**CONSIDER THIS**
What factors will likely lead to larger or smaller numbers of children being identified as having emotional and behavioral disorders?

Because of the difficulty in defining and identifying emotional and behavioral disorders, the range of estimates of the prevalence of the disorder is great (Knitzer et al., 1990). The U.S. Department of Education estimates that 2% of students are emotionally disturbed (National Center for Education Statistics, 1991). This contrasts rather sharply with the 22% estimated by Cotler (1986); and the 14% to 20% estimated by Brandenburg, Friedman, and Silver (1990) as having moderate to severe behavioral disorders. Although a specific prevalence rate has not been established,

*Depression is a characteristic of students with emotional and behavioral disorders.*

the 2% rate used by the federal government is generally considered too low (Center, 1985; Center & Eden, 1989–1990; Center & Obringer, 1987). The specific number depends on the definition used and the interpretation of the definition by individuals who classify students.

Students with emotional and behavioral disorders are typically the most under-identified in the school. Lambros, Ward, Bocian, MacMillan, and Gresham (1998) indicate that the reasons for this include the ambiguity of definitions used by states; lack of training of school psychologists in conducting assessments for these students; the financial limitations of districts; and the general hesitation to apply labels such as behavior disorder or seriously emotionally disturbed.

Among students classified as having emotional and behavioral disorders, the majority are males. Some studies have revealed that as many as 10 times more boys than girls are found in special classes for students with behavior disorders (Rosenberg, Wilson, Maheady, & Sindelar, 1992; Smith, Price, & Marsh, 1986).

Many different factors can cause students to display emotional and behavioral disorders. These can be found in five different theoretical frameworks, including biological, psychoanalytical, behavioral, phenomenological, and sociological/ecological. Within each framework are numerous specific causal factors. Table 6.2 summarizes some of these variables by theoretical framework.

| **TABLE 6.2** | **Causes of Serious Emotional and Behavioral Disorders** |
|---|---|
| **Theoretical Framework** | **Etiologies/Causal Factors** |
| BIOLOGICAL | Genetic inheritance<br>Biochemical abnormalities<br>Neurological abnormalities<br>Injury to the central nervous system |
| PSYCHOANALYTICAL | Psychological processes<br>Functioning of the mind: id, ego, and superego<br>Inherited predispositions (instinctual process)<br>Traumatic early-childhood experiences |
| BEHAVIORAL | Environmental events<br>1. Failure to learn adaptive behaviors<br>2. Learning of maladaptive behaviors<br>3. Developing maladaptive behaviors as a result of stressful environmental circumstances |
| PHENOMENOLOGICAL | Faulty learning about oneself<br>Misuse of defense mechanisms<br>Feelings, thoughts, and events emanating from the self |
| SOCIOLOGICAL/ECOLOGICAL | Role assignment (labeling)<br>Cultural transmission<br>Social disorganization<br>Distorted communication<br>Differential association<br>Negative interactions and transactions with others |

From *Human Exceptionality* (p. 148), by M. L. Hardman, C. J. Drew, M. W. Egan, and B. Wolf, 1993, Boston: Allyn and Bacon. Used by permission.

## Characteristics of Students with Emotional and Behavioral Disorders

Students with emotional and behavioral problems exhibit a wide range of characteristics that differ in type as well as intensity. This wide range of behaviors and emotions experienced by all individuals reflects the broad variety of characteristics associated with individuals with emotional and behavior problems (Bullock, Zagar, Donahue, & Pelton, 1985).

Problems typically associated with children with emotional and behavioral disorders include the following:

*CONSIDER THIS*
Do students without disabilities ever exhibit these characteristics? What differentiates nondisabled students from those classified as E/BD?

◢ Aggressive/acting-out behaviors (Grosenick, George, George, & Lewis, 1991; Kauffman, Lloyd, Baker, & Riedel, 1995)
◢ Social deficits (Smith & Luckasson, 1995)
◢ Irresponsibility (Smith, Finn, & Dowdy, 1993)
◢ Inadequate peer relationships (Searcy & Meadows, 1994)
◢ Hyperactivity/distractibility
◢ Lying, cheating, and stealing (Rosenberg et al., 1992)
◢ Academic deficits (Bullock, 1992)
◢ Anxiety (Kauffman et al., 1995; Wicks-Nelson & Israel, 1991)

One problem too often overlooked is depression. According to national estimates, approximately 2–4% of elementary school children and 4–8% of adolescents suffer from depression (CEC, 1999). Further, Forness (cited by CEC, 1999) has estimated that between 30–40% of students in E/BD classes suffer from depression. Issues such as the stigma of being labeled, biological factors related to the causation of the disability, and failure experiences can all promote feelings of depression. Teachers should be alert to signs of depression in order to assist students in general and specifically to prevent suicide, estimated to be the third leading cause of death for adolescents and young adults.

All children classified as having emotional and behavioral disorders do not exhibit all of these characteristics. The ones exhibited by a particular child will depend on the nature of the emotional or behavioral problem.

**OUTCOMES AND POST-SCHOOL ADJUSTMENT**    A critical concern for students with emotional and behavioral disorders is the determination of outcomes. In a comprehensive, longitudinal study of such students, Greenbaum and colleagues (1999) reported on students who were identified as SED who were served in either a publicly funded residential mental health facility or a community-based special education program. While the severity of the disorders that these students experienced is likely to be greater than those of students in general education classrooms, this information should alert educators to the challenges that these students face.

Greenbaum et al. (1999) reported that approximately two-thirds (66.5%) of the individuals had at least one contact with police in which he or she was believed to be the perpetrator of a crime and 43.3% had been arrested at least once. In general, the most commonly reported crimes were property-related.

For this same sample of students, educational outcomes were generally poor. For those who were young adults (over 18 years of age) at the time of the follow-up, 75.4% were assessed to be below their appropriate reading grade levels, and 96.9% were below appropriate levels in math achievement. Only one in four had obtained a regular high school diploma; an additional 17.4% had completed a GED. Approximately 43% had dropped out of school programs. Risk indicators included lower IQ, a pattern of aggressive behaviors, a history of criminal offenses, and a family history of social, emotional, behavioral, and/or substance abuse-related problems. These data confirm annual federal reports that indicate that students with E/BDs are the most likely to drop out of school and the least likely to receive a high school diploma or certificate (U.S. Department of Education, 1998). As Burns, Hoagwood, and Maultsby (1999) noted, "Consensus about the critical outcomes for children with serious emotional and behavioral disorders—at home, in school, and out of trouble—is not difficult to obtain. Achieving such outcomes and more is the challenge!" (p. 685).

Students with emotional and behavioral disorders often have significant challenges in adjustment within the community. As Maag and Katisyannis (1998) noted, successful adjustment is certainly discouraged by the high dropout rate, which makes it difficult to establish and address transition goals within the student's IEP and individual transition plan. In addition, successful transition is affected by the high rates of unemployment, increased likelihood of incarceration, and the persistence of mental health problems in adulthood for individuals with E/BD.

In the area of employment, critical to successful transition, Rylance (1998) reported that the key variables that increase an individual's chances of employment included basic academic skills, higher functional competence levels in school-related areas, and high school graduation. Successful school programs for these students tended to be ones that included effective vocational education and counseling programs and that motivated students to persist in school and obtain a diploma. Chapter 15 provides more information about preparing students with disabilities for successful transitions to adult life.

## Manifestation of the Disability

A key issue in the field of emotional and behavioral disorders is the relationship between the disability itself and the behaviors that are exhibited in school. Under IDEA guidelines, educators must determine whether the behavior in question functions as a manifestation of the student's disability. The key question is whether the student's disability impairs his or her ability to control the behavior and/or interferes with his or her awareness of the possible disciplinary action that may follow. The function of the guidelines is neither to exclude students with disabilities from normal disciplinary routines, nor to prevent educators from taking action to redirect troublesome behavior. Rather, the purpose is to prevent the misapplication of disciplinary actions that, owing to the student's particular disability, may fail to achieve the desired objective and create needless frustration for everyone involved (Buck, Polloway, Kirkpatrick, Patton, & Fad, 1999).

To complete a manifestation determination for students with emotional and behavioral disorders (as well as for other disabilities), school personnel should carefully consider the disability and the nature of the behavior to determine a possible relationship. Polloway et al. (1999) suggest the following representative questions:

- Does the student know right from wrong?
- Does the disability limit the student's ability to handle stressful situations?
- Does the disability interfere with the student's ability to build or maintain appropriate peer and/or teacher relationships?
- Does the disability interfere with the student's ability to learn how to appropriately express his or her feelings?

To explore the concept of manifestation determination further, a guide to its implementation is in Fad, Patton, and Polloway (2000).

## Manifestation Determination: What Does Federal Law Say?

A key question that educators must ask when dealing with issues related to discipline concerns and students with behavioral disorders is this: is the behavior observed a manifestation of the disability? Careful consideration of federal law (and any relevant state statutes) is essential for prudent decision-making in the schools.

Under P.L. 105-17, the following guidelines (as adapted) apply:

> If an action is contemplated regarding [a problem] behavior or involving a removal [from school] that constitutes a change of placement for a child with a disability [then] no later than the date on which the decision to take that action is made, the parents must be notified of that decision and of all procedural safeguards. [Further], immediately, if possible, but in no case later than 10 school days after the date on which the decision to take that action is made, a review must be conducted of the relationship between the child's disability and the behavior subject to the disciplinary action.

A review must be conducted by the IEP team and other qualified personnel in a meeting. In carrying out [the] review, the IEP team and other qualified personnel may determine that the behavior of the child was not a manifestation of the child's disability only if the IEP team and other qualified personnel—

1. first consider, in terms of the behavior subject to disciplinary action, all relevant information, including: evaluation and diagnostic results, including the results or other relevant information supplied by the parents of the child; observations of the child; and the child's IEP and placement; and

2. then determine that—

   - In relationship to the behavior subject to disciplinary action, the child's IEP and placement were appropriate and the special education services, supplementary aids and services, and behavior intervention strategies were provided consistent with the child's IEP and placement.

   - The child's disability did not impair the ability of the child to understand the impact and consequences of the behavior subject to disciplinary action; and

   - The child's disability did not impair the ability of the child to control the behavior subject to disciplinary action.

If the IEP team and other qualified personnel determine that any of the [preceding] standards were not met, the behavior must be considered a manifestation of the child's disability. However, if the result of the review is a determination that the behavior of the child with a disability was not a manifestation of the child's disability, the relevant disciplinary procedures applicable to children without disabilities may be applied to the child in the same manner in which they would be applied to children without disabilities.

Classroom teachers should be aware of the concept of manifestation of disability within the continuing debate about disciplinary procedures for students with disabilities, including those with emotional and behavioral disorders. The debate revolves around the issues of equity, discipline, school safety, and the legal rights of students with disabilities for a free and appropriate public education with accommodations designed to be consistent with students' individual needs. The nearby Rights and Responsibilities feature highlights this issue.

A survey reported by Butera, Klein, McMullen, and Wilson (1998) underscores the disciplinary issues in schools. While it might be assumed that special education teachers are likely to be strong advocates of students with disabilities, Butera et al. noted that

> General and special educators interviewed did not differ in their opinions about the need for clearer school-wide discipline policies applied in an equitable fashion to all students. Special educators as well as general educators did not value IEP

protection of students' rights. Especially noteworthy is our finding that schools did not often examine IEPs when making discipline decisions. Apparently educators do not see the necessity for individualized discipline procedures for students with disabilities nor do they readily acknowledge a relationship between disability and student misconduct. (p. 113)

As can be noted from this summary of Butera et al.'s research, educators in general seem to reflect a consistent concern for discipline issues that do not clearly follow the issue of manifestation determination in the preceding discussion. Teachers are encouraged to closely follow the continuing discussions in the area of discipline. Real concerns for school safety, particularly following the 1999 tragedy at Columbine High School in Colorado, further exacerbate the resolution of this issue.

## Identification, Assessment, and Eligibility

Students with emotional and behavioral disorders are evaluated for several purposes, including identification, assessment to determine appropriate intervention strategies, and determination of eligibility for special education services. The first step is for students to be identified as potentially having emotional and behavioral problems. Teachers' awareness of the characteristics of students with these problems is critical in the identification process. Behavioral checklists can be used to identify students for possible referral.

Once students are identified as possibly having emotional and behavioral problems, they are referred for formal assessment to determine their eligibility for special education programs and to ascertain appropriate intervention strategies. Kaplan (1996) lists clinical interviews, observations, rating scales, personality tests, and neurological examinations as methods for obtaining information for assessment and determining eligibility. Table 6.3 summarizes these procedures.

*TEACHING TIP*

When you suspect a student of having an emotional or behavioral disorder, develop a systematic method of collecting information during observations of the student.

One encouraging new approach to the assessment of students with emotional and behavioral disorders is through the use of strength-based assessment. Unlike widely used deficit-oriented assessment models, strength-based assessment focuses on the student and his or her family "as individuals with unique talents, skills, and life events as well as with specific unmet needs. Strength-based assessment recognizes that even the most challenged children in stressed families have strengths, competencies, and resources that can be built on in developing a treatment approach" (Epstein, 1998, p. x).

Epstein and Charma (1998) have developed a scale that complements the other assessment instruments that tend to focus on difficulties experienced by the student in the school or home setting. As noted by Epstein and Charma (1998, p. 3): "Strength-based assessment is defined as the measurement of those emotional/ behavioral skills and characteristics that create a sense of personal accomplishment; contribute to satisfying relationships with family members, peers, and adults; enhance one's ability to deal with adversity and stress; and promote one's personal, social, and academic development."

**FUNCTIONAL BEHAVIORAL ASSESSMENT** One important approach to assessment warrants separate consideration because of its clear implications for intervention efforts. *Functional behavioral assessment (FBA)* provides a consideration of specific behaviors and behavioral patterns set within an environmental context. It has been defined as "an analysis of the contingencies responsible for behavioral problems" (Malott, Whaley, & Malott, 1997, p. 433).

| TABLE 6.3 | Assessment Procedures Used for Students with Emotional and Behavioral Disorders |
|---|---|
| CLINICAL INTERVIEW | ■ The clinical interview is the most common tool for assessment. <br> ■ Questions are directed to the child and others regarding behaviors and any relevant relationships. <br> ■ Some questions are planned; some are developed as the interview progresses. <br> ■ The interview can be highly structured, using questions generated from the *DSM-IV* criteria. |
| OBSERVATION | ■ The observation can be structured with time limitations, or unstructured. <br> ■ Observations should occur in a variety of different settings and at different times. |
| RATING SCALES | ■ A rating scale contains a listing of behaviors to note. <br> ■ It provides for much more structure than simple observation. <br> ■ It ensures that certain behaviors are observed or asked about. |
| PERSONALITY TESTS | ■ The two kinds of personality tests include self-completed inventories and projective tests. <br> ■ Both kinds of personality tests can provide insightful information. <br> ■ Interpretation of personality tests is subjective and needs to be done by a trained professional. |

From *Pathways for Exceptional Children: School, Home, and Culture,* by P. Kaplan, 1996, St. Paul, MN: West Publishing.

When determining appropriate intervention strategies, *functional behavioral assessment* provides extensive information for teachers. A functional assessment helps teachers better understand disruptive behaviors, which can lead to an insightful intervention approach. Foster-Johnson and Dunlap (1993) list the following variables that may influence behavior:

1. Physiological factors
   - Sickness or allergies
   - Side effects of medication
   - Fatigue
   - Hunger or thirst
   - Frustration due to a fight, missing the bus, a disrupted routine
2. Classroom environment
   - High noise level
   - Uncomfortable temperature
   - Over- or understimulation
   - Poor seating arrangement
   - Frequent disruptions
3. Curriculum and instruction
   - Few opportunities for making choices
   - Lack of predictability in the schedule
   - Inadequate level of assistance provided to the student
   - Unclear directions provided for activity completion
   - Few opportunities for the student to communicate
   - Activities that are too difficult
   - Activities that take a long time to complete
   - Activities that the student dislikes
   - Activities for which the completion criterion is unclear
   - Activities that might not be perceived as being relevant or useful by the student

After reviewing these variables with a particular child in mind, teachers can devise interventions that target a specific variable to alter a particular behavior (Foster-Johnson & Dunlap, 1993). McConnell, Hilvitz, and Cox (1998) present a 10-step procedure for conducting a functional behavioral assessment. Their approach shows how writing a behavioral intervention plan is a direct outgrowth of the assessment process. McConnell et al. (1998) stress that while an evaluation of the environmental context within which a problem behavior occurs is necessary for developing hypotheses regarding the causes of the behavior, the only valid way to reach a conclusion about behavioral influence is to change the environmental setting and/or the events associated with the behavior, and to observe whether or not a change in behavior results.

## STRATEGIES FOR CURRICULUM AND INSTRUCTION

Students with emotional and behavioral disorders typically present significant problems for teachers in general education settings. Their behavior frequently affects not only their own learning but often the learning of others as well.

The challenges of appropriately serving students with emotional and behavioral disorders are emphasized by the realities of how schools respond to these students. The nearby Personal Spotlight highlights one educator's experience with these challenges. A major national study, *At the Schoolhouse Door* (Knitzer et al., 1990), illustrates these challenges.

The following are examples of findings from the study:

◢ Over 80% of students classified as E/BD are educated in general education schools.

◢ Approximately 50% of students classified as E/BD are educated for at least a portion of each school day in general education classrooms by general education classroom teachers.

◢ There is limited or no mental health presence in most special education programs for E/BD students.

◢ Children and adolescents with E/BD get limited transition services.

◢ Parents of students with E/BD often encounter great difficulties in securing appropriate educational programs for their children.

◢ School-based mental health services are being introduced in many schools across the country.

◢ Social skills training is nearly nonexistent in many schools.

◢ Efforts to extend families' involvement in students' programs are increasing.

**CONSIDER THIS**
What role should mental health professionals play in serving students with E/BD? How can schools involve mental health professionals more?

Although not all the findings are negative, this study reveals significant gaps in educational services for students with E/BD. However, the study also suggests that improvements are being made in many school districts in providing appropriate services to this large group of students.

### Educational Placements

Students with emotional and behavioral disorders are commonly included in general education classrooms, albeit to a lesser extent than students with other types of disabilities. According to the *20th Annual Report to Congress on the Implementation of IDEA* (1998), 23.5% of all students identified as emotionally disturbed were taught primarily in regular class (i.e., general education) settings while an additional 23.7%

## *personal* SPOTLIGHT

### Elementary Principal

**MIKE KELLY**
*Bedford County, Virginia*

Mike Kelly took a somewhat unusual route to becoming a school administrator. After completing his undergraduate degree in special education, Mike taught for 11 years in both self-contained classrooms and resource rooms, primarily working with students with learning, and emotional and behavioral problems. He then completed two master's degrees, one in school administration and the other in special education. Mike has now served for eight years as an elementary school principal. He finds that inclusion is a wonderful concept because it provides excellent learning opportunities for all students. At the same time, his experiences as a teacher and administrator reinforce the fact that successful inclusion stands or falls on access to necessary resources and supports. Reflecting back on his own teaching experience, he wishes there were more opportunities for his own students to have experienced inclusion when he was teaching elementary and middle school children with disabilities.

As a principal, Mike has seen a number of successes that relate to inclusion. In particular, with students with emotional and behavioral disorders, the benefits of inclusion are most clearly seen when a student's behavior begins to change as a result of interaction with nondisabled peers. While he would be reluctant to extol the virtues of inclusion for all students with severe behavior disorders, in many instances he found that there were dramatic changes, after inclusion, in terms of appropriate behavior. "For example, one student identified as ED was placed in a general education classroom and initially continued the kinds of behaviors that characterize ED. After a while, however, he seemed to realize that he was not getting the 'audience' that he had anticipated and consequently, his inappropriate behaviors began to decrease and his prosocial interactions began to increase. He became a real success story." Mike continues, "While some indicate that inclusion may be difficult in schools with academically talented students, I believe that there are some special advantages in such a school. The students really are quite committed to the learning process and consequently serve as very effective models for students who are experiencing both learning and behavioral difficulties."

Mike finds that the challenges for inclusion are more often in the academic domain. While some students have made remarkable progress in social adjustment, there is a significant need for supports in the classroom in order to make it work from an academic perspective. Paraprofessionals and substantive involvement of special educators can make the difference between successful and not-so-successful inclusion experiences for individual learners as well as for their nondisabled peers.

were served through resource room programs. Combining these figures, we can conclude that approximately half of all students identified as E/BD will spend most of their time in general education-based programs. For those students who are placed in more restrictive settings, 34.3% were placed in separate classes, 13.9% in separate public or private day facilities, 3.1% in public or private residential facilities, and 1.6% in home or hospital environments.

Because many students with EB/D are included in general education classrooms, teachers and special education teachers need to collaborate in developing and implementing intervention programs. Without this collaboration, appropriate interventions will be very difficult to provide. Consistency in behavior management and other strategies among teachers and family members is critical. If students receive feedback from the special education teacher that significantly differs from the feedback received from the classroom teacher, confusion often results.

As more students with disabilities are included in general education classrooms, many students with serious emotional disturbance and behavioral disorders are being reintegrated into general classrooms from more restrictive settings. The ability of students and teachers to deal effectively with behavior problems is critical for successful reintegration (Carpenter & McKee-Higgins, 1996). Rock, Rosenberg, and Carran (1995) studied the variables that affected this reintegration. Their findings indicate that success can be predicted when reintegration orientation, demographic characteristics of restrictive programs, and particular experiences and training of special educators are features of the reintegration process. Programs that were more likely to have better success at reintegration include those with a more positive reintegration orientation; those with certain demographic characteristics, such as being located in a wing of the general classroom building; and particular training experiences of teachers, such as having reintegration training in several sites. Administrators might want to take these variables into consideration when planning the reintegration of students with emotional and behavior disorders into general education programs.

## EFFECTIVE INSTRUCTION

Teaching students with emotional and behavioral disorders is clearly challenging. Research, however, does offer some direction for effective instructional practices. As summarized by Wehby, Symons, Canale, and Go (1998), these practices include:

- ◢ providing appropriate structure and predictable routines
- ◢ establishing a structured and consistent classroom environment
- ◢ establishing a consistent schedule with set rules and consequences and clear expectations
- ◢ fostering positive teacher-student interaction with adequate praise and systematic responses to problem behaviors
- ◢ frequently implementing instructional sequences that promote high rates of academic engagement
- ◢ creating a classroom environment in which independent seat work is limited and sufficient time is allotted for establishing positive social interaction. (p. 52)

### Social Skills Instruction

Students with emotional and behavioral disorders frequently display deficits in social skills (Knitzer, 1990; Rosenberg et al., 1992). Elksnin and Elksnin (1998) stress the complexity of social skills, indicating that they include both more overt, observable type behaviors as well as covert actions that may relate more to problem solving. A list of typical social skills is presented in Table 6.4.

Although many schools do not offer extensive opportunities for students to learn appropriate social skills (Knitzer et al., 1990), such instruction can be quite beneficial. Social skills are probably best learned from observing others who display appropriate skills, but there are times when a more formal instructional effort must be made. When using a formal instructional process to teach social skills, the first step is to determine the student's level of social competence. Assessing social skills requires eliciting informed judgments from persons who interact regularly with the student (Smith et al., 1993). Many different checklists are available to assist in assessing social competence. In addition, self-monitoring charts and sociometric measures may be used (Smith et al., 1993).

Following the assessment process, an instructional approach to teach solutions to deficiencies in social skills must be developed. Numerous methods may be used

| TABLE 6.4 | Types of Social Skills |
|---|---|
| INTERPERSONAL BEHAVIORS | "Friendship-making skills," such as introducing yourself, joining in, asking a favor, offering to help, giving and accepting compliments, and apologizing. |
| PEER-RELATED SOCIAL SKILLS | Skills valued by classmates and associated with peer acceptance. Examples include working cooperatively, asking for and receiving information, and correctly assessing another's emotional state. |
| TEACHER-PLEASING SOCIAL SKILLS | School success behaviors, including following directions, doing your best work, and listening to the teacher. |
| SELF-RELATED BEHAVIORS | Skills that allow a child to assess a social situation, select an appropriate skill, and determine the skill's effectiveness. Other self-related behaviors include following through, dealing with stress, understanding feelings, and controlling anger. |
| ASSERTIVENESS SKILLS | Behaviors that allow children to express their needs without resorting to aggression. |
| COMMUNICATION SKILLS | Listener responsiveness, turn taking, maintaining conversational attention, and giving the speaker feedback. |

From "Teaching Social Skills to Students with Learning and Behavioral Problems" by L. K. Elksnin and N. Elksnin, 1998, *Intervention in School and Clinic, 33,* p. 132.

to teach social skills and promote good social relations, including modeling, direct instruction, prompting, and positive practice (Searcy & Meadows, 1994). Teachers must determine the method that will work best with a particular student. Table 6.5 summarizes the predominant methods of teaching social skills.

Hetfield (1994) suggests improving social skills by having students work on the student newspaper. The work requires students to work interdependently and cooperatively in both small and large groups. By completing their own jobs and working with other newspaper staff members to produce the entire product, students with emotional and behavioral problems share in a sense of group and individual accomplishment while learning important skills. This helps students meet their needs for belonging to a social group (Rockwell & Guetzloe, 1996).

Quinn, Kavale, Mathur, Rutherford, and Forness (1999) reported a comprehensive research analysis of the use of social skills training with students with E/BD. In general, they caution that only about half of students with E/BD have been demonstrated to benefit from social skills training, particularly when the focus was on the broader dimensions of the social domain. Greater success was obtained when the focus was on specific social skills (e.g., social problem solving, social interaction, cooperation). Kavale and Forness (1999) hypothesize that the reason why more substantive positive effects have not been obtained from social skills training may be due to the fact that the training programs within the research studies may have been of too limited duration and intensity.

One reason why social skills instruction may be problematic is that its effectiveness as an intervention is challenged by the difficulty in achieving generalization across settings. Scott and Nelson (1998) cautioned teachers to realize that educational practices that may achieve generalization and academic instruction have not often been sufficient to achieve similar outcomes for social skills instruction. They stress that any such instruction in artificial contexts will create difficulty in generalization and therefore school-wide instruction, modeling, and the reinforcement of appropriate social behaviors taught within the context of the classroom are likely to be most effective. This instruction may be more effective when nondisabled students are involved in the training. While they stress the complexity of teaching social skills, Scott and Nelson (1998) also similarly stress the critical nature of learning within this area. Teachers are advised to consider social skills programs cautiously and determine that positive outcomes are obtained.

| TABLE 6.5 | Tactics to Teach Social Skills | | |
|---|---|---|---|
| **Instructional Strategy** | **Description** | **Advantages** | **Disadvantages** |
| MODELING | Exposing target student to display of prosocial behavior. | Easy to implement. | Not sufficient if used alone. |
| STRATEGIC PLACEMENT | Placing target student in situations with other students who display prosocial behaviors. | Employs peers as change agents. Facilitates generalization. Is cost effective. | Research data inconclusive when used alone. |
| INSTRUCTION | Telling students how and why they should behave a certain way, and/or giving rules for behavior. | Overemphasizes norms and expectations. | Not sufficient if used alone. |
| CORRESPONDENCE TRAINING | Students are positively reinforced for accurate reports regarding their behavior. | Facilitates maintenance and generalization of training. Is cost effective. | Very little documentation of effectiveness. |
| REHEARSAL AND PRACTICE | Structured practice of specific prosocial behavior. | Enhances skill acquisition. | Not sufficient to change behavior if used alone. |
| POSITIVE REINFORCEMENT OR SHAPING | Prosocial behaviors or approximations are followed by a reward or favorable event. | Strong research support for effectiveness. | Maintenance after treatment termination is not predictable. |
| PROMPTING AND COACHING | Providing students with additional stimuli or prompts that elicit the prosocial behavior. | Particularly effective after acquisition to enhance transfer to natural settings. | Maintenance after treatment termination is not predictable. |
| POSITIVE PRACTICE | A consequence strategy in which student repeatedly practices correct behavior. | May produce immediate increases in prosocial behavior. | Long-term effectiveness not documented. Less restrictive approaches should be used first. |
| MULTIMETHOD TRAINING PACKAGES | Multicomponent instructional package that incorporates several behavioral techniques. | Greater treatment strength and durability. Applicable to a wide range of children and settings. | |

From "Social Skills Curriculum Analysis" by J. Carter and G. Sugai, 1989, *Teaching Exceptional Children, 22,* p. 38. Used by permission.

## CLASSROOM AND BEHAVIORAL MANAGEMENT

Teachers can help students improve their behavior in many different ways, from preventive measures to direct confrontation with the students. Chapter 13 discusses ways to implement classroom management techniques. The level of collaboration among professionals involved in providing services to this group of students is critical. Mental health professionals should be involved with services to these students, and in some cases, personnel from the juvenile justice system, child welfare system, and social work agencies should also collaborate. *Without a close working relationship among the many groups involved in serving children and adolescents with E/BD, services will be fragmented and disorganized.*

### Classroom Management Accommodations

**CROSS-REFERENCE**
For more information on management considerations, refer to Chapter 13.

Effectively managing the classroom is critical for teachers with students with emotional and behavioral disorders because of the potential disruptiveness of this group of students and their impact on the learning of other students.

**STANDARD OPERATING PROCEDURES**   Classroom rules and procedures are a critical management tool for students with E/BD. Rules should be developed with the input of students and should be posted in the room. Remember that "the process of determining rules is as important as the rules themselves" (Zabel & Zabel, 1996, p. 169). Walker and Shea (1995) give the following examples of rules:

- General classroom rules:
  - Be polite and helpful.
  - Keep your space and materials in order.
  - Take care of classroom and school property.
- More specific rules:
  - Raise your hand before speaking.
  - Leave your seat only with permission.
  - Only one person in the rest room at a time. (p. 252)

**CONSIDER THIS**
How can classroom rules and procedures result in improved behavior for children with emotional and behavioral disorders? Are they also effective with nondisabled students?

Teachers should establish classroom procedures to ensure an orderly environment. These could include procedures for using classroom space and equipment, procedures for nonclassroom space and facilities, and procedures for group and individual activities (Walker & Shea, 1995).

### Physical Accommodations

The physical arrangement of the classroom has an impact on the behaviors of students with emotional and behavioral disorders. Attention to the classroom arrangement can both facilitate learning and minimize disruptions (Zabel & Zabel, 1996). The following considerations can help in maintaining an orderly classroom:

- Arranging traffic patterns to lessen contact and disruptions
- Arranging student desks to facilitate monitoring of all students at all times
- Physically locating students with tendencies toward disruptive behaviors near the teacher's primary location
- Locating students away from stored materials that they may find tempting
- Creating spaces where students can do quiet work, such as a quiet reading area

## Preventive Discipline

Probably the most effective means of working with students who display emotional and behavior problems is preventive in nature. If inappropriate behaviors can be prevented, then disruptions will be minimal, and the student can attend to the learning task at hand. **Preventive discipline** can be described as "the teacher's realization that discipline begins with a positive attitude that nurtures students' learning of personal, social, and academic skills" (Sabatino, 1987, p. 8). Rather than wait to respond to inappropriate behaviors, adherents to positive discipline take the initiative by interacting with students in a positive manner that removes the need for inappropriate behaviors.

*PREVENTIVE DISCIPLINE* refers to the utilization of methods that prevent disciplinary problems from manifesting.

Sabatino (1987) describes 10 components of a preventive discipline program:

1. Inform pupils of what is expected of them.
2. Establish a positive learning climate.
3. Provide a meaningful learning experience.
4. Avoid threats.
5. Demonstrate fairness.
6. Build and exhibit self-confidence.
7. Recognize positive student attributes.
8. Recognize student attributes at optimal times.
9. Use positive modeling.
10. Structure the curriculum and classroom environment.

Teacher behavior can greatly facilitate preventive discipline. Teachers have to be consistent in meting out discipline; they must not treat inappropriate behaviors from one student differently than they treat misbehavior from other students. Teachers must also apply consequences systematically. Disciplining a student for an inappropriate behavior one time and ignoring the same behavior another time will only cause the student to be confused over expectations.

*The behaviors of teachers can greatly impact effective behavior management.*

## General Behavior Management Strategies

Numerous strategies are referred to as **behavior management** techniques. (They will be described in detail in Chapter 13.) Table 6.6 shows the types of interventions used in 145 school districts included in a study by Grosenick et al. (1991). The wide variety of techniques spans behavioral and cognitive strategies, psychological interventions, and reactive interventions. Behavioral and cognitive strategies include common behavior management techniques such as positive reinforcement, time out, and teaching self-control strategies. Psychological interventions focus on counseling and the use of medication, whereas reactive strategies include methods of responding to inappropriate behaviors.

Of the different approaches, behavior management strategies appear to be the most common methods relied upon by teachers. These approaches, similar to assertive discipline, focus on preventing inappropriate behaviors from occurring. They differ from assertive discipline by emphasizing the reinforcement of students for desired behaviors, as opposed to reacting to behaviors after they are displayed. Good-behavior games, contracting, and individual behavior management plans are additional examples.

Webber and Scheuermann (1991) provide several suggestions for reinforcing positive behaviors that can eliminate inappropriate behaviors. These examples utilize

| **TABLE 6.6** | **Interventions Used in Programs for Students with Emotional and Behavioral Disorders** | | |
|---|---|---|---|
| Type of Intervention | Not at All Used | Used in Some Classrooms/Caseloads | Used in Most or All Classrooms/Caseloads |
| **BEHAVIORAL/COGNITIVE STRATEGIES** | | | |
| Positive reinforcement | 0 | 5 | 95 |
| Social skills training | 1 | 18 | 81 |
| Environmental management | 9 | 23 | 68 |
| Modeling | 4 | 7 | 89 |
| Self-control strategies | 2 | 12 | 86 |
| Time out | 4 | 27 | 69 |
| Generalization training | 16 | 43 | 41 |
| Use of aversives | 33 | 40 | 27 |
| **PSYCHOLOGICAL INTERVENTIONS** | | | |
| Counseling | 1 | 24 | 75 |
| Peer group processes | 5 | 34 | 61 |
| Managing surface behaviors | 0 | 11 | 89 |
| Life space interviewing | 38 | 31 | 31 |
| Psychotherapy | 49 | 30 | 21 |
| Medication | 31 | 55 | 14 |
| **REACTIVE STRATEGIES** | | | |
| Crisis management | 0.7 | 21 | 78 |
| Physical restraint | 25 | 52 | 23 |
| Suspension/expulsion | 10 | 56 | 34 |

From "Public School Services for Behaviorally Disordered Students: Program Practices in the 1980s" by J. K. Grosenick, N. L. George, M. P. George, and T. J. Lewis, 1991, *Behavior Disorders, 16,* p. 92. Used by permission.

*differential reinforcement of zero rates of undesirable behaviors (DRO), differential reinforcement of incompatible behaviors (DRI), differential reinforcement of lower rates of behaviors (DRL), and differential rates of communicative behaviors (DRC).* The nearby Inclusion Strategies feature provides examples of these techniques.

Another technique, the use of peer behavior modifiers, has been reviewed for use with students with emotional and behavioral disorders. When using peer behavior modifiers, a student's peer is responsible for providing reinforcers or monitoring behaviors. Gable, Arllen, and Hendrickson (1994) note that most behavior management programs rely on adults to monitor and provide reinforcement for desirable behaviors; this technique instead relies on peers. After reviewing peer interaction studies, they conclude that peer behavior modifiers could be effective among students with emotional and behavioral problems: "The generally positive results surfacing

**TEACHING TIP**
When using peers to assist with behavior changes, make sure that the students involved in the process are appropriately trained.

---

# INCLUSION STRATEGIES

## Problem Classroom Behaviors and Differential Reinforcement Strategies

| Problem Behavior | Differential Reinforcement Strategy |
| --- | --- |
| TALKING BACK | Reinforce each 15- or 30-minute or 1-hour period with no talking back (DRO). Or reinforce each time that the student responds to the teacher without talking back (DRI). |
| CAUSING PROPERTY DAMAGE | For each day that no property is damaged, reinforce the student and/or the class (DRO). |
| CURSING | Reinforce each 15- or 30-minute or 1-hour period with no cursing (DRO). Reinforce use of appropriate adjectives and exclamations (DRC). |
| BEING OFF TASK | Reinforce each 5-, 10-, 15-, or 30-minute period of continuous in-seat behavior (DRI). |
| FAILING TO COMPLETE TASKS | Reinforce each task that is completed, half completed, or started (DRI). |
| TARDINESS | Reinforce each day or period that the student is on time (DRI). |
| BEING OUT OF SEAT | Reinforce 5-, 10-, 15-, or 30-minute periods of continuous in-seat behavior (DRI). |
| FIGHTING | Reinforce the student after each hour or 1/2 hour that the student does not fight (DRO). Reinforce talking about feelings (DRC). |
| PICKING ON OTHERS, NAME CALLING, TEASING | Reinforce the student each time he or she interacts appropriately with another student (DRI). Or reinforce the student each hour that he or she does not tease, pinch, etc. (DRO). |
| NONCOMPLIANCE | Reinforce the student for each direction that he or she follows within 5 seconds (DRI). The schedule can be thinned to every 3 directions followed, 8, 10, etc. |
| TALKING OUT | Reinforce the student each time that he or she raises a hand and waits to be called on (DRI). Thin the schedule to 3, 5, 10 times, etc. Or reinforce progressively less talking out (DRI). |

From "Accentuate the Positive . . . Eliminate the Negative!" by J. Webber and B. Scheuermann, 1991, *Teaching Exceptional Children, 24,* p. 16. Used by permission.

from the modest number of investigations in which E/BD students have served as behavior modifiers underscore the relevance of this procedure for those facing the daunting task of better serving students with emotional/behavioral disorders" (p. 275).

## INTERVENTIONS BASED ON FUNCTIONAL BEHAVIORAL ASSESSMENT

**CONSIDER THIS**
How can using functional behavioral assessment help teachers focus on specific issues related to inappropriate behaviors?

Functional assessment is a technique used to determine hypotheses about a student's inappropriate behaviors. For example, an analysis of a student's acting-out behaviors could indicate that the student could not perform the required academic task and became disruptive as a result. Cipani (1995) refers to this process as behavioral diagnostics. The nearby Inclusion Strategies feature discusses this concept. In using behavioral diagnostics (also called functional assessment procedures), teachers should

1. collect information about the behavior.
2. develop hypothesis statements about the behavior.
3. develop intervention strategies. (Foster-Johnson & Dunlap, 1993)

Table 6.7 provides some sample hypothesis statements and possible interventions. Such an approach does not lock teachers into specific strategies, allowing them to tailor interventions to specific behaviors and causes (Kauffman et al., 1995). Figure 6.2 presents a sample functional behavioral assessment.

Functional behavioral assessment is also an important basis for the development of positive behavioral supports (PBS). PBS interventions have developed as an alter-

## INCLUSION STRATEGIES

### Behavioral Diagnostics

Through behavioral diagnostics, a teacher develops hypotheses about the environmental reasons for a student's problem behavior. Such a diagnosis is similar to what professionals in many fields do before solving a problem that arises. For example, a good auto mechanic collects information about your car's performance by interviewing you and running tests on your car. Using that information, the mechanic makes a diagnosis about the probable cause of the problem before he or she makes any repairs. In a similar way, a teacher attempts to make a diagnosis about why a student's problem behavior is occurring, and based on that diagnosis, designs a strategy that addresses the underlying cause of the behavior.

*An accurate diagnosis of why the problem behavior is occurring will mean the difference between an effective* *and an ineffective solution.* A specific behavioral prescription can be either right or wrong, depending on the diagnosis.

If the child's problem behavior is being maintained by teacher attention, then some form of time out away from the teacher's attention would be an appropriate strategy for eliminating the behavior. Of course, the teacher should also design an overall strategy to help the child develop more productive behavior (Cipani, 1990, 1994; Cipani & Trotter, 1991; LaVigna, Willis, & Donnellan, 1989; Sulzer-Azaroff & Mayer, 1977). However, if the same problem behavior is maintained by time out—escape/avoidance of task or instruction—then time out (in the form of task withdrawal) is contraindicated and will, in all likelihood, increase the very behavior the teacher has targeted to decrease.

From "Be Aware of Negative Reinforcement" by E. C. Cipani, 1995, *Teaching Exceptional Children, 27,* p. 39. Used by permission.

| TABLE 6.7 | Sample Hypothesis Statements and Possible Interventions |
|---|---|

| | INTERVENTION | |
|---|---|---|
| **HYPOTHESIS STATEMENTS** | **Modify Antecedents** | **Teach Alternative Behavior** |
| Suzy pinches herself and others around 11:00 A.M. every day because she gets hungry. | Make sure Suzy gets breakfast.<br><br>Provide a snack at about 9:30 A.M. | Teach Suzy to ask for something to eat. |
| Jack gets into arguments with the teacher every day during reading class when she asks him to correct his mistakes on the daily reading worksheet. | Get Jack to correct his own paper.<br><br>Give Jack an easier assignment. | Teach Jack strategies to manage his frustration in a more appropriate manner.<br><br>Teach Jack to ask for teacher assistance with the incorrect problems. |
| Tara starts pouting and refuses to work when she has to sort a box of washers because she doesn't want to do the activity. | Give Tara half of the box of washers to sort.<br><br>Give Tara clear directions about how much she has to do or how long she must work. | |
| Frank kicks other children in morning circle time and usually gets to sit right by the teacher. | Give each child a clearly designated section of the floor that is his or hers. | Teach Frank how to ask the children to move over.<br><br>Teach Frank how to ask the teacher to intervene with his classmates. |
| Harry is off task for most of math class when he is supposed to be adding two-digit numbers. | Ask Harry to add the prices of actual food items.<br><br>Intersperse an easy activity with the more difficult math addition so Harry can experience some success. | Teach Harry how to ask for help.<br><br>Teach Harry how to monitor his rate of problem completion, and provide reinforcement for a certain number of problems. |

From "Using Functional Assessment to Develop Effective, Individualized Interventions for Challenging Behaviors" by L. Foster-Johnson and G. Dunlap, 1993, *Teaching Exceptional Children, 25,* p. 49. Used by permission.

native to an emphasis on punitive disciplinary strategies and as a way to provide guidance to students with behavioral problems to make appropriate changes in their behavioral patterns. PBS emphasizes proactive, preventative strategies and early intervention with students deemed to be at risk.

As described by Lewis and Sugai (1999), an effective positive behavioral support program for a school should include the following components:

▲ specialized individual behavior support for students with chronic behavior problems
▲ specialized group behavior support for students without-risk problem behavior
▲ universal group behavior support for most students. (p. 4)

The system that Lewis and Sugai have developed emphasizes school-wide programs that put in place a preventative, proactive system and provide a foundation for the appropriate design of programs for individuals experiencing significant behavior problems.

**TEACHING TIP**
Whenever possible, teach appropriate social skills in the context in which they will be used. If they must be taught in a different context, plan for their transfer to more typical settings.

## III. Functional Behavioral Assessment (FBA)

The Functional Behavioral Assessment (FBA) addresses the relationship among precipitating conditions, the behavior, its consequences, and the function of the behavior. The FBA also reflects a consideration of all relevant data gathered, both as background information and by using specific assessment techniques. Refer to the Functional Behavioral Assessment Discussion Guide (found on page 16 of the manual) for assistance in completing this form.

**Behavior #** ___3___    Physical aggression/fighting

| Precipitating Conditions (Setting, time, or other situations typically occurring *before* the behavior) | Specific Behavior (*Exactly* what the student does or does not do) | Consequences (Events that typically *follow* the behavior) | Function of the Behavior (*Hypothesized purpose[s]* the behavior serves) |
|---|---|---|---|
| ☒ unstructured time in hallways/on the bus | Casey pushes, hits, trips other students, often students who are smaller; Casey's aggression occurs more often when no adults are watching her (on bus; in halls). | ☒ teacher attention | ☐ escape/avoidance |
| ☐ academic instruction in _____ | | ☒ peer attention | ☐ gaining attention |
| ☐ when given a directive to _____ | | ☒ verbal warning/reprimand | ☒ expression of anger |
| | | ☐ loss of privilege (what kind?) | ☐ frustration |
| ☒ when close to smaller students | | | ☒ vengeance |
| ☐ when provoked by _____ | | ☐ time out (where/how long?) | ☒ seeking of power/control |
| | | | ☒ intimidation |
| ☐ when unable to _____ | | ☒ detention (how long?) after school | ☐ sensory stimulation |
| ☒ other when unsupervised | | ☐ removal from class | ☐ relief of fear/anxiety |
| ☐ none observed | | ☒ in-school suspension (how long?) 3 days | ☐ other _____ |
| | | ☐ other _____ | |

### Specific Assessment Techniques Used to Analyze This Behavior

☒ Observation  ☐ Student Interview  ☒ Administrative Interview  ☒ Parent Interview
☒ Behavior Checklist/Rating Scale  ☐ Video/Audio Taping  ☒ Teacher Interview  ☐ Other _____

### Relating Information/Considerations

Academic: ___Low grades—homework not turned in___

Social/Peer: ___Few friends___

Family: ___Casey's behavior has disrupted family life. Mother reports she is afraid of Casey.___

Other: _____

## Behavioral Intervention Planning

According to federal guidelines under the 1997 amendments to IDEA, school district personnel are required to address the strategies to be employed for students with disabilities who exhibit significant behavioral problems. The required component is the development of a behavioral intervention plan (BIP). This plan is required in certain instances of serious misbehavior (e.g., using weapons or drugs) but also may be effectively used as a response to other significant behavioral problems. The development of the behavioral intervention plan parallels the development of the IEP and includes input from multiple professionals and parents. Further discussion on the development of BIPs follows in Chapter 13.

## Medication

Many students with emotional and behavioral problems experience difficulties in maintaining attention and controlling behavior. Although many students with attention deficits and hyperactivity do not have emotional and behavior problems, many do. For students experiencing these problems, "medication is the most frequently used (and perhaps overused) intervention" (Ellenwood & Felt, 1989, p. 16). Many different kinds of medication have been found to be effective with students' behavior problems (Forness & Kavale, 1988) including stimulants, tranquilizers, anticonvulsants, antidepressants, and mood-altering drugs.

The use of medication to help manage students with emotional and behavior problems is controversial and has been investigated extensively. Findings include the following:

1. Medication can result in increased attention of students.
2. Medication can result in reduced aggressive behaviors.
3. Various side effects can result from medical interventions.
4. The use of medication for children experiencing emotional and behavioral problems should be carefully supervised and monitored. (Smith et al., 1993)

When medication is used, the teacher must closely monitor the child. Teachers need to have knowledge of the medication and its possible side effects. On a regular basis, the teacher should report observations to the parents or the student's physician to ensure that negative side effects are not beginning to appear. If the level or kind of medication is changed, the teacher needs to be informed immediately and given information about possible side effects.

Numerous side effects may accompany medications taken by children for emotional and behavioral problems. Ritalin is commonly prescribed to help students with attention and hyperactivity problems. Several potential side effects of Ritalin include nervousness, insomnia, anorexia, dizziness, blood pressure and pulse changes, abdominal pain, and weight loss. Teachers can monitor side effects by keeping a daily log of student behaviors that could be attributed to the medication (Dowdy, Patton, Smith, & Polloway, 1997).

**FIGURE 6.2**
Sample Functional Behavioral Assessment
From *Behavioral Intervention Planning: Completing a Functional Behavioral Assessment and Developing a Behavioral Intervention Plan* (2nd ed.) (p. 38), by K. Fad, J. R. Patton, and E. A. Polloway, 2000, Austin, TX: Pro-Ed.

# TECHNOLOGY TODAY

## Uses of Videotaping in Classrooms Serving Youth with Behavioral Disorders

1. To provide a permanent antecedent-behavior-consequence (ABC) analysis.
2. To self-monitor one's behavioral strengths and weaknesses.
3. To evaluate peer behavioral strengths and weaknesses.
4. To provide reality replay on facial expressions, body language, expressions of feelings, tone of voice, and other hard-to-define performance criteria.
5. To provide motivation and enthusiasm for group sessions.
6. To add vitality to simulations and role playing.
7. To reinforce shared experience.
8. To "catch" unobserved misbehavior or adaptive behaviors.
9. To provide a less intrusive consequence for misbehavior.

*Videotaping can be used as an effective management tool by teachers.*

10. To give parents and other agencies a realistic perspective on child misbehavior and classroom interventions.
11. To build cooperation and trust.
12. To plan for inclusion.

From "The Many Uses of Videotape in Classrooms Serving Youth with Behavioral Disorders" by S. A. Broome and R. B. White, 1995, *Teaching Exceptional Children, 27,* pp. 10–13.

## Technology

Technology offers ways for teachers to deal effectively with students with emotional and behavioral disorders. Technological devices, including wrist counters, golf counters, grocery counters, index cards for tally marks, beads-in-pocket, and printing calculators, can assist teachers in recording student behaviors. Broome and White (1995) suggest the use of videotaping to help manage students with emotional and behavioral problems. The nearby Technology Today feature describes different ways that videotaping can be used for this purpose.

## ENHANCING INCLUSIVE CLASSROOMS FOR STUDENTS WITH EMOTIONAL AND BEHAVIORAL DISORDERS

Classroom teachers usually make the initial referral for students with emotional and behavioral problems. Unless the problem exhibited by the student is severe, it has usually gone unnoticed until the school years. In addition to referring students, classroom teachers must be directly involved in implementing the student's IEP because the majority of students in this category receive a portion of their educational program in general education classrooms. General education classroom teachers must deal with behavior problems much of the time since in addition to E/BD students there are large numbers of students who from time to time display inappropriate behaviors, although they have not been identified as having emotional and behavioral problems.

Kauffman and Wong (1991) point out that "effective teaching of behaviorally disordered students may require skills, attitudes, and beliefs different from those of teachers who work effectively with more ordinary students" (p. 226). However, no single characteristic will guarantee success for teachers dealing with students who are experiencing emotional and behavioral problems.

**CONSIDER THIS**

Can general classroom teachers effectively deal with students with emotional and behavioral disorders in their classrooms? What factors will enhance the likelihood of success?

## Promoting a Sense of Community and Social Acceptance

Students with emotional and behavioral disorders are generally placed in general education classrooms rather than in isolated special education settings. Therefore, teachers must ensure the successful inclusion of these students. Several tactics that teachers can use to accomplish this include:

◢ Using programs in which peers act as buddies or tutors
◢ Focusing on positive behaviors and providing appropriate reinforcements
◢ Using good-behavior games in which all students work together to earn rewards

Teachers must make a special effort to keep themselves, as well as other students, from developing a negative attitude toward students with E/BD. The nearby Diversity Forum feature describes precautions that teachers can take to keep from discriminating against this challenging group of children.

# DIVERSITY FORUM

## Ways for Teachers to Lessen Discrimination

### WHAT CAN YOU DO?

☑ Create class rules with your students. Think how they may be stated in positive rather than negative terms. Focus on privileges rather than on punitive consequences.

☑ Monitor your own behavior with your students. Do you tend to be more patient with some students than with others? Are you quicker to assign detentions or take other disciplinary measures with some students than with others? Do you use sarcastic, menacing, or negative language with some students? Ask a colleague to help you identify these incidents.

☑ Be sensitive to how some students are more negatively affected by some disciplinary prac-

tices than others. For example, if a student is consistently assigned to detention after school and misses work as a result, he or she might be losing needed family income. Think of a number of alternative and more positive strategies for influencing behavior.

☑ Encourage parents and other community members to participate on committees in which disciplinary policies are discussed. In your own classroom, invite parents to talk about their perceptions of school policies with you.

From *Affirming Diversity* (2nd ed.) (p. 376), by S. Nieto, 1996, White Plains, NY: Longman. Used by permission.

# SUPPORTS FOR GENERAL EDUCATION TEACHERS

Since most students with emotional and behavioral disorders are educated in general classrooms, classroom teachers are the key to the success of these students. Too often, if these students do not achieve success, the entire classroom will be disrupted and all students will suffer. Therefore, appropriate supports must be available to teachers. They include special education personnel, psychologists and counselors, and mental health service providers.

Special educators should consult with teachers regarding behavior management as well as instructional support. These teachers may provide this support in the classroom or confer with teachers in a different setting. A particularly helpful way to assist classroom teachers involves modeling methods of dealing with behavior problems. At times, it is best for students with emotional and behavioral problems to leave the general education setting and receive instruction from special educators. School psychologists and counselors can provide intensive counseling to students with emotional and behavioral disorders; they may also consult with teachers on how to implement specific programs, such as a student's individual behavior management plan.

Finally, mental health personnel can provide helpful supports for teachers. Too often, mental health services are not available in schools; however, some schools are beginning to develop school-based mental health programs that serve students with emotional and behavioral disorders. These programs are jointly staffed by school personnel and mental health staff and provide supports for teachers as well as direct interventions for students. If mental health services are not available in a particular school, teachers should work with school administrators to involve mental health specialists with students who display emotional and behavioral problems.

# Summary

## Basic Concepts about Emotional and Behavioral Disorders

◢ Most children and youths are disruptive from time to time, but most do not require interventions. Some students' emotional or behavioral problems are severe enough to warrant interventions.

◢ Many problems complicate serving students with emotional and behavioral disorders, including inconsistent definitions of the disorder, numerous agencies involved in defining and treating it, and limited ways to objectively measure the extent and precise parameters of the problem.

◢ Definitions for emotional disturbance and behavioral disorders are generally vague and are typically subject to alternative explanations.

◢ There is limited consistency in classifying persons with emotional and behavioral problems.

◢ Determining the eligibility of students with E/BD is difficult because of problems with identification and assessment.

◢ The estimated prevalence of students with emotional and behavioral problems ranges from a low of 1% or 2% to a high of 30%.

◢ Students with emotional and behavioral problems are significantly underserved in schools.

## Strategies for Curriculum and Instruction

◢ Students with E/BD are commonly included in general education classes and may present significant problems for general education teachers.

◢ General education teachers and special education teachers must collaborate so that there is consistency in the development and implementation of intervention methods.

## Effective Instruction

◢ A variety of curricular, classroom, and behavioral management strategies are available to enhance the educational programs for students with E/BD.

▲ Social skills instruction is very important for students with E/BD.

▲ Although this treatment is highly controversial, many students with E/BD problems receive medication in an attempt to control their behaviors.

## Interventions Based on Functional Behavioral Assessment

▲ Interventions based on functional behavioral assessment and preventative discipline are important methods for reducing the impact of problems or to keep problems from occurring.

▲ Functional behavioral assessment is also important for the development of positive behavioral supports.

### Enhancing Inclusive Classrooms for Students with Emotional and Behavioral Disorders

▲ General education teachers must realize that the skills, attitudes, and beliefs needed to work effectively with students with E/BD may vary from those that are effective for nondisabled students.

▲ Positive reinforcement and peer tutoring are possible tactics for preventing students with E/BD from feeling isolated in the general education classroom.

### Supports for General Education Teachers

▲ Special education teachers and mental health personnel need to be available to provide guidance for general education teachers who are implementing a student's behavior management plan.

# *Further Readings*

American Psychiatric Association. *Diagnostic and statistical manual (DSM-IV)* (1994). Washington, DC: Author.

Rock, E. E., Rosenberg, M. S., & Carran, D. T. (1995). Variables affecting the reintegration rate. *Exceptional Children, 61.*

Skiba, R., Grizzle, K., & Minke, K. M. (1994). Opening the floodgates? The social maladjustment exclusion and state SED prevalence rates. *Journal of School Psychology, 32,* 267–283.

U. S. Department of Education. *Annual report to Congress on the implementation of IDEA* (1999). Washington, DC: U.S. Government Printing Office.

Woods, F. H. (1995). Emotional/behavioral disorders and the Ziegarnik effect. *Education and Treatment of Children,* August.

Zabel, R. H., and Zabel, M. K. (1996). *Classroom management in context.* Boston: Houghton Mifflin.

# Chapter 7

# Teaching Students with Mental Retardation

*After reading this chapter, you should be able to:*

◢ Describe the concept of mental retardation

◢ Provide personal perspectives on mental retardation

◢ Summarize key definitions and classifications

◢ Identify the instructional implications of common characteristics of students with mild mental retardation

◢ Describe the transitional needs of students with mild mental retardation

◢ Apply considerations of the needs of students with mental retardation to curriculum design

◢ Enhance the inclusion of students with mental retardation

The phrase "persons who are retarded are far more like us than different from us" has been central to efforts to enhance life experiences for individuals with mental retardation. Sometimes events dramatically underscore this point. An interchange that took place on a college campus provides a good illustration.

Several years ago, the Student Council for Exceptional Children (SCEC) invited about 20 adolescents and adults who were residents of a state institution for persons with mental retardation to a campus dance attended by many members of the college community. By all accounts, the evening went quite well. A highlight of the evening occurred when one zealous SCEC member asked one of the apparently more withdrawn adults to dance. He hesitated, somewhat surprised at the invitation. After coaxing and cajoling, however, he agreed. After the dance, the college student inquired, "Where do you live?"

"Lynchburg," was the reply.

"Oh, and where do you work?"

"I work here at Lynchburg College," he indicated.

Perhaps sensing that this might be a prime example of the college's commitment to hire people with disabilities, the student questioned further, "What do you do on campus? I've not seen you around."

"I'm the chair of the anthropology department," came the response.

## QUESTIONS TO CONSIDER

1. How do we learn to accept people with mental retardation and ensure that they occupy a respected place in society?
2. What opportunities are central to attaining a positive quality of life?
3. What supports can enhance inclusion in schools and communities?

*M*ental retardation is a powerful term used to describe a level of functioning significantly below what is considered to be "average." It conjures up a variety of images including a stereotypical photo of an adolescent with Down syndrome, a young child living in poverty and provided with limited experience and stimulation, and an adult striving to adjust to the demands of a complex society. Since it is a generic term representing a highly diverse group of individuals, all of the images and, at the same time, none of these images, can be assumed to be accurate ones. The vignette at the beginning of this chapter emphasizes this point.

**CONSIDER THIS**
Why do you think the prevalence of mental retardation varies so much from state to state?

In the public schools, the most recent national database (for 1996–1997) indicates that 0.96% of the estimated student population (ages 6–21) is identified as mentally retarded (U.S. Department of Education, 1998). However, a closer look at these data reveals a substantial variance in prevalence from 2.40% in Alabama to 1% in Virginia to 0.419% in California. Even a naive observer would at once conclude that the concept is not defined, or the condition is not conceptualized, in the same way across the states. For that matter, the term itself may be eschewed in many areas. For example, *intellectually impaired* or *educationally handicapped* may be the preferred description in a given state, or even in a specific geographical area within a state. Although the term mental retardation has been widely criticized and proposals periodically forthcoming for alternative terms (e.g., *cognitive delay, educational disability*) state educational departments in 26 states (51%) continue to use the term, while an additional 14 states (28.4%) use similar terms (e.g., *mental disability, mental impairment*) (Denning, Chamberlain, & Polloway, 2000). This finding is consistent with a broad survey by Sandieson (1998) that looked at worldwide trends. For this reason we continue to use the term mental retardation in this text, although we caution the reader that it is a value-laden term. Indeed, the underlying message is clear: Being labeled mentally retarded can be stigmatizing. Avoiding labels or using more positive labels, as well as providing opportunities to be with peers who are not disabled, must be considered in order to ensure the prospect of a high quality life for those people who are labeled mentally retarded.

In the field of mental retardation, the late twentieth century witnessed momentous changes. Shifts in public attitudes toward persons with mental retardation and the resulting development and provision of services and supports for them have been truly phenomenal. Consequently, this is an exciting time to be participating in the changing perspectives on mental retardation.

## BASIC CONCEPTS ABOUT MENTAL RETARDATION

**T**he concept of mental retardation is a broad one. It includes a wide range of functioning levels, from mild disabilities to more severe limitations. The discussion in this chapter initially addresses the global concept of mental retardation. Then the remainder of the chapter focuses on the educational implications of mild mental retardation. More severe disabilities receive detailed attention in Chapter 9, which focuses on low-incidence disabilities.

## Mental Retardation Defined

It has been difficult for professionals to formulate definitions of mental retardation that could then be used to govern practices such as assessment and placement. Mental retardation has been most often characterized by two dimensions: limited intellectual ability and difficulty in coping with the social demands of the environment. Greenspan (1996) views mental retardation primarily as a problem in "everyday intelligence"; thus persons with retardation can be viewed as those who are challenged by adapting to the demands of daily life in the community. Thus, all individuals with mental retardation must, by most definitions, demonstrate some degree of impaired mental abilities, most often reflected in an intelligence quotient (IQ) significantly below average. In addition, these individuals would necessarily demonstrate less mature adaptive skills, such as social behavior or functional academic skills, when compared to their same-age peers. For individuals with mild disabilities, this discrepancy can be relatively subtle and not be readily apparent in a casual interaction in a nonschool setting. These individuals may be challenged most dramatically by the school setting, and thus between the ages of 6 and 21 their inability to cope may be most evident—for example, in problems with peer relationships, difficulty in compliance with adult-initiated directions, or academic challenges.

**1983 AAMD DEFINITION**   The American Association on Mental Deficiency (AAMD) (Grossman, 1983) concerned itself for decades with developing and revising the definition of mental retardation. This organization's efforts are broadly recognized, and their definitions were often incorporated, with modifications, into state and federal statutes. Although usage in the states in terms of educational regulations and practice has been uneven (Frankenberger & Harper, 1988), the organization's definitions frequently have been considered the basis for diagnosis in the field.

The Grossman (1983) AAMD definition was as follows:

> Mental retardation refers to significantly subaverage general intellectual functioning resulting in or associated with concurrent impairments in adaptive behavior and manifested during the developmental period. (p. 11)

Three concepts are central to this definition: intellectual functioning, adaptive behavior, and the developmental period.

*Intellectual functioning* is intended as a broad summation of cognitive abilities, such as the capacity to learn, solve problems, accumulate knowledge, adapt to new situations, and think abstractly. Operationally, however, it has often been reduced to performance on a test of intelligence. "Significantly below average" is defined in the 1983 AAMD definition as below a flexible upper IQ range of 70 to 75. Research indicates that this approximate IQ range remains a common component of state identification practices if an IQ cut-off score is required at all (Denning et al., 2000).

It is worth considering how an IQ score relates to this first criterion for diagnosis. Since an IQ of 100 is the mean score on such tests, a person receiving a score of 100 is considered to have an average level of cognitive functioning. Based on statistical analysis, approximately 2.3% of IQs would be expected to lie below 70 and a like percentage above 130. Thus, to limit the diagnosis of mental retardation to persons with

**CONSIDER THIS**
What are some of the dangers in relating the concept of mental retardation to a numerical index, such as IQ?

| TABLE 7.1 | Key Adaptive Skill Areas | | |
|---|---|---|---|
| Communication | Social skills | Health and safety | Leisure |
| Self-care | Community use | Functional academics | Work |
| Home living | Self-direction | | |

From *Mental Retardation: Definition, Classification, and Systems of Supports* (p. 1), by R. Luckasson, E. L. Coulter, E. A. Polloway, S. Reiss, R. L. Schalock, M. E. Snell, D. M. Spitalnik, and J. A. Stark, 1992, Washington, DC: American Association on Mental Retardation. Used by permission.

IQs of about 70 or below is to suggest that, hypothetically, about 2%–3% of the tested population may have significantly subaverage general intellectual functioning. However, as the definition clearly states, low IQ scores alone are not sufficient for diagnosis. Hence, we must next consider the adaptive dimension.

**CONSIDER THIS**
Without an operational definition derived from the 1983 AAMD definition, could you identify a person as having mental retardation?

An individual's *adaptive behavior* represents the degree to which the individual meets "the standards of maturation, learning, personal independence, and/or social responsibility that are expected for his or her age level and cultural group" (Grossman, 1983, p. 11). Continuing with this concept, Grossman (1983) emphasizes the idea of coping: "*Adaptive behavior* refers to the quality of everyday performance in coping with environmental demands. . . . adaptive behavior refers to what people do to take care of themselves and to relate to others in daily living rather than the abstract potential implied by intelligence." Particularly important to the concept of adaptive behavior are the skills necessary to function independently in a range of situations and to maintain responsible social relationships. The importance of adaptive behavior is reflected in the fact that currently 98% of all states require consideration of this dimension for eligibility (Denning et al., 2000). Table 7.1 lists key adaptive skill areas.

The **DEVELOPMENTAL PERIOD** is the period between conception and 18 years of age that is used for the purposes of determining mental retardation.

The third component of the definition is the **developmental period.** It is typically defined as the period of time between conception and 18 years of age. Below-average intellectual functioning and disabilities in adaptive behavior must appear during this period in order for an individual to be considered to have mental retardation.

**AAMR DEFINITION, 1992**    The American Association on Mental Deficiency, now the American Association on Mental Retardation (AAMR), has continued to be the leading professional organization in developing definitions of mental retardation. In 1992, the AAMR revised its definition in order to reflect changes in current thinking about persons with mental retardation. According to Luckasson et al. (1992),

> Mental retardation refers to substantial limitations in present functioning. It is manifested by significantly subaverage intellectual functioning, existing concurrently with related limitations in two or more of the following applicable adaptive skill areas: communication, self-care, home living, social skills, community use, self-direction, health and safety, functional academics, leisure, and work. Mental retardation begins before age 18. (p. 8)

**CONSIDER THIS**
What are some reasons for subclassifying the category of mental retardation into levels of severity?

Luckasson et al. (1992) provide a further context for the definition. The appropriate application of the definition requires consideration of four key assumptions. These are detailed in Figure 7.1. Note that these elements are deemed essential to the use of the 1992 definition.

The following four assumptions are *essential* to the application of the definition.

1. Valid assessment considers cultural and linguistic diversity, as well as differences in communication and behavioral factors.
2. The existence of limitations in adaptive skills occurs within the context of community environments typical of the individual's age peers and is indexed to the person's individualized needs for supports.
3. Specific adaptive limitations often coexist with strengths in other adaptive skills or other personal capabilities.
4. With appropriate supports over a sustained period, the life-functioning of the person with mental retardation will generally improve.

**FIGURE 7.1**

Four Assumptions Essential to the Application of the Definition of Mental Retardation

From *Mental Retardation: Definition, Classification, and Systems of Supports* (p. 1), by R. Luckasson, D. L.. Coulter, E. A. Polloway, S. Reiss, R. L. Schalock, M. E. Snell, D. M. Spitalnik, and J. A. Stark, 1992, Washington, DC: American Association on Mental Retardation. Used by permission.

*MILD MENTAL RETARDATION* is the highest functioning level of mental retardation; individuals usually have IQ scores in the 55–70 range.

*MODERATE MENTAL RETARDATION* is the level of mental retardation that includes persons with an IQ range of 35/40–55.

*SEVERE MENTAL RETARDATION* is the level of mental retardation that includes persons with an IQ range of 20–35/40.

*PROFOUND MENTAL RETARDATION* is the lowest functioning level of mental retardation.

*EDUCABLE MENTAL RETARDATION* is a classification previously used in schools to identify students with high ranges of mental retardation who could learn academic skills.

*TRAINABLE MENTAL RETARDATION* is a level of mental retardation that schools used to identify students who needed a curriculum more focused on adaptive behavior skills rather than academic skills.

The 1992 definition retains the focus of earlier AAMR definitions on the two key dimensions of intelligence and adaptation as well as the modifier of age of onset. However, the conceptual basis varies from those earlier efforts. The 1992 definition reflects a more *functional approach,* thus shifting focus to the individual's functioning within the community rather than giving weight mainly to the psychometric and clinical aspects of the person (e.g., IQ scores, limited adaptive behavior evaluations). Denning et al. (2000) reported on the definitional basis for state guidelines across the 50 states and the District of Columbia. They found that the Grossman (1983) definition continued to be used by 35 (68.6%) states in an adapted version and by 9 (17.6%) verbatim. On the other hand, the Luckasson et al. (1992) definition was reported to be used by only 3 states in either the verbatim or adapted form. Table 7.2 provides a summary of the findings by state.

For a fuller appreciation of the Luckasson et al. (1992) definitional system, the reader should consult the AAMR manual. It remains to be seen if the 1992 definition will eventually become the basis for state and federal statutes for educational, psychological, medical, and legal practice. Consult Schalock et al. (1994), MacMillan, Gresham, and Siperstein (1993), Polloway (1997), Luckasson, Schalock, Snell, and Spitalnik (1996), and Smith (1994) for a discussion of the uses of this definition as well as a review of the questions that have been raised about the 1992 manual.

## Classification of Mental Retardation

Historically, classification in this field has been done by both etiology (i.e., causes) and level of severity. While the former has limited application to nonmedical practice, the latter has been used by a range of disciplines, including education and psychology. The classification system cited most often in the professional literature is one recommended by Grossman (1983). This system uses the terms **mild, moderate, severe,** and **profound mental retardation,** which are summative judgments based on both intelligence and adaptive behavior assessment. Often, however, the emphasis has been on the former only, so IQ scores have frequently and unfortunately been equated with level of functioning.

Terms such as **educable** and **trainable** reflect an alternative system that has been used in school environments. These terms remain in use today in many places; it is not

| TABLE 7.2 | State Guidelines for Mental Retardation: Definition and Classification |

| State | Term[1] | Definition[2] | IQ Cut-off | Require Adaptive Behavior? | Age Ceiling | Classification System[3] |
|---|---|---|---|---|---|---|
| Alabama | MR | GV | 70 | YES | NO | NO |
| Alaska | MR | GA | 2 SD | YES | NO | NO |
| Arizona | MR | GA | 2 SD | YES | NO | M/M/S/P |
| Arkansas | MR | GA | NO | YES | NO | NO |
| California | MR | GA | NO | YES | NO | M/M/S/P |
| Colorado | SLIC | GA | 2 SD | YES | NO | NO |
| Connecticut | MR | GA | 2 SD | YES | NO | NO |
| Delaware | MD | GA | 70 | YES | NO | EMR/TMR/S |
| District of Columbia | MR | GA | 70 | YES | NO | M/M/S/P |
| Florida | MH | GV | 2 SD | YES | NO | EMR/TMR/P |
| Georgia | ID | GV | 70 | YES | NO | M/M/S/P |
| Hawaii | MR | GA | 2 SD | YES | NO | M/M/S |
| Idaho | MR | GA | 70 | YES | NO | NO |
| Illinois | MI | GA | NO | YES | NO | M/M/S/P |
| Indiana | MH | GA | 2 SD | YES | 18 | M/M/S |
| Iowa | MD | GV | 75 | YES | 21 | NO |
| Kansas | MR | LV | 2 SD | YES | NO | MR/SMD |
| Kentucky | MD | O | 2 SD | YES | 21 | M/FMD |
| Louisiana | MD | GA | 70 | YES | NO | M/M/S/P |
| Maine | MR | GA | NO | YES | NO | NO |
| Maryland | MR | GV | NO | YES | NO | NO |
| Massachusetts | II | O | NO | NO | NO | NO |
| Michigan | MI | O | 2 SD | YES | NO | EMR/TMR/S/P |
| Minnesota | MI | GA | 70 | YES | NO | M/M/S/P |
| Mississippi | ED | GA | 2 SD | YES | NO | EMR/TMR/S |
| Missouri | MR | GA | 2 SD | YES | 18 | M/M/S/P |
| Montana | CD | GA | NO | YES | 18 | NO |
| Nebraska | MH | GA | 2 SD | YES | NO | M/M/S/P |
| Nevada | MR | GA | NO | YES | 21 | M/M/S/P |
| New Hampshire | MR | GA | NO | YES | NO | NO |
| New Jersey | CI | LA | 2 SD | YES | NO | M/S CI |
| New Mexico | ID | GA | NO | YES | NO | NO |
| New York | MR | GA | 1.5 SD | YES | NO | NO |
| North Carolina | MD | GA | 70 | YES | NO | EMR/TMR |
| North Dakota | MR | GV | 70 | YES | NO | EMR/TMR |
| Ohio | DH | GV | 80 | YES | NO | DH |
| Oklahoma | MR | GA | 2 SD | YES | 18 | NO |
| Oregon | MR | GA | 2 SD | YES | NO | NO |
| Pennsylvania | MR | GA | 80 | YES | NO | NO |
| Rhode Island | MR | GA | 70 | YES | YES | M/M/S/P |
| South Carolina | MD | GV | 70 | YES | 18 | EMR/TMR |
| South Dakota | MR | GA | 70 | YES | 18 | NO |

| TABLE 7.2 | | *continued* | | | | |
|---|---|---|---|---|---|---|
| **State** | **Term**[1] | **Definition**[2] | **IQ Cut-off** | **Require Adaptive Behavior?** | **Age Ceiling** | **Classification System**[3] |
| Tennessee | MR | LA | 74 | YES | NO | NO |
| Texas | MR | GA | 2 SD | YES | NO | NO |
| Utah | ID | GA | NO | YES | NO | NO |
| Vermont | LI | GA | 70 | YES | NO | NO |
| Virginia | MR | GA | NO | YES | NO | EMR/TMR |
| Washington | MR | GA | 2 SD | YES | NO | NO |
| West Virginia | MI | LA | 70–75 | YES | 18 | M/M/S/P |
| Wisconsin | CD | GV | 70–75 | YES | NO | M/M/S/P |
| Wyoming | MD | GA | NO | YES | NO | NO |

1. CD=cognitively delayed/cognitive disability, CI=cognitive impairment, DH=developmentally handicapped, ED=educational disability, ID=intellectual disability, II=intellectual impairment, LI=learning impairments, MD=mental disability, MH=mentally handicapped, MI=mental impairment, MR=mental retardation, SLIC=significantly limited intellectual capacity.

2. GA=Grossman adapted, GV=Grossman verbatim, LA=Luckasson adapted, LV=Luckasson verbatim, O=other.

3. EMR=educable mentally retarded, M/FMD=mild and functional mental disability, M/M=mild/moderate, M/SCD=mild and severe cognitive disability, P=profound, S=severe, SMD=severe multiple disabilities, TMR=trainable mentally retarded.

From "An Evaluation of State Guidelines for Mental Retardation: Focus on Definition and Classification Practices," by C. Denning, J. Chamberlain, and E. A. Polloway, 2000, *Education and Training in Mental Retardation and Developmental Disabilities, 35,* 111–119.

uncommon to hear students referred to as EMR (educable mentally retarded) and TMR (trainable mentally retarded). The terms roughly correspond somewhat to the 1983 AAMR terms *mild* and *moderate/severe* retardation, respectively. However, by nature, these terms are inherently stereotypical and prejudicial, and consequently (and appropriately) have often been criticized, thus leading to decreased use, although some derivatives of this system continue to be reflected in state guidelines (see Table 7.2).

One alternative has been to classify mental retardation according to only two levels of functioning (i.e., mild and severe) and to avoid sole reliance on IQ scores in considerations of level of severity. Consideration of level of adaptive skills would thus be used as a yardstick for determining level of retardation, resulting in a more meaningful, broad-based system of classification.

Finally, an alternative is the classification system of Luckasson et al. (1992), which has particular merit for use in inclusive settings. According to this system, classification is not derived from levels of disability, or deficit, but rather from needed **levels of support.** Thus, this system would classify the *needs* rather than the *deficits* of the individual. Individuals would be designated as needing intermittent, limited, extensive, or pervasive levels of support as related to each of the adaptive skills areas

**LEVELS OF SUPPORT** is the terminology used by the AAMR to identify levels of services needed by various persons with mental retardation.

**CONSIDER THIS**
What are some advantages to using a classification system based on levels of support rather than levels of deficit?

*T*erms such as educable *and* trainable *have often been used to categorize students with mental retardation.*

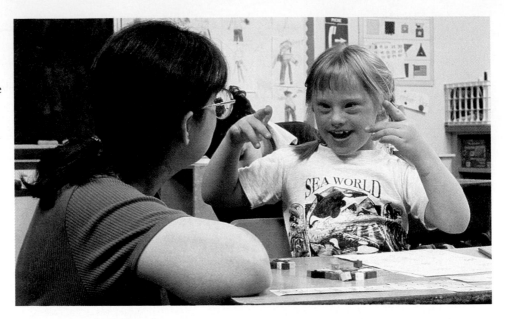

(see Table 7.1). Of course, in a given area, an individual may also not need any support to function successfully. These levels of support are defined as follows:

*Intermittent:* Supports on an "as needed" basis; episodic in nature. Short-term supports may be needed during lifespan transitions (e.g., job loss or an acute medical crisis).

*Limited:* Supports are consistent over time, are time-limited but not intermittent, and may require fewer staff and less cost than more intense levels of support (e.g., employment training or transitional supports during the school-to-adult period).

*Extensive:* Supports characterized by regular involvement (e.g., daily) in at least some environments (e.g., long-term support and long-term home living support).

*Pervasive:* Supports characterized by their constancy and high intensity; provided across environments; potentially life-sustaining in nature. Pervasive supports typically involve more staff and intrusiveness than extensive or limited supports. (Adapted from Luckasson et al., 1992, p. 26)

The supports classification system of the AAMR manual (Luckasson et al., 1992) was further explicated in a publication by Luckasson et al. (1996). Table 7.3 presents a grid showing different levels of intensity of supports to illustrate the way that this classification system can be put into practice.

To date, the Luckasson et al. (1992) classification has received general support in the field, particularly in the area of programs for adults with mental retardation but it has yet to make a significant impact on research and school practices. Polloway, Smith, Chamberlain, Denning, and Smith (1999) found that 99% of research papers published in three mental retardation journals (1993–1997), which relied on a system, continued to use the levels of deficit model from the Grossman (1983) manual rather than relying on the levels of support system. More importantly, in their review of state educational guidelines, Denning et al. (2000) reported that no states were currently using the levels of support model as their classification system. Most commonly used were a variety of deficit models based on either the AAMR system of mild/moderate/severe/profound or the traditional school-based system of educable/trainable (see Table 7.2).

| TABLE 7.3 | Levels of Supports × Intensity Grid | | | |
|---|---|---|---|---|
| | **Intermittent** | **Limited** | **Extensive** | **Pervasive** |
| **TIME:** Duration | As needed | Time limited, occasionally ongoing | Usually ongoing | Possibly lifelong |
| **TIME:** Frequency | Infrequent, low occurrence | Regular, anticipated, could be high frequency | | High rate, continuous, constant |
| **SETTINGS:** Living, Work, Recreation, Leisure, Health, Community, etc. | Few settings, typically one or two settings | Across several settings, typically not all settings | | All or nearly all settings |
| **RESOURCES:** Professional/ Technological Assistance | Occasional consultation or discussion, ordinary appointment schedule, occasional monitoring | Occasional contact or time limited but frequent regular contact | Regular, ongoing contact or monitoring by professionals typically at least weekly | Constant contact and monitoring by professionals |
| **INTRUSIVENESS** | Predominantly all natural supports, high degree of choice and autonomy | Mixture of natural and service-based supports, lesser degree of choice and autonomy | | Predominantly service-based supports, controlled by others |

From "The 1992 AAMR Definition and Preschool Children: Response from the Committee on Terminology and Classification," by R. Luckasson, R. Schalock, M. Snell, and D. Spitalnik, 1996, *Mental Retardation, 34,* p. 250.

## Prevalence, Causes, and Characteristics of Mental Retardation

As discussed previously, data based on the 20th report from the U.S. Department of Education for IDEA indicated that 0.96% of the estimated student population (ages 6–21) was identified as having mental retardation in school year 1996–1997 (U.S. Department of Education, 1998). This represents a significant change from the time when mental retardation was one of the two largest categories of disabilities and when mild retardation, in particular, was the most significant high-incidence disability related to learning problems in the schools. Currently, it is likely that of the approximately 1% of the school population that is identified with mental retardation, approximately 60% might be viewed as mildly retarded with the remainder having more severe disabilities.

This numerical "cure" (Reschly, 1988) reflects both the declassification of many students previously described as most "adaptive" in educable mentally retarded programs and the restrictiveness in eligibility procedures for subsequently referred children who

**CROSS-REFERENCE**
Review the causes of other disabilities (see Chapters 4–10) to determine the overlap of etiological factors.

might have been considered borderline cases (MacMillan, 1989; Mascari & Forgnone, 1982; Polloway, 1984). In general, research trends indicate that the majority of students declassified have not been relabeled learning disabled and are increasingly served in general education classrooms.

A key reason for the decrease in the reported incidence of mild mental retardation is the concern about the overrepresentation of minority children under this label. However, while effort has been made to prevent potential bias in the system (see MacMillan & Forness, 1998), the fact remains that African American students are 2.4 times more likely to be identified as having mild mental retardation than their non–African American peers (Oswald, Coutinho, Best, & Singh, 1999).

There are hundreds of known causes of retardation, and at the same time, numerous cases for which the cause is unknown. Table 7.4 outlines some representative causes to show the complexity of this area of concern. Mental retardation is associated with a number of challenges to learning. Table 7.5 identifies the most significant learning domains, lists representative problem areas, and notes certain instructional implications. In addition, the table focuses on related concerns for cognitive, language, and sociobehavioral development.

Recent research on learning in students with mental retardation has been limited. For example, Kavale and Forness (1999), reported that the majority of the studies in this area were more than 25 years old. Thus, while the population has changed over time, there has been rather limited attention to the study of these changes.

An important area of the study with direct implications for instruction is strategy training. Clearly it remains critical for teachers of students with mental retardation to focus not only on the content to be learned but also on the learning process itself so that students can lessen their learning deficits through systematic strategy training. Kavale and Forness (1999) underscore the importance of focusing on strategy training so that students learn effective ways to acquire, retain, and master relevant skills within the curriculum.

While the obvious focus in the field of mental retardation is on the cognitive characteristics of students with mental retardation, practitioners should not overlook the fact that socioemotional factors are also critical to successful functioning. For example, Masi, Mucci, and Favilla (1999) studied a group of adolescents with mild mental retardation and found depressed moods, psychomotor agitation, and loss of energy and interest as the more common problems experienced by these students.

## Identification, Assessment, Eligibility, and Placement

Procedures for the identification of mental retardation proceed directly from the specific AAMR scheme that is followed. For the 1992 manual, the diagnostic process, and hence the eligibility for services, is based on the model presented in Table 7.6.

The challenges of accurate identification, assessment, and eligibility criterion procedures have been faced by the field for many years. The nearby Personal Spotlight feature (on p. 212) provides a perspective on this process by offering a biographical sketch of an individual who was misdiagnosed as having severe mental retardation.

Students with mental retardation typically represent the category that is least likely to be included within general education classrooms. According to the U.S. Department of Education (1998), during the 1995–1996 school year, 12.7% of the students were served in regular classes and 27.5% in resource rooms, but 55.6% in separate, special education classes. An additional 4.2% were served in alternative settings. When these numbers are compared with other areas of exceptionality, it is apparent

| TABLE 7.4 | Selected Causes of Mental Retardation | |
| --- | --- | --- |
| **Cause** | **Nature of Problem** | **Considerations** |
| DOWN SYNDROME | Trisomy 21 (3 chromosomes on this pair) | IQ range from severe retardation to nonretarded<br>Wide variance in learning characteristics<br>Classic physical signs |
| ENVIRONMENTAL DISADVANTAGE | Elements of poverty environment | Can result in mild retardation<br>Commonly associated with school failure |
| FETAL ALCOHOL SYNDROME | Caused by drinking during pregnancy<br>Related to toxic effects of alcohol | Associated with varying degrees of disability<br>Often accompanied by facial and other malformations |
| FRAGILE X SYNDROME | Related to a "fragile site" on the X chromosome<br>Most often transmitted from mother to son | Associated with retardation in males and learning disabilities in females (in some instances)<br>May be accompanied by variant patterns of behavior, social skills, language |
| HYDROCEPHALUS | Multiple causes<br>Disruption in appropriate flow of cerebrospinal fluid on the brain | Previously associated with enlarged head and brain damage<br>Controlled by the implantation of a shunt |
| PHENYLKETONURIA | Autosomal recessive genetic disorder | Associated with metabolic problems in processing high protein foods<br>Can be controlled via restrictive diets |
| PRADER-WILLI SYNDROME | Chromosomal error of the autosomal type | Associated with biological compulsion to overeat<br>Obesity as a common secondary trait to retardation |
| TAY-SACHS DISEASE | Autosomal recessive genetic disorder | Highest risk for Ashkenazic Jewish persons<br>Associated with severe disabilities and early death<br>No known cure |

that students with other kinds of disabilities are more likely to be served in general education classrooms than are students with mental retardation.

When evaluating placement considerations for students with mental retardation (as well as with other disabilities) educators should realize that setting alone does not represent effective "treatment" for the students. As Kavale and Forness (1999) noted, too much of the current debate in special education has concerned placement to the exclusion of a careful analysis of what constitutes effective instructional practices. In fact, it is quite likely that "features of instruction are probably the major influence on outcomes, but these are not unique to setting. Setting is thus a macro variable; the real question becomes one of examining what happens in that setting" (p. 70).

**CONSIDER THIS**

Why do you think the prevalence of students identified as having mental retardation has declined over the past 25 years?

| TABLE 7.5 | Characteristics and Implications of Mental Retardation | |
|---|---|---|
| **Domain** | **Representative Problem Areas** | **Instructional Implications** |
| ATTENTION | Attention span (length of time on task) Focus (inhibition of distracting stimuli) Selective attention (discrimination of important stimulus characteristics) | Train students to be aware of the importance of attention. Teach students how to actively monitor their attention (i.e., self-monitoring). Highlight salient cues. |
| USE OF MEDIATIONAL STRATEGIES | Production of strategies to assist learning Organizing new information | Teach specific strategies (rehearsal, labeling, chunking). Involve student in active learning process (practice, apply, review). Stress meaningful content. |
| MEMORY | Short-term memory (i.e., over seconds, minutes)—common deficit area Long-term memory—usually more similar to that of persons who are nondisabled (once information has been learned) | Because strategy production is difficult, students need to be shown how to use specific strategies in order to proceed in an organized, well-planned manner. Stress meaningful content. |
| GENERALIZED LEARNING | Applying knowledge or skills to new tasks, problems, or situations Using previous experience to formulate rules that will help solve problems of a similar nature | Teach in multiple contexts. Reinforce generalization. Remind students to apply what they have learned. |
| MOTIVATIONAL CONSIDERATIONS | External locus of control Outerdirectedness Lack of encouragement to achieve Failure set (expectancy of failure) | Create environment focused on success opportunities. Emphasize self-reliance. Promote self-management strategies. Encourage problem-solving strategies (vs. only correct responses). |
| COGNITIVE DEVELOPMENT | Ability to engage in abstract thinking Symbolic thought, as exemplified by introspection and hypothesizing | Provide concrete examples in instruction. Encourage interaction between students and the environment, being responsive to their needs so that they may learn about themselves as they relate to the people and objects around them. |
| LANGUAGE DEVELOPMENT | Delayed acquisition of vocabulary and language rules Possible interaction with cultural variance and language dialects Speech disorders (more common than in general population) | Create environment that facilitates development and encourages verbal communication. Provide opportunities for students to interact with language. Provide opportunities for students to use language for a variety of purposes and with different audiences. Encourage student speech and active participation. |
| SOCIOBEHAVIORAL CONSIDERATIONS | Social adjustment Problems in "everyday intelligence" (Greenspan, 1996) Self-concept Social acceptance Classroom behavioral difficulties (e.g., disruptions) | Promote social competence through direct instruction in social skills. Reinforce appropriate behaviors. Seek an understanding of reasons for inappropriate behavior. Involve peers as classroom role models. Program for social acceptance. Use peers in reinforcing. |

| TABLE 7.6 | Diagnostic System for Mental Retardation |
|---|---|
| **Dimensions** | **Steps** |

| Dimensions | Steps |
|---|---|
| **DIMENSION I:**<br>Intellectual Functioning and Adaptive Skills | **STEP 1.  DIAGNOSIS OF MENTAL RETARDATION**<br>*Determines Eligibility for Supports*<br><br>Mental retardation is diagnosed if:<br><br>1. The individual's intellectual functioning is approximately 70 to 75 or below.<br>2. There are significant disabilities in two or more adaptive skill areas.<br>3. The age of onset is below 18. |
| **DIMENSION II:**<br>Psychological/Emotional Considerations<br><br>**DIMENSION III:**<br>Physical Health/Etiology Considerations<br><br>**DIMENSION IV:**<br>Environmental Considerations | **STEP 2.  CLASSIFICATION AND DESCRIPTION**<br>*Identifies Strengths and Weaknesses and the Need for Supports*<br><br>1. Describe the individual's strengths and weaknesses in reference to psychological/emotional considerations.<br>2. Describe the individual's overall physical health and indicate the condition's etiology.<br>3. Describe the individual's current environmental placement and the optimal environment that would facilitate his/her continued growth and development. |
| | **STEP 3.  PROFILE AND INTENSITIES OF NEEDED SUPPORTS**<br>*Identifies Needed Supports*<br><br>Identify the kind and intensities of supports needed for each of the four dimensions.<br><br>1. Dimension I:  Intellectual Functioning and Adaptive Skills<br>2. Dimension II:  Psychological/Emotional Considerations<br>3. Dimension III:  Physical Health/Etiology Considerations<br>4. Dimension IV:  Environmental Considerations |

From *Mental Retardation: Definition, Classification, and Systems of Supports* (p. 24), by R. Luckasson, D. L. Coulter, E. A. Polloway, S. Reiss, R. L. Schalock, M. E. Snell, D. M. Spitalnik, and J. A. Stark, 1992, Washington, DC: American Association on Mental Retardation. Used by permission.

## *TRANSITION CONSIDERATIONS*

Occupational success and community living skills are among the critical life adjustment variables that ensure successful transition into adulthood. The research on these variables does not inspire overconfidence regarding students with mild mental retardation. Two general and equally critical considerations are: (1) Through which means do students exit special education? and (2) What opportunities and supports are available to them during adulthood?

The U.S. Department of Education (1998) tracks exit data on all students who leave special education (with the most recent data available from the 1995–1996 school

**TEACHING TIP**
Students with mental retardation should be taught functional skills that will prepare them for success as adults.

## *personal* SPOTLIGHT

### Sibling

Max Lewis is a clinical psychologist. He has a 51-year-old sister, Judy, with mental retardation. Because Judy is older than Max, he only remembers her as having mental retardation; she was diagnosed in her first few years. Many professionals told Max's parents that Judy should be institutionalized. Despite these recommendations, Judy's parents kept her at home and struggled to obtain an appropriate education for her in public schools, but most public schools did not have programs for Judy. It was not until she was in the eighth grade that she actually went to a public school. Prior to this time, Judy attended segregated programs that focused on children with developmental disabilities.

**MAX LEWIS**
*Bellingham, Washington*

During the few years that Judy attended public schools, she was still very segregated from nondisabled children. "The students with disabilities were segregated to the point," notes Max, "that they were allowed to leave their classrooms only when the other students were not around." The students with disabilities were treated nearly like "untouchables." Max says that as an adolescent, his sister was somewhat of an embarrassment to him. He rarely told his friends that he had a sister with mental retardation for fear of their rejecting him.

Judy is now living with her parents, which is a concern for all the family. Max and his brother are both aware that when their parents die, Judy will be without a home. Although the family will provide whatever supports are necessary for Judy, they are concerned that she will have a very difficult time adjusting to any new living situation. Max believes that had there been other alternatives for Judy while she was growing up, this would not be a problem now. Had she been more involved with nondisabled students, she very likely would be more independent now.

Max believes that current practices in public schools for students with disabilities are significantly superior to the situation that existed when Judy was growing up. He states that "schools are so much better now simply because they are trying to deal with the problems of these children." Unfortunately for Judy, and for thousands of children who grew up before special education services were expanded, many opportunities for individual growth and development were simply not available.

year). For students with mental retardation, the data on special education exits are not encouraging. However, they do illustrate some interesting points. Removing from the total data those who move from a school division but are continuing in another location, the reasons for exit include the following: graduated with diploma (32.2%), graduated through certificate of completion (21.0%), "aged-out" of education (4.7%), died (0.75%), moved and were not known to continue their education (13.5%), and dropped out (22.4%). The key conclusion that can be drawn is that too few students with mental retardation complete the designated academic curriculum with either a diploma or a certificate and too many students either leave because of age or formally or less formally (i.e., moved, not known to continue) drop out of school.

In terms of postschool adjustment, Polloway, Patton, Smith, and Roderique (1992) posed the question: "What happens when students who are mildly retarded get older?" They considered in particular the data that Edgar (1987, 1988, 1990) and Affleck, Edgar, Levine, and Kortering (1990) reported, indicating that students who went through special education programs have not fared well. Less than one half were either working or involved in training programs. Although few dropped out of school, this additional time in school had not been productive in terms of employment outcomes (Edgar,

1987). Only 21% were living independently 30 months after completion of secondary school, a figure that compares poorly to data on individuals without disabilities. The transition period can be seen as a time of "floundering" (Edgar, 1988); it is clearly more so for students with mild retardation. Unfortunately, "productive adulthood" has been an elusive goal for these students (Edgar, 1990). The challenge of productive adulthood is clearly demonstrated in Table 7.7, which identifies adult domains and relates them to Knowles's (1984) traditional life problems areas.

In general, the vast majority of adults with mental retardation can make successful transitions and obtain and maintain gainful employment. A number of critical factors, however, influence their success. First, postschool adjustment hinges on their ability to demonstrate personal and social behaviors appropriate to the workplace. Second, the quality of the transition programming provided will predict subsequent success. Such programs recognize that programming must reflect a top-down perspective (i.e., from community considerations to school curriculum) that bases curriculum on the demands of the next environment in which the individual will live, work, socialize, and recreate.

| TABLE 7.7 | Demands of Adulthood | |
|---|---|---|
| **Adult Domains** | **Knowles' Domains** | **Examples** |
| VOCATION AND EDUCATION | Vocation and career | Being interviewed<br>Getting along at work<br>Changing jobs |
| HOME AND FAMILY | Home and family living | Dating<br>Family planning<br>Raising children<br>Solving marital problems<br>Financial planning |
| RECREATION AND LEISURE | Enjoyment of leisure | Choosing hobbies<br>Buying equipment<br>Planning recreational outings |
| COMMUNITY INVOLVEMENT | Community living | Using community resources<br>Voting<br>Getting assistance |
| EMOTIONAL AND PHYSICAL HEALTH | Health | Exercising<br>Treating medical emergencies<br>Understanding children's diseases |
| PERSONAL DEVELOPMENT | Personal development | Making decisions<br>Dealing with conflict<br>Establishing intimate relationships<br>Understanding oneself |

From "Curricular Considerations: A Life Skills Orientation," by J. R. Patton, M. E. Cronin, E. A. Polloway, D. Hutchinson, and G. A. Robinson (p. 27), in *Best Practices in Mild Mental Retardation,* edited by G. A. Robinson, J. R. Patton, E. A. Polloway, and L. Sargent, 1989, Reston, VA: CEC-MR. Used by permission.

# TECHNOLOGY TODAY

## Assistive Technology

Assistive technology can be low- or high-tech devices designed to remove barriers or provide practical solutions to common everyday problems. . . . [Such] devices can be applied in the classroom to assist a student with learning curriculum content or in a community setting to promote skill development and participation.

Assistive technology can include such complex devices as (1) an environmental control unit to allow an individual with little or no mobility to control his or her environment (e.g., turn on the lights), (2) a voice-activated computer to allow an individual with mobility or sensory impairments to input data on a computer and receive output information, (3) augmentative communication systems to allow an individual with poor speech to be able to communicate with others (e.g., electronic communication aids), and (4) microswitches to allow an individual to perform a more complex task by reducing the number of steps to complete it to one press on the switch or to allow someone with poor motor skills to access something by touching a very large switch pad as opposed to a small button or lever. In addition, switches can be activated by a number of means, such as sound, air, light, or movement, and are very versatile as to the functions they can perform.

Assistive technology can also include low-tech devices or modifications that can be very inexpensive and easy to apply, such as (1) a reach device to assist an individual with picking things off the floor or taking something off a high shelf, (2) a precoded push button phone to allow an individual with poor memory to complete a call to an important or frequently used number by lightly touching a large color-coded button, (3) audiotape instruction to allow an individual with cognitive or sensory impairments to have access to the instructions, directions, or classroom materials in a format that can be repeated as often as necessary to either learn or perform a task, and (4) a holder made out of wood with suction cups on the bottom that will keep a bowl or pan in place to allow an individual to mix ingredients using only one hand.

The range of high- and low-tech devices to assist with completing an activity or just to make the task easier is virtually endless. Many of these devices are commercially available while others can oftentimes be developed by any interested persons. The major ingredients for developing useful assistive technology devices are creativity, open-mindedness, and resourcefulness.

Adapted from "Severe Mental Retardation," by P. Wehman and W. Parent (pp. 170–171), in *Exceptional Individuals in School, Community, and Work,* edited by P. Wehman, 1997, Austin, TX: Pro-Ed. Used by permission.

---

The challenge for teachers seeking to successfully include students with mental retardation thus reaches beyond the students' acquisition of, for example, specific academic skills. Rather, it requires finding ways to provide a "belonging place" for them in the general education classroom. Such a place is created through friendships. Despite the broad support for inclusion—in fact, parents of students with mental retardation have, in general, been its primary proponents (see Arc, 1993)—inclusion does bring with it the potential loss of friendships present in traditional, self-contained classes. For example, Stainback, Stainback, East, and Sapon-Shevin (1994) note the concern of adolescents (and their parents) over finding dating partners in general education classes. Teachers should be sensitive to this consideration and promote an environment in which the benefits of friendships can be realized. The nearby Inclusion Strategies feature underscores the importance of this point.

A helpful strategy for promoting social acceptance for students (and young adults) with mental retardation involves "circles of support," or "circles of friends." The nearby Inclusion Strategies feature discusses an example of such a program.

## INCLUSION STRATEGIES

### Why Friends Are Important

Friendships are such an everyday thing, we just take them for granted. They are like electricity, telephone, clothing, and three meals a day—we languish only when we are deprived of them.

And yet we have just begun to sense the pain experienced by people with disabilities when they are deprived of mutually satisfying friendships with ordinary people. We suddenly see that family support, regular schooling, and community living programs are not enough. Those people need friends just as we do. Consider these facts:

▲ *Friendship is a familiar but elusive term.* Researchers reduce their focus to specific *relationships* or *social interactions,* classifying, counting, and analyzing them. But the rest of us need to view a good friendship the way we look at a sunrise, seeing it in all its radiance.

▲ *Friends help us stretch beyond our families.* In *Just Friends,* social scientist Lillian Rubin illustrates vividly that young people turn more to friends than to family when they seek to be affirmed as adults.

▲ *Friends help us move beyond human-service goals.* Friends provide us with myriad options that never could be programmed.

▲ *Friends help us rehearse adult roles.* You and I are the way we are largely because we rehearse our actions and attitudes with friends—things we wouldn't think of saying or doing with family or human-service workers.

▲ *Friends serve as fresh role models.* We often choose certain friends because we see something in them that we wish for ourselves.

▲ *Good friendships are a mystery.* There's no ritual or program for starting them. Sometimes they thrive and sometimes they fade.

▲ *Good friendships are attractive.* Others watch interactions between friends with great interest.

▲ *Friendships generate their own energy.* Quite often, when two people do things together, their zest and success equal much more than the sum of two people's efforts.

▲ *Friendships become a haven from stress.* When things get tough, many of us have good friends "on call."

▲ *Friendships are reciprocal.* Both parties receive enrichment from the relationship.

▲ *Friends can demystify strange behaviors.* While I visited two friends in a print shop in Rockville, Maryland, one friend—during a moment of boredom—began to move his arms and fingers in patterns professionals call "autistic." When I asked the other friend what he thought about such movements, he replied, "Hey man, if you think that's weird, you should come with me to my favorite tavern on Friday nights."

▲ *Every friendship is unique and unrepeatable.* Each relationship is as vivid as a fingerprint.

▲ *One can learn much from good friendships.* A good friendship can become a living document. With great interest, we can study the remarkable things friends do with each other. And it doesn't matter whether society has imaged us as a so-called normal or as a person with a disability, good friendships can inspire us to try refreshing new interpersonal activities in our own lives—things we've never done before.

Adapted from *Circles of Friends: People with Disabilities and Their Friends Enrich the Lives of One Another* (pp. 12–13), by R. Perske, 1988, Nashville, TN: Abingdon Press.

---

Another concern relates to policy issues and procedures related to inclusion. Polloway et al. (1996) pose questions valid for students with mild retardation and other students as well:

▲ Is inclusion achieved via teacher and parental involvement or solely via administrative decision?

▲ Is it selected because it is considered a less costly form of intervention or chosen for its value in spite of potentially being more costly?

▲ Are sufficient numbers of properly trained paraprofessionals available to assist special education teachers in providing supports within general education?

▲ Has training been provided to all staff regarding collaborative relationships?

▲ Has training been provided to general educators regarding meeting the needs of students with diverse abilities?

▲ Is there attention to appropriate adaptations in instructional practices?

**TEACHING TIP**
Curricular decisions for students with mental retardation should always be made with the student's future needs in mind.

## INCLUSION STRATEGIES

### Circle of Friends in Schools

Marsha Forest came away from her Joshua Committee experiences as if she had put on a better pair of glasses. Her position as a professor of special education suddenly seemed less important to her. She spent long hours on the road helping school boards, principals, and teachers to see how everybody can experience richness when someone with a disability is placed in a regular classroom and the so-called regular students are encouraged to form a circle of friends around that person.

Forest always believed in getting teaching down to meticulous detail when it came to educating persons with disabilities. Now, however, she saw that some of the most valuable educational steps can come *naturally* from regular classmates, if the right conditions exist in the classroom.

She also knew that parents and teachers fear peer group pressure. After all, when kids get together these days, they can give themselves quite an education—one that often shapes lives more powerfully than adults can shape them. But peer group education doesn't always lead to belligerence and destruction and drugs. It can lead to caring and nurturing and helping others do healthy things they had never done before.

This twist, however, generated fears in some teachers when it dawned on them that a circle of friends might foster better growth and development in a student than they were capable of teaching.

And so Marsha moved into regular schools and worked hard at

1. helping boards and principals understand the circles-of-friends process.
2. finding a teacher and class willing to include a person with a disability.
3. helping the regular teacher handle any initial fears about the venture.
4. letting the teacher and class call the shots as much as possible.
5. providing strong support persons who would assist only when they really were needed.
6. then finding a handful of kids willing to work at being friends with their classmate with the disability.

"The first placement in a school is the toughest," she said. "After that, it's usually easy to include others."

Forest sees building a circle of friends as a person-by-person process, not an all-encompassing program. So she focuses on students with disabilities one at a time, and sets up a framework that enables a circle to surround that person.

Because no two settings are alike, she watches as the circle, the regular teacher, and the rest of the students develop and coordinate their own routines for helping. Then, never predicting an outcome, she waits. And when new learning takes place in the person with the disability, Forest moves in and makes all the students, the teacher, the principal—even the board members—feel simply great.

According to her, the average school can handle up to twelve of these arrangements. After that, the efficiency of the process may diminish.

She doubts that circles of friends will work in every school. "If a school is all screwed up," she said, "and if it has lost its zest and commitment for really helping kids learn—forget it. On the other hand, I'm sure that circles of friends can help make a good school—and especially the kids—better. Then coming to school takes on fresh values and meaning. Some enjoy coming to school as they never did before."

Adapted from *Circles of Friends: People with Disabilities and Their Friends Enrich the Lives of One Another* (pp. 39–40), by R. Perske, 1988, Nashville, TN: Abingdon Press.

*Teachers need to promote an environment where social relationships can be developed.*

## FINAL THOUGHTS

As special and general education teachers jointly develop and implement educational programs for students with mental retardation, they should keep in mind that these students require a comprehensive, broad-based curriculum to meet their needs. The most effective programs will provide appropriate academic instruction, adapted to facilitate learning. However, the curriculum cannot solely be academic in orientation, but rather should focus on developing social skills and transition skills to facilitate the students' success in general education classrooms and subsequent integration into community settings.

In making curriculum choices, teachers will have to consider how responsive the general education classroom can be to the needs of students with mental retardation. The ultimate goal is not simply school inclusion but rather community or "life" inclusion; whichever curriculum achieves that purpose most effectively is the most appropriate one. As Cassidy and Stanton (1959) suggested over four decades ago, the key question in evaluating the effectiveness of programs is *effective for what?* What is it that the schools are to impart to the students? Affleck et al. (1990) argue that educators must design programs that provide the instructional intensity to meet skill needs while addressing the long-term needs of students. The challenge of inclusion for students with mental retardation is to ensure that the curriculum they pursue prepares them for their future. The nearby Rights and Responsibilities feature provides a Disabled Manifesto that outlines how individuals with mental retardation feel about their legal rights.

### A Disabled Manifesto

We proclaim that we are born free and equal human beings; that our disabilities are limitations only, and that our identity does not derive from being disabled.

We proclaim that we have the same value as people who are not disabled, and we reject any scheme of labeling or classifying us that encourages people to think of us as having diminished value.

We reject the idea that institutions must be created to "care" for us, and proclaim that these institutions have been used to "manage" us in ways that nondisabled people are not expected to accept. We particularly denounce institutions whose purpose is to punish us for being disabled, or to confine us for the convenience of others.

We reject the notion that we need "experts," to tell us how to live, especially experts from the able-bodied world. We are not diagnoses in need of a cure or cases to be closed. We are human, with human dreams and ambitions.

We deny that images of disability are appropriate metaphors for incompetence, stupidity, ugliness or weakness.

We are aware that as people with disabilities, we have been considered objects of charity and we have been considered commodities. We are neither. We reject charitable enterprises that exploit our lifestyle to titillate others, and which purpose to establish the rules by which we must live without our participation. We also reject businesses that use us as "warm bodies" to provide a passive market for their services, again laying down rules by which we must live for their profit. We recognize that the lines between charities and businesses are blurred in the disability industry, and we do not accept services from either if their essential function is to exploit us.

We assert our rights of self-determination in the face of barriers, and we pledge not to allow any authority or institution to deprive us of our freedom of choice.

Finally, we assert that any service we need, from specialized teaching to personal care, can be provided to us in the community among our nondisabled peers. Segregated institutions are not necessary to serve us, and they have been the greatest source of our oppression, especially when they have been run by able-bodied people without our participation.

All human beings are more alike than we are different. We recognize that when we assert this belief we will find ourselves in conflict with regressive institutions and their supporters, some of whom may be disabled themselves. We do not expect thousands of years of stereotyping to dissipate quickly. We commit ourselves and those who come after us to challenge our oppression on every level until we are allowed to be fully human and assert our individuality ahead of our disability.

By John R. Woodward, M.S.W.
Center for Independent Living of
North Florida, Inc.
[content public domain]

This document may be distributed freely in electronic format. URL: http://www.dimenet.com/cgibin/ilrulib/getlink?ilrulib/ilruilhistory,6

(For further information contact: Access Center for Independent Living, Inc.; 35 S. Jefferson Street, Dayton, OH 45402; 937-341-5202.)

## Summary

### Basic Concepts about Mental Retardation

▲ The concept of mental retardation has variant meanings to professionals and the public.

▲ The three central dimensions of the definition are lower intellectual functioning, deficits or limitations in adaptive skills, and an onset prior to age 18.

▲ The 1992 AAMR definition retains the three dimensions, but also stresses the importance of four assumptions: cultural and linguistic diversity, an environmental context for adaptive skills, the strengths of individuals as well as their limitations, and the promise of improvement over time.

▲ Common practice in the field has been to speak of two general levels of mental retardation, mild and severe, but emerging efforts in classification stress levels of needed supports rather than levels of disability.

- The prevalence of mental retardation in schools decreased dramatically throughout the 1980s and early 1990s but has now stabilized at approximately 1%.

## Transition Considerations

- Social competence is a critical component of instructional programs for students with mental retardation. Teaching social skills can have a positive effect on successful inclusion both in school and in the community.
- Educational programs must be outcome-oriented and attend to transitional concerns so that students receive the appropriate training to prepare them for subsequent environments. The curriculum should thus have a top-down orientation.

## Strategies for Curriculum and Instruction

- Teachers should teach not only content but also mediation strategies that facilitate learning. Examples include rehearsal, classification, and visual imagery.
- Attention difficulties can be addressed by modifying instruction to highlight relevant stimuli and by training students to monitor their own attention.

- Memory problems respond to mediation strategies (see previous point) and to an emphasis on content that is meaningful and relevant.
- Cognitive development for students with mental retardation can be enhanced by emphasizing active interaction with the environment and the provision of concrete learning experiences.

## Classroom Accommodations

- Many students with a history of failure have an external locus of control, which can be enhanced by an emphasis on success experiences and by reinforcement for independent work.
- To enhance language development, teachers should provide a facilitative environment, structure opportunities for communication, and encourage verbal language.

## Enhancing Inclusive Accommodations

- Opportunities for inclusion are essential and should focus on social benefits such as friendship while not neglecting critical, functional curricular needs.

# Further Readings

Luckasson, R., Coulter, D., Polloway, E. A., Reiss, S., Schalock, R., Snell, M., Spitalnik, D., & Stark, J. (1992). *Mental retardation: Definition, classification and systems of supports.* Washington, DC: American Association on Mental Retardation.

Patton, J. R., Polloway, E. A., Smith, T. E. C., Edgar, E., Clark, G. M., & Lee, S. (1996). Individuals with mild mental retardation: Post-secondary outcomes and implications for educational policy. *Education and Training in Mental Retardation and Development Disabilities, 31,* 77–85.

Polloway, E. A., Smith, T. E. C., Patton, J. R., & Smith, J. D. (1996). Historical perspectives in mental retar-

dation. *Education and Training in Mental Retardation and Developmental Disabilities, 31,* 3–12.

Sargent, L. R. (1991). *Social skills for school and community.* Reston, VA: CEC-MR.

Smith, T. E. C., & Dowdy, C. A. (1992). Future-based assessment for persons with mental retardation. *Education and Training in Mental Retardation and Developmental Disabilities, 27,* 255–260.

Smith, T. E. C., & Puccini, I. K. (1996). Secondary programming issues. *Education and Training in Mental Retardation and Developmental Disabilities, 35,* 320–327.

# 8 Teaching Students with Sensory Impairments

*After reading this chapter, you should be able to:*

◢ explain the nature of low-incidence disabilities

◢ define hearing impairment and visual impairment

◢ describe educationally relevant characteristics of students with hearing impairments and visual impairments

◢ describe accommodations and modifications for students with hearing impairments and visual impairments

It was only the end of September, but Ana was already beginning to fall behind most of her peers in the second grade. Although she was promoted at the end of the first grade, she did not acquire most of the skills necessary for success in the second grade.

For the first half of the first grade, Ana had tried very hard. She wanted to learn to read like her classmates, but seemed always to miss out on sounding letters and words correctly. According to her teacher, Ms. Pryor, Ana also appeared to daydream a lot. The teacher frequently had to go to Ana's desk to get her attention when giving directions and assignments. By the middle of the first grade, Ana seemed to be giving up. Her efforts always seemed to end in failure. Her spelling was poor, and her reading skills were not improving. She began having behavior problems, which Ms. Pryor attributed to the influence of her older brother, who was always getting into trouble. Ana's parents were interested but did not have any answers. They said that Ana was in her own world at home and often did not respond to what was happening around her. In addition to Ana's poor academic skills and behavior problems, she also had difficulties with her peers. She was not very popular, and some of the other students made fun of her poor articulation of certain words.

Ms. James, Ana's new second-grade teacher, decided to refer Ana for vision and hearing screening. Ana had been absent from school when the routine screening was done in the first grade, and there was no record of Ana's having had a screening in kindergarten. Sure enough, Ana was found to have a hearing loss in both ears. Although the loss was not significant enough to warrant specialized placement, it did suggest that a hearing aid might be useful.

Thanks to the awareness of Ms. James, Ana's hearing loss was detected before she experienced more failure. Unfortunately, she had missed much of what she should have learned during the first grade and kindergarten, probably because of the hearing impairment.

## QUESTIONS TO CONSIDER

1. Should schools routinely screen kindergarten and first-grade students for hearing and vision problems? Why or why not?
2. What can Ana's second-grade teacher do to help her overcome the problems created by the late identification of her hearing impairment?

Although there remains some debate regarding the best setting in which to provide services to students with **sensory impairments,** many students with these conditions are placed in general education settings. Most are capable of handling the academic and social demands of these settings. However, for these students to receive an appropriate education, a variety of accommodations may be needed, ranging from minor seating adjustments to the use of sophisticated equipment for communicating, listening, or navigating. Students with these impairments may also need the support of additional personnel (e.g., an *interpreter* or *braille instructor*).

To provide appropriate accommodations, teachers must have accurate information about how to modify their classrooms and adapt instruction to meet student needs. In addition, they need to understand the psychosocial aspects of these types of disabilities. Ultimately, teachers must feel comfortable and confident that they can address the range of needs these students present.

Sensory impairments are considered *low-incidence disabilities*, since there are not large numbers of these students in the school population. The number of students (ages 6 to 21) with hearing or visual impairments who were officially identified and provided with special education or related services nationally for the school year 1996–1997 is reported in Figure 8.1. These are small numbers, considering the total number of students in this age range. Furthermore, these groups represent a very small percentage of all students who are disabled.

However, having only one of these students in a classroom may seem overwhelming, as he or she may require a variety of modifications in the way a classroom is managed and how certain instructional practices are implemented. Students who have both vision and hearing losses present significant challenges for educators; *deaf-blindness* is covered in Chapter 9.

**FIGURE 8.1**

Students of Ages 6 through 21 Served under IDEA and Chapter 1 in 1996–1997*

*Note: For comparative purposes, 2.6 million students with learning disabilities and 594,000 students with mental retardation were served during the same period.

From *20th Annual Report to Congress on the Implementation of IDEA* (p. 11), by U.S. Department of Education, 1998, Washington, DC: Author.

**Students by Disability Area**

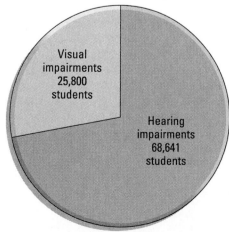

Visual impairments 25,800 students

Hearing impairments 68,641 students

## BASIC CONCEPTS ABOUT HEARING IMPAIRMENT

**H**earing impairment is a hidden disability—an observer typically cannot tell from looking at physical features alone that a person's hearing is impaired. However, in any context where communicative skills are needed, hearing limitations become evident.

Students with a hearing disability pose a variety of challenges to the general classroom teacher. Although their numbers are increasing, relatively few students with profound hearing loss (deafness) are educated in general education settings (Brackett, 1997). When these students are placed in general education classes, they need major accommodations (e.g., an interpreter).

The number of students who have some degree of hearing loss (i.e., mild to severe) is more noteworthy, because these students can function in general education settings more easily when certain accommodations are provided. For this to happen, it is critical for teachers to understand the nature of hearing impairments and to know how to address the needs associated with these conditions.

The importance of language acquisition and usage to the development of cognitive abilities and achievement in academic subject areas is unassailable (Polloway & Smith, 2000). While the greatest effect of a hearing impairment is on a students' ability to hear someone speak, "its impact on communication development dramatically alters social and academic skill acquisition" (Brackett, 1997, p. 355).

The following sections provide basic information on hearing impairments. Teachers who build a solid working knowledge in this area can teach more effectively and communicate more clearly with other professionals and with families.

*HEARING IMPAIRMENTS* affect an individual's ability to perceive and/or distinguish among sounds. *Deaf* or *hard of hearing* are two terms that are often used to describe individuals with this disability.

### Hearing Impairment Defined

A number of different terms are associated with hearing loss, which often causes confusion. Three terms frequently encountered in print and in professional conversation are *hearing impairment, deafness,* and *hard of hearing.*

▲ *Hearing impairment* is the generic term used to describe any level of hearing loss, ranging from mild to profound.
▲ *Deafness* describes a hearing loss that is so profound, the auditory channel (the ear) cannot function as the primary mode for perceiving and monitoring speech or acquiring language.
▲ *Hard of hearing* describes individuals who have a hearing loss, but are able to use the auditory channel as their primary mode for perceiving and monitoring speech or acquiring language. (Diefendorf, 1996)

*CONSIDER THIS*
Do some of the terms used in this chapter—for example, hearing impairment—convey a clear understanding of a particular hearing disability? Which terms in the text are the most descriptive and useful to teachers?

Some school systems do use other terminology, such as *auditorily impaired,* to describe hearing loss.

Hearing loss is often measured in decibel (dB) loss. Individuals with losses from 25 to 90 dB are considered hard of hearing, whereas those with losses greater than 90 dB are classified as deaf.

### Classification of Hearing Impairment

Hearing loss can be categorized in several different ways. Diefendorf (1996) organized hearing loss into four different groups: conductive hearing loss (mild loss in both ears),

| TABLE 8.1 | Symptoms Associated with Conductive Hearing Loss; Unilateral Hearing Loss; Mild, Bilateral Sensorineural Hearing Loss; and Moderate-to-Severe Bilateral Sensorineural Hearing Loss |

| | Audiological | Communicative | Educational |
|---|---|---|---|
| **CONDUCTIVE HEARING LOSS** | ■ Hearing loss 30 dB (range 10–50 dB)<br>■ Poor auditory reception<br>■ Degraded and inconsistent speech signal<br>■ Difficulty understanding under adverse listening conditions<br>■ Impaired speech discrimination<br>■ HL overlays developmental requirement for greater stimulus intensity before infants can respond to and discriminate between speech<br>■ Inability to organize auditory information consistently | ■ Difficulty forming linguistic categories (plurals, tense)<br>■ Difficulty in differentiating word boundaries, phoneme boundaries<br>■ Receptive language delay<br>■ Expressive language delay<br>■ Cognitive delay | ■ Lower achievement test scores<br>■ Lower verbal IQ<br>■ Poorer reading and spelling performance<br>■ Higher frequency of enrollment in special support classes in school<br>■ Lower measures of social maturity |
| **UNILATERAL HEARING LOSS** | ■ Hearing loss moderate to profound<br>■ Impaired auditory localization<br>■ Difficulty understanding speech in presence of competing noise<br>■ Loss of binaural advantage: binaural summation, binaural release from masking | ■ Tasks involving language concepts may be depressed | ■ Lags in academic achievement: reading, spelling, arithmetic<br>■ Verbally based learning difficulties<br>■ High rate of grade repetition<br>■ Self-described: embarrassment, annoyance, confusion, helplessness<br>■ Less independence in the classroom |
| **MILD BILATERAL SENSORINEURAL HEARING LOSS** | ■ Hearing loss 15–20 dB<br>■ Speech recognition depressed<br>■ Auditory discrimination depressed<br>■ Amplification considered: FM systems, classroom amplification | ■ Potential problems in articulation<br>■ Problems in auditory attention<br>■ Problems in auditory memory<br>■ Problems in auditory comprehension<br>■ Possible delays in expressive oral language<br>■ Impact on syntax and semantics | ■ Impact on vocabulary development<br>■ Lowered academic achievement: arithmetic problem solving, math concepts, vocabulary, reading comprehension<br>■ Educational delays progress systematically with age |
| **MODERATE-TO-SEVERE BILATERAL SENSORINEURAL HEARING LOSS** | ■ Hearing loss 41 dB–90 dB<br>■ Noise and reverberation significantly affect listening and understanding<br>■ Audiologic management: essentials, amplification recommendations, monitor hearing for:<br>–otitis media<br>–sudden changes in hearing<br>–progressive hearing loss | ■ Deficits in speech perception<br>■ Deficits in speech production (mild-to-moderate articulation problems)<br>■ Language deficits from slight to significant: syntax, morphology, semantics, pragmatics<br>■ Vocabulary deficits | ■ Slight to significant deficits in literacy (reading and writing)<br>■ Deficits in academic achievement<br>■ High rate of academic failure<br>■ Immaturity<br>■ Feelings of isolation and exclusion<br>■ Special education supports needed |

From "Hearing Loss and Its Effect" (p. 5), by A. O. Diefendorf, in *Hearing Care for Children,* edited by F. N. Martin and J. G. Clark, 1996, Boston: Allyn and Bacon. Used by permission.

unilateral hearing loss (loss only in one ear), mild bilateral sensorineural hearing loss (caused by sound not being transmitted to the brain), and moderate-to-severe bilateral sensorineural hearing loss (more severe loss in both ears). Table 8.1 summarizes the audiological, communicational, and educational implications for each type of loss. Each specific type and degree of loss poses challenges in learning and communicating.

**CONSIDER THIS**
Is it important for teachers to know the type of hearing loss experienced by a student? Why or why not?

## Prevalence and Causes of Hearing Impairment

As noted in Figure 8.1, more than 68,000 students are served in special education programs for students with hearing impairments. This represents only about 0.11% of the total school population. While the number of children with hearing impairments significant enough to be eligible for special education is small, the Centers for Disease Control and Prevention (CDC) have estimated that as many as 15% of all children experience some degree of hearing loss (Crawford, 1998).

Many different factors can lead to hearing impairments. These include genetic causes (Arnos, Israel, Devlin, & Wilson, 1996); developmental anomalies (Clark & Jaindl, 1996); and toxic reaction to drugs, infections, trauma, premature birth, anoxia (lack of oxygen for a period of time), birth trauma (Chase, Hall, & Werkhaven, 1996), and allergies (Lang, 1998). Knowing the specific cause of a hearing impairment is usually not important for school personnel, since the cause rarely affects interventions needed by students.

## Characteristics of Students with Hearing Impairment

The characteristics of students with hearing impairment vary greatly. Four categories of characteristics are especially meaningful to the classroom setting: (1) psychological, (2) communicational, (3) academic, and (4) social–emotional. Specific characteristics that fall into each of these general categories are listed in Table 8.2. (Table 8.1 listed characteristics associated with types and degrees of hearing losses.)

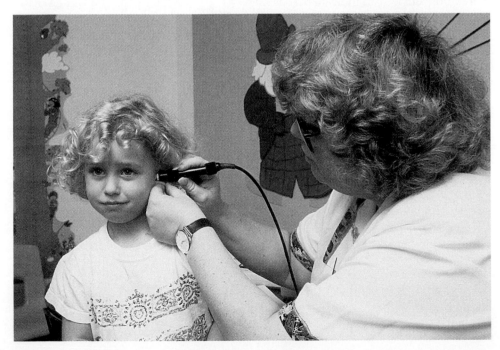

*Some children may require an audiological evaluation to determine the nature of their hearing loss.*

| TABLE 8.2 | Possible Characteristics of Students with Hearing Impairments |
|---|---|
| **Area of Functioning** | **Possible Effects** |
| PSYCHOLOGICAL | ■ Intellectual ability range similar to hearing peers<br>■ Problems with certain conceptualizations |
| COMMUNICATIONAL | ■ Poor speech production (e.g., unintelligibility)<br>■ Tested vocabulary limited<br>■ Problems with language usage and comprehension, particularly abstract topics<br>■ Voice quality problems |
| SOCIAL–EMOTIONAL | ■ Less socially mature<br>■ Difficulty making friends<br>■ Withdrawn behavior—feelings of being an outsider<br>■ Possible maladjustment problems<br>■ May resent having to wear a hearing aid or use other amplification devices<br>■ May be dependent on teacher assistance |
| ACADEMIC | ■ Achievement levels significantly below those of their hearing peers<br>■ Reading ability most significantly affected<br>■ Spelling problems<br>■ Limited written language production<br>■ Discrepancy between capabilities and performance in many academic areas |

## Identification, Assessment, and Eligibility

The ease of identifying students with hearing impairment is related to the degree of hearing loss. Students with severe losses are more easily recognized, while those with mild losses may go unrecognized for many years. In fact, the prevalence of hearing loss among children is higher than cited in previous reports because of delayed identification, which often results in serious consequences for children. As noted previously, data indicate that as many as 15% of children in the United States have low- or high-frequency hearing loss that is often too mild to easily identify (Herer & Reilly, 1999). Teachers should be aware of certain indicators of possible hearing loss and refer students who show these signs for a comprehensive assessment (Kuster, 1993). Teachers should consider referring a student for a comprehensive audiological evaluation if any of these behaviors are present:

*TEACHING TIP*
Teachers should keep records of students who display these types of behaviors to determine whether there is a pattern that might call for a referral.

◢ Turns head to position an ear in the direction of the the speaker
◢ Asks for information to be repeated frequently
◢ Uses a loud voice when speaking
◢ Does not respond when spoken to
◢ Gives incorrect answers to questions
◢ Has frequent colds, earaches, or infections
◢ Appears inattentive and daydreams
◢ Has difficulty following directions
◢ Is distracted easily by visual or auditory stimuli
◢ Misarticulates certain speech sounds or omits certain consonant sounds
◢ Withdraws from classroom activities that involve listening
◢ Has a confused expression on face
◢ Has a restricted vocabulary

A teacher's careful observations and referral can spare a student months or years of struggle and frustration.

**FORMAL ASSESSMENT**   The assessment of hearing ability requires the use of various audiological techniques. The most common method of evaluating hearing is the use of **pure-tone audiometry,** in which sounds of different frequencies are presented at increasing levels of intensity. Bone conduction hearing (related to the outer and middle ear) can also be assessed to determine if there are problems in the sensorineural portion of the hearing mechanism (occurring in the inner ear). The role of pediatric audiology has grown significantly in the past years. With new technology, audiologists are going to be more involved in assessment (Herer & Reilly, 1999).

*PURE-TONE AUDIO-METRY* is a method of evaluating hearing loss by examining how sounds are heard at different frequencies.

**INFORMAL ASSESSMENT**   In addition to the formal assessment conducted by audiologists, teachers and other school personnel should engage in informal assessment of students, especially those suspected of having a hearing impairment. Informal assessment focuses on observing students for signs that might indicate a hearing loss. Tables 8.1 and 8.2 list indicators that, if recorded over a period of time, show that a student may need formal assessment.

**ELIGIBILITY**   The eligibility of students for special education and related services is determined by individual state departments of education. Most states follow the federal guidelines for eligibility, which are based on certain levels of decibel loss. Teachers should not be concerned about specific eligibility criteria, but should refer students who display characteristics suggesting the presence of a hearing loss.

## STRATEGIES FOR CURRICULUM AND INSTRUCTION

Students with hearing impairment may present a significant challenge for general education teachers. Language is such an important component of instruction that students who have problems processing language because of hearing losses make it difficult for teachers to use standard instructional methods effectively. Teachers have to rely on the supports provided by special education staff and specialists in hearing impairments to assist them in meeting the needs of these students.

*CONSIDER THIS*
How do educational needs differ for these two students: one with a mild hearing loss who can effectively use a hearing aid and one who is not disabled?

### Realities of the General Education Classroom

Students with hearing impairments vary greatly in their need for supports in the general education classroom. Students with mild losses, generally classified as hard of hearing, need minimal supports. In fact, these students resemble their nondisabled peers in most ways. If amplification assistance can enable these students to hear clearly, they will need little specialized instruction (Dagenais, Critz-Crosby, Fletcher, & McCutcheon, 1994).

Students with severe hearing impairments, those classified as deaf, present unique challenges to teachers. Specialized instructional techniques usually involve alternative communication methods; the use of interpreters is typically a necessity for these students. Consider the following when using an interpreter:

**GENERAL GUIDELINES**
◢ Include the interpreter as a member of the IEP team to help determine the communication needs of the student.
◢ Request an interpreter (i.e., do not let parents interpret for their children) for certain important situations (e.g., transition planning meetings).

◢ Supervise the interpreter if this person is involved with additional classroom tasks.

◢ Meet with the interpreter regularly to discuss the needs of the student and to review ongoing communication patterns.

◢ Evaluate the effectiveness of interpreters.

**SPECIFIC SUGGESTIONS**

◢ Allow the interpreter to be positioned so that the student can easily see both the teacher (or media) and the interpreter.

◢ Prepare the interpreter for the topic(s) that will be covered and the class format that will be followed.

◢ Provide copies of all visual materials (e.g., overhead transparencies) before class begins.

◢ Be sensitive to the "time-lag" factor associated with interpreting—the few-word delay that the interpreter lags behind the spoken message.

◢ Program breaks in lecturing if at all possible.

◢ Limit movement so that the student can see the interpreter and teacher without difficulty.

◢ Check student understanding regularly—ensure that the student does not fake understanding.

**CONTINUUM-OF-PLACEMENT OPTIONS** Students with hearing impairments are educated in the complete continuum-of-placement options, depending on their individual needs. These range from general education classrooms to residential schools for the deaf. "The topic of educational placement has generated more controversy in the education of children who are hard of hearing and deaf than any issue in the curriculum" (Edwards, 1996, p. 403). No single educational setting is best for all students with hearing impairments. Like students with other disabilities, a student with hearing impairments will be placed according to decisions made during the IEP process (Edwards, 1996).

Still, the trend continues toward educating more students with hearing impairments in the general education classroom. During the 1995–1996 school year, 55% of all students with hearing impairments were educated, for at least part of each school day, in general education classrooms (U.S. Department of Education, 1998). This compares with approximately 44% served in the same types of settings during the 1986–1987 school year (U.S. Department of Education, 1989). The trend, therefore, favors inclusion, which in turn signals a need for supports and services to help students succeed. Figure 8.2 describes the types of supports that students with hearing impairments will need in inclusive settings. They resemble those needed by students with other disabilities, except for a few services specific to students with hearing problems.

*CONSIDER THIS*
What are some obvious advantages and disadvantages to the different placement options for students with hearing impairments?

# CLASSROOM ACCOMMODATIONS FOR STUDENTS WITH HEARING IMPAIRMENTS

**A**s mentioned before, the general education setting is appropriate for most students who are hard of hearing and for many students who are deaf. However, this statement is true only if the specific needs of these students are taken into consideration.

**■ FIGURE 8.2**    Types of Supports for Students with Hearing Impairments in Inclusive Settings

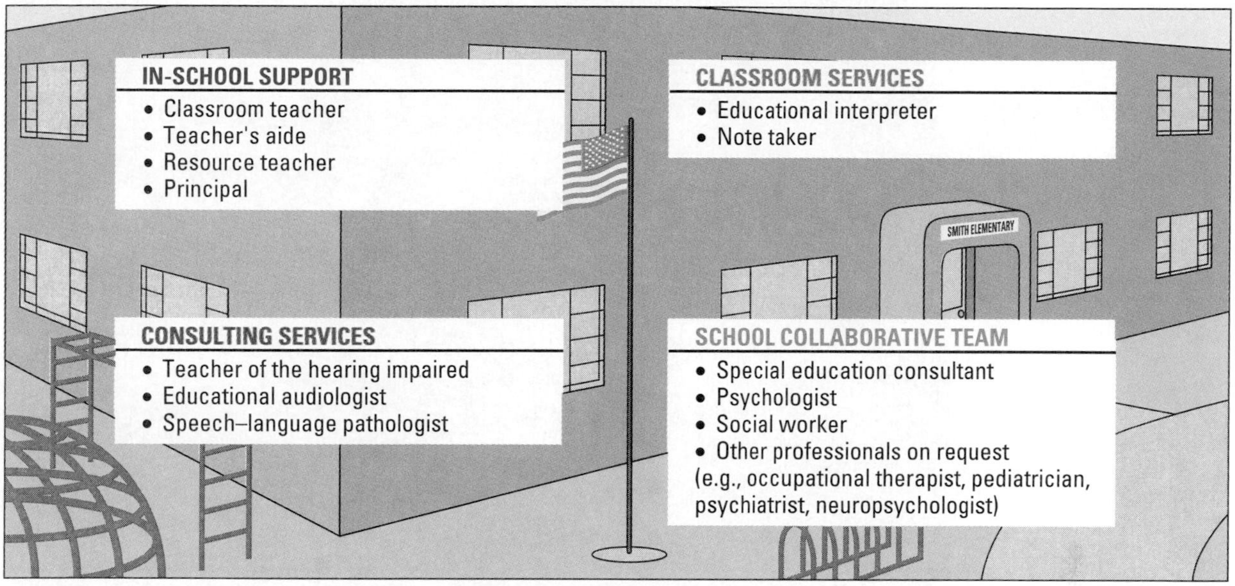

**IN-SCHOOL SUPPORT**
- Classroom teacher
- Teacher's aide
- Resource teacher
- Principal

**CLASSROOM SERVICES**
- Educational interpreter
- Note taker

**CONSULTING SERVICES**
- Teacher of the hearing impaired
- Educational audiologist
- Speech–language pathologist

**SCHOOL COLLABORATIVE TEAM**
- Special education consultant
- Psychologist
- Social worker
- Other professionals on request (e.g., occupational therapist, pediatrician, psychiatrist, neuropsychologist)

From "Educational Management of Children with Hearing Loss" (p. 306), by C. Edwards, in *Hearing Care for Children,* edited by F. N. Martin and J. G. Clark, 1996, Boston: Allyn and Bacon. Used by permission.

The following sections provide recommendations for accommodating these students in general education classrooms. Specific suggestions are also given. Both general recommendations and specific suggestions are clustered under three major areas: management considerations, curricular and instructional accommodations, and social–emotional interventions.

## Management Considerations

The effective management of a classroom is critical to maximizing the potential for learning. This important topic is covered in detail in Chapter 13. Attention to classroom management can help include students with various degrees of hearing impairment in general education settings.

**STANDARD OPERATING PROCEDURES**  This dimension refers to the rules, regulations, and procedures that operate in a classroom. Students who have hearing impairments must be subject to the same requirements as other students. Some procedures may have to be modified to accommodate special needs. For instance, students may be allowed to leave their seats to get the attention of a student who cannot hear a spoken communication.

Teachers should always confirm that students understand the rules and procedures developed for the classroom. Teachers may also want to establish a buddy system (i.e., a peer support system). With such a system, a student with normal hearing is assigned to assist the student with a hearing impairment in, for example, following procedures for a fire drill or helping the student take notes during a class lecture.

**PHYSICAL CONSIDERATIONS**  Seating is the major consideration related to the physical setup of the classroom. Teachers need to ensure that students are seated to maximize

***CROSS-REFERENCE***
Preview the section in Chapter 13 on rules and procedures appropriate for all students with disabilities and for students without disabilities.

*S*tudents with hearing impairments should be seated near the front of the class.

the use of their residual hearing or to have an unobstructed view of an interpreter. Since information presented visually is extremely helpful to these students, they need to be positioned to take advantage of all visual cues (Berry, 1995). Following are some specific suggestions:

**CONSIDER THIS**
How can teachers use seating as an effective accommodation even when there is a great deal going on in different parts of the room?

◢ Seat students near the teacher or source of orally presented information.
◢ Seat students so they can take advantage of their residual hearing, avoid being distracted either visually or auditorily, and follow different speakers during class discussions.
◢ Seat students who use interpreters so that they can easily see the interpreter, the teacher, and any visual aids that are used.

Unfortunately, seating a student with a hearing loss near the front of the class is rarely the only modification that needs to be made. As opposed to how teachers taught in the past, today very little may happen at the front of the room (Crawford, 1998).

**CREATING A FAVORABLE ENVIRONMENT FOR STUDENTS**    As noted in the preceding section, more than preferential seating is necessary for students with a hearing loss. Attention must be given to creating a supportive acoustical environment throughout the classroom. Modifications that can be made to provide an accommodating acoustical environment include the following (Scott, 1997):

◢ acoustical ceiling tiles
◢ carpeting
◢ thick curtains
◢ rubber tips on chair and table legs
◢ proper maintenance of ventilation systems, lighting, doors, and windows

**PREINSTRUCTIONAL CONSIDERATIONS**　Teachers must also carefully plan ahead to deliver instruction in a way that will benefit students with hearing impairments. The following list gives many practical suggestions:

◢ Allow students to move about the classroom to position themselves for participation in ongoing events.

◢ Let students use swivel chairs.

◢ Reduce distracting and competing noise by modifying the classroom environment (e.g., carpeting on floor, corkboard on walls).

◢ Ensure that adequate lighting is available.

◢ Provide visual reminders indicating the amount of time left for an activity or until the end of class.

◢ Use cooperative learning arrangements to facilitate student involvement with hearing peers.

◢ Include a section of the lesson plan for special provisions for students with hearing impairments.

◢ Acquire or develop visually oriented materials to augment orally presented topics—use overhead projection systems when appropriate.

◢ Use homework assignment books and make sure that students understand their assignments.

Specific suggestions related to grouping, lesson planning, materials acquisition and adaptation, and homework systems can be found in Chapter 14.

## Curricular and Instructional Considerations

All basic elements of effective instructional practice will benefit students with hearing impairment. However, certain specific ideas will enhance their learning experiences.

**COMMUNICATION**　Perhaps the most challenging aspect of teaching students whose hearing is impaired is making sure that (1) they participate in communicational activities (i.e., teacher to student, student to teacher, student to student) that are occurring in the classroom and (2) they are able to handle the reading and writing demands of the class.

Students who have profound hearing loss must rely on alternative methods of communication such as sign language or speech reading. Because these students typically do not become facile with standard forms of English, they can have significant problems in the areas of reading and writing. Sign language does not follow the grammatical conventions of English. (See the nearby Rights and Responsibilities feature.)

When students using some form of manual communication, usually **American Sign Language (ASL),** are in general education classrooms, teachers are not required to learn this language. However, teachers should make an effort to know some of the more common signs and to be able to finger-spell the letters of the alphabet as well as the numbers one to ten. If students can communicate only by using sign language, an interpreter will most likely need to be present. Teachers should know basic information about the role and functions of an interpreter.

Still another form of communication that may be effective is **cued speech.** Cued speech is a system of hand cues that enhances lipreading. Eight different handshapes represent consonant sounds and four hand positions represent vowel sounds. By using the hand signs near the lips, students have cues that help with their lipreading (Blasi & Priestley, 1998).

*AMERICAN SIGN LANGUAGE* is a particular form of sign language used by many individuals with severe hearing impairments.

*CUED SPEECH* uses both signs and lipreading for communication purposes.

## RIGHTS & RESPONSIBILITIES

### Legal Requirements for Sign Language Interpreters

Several court cases have ruled on the requirement for schools to provide sign language interpreters for students with hearing impairments. While sign language interpreters may be required as a related service for students with hearing impairments in cases where these services are legitimate related services, there are instances when the services do not have to be provided. The following summarizes two of these cases:

*Cefalu v. East Baton Rouge School Bd., 117F.3d 231 (5th Cir.1997).* In this case, the U.S. District Court for the Middle District of Louisiana ruled in favor of the parents who had requested that the local school provide a sign language interpreter for their 14-year-old son who was attending a parochial school. On appeal, the appeals court determined that because the district had offered interpreter services at the public school, it did not have to provide such services at the private school.

*Fowler v. Unif. School Dist. No. 259, Sedgwick County, Kansas, 128F.3d 1431 (10th Cir.1997).* In this case, the parents of a student with profound hearing loss moved him from a public school, where he was receiving interpreter services, to a private school. The parents then requested the interpreter services be provided at the private school site. The federal appeals court ruled that the state would not be required to pay for the interpreter services as long as the public school offered an appropriate education at its location.

From *Special Education Law Update,* 1998, Rosemount, MN: Data Research Inc. Used by permission.

Teachers should be conscious of how well they are communicating with their students. The teacher's speech, location, and movement in the classroom can affect the facility with which a student with a hearing impairment can follow a discussion or lecture. The proper use of assistive equipment (e.g., amplification devices) can also make a difference. This topic is covered in a subsequent section.

**DELIVERY OF INSTRUCTION**    Teachers need to utilize a host of practices that allow students to learn more effectively and efficiently. One suggestion already mentioned, the use of visually oriented material, is especially valuable for students with hearing problems. The following are additional suggestions:

- Make sure students are attending.
- Provide short, clear instructions.
- Speak clearly and normally—do not exaggerate the pronunciation of words.
- Keep your face visible to students.
- Avoid frequent movement around the classroom, turning your back on students while talking, and standing in front of a bright light source.
- Use gestures and facial expressions.
- If the student reads speech, make sure that your mustache and beard are trimmed to maximize visibility.
- Maintain eye contact with the student, not the interpreter.
- Check with students to confirm that they are understanding what is being discussed or presented.
- Encourage students to request clarification and to ask questions.
- Identify other speakers by name so that students can more easily follow a discussion among more than one speaker.
- Repeat the comments of other students who speak.
- Paraphrase or summarize discussions at the end of a class session.
- Write information when necessary.
- Have students take responsibility for making themselves understood.
- Provide students with advance organizers such as outlines of lectures and copies of overhead transparencies.

- Preview new vocabulary and concepts prior to their presentation during a lecture.
- Use the demonstration-guided practice–independent practice paradigm as often as possible (see Polloway & Patton, 1993, for a comprehensive discussion of this paradigm).
- Utilize a variety of instructional formats, including demonstrations, experiments, and other visually oriented activities.
- Emphasize the main points covered in a lecture both verbally and visually.
- Use lots of visual aids (e.g., overhead transparencies, slides, diagrams, charts, multimedia) to explain material.
- Provide summaries, outlines, or scripts of videotapes, videodiscs, or films.
- Let students use microcomputers for word processing and for checking their spelling and grammar.

Teaching secondary-level content classes to students with hearing impairments is uniquely challenging. The nearby Inclusion Strategies feature provides suggestions for teaching science to students who are deaf. Co-teaching has been shown to be one effective method for teaching students with hearing losses in general education classes. Using this model encourages general classroom teachers and teachers of students with hearing losses to combine their skills in an inclusive setting. "Coteaching allows teachers to respond to the diverse needs of all students, provides another set of hands and eyes, lowers the teacher-student ratio, and expands the amount of professional expertise that can be directed to student needs" (Luckner, 1999, p. 150).

## Social–Emotional Considerations

Classrooms constitute complex social systems. In addition to development of scholastic abilities and academic support skills, personal development is also occurring.

---

## INCLUSION STRATEGIES

### Teaching Science to Deaf Students

The following are several suggestions on how to give better individual attention in teaching science to deaf students:

1. Individualize assignments so that students progress at their own rate and at the end of the period, hand in what they have accomplished. This may be a laboratory or written assignment.

2. Extend special recognition to a student who goes beyond minimum acceptance level for doing and formulating laboratory investigation.

3. Use multiple resources, including texts, in class. If a slow student has difficulty reading one text, endeavor to find another or attempt to help him or her learn the material in ways other than through books.

4. Offer special activities for the academically talented. Let them assist you in preparing solutions and materials for laboratory work. They should be involved in experiences that are educationally desirable and not just prepared for a future working at a menial job.

5. Encourage students to do research. They should consult with a scientist or engineer in the community on their research problem. Local industries, museums, zoos, botanical gardens, and hospitals have resource people who will often help.

6. Have students from the upper grades go to some of the lower grades and demonstrate a scientific principle or explain a science project. This approach has the advantage of giving recognition to the younger students and motivating them to greater achievement.

7. Encourage parents to obtain books and to take trips advantageous to science students. Parents often welcome a suggestion from the teacher about books and type of trips to help enrich their children's science education.

# *T*ECHNOLOGY *T*ODAY

## ALDs at a Glance

Assistive devices, whether used as stand-alone systems or in conjunction with hearing aids, amplify voices and sounds, communicate messages visually, or alert users to environmental sounds. Subcategories within the major classifications address a variety of hearing needs in different situations.

The ability of a device to perform in a specific setting can be determined by studying the specifications of the individual product in conjunction with a patient's case history.

In general, dispensers interested in expanding their scope of practice to include assistive technology, or those who want to broaden their involvement in this area, can use the following overview as a guide to the kinds of technology available in the field.

### AMPLIFICATION

In some settings, hearing aids alone are less effective than ALDs in discerning voices in the presence of background noise or picking up speech clearly from a distance. Large-area amplification systems as well as portable personal devices improve the signal-to-noise ratio at the listener's ear, making it easier for users to hear and understand speech, whether watching television at home or listening to a lecture in a public auditorium.

Amplification devices can be further divided into hard-wired or wireless systems.

▲ In hard-wire devices, the user is connected to the sound source by a wire and, consequently, limited in movement by the length of the cord connected to an earphone headset, hearing aid, or

*Assistive learning devices can greatly facilitate the inclusion of students with hearing impairments in general education classrooms.*

neck loop. Hard-wired systems are more appropriate for television watching and small-group business or social settings than for listening in large public areas.

---

Students need to learn how to get along with their peers and authority figures while they learn how to deal with their beliefs and emotions. Teachers should help students develop a realistic sense of their abilities, become more responsible and independent, interact appropriately with their peers, and enhance their self-concept and sense of belonging (Luckner, 1994). The following are some specific suggestions:

▲ Create a positive, supportive, and nurturing classroom environment.

▲ Encourage class involvement through active participation in classroom activities and interaction in small groups.

▲ Let students know that you are available if they are experiencing problems and need to talk.

▲ Help the students with normal hearing understand the nature of hearing impairment and what they can do to assist.

▲ Practice appropriate interactive skills.

▲ Encourage and assist students to get involved in extracurricular activities.

Wireless systems, in which sound is transmitted from the source to the listener's ear by means of electromagnetic energy, invisible light waves, or on radio bands, are more practical in large public areas, like theaters and lecture halls. Typically, users access the system from a telecoil circuit built into their hearing aids or from a receiver attached to a headset.

(1) An induction loop wireless system transmits sound in the form of electromagnetic energy. A loop of wire that encircles a room receives the signal from an amplifier connected to a lecturer's microphone or, in small settings, to a tape recorder or television.

(2) An infrared wireless system transmits sound via light waves. A photo detector diode picks up infrared light and changes the information into sound, which users hear with a hearing aid, telecoil feature, or earphones.

(3) In an FM wireless system, sound is transmitted and received via radio waves.

## COMMUNICATIONS

Assistive technology facilitates communication by telephone for deaf and hard-of-hearing people. Cost and the degree of hearing loss determine appropriateness of products, which are available in a number of forms. Consult manufacturers for advantages and limitations of individual products.

*Amplified replacement handsets* are available for most telephone models, for use at home and at work.

*In-line telephone amplifiers* splice an existing handset and telephone base to a device that amplifies a voice. Portable, strap-on amplifiers can be attached directly to the handset.

*TDD (telecommunications devices for the deaf)*, also known as *TTs (text telephones)*, supply a visual medium for communication. A TDD user types a message that is translated into electrical pulses and sent over a telephone line to the receiving TDD or to an intercept operator. Some TDDs can be used in conjunction with personal computers.

*Decoders* provide closed captioning subtitles for television and VCR viewing.

## ALERTING

Alerting devices signal users to sound by means of visual, auditory, or vibrotactile stimuli. In general, alerting devices detect sound (e.g., a telephone, doorbell, or smoke alarm) and either amplify the sound or convert it to another signal, such as a flashing light, to make the person aware of the sound.

*Visual* alerting devices connected to lamps flash different patterns to differentiate among sounds. One pattern can be programmed to signal that the telephone is ringing, while another indicates the doorbell.

*Auditory* alerting devices amplify the sound or convert it to a lower pitch, which is more easily audible than high-frequency sound.

*Vibrotactile* devices respond to sound with a gentle shaking motion. The ringing of an alarm clock or smoke detector, for instance, makes the mattress vibrate. Body-worn vibrotactile devices are available also.

From "ALDs at a Glance," 1996, *The Hearing Journal, 49,* p. 21. Used by permission.

---

Help them develop problem-solving abilities.

Help students develop realistic expectations.

Prepare students for dealing with the demands of life and adulthood.

## Technology

Students with hearing impairments placed in general education classrooms often use devices to help them to maximize their communicational abilities (Easterbrooks, 1999), and they need a supportive environment in which to use these devices (McAnally, Rose, & Quigley, 1999). Teachers need a working knowledge of these devices so that they can ensure that the student benefits from the equipment.

**ASSISTIVE LISTENING DEVICES** *Assistive listening devices (ALDs)* include hearing aids and other devices that amplify voices and sounds, communicate messages visually, or alert users to environmental sounds (Bloom, 1996). Children with even small losses, those

*TEACHING TIP*
When students in your classroom use assistive listening devices, learn as much about the devices as possible so that you will be able to maximize their use.

in the 16dB to 25dB range, may have problems hearing faint or distant speech without some amplification (Iskowitz, 1998). Hearing aids are the predominant ALDs found in schools. These devices pick up sound with a microphone, amplify and filter it, and then convey that sound into the ear canal through a loudspeaker, also called a receiver (Shimon, 1992, p. 96). They work very well with students who experience mild-to-severe hearing losses (Iskowitz, 1997). The preceding Technology Today feature (on pp. 240–241) describes hearing aids and other ALDs that can be used in school programs.

To assist students in maximizing the use of their ALDs, teachers should

◢ know what type of ALD a student uses.
◢ understand how the device works: on/off switch, battery function (e.g., selection, lifespan, insertion), volume controls.
◢ be able to determine whether a hearing aid is working properly.
◢ help students keep their hearing aids functioning properly (e.g., daily cleaning, appropriate storage).
◢ make sure students avoid getting their hearing aids wet, dropping or jarring them, spraying hairspray on them, and exposing them to extreme heat (Shimon, 1992).
◢ keep spare batteries on hand.
◢ ensure that the system is functioning properly.
◢ be sure that students turn the transmitter off when not engaged in instructional activities to prevent battery loss.
◢ perform daily troubleshooting of all components of the system (Brackett, 1990).
◢ make sure background noises are minimized.

Table 8.3 includes a list of media, materials, and technology available for students with hearing losses.

This information should provide teachers with a beginning understanding of how to meet the needs of students with hearing loss. We strongly recommend that teachers consult with a hearing specialist to determine the best possible accommodations to provide an appropriate educational environment for students with hearing problems.

| **TABLE 8.3** | **Media, Materials, and Technology for Students with Hearing Losses** |
|---|---|
| **VISUAL TECHNOLOGY, MEDIA, AND MATERIALS** | ■ Microcomputers and computer systems such as ENFI<br>■ Captioning systems<br>■ Computer-assisted notetaking<br>■ Videotapes and interactive video discs<br>■ Instructional CDs and software<br>■ Telecommunication technology<br>■ Printed materials, programs, and packages |
| **AUDITORY TECHNOLOGY, MEDIA, AND MATERIALS** | ■ Induction loops<br>■ FM systems<br>■ Programmable hearing aids<br>■ Soundfield amplification systems<br>■ Cochlear implants<br>■ Instructional CDs, interactive listening developmental program, and software<br>■ Audiocassette programs<br>■ Computer-based speech training systems |

From Bruce, Peyton, & Batson (1993); Kaplan, Mahshie, Moseley, Singer, & Winston (1993).

# PROMOTING A SENSE OF COMMUNITY AND SOCIAL ACCEPTANCE FOR STUDENTS WITH HEARING IMPAIRMENTS

**B**eing an integral part of the inclusive school community is important for students with hearing impairments who receive their educational programs in public schools, especially for those placed in general education classrooms. Simply physically situating students in classrooms does not automatically result in their being an included member of the class. Therefore, teachers must ensure that these students become part of the community of the school and class and are socially accepted by their peers.

Teachers may have to orchestrate opportunities for interaction between students with hearing impairments and their nondisabled peers. This could include grouping, pairing students for specific tasks, assigning buddies, and establishing a circle of friends. Kluwin (1996) suggests using dialogue journals to facilitate this interaction. Students are paired (one hearing and one nonhearing) to make journal entries and then exchange them. Rather than assign deadlines, allow students to exchange journal entries whenever they want to. You may need to give them ideas appropriate for sharing to get them started. Reward students for making and exchanging journal entries. This approach encourages interactions between students with hearing impairments and their nondisabled peers without using a rigidly structured activity or assignment.

**CONSIDER THIS**
Do you think that students with hearing impairments can be included and accepted in the classroom by their peers in spite of their differing language skills? Should students with hearing impairments be isolated in institutions with other students who have hearing losses? Why or why not?

## Supports for the General Education Teacher

Students with hearing impairments often create major challenges for general classroom teachers, primarily because of the language barrier that hearing loss often creates. Therefore, teachers must rely on support personnel such as educational consultants who specialize in the area of hearing impairment, as well as interpreters, audiologists, and medical personnel to assist them in their efforts to provide appropriate educational programs.

# BASIC CONCEPTS ABOUT VISUAL IMPAIRMENTS

**S**tudents with visual impairments also pose unique challenges to teachers in general education classrooms. Although the number of students whose vision creates learning-related problems is not large (see Figure 8.1), having one such student in a classroom may require a host of accommodations.

Vision plays a critical role in the development of concepts, the understanding of spatial relations, and the use of printed material. Thus children with visual problems have unique educational needs. "Learning the necessary compensatory skills and adaptive techniques—such as using braille or *optical devices* for written communication—requires specialized instruction from teachers and parents who have expertise in addressing disability-specific needs" (Corn, Hatlen, Huebner, Ryan, & Siller, 1995, p. 1). Teachers may be able to use their usual instructional techniques with some modifications with students who have some functional vision. But for students who have very little or no vision, teachers will need to implement alternative techniques to provide effective educational programs.

**TEACHING TIP**
Try using an idea from a children's game to work with children with visual impairments. Just as you would ask a blindfolded child what information he or she needs to make progress in the game, ask the children with visual impairments what assistance or information they need in order to benefit from your teaching.

General education classes are appropriate settings for many students with visual impairments. However, teachers working with these students need to understand the nature of a particular student's vision problem to be able to choose appropriate accommodative tactics. They need basic information related to four categories: (1) fundamental concepts of vision and visual impairment, (2) signs of possible visual problems, (3) typical characteristics of students with visual problems, and (4) specific accommodative techniques for meeting student needs.

## Visual Impairments Defined

Because a number of different terms are associated with this concept, confusion regarding the exact meaning of visual terminology is often a problem. These are the most frequently used terms and their definitions:

**CONSIDER THIS**
Some students who are classified as blind are actually able to read print and do not need to use braille. Are there descriptors other than *blind* and *low vision* that would better describe students with visual impairments for educational purposes?

◢ *Visual impairment* is a generic term that includes a wide range of visual problems.
◢ *Blindness* has different meanings depending upon context, resulting in some confusion. *Legal blindness* refers to a person's visual acuity and field of vision. It is defined as a visual acuity of 20/200 or less in the person's better eye after correction, or a field of vision of 20° or less. An educational definition of *blindness* implies that a student must use braille (a system of raised dots that the student reads tactilely) or aural methods in order to receive instruction (Heward, 2000).
◢ *Low vision* indicates that some functional vision exists to be used for gaining information through written means with or without the assistance of optical, nonoptical, or electronic devices (Kirk, Gallagher, & Anastasiow, 2000).

Students with low vision are capable of handling the demands of most classroom settings. However, they will need some modifications to perform successfully. Students who are blind (i.e., have very little or no vision) will need major accommodations to be successful in general education settings.

## Classification of Visual Impairments

Visual problems can be categorized in a number of ways. One typical method organizes visual problems as refractive errors (e.g., farsightedness, nearsightedness, and astigmatism); retinal disorders; disorders of the cornea, iris, and lens; and optic nerve problems. In addition to common refractive problems, which usually can be improved with corrective lenses, other visual problems include the following:

◢ *Strabismus*—improper alignment of the eyes
◢ *Nystagmus*—rapid involuntary movements of the eye
◢ *Glaucoma*—fluid pressure buildup in the eye
◢ *Cataract*—cloudy film over the lens of the eye
◢ *Diabetic retinopathy*—changes in the blood vessels of the eye caused by diabetes
◢ *Macular degeneration*—damage to the central portion of the retina, causing central vision loss
◢ *Retinitis pigmentosa*—genetic eye disease leading to total blindness (Smith & Luckasson, 1998)

*Tunnel vision* denotes a condition caused by deterioration of parts of the retina, which leaves the person with central vision only. Individuals who have tunnel vision can see as if they are looking through a long tube; they have little or no peripheral vision.

Regardless of the cause of the visual problem, educators primarily have to deal with its functional result. Whether or not the student has usable residual vision is an important issue, as is the time at which the vision problem developed. Students who are born with significant visual loss have a much more difficult time understanding some concepts and developing basic skills than students who lose their vision after they have established certain concepts (Warren, 1994).

## Prevalence and Causes of Visual Impairments

Vision problems are common in our society. Fortunately, corrective lenses allow most individuals to see very efficiently. However, many individuals have vision problems that cannot be corrected in this way. Like persons with hearing impairments, the number of individuals who have visual impairments increases with age as a result of the aging process. In the school-age population, approximately 0.1% of students are classified as visually impaired. During the 1996–1997 school year, 25,800 students, ages 6–21, were classified as having visual impairments in the United States (U.S. Department of Education, 1998).

Etiological factors associated with visual impairments include genetic causes, physical trauma, infections, premature birth, anoxia, and retinal degeneration. *Retrolental fibroplasia (RLF)* was a common cause of blindness in the early 1950s, resulting when premature infants were exposed to too much oxygen in incubators. Once the cause of this problem was understood, it became nearly nonexistent. However, this cause of blindness is reasserting itself as medical science faces the challenge of providing care to infants born more and more prematurely. Blindness sometimes accompanies very premature birth.

*CONSIDER THIS*
How does the low incidence of visual impairments affect a school's ability to provide appropriate services? How can small systems meet the needs of these children when there may be only one child with a visual impairment in their district?

## Characteristics of Students with Visual Impairments

The most educationally relevant characteristic of students who have visual impairments is the extent of their visual efficiency. More specific characteristics can be categorized as psychological, communicational, academic, and social–emotional. These characteristics are listed in Table 8.4.

| TABLE 8.4 | Possible Characteristics of Students with Visual Impairments |
|---|---|
| **Area of Functioning** | **Possible Effects** |
| PSYCHOLOGICAL | ■ Intellectual abilities similar to those of sighted peers<br>■ Concept development can depend on tactile experiences (i.e., synthetic and analytic touch)<br>■ Unable to use sight to assist in the development of integrated concepts<br>■ Unable to use visual imagery |
| COMMUNICATIONAL | ■ Relatively unimpaired in language abilities |
| SOCIAL/EMOTIONAL/<br>BEHAVIORAL | ■ May display repetitive, stereotyped movements (e.g., rocking or rubbing eyes)<br>■ Socially immature<br>■ Withdrawn<br>■ Dependent<br>■ Unable to use nonverbal cues |
| MOBILITY | ■ Distinct disadvantage in using spatial information<br>■ Visual imagery and memory problems with functional implications |
| ACADEMIC | ■ Generally behind sighted peers |

## Identification, Assessment, and Eligibility

Students with visual impairments can be easily identified if their visual loss is severe. However, many students have milder losses that are much more difficult to identify and may go several years without being recognized. Teachers must be aware of behaviors that could indicate a vision problem. Table 8.5 summarizes possible symptoms of vision problems.

**FORMAL ASSESSMENT**   Students are screened for vision problems in schools, and when problems are suspected, a more in-depth evaluation is conducted. The typical eye examination assesses two dimensions: visual acuity and field of vision. Visual acuity is most often evaluated by the use of a **Snellen chart.** As Smith and Luckasson (1995) note, two versions of this chart are available: the traditional version using alphabetic letters of different sizes, and the other version using the letter *E* presented in different spatial arrangements and sizes. Regardless of the assessment used, the person conducting it should have expertise in the area of visual impairment (Corn et al., 1995).

Once students are identified as having possible vision problems, they should be referred for more extensive evaluations. Ophthalmologists, medical doctors, and optometrists (who specialize in evaluating vision and prescribing glasses) are typically involved in this more extensive evaluation. These specialists determine the specific nature and extent of any vision problem.

**INFORMAL ASSESSMENT**   A great deal of informal assessment should be completed by school personnel. Like that of students with hearing impairments, the informal assessment of students with visual impairments focuses on observation. Teachers and other school personnel note behaviors that might indicate a vision loss or change

*SNELLEN CHART* is the letter chart used to check eyesight, in which individuals have to read letters of declining size.

*TEACHING TIP*
For students who are not doing well academically and who display symptoms of visual impairment, conduct a functional visual screening to determine whether the child should be referred for more formal screening.

| TABLE 8.5 | Symptoms of Possible Vision Problems |
|---|---|
| BEHAVIOR | ■ Rubs eyes excessively<br>■ Shuts or covers one eye, tilts head, or thrusts head forward<br>■ Has difficulty in reading or in other work requiring close use of the eyes<br>■ Blinks more than usual or is irritable when doing close work<br>■ Holds books close to eyes<br>■ Is unable to see distant things clearly<br>■ Squints eyelids together or frowns |
| APPEARANCE | ■ Crossed eyes<br>■ Red-rimmed, encrusted, or swollen eyelids<br>■ Inflamed or watery eyes<br>■ Recurring styes |
| COMPLAINTS | ■ Eyes that itch, burn, or feel scratchy<br>■ Cannot see well<br>■ Dizziness, headaches, or nausea following close eye work<br>■ Blurred or double vision |

From *Exceptional Learners: Introduction to Special Education* (7th ed.) (p. 358), by D. P. Hallahan and J. M. Kauffman, 1997, Boston: Allyn & Bacon. Used by permission.

in the vision of the child. Once students are identified as having a problem, school personnel must be alert to any changes in the student's visual abilities.

**ELIGIBILITY**    Most states adhere to the eligibility guidelines established in IDEA for students with visual impairments. These guidelines focus on the visual acuity of students. Students with a 20/200 acuity or worse, in the better eye with best correction, are eligible as blind students, whereas those with a visual acuity of 20/70 to 20/200 are eligible as low-vision students. Like all other students with disabilities served under IDEA, these students must evidence need of special education services in order to be eligible for them.

## STRATEGIES FOR CURRICULUM AND INSTRUCTION

Students with visual impairments need specific curricular and instructional modifications. For students with low vision, these modifications may simply mean enlarging printed materials to sufficient size so that the student can see them. For students with little or no vision, modifications must be more extensive.

### Realities of the General Education Classroom

Students with visual impairments present a range of needs. Those who are capable of reading print, with modifications, often require minimal curricular changes; those who must read using braille require significant changes. Teachers should remember that even students who are capable of reading print may need modifications in many day-to-day activities. These may be as simple as ensuring appropriate contrast in printed materials and having students sit in a place that will optimize their vision.

### Continuum-of-Placement Options

Like students with hearing impairments, students with visual problems may be placed anywhere on the full continuum-of-placement options, ranging from general education classrooms to residential schools for students with visual impairments. *The National Agenda for the Education of Children and Youth with Visual Impairments, Including Those with Multiple Disabilities,* calls for all schools to offer programs that will give all students a full array of placement options (Corn et al., 1995). Students must be evaluated individually to determine the appropriate educational placement. Although some totally blind students function very well in general education settings, many are placed in residential schools where they receive more extensive services. (See the nearby Personal Spotlight.)

**CONSIDER THIS**
What are some typical reasons a teacher might give for not wanting children with visual impairments in his/her general classroom? Can these reasons be overcome or not?

## CLASSROOM ACCOMMODATIONS FOR STUDENTS WITH VISUAL IMPAIRMENTS

Certain classroom accommodations will enhance the quality of programs for students with visual problems. This section recommends ways to address the needs of these students, organized according to four categories: general considerations, management considerations, curricular and instructional accommodations, and social–emotional interventions.

## *personal* SPOTLIGHT

### Mother

Gloria Jordan is the mother of Michelle, who was diagnosed at birth with congenital blindness caused by Peter's anomaly. Michelle is now 15 years old and in the 10th grade. She has never attended a school specifically for students with visual problems

**GLORIA JORDAN**
*Pine Bluff, Arkansas*

or any other disability. Although there have been many challenges along the way, Michelle is currently included in most of her classes.

Gloria says that there are some very good things about Michelle's inclusion. First of all, notes Gloria, Michelle is learning about the real world. Since life after public school will include a variety of different people, some with disabilities but most without, Gloria thinks it is important for Michelle to experience this "sighted" world throughout her life. Gloria also notes that some of

Michelle's teachers have said that "she is an encouragement to me and other students. By seeing her work hard to achieve, despite her disability, other students are actually motivated." Gloria sees another benefit of inclusion as being her ability to interact with nondisabled peers, especially in social settings like lunch period.

Although Gloria strongly supports inclusion, she notes that there are some drawbacks to the model. For one thing, she says that it is often hard to get some teachers to understand just how difficult it is to do some academic work without vision. "Some teachers simply do not understand; they think that Michelle is using her blindness as an excuse." Gloria notes that for some subjects, such as algebra and chemistry, it is very difficult for Michelle to understand because of the symbols, graphs, and other materials that do not translate well verbally.

Gloria believes that Michelle is much better adjusted because she has been included in public schools. There are some teachers, she says, who obviously wish they did not have to deal with a student who is blind, but there are many other teachers who are extremely supportive and willing to do whatever it takes to make the class a successful opportunity for Michelle.

## General Considerations

When educating students with visual impairments, the unique needs of each student must be considered (Desrochers, 1999). However, some general practices apply for most, if not all, students with these problems. These practices include the following:

- ▲ Ask the student if assistance is needed.
- ▲ Do not assume that certain tasks and activities cannot be accomplished without accommodations or modifications.
- ▲ Include students with visual impairments in all activities that occur in the class.
- ▲ Use seating arrangements to take advantage of any vision the child can use.
- ▲ Encourage the use of residual vision.
- ▲ Remember that many characteristics of students with visual impairment (e.g., intelligence, health) may not be negatively affected by the vision problem.

## Management Considerations

A variety of classroom management tactics can be helpful to students who have vision problems. Classroom management is discussed in detail in Chapter 13. When students with vision problems are present, attention needs to be given to standard operating procedures, physical considerations, and preinstructional considerations.

**STANDARD OPERATING PROCEDURES**   The same standards of expected behavior should be applied to all students, including those who have visual problems. However, students with visual limitations may need special freedom to move around the classroom, to find the place where they can best see demonstrations or participate in activities.

**PHYSICAL CONSIDERATIONS**   Students with visual problems need to know the physical layout of the classroom so that they can navigate through it without harming themselves. This requires orienting them to the classroom. This can be accomplished by taking students around the classroom and noting certain features, such as the location of desks, tables, and materials. Use a clock orientation approach, such as the front of the class is 12 o'clock, at 3 o'clock is the teacher's desk, at 6 o'clock is the reading table, and at 9 o'clock is the area for students' coats and backpacks. Appropriate seating is extremely important for students who are able to use their existing vision. Placement of the student's desk, lighting, glare, and distractions should be considered when situating such students in the classroom.

**PREINSTRUCTIONAL CONSIDERATIONS**   Teachers should plan ahead to adapt instruction to the needs of students with visual impairments. Class schedules must allow extra time for students who use large-print or braille materials, as it takes longer to use these materials.

Test-taking procedures may need to be modified. This might involve preparing an enlarged version of the test, allowing extra time, or arranging for someone to read the test to the student.

Some students may need special instruction in study skills such as note taking, organizational skills, time management, and keyboarding. These become increasingly important as students move to middle school and high school.

*Classmates can assist students with visual problems in areas such as mobility.*

**TEACHING TIP**
Have vision specialists, such as an orientation and mobility specialist, visit your class to demonstrate sighted guide techniques that provide support for students with visual impairments.

The following are some specific accommodation suggestions:

◢ Assign a classmate to assist students who may need help with mobility in emergency situations.
◢ Teach all students in the class the proper techniques of being a sighted guide.
◢ In advance, inform staff members at fieldtrip sites that a student with a visual problem will be part of the visiting group.
◢ Tell students with visual problems that you are entering or leaving a room so that they are aware of your presence or absence.
◢ Have all students practice movement patterns that you expect of them, to maintain an orderly classroom.
◢ Orient students to the physical layout and other distinguishing features of the classroom.
◢ Maintain consistency in the placement of furniture, equipment, and instructional materials—remove all dangerous obstacles.
◢ Keep doors to cabinets, carts, and closets closed.
◢ Assist students in getting into unfamiliar desks, chairs, or other furniture.
◢ Eliminate auditory distractions.
◢ Seat students to maximize their usable vision and listening skills—often a position in the front and center part of the room is advantageous.
◢ Seat students so that they are not looking into a source of light or bothered by glare from reflected surfaces.
◢ Ensure that proper lighting is available.
◢ Create extra space for students who must use and store a piece of equipment (e.g., brailler, notebook computer).
◢ As a special section of the lesson plan, include notes for accommodating students with visual problems.

## Curricular and Instructional Considerations

**TEACHER-RELATED ACTIVITIES**   As the principal agents in delivering instruction, teachers should use techniques that will ensure success for students who have visual problems. A special challenge involves conveying primarily visual material to those who cannot see well. For example, it will require some creativity on the part of the teacher to make a graphic depiction of the circulatory system in a life science book (a two-dimensional illustration) accessible to a student who can see little or not at all. Three-dimensional models or illustrations with raised features might address this need.

Teachers have to decide what should be emphasized in the curriculum when students with visual impairments are in their classes. As a result of the wide array of curricular options for these student, teachers must "(a) address the multi-faceted educational requisites of their students, (b) ensure that instruction occurs in all areas of greatest need and (c) ensure that sufficient instructional time is allocated for identified educational priorities" (Lueck, 1999, p. 54).

**MATERIALS AND EQUIPMENT**   Special materials and equipment can enhance the education of students who have visual impairments. Some materials (e.g., large-print materials) are not appropriate for all and must be considered in light of individual needs. Vision specialists can help teachers select appropriate materials and equipment.

**TEACHING TIP**
Make sure that students with visual impairments have ample storage areas near their desks for materials such as large-print or braille books and other equipment.

Many materials found in general education classrooms may pose difficulties for students with vision problems. For instance, the *size* and *contrast* of print materials have a real effect on students with visual problems. Print size can generally be taken care of with magnification devices; however, little can be done to enhance the poor contrast often found on photocopies. Consider these points when using photocopies.

◢ Avoid using both sides of the paper (ink often bleeds through, making it difficult to see either side).

◢ Avoid old or light worksheet masters.

◢ Avoid worksheet masters with missing parts or creases.

◢ Give the darkest copies of handouts to students with visual problems.

◢ Do not give a student with a visual impairment a poor copy and say, "Do the best you can with this."

◢ Copy over lines that are light with a dark marker.

◢ Make new originals when photocopies become difficult to read.

◢ Avoid the use of colored inks that may produce limited contrast.

◢ Do not use colored paper—it limits contrast.

Although large-print materials seem like a good idea, they may be used inappropriately. Barraga and Erin (1992) recommend that these materials be used only as a last resort, since they may not be readily available. They believe that large-print materials should be utilized only after other techniques (e.g., optical devices or reduction of the reading distance) have been tried.

Teachers also may want to use concrete materials (i.e., realia—realistic representations of actual items). However, concrete representations of large real-life objects may not be helpful for young students, who may not understand the abstract notion of one thing representing another. Teachers must carefully ensure that all instructional materials for students with visual impairments are presented in the appropriate medium for the particular student (Corn et al., 1995).

Various optical, nonoptical, and electronic devices are also available for classroom use. These devices help students by enlarging existing printed images. If these devices are recommended for certain students, teachers will need to learn about them to ensure that they are used properly and to recognize when there is a problem. Teachers should practice the use of optical and electronic devices with students after consultation with a vision specialist.

Some students with more severe visual limitations may use braille as the primary means of working with written material. They may use instructional materials that are printed in braille and may also take notes using it. Through the use of computers, a student can write in braille and have the text converted to standard print. The reverse process is available as well. If a student uses this system of communication, the teacher should consult with a vision specialist to understand how it works.

Following are some specific accommodation suggestions:

◢ Call students by name, and speak directly to them.

◢ Take breaks at regular intervals to minimize fatigue in listening or using a brailler or optic device.

◢ Ensure that students are seated properly so that they can see you (if they have vision) and hear you clearly.

◢ Vary the type of instruction used, and include lessons that incorporate hands-on activities, cooperative learning, or the use of real-life materials.

◢ Use high-contrast materials, whether on paper or on the chalkboard—dry-erase boards may be preferable.

◢ Avoid using materials with glossy surfaces and, if possible, dittoed material.

◢ Use large-print materials only after other methods have been attempted and proved unsuccessful.

◢ Use environmental connectors (e.g., ropes or railing) and other adaptations for students with visual problems for physical education or recreational activities (Barraga & Erin, 1992).

◢ Avoid using written materials with pages that are too crowded.

***TEACHING TIP***
Have a student who uses a braille writer demonstrate the braille code and methods of writing braille to members of the class so they can understand the learning medium used by their classmates.

## Social–Emotional Considerations

Although the literature is mixed on whether students with visual impairments are less well adjusted than their sighted peers (Hallahan & Kauffman, 1997), there is evidence that some students with this disability experience social isolation (Huurre, Komulainen, & Aro, 1999). As a result, many students with visual problems will benefit from attention to their social and emotional development. Social skill instruction may be particularly useful (Sacks, Wolffe, & Tierney, 1998). However, because social skills are typically learned through observing others and imitating their behaviors, it is difficult to teach these skills to students who are not able to see.

Concern about emotional development is warranted for all students, including those with visual problems. Teachers should make sure that students know that they are available to talk about a student's concerns. A system can be developed whereby a student who has a visual impairment can signal the need to chat with the teacher. Being accessible and letting students know that someone is concerned about their social and emotional needs are extremely important.

The following are some specific accommodation suggestions:

◢ Encourage students with visual problems to become independent learners and to manage their own behaviors.
◢ Create opportunities for students to manipulate their own environment (Mangold & Roessing, 1982).
◢ Reinforce students for their efforts.
◢ Help students develop a healthy self-concept.
◢ Provide special instruction to help students acquire social skills needed to perform appropriately in classroom and social situations.
◢ Teach students how to communicate nonverbally (e.g., use of hands, etc.).
◢ Work with students to eliminate inappropriate mannerisms that some students with visual impairments display.

## Technology

Like students with hearing impairments, those with visual problems often use technological devices to assist them in their academic work and daily living skills. Low-vision aids include magnifiers, closed-circuit televisions, and monoculars. These devices enlarge print and other materials for individuals with visual impairments. The nearby Technology Today feature describes some basic considerations for educators when working with a child using a *monocular,* a small telescope that enables a student to see print, pictures, diagrams, maps, and people.

Many other technological devices are used by students with visual impairments. The following list notes some of them:

*Talking calculator:* A hand-held calculator that provides voice output of information put into the calculator and the solution
*Optacom:* A machine that scans printed material and transforms it into raised dot configurations that can be read with the fingertips
*Speech synthesizers:* An adaptation to a computer that provides voice output of material presented on the computer
*Braille embossers:* Computer printers that produce material from the computer in braille
*Software programs:* Numerous software programs for both DOS and Apple computers that produce voice output, large print, or both (Torres & Corn, 1990)

# TECHNOLOGY TODAY
## Using a Monocular

1. A monocular severely restricts the visual field. Students will be taught by the vision teacher to scan to pick up all visual information and increase their visual memory so they can copy more quickly and efficiently.

2. A monocular is typically used for distance tasks only.

3. Copying while using a monocular is laborious, and it will take the student with low vision longer to copy from the board or chart. You can adapt the assignment by providing a copy of the material to be copied or by modifying its length. Some ways of doing this include
   - Assigning even or odd numbers of items.
   - Allowing the student to write only the answers to questions rather than recopy entire sentences, questions, and/or paragraphs.

4. When a student is using a monocular, walking up to the board or chart should be discouraged. This annoys other students and severely hinders speed, continuity of thought, and proficiency when reading or completing an assignment.

5. Singling out the desk of a student with low vision (to place him or her closer to the board) is discouraged for social reasons. A monocular will enable the child to sit within the group at all times.

6. Monoculars break easily and should be worn around the neck when in use and stored in a case at other times. Encourage students to keep their monoculars out of sight when the room is empty.

7. Encourage the student to take the monocular to other school events, such as assemblies, film presentations, and so on.

8. Do not allow other students to handle the monocular.

*Monoculars and other forms of technology enhance educational opportunities for students with visual impairments.*

9. Do not allow the monocular to be taken home with younger students unless arrangements have been made with the itinerant vision teacher.

10. A student who is using the monocular should be seated facing the board or chart to allow straight-on viewing. This also enables the student to rest the elbow on the desk while looking through the monocular.

While access to the Internet is relatively easy for students without visual problems, many students with visual impairments may have difficulty. Certain technological devices can make access to the Internet available. Braille printers and speech input/output devices can help achieve access. Access and computer training can give students with visual impairments a vast resource that can have a profound positive impact on their education (Heinrich, 1999).

## PROMOTING A SENSE OF COMMUNITY AND SOCIAL ACCEPTANCE FOR STUDENTS WITH VISUAL IMPAIRMENTS

Students with visual impairments, like those with hearing impairments, need to be part of the school community. Many can be included without special supports. However, for others, teachers may need to consider the following (Amerson, 1999; Desrochers, 1999; Torres & Corn, 1990):

1. Remember that the student with a visual impairment is but one of many students in the classroom with individual needs and characteristics.
2. Use words such as *see, look,* and *watch* naturally.
3. Introduce students with visual impairments the same way you would introduce any other student.
4. Include students with visual impairments in all classroom activities, including physical education, home economics, and so on.
5. Encourage students with visual problems to seek leadership and high-visibility roles in the classroom.
6. Use the same disciplinary procedures for all students.
7. Encourage students with visual problems to move about the room just like other students.
8. Use verbal cues as often as necessary to cue the student with a visual impairment about something that is happening.
9. Provide additional space for students with visual impairments to store materials.
10. Allow students with visual impairments to learn about and discuss with other classmates special topics related to visual loss.
11. Model acceptance of visually impaired students as an example to other students.
12. Encourage students with visual impairments to use their specialized equipment, such as a braille writer.
13. Discuss special needs of the child with a visual impairment with specialists, as necessary.
14. Always tell a person with a visual impairment who you are as you approach.
15. Help students avoid inappropriate mannerisms associated with visual impairments.
16. Expect the same level of work from students with visual impairments as you do from other students.
17. Encourage students with visual impairments to be as independent as possible.
18. Treat children with visual impairments as you treat other students in the classroom.
19. Provide physical supports for students with concomitant motor problems.
20. Include students with visual impairments in outdoor activities and team sports.

In your efforts to promote a sense of community, consider that some students with visual impairments may have different cultural backgrounds than the majority of students in the school. School personnel must be sensitive to different cultural patterns. Bau (1999) noted 7 different cultural values that could have an impact on the provision of services to students with visual impairments. These include communication, health beliefs, family structure, attitude toward authority, etiquette, expectations of helping, and time orientation. To communicate clearly with a family that speaks a different language, you may need to use a language interpreter. Lynch and

# DIVERSITY FORUM   Suggestions for Working with Language Interpreters

▲ Introduce yourself and the interpreter, describe your respective roles, and clarify mutual expectations and the purpose of the encounter.

▲ Learn basic words and sentences in the family's language and become familiar with special terminology they may use so you can selectively attend to them during interpreter–family exchanges.

▲ During the interaction, address your remarks and questions directly to the family (not the interpreter); look at and listen to family members as they speak and observe their nonverbal communication.

▲ Avoid body language or gestures that may be offensive or misunderstood.

▲ Use a positive tone of voice and facial expressions that sincerely convey respect and your interest in the family, and address them in a calm, unhurried manner.

▲ Speak clearly and somewhat more slowly, but not more loudly.

▲ Limit your remarks and questions to a few sentences between translations and avoid giving too much information or long complex discussions of several topics in a single session.

▲ Avoid technical jargon, colloquialisms, idioms, slang, and abstractions.

▲ Avoid oversimplification and condensing important explanations.

▲ Give instructions in a clear, logical sequence; emphasize key words or points; and offer reasons for specific recommendations.

▲ Periodically check on the family's understanding and the accuracy of the translation by asking the family to repeat instructions or whatever has been communicated in their own words, with the interpreter facilitating. But avoid literally asking, "Do you understand?"

▲ When possible, reinforce verbal information with materials written in the family's language and visual aids or behavioral modeling if appropriate. Before introducing written materials, tactfully determine the client's literacy level through the interpreter.

▲ Be patient and prepared for the additional time that will inevitably be required for careful interpretation.

▲ Learn proper protocols and forms of address (including a few greetings and social phrases) in the family's primary language, the name they wish to be called, and the correct pronunciation.

From "From Culture Shock to Cultural Learning," by E. W. Lynch (p. 56), in *Developing Cross-Cultural Competence,* edited by W. E. Lynch and M. J. Hanson, 1992, Baltimore: Brookes. Used by permission.

Hansen (1992) offer guidelines to use when working with a language interpreter; they are summarized in the nearby Diversity Forum feature. Being sensitive to the culture and family background of students with visual impairments facilitates the delivery of appropriate services.

## Supports for the General Education Teacher

As noted earlier, general education teachers can effectively instruct most students with visual impairments, with appropriate supports. A vision specialist may need to work with students on specific skills, such as braille; an orientation and mobility instructor can teach students how to travel independently; an adaptive physical education instructor can help modify physical activities for the student with visual impairment. Counselors, school health personnel, and vocational specialists may also provide support services for general education teachers. School personnel should never forget to include parents in helping develop and implement educational supports for students with visual impairments. In a recent study, McConnell (1999) found that a model program that included family involvement and support greatly

**CONSIDER THIS**
Students with visual impairments may not be able to monitor visual cues from peers regarding social behaviors. How can you teach students with visual impairments to understand these visual cues?

assisted adolescents with visual impairments to develop career choices and values. Other ways to enhance the education of students with visual impairments are:

▲ Get help from others. Teach other students to assist in social as well as academic settings. Call parents and ask questions when you don't understand terminology, equipment, or reasons for prescribed practices.

▲ Learn how to adapt and modify materials and instruction.

▲ Learn as much as you can, and encourage the professionals you work with to do the same. Find out about training that may be available and ask to go.

▲ Suggest that others become informed, especially students. Use your local library and bookstores to find print material that you can read and share. (Viadero, 1989)

# Summary

## Basic Concepts about Hearing Impairment

▲ Many students with sensory deficits are educated in general education classrooms.

▲ For students with sensory impairments to receive an appropriate education, various accommodations must be made.

▲ Students with hearing and visual problems represent a very heterogeneous group.

▲ Most students with hearing problems have some residual hearing ability.

▲ The term *hearing impairment* includes individuals with deafness and those who are hard of hearing.

## Strategies for Curriculum and Instruction

▲ The effect of a hearing loss on a student's ability to understand speech is a primary concern of teachers.

▲ An audiometric evaluation helps to determine the extent of a hearing disorder.

▲ Several factors should alert teachers to a possible hearing loss in a particular student.

## Classroom Accommodations for Students with Hearing Impairments

▲ Teachers in general education classrooms must implement a variety of accommodations for students with hearing impairments.

▲ The seating location of a student with hearing loss is critical for effective instruction.

▲ Specialized equipment, such as hearing aids, may be necessary to ensure the success of students with hearing losses.

## Promoting a Sense of Community and Social Acceptance for Students with Hearing Impairments

▲ The most challenging aspect of teaching students with hearing problems is making sure that they participate in the communicational activities that occur in the classroom.

▲ Teachers need to encourage interaction (e.g., grouping, assigning buddies) between students with hearing impairments and their nondisabled classmates.

## Basic Concepts about Visual Impairment

▲ Vision plays a critical role in the development of concepts such as understanding the spatial relations of the environment.

▲ Teachers must use a variety of accommodations for students with visual disabilities.

▲ Most students with visual disabilities have residual or low vision.

▲ Refractive errors are the most common form of visual disability.

▲ Visual problems may be congenital or occur later in life.

## Strategies for Curriculum and Instruction

▲ The most educationally relevant characteristic of students who have visual impairments is the extent of their visual efficiency.

▲ Special materials may be needed when working with students with visual problems.

▲ Using large-print and nonglare materials may be sufficient accommodation for many students with visual disabilities.

▲ Provide ample storage space for students' materials.

▲ Allow students additional time as braille and large print reading is slower than regular print reading.

**Classroom Accommodations for Students with Visual Impairments**

▲ A very small number of students require instruction in braille.

▲ Specialists to teach braille and develop braille materials may be needed in order to successfully place students with visual disabilities in general education classrooms.

▲ Academic tests may need to be adapted when evaluating students with visual disabilities.

▲ Allow students to hold materials as close as necessary.

▲ Facilitate all technology needed by students.

**Promoting a Sense of Community and Social Acceptance for Students with Visual Impairments**

▲ It is critical that students with visual impairments be socially accepted in their general education classrooms.

▲ Orchestrate social opportunities for students.

▲ Encourage students with visual impairments to demonstrate any specialized equipment they may use.

# urther Readings

American Foundation for the Blind. (1998). *AFB director of services for blind and visually impaired persons in the United States and Canada* (27th ed.). New York: Author.

Beukelman, D. R., & Mirenda, P. (1998). *Augmentative and alternative communication* (2nd ed.). Baltimore: Brookes.

Caton, H. (Ed.). (1997). *Tools for selecting appropriate learning media.* Louisville, KY: American Printing House for the Blind.

Corn, A. L., & Koening, A. J. (Eds.). *Foundations of low vision: Clinical and functional perspectives.* New York: American Foundation for the Blind.

Jahoda, G. (1993). *How can I do this if I can't see what I'm doing?* Washington, DC: National Library Service for the Blind and Physically Handicapped.

Kluwin, T. N., Moores, D. F., & Gaustad, M. G. (Eds.). (1998). *Toward effective public school programs for deaf students: Context, process, & outcomes.* New York: Teachers College Press.

Koenig, A. J., & Holbrook, M. C. (1995). *Learning media assessment of students with visual impairments: A resource guide for teachers* (2nd ed.). Austin, TX: Pro-Ed.

Lucas, C. (Ed.). (1990). *Sign language research.* Washington, DC: Gallaudet University Press.

Martin, D. S. (1991). *Advances in cognition, education, and deafness.* Washington, DC: Gallaudet University Press.

Moores, D. (1999). *Educating the deaf: Psychology, principles, and practices* (5th ed.). Columbus, OH: Merrill.

Paul, P. V. (1998). *Literacy and deafness: The development of reading, writing, and literate thought.* Boston: Allyn and Bacon.

Sacks, S. Z., & Silberman, R. K. (1998). *Educating students who have visual impairments with other disabilities.* Baltimore: Brookes.

Smith, A., & Cote, K. S. (1983). *Look at me. A resource manual for the development of residual vision in multiple impaired children.* Philadelphia: College of Optometry Press.

Articles in *American Annals of the Deaf*

Articles in *Journal of Visual Impairment and Blindness*

Articles in *RE:view*

# Chapter 9

# Teaching Students with Autism, Traumatic Brain Injury, and Other Low-Incidence Disabilities

*After reading this chapter, you should be able to:*

▲ Define and describe students with autism and Asperger's syndrome

▲ Define and describe students with traumatic brain injury

▲ Define and describe students with health problems and physical disabilities

▲ Describe various intervention strategies for students with autism, traumatic brain injury, health problems, and physical disabilities

While riding his bicycle at age 7, Bob struck a tree. He was not wearing a helmet at the time of the accident. His head struck the tree near the right temple just above the ear. Doctors found a bruise the size of a quarter. Bob experienced a closed head injury (CHI); his skull was not penetrated. Bob's skull was cracked in several different areas. In addition, he had internal damage and bleeding in the left stomach region.

Doctors observed considerable swelling, and Bob experienced generalized tonic–clonic seizures soon after the impact. He lapsed into a coma and was airlifted to a hospital. Doctors performed emergency surgery to control the rising intracranial pressure in his brain, as well as the abdominal bleeding. After surgery, doctors medically maintained a coma state to control the seizures. During his 11-day hospital stay, Bob was in a coma for the first 5 days and went from intensive care to constant care during that time. Seizure medication was required following the accident; however, Bob has not had another seizure for the past 2 years.

Adapted from "Meet Bob," by C. White, 1998, *Teaching Exceptional Children, 30,* p. 56. Used by permission.

## QUESTIONS TO CONSIDER

1. In what ways does a child like Bob impact his or her family?
2. What kinds of planning need to take place for Bob to make a transition from a hospital setting to a school setting?

¶he previous chapter dealt with students with sensory impairments, typically considered low-incidence disabilities because they do not occur in many children. In addition to these two categories of disabilities, many other conditions that occur relatively rarely in children can result in significant challenges for these students, their families, school personnel, and other professionals. These conditions include autism, traumatic brain injury (TBI), and a host of physical and health problems that may be present in school-age children, such as cerebral palsy, spina bifida, AIDS, cystic fibrosis, epilepsy, and diabetes.

**CONSIDER THIS**
What are some problems that may be encountered by general classroom teachers with which specialists could provide assistance?

Many general education classroom teachers will teach their entire careers without encountering children with these problems. However, because children with these kinds of conditions might be included in their future classrooms, teachers need to generally understand the conditions and how to support these students in the classroom. This chapter will provide substantial information on autism and traumatic brain injury, two disability categories recognized in the Individuals with Disabilities Education Act (IDEA). Other conditions, primarily subsumed under the *other health impaired* and *orthopedically impaired* categories in IDEA, will be presented more briefly. Often, schools and state education agencies provide support personnel for teachers and students with these types of problems. Therefore, teachers should not have to "go it alone" when working with students with these disabilities. Behavioral specialists, psychologists, physical therapists, occupational therapists, nurses, and other health personnel are often available to provide services to students and supports to their teachers (Wadsworth & Knight, 1999). The fact that many different professionals are involved in providing services for some of these children may have repercussions for students of certain cultural backgrounds. Individuals from some cultures, for example, prefer to interact with only one person at a time, rather than a team of individuals. Professionals providing services must be sensitive to the cultural traits that characterize different families. The nearby Diversity Forum summarizes some contrasting beliefs, values, and practices that distinguish mainstream U.S. culture from Latino cultures. Professionals should consider the unique characteristics of each student's cultural background.

Describing every aspect of autism, TBI, and other low-incidence disabilities is not possible here. However, this chapter discusses the more common and in some cases, unique, aspects of these conditions. Figure 9.1 shows the number of children in each group served in special education programs.

## BASIC CONCEPTS ABOUT AUTISM

*AUTISM* is an organic disorder of communication and social interactions.

**A**utism is a pervasive developmental disorder that primarily affects social interactions, language, and behavior. Although autism has been glamorized by several movies, such as *Rain Man* (1988) (see the nearby Personal Spotlight), it still has a significant impact on individuals and their families. The characteristics displayed by individuals with autism vary significantly; some individuals are able to assimilate

# DIVERSITY FORUM

## Contrasting Beliefs, Values, and Practices

| Latino Cultures | Mainstream Culture |
|---|---|
| Collective orientation | Individual orientation |
| Interdependence | Independence |
| Collective, group identity | Individual identity |
| Cooperation | Competition |
| Saving face | Being direct |
| Relaxed with time | Time sensitive |
| Emphasis on interpersonal relations | Emphasis on task orientation |
| Spiritual/magical belief orientation | Rational/empirical orientation |
| More recent agrarian influence | More urbanized/industrialized mode |
| Tendency toward more patriarchal family structure | Tendency toward more democratic family structure |
| More relaxed with child development | Strong expectations for child development |
| More overt respect for the elderly | Less value/respect toward the elderly |
| Extended family systems more pronounced | Nuclear family systems more pronounced |

From "Families with Latino Roots" (p. 176), by M. Zuniga, in *Developing Cross-Cultural Competence,* edited by E. W. Lynch and M. J. Hansen, 1992, Baltimore: Brookes. Used by permission.

into community settings and activities, whereas others have major difficulties achieving such *normalcy.*

The study of autism has had a confusing and controversial history since the condition was first described less than 50 years ago by Dr. Leo Kanner (Eaves, 1992). Some of the early controversy centered on attempts to relate the cause of autism to poor mother–child bonding. Eventually this hypothesis was disproved, but it caused a great deal of misunderstanding. Many professionals once thought that children with autism made a conscious decision to withdraw from their environment because of its hostile nature. During the past two decades, autism has been found to be an organic disorder, laying to rest much of this speculation (Eaves, 1992). Until 1990, autism was not a separate category under IDEA, and children with autism were eligible for

**CONSIDER THIS**

How can movies that depict persons with disabilities help, as well as hurt, the cause of providing appropriate educational opportunities to students with disabilities?

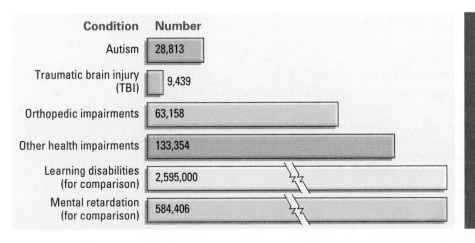

| Condition | Number |
|---|---|
| Autism | 28,813 |
| Traumatic brain injury (TBI) | 9,439 |
| Orthopedic impairments | 63,158 |
| Other health impairments | 133,354 |
| Learning disabilities (for comparison) | 2,595,000 |
| Mental retardation (for comparison) | 584,406 |

*FIGURE* **9.1**

Number of Students, Ages 6–21, with Autism, TBI, and Health and Physical Disabilities Served in Public Schools during the 1996–1997 School Year

From *20th Annual Report to Congress on the Implementation of the Individuals with Disabilities Education Act* (p. 11), U.S. Department of Education, 1998, Washington, DC: Author.

## *personal* SPOTLIGHT

### The *Real* Rain Man

**KIM PEEK**
*Interviewed by
Marcy Mezzano*

For all appearances, Kim Peek seems to be just an overgrown kid. With a perpetual pouty lip, a cranky attitude when he's tired, and a reliance on his father, Fran, to help him with the little things in life, he is just like any other kid. His dad helps him get dressed, brush his teeth, and communicate with others. He wants to answer every question he is asked in order to show off what he knows, and he becomes excited when he has given you information. Kim, however, is not a kid. Rather, he is a 45-year-old man whose innocent, honest, and vibrant personality belies the cynicism that too often is associated with his age.

Kim is a *mega*savant and perhaps the only megasavant in the world. His IQ is estimated at over 180 (Einstein's was measured at 149). Despite having almost total recall of everything he reads, Kim is challenged to think in abstract terms. He has difficulties in problem solving, motor control, and social relationships. However, he does have some remarkable skills. He can read "faster than a speeding bullet," with his left eye reading the left page of a book while his right eye is reading the right side. Kim read Tom Clancy's *Hunt for Red October* in about one hour and twenty minutes. He can quote passages from it if you give him the page number. (If you tell Kim your birthdate, for example, July 19, 1974, he will tell you that you were born on a Friday, the years the date falls on Saturday, and that you will retire on Tuesday in the year 2039.)

Although Kim Peek's name may not be familiar, many people know about him. Kim was the inspiration for the Oscar-winning best picture of 1988, *Rain Man*. Unlike the character in the movie, Kim does not have autism. Rather, he has deficiencies in social and motor skill areas. He easily talks to whomever he meets and is not shy about telling people exactly what he is thinking. Kim and his father travel around the country in an effort to educate people, not merely about his disability, but about a universal problem—intolerance. While he always knew his son was special, it wasn't until the movie *Rain Man* that Fran knew exactly how bright his son was.

Kim is truly a remarkable individual. He is a great example about how being different, significantly different, does not mean that you are incapable of doing incredible things. All educators should remember Kim Peek when they are dealing with students with special needs. Accepting people for who they are and what they can do is a quality we all need to enhance.

special education services only as *other health impaired*. This changed with the 1990 reauthorization of IDEA, when autism became a separate category (Kaplan, 1996).

### Autism Defined

Although many definitions of autism have been developed, no single definition has been universally accepted. However, it is important to be familiar with two definitions: the one in IDEA, primarily used by educators, and the one found in the *Diagnostic and Statistical Manual,* Fourth Edition (*DSM-IV*), used by psychologists and medical professionals. IDEA defines autism as "a developmental disability that primarily results in significant deficits in verbal and non-verbal communication and social interactions." The condition generally presents itself before the age of 3 years and adversely affects the child's educational performance once school age is reached. Knoblock (1982) describes autism as a lifelong, severely disabling condition. It is typically marked by significant impairments in intellectual, social, and emotional functioning (McEachlin, Smith, & Lovaas, 1993). This definition differs substantially from the one found in the *DSM-IV,* which uses a multitude of criteria. Figure 9.2 provides the *DSM-IV* definition and diagnostic criteria.

A. A total of six (or more) items from (1), (2), and (3), with at least two from (1), and one each from (2) and (3):

  (1) qualitative impairment in social interaction, as manifested by at least two of the following:

    (a) marked impairment in the use of multiple nonverbal behaviors such as eye-to-eye gaze, facial expression, body postures, and gestures to regulate social interaction

    (b) failure to develop peer relationships appropriate to developmental level

    (c) a lack of spontaneous seeking to share enjoyment, interests, or achievements with other people (e.g., by a lack of showing, bringing, or pointing out objects of interest)

    (d) lack of social or emotional reciprocity

  (2) qualitative impairments in communication as manifested by at least one of the following:

    (a) delay in, or total lack of, the development of spoken language (not accompanied by an attempt to compensate through alternative modes of communication such as gesture or mime)

    (b) in individuals with adequate speech, marked impairment in the ability to initiate or sustain a conversation with others

    (c) stereotyped and repetitive use of language or idiosyncratic language

    (d) lack of varied, spontaneous make-believe play or social imitative play appropriate to developmental level

  (3) restricted repetitive and stereotyped patterns of behavior, interests, and activities, as manifested by at least one of the following:

    (a) encompassing preoccupation with one or more stereotyped and restricted patterns of interest that is abnormal either in intensity or focus

    (b) apparently inflexible adherence to specific, nonfunctional routines or rituals

    (c) stereotyped and repetitive motor mannerisms (e.g., hand or finger flapping or twisting, or complex whole-body movements)

    (d) persistent preoccupation with parts of objects

B. Delays or abnormal functioning in at least one of the following areas, with onset prior to age 3 years: (1) social interaction, (2) language as used in social communication, or (3) symbolic or imaginative play.

C. The disturbance is not better accounted for by Rett's Disorder or Childhood Disintegrative Disorder (two pervasive developmental disorders characterized by impairment in the development of reciprocal social interaction).

**FIGURE 9.2**
Definition of Autism Using *DSM-IV*
From *Diagnostic and Statistical Manual of Mental Disorders* (4th ed.) (p. 32), American Psychiatric Association, 1994, Washington, DC: Author. Used by permission.

Just as autism is hard to define, children with autism are difficult to identify. Problems related to the identification of these children include the following:

◢ Children with autism display many characteristics exhibited by individuals with other disabilities, such as speech and language disorders.

◢ Many children with autism, because they exhibit disorders across multiple domains, are mistakenly classified as having multiple disabilities.

◢ No stable classification system is used among educators and other professionals who encounter children with autism. (Eaves, 1992)

Still another problem in identifying children with autism is the large, diverse group of professionals involved in the evaluation and diagnosis. In diagnosing some disabilities, educators function as the lead professionals; in the area of autism, pediatricians, speech–language pathologists, psychologists, audiologists, and social workers are typically involved as well (Powers, 1989). Working with such a large group of individuals can cause difficult logistical problems. Diverse definitions and eligibility criteria, different funding agencies, and varying services complicate the process of identifying and serving these children and adults. The nearby Rights and Responsibilities feature summarizes some of the legal decisions concerning the rights of students with autism.

## Prevalence and Causes of Autism

There is no single specific cause of autism, but a variety of factors can result in this disability. Organic factors such as brain damage, genetic links, and complications during pregnancy may cause this condition, though in most cases, no cause can be confirmed (Kaplan, 1996). Some children have a higher risk for autism than others. For example, children who are born with rubella and those classified as having fragile X syndrome are more likely to develop autism than other children (Blackman, 1990). In general, however, autism strikes randomly in all segments of society.

Autism is a relatively rare condition. The incidence of autism varies directly with the definition used. More restricted definitions result in approximately 0.7 to 2.3 individuals per 10,000 being identified, while less restrictive definitions may result in the identification of as many as 7 to 14 per 10,000 (Koegel et al., 1995; Locke, Banken, & Mahone, 1994). Regardless of the definition used, however, autism represents a very low incidence disability. During the 1996–1997 school year, 29,057 children were classified as having autism for IDEA reporting purposes. This accounted for only 0.07% of children in public schools, making it one of the smallest disability categories recognized in schools (U.S. Department of Education, 1999).

# RIGHTS & RESPONSIBILITIES

### Court Decisions Related to Interventions and Treatment Programs for Students with Autism

*Delaware County IU#25* v. *Martin K.* (1993)   When programs are new or considered pilot programs, programs with documented benefits (e.g., the program developed by Lovaas) will be considered more effective.

*Mark Hartmann* v. *Loudoun County Board of Education* (1997)   A student's IEP should reflect individual needs; an IEP that strictly focuses on a singular emphasis, such as social skills training, will likely be considered inappropriate.

*Cordrey* v. *Euckert* (1990)   Benefit alone is insufficient to justify extended school year services. Parents

may be required to show that regression will occur without extended services.

*Johnson* v. *Independent School District No. 4 of Bixby* (1990)   In addition to regression/recoupment, other factors that must be included when determining the need for an extended school year for students with autism are the degree of impairment, the ability of the child to interact with others, the child's rate of progress, and professional opinion predicting the student's progress toward goals.

How might these court decisions affect the classroom teacher who has a student with autism?

From "Interventions for Children and Youth with Autism: Prudent Choices in a World of Exaggerated Claims and Empty Promises," Heflin and Simpson, 1998, *Focus on Autism and Other Developmental Disabilities, 13,* pp. 212–220.

## Characteristics of Individuals with Autism

A wide variety of characteristics are associated with autism. Some of the more pervasive include verbal and nonverbal communication impairments (Dyches, 1998), auditory-based sensory impairments (Orr, Myles, & Carlson, 1998), and problems relating to other individuals (NICCHY, 1993). Eaves (1992) defined five major areas of impairment. These areas and the conditions associated with each one are as follows:

1. Affective and cognitive indifference
   - Avoids eye contact
   - Presents a blank expression
   - Does not like to be hugged
   - Displays self-stimulating behavior, such as finger flicking, hand shaking, rocking, head banging, and staring at hands
   - Likes to spin jars, lids, tops, and other objects
   - Has a fascination for crinkly sounds
   - Enjoys dangling objects
   - Mouths objects
2. Expressive affect
   - Cries on happy occasions
   - Hits, bites, or scratches others
   - Cries and screams when desires are not met
   - Smiles or laughs for no apparent reason
   - Hallucinates
   - Masturbates
   - Is overly sensitive to certain smells and odors
3. Passive affect
   - Collects and hoards things of no apparent value
   - Is compulsive about cleanliness and orderliness
   - Walks on tiptoes, twirls, and overreacts to any environmental changes
4. Anxiety and fears
   - Is fearful of nonfrightening things
   - Has excessive fear of loud sounds or noises
   - Fears water
   - Fears crowds
5. Cognition
   - Displays savant behaviors in some areas, such as number counting, memorizing, spelling
   - Exhibits unique speech patterns, such as one that is flat and monotonal in quality
   - Has uneven skill development
   - Has recorded low intellectual levels

**CROSS-REFERENCE**
Review Chapter 6 on children with serious emotional disturbance (SED). Compare the characteristics of children with autism and those with SED. How are these children similar and different?

Although most of these characteristics are negative, some children with autism present some positive, as well as unexpected, characteristics. For example, Tirosh and Canby (1993) describe children with autism who also have hyperlexia, which is defined as "an advance of at least one standard deviation (SD) in the reading over the verbal IQ level" (p. 86). For these children, spelling and contextual reading also appeared to be advanced.

In some cases, children with autism display unique **splinter skills**. Some are incredible spellers, some artists, and some have calendar skills that allow them to always know what day of the week a certain date will fall on. These types of skills are found in only a small number of children with autism.

**SPLINTER SKILLS** are skills that individuals exhibit that go well beyond their presumed capability.

# CLASSROOM ACCOMMODATIONS FOR STUDENTS WITH AUTISM

*CONSIDER THIS*
How do splinter skills often confuse family members concerning the abilities and capabilities of a child with autism?

*TEACHING TIP*
Peer buddies can be very useful when a student with autism is included in a general classroom. Peers can serve as excellent role models and provide support for these students.

Formerly, the prognosis for individuals with autism was pessimistic; most children with autism would grow into adulthood with severe impairments. However, intensive intervention programs have been somewhat effective with this group. No single method is effective with all children with autism, partly because these children display widely variable characteristics (Heflin & Simpson, 1998). However, several different techniques have shown positive results (Kaplan, 1996). Table 9.1 summarizes some of these techniques.

Growing evidence shows that placing children with autism with their nondisabled peers in general education settings, with appropriate supports, can make a significant difference in their behaviors. Appropriate role models appear to be very important. Recent research also indicates that behavioral treatment of children with autism, especially young children, may result in significant long-term gains in intellectual and adaptive behavior areas (McEachlin et al., 1993). Also, social skills training has been shown

| TABLE 9.1 | Classroom Tips for Teaching Children with Autism |
|---|---|
| **Tip** | **Reason** |
| 1. Teaching a child with autism should be seen as a team approach with many professionals helping the classroom teacher. | The child with autism being educated in a regular class has probably been treated by many professionals who have extensive experience with the child. Their experiences and suggestions are of great help to the teacher. Regular consultations should be scheduled. |
| 2. Learn everything possible about the child's development, behavior, and what services the child has received. | Understanding the nature of the child's difficulties and what has been accomplished previously can serve as a beginning for designing a program that will enable the child to learn. |
| 3. Try to foster an atmosphere of shared decision making with other professionals responsible for the child's progress. | Successful models for integration of children with autism into regular classes show that shared decision making among all professionals leads to superior results. |
| 4. Do not assume that children with autism have mental retardation. | The serious behavioral and linguistic difficulties of these children may lead to the assumption that they have mental retardation. The meaning of intelligence tests for children with autism is subject to question. |
| 5. Beware of even suggesting that parents have caused their children's difficulties. | Blaming parents is counterproductive since parental help is so often required. However, in the case of autism, old discredited theories did suggest such a connection. Even though these ideas have been proven false, parental guilt may be present. |
| 6. Prepare the class for the child with autism. | Discussing the nature of autism and some behaviors, such as rocking, may help allay the concerns of other children in the class. |

From *Pathways for Exceptional Children* (p. 595), by P. S. Kaplan, 1996, St. Paul, MN: West Publishing. Used by permission.

to be effective for this group of children (Kamps et al., 1992) (see Chapter 6 for more information on behavior management and social skills instruction).

Regardless of the specific intervention used, professionals developing programs for children with autism should ask these questions (Heflin & Simpson, 1998):

1. What are the anticipated outcomes of the programming option?
2. What are the potential risks?
3. How will the option be evaluated?
4. What proof is available that the option is effective?
5. What other options would be excluded if this option is chosen?

Since there is no single, best method for teaching students with autism, school personnel must have available a variety of intervention strategies. Hardman et al. (1996) suggest a variety of tips that general and special education teachers should consider when working with students with autism. These are listed in Table 9.2.

In addition, Egel (1989) has emphasized two important principles that should inform educational programs for children with autism: the use of functional activities and an effort to make programs appropriate for the student's developmental level and chronological age. Children with autism grow up to be adults with autism; the condition cannot be cured. As a result, educational programs should help them deal with the daily needs that will extend throughout their lives. To help educators focus more on the functionality of curriculum choices, they should ask themselves the following questions:

1. Does the program teach skills that are immediately useful?
2. Will the materials used be available in the student's daily environment?
3. Will learning certain skills make it less likely that someone will have to do the task for the student in the future?

If the answer to any of these questions is no, then the instructional program should be changed.

**TEACHING TIP**
Always remember that students with autism present a wide range of characteristics, strengths, and weaknesses. Treat each child as a unique individual, and do not expect them all to need the same kinds of services.

**CONSIDER THIS**
How should the curriculum for students with autism be balanced between academic skills and functional life skills? Should skills from both areas be taught to all students with autism?

**CROSS-REFERENCE**
Review program recommendations for students with mental retardation found in Chapter 7. How are programs for these two groups of students similar and different?

*Self-management is a promising intervention strategy for children with autism.*

| TABLE 9.2 | Tips for Teaching Students with Autism |

| Tips for the Regular Classroom Teacher | Tips for School Personnel |
|---|---|
| ■ Help with organizational strategies, assisting the student with autism with matters that are difficult for him or her (e.g., remembering how to use an eraser). Keep instruction as unrestrictive as possible, perhaps a prompting note or picture somewhere.<br><br>■ Avoid abstract ideas unless they are necessary in instruction. Be as concrete as possible.<br><br>■ Communicate with specific directions or questions, not vague or open-ended statements.<br><br>■ If the child becomes upset, he or she may need to change activities or go to a place in the room that is "safe" for a period of time.<br><br>■ If the child is not learning a particular task, it may need to be broken down into smaller steps or presented through more than one medium (e.g., visual and verbal).<br><br>■ Begin preparing the child with autism for a more variable environment by programming and teaching adaptation to changes in routine. Involve him or her in planning for the changes, mapping out what they might be.<br><br>■ Gradually increase the level of abstraction in teaching, remaining aware of the individual limitations the child with autism has.<br><br>■ Continue preparing the student for an increasingly variable environment through instruction and example.<br><br>■ Focus increasingly on matters of vital importance to the student as he or she matures (e.g., social awareness and interpersonal issues between the sexes).<br><br>■ Teach the student with an eye toward postschool community participation, including such matters as physically navigating the community, participating in activities, and seeking and maintaining employment. Teach the student about interacting with police in the community, since they require responses different than those appropriate for other strangers. | ■ To the degree possible for children with autism, promote involvement in social activities and clubs that enhance interpersonal interaction.<br><br>■ Encourage the development of functional academic programs for students with autism that are combined with transition planning and programs.<br><br>■ Promote a continuing working relationship with school staff and other agency personnel that might be involved in the student's overall treatment program (e.g., health care providers, social service agencies, and others).<br><br>■ Work with other agencies that may encounter the child in the community (e.g., law enforcement). Provide workshops, if possible, to inform officers regarding behavioral characteristics of people with autism that might be misinterpreted.<br><br>■ Promote an all-school environment where children model appropriate behavior and receive reinforcement for it.<br><br>■ Develop peer-assistance programs, where older students can help tutor and model appropriate behavior for children with autism.<br><br>■ Encourage the development of strong, ongoing, school-parent relationships and support groups working together to meet the child's needs. Consistent expectations are important.<br><br>■ Do not depend on the child with autism to take messages home to parents unless you are trying this out as a skill for him or her to learn; communication is a major problem, and even a note may be lost. |

From *Human Exceptionality: Society, School, and Family* (4th edition) (pp. 270–271), by M. L. Hardman, C. J. Drew, M. W. Egan, and B. Wolf, 1996, Boston: Allyn and Bacon. Used by permission.

Programs for students with autism should also be age appropriate and **developmentally appropriate.** The individual's chronological age and developmental status must be considered together. Sometimes a real incongruence exists between these two realms, making program planning a challenge (McDonnell, Hardman, McDonnell, & Kiefer-O'Donnell, 1995). In this case, developmentally appropriate materials must be modified to make them as age appropriate as possible.

A promising intervention strategy for children and adults with autism is **self-management**—implementing a variety of techniques that assist in self-control. Although total self-management is not possible for many students with autism, most can be taught to improve their skills in this area (Alberto & Troutman, 1995). Koegel et al., (1992) studied four children with autism who displayed a variety of inappropriate behaviors, including **self-injurious behaviors** (or self-abusive behaviors), running away from school personnel, delayed echolalic speech (repeating what is said to them), hitting objects, and stereotypical twirling of hair. After several sessions in which the children were taught how to use self-management strategies, such as **self-recording** (documenting their own behavior) and **self-reinforcement** (giving themselves reinforcers), marked improvement occurred. The results indicate that "the lack of social responsivity that is so characteristic in autism can be successfully treated with self-management procedures, requiring minimal presence of a treatment provider in the children's natural environments" (p. 350). This particular study focused on self-management related to social skills, yet hints at the possibility that such interventions could be successful in other areas.

Over the past several years, a major controversy has erupted in the education of children with autism over the use of **facilitated communication,** a process in which a facilitator helps the person with autism (or some other disability related to expressive language) type or use a keyboard for communication purposes. The process is described by Biklen et al. (1992) as follows:

> Facilitated communication involves a series of steps. The communicator types with one index finger, first with hand over hand or hand-at-the-wrist support and then later independently or with just a touch to the elbow or shoulder. Over time, the communicator progresses from structured work such as fill-in-the-blanks/cloze exercises and multiple-choice activities to open-ended, typed, conversational text. (p. 5)

Although this method was once touted as the key to establishing communication with children with autism, recent studies have cast doubt on its authenticity. The heart of the controversy concerns how to validate the technique. Advocates of the method offer numerous qualitative research studies as proof of success, yet recent quantitative research raises significant questions about the program. After reviewing much of the empirical research related to facilitated communication, Kaplan (1996) reported that evidence often shows that the facilitator influences the person with autism, though the facilitator may be unaware of it. Yet despite the growing evidence questioning the efficacy of facilitated communication, Kaplan says that "it would be incorrect to suggest that because excesses sometimes creep into the way the method is used, it should completely be abandoned" (p. 585). In other words, although little empirical evidence supports facilitated communication, it could still be an effective means of communication for some individuals and should not be abandoned totally until more study is done. It is unlikely, however, that facilitated communication is the miracle many people had hoped it would be.

**DEVELOPMENTALLY APPROPRIATE** is the level of instruction that is appropriate for a student's current developmental status.

**SELF-MANAGEMENT SKILLS** enable a student to manage his or her own behaviors.

**SELF-INJURIOUS BEHAVIOR** is behavior exhibited by an individual that result in injuries to him- or herself.

**SELF-RECORDING** involves keeping track of data on your own behavior.

**SELF-REINFORCEMENT** is a reinforcement system totally controlled by the individual being reinforced.

**FACILITATED COMMUNICATION** is a controversial approach to assist individuals with autism communicate by providing a physical assist when they use a communication device.

**CONSIDER THIS**
How can the use of invalidated procedures harm students? Why do some of these ideas become so popular with some educators and family members before they are proven effective?

# ASPERGER SYNDROME

*ASPERGER SYNDROME*
is a disorder similar
to autism that results
in impairments in social
interactions.

During the past few years a condition associated with autism has received a great deal of attention. This condition, called **Asperger syndrome,** was first included in the 4th edition of the *Diagnostic and Statistical Manual of Mental Disorders (DSM-IV)* (Stoddart, 1998). In general, students classified as having Asperger syndrome share many of the same characteristics of children with autism, but also display some unique features. "Clinical features of Asperger syndrome include social interaction impairments, speech and communication characteristics, cognitive and academic characteristics, sensory characteristics, and physical and motor-skill anomalies" (Myles & Simpson, 1998, p. 3). These characteristics, for the most part, are the same as those found in children with autism (McLaughlin-Cheng, 1998). Children with Asperger syndrome differ from those with autism in having higher cognitive development and more typical communication skills.

| TABLE 9.3 | Behavioral Comparison of Asperger Syndrome and Autism | |
|---|---|---|
| | **Asperger Syndrome** | **Autistic Syndrome** |
| 1. Intelligence measures | | |
| Standardized scores | Average to high average range | Borderline through average range |
| 2. Language | | |
| Development | Normal development | Delayed onset, deficits |
| Pragmatic language | | |
| a. Verbal | Deficits can be observed | Delayed and disordered |
| b. Nonverbal | Deficits (e.g., odd eye gaze) | Deficits can be severe |
| 3. Communication | | |
| Expressive | Within normal limits | Deficits can be observed |
| Receptive | Within normal limits | Deficits can be observed |
| 4. Social responsiveness | | |
| Attachment | | |
| a. Parents | Observed responsiveness | Lack responsiveness |
| b. Caregivers | Observed responsiveness | Lack responsiveness |
| c. Peers | Observed responsiveness | Lack responsiveness |
| Interactions | | |
| a. Initiations to peers | Frequent, poor quality | Minimal frequency |
| b. Positive responses to peers | Frequent, awkward, and pertains to self-interests | Minimal frequency |
| c. Symbolic play | No impaired symbolic play | Absence of symbolic play |
| d. Reciprocal play | Observed but awkward | Minimal frequency |
| e. Coping | Deficits observed in quality | |
| f. Friendships | Minimal frequency | Minimal frequency |
| g. Requests for assistance | Observed but awkward | Minimal frequency |
| Emotional self-regulation | | |
| a. Emotional empathy | Observed but awkward | Deficits can be observed |
| b. Emotional responsiveness | Observed but could be extreme | Aloof, indifferent |
| 5. Physical/motor | | |
| a. Gross motor | Observed deficits—controversial | No observed deficits |
| b. Repetitive behavior | Observed | Observed |

From "Asperger Syndrome and Autism: A Literature Review and Meta-analysis," by E. McLaughlin-Cheng, 1998, *Focus on Autism and Other Developmental Disabilities, 13,* p. 237. Used by permission.

Table 9.3 shows the similarities and differences of the behavioral characteristics of children with Asperger syndrome and children with autism.

Just as there is no single method to teach children with autism, there is also not a preferred educational intervention for children with Asperger syndrome. Teachers must address several issues when dealing with these children and develop effective strategies for each child on an individual basis. Areas that should be considered include using visual strategies, which takes advantage of their more intact learning modality; using structural strategies, such as preparing students for changes in schedules and routines; and providing an instructional sequence that follows a logical progression for learning (Myles & Simpson, 1998).

## BASIC CONCEPTS ABOUT TRAUMATIC BRAIN INJURY

**Traumatic brain injury (TBI)** was added to the special education categories under IDEA in 1990. The condition is defined in the law as an acquired injury to the brain caused by an external physical force, resulting in total or partial functional disability or psychosocial impairment, or both, that adversely affects a child's educational performance. The term applies to open or closed head injuries resulting in impairments in one or more areas, such as cognition, language, memory, attention, reasoning, abstract thinking, judgment, problem solving, sensory, perceptual and motor abilities, psychosocial behavior, physical functions, information processing, and speech. The term does not apply to brain injuries that are congenital, degenerative, or induced by birth trauma (IDEA, 1997).

*TRAUMATIC BRAIN INJURY* is an acquired injury to the brain caused by an external physical force.

Traumatic brain injury can result from a wide variety of causes, including falls, vehicle accidents, and even abuse. It can also be caused by lack of oxygen to the brain, infections, tumors and strokes (Garcia, Krankowski, & Jones, 1998). Save (1997) reported that about 30,000 children suffer permanent brain injury each year.

Information about the severity of a traumatic brain injury is important for teachers to know, as it can provide a sense of the expected long-term outcomes for a student. Although no standardized system has been developed to describe levels of severity, Mira, Tucker, & Tyler (1992) offer the following system, which is derived from a variety of sources:

*Mild:* Signs of concussion or a blow resulting in some aftereffects, such as dizziness or loss of consciousness, for less than an hour; no skull fracture; majority of brain injuries are mild.

*Moderate:* Loss of consciousness for from 1 to 24 hours or evidence of a skull fracture; may develop secondary neurological problems such as swelling within the brain and subsequent complications; neurosurgery may be required.

*Severe:* Loss of consciousness for more than 24 hours, or evidence of contusion (actual bruising of brain tissue) or intracranial hematoma (bleeding within the brain); long-term medical care is likely; typical sequelae (consequences) include motor, language, and cognitive problems.

The social–emotional and cognitive deficits caused by the injury may persist long after physical capabilities recover. Students with TBI can experience a host of confusing and frustrating symptoms. "There is an inability to concentrate; short-term memory is affected; one's self-confidence is undermined; self-esteem is diminished; the personality changes; . . . the family and friends are affected" (Infusini, 1994, pp. 4–5). Teachers must guard against minimizing an injury because it presents no visible

| TABLE 9.4 | Persisting Features of Traumatic Brain Injury |
|---|---|
| **Area of Functioning** | **Possible Effects** |
| PHYSICAL/MEDICAL | ■ Reduced stamina and fatigue<br>■ Seizures (5%)<br>■ Headaches<br>■ Problems with regulation of various functions (e.g., growth, eating, body temperature) |
| SENSORY | ■ Hearing problems (e.g., conductive and/or sensorineural loss)<br>■ Vision problems (e.g., blurred vision, visual field defects) |
| COGNITIVE | ■ Memory problems (e.g., storage and retrieval)<br>■ Attentional difficulties<br>■ Intellectual deficits<br>■ Reasoning and problem-solving difficulties |
| LANGUAGE-RELATED | ■ Word retrieval difficulties<br>■ Motor-speech problems (e.g., dysarthria)<br>■ Language comprehension deficits (e.g., difficulty listening)<br>■ Difficulty acquiring new vocabulary and learning new concepts<br>■ Socially inappropriate verbal behavior |
| BEHAVIORAL/EMOTIONAL | ■ Problems in planning, organizing, and problem solving<br>■ Disinhibition<br>■ Overactivity<br>■ Impulsivity<br>■ Lack of self-direction<br>■ Helplessness or apathy<br>■ Inability to recognize one's injury |

From *Traumatic Brain Injury in Children and Adolescents: A Sourcebook for Teachers and Other School Personnel* (pp. 71–72), by M. P. Mira, B. F. Tucker, and J. S. Tyler, 1992, Austin, TX: Pro-Ed. Used by permission.

evidence. Many teachers doubt the severity of the cognitive deficits of a student who has experienced mild TBI because the child seems normal. Table 9.4 lists possible lingering effects of TBI that can have an impact on a student's education.

The prognosis for recovery depends on many variables. Initially, it is "influenced by the type of injury and the rapidity and quality of medical and surgical care" (Bigge, 1991, p. 197). Later, it will be influenced by the nature of rehabilitative and educational intervention.

*CONSIDER THIS*
What can school personnel do to facilitate the transition of children with TBI from hospital and residential settings to public school? What kind of relationship should school personnel and hospital personnel maintain after the transition is completed?

# CLASSROOM ACCOMMODATIONS FOR STUDENTS WITH TRAUMATIC BRAIN INJURY

The reentry of students with TBI to school settings needs to be coordinated among a number of people. Intervention involves the efforts of professionals from many different disciplines, including teachers (Bergland & Hoffbauer, 1996). In addition to the injury itself and its implications on functioning and potential learning, students probably will have missed a significant amount of schooling. All of these factors can have a significant impact on educational performance. An effective educational program creates a positive attitude about the student's prognosis. This reaches beyond just speaking positively. Teachers communicate a positive attitude by the type of programming they present and by the level of expectations they establish. Remember to "keep expectations for students' performance high. Often, this means providing students with mild TBI with multiple opportunities for practice that do not carry penalties for inaccuracy" (Hux & Hackley, 1996). This will show the students that programs and instruction are designed to support them and not just to give them a grade. They will respond better when programs do not seem punitive.

Under the Individuals with Disabilities Education Act of 1997, TBI is a distinct category of disability, although some students may be provided services under Section 504. If they are identified under IDEA, they will have a written individual educational program (IEP); if served under Section 504, they will have an appropriate accommodation plan. Whatever plan is used, teachers will need to address the specific areas that have been identified as problematic. Table 9.5 gives ideas for helping students with problems that may result from TBI.

A well-planned program of instruction should focus on "retaining impaired cognitive processes, developing new skills or procedures to compensate for residual deficits, creating an environment that permits effective performance, identifying effective instructional procedures, and improving metacognitive awareness" (Ylvisaker et al., 1994, p. 17). The impact of the injury may require that the student learn compensatory strategies to make up for deficits. Such strategies can address problems with attending, language comprehension, memory, sequencing, and thought organization.

The following suggestions will help provide a positive learning program and environment for students with TBI:

▲ Prepare classmates for the reentry of a fellow student who has sustained a traumatic brain injury—it is important to discuss changes in physical functioning and personality.
▲ Modify the classroom to ensure safety and to address any specific needs of the student.
▲ Be familiar with any special equipment that might be needed (e.g., augmentative communication devices).
▲ Be familiar with the effects and administration procedures of prescribed medications.
▲ Assist students who are having difficulty with organization.
▲ Break down learning tasks into substeps.
▲ Create many opportunities for the student to use problem-solving skills.
▲ Allow extra time for students to respond to questions, take tests, complete assignments, and move from one setting to another.
▲ Teach students social skills appropriate for their age and needs.
▲ Implement behavior reduction techniques to eliminate inappropriate and undesirable behaviors.
▲ Help students to understand the nature of their injury.
▲ Provide information about academic, social, and psychomotor progress to families on a regular basis. Describe the nature of the educational program to them.

**TEACHING TIP**
Develop and implement intervention programs based on the student's specific needs. TBI results in a wide variety of deficits resulting in a great diversity of intervention needs.

## LOW-INCIDENCE HEALTH PROBLEMS AND PHYSICAL DISABILITIES

As noted in the beginning of this chapter, many health and physical disabilities may be present in children that result in a need for special education and related services. The remainder of this chapter will provide a quick guide to some of these

| TABLE 9.5 | Suggestions for Teaching Students with Traumatic Brain Injury |
|---|---|
| **Area of Functioning** | **Suggestion** |
| RECEPTIVE LANGUAGE | ■ Limit the amount of information presented at one time.<br>■ Provide simple instructions for only one activity at a time.<br>■ Have the student repeat instructions.<br>■ Use concrete language. |
| EXPRESSIVE LANGUAGE | ■ Teach the student to rehearse silently before verbally replying.<br>■ Teach the student to look for cues from listeners to ascertain that the student is being understood.<br>■ Teach the student to directly ask if he or she is being understood. |
| MAINTAINING ATTENTION | ■ Provide a study carrel or preferential seating.<br>■ After giving instructions, check for proper attention and understanding by having the student repeat them.<br>■ Teach the student to use self-regulating techniques to maintain attention (e.g., asking "Am I paying attention?" "What is the required task?"). |
| IMPULSIVENESS | ■ Teach the student to mentally rehearse steps before beginning an activity.<br>■ Reduce potential distractions.<br>■ Frequently restate and reinforce rules. |
| MEMORY | ■ Teach the student to use external aids such as notes, memos, daily schedule sheets, and assignment sheets.<br>■ Use visual imagery, when possible, to supplement oral content.<br>■ Teach visual imaging techniques for information presented.<br>■ Provide repetition and frequent review of instruction materials.<br>■ Provide immediate and frequent feedback to enable the student to interpret success or failure. |
| FOLLOWING DIRECTIONS | ■ Provide the student with both visual and auditory directions.<br>■ Model tasks, whenever possible.<br>■ Break multistep directions into small parts and list them so that the student can refer back when needed. |
| MOTOR SKILLS | ■ Allow the student to complete a project rather than turn in a written assignment.<br>■ Have the student use a typewriter or word processor to complete assignments.<br>■ Allow extra time for completing tasks requiring fine-motor skills.<br>■ Assign someone to take notes for the student during lectures. |

Adapted from *Traumatic Brain Injury in Children and Adolescents: A Sourcebook for Teachers and Other School Personnel* (pp. 71–72), by M. P. Mira, B. F. Tucker, and J. S. Tyler, 1992, Austin, TX: Pro-Ed. Used by permission.

disabilities and some considerations for educators. Teachers who work with children with one of these conditions should refer to a more thorough reference work to learn more about it. A Further Readings list at the end of this chapter suggests such sources of information.

## Asthma

**ASTHMA** is a chronic respiratory disorder characterized by episodic breathing difficulty.

**Asthma** is the most common chronic illness in children, affecting approximately 3 million children and youth under the age of 15 (American Academy of Allergy and Immunology, 1991; Bauer et al., 1999).

It is characterized by repetitive episodes of coughing, shortness of breath, and wheezing, resulting from the narrowing of small air passages, caused by irritation of the bronchial tubes by allergic reactions to various substances, such as animal dander, air pollutants, and pollens (McEwen et al., 1998). Asthma attacks can be very dangerous and should be taken seriously by school personnel. Specific suggestions for teachers include the following:

- Know the signs and symptoms of respiratory distress (Getch & Neuharth-Pritchett, 1999).
- Ensure that students have proper medications and that they are taken at the appropriate times.
- Allow students to rest when needed, as they often tire easily.
- Eliminate any known allergens found in the classroom.
- Determine what types of physical limitations might have to be set (e.g., restriction of a certain physical activity that can induce attacks), but otherwise encourage students to play games and participate in activities.
- Recognize the side effects of prescribed medication.
- Remain calm if an attack occurs.
- Allow the student to participate in nonstressful activity until an episode subsides.
- Introduce a vaporizer or dehumidifier to the classroom when recommended by the student's physician.
- Work on building up the student's self-image.
- Sensitize other students in the class to the nature of allergic reactions.
- Develop an effective system for helping the student keep up with schoolwork, as frequent absences may occur.

Educators can ask the following questions to determine whether a school is prepared to deal with students with asthma (National Heart, Lung, and Blood Institute, 1998):

1. Is the school free of tobacco smoke all of the time, including during school-sponsored events?
2. Does the school maintain good indoor air quality?
3. Is a school nurse in the school all day, every day?
4. Can children take medicines at school as recommended by their doctor and parents?
5. Does the school have an emergency plan for taking care of a child with a severe asthma attack?
6. Does someone teach school staff about asthma, asthma management plans, and asthma medicines?
7. Do students with asthma have good options for fully and safely participating in physical education class and recess?

## Childhood Cancer

**Childhood cancer** occurs in approximately 1 in 330 children prior to the age of 19 years (National Cancer Foundation, 1997). Childhood cancer can take several different forms, including leukemia, lymphoma, tumors of the central nervous system, bone tumors, tumors affecting the eyes, and tumors affecting various organs (Heller, Alberto, Forney, & Schwartzman, 1996). Treatment of cancer includes chemotherapy, radiation, surgery, and bone marrow transplantation. Suggestions for teachers and administrators who have students with cancer include the following:

**CHILDHOOD CANCER** is any form of cancer contracted during childhood.

- Express your concern about a student's condition to the parents and family.
- Learn about a student's illness from hospital personnel and parents.

**CONSIDER THIS**
What are some ways that teachers can maintain contact with students with cancer during their extended absences from the classroom? How can the teacher facilitate contact between classmates and the student with cancer?

◢ Inquire about the type of treatment and anticipated side effects.
◢ Refer the student for any needed special education services.
◢ Prepare for a student's terminal illness and possible death.
◢ Encourage discussion and consideration of future events.
◢ Allow for exceptions to classroom rules and procedures when indicated (e.g., wearing a baseball cap to disguise hair loss from chemotherapy).
◢ Be available to talk with a student when the need arises.
◢ Share information about the student's condition and ongoing status with teachers of the student's siblings.
◢ Be prepared to deal with issues concerning death and dying with students. See the nearby Inclusion Strategies feature for ideas.
◢ Provide information to school staff and parents, as needed (Hoida & McDougal, 1998).
◢ Facilitate the student's reentry into school after an extended absence.

## Cerebral Palsy

*CEREBRAL PALSY* is a disorder of movement or posture resulting from brain injury.

**Cerebral palsy** is a disorder of movement or posture that is caused by brain damage. It affects the voluntary muscles and often leads to major problems in communication and mobility. Cerebral palsy is neither progressive nor communicable (Gersh, 1991; Schleichkorn, 1993). It is also not "curable" in the usual sense of the word although education, therapy, and applied technology can help persons with cerebral palsy lead productive lives.

Between 6 and 10 individuals for every 10,000 in the population have cerebral palsy (Eaves, 1992). There are three primary methods for classifying individuals with cerebral palsy: by type (physiological), by distribution (topological) (Inge, 1992), and by degree of severity (Bigge, 1991). Table 9.6 describes the different types of cerebral palsy according to two classification systems. The primary intervention approach for children with cerebral palsy focuses on their physical needs. Physical therapy,

**TABLE 9.6    Classification of Cerebral Palsy**

| Topographical Classification System | Classification System by Motor Symptoms (Physiological) |
|---|---|
| A. *Monoplegia:* one limb | A. Spastic |
| B. *Paraplegia:* legs only | B. Athetoid |
| C. *Hemiplegia:* one-half of body |   1. Tension |
| D. *Triplegia:* three limbs (usually two legs and one arm) |   2. Nontension<br>  3. Dystonic<br>  4. Tremor |
| E. *Quadriplegia:* all four limbs | C. Rigidity |
| F. *Diplegia:* more affected in the legs than the arms | D. Ataxia |
| | E. Tremor |
| G. *Double hemiplegia:* arms more involved than the legs | F. Atonic (rare) |
| | G. Mixed |
| | H. Unclassified |

From *Understanding Physical, Sensory, and Health Impairments* (p. 95), by K. W. Heller, P. A. Alberto, P. E. Forney, and M. N. Schwartzman, 1996, Pacific Grove, CA: Brooks/Cole. Used by permission.

*Teachers who have students with cancer should learn about the child's illness from medical personnel.*

## INCLUSION STRATEGIES

### How to Handle the Issue of Death

Almost all students will want to know, but be afraid to ask, whether their classmate can die from cancer. If a classmate asks, respond honestly with something like "Nobody knows. Some children as sick as _____ have died, some other children have gotten better and are just fine. We don't know what will happen to _____, but [she/he] and [her/his] doctors are working very hard to make [her/him] well." If the class does not raise the issue of death, you *should* bring it up. Ask a question such as "Have any of you known anyone who has died from cancer?" (You will get nods.) Once you have raised the question, you can address it. "Cancer is a very serious disease and people do die from it." Then proceed with, "Nobody knows . . ."

Remember that elementary school children do not have the philosophical understanding of death that teenagers and adults do. Until children are capable of formal operational thought, they cannot truly conceptualize the finality of death. As educators we know that it is futile to try to teach history with concepts of past and future generations until children are 11 or 12 years old. Most elementary school students have had some experience with a pet or older relative who has died. They do understand that it means that the person does not come back. Be careful of the language you use. One child thought he was going to die when he was told he would be "put to sleep" for his operation. He knew his dog had been "put to sleep" and never came back. By having a discussion, you may be able to clarify such misconceptions. Generally, children are much more concerned with the concrete and immediate consequences to themselves and their friend. The classmates and friends of the ill student will understand that their friend is worried about physical pain, needles, and bodily harm. Some children will view their friend as a hero for having conquered forces they all fear. Children of this age are able to feel for another's pain. Most children have had flu, viruses, mouth sores, nausea, and even hospital experiences from which they are able to relate personal pain to that of another. The more you emphasize things children understand, the more you will tap into their altruism in helping their ill classmate.

Older children (and sometimes teachers) may be worried that their friend might die suddenly while they are together. The basic fear is that they would not know what to do or how to handle the situation. Assure them that children do not die suddenly. They get much sicker first. Their doctors and parents would be taking care of them, and they would not be in school.

From "Children with Cancer in the Classroom," by V. C. Peckham, 1993, *Teaching Exceptional Children, 26,* p. 31. Used by permission.

occupational therapy, and even surgery often play a part. Specific suggestions for teachers include the following:

*TEACHING TIP*
Develop some simulation activities for nondisabled students that will help them understand mobility problems. The use of wheelchairs and restricting the use of students' arms or hands will help them understand the problems experienced by some students with CP.

▲ Create a supportive classroom environment that encourages participation in every facet of the school day.
▲ Allow extra time for students to move from one location to another.
▲ Ask students to repeat verbalizations that may be hard to understand because of their speech patterns.
▲ Provide many real-life activities.
▲ Learn the correct way for the student to sit upright in a chair or wheelchair and how to use adaptive equipment (e.g., prone standers).
▲ Understand the functions and components of a wheelchair and any special adaptive pieces that may accompany it.
▲ Consider the use of various augmentative communication techniques with students who have severe cerebral palsy (Musselwhite, 1987).
▲ Encourage students to use computers that are equipped with expanded keyboards if necessary or other portable writing aids for taking notes or generating written products.
▲ Consult physical and occupational therapists to understand correct positioning, posture, and other motor function areas.

## Cystic Fibrosis

*CYSTIC FIBROSIS* is a genetically transmitted disorder that results in extreme breathing difficulty due to an over production of mucus.

**Cystic fibrosis** is an inherited, fatal disease that results in an abnormal amount of mucus throughout the body, most often affecting the lungs and digestive tract. It occurs in approximately 1 in 2,000 live births (Hill et al., 1993). On the average, children with the disease will live to their midteens. Teachers must make sure that children with cystic fibrosis take special medication before they eat. As the disease progresses, it greatly affects stamina and the student's physical condition. Specific suggestions for dealing with students with this disease include:

▲ Prepare students in class for the realities of this disease (e.g., coughing, noncontagious sputum, gas).
▲ Learn how to clear a student's lungs and air passages, as such assistance may be needed after certain activities.
▲ Know the medications a student must take and be able to administer them (e.g., enzymes, vitamins).
▲ Consider restricting certain physical activities.
▲ Inquire about the therapies being used with the student.
▲ Support the implementation of special diets if needed.
▲ Provide opportunities for students to talk about their concerns, fears, and feelings.
▲ Ensure that the student is included in all class activities to whatever extent is possible.
▲ Prepare students for the eventual outcome of the disease by raising the topic of death and dying.

## Deaf–Blind

*DEAF–BLIND* is the condition in which an individual has disorders of vision and hearing simultaneously.

Students who have visual impairments or auditory impairments create unique problems for educators. When students present deficits in both sensory areas, resulting in their being **deaf–blind**, their needs become extremely complex. Although the term *deaf–blind* continues to be found in federal legislation and regulations, including IDEA, the terms *dual sensory impairment* or *multiple sensory impairments* are considered more appropriate (Marchant, 1992). For purposes of being eligible for special education services under IDEA, deaf–blind is still the label for such students.

Students who are classified as being deaf–blind may be blind or deaf, or they may have degrees of visual and auditory impairments that do not classify as blindness or deafness. "The Helen Keller National Center estimates that about 94% of such individuals have residual hearing or residual sight that can facilitate their educational programs" (Marchant, 1992, p. 114). Obviously, individuals classified as being deaf–blind present a variety of characteristics. While these characteristics represent those exhibited by students who only have visual or hearing impairments, the overlap of these two disabilities results in significant educational needs. Wolfe (1997) suggests the following educational techniques for teachers to use when working with students classified as deaf–blind:

- Use an ecological approach to assessment and skill selection to emphasize functional needs of students. (See Chapter 3.)
- Use a variety of prompts, cues, and reinforcement strategies in a systematic instructional pattern.
- Use time delay prompting, where time between prompts is increased.
- Use groups and cooperative learning strategies.
- Implement environmental adaptations, such as enlarging materials, using contrasting materials, altering seating arrangements, and reducing extraneous noises to maximize residual hearing and vision of the student.

## Diabetes (Juvenile Diabetes)

Affecting nearly 8 million people in the United States, diabetes is a metabolic disorder in which the pancreas cannot produce sufficient insulin to process food (Holcomb et al., 1998). Teachers should be alert to possible symptoms of diabetes, including increased thirst, appetite, and urination; weight loss; fatigue; and irritability. Children with type I **(insulin-dependent) diabetes** must take daily injections of insulin. School personnel must have knowledge of the special dietary needs of these children and understand their need for a daily activity regimen. Some specific suggestions on dealing with diabetic students follow:

- Communicate regularly with the family to determine any special needs the student may have.
- Schedule snacks and lunch at the same time every day.
- Be prepared for hypoglycemia—a situation in which the student needs to have sugar.
- Help the student deal with the disease.
- Understand the distinction between having too much insulin in the body and not having enough. Table 9.7 describes both of these conditions and actions to address them.

## Epilepsy

**Epilepsy** is a series of recurrent convulsions, or seizures, that are caused by abnormal electrical discharges in the brain (Smith, 1998). There are several different types of epilepsy, determined by the impact of abnormal brain activity. Table 9.8 describes four types. Approximately 1% of the population of the United States has epilepsy (Jan, Ziegler, & Erba 1991). No common characteristics are shared by individuals

*INSULIN-DEPENDENT DIABETES* is type I diabetes that requires daily insulin injections.

*TEACHING TIP*
Be prepared to deal with students with diabetes in your classroom before an emergency develops. Keep a list of symptoms and things to do if a student has too much insulin and if a student has too little insulin readily available.

*EPILEPSY* is characterized by seizure disorders that result in loss of motor or muscular control.

| TABLE 9.7 | Hyperglycemia and Hypoglycemia | | |
|---|---|---|---|
| **Category** | **Possible Symptoms** | **Cause** | **Treatment** |
| Ketoacidosis; hyperglycemia (too much sugar) | Symptoms occur gradually (over hours or days): polyuria; polyphagia; polydipsia; fatigue; abdominal pain; nausea; vomiting; fruity odor on breath; rapid, deep breathing; unconsciousness | Did not take insulin; did not comply with diet | Give insulin; follow plan of action |
| Insulin reaction; hypoglycemia (too little sugar) | Symptoms occur quickly (in minutes): headache; dullness; irritability; shaking; sweating; lightheadedness; behavior change; paleness; weakness; moist skin; slurred speech; confusion; shallow breathing; unconsciousness | Delayed eating; participated in strenuous exercise; took too much insulin | Give sugar; follow plan of action |

From *Understanding Physical, Sensory, and Health Impairments* (p.78), by K. W. Heller, P. A. Alberto, P. E. Forney, and M. N. Schwartzman, 1996, Pacific Grove, CA: Brooks/Cole. Used by permission.

| TABLE 9.8 | Four Types of Seizures |
|---|---|
| **GENERALIZED (GRAND MAL)** | ■ Sudden cry, fall, rigidity, followed by muscle jerks<br>■ Shallow breathing, or temporarily suspended breathing, bluish skin<br>■ Possible loss of bladder or bowel control<br>■ Usually lasts 2–3 minutes |
| **ABSENCE (PETIT MAL)** | ■ Blank stare, beginning and ending abruptly<br>■ Lasting only a few seconds<br>■ Most common in children<br>■ May be accompanied by blinking, chewing movement<br>■ Individual is unaware of the seizure |
| **SIMPLE PARTIAL** | ■ Jerking may begin in one area of body, arm, leg, or face<br>■ Cannot be stopped but individual is aware<br>■ Jerking may proceed from one area to another area |
| **COMPLEX PARTIAL** | ■ Starts with blank stares, followed by chewing and random activity<br>■ Individual may seem unaware or dazed<br>■ Unresponsiveness<br>■ Clumsy actions<br>■ May run, pick up objects, take clothes off, or other activity<br>■ Lasts a few minutes<br>■ No memory of what occurred |

From *Understanding Physical, Sensory, and Health Impairments* (p. 78), by K. W. Heller, P. A. Alberto, P. E. Forney, and M. N. Schwartzman, 1996, Pacific Grove, CA: Brooks/Cole. Used by permission.

with epilepsy. The Epilepsy Foundation of America (1992) notes the following significant signs of the disorder: (1) staring spells, (2) tic-like movements, (3) rhythmic movements of the head, (4) purposeless sounds and body movements, (5) head drooping, (6) lack of response, (7) eyes rolling upward, and (8) chewing and swallowing movements. Medical intervention is the primary recourse for individuals with epilepsy. Most people with epilepsy are able to control their seizures with the proper regimen of medical therapy (Agnew, Nystul, & Conner, 1998).

Even persons who respond very well to medication have occasional seizures. Therefore teachers and other school personnel must know what actions to take should a person experience a generalized seizure. Figure 9.3 summarizes the steps that should be taken when a child has a seizure. Teachers, parents, or others need to record behaviors that occur before, during, and after the seizure because they may be important to treatment of the disorder.

---

In a generalized tonic–clonic seizure, the person suddenly falls to the ground and has a convulsive seizure. It is essential to protect him or her from injury. Cradle the head or place something soft under it—a towel or your hand, for example. Remove all dangerous objects. A bystander can do nothing to prevent or terminate an attack. At the end of the episode, make sure the mouth is cleared of food and saliva by turning the person on his or her side to provide the best airway and allow secretions to drain. The person may be incontinent during a seizure. If the assisting person remains calm, the person will be reassured when he or she regains consciousness.

Breathing almost always resumes spontaneously after a convulsive seizure. Failure to resume breathing signals a complication of the seizure such as an aspiration of food, heart attack, or severe head or neck injury. In these unusual circumstances, cardiopulmonary resuscitation must start immediately. If repeated seizures occur, or if a single seizure lasts longer than five minutes, the person should be taken to a medical facility immediately. Prolonged or repeated seizures may suggest *status epilepticus* (nonstop seizures), which requires emergency medical treatment. In summary, *first aid for generalized tonic–clonic seizures is similar to that for other convulsive seizures.*

◢ Prevent further injury. Place something soft under the head, loosen tight clothing, and clear the area of sharp or hard objects.

◢ Force no objects into the person's mouth.

◢ Do not restrain the person's movements unless they place him or her in danger.

◢ Turn the person on his or her side to open the airway and allow secretions to drain.

◢ Stay with the person until the seizure ends.

◢ Do not pour any liquids into the person's mouth or offer any food, drink, or medication until he or she is fully awake.

◢ Start cardiopulmonary resuscitation if the person does not resume breathing after the seizure.

◢ Let the person rest until he or she is fully awake.

◢ Be reassuring and supportive when consciousness returns.

◢ A convulsive seizure is not a medical emergency unless it lasts longer than five minutes or a second seizure occurs soon after the first. In this situation, the person should be taken to an emergency medical facility.

*FIGURE* **9.3**

Steps to Take When Dealing with a Seizure

From *Seizure Recognition and Observation: A Guide for Allied Health Professionals* (p. 2), Epilepsy Foundation of America, 1992, Landover, MD: Author. Used by permission.

## HIV and AIDS

**Human immunodeficiency virus (HIV)** infection occurs when the virus attacks the body's immune system, leaving an individual vulnerable to infections or cancers. In its later stages, HIV infection becomes **acquired immunodeficiency syndrome (AIDS).** Two of the fastest-growing groups contracting HIV are infants and teenagers. HIV/AIDS is transmitted only through the exchange of blood or semen. As of September 1996, 7,472 cases of AIDS in children under 13 years of age, were reported to the Centers for Disease Control (Centers for Disease Control, 1997). Students with HIV/AIDS may display a variety of academic, behavioral, and social–emotional problems. Teachers need to take precautions when dealing with children with HIV/AIDS, hepatitis B, or any other blood-borne pathogen. See Figure 9.4 for specific precautions. Some specific suggestions for teachers include:

◢ Follow the guidelines (universal precautions) developed by the Centers for Disease Control and the Food and Drug Administration for working with HIV-infected individuals (see Figure 9.4).

◢ Ask the student's parents or physician whether there are any special procedures that must be followed.

◢ Discuss HIV/AIDS with the entire class, providing accurate information, dispelling myths, and answering questions.

◢ Discuss with students in the class that a student's skills and abilities will change over time if he or she is infected with HIV/AIDS.

◢ Prepare for the fact that the student may die, especially if AIDS is present.

◢ Ensure that the student with HIV/AIDS is included in all aspects of classroom activities.

◢ Be sensitive to the stress that the student's family is undergoing.

**FIGURE** **9.4**
Universal Precautions for Prevention of HIV, Hepatitis B, and Other Blood-Borne Pathogens

From *AIDS Surveillance Report* (p. 7), Centers for Disease Control, 1988, Atlanta, GA: Author. Used by permission.

The Centers for Disease Control and the Food and Drug Administration (1988) published guidelines designed to protect health care workers and to ensure the confidentiality of patients with HIV infection. These guidelines include the following information that is useful for classroom teachers.

◢ Blood should always be handled with latex or nonpermeable disposable gloves. The use of gloves is not necessary for feces, nasal secretions, sputum, sweat, saliva, tears, urine, and vomitus unless they are visibly tinged with blood. Handwashing is sufficient after handling material not containing blood.

◢ In all settings in which blood or bloody material is handled, gloves and a suitable receptacle that closes tightly and is child-proof should be available. Although HIV does not survive well outside the body, all spillage of secretions should be cleaned up immediately with disinfectants. This is particularly important for cleaning up after a bloody nose or a large cut. Household bleach at a dilution of 1:10 should be used. Only objects that have come into contact with blood need to be cleaned with bleach.

◢ When intact skin is exposed to contaminated fluids, particularly blood, it should be washed with soap and water. Handwashing is sufficient for such activities as diaper change; toilet training; and clean-up of nasal secretions, stool, saliva, tears, or vomitus. If an open lesion or a mucous membrane appears to have been contaminated, AZT therapy should be considered.

*Children in wheelchairs need opportunities for social interactions.*

## Muscular Dystrophy

**Muscular dystrophy** is an umbrella term used to describe several different inherited disorders that result in progressive muscular weakness (Tver & Tver, 1991). The most common and most serious form of muscular dystrophy is **Duchenne dystrophy.** In this type of muscular dystrophy, fat cells and connective tissue replace muscle tissue. Individuals with Duchenne dystrophy ultimately lose their ability to walk, typically by age 12. Functional use of arms and hands will also be affected. Muscle weakness will also result in respiratory complications. Teachers must adapt their classrooms to accommodate the physical needs of these students. Most individuals with this form of muscular dystrophy die during young adulthood. Specific suggestions for teachers include the following:

◢ Be prepared to help the student deal with the loss of various functions.
◢ Involve the student in as many classroom activities as possible.
◢ Using assistive techniques that do not hurt the individual, help the student as needed in climbing stairs or in getting up from the floor.
◢ Understand the functions and components of wheelchairs.
◢ Monitor the administration of required medications.
◢ Monitor the amount of time the student is allowed to stand during the day.
◢ Be familiar with different types of braces (e.g., short leg, molded ankle-foot) students might use.
◢ Prepare other students in class for the realities of the disease.

## Prader-Willi Syndrome

**Prader-Willi syndrome** is a condition characterized by compulsive eating, obesity, and mental retardation (Silverthorn, & Hornak, 1993). Other characteristics include hypotonia (deficient muscle tone), slow metabolic rate, small or underdeveloped testes and penis, excessive sleeping, round face with almond-shaped eyes, nervous picking of skin, and stubbornness (Davies & Joughin, 1993; Silverthorn & Hornak, 1993; Smith & Hendricks, 1995). The only effective treatment for persons with Prader-Willi syndrome is weight management through diet and exercise.

**MUSCULAR DYSTROPHY** is an hereditary disorder characterized by weakening of the muscles.
**DUCHENNE DYSTROPHY** is the form of muscular dystrophy that is most severely disabling.

**CONSIDER THIS**
Should students who require extensive physical accommodations be placed in the same school, so that all schools and classrooms do not have to be accessible? Defend your response.

**TEACHING TIP**
Get in a wheelchair and try to move about your classroom to see whether it is fully accessible; often, areas that look accessible are not.

**PRADER-WILLI SYNDROME** is a chromosomal disorder that results in mental retardation and obsessive eating.

## Spina Bifida

**Spina bifida** is a "congenital condition characterized by a malformation of the vertebrae and spinal cord" (Gearheart, Weishahn, & Gearheart, 1996). It affects about 1 in 2,000 births (Bigge, 1991). There are three different types of spina bifida: spina bifida occulta, meningocele, and myelomeningocele (Gearheart et al., 1996; Robertson et al., 1992).

*SPINA BIFIDA is a birth defect in which the spinal column does not close properly.*

The least serious form of spina bifida is spina bifida occulta. In this type, the vertebral column fails to close properly, leaving a hole in the bony vertebrae that protect the delicate spinal column. With this form of spina bifida, surgically closing the opening to protect the spinal column is generally all that is required and does not result in any problems. **Meningocele** is similar to spina bifida occulta in that the vertebral column fails to close properly, leaving a hole in the bony vertebrae. Skin pouches out in the area where the vertebral column is not closed. In meningocele, the outpouching does not contain any nerve tissue. Surgically removing the outpouching and closing the opening usually result in a positive prognosis without any problems. **Myelomeningocele** is the most common and most severe form of spina bifida. Similar to meningocele, it has one major difference: nerve tissue is present in the outpouching. Because nerve tissue is involved, this form of spina bifida generally results in permanent paralysis and loss of sensation. Incontinence is also a possible result of this condition (Bigge, 1991; Robertson et al., 1992). School personnel must ensure appropriate use of wheelchairs (see the nearby Technology Today feature) and make accommodations for limited use of arms and hands. Teachers should do the following when working with a child with spina bifida:

*MENINGOCELE is a form of spina bifida in which there is an out-pouching but usually not paralysis.*

*MYELOMENINGOCELE is the most serious form of spina bifida that results in paralysis.*

◢ Inquire about any acute medical needs the student may have.
◢ Learn about the various adaptive equipment a student may be using (see Baker & Rogosky-Grassi, 1993).
◢ Maintain an environment that assists the student who is using crutches by keeping floors from getting wet and removing loose floor coverings.
◢ Understand the use of a wheelchair as well as its major parts.
◢ Learn how to position these students to develop strength and to avoid sores from developing in parts of their bodies that bear their weight, or that receive pressure from orthotic devices they are using. Because they do not have sensation, they may not notice the sores themselves. Healing is complicated by poor circulation.
◢ Understand the process of **clean intermittent bladder catheterization (CIC),** as some students will be performing this process to become continent and avoid urinary tract infections—the process involves insertion of a clean catheter through the urethra and into the bladder, must be done four times a day, and can be done independently by most children by age 6.
◢ Be ready to deal with the occasional incontinence of students. Assure the student with spina bifida that this is not a problem and discuss this situation with other class members.
◢ Learn how to deal with the special circumstances associated with students who use wheelchairs and have seizures.
◢ Ensure the full participation of the student in all classroom activities.
◢ Help the student with spina bifida develop a healthy, positive self-concept.
◢ Notify parents if there are unusual changes in the student's behavior or personality or if the student has various physical complaints such as headaches or double vision—this may indicate a problem with increased pressure on the brain (Deiner, 1993).

*CLEAN INTERMITTENT BLADDER CATHETERIZATION is the health procedure used to assist individuals who cannot urinate naturally.*

# *T*ECHNOLOGY *T*ODAY

## Pushing a Wheelchair

1. Over rough terrain or a raised area:
   a. Tilt the wheelchair by stepping down on tipping lever with foot as you pull down and back on hand grips.
   b. Continue to tilt chair back until it requires little or no effort to stabilize it.
   c. When the wheelchair is at the balance point, it can then be pushed over obstacles or terrain.
   d. Reverse the procedure and lower slowly. Make sure the wheelchair does not slam down or drop the last few inches.
2. Over curbs and steps:
   a. As you approach the curb or step, pause and tilt the wheelchair back to the balance point.
   b. When the wheelchair is stabilized, move toward curb until casters are on curb, and rear wheels come in contact with the curb.
   c. Move in close to the chair and lift the chair up by the handles. Roll the wheelchair up over the curb and push it forward.
   d. To go down, reverse the steps—back the wheelchair down off the curb without allowing it to drop down. Once rear wheels are down, step down on tipping lever and slowly lower casters.
3. Down a steep incline:
   a. Take the wheelchair down backward.
   b. The wheelchair can pick up speed too easily, and you can lose control if the wheelchair goes down first.
   c. Turn the chair around until your back is in the direction you plan to go.
   d. Walk backward, and move slowly down the ramp.
   e. Look backward occasionally to make sure you are staying on track and to avoid collisions.

*With proper planning, a student in a wheelchair can participate in fieldtrips and outings.*

4. Tips for a motorized wheelchair:
   a. Ensure that the child's hands are free in order to manipulate the controls.
   b. Know how to check the battery to ensure that there is sufficient charge for the day.
   c. Have someone from the family or company provide some training on trouble shooting problems that the student may experience with the wheelchair.
   d. Ensure that the child has sufficient room to maneuver the chair, which may require more room than a nonmotorized chair.
   e. Coordinate with the family to ensure that the wheelchair is maintained properly to avoid out-of-control movements.
   f. Make sure that sites visited on fieldtrips have accessible features since motorized wheelchairs are too heavy to lift or pull up stairs.
   g. Ensure that the student in the wheelchair, as well as students in the environment, do not play with the wheelchair.
   h. Explain to other students that the motorized wheelchair is a necessary support for the student and is not a toy.

## Tourette Syndrome

**Tourette syndrome** is a neuropsychiatric disorder that occurs in males three times as often as in females, resulting in a prevalence rate for males as high as 1 in 1,000 individuals (Hansen, 1992). The syndrome is "characterized by multiple motor and one or more vocal tics, which occur many times a day, nearly every day or intermittently, throughout a period of more than one year" (Crews et al., 1993, p. 25). Characteristics include various motor tics; inappropriate laughing; rapid eye movements;

*TOURETTE SYNDROME* is a disorder characterized by motor and vocal tics.

**CONSIDER THIS**
How should students with Tourette syndrome be dealt with when they shout obscenities and display other inappropriate disruptive behaviors?

winks and grimaces; aggressive behaviors; in infrequent cases, mental retardation; mild to moderate incoordination; and peculiar verbalizations (Wodrich, 1998). Most important, school personnel should be understanding with children who have Tourette syndrome. Monitoring medication and participating as a member of the interdisciplinary team are important roles for teachers and other school personnel.

# Summary

- Children with physical and health needs are entitled to an appropriate educational program as a result of IDEA.
- Physical and health impairments constitute low-incidence disabilities.
- The severity, visibility, and age of acquisition affect the needs of children with physical and health impairments.
- Students with physical and health problems display a wide array of characteristics and needs.
- Students with physical problems qualify for special education under the *orthopedically impaired* category of IDEA.
- Students with health problems qualify for special education under the *other health impaired* category of IDEA.

## Basic Concepts about Autism

- Autism is a pervasive developmental disability that primarily affects social interactions, language, and behavior.
- Although originally thought to be caused by environmental factors, autism is now considered to be caused by organic factors, including brain damage and complications during pregnancy.

## Classroom Accommodations for Students with Autism

- Growing evidence suggests that placing students with autism in general education classrooms with their nondisabled peers results in positive gains for them.

## Asperger Syndrome

- A condition associated with autism, Asperger syndrome was first included in the fourth edition of the *Diagnostic and Statistical Manual of Mental Disorders.*
- Although many of the behavioral characteristics displayed by children with Asperger syndrome are similar to those displayed by children with autism, the former generally have higher cognitive development and more typical communication skills.

## Basic Concepts about Traumatic Brain Injury

- Traumatic brain injury (TBI) is one of the newest categories recognized by IDEA as a disability category eligible for special education services. Children with TBI exhibit a wide variety of characteristics, including emotional, learning, and behavior problems.

## Classroom Accommodations for Students with Traumatic Brain Injury

- Teachers need to maintain as high a level of expectation as possible for students with TBI.
- Teachers must familiarize themselves with any specific equipment or medications students with TBI might need and modify the classroom accordingly.

## Low-Incidence Heath Problems and Physical Disabilities

- Asthma affects many children; teachers primarily need to be aware of medications to control asthma, side effects of medication, and the limitations of students with asthma.
- The survival rates for children with cancer have increased dramatically over the past 20 years. Teachers need to be prepared to deal with the emotional issues surrounding childhood cancer, including death issues. Children with cancer may miss a good deal of school; the school should make appropriate arrangements in these situations.
- Cerebral palsy is a condition that affects muscles and posture; it can be described by the way it affects movement or which limb is involved.
- Physical therapy is a critical component of treatment for children with cerebral palsy. Accessibility, communication, and social–emotional concerns are the primary areas that general educators must attend to.
- Cystic fibrosis is a terminal condition that affects the mucous membranes of the lungs.
- Juvenile diabetes results in children having to take insulin injections daily. Diet and exercise can help children manage their diabetes.

◢ Epilepsy is caused by abnormal activity in the brain that is the result of some brain damage or insult. Teachers must know specific steps to take in case children have a generalized tonic-clonic seizure in their classrooms.

◢ Infants and teenagers are two of the fastest-growing groups to contract HIV. Teachers need to keep up to date with developments in HIV/AIDS prevention and treatment approaches.

◢ Muscular dystrophy is a term used to describe several different inherited disorders that result in progressive muscular weakness and may cause death.

◢ Prader-Willi syndrome is a condition caused by a defect in the number 15 chromosome pair and is characterized by excessive overeating and mild mental retardation.

◢ Spina bifida is caused by a failure of the spinal column to close properly; this condition may result in paralysis of the lower extremities.

◢ Tourette syndrome is a neuropsychiatric disorder that is characterized by multiple motor tics, inappropriate laughter, rapid eye movements, winks, and grimaces, and aggressive behavior.

# *urther Readings*

Batshaw, M. L., & Parret, Y. M. (1986). *Children with handicaps: A medical primer.* Baltimore: Brookes.

Blackman, J. A. (Ed.). (1984). *Medical aspects of developmental disabilities in children birth to three.* Rockville, MD: Aspen.

Gillberg, C. (Ed.). (1989). *Diagnosis and treatment of autism.* New York: Plenum Press.

Koegel, R. L., & Koegel, L. K. (1995). *Teaching children with autism.* Baltimore: Brookes.

National Head Injury Foundation. (1988). *An educator's manual: What educators need to know about students with traumatic brain injury.* Southborough, MA: Author.

Pless, I. B. (Ed.). *The epidemiology of childhood disorders.* New York: Oxford Press.

Savage, R. C., & Wolcott, G. F. (Eds.). *Educational dimensions of acquired brain injury.* Austin, TX: Pro-Ed.

Schopler, E., & Mesibov, G. B. (Eds.). *Learning and cognition in autism.* New York: Plenum Press.

Smith, M. D., Belcher, R. G., & Juhrs, P. D. (1995). *A guide to successful employment for individuals with autism.* Baltimore: Brookes.

Wetherby, A. M., & Prizant, B. M. (Eds.). (2000). *Autism spectrum disorders: A transactional developmental perspective.* Baltimore: Brookes.

# Chapter 10

# Teaching Students with Communication Disorders

*by Kathleen McConnell Fad and Peggy Kipping*

*After reading this chapter, you should be able to:*

◢ Define the concept of communication and describe its major components, language, and speech

◢ Discuss communication disorders, including the different types of disorders and some of their characteristics

◢ Describe various classroom accommodations appropriate for students with speech and language disorders

◢ Describe typical speech and language development in children

◢ Discuss language differences that are due to culture and ways that teachers can deal with these differences

◢ Discuss augmentative and alternative communication techniques.

*I* got help for my speech from the time I was in kindergarten until third or fourth grade. Now my speech is as normal as anyone else's. When I get excited, I still stutter and mispronounce words as anyone does.

A lot of what has happened to me is reflected in the way I am today. I have never been one to make a lot of friends. I have a lot of associates, but only one or two close friends. It was the same in kindergarten. It might be a habit from not having lots of friends then. I had one or two, maybe three friends who could understand me and who took the time to listen to me. They were what you'd call good active listeners who would try to understand me.

That time ties into today and the way I make speeches. Once you know how to do something, you enjoy doing it. I know people who were called dyslexic and now love to read. I will give a presentation in front of a crowd—no problem. I like to talk in public.

I can't remember any bad things about special ed or speech therapy. I thought I was the cream of the crop. I didn't feel bad at all. There were a lot of good, positive things. My teachers did things in an encouraging way. They really made the kids feel comfortable. I think they got better results that way. I liked my resource time and looked forward to it. I think that my experiences have helped me make some positive relationships. I am a lot more self-reliant.

Don Ayers
Southwestern University

## QUESTIONS TO CONSIDER

1. In what ways did the special services provided to Don have an impact on his life as an adult?

2. Why is it important to be concerned with a student's self-concept? What kind of atmosphere helped Don have such a positive view of himself?

**F**or most of us, the ability to communicate is a skill we take for granted. Our communication is effortless and frequent. In one day, we might share a story with family members, discuss problems with our coworkers, ask directions from a stranger on the street, and telephone an old friend. When we are able to communicate easily and effectively, it is natural to participate in both the commonplace activities of daily living and the more enjoyable experiences that enrich our lives.

**CONSIDER THIS**
How would your life be different if you could not talk? If you could not write? If you could not hear?

However, when communication is impaired, absent, or qualitatively different, the simplest interactions may become difficult or even impossible. Moreover, because the communication skills that most of us use fluently and easily almost always involve personal interactions with others, disorders in speech or language may also result in social problems. For children, these social problems are most likely to occur in school. School is a place not only for academic learning, but also for building positive relationships with teachers and enduring friendships with peers. When a student's communication disorder, however mild, limits these experiences, makes him or her feel different and inadequate, or undermines confidence and self-esteem, the overall impact can be devastating.

Communication problems are often complex. There are many types of communication disorders, involving both speech and language. This chapter describes strategies that teachers can use with students who have such disorders. Suggestions will address specific communication disorders as well as associated problems in socialization and adjustment.

## BASIC CONCEPTS ABOUT COMMUNICATION DISORDERS

### Communication Disorders Defined

**SPEECH** and **LANGUAGE** are interrelated tools used to communicate among individuals.

**Speech** and **language** are interrelated skills, tools that we use to communicate. Heward (1995) defines the related terms this way:

> *Communication* is the exchange of information and ideas. Communication involves encoding, transmitting, and decoding messages. It is an interactive process requiring at least two parties to play the roles of both sender and receiver. . . . *Language* is a system used by a group of people for giving meaning to sounds, words, gestures, and other symbols to enable communication with one another. . . . *Speech* is the actual behavior of producing a language code by making appropriate vocal sound patterns. Although it is not the only possible vehicle for expressing language (gestures, manual signing, pictures, and written symbols can also be used to convey ideas and intentions), speech is a most effective and efficient method. Speech is also one of the most complex and difficult human endeavors. (pp. 234–236)

The **AMERICAN SPEECH-LANGUAGE-HEARING ASSOCIATION** is the predominant professional organization for individuals working in speech and language areas.

Various cultures develop and use language differently, and the study of language is a complex topic. The **American Speech-Language-Hearing Associa-**

290

tion (ASHA) (1982) includes the following important considerations in its discussion of language: (1) language evolves within specific historical, social, and cultural contexts; (2) language is rule-governed behavior; (3) language learning and use are determined by the interaction of biological, cognitive, psychosocial, and environmental factors; and (4) effective use of language for communication requires a broad understanding of human interactions, including associated factors such as nonverbal cues, motivation, and sociocultural roles (p. 949).

Because language development and use are such complicated topics, determining what is *normal* and what is *disordered* communication is also difficult. According to Emerick and Haynes (1986), a communication difference is considered a disability when

- the transmission or perception of messages is faulty.
- the person is placed at an economic disadvantage.
- the person is placed at a learning disadvantage.
- the person is placed at a social disadvantage.
- there is a negative impact upon the person's emotional growth.
- the problem causes physical damage or endangers the health of the person. (pp. 6–7)

In order to better understand communication disorders, it is helpful to be familiar with the dimensions of communication and the terms used to describe related disorders.

**TYPES OF COMMUNICATION DISORDERS**  In its definition of communicative disorders, ASHA (1982) describes both speech disorders and language disorders. **Speech disorders** include impairments of *voice, articulation,* and *fluency.* **Language disorders** are impairments of *comprehension* or *use of language,* regardless of the symbol system used. A language disorder may involve the *form* of language, the *content* of language, or the *function* of language. Specific disorders of language form include **phonologic, syntactic,** and **morphologic impairments. Semantics** refers to the content of language, and **pragmatics** is the system controlling language function. Figure 10.1 contains the definitions of communication disorders as described by ASHA. The terms in this figure are discussed in more detail later in the chapter. The category of communication disorders is broad in scope and includes a wide variety of problems, some of which may overlap. It is not surprising that this group of disorders includes a large proportion of all students with disabilities.

## Prevalence and Causes of Communication Disorders

Approximately 1,049,075 children and youth, about 2% of the school-age population, were classified as having speech or language impairments (SLI) during the 1996–1997 school year (U.S. Department of Education, 1998). These students have impairments in their ability to send or receive a message, to articulate clearly or fluently, or to comprehend the pragmatics of social interactions. Because many other students have other conditions as their primary disability but still receive speech–language services, the total number of students served by **speech–language pathologists** is about 5% of all school-age children. Students with communication disorders constitute about 20% of all students with disabilities. The number of students in this classification increased during the 1996–1997 school year (U.S. Department of Education, 1998). Of the estimated 1 million students identified as speech- or language-impaired, about 90% (over 900,000) are 6 to 12 years of age (U.S.

*CONSIDER THIS*
Can you think of instances in which you have been involved when communication between two or more persons was so poor that problems resulted?

*SPEECH DISORDERS* are impairments of voice, articulation, and fluency.

*LANGUAGE DISORDERS* are impairments of comprehension or use of language.

*PHONOLOGIC IMPAIRMENTS* are impairments in the sounds exhibited.

*SYNTACTIC IMPAIRMENTS* are impairments in syntax or the ordering of words.

*MORPHOLOGIC IMPAIRMENTS* are impairments in the structure of the words used.

*SEMANTICS* is the content of language.

*PRAGMATICS* is the system that controls language function.

*SPEECH–LANGUAGE PATHOLOGISTS* are professionals who provide therapy for individuals with speech and language disorders.

*FIGURE* **10.1**

Definitions of Communication Disorders from ASHA

From "Definitions: Communicative Disorders and Variations," by the American Speech-Language-Hearing Association, 1982, *ASHA, 24,* pp. 949–950. Reprinted by permission of the American Speech-Language-Hearing Association.

## COMMUNICATION DISORDERS

A.  A *speech disorder* is an impairment of voice, articulation of speech sounds, and/or fluency. These impairments are observed in the transmission and use of the oral symbol system.

  1.  A *voice disorder* is defined as the absence or abnormal production of voice quality, pitch, loudness, resonance, and/or duration.

  2.  An *articulation disorder* is defined as the abnormal production of speech sounds.

  3.  A *fluency disorder* is defined as the abnormal flow of verbal expression, characterized by impaired rate and rhythm, which may be accompanied by struggle behavior.

B.  A *language disorder* is the impairment or deviant development of comprehension and/or use of a spoken, written, and/or other symbol system. The disorder may involve (1) the form of language (phonologic, morphologic, and syntactic systems), (2) the content of language (semantic system), and/or (3) the function of language in communication (pragmatic system) in any combination.

  1.  Form of language

    a.  *Phonology* is the sound system of a language and the linguistic rules that govern the sound combinations.

    b.  *Morphology* is the linguistic rule system that governs the structure of words and the construction of word forms from the basic elements of meaning.

    c.  *Syntax* is the linguistic rule governing the order and combination of words to form sentences, and the relationships among the elements within a sentence.

  2.  Content of language

    a.  *Semantics* is the psycholinguistic system that patterns the content of an utterance, intent, and meanings of words and sentences.

  3.  Function of language

    a.  *Pragmatics* is the sociolinguistic system that patterns the use of language in communication, which may be expressed motorically, vocally, or verbally.

## COMMUNICATION VARIATIONS

A.  *Communicative difference/dialect* is a variation of a symbol system used by a group of individuals that reflects and is determined by shared regional, social, or cultural/ethnic factors. Variations or alterations in use of a symbol system may be indicative of primary language interferences. A regional, social, or cultural/ethnic variation of a symbol system should not be considered a disorder of speech or language.

B.  *Augmentative communication* is a system used to supplement the communicative skills of individuals for whom speech is temporarily or permanently inadequate to meet communicative needs. Both prosthetic devices and/or nonprosthetic techniques may be designed for individual use as an augmentative communication system.

## RIGHTS & RESPONSIBILITIES

### The Right to "Related Services" for Students with Speech Impairments

Students with speech impairments are generally served in general education classes. They are usually in need of related services. Related services are "to benefit the student" so that he or she may

▲ Advance appropriately toward attaining annual goals;

▲ Be involved and progress in the general curriculum and to participate in extracurricular activi-

ties and other nonacademic activities; and

▲ Be educated and participate with other children with disabilities and nondisabled children in those extracurricular and nonacademic activities. (Turnbull & Turnbull, 2000, p. 193)

Related services include speech pathology and speech–language pathology. IDEA defines these as "identification, diagnosis, and appraisal of specific speech or language impairments; referral to or provision of speech and language, medical, or other services; and counseling and guidance of parents, children, and teachers regarding speech and language impairments" (34 C.F.R., 300.24 (b)(14).

---

Department of Education, 1998). For this reason, most of the suggestions in this chapter focus on that age group, although many of the language development activities would also be useful for older students.

### Identification, Assessment, and Eligibility

Placement patterns for students with disabilities vary by disability, according to students' individual needs. Usually, the milder the disability, the less restrictive the placement. Students with speech or language impairments are the most highly integrated of all students with disabilities. Since 1985, most students with SLI have been served in either general education classes or resource rooms. During the 1995–1996 school year, 88.6% of students with communication disorders were served in general education classroom placements and 6.5% were served in resource rooms (U.S. Department of Education, 1998). The small proportion served in separate classes most likely represents students with severe language delays and disabilities. For classroom teachers, having students with communication disorders in their classes is more the rule than the exception. The nearby Rights and Responsibilities feature highlights students with speech impairments rights to related services when they are in the general education classroom.

Because so many students with communication disorders are in general education, it is important that teachers be able to identify those students who may have speech or language problems, be familiar with common causes of communication disorders, know when problems are serious enough to require referral to other resources, and have some effective strategies for working with students in the general education environment.

**CONSIDER THIS**

What are the advantages of serving most of the students with communication disorders in general education classrooms? When would pull-out services be appropriate?

## SPEECH DISORDERS

This section of the chapter discusses speech disorders that include problems in *articulation, voice,* and *fluency.* The discussion includes (1) a description and definition, (2) a brief explanation of causes, and (3) information related to identifying problems serious enough to require a referral for possible assessment or remediation.

| TABLE 10.1 | The Four Kinds of Articulation Errors | |
|---|---|---|
| **Error Type** | **Definition** | **Example** |
| SUBSTITUTION | Replace one sound with another sound. | Standard: The ball is red. Substitution: The ball is wed. |
| DISTORTION | A sound is produced in an unfamiliar manner. | Standard: Give the pencil to Sally. Distortion: Give the pencil to Sally. (the /p/ is nasalized) |
| OMISSION | A sound is omitted in a word. | Standard: Play the piano. Omission: P_ay the piano. |
| ADDITION | An extra sound is inserted within a word. | Standard: I have a black horse. Addition: I have a balack horse. |

From *Human Communication Disorders* (3rd edition), by G. H. Shames and E. H. Wiig, 1990, New York: Macmillan. Copyright © 1990 by Macmillan Publishing Company. Reprinted by permission.

## Articulation Disorders

*ARTICULATION DISORDERS* are disorders in making sounds.

*DISTORTIONS* involve producing a sound in an unfamiliar manner.

*SUBSTITUTIONS* occur when one sound is replaced with another sound.

*OMISSIONS* are caused by leaving a sound out of a word.

*ADDITIONS* are caused by adding a sound in a word.

*CROSS-REFERENCE* Review Chapter 8 on sensory impairments to see the impact of a hearing loss on articulation skills.

**Articulation disorders** are the most common speech disorder representing more than 75% of all speech disorders in children (ASHA, 1999). The ability to articulate clearly and correctly is a function of many variables, including a student's age and culture. Although some articulation errors are normal and acceptable at young ages, when students are older these same errors may be viewed as developmentally inappropriate and problematic. McReynolds (1990) has described the most common types of articulation errors: **distortions, substitutions, omissions,** and **additions.** (See Table 10.1.)

CAUSES OF PROBLEMS IN ARTICULATION   Speech impairments can be either *organic* (i.e., having a physical cause) or *functional* (i.e., having no identifiable organic cause). Children with functional communication disorders account for 99% of the articulation caseloads of speech–language pathologists in the schools (ASHA, 1999). When you encounter a child with articulation disorders, consider the child's environment. Many functional disorders may be related to the student's opportunities to learn appropriate and inappropriate speech patterns, including opportunities to practice appropriate speech and the absence or presence of good speech models. Many functional articulation problems have causes that may be related to complex neurological or neuromuscular activities and might never be understood. Differences in speech can also be related to culture. These differences often do not constitute a speech disorder and will be discussed later in the chapter.

Organic articulation disorders are related to the physical abilities required in the process of producing speech sounds, which is a highly complex activity involving numerous neurological and muscular interactions. According to Oyer, Crowe, and Haas (1987), organic causes of speech impairments may include cleft palate, dental malformations, or tumors. Hearing loss, brain damage, or related neurological problems may also result in disorders of speech. The severity of articulation disorders can vary widely, depending in part on the causes of the disorders.

**WHEN ARTICULATION ERRORS ARE A SERIOUS PROBLEM**  Because we know the developmental patterns for normal sound production, we can recognize those children who are significantly different from the norm. According to Sander (1972), the normal pattern of consonant sound production falls within relatively well-defined age limits. For example, children usually master the consonant *p* sound by age 3, but may not produce a correct *s* sound consistently until age 8. Although young children between ages 2 and 6 often make articulation errors as their speech develops, similar errors in older students would indicate an articulation problem. At age 3 it might be normal for a child to say *wabbit* instead of *rabbit*. If a 12-year-old made the same error, it would be considered a problem, and the teacher might want to refer the student to a speech–language pathologist for evaluation. Figure 10.2 presents this pattern of normal development.

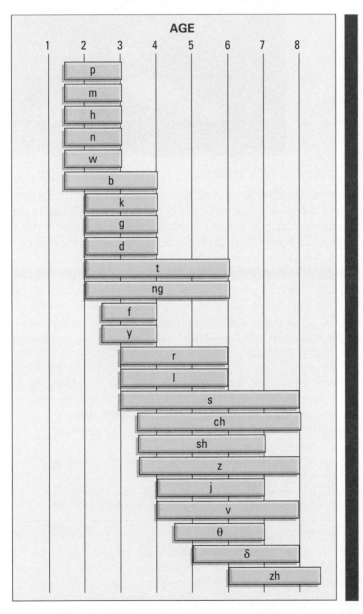

**FIGURE 10.2**

Ages at Which 90% of All Children Typically Produce a Specific Sound Correctly

Note: Average estimates and upper age limits of customary consonant production. The solid bar corresponding to each sound starts at the median age of customary articulation; it stops at an age level at which 90% of all children are customarily producing the sound. The q symbol stands for the breathed "th" sound, as in *bathroom,* and the ∂ symbol stands for the voiced "th" sound, as in feather (Smith and Luckasson, 1992, p. 168).

From "When Are Speech Sounds Learned?" by E. K. Sander, 1972, *Journal of Speech and Hearing Disorders,* 37, p. 62. Reprinted by permission of the American Speech-Language-Hearing Association.

**CONSIDER THIS**
How could cultural differences influence a child's development of the specific sounds listed in Figure 10.2?

*A*rticulation problems can result in problems in socialization or adjustment.

For a general education teacher, evaluating a student's articulation errors involves looking at the big picture, that is, how well the student is doing in class and whether the articulation disorder is interfering with either overall academic performance or social adjustment. A few common sense considerations may give some insight into whether the student has a serious problem and what, if anything, should be done about it:

▲ *Take note of how understandable or intelligible the student's speech is.* This factor may vary over time. Sometimes, the context of the student's speech will make it easier for listeners to understand her or him. Also, some errors are easier to understand than others. For example, omissions of sounds are usually more difficult to understand than distortions or substitutions.

▲ *Consider how many different errors the student makes.* If the errors are consistent, that is, if the student repeats the same error rather than numerous different errors, he or she will be easier to understand. Peers and teachers will become familiar with these speech problems, and the student will have less of a problem relating to others. However, the problem should still be addressed so that the student's speech is intelligible to strangers.

▲ *Observe whether the articulation errors cause the student problems in socialization or adjustment.* If a student with articulation problems is ridiculed, excluded, or singled out because of a speech problem, then the teacher may want to refer the student for a speech-language evaluation. Likewise, if a student is reluctant to speak in class, or seems self-conscious or embarrassed by articulation errors, the general education teacher should seek an evaluation.

▲ *Consider whether the errors are due to physical problems.* If they are, be sure that the student is referred to a physician. Some articulation problems are due to malformations of the mouth, jaw, or teeth. When the problems are structural, such as cleft lip or palate, they can often be corrected surgically. Likewise, dental malocclusions (abnormal closures and fit of the teeth) can be corrected with orthodontic treatment.

**TEACHING TIP**
General classroom teachers should screen all students in their classes, especially during the early elementary grades, to determine which students have articulation problems that might require intervention.

## Voice Disorders

**Voice disorders** are abnormalities of speech related to volume, quality, or pitch. Voice problems are not very common in children, and it is difficult to distinguish an unpleasant voice from one that would be considered disordered. People generally tolerate a wide range of voices. Because our voices are related to our identities and are an integral part of who we are and how we are recognized, we usually allow for individual differences in voice.

According to Heward (1995), there are two basic types of voice disorders, **phonation** and **resonance.** Phonation refers to the production of sounds by the vocal folds. Humans have two vocal folds, which are located in the larynx and lie side by side. When we speak, healthy vocal folds vibrate, coming together smoothly along the length of their surfaces, separating, and then coming together again. These movements are usually very rapid and are controlled by the air pressure coming from the lungs. If the vocal folds do not meet and close together smoothly, the voice is likely to sound breathy, hoarse, husky, or strained.

Disorders of resonance involve either too many sounds coming out through the air passages of the nose (hypernasality) or the opposite, too little resonance of the nasal passages (hyponasality). Hypernasality sounds like talking through one's nose or with a "twang," and hyponasality sounds like one has a cold or a stuffy nose. Because resonance is related to what happens to air that travels from the vocal folds into the throat, mouth, and nasal cavity, when there are abnormalities in any of these structures, resonance problems can result.

**CAUSES OF VOICE DISORDERS**　Voice disorders can result from vocal abuse and misuse, trauma to the larynx from accidents or medical procedures, congenital malformations of the larynx, nodules, or tumors. Disorders caused by abuse or misuse are the most common and most easily prevented voice disorders in school-aged children (ASHA, 1999). Sometimes, voice disorders are related to other medical conditions, so that when students evidence a voice disorder, the speech–language pathologist will refer them to an otolaryngologist (ear, nose, and throat doctor). Some examples of organic problems related to voice disorders include congenital anomalies of the larynx, Reye's syndrome, juvenile arthritis, psychiatric problems, or Tourette syndrome. Because most of these conditions are relatively rare, it may be more likely that the student's voice disorder is a functional problem, perhaps resulting from learned speech patterns (Oyer et al., 1987).

**WHEN VOICE DISORDERS ARE A SERIOUS PROBLEM**　A student who has a voice disorder should be observed over the course of several weeks, since many symptoms of voice disorders are similar to other temporary conditions such as colds, seasonal allergies, or minor respiratory infections (Oyer et al., 1987). One way to get a meaningful measure of the student's speech during this time is to tape record him or her several times during the observation period. The tape recordings will be helpful to the speech–language pathologist and will provide a basis for comparison. Again, our voices are part of our identity, and, quite often, differences in voice quality, volume, or pitch may be considered to be part of who we are, rather than a problem that requires correction. Teachers might ask themselves the following questions before referring a student for evaluation of a voice disorder:

◢　Is the student's voice having such an unpleasant effect on others that the student is excluded from activities?

---

**VOICE DISORDERS** are speech abnormalities that affect volume, quality, or pitch.

**PHONATION** is the production of sounds by the vocal folds.

**RESONANCE** is determined by what happens to the air that travels from the vocal folds into the throat, mouth, and nasal cavity.

**CONSIDER THIS**
How can a student's voice quality affect classroom and peer acceptance? What are some things that teachers can do to influence this impact?

◢ Is there a possibility that the voice disorder is related to another medical condition?

◢ Might the voice quality be related to a hearing loss?

## Fluency Disorders

**FLUENCY** is the rate and flow of a person's speech.

**Fluency** refers to the pattern of the rate and flow of a person's speech. Normal speech has a rhythm and timing that is regular and steady; however, normal speech patterns also include some interruptions in speech flow. We all sometimes stumble over sounds, repeat syllables or words, mix up speech sounds in words, speak too fast, or fill in pauses with "uh" or "you know." Often normal dysfluencies of speech are related to stressful or demanding situations. When the interruptions in speech flow are so frequent or pervasive that a speaker cannot be understood, when efforts at speech are so intense that they are uncomfortable, or when they draw undue attention, then the dysfluencies are considered a problem (Hallahan & Kauffman, 1995).

Many young children, especially those between ages 3 and 5, demonstrate dysfluencies in the course of normal speech development. Parents and teachers may become concerned about young children's fluency problems, but most of these dysfluencies of early childhood begin to disappear by age 5. The most frequent type of fluency disorder is **stuttering**, which affects about 2% of school-age children, more often boys than girls (Smith & Luckasson, 1992).

**STUTTERING** is interruptions in the flow of speech.

Fluency problems usually consist of blocking, repeating, or prolonging sounds, syllables, words, or phrases. In *stuttering,* these interruptions are frequently obvious to both the speaker and the listener. Often, they are very disruptive to the act of speaking, much more so than disorders of articulation or voice. When the speech dysfluencies occur, listeners may become uncomfortable and try to finish the speaker's words, phrases, or sentences. This discomfort is exacerbated when a speaker's stuttering is accompanied by gestures, facial contortions, or physical movements. Because stuttering is such a pronounced interruption of normal speech and also has a profound impact on listeners, the disorder receives a lot of attention, even though it is not as prevalent as other communication disorders (Hardman, Drew, Egan, & Wolf, 1993).

**CAUSES OF STUTTERING**    Although many causes of stuttering have been suggested over the years, the current thinking among professionals in the field of communication disorders is that there may be many different causes of the disorder. According to Van Riper and Emerick (1984), these theories include (1) the view that stuttering is related to emotional problems, (2) the idea that stuttering is the result of a person's biological makeup or of some neurological problem, and (3) the view that stuttering is a learned behavior. The most persistent theory is that stuttering is a learned behavior resulting from normal dysfluencies evident in early speech development. Also, the role that heredity plays in the development of stuttering remains interesting, in light of the fact that males who stutter outnumber females who stutter by a ratio of four to one (Hardman et al., 1990).

**TEACHING TIP**
Teachers who have students who stutter should attempt to reduce the stress on these students and create an accepting atmosphere.

There seems to be no doubt that the children who stutter are very vulnerable to the attitudes, responses, and comments of their teachers and peers. When considerable attention is focused on normal dysfluencies or when students begin to have negative feelings about themselves because of their stuttering, they may become even more anxious and their stuttering may get worse. Most students who stutter will require therapy by a speech–language clinician if they hope to avoid a lifelong problem that will affect their ability to communicate, learn, work, and develop positive interpersonal relationships.

**WHEN FLUENCY DISORDERS ARE A SERIOUS PROBLEM**   We know that many children outgrow their speech dysfluencies. However, classroom teachers should be sensitive to students' problems and be sure to refer children who stutter so that they receive speech therapy. Teachers may wish to consider the following questions when deciding whether speech dysfluencies are serious:

**TEACHING TIP**
Teachers should keep a log to record instances of stuttering and the activities occurring with the student and the rest of the class when stuttering occurs and when it does not occur.

▲ *Is there a pattern to situations in which the student stutters?* Collect information about the student related to his stuttering. With careful observation, teachers may be able to determine if a student's stuttering occurs under specific conditions, that is, with certain individuals, in particular settings, or when in stressful situations.

▲ *Is the student experiencing social problems?* Carefully monitor unstructured situations to determine the level of the student's acceptance by peers. Much of the socialization that occurs in school takes place in the cafeteria, on the playground, in the halls, on the bus, and in other nonacademic settings. When students are not successfully relating to peers in these environments because of a stuttering problem, then the problem is likely to grow worse.

▲ *Is the student confident?* Talk to the student to ascertain his or her level of confidence and self-esteem. One of the biggest problems facing children who stutter is the interactive effect of the disorder. The more they stutter, the more anxious, fearful, or nervous they become when they speak, thereby increasing the likelihood of stuttering. Children caught in this cycle of behavior may be so self-conscious that they avoid situations in which they are required to speak and thus become isolated from peers and teachers.

## CLASSROOM ACCOMMODATIONS FOR STUDENTS WITH SPEECH DISORDERS

### Build a Positive Classroom Climate

Regardless of the type of speech disorder that students in general education classes demonstrate, it is crucial that teachers make every effort to create a positive, accepting, and safe climate. The following points are helpful to remember when dealing with children who have speech disorders:

▲ Don't think of or refer to students with speech disorders in terms of their behaviors ("students," not "stutterers").

▲ Work closely with the speech–language pathologist, following suggestions and trying to reinforce specific skills.

▲ Encourage the student.

▲ Be positive.

▲ Accept the child just as you would any other student in the class.

▲ Provide lots of opportunities for students to participate in oral group activities.

▲ Give students lots of chances to model and practice appropriate speech.

▲ Maintain eye contact when the student speaks.

▲ Be a good listener.

▲ Don't interrupt or finish the student's sentence for him or her.

▲ When appropriate, educate other students in the class about speech disorders and about acceptance and understanding.

▲ Reward the child just as you would reward any student.

**TEACHING TIP**
Self-monitoring strate-
gies, such as record
keeping, can facilitate a
student's attempts to
monitor his or her own
speech.

## Help Students Learn to Monitor Their Own Speech

By using simple contract formats, teachers can help students focus on using the skills they learn in speech therapy. When students are aware of how to make sounds correctly, they can then practice, monitor their own performance, and earn reinforcement from the teacher or parents whenever specific criteria are met.

## Pair Students for Practice

If students are to master articulation skills, they will need to practice the skills taught by the speech–language pathologist. One way for students to practice specific sounds is to

**FIGURE 10.3**

Sample Form for
Articulation Practice

From *Hall's Articulation
Remediation Training Sheets
(HARTS)* (p. 3), by B.
Butler-Hall, 1987,
Henderson, TX:
Creations Publications.
Used by permission.

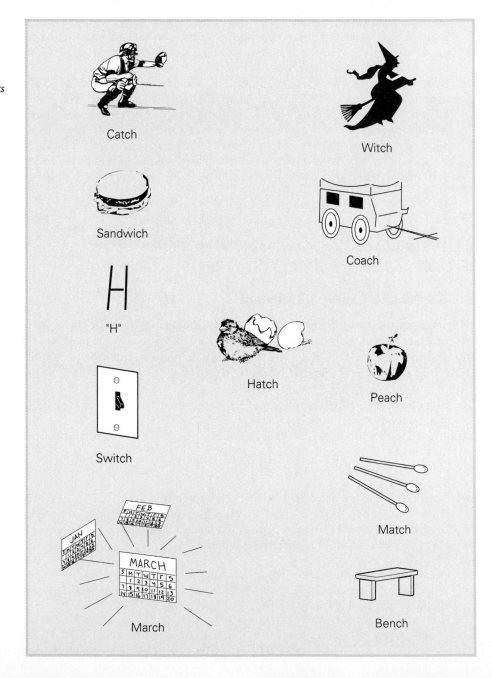

Catch

Witch

Sandwich

Coach

"H"

Hatch

Peach

Switch

Match

March

Bench

use practice exercises like those in *Hall's Articulation Remediation Training Sheets (HARTS)* (Butler-Hall, 1987). (See Figure 10.3.) With a partner, students can use short periods of downtime such as those between or before classes to work on their articulation. First, the student is trained in the speech therapy setting on a specific phoneme in a key word, for example, the *ch* sound in *hatch*. After the student has reached 90% mastery of the sound in the key word, she or he then reads the key word and every other word on the skill sheet, in alternating sequence (*hatch, catch, hatch, witch, hatch, sandwich,* etc.). Each practice session should take no more than five minutes and will provide students with practice that is simple and fun. Both partners should be reinforced for their participation. This practice format can also be used at home with parents.

## Teach Students Affirmations and Positive Self-Talk

For students with speech disorders, especially stuttering, confidence and attitudes are as important as specific speech skills. Some research has supported the premise that we all talk to ourselves all of the time, and the more we talk to ourselves in certain ways, the more we think about ourselves in those same ways. Although negative **self-talk** is common among individuals who have speech disorders, it is possible to change negative patterns to more positive ones.

*SELF-TALK* is the process of talking to one's self.

Affirmations like those suggested by Daly (1991) can enable students to build their confidence. The goal of positive self-talk is to replace negative patterns, which might include the statements "I could never do that" or "I can never talk on the phone without stuttering" with positive statements such as "I am positive and confident. I know that I can handle any speaking situation by being in control of my speech" and "I enjoy saying my name clearly and smoothly when answering the telephone." Whenever a student slips back into a negative frame of mind, encourage him or her to mentally erase the negative ideas and immediately think of something positive. Students should also write their affirmations in their own words, so that they will remember them easily and will more likely use them.

## Modify Instruction and Materials

*The Pre-Referral Intervention Manual (PRIM)* (McCarney & Wunderlich, 1988) presents numerous ways of intervening with students who demonstrate speech errors. Some of the suggestions include the following:

- ▲ Set up a system of motivators to encourage students' efforts.
- ▲ Highlight material to identify key syllables and words in a passage.
- ▲ Give students practice listening so that they can learn to discriminate sounds.
- ▲ Tape record the students' reading so that they can evaluate themselves concerning omissions, additions, distortions, substitutions, or reversals (saying words backwards).
- ▲ Reduce the emphasis on competition. Competitive activities may increase students' stress and result in even more speech errors.

## Encourage Parents to Work with Their Children

There are many ways to structure practice activities so that students can work at home with their parents. One program is described in the book *Weekday Speech Activities to Promote Carryover* (Fehling, 1993; see Figure 10.4). This series of activities is designed for the carryover phase of an articulation program. There are 36 worksheets for summer activities. They are designed to be an enjoyable approach to maintenance and generalization of sounds into everyday conversation. By completing the activities, students

FIGURE **10.4**   Speech Activities That Parents Can Use

**Sample Worksheet #1 (front)**

Sample Worksheet #1 (front)

Student's Name ___Eric___   Date __Oct. 7__

Sound ___S, Z___

__Mon.__ —Look for two street or road signs that have your sound.

   *1. Countryway Street*

   *2. STOP Sign*

__Tues.__ —What letters of the alphabet have your sound as you pronounce the names of those letters? Write them down here.

   *C, S, X, Z*

__Wed.__ —Who are two relatives or neighbors with your sound in their names?

   *1. Elizabeth*

   *2. Robyn Pearse*

__Thurs.__ —Tell how you get over the hiccups. Be sure to use at least one word with your sound.

   *drink a glass of water*

__Fri.__ —On the back of this paper draw something with your sound that is COLD.

*Comments:*

   *Eric seems to be doing better making his sound at home.*

Please return ___Mon., Oct. 14___

      *Susan Garrison*

      **Parent Signature**

**Sample Worksheet #1 (back)**

*Ice Cream Cone*

From *Weekday Speech Activities to Promote Carryover* (p. 117), by R. H. Fehling, 1993, Austin, TX: Pro-Ed. Used by permission.

assume responsibility for correct production of sounds in environments other than the speech therapy room. It is suggested that students complete one activity per day and then have their parents discuss it with them and provide feedback and guidance.

## Teach Students Their Own Strategies

Many of the speech problems that students demonstrate while young can be corrected and modified with therapy. While the therapy is going on, the teacher should focus on giving students strategies for successful learning. The strategies are little "tricks of the trade" that students can use to maximize their academic and social strengths. Some of these strategies also require accommodations on the part of the teacher in structuring situations and requirements.

⏺ Teach them to relax with breathing exercises or mental imagery.

⏺ Encourage them to participate in groups in which responses do not have to be individually generated.

⏺ Teach them to reinforce themselves by recognizing when they are doing well and by appreciating themselves.

⏺ Let them practice skills with a friend in real situations so that they are not afraid or nervous when it's the "real thing."

⏺ Let them tape record their own speech and listen carefully for errors so that they can discriminate between correct and incorrect sounds.

⏺ Help them come up with strategies for dealing with specific people or situations that make them nervous (walking away, counting to 10 before they speak, deep breathing, etc.).

## LANGUAGE DISORDERS

Language is the system we use to communicate our thoughts and ideas to others. According to Lahey (1988), language is a code "whereby ideas about the world are expressed through a conventional system of arbitrary signals for communication" (p. 2). The interrelationships of what we hear, speak, read, and write become our format for sharing information.

For most of us, spoken language is the tool we use to communicate our ideas, but even the most articulate, fluent, pleasant speech would be useless without a language system that enables us to understand and be understood. Language is an integral component of students' abilities in reading, writing, and listening. Disorders of language may have a serious impact on academic performance. In recent years, the emphasis in the field of communication disorders has shifted away from remediation of speech problems to an increased focus on language disorders. Estimates today are

**CONSIDER THIS**
Try to go through a social situation without using oral language. Did you become frustrated when attempting to make your needs or ideas known to other people? How did you deal with the frustrations?

*Students with speech disorders can learn tricks and strategies that will help them to maximize their social strengths.*

that 50% to 80% of the children seen by speech–language pathologists have language disorders (Wiig, 1986).

More important for classroom teachers, however, is the fact that remediation of language disorders will often be as much their responsibility as it is the speech–language pathologist's. Although remediation of speech problems is provided primarily in a therapeutic setting and then supported and reinforced by the classroom teacher, teachers will often direct and manage overall language development.

We know that humans can communicate in several ways. Heward (1995) describes a child's process for learning language this way: "A child may learn to identify a familiar object, for example, by hearing the spoken word *tree,* by seeing the printed word *tree,* by viewing the sign language gesture for *tree,* or by encountering a combination of these signals" (p. 235). We generally describe modes of communication as either **receptive language,** which involves receiving and decoding or interpreting language, or **expressive language,** which is the encoding or production of a message. Reading and listening are examples of receptive language; writing and speaking are forms of expressive language.

*RECEPTIVE LANGUAGE* involves receiving and interpreting language.

*EXPRESSIVE LAN-GUAGE* is the encoding and production of a message.

As with speech disorders, knowing the normal sequence of language development is important in working with students with language disorders. Some children may be delayed in their development of language but still acquire skills in the same sequence as other children. Other children may acquire some age-appropriate language skills but have deficits in other specific areas. Table 10.2 shows the normal patterns of language development for children with language disorders and children without language disorders. Although they may refer to these general patterns of language development to judge students' overall progress, teachers should not expect every child to follow this precise sequence on these exact timelines.

## Dimensions of Language

Earlier in the chapter, some terminology related to language disorders was introduced. In addition, we refer to the dimensions of language and their related impairments in terms of form, content, and function (or use). Students can demonstrate impairments in any or all of these areas.

*FORM* describes rules that are used in oral language.

*PHONOLOGY* is the system that governs individual and combined sounds of a language.

*MORPHOLOGY* is the system that controls the structure of words.

*SYNTAX* is the system that orders or places words in an understandable sequence.

**FORM**   **Form** describes the rule systems used in oral language. Three different rule systems are included when we discuss form: **phonology, morphology,** and **syntax.**

Phonology is the rule system that governs the individual and combined sounds of a language. Phonological rules vary from one language to another. For example, some of the guttural sounds heard in German are not used in English, and some of the vowel combinations of English are not found in Spanish.

Morphology refers to the rule system controlling the structure of words. Because the structures of words govern their meanings, comparative suffixes such as *-er* or *-est* and plural forms such as the *s* that changes *book* to *books* are important. Oyer et al. (1987) provide an example of how morphemes (units of meaning) can change a basic word into similar words with many different meanings:

The word "friend" is composed of one free morpheme that has meaning. One or more bound morphemes may be added, making "friend*ly,*" "*un*friendly," "friend-*less,*" "friend*liness,*" "friend*ship,*" and "friend*lier.*" There are rules for combining morphemes into words that must be followed (e.g., "*dis*friend" is not an allowable word and thus has no meaning). (p. 61)

| TABLE 10.2 | Language Development for Children with Language Disorders and without Language Disorders |
|---|---|

| LANGUAGE-DISORDERED CHILD | | | NORMALLY DEVELOPING CHILD | | |
|---|---|---|---|---|---|
| **Age** | **Attainment** | **Example** | **Age** | **Attainment** | **Example** |
| 27 MONTHS | First words | *this, mama, bye bye, doggie* | 13 MONTHS | First words | *here, mama, bye bye, kitty* |
| 38 MONTHS | 50-word vocabulary | | 17 MONTHS | 50-word vocabulary | |
| 40 MONTHS | First two-word combinations | *this doggie more apple this mama more play* | 18 MONTHS | First two-word combinations | *more juice here ball more TV here kitty* |
| 48 MONTHS | Later two-word combinations | *Mimi purse Daddy coat block chair dolly table* | 22 MONTHS | Later two-word combinations | *Andy shoe Mommy ring cup floor keys chair* |
| 52 MONTHS | Mean sentence length of 2.00 words | | 24 MONTHS | Mean sentence length of 2.00 words | |
| 55 MONTHS | First appearance of -*ing* | *Mommy eating* | 24 MONTHS | First appearance of -*ing* | *Andy sleeping* |
| 63 MONTHS | Mean sentence length of 3.10 words | | 30 MONTHS | Mean sentence length of 3.10 words | |
| 66 MONTHS | First appearance of *is* | *The doggie's mad* | 30 MONTHS | First appearance of *is* | *My car's gone!* |
| 73 MONTHS | Mean sentence length of 4.10 words | | 37 MONTHS | Mean sentence length of 4.10 words | |
| 79 MONTHS | Mean sentence length of 4.50 words | | 37 MONTHS | First appearance of indirect requests | *Can I have some cookies?* |
| 79 MONTHS | First appearance of indirect requests | *Can I get the ball?* | 40 MONTHS | Mean sentence length of 4.50 words | |

From "Language Disorders in Preschool Children," by L. Leonard, in *Human Communications Disorders: An Introduction* (4th edition) (p. 179), edited by G. H. Shames, E. H. Wiig, and W. A. Second, 1994, New York: Macmillan. Copyright © 1994. Reprinted with permission of Merrill, an imprint of Macmillan Publishing Company.

Syntax is the ordering of words in such a way that they can be understood. Syntax rules determine where words are placed in a sentence. Just like phonology, syntax rules vary from one language to another. Rules governing negatives, questions, tenses, and compound or simple sentences determine the meanings of word combinations. For example, the same words used in different combinations can mean very different things: *The boy hit the ball* is not the same as *The ball hit the boy*.

All of these rule systems affect how we use and understand language. Children's abilities to understand and correctly use all of these rules related to form develop sequentially as their language skill develops. Form is important not only in spoken language, but in written language and in sign language systems, too.

**CONTENT**   *Content* refers to the intent and meaning of language and its rule system; *semantics* deals with the meaning of words and word combinations. Without specific words to label and describe objects or ideas, our language would have no meaning. When students fail to comprehend concrete and abstract meanings of words, inferences, or figurative phrases, it is difficult for them to understand more subtle uses of language such as jokes, puns, similes, proverbs, or sarcasm. As children mature, they are better able to differentiate meanings of similar words, classify them by similarities, and understand abstract meanings of words.

**TEACHING TIP**
Teaching students appropriate social skills has a link to pragmatics and helps them understand when to modify language in different situations.

**USE**   When we use language in various social contexts, we follow another set of rules, *pragmatics*. The purpose and setting of our communication as well as the people with whom we are communicating determine the language we use. If children are to build and maintain successful relationships with others, it is important that they understand and effectively use skills appropriate to the context. For example, when children speak to adults, it is helpful if they use polite, respectful language; when they speak to their friends, they will most likely use less formal spoken language, demonstrate more relaxed body language, and take turns while talking (Owens, 1984).

| **TABLE 10.3** | **Types of Language Disorders and Their Causes** |
|---|---|
| **Type** | **Commonly Suspected Causative Factors or Related Conditions** |
| **NO VERBAL LANGUAGE**<br>Child does not show indications of understanding or spontaneously using language by age 3. | ■ Congenital or early acquired deafness<br>■ Gross brain damage or severe mental retardation/developmental disabilities<br>■ Severe emotional disturbance |
| **QUANTITATIVELY DIFFERENT LANGUAGE**<br>Child's language is different from that of nondisabled children at any stage of development—meaning and usefulness for communication are greatly lessened or lost. | ■ Inability to understand auditory stimuli<br>■ Severe emotional disturbance<br>■ Learning disability<br>■ Mental retardation/developmental disabilities<br>■ Hearing loss |
| **DELAYED LANGUAGE DEVELOPMENT**<br>Language follows normal course of development, but lags seriously behind that of most children who are the same chronological age. | ■ Mental retardation<br>■ Experiential deprivation<br>■ Lack of language stimulation<br>■ Hearing loss |
| **INTERRUPTED LANGUAGE DEVELOPMENT**<br>Normal language development begins but is interrupted by illness, accident, or other trauma; language disorder is acquired. | ■ Acquired hearing loss<br>■ Brain injury due to oxygen deprivation, physical trauma, or infection |

Adapted from "Language Disorders in Children," by R. C. Naremore. In *Introduction to Communication Disorders* (p. 224), edited by T. J. Hixon, L. D. Shriberg, and J. H. Saxman, 1980, Englewood Cliffs, NJ: Prentice-Hall. Used by permission.

## Types and Causes of Language Disorders

Hallahan and Kauffman (1991) have described four basic categories of language disorders: absence of verbal language, qualitatively different language, delayed language development, and interrupted language development. Table 10.3 from Naremore (1980) summarizes these four categories and includes some suspected causes of each. For children who are not deaf, a complete absence of language would likely indicate severe emotional disturbance or a severe developmental disorder. Qualitatively different language is also associated with developmental disorders and emotional disturbance. A good example of this type of problem is the echolalic speech of children with autism, who may repeat speech they hear in a singsong voice and fail to use their spoken language in a meaningful way. Delayed language occurs when a child develops language in the same sequence as other children, but at a slower rate. Causes of delayed language include mental retardation, hearing loss, or lack of stimulation or appropriate experiences. Sometimes language development is interrupted by illness or physical trauma. This type of language problem is increasingly common among children as a result of traumatic brain injury (TBI). In general education classrooms, teachers may encounter any or all of these types of language disorders at ranges from very mild to severe.

## Indicators of Language Impairments

Some teachers may have an overall sense that a student is demonstrating language problems; others may not notice anything amiss. Wiig and Semel (1984) have identified some indicators of language problems by grade levels.

▲ Primary grades:
- Problems in following verbal directions
- Difficulty with preacademic skills
- Phonics problems
- Poor word-attack skills
- Difficulties with structural analysis
- Problems learning new material

▲ Intermediate grades:
- Word substitutions
- Inadequate language processing and production that affects reading comprehension and academic achievement

▲ Middle and high school:
- Inability to understand abstract concepts
- Problems understanding multiple word meanings
- Difficulties connecting previously learned information to new material that must be learned independently
- Widening gap in achievement when compared to peers

> **TEACHING TIP**
> If you suspect a child of having language problems, keep a record of the problems to better determine if a referral for services is warranted.

In addition, teachers can check for the following list of behaviors that may indicate either speech or language problems.

### SPEECH
▲ Poor articulation
▲ Different voice quality
▲ Dysfluencies
▲ Slurred conversational speech

**LANGUAGE**

◢ Has problems following oral directions
◢ Speech rambles; isn't able to express ideas concisely
◢ Appears shy, withdrawn, never seems to talk or interact with others
◢ Asks questions that are off-topic
◢ Has a poor sense of humor
◢ Has poor comprehension of material read
◢ Doesn't plan ahead in pencil/paper activities
◢ Takes things literally
◢ Is not organized; appears messy
◢ Doesn't manage time well; has to be prodded to complete assignments

Children who have language disorders sometimes develop patterns of interaction with peers, teachers, and family members that may result in behavior problems. The behavior problems might seem to have nothing to do with language problems but may in fact have developed in response to inabilities to read, spell, talk, or write effectively.

## CLASSROOM ACCOMMODATIONS FOR STUDENTS WITH LANGUAGE DISORDERS

Numerous strategies can be used in general education classrooms to improve students' language skills and remedy language deficits. The following sections present some ways of structuring learning situations and presenting information to enhance communication.

### Teach Some Prerequisite Imitation Skills

Nowacek and McShane (1993) recommend the following activities:

◢ Show a picture (of a girl running) and say, "The girl is running."
◢ Ask the student to repeat a target phrase.
◢ Positively reinforce correct responses.
◢ Present a variety of subject/verb combinations until the student correctly and consistently imitates them.

### Increase Receptive Language in the Classroom

***CROSS-REFERENCE***
When reading Chapters 14 and 15, consider specific activities that could be used to teach listening skills to elementary students and secondary students.

Clary and Edwards (1992) suggest some specific activities to improve students' receptive language skills:

◢ *Give students practice in following directions.* Begin with one simple direction, and then increase the length of the list of directions. Have the student perform a simple task in the classroom such as closing the door, turning around, and so on.
◢ *Have students pair up and practice descriptions.* Place two students at a table separated by a screen. Place groups of identical objects in front of both students. Have one describe one of the objects; the other must determine which object is being described. Reverse roles with new sets of objects.
◢ *Let students work on categorizing.* Orally present a list of three words. Two should be related in some way. Ask a student to tell which two are related and why (e.g., horse, tree, dog).

# INCLUSION STRATEGIES

## Teaching Listening Skills for Class Discussions

### ENCOURAGE ACTIVE LISTENING DURING DIRECTIONS
You can do this in several ways:

1. Restate the directions in question form. "How many problems are you supposed to do?"
2. Ask a student to rephrase the direction. "Tell the class what page we need to read."
3. Write the key words from the direction on the board (not the entire direction; it discourages listening).

### USE LISTENING BUDDIES
Students can rephrase information for each other in a cooperative structure. ("Turn to your partner and explain what the first step is.") Students could also quiz each other at regular intervals, either for test reviews or less formal checks for understanding.

### ENCOURAGE LISTENING DURING LECTURES
After stating the objectives for the lesson, one way to encourage good active listening is to make use of students' prior knowledge. Let students begin discussion of a topic with a brainstorming session. Brainstorming ideas is fun for students. Students can generate ideas and share information; teachers can acknowledge students' input and remind them of how much they already know.

### AROUSE STUDENT CURIOSITY
There are numerous questioning strategies that arouse students' interest in various topics. At the beginning of a lesson, let students generate a list of questions about the topic. As the lesson progresses, return to the students' questions. Point out the ones that have been answered, and, if there are still some questions unanswered at the end of the lesson, allow students to work independently or in cooperative groups to locate the information. Always try to encourage some higher-level *thinking questions* that call for creative, open-ended responses.

From *Listen to Learn* (p. 10), by L. K. Pruden, 1992, Bedford, TX: GG Publishing. Used by permission.

---

The nearby Inclusion Strategies feature provides some additional suggestions for teaching listening skills.

## Give Students Opportunities for Facilitative Play

This type of interaction provides modeling for the students so that they can imitate and expand their own use of language. The following is an abbreviated sequence for facilitative play:

▲ The teacher models self-talk in a play activity. ("I'm making the cars go.")
▲ The teacher elicits comments from the student and then expands on them. ("Yes, the cars are going fast.")
▲ The teacher uses "buildups" and "breakdowns" by expanding on a student's ideas, breaking them down, and then repeating them. ("Red car go? Yes, look at the red car. It's going fast on the road. It's going to win the race.") (Nowacek & McShane, 1993)

## Elicit Language from Students

Sometimes students who are reluctant to speak require encouragement. In addition to encouraging them with positive social interactions, teachers might also have to structure situations in which students must use language to meet some of their needs in the classroom. The strategies that follow should prompt students to use language when they otherwise might not.

◢ Place items out of reach so that the child has to ask for them.

◢ When a child asks for an item, present the wrong item (e.g., the child asks for a spoon and you present a fork).

◢ Give a child an item that is hard to open so that he or she has to request assistance.

◢ When performing a task, do one step incorrectly (forget to put the milk in the blender with the pudding mix).

◢ Make items difficult to find.

◢ Give students an item that requires some assistance to work with (e.g., an orange that needs peeling).

## Use Naturalistic Techniques and Simulated Real-Life Activities to Increase Language Use

*CONSIDER THIS*
When using some of these strategies that encourage students to speak, what can you do to make it more likely that the student will continue to speak without these strategies?

Often, the most effective techniques to instill language acquisition and use are those that will be easy for teachers to use and easy for students to generalize to everyday situations. Teachers can encourage generalization by using naturalistic and situational strategies and real-life activities.

◢ Naturalistic Techniques
  • Try cloze activities. ("What do you need? Oh, you need paint and a _____. That's right, you need paint and a brush.")
  • Emphasize problem solving. ("You can't find your backpack? What should you do? Let's look on the hook. Is your coat there? What did we do to find your coat? That's right, we looked on the hook.")
  • Use questioning techniques. ("Where are you going? That's right, you are going to lunch.")

◢ Simulated Real-Life Activities
  • Let students simulate a newscast or commercial.
  • Have students write and follow their own written directions to locations in and around the school.
  • Play "social charades" by having students act out social situations and decide on appropriate responses.
  • Have one student teach an everyday skill to another (e.g., how to shoot a basket).
  • Using real telephones, give students opportunities to call each other, and to give, receive, and record messages.

## Encourage Students' Conversations through Story Reading

McNeill and Fowler (1996) give some excellent suggestions for helping students with delayed language development. Since students with language development problems often do not get the results they want through their ordinary conversations, they need more practice. What better way to practice effective language skills than through story reading! Students of all ages enjoy being read to, whether individually or in small groups while students are young, or in larger classes when they are in intermediate or secondary grades.

These authors suggest four specific strategies for teachers to use when reading stories aloud: (1) praise the students' talk, (2) expand on their words, (3) ask open-ended questions, and (4) pause long enough to allow students to initiate speaking. In addition, they emphasize taking turns, so that students have an opportunity to clarify their messages, hear appropriate language models, and practice the unspoken rules of communication.

McNeill and Fowler (1996) also recommend coaching parents in how to give their children opportunities to talk and how to respond when their children *do* talk. When parents pause, expand on answers, and ask open-ended questions that require more than just "yes" or "no" responses, they can become their children's best teachers.

## Use Music and Play Games to Improve Language

Teachers should always try to have some fun with students. Using music and playing games are two ways language can be incorporated into enjoyable activities.

◢ Music
  • Use songs that require students to request items (e.g., rhythm sticks or tambourines passed around a circle).
  • Have picture symbols for common songs so that students can request the ones they like.
  • Use props to raise interest and allow students to act out the story (e.g., during "Humpty Dumpty" the student falls off a large ball).
  • Use common chants such as "When You're Happy and You Know It," and let students choose the action (e.g., clap your hands).
◢ Games That Require Receptive or Expressive Language
  • Do "Simon Says."
  • Play "Musical Chairs" with words. (Pass a ball around a circle. When the teacher says a magic word, the student with the ball is out.)
  • Use key words to identify and organize students. ("All of the boys with red hair stand up. Everyone who has a sister sit down.")
  • Play "Twenty Questions." ("I'm thinking of a person." Students ask yes-or-no questions.)

## Arrange Your Classroom for Effective Interactions

For students who have either speech or language problems, the physical arrangement of the classroom can contribute to success. The following guidelines may improve students' language development:

◢ Give instructions and important information when distractions are at their lowest.
◢ Use consistent attention-getting devices, either verbal, visual, or physical cues.
◢ Be specific when giving directions.
◢ Write directions on the chalkboard, flipchart, or overhead so that students can refer to them.
◢ Use students' names frequently when talking to them.
◢ Emphasize what you're saying by using gestures and facial expressions.
◢ Pair students up with buddies for modeling and support.
◢ Allow for conversation time in the classroom so that students can share information and ideas.
◢ Encourage students to use calendars to organize themselves and manage their time. (Breeding, Stone, & Riley, n.d.)

## Use Challenging Games with Older Students

Older students may require continued intervention to improve language skills. However, the activities chosen must be appropriate and not seem like "baby" games.

Thomas and Carmack (1993) have collected ideas to involve older students in enjoyable, interactive tasks:

- ◢ Read fables or stories with morals. Discuss outcomes and focus on the endings.
- ◢ Do "Explain That." Discuss common idiomatic phrases, and help students discover the connection between the literal and figurative meanings (e.g., *She was on pins and needles*).
- ◢ "Riddlemania" presents riddles to students and has them explain what makes them humorous.
- ◢ Have "Sense-Able Lessons." Bring objects to see, taste, hear, and smell, and compile a list of students' verbal comments. (p. 155)

## Modify Strategies to Develop Students' Learning Tools

When facilitating language development for older students, help them develop their own strategies to use in challenging situations (Thomas & Carmack, 1993). Requiring them to use higher-order thinking skills will both require and stimulate higher-level language.

- ◢ Pair students to find word meanings. Use partners when working on categories such as synonyms or antonyms. Let students work together to master using a thesaurus.
- ◢ Teach students to categorize. Begin with concrete objects that they relate to easily, such as types of cars or names of foods, and then move to more abstract concepts such as feelings or ideas.
- ◢ Play reverse quiz games like "Jeopardy!" in which students have to work backward to think of questions for answers. (pp. 155–163)

## Work Collaboratively with the Speech–Language Pathologist

LINC (Language IN the Classroom) is a program adapted for use in many school districts (Breeding et al., n.d.). The program philosophy holds that language learning should occur in the child's most natural environment and in conjunction with other content being learned. The development of students' language should relate to their world and should be a learning experience, not a teaching experience.

The purpose of the program is to strengthen the language system of those students in general education classrooms who need to develop coping and compensatory skills to survive academically. Another goal is to transfer language learned from the therapy setting to the classroom, thereby allowing children to learn to *communicate,* rather than merely *talk.* The teacher and the speech–language pathologist must both be present for the approach to be successful. The two professionals work together to plan unit lessons that develop language skills in students.

Hiller (1990) presents an example of how LINC works. His elementary school implemented classroom-based language instruction. At the beginning of the program, the speech–language pathologist visited each classroom for a specified amount of time each week (90 minutes) during the language arts period. The first 45 minutes were used for an oral language activity, often a cooking activity from the *Blooming Recipes* workbook (Tavzel, 1987). During the second 45 minutes, students wrote paragraphs. For example, after preparing peanut butter and raisins on celery ("Bumps on a Log"), students responded to the following questions.

What was the name of the recipe we made?
Where did we do our preparing?
Who brought the peanut butter, celery, and raisins?
How did we make "Bumps on a Log"?
When did we eat "Bumps on a Log"?
Why do you think this recipe is called "Bumps on a Log"?

Responses were written on the board or on an overhead transparency. Students copied the responses in paragraph format.

Teachers and speech–language pathologists later extended the activities to teaching language lessons on current topics, team-teaching critical thinking activities during science experiments, and team planning and teaching social studies units. Reports from Hiller's and other schools using LINC programs described better collaboration among professionals, more accurate language referrals, and increased interest in speech–language activities among the entire staff. The nearby Personal Spotlight describes how a speech–language pathologist views collaboration.

## *personal* SPOTLIGHT

### Speech–Language Pathologist

Martha Drennan has been a speech–language pathologist for five years. She has been employed in both a large, urban district and a small, rural district. Currently she works for the Rison School District in Rison, Arkansas. One of

*MARTHA DRENNAN*

the most significant changes Martha has observed in her field is that many children now receive speech–language services in a general education setting rather than being pulled out for services in a segregated, speech classroom. Martha likes this change. She notes that there are several advantages to providing services to these children in general classrooms rather than pulling them out. Among these advantages are that

▲ More students can be served because the speech–language pathologist can work with several students at the same time. Often an entire class is the target of a lesson conducted by the speech–language pathologist so that all students benefit.

▲ Some students, especially older ones, do not feel the stigma of receiving services as part of their general education classroom whereas they did when they had to leave the room for speech.

Martha notes that many older students really resent having to go to the speech room. She especially sees serving students in the general education setting as beneficial for this group of students.

Despite benefits, there are also some negative factors associated with this newer service delivery model. Martha said that "some teachers would simply rather teach all the lessons in their classroom themselves because they feel like they do not have the luxury to give another teacher time." Another negative to providing services in the general education classroom is that students with speech–language needs do not get the individual attention in general education classes that they would if they were to receive their services in the speech room.

Overall, Martha is very pleased with serving students with speech and language needs in general education classes. She noted that "virtually all general education teachers are very happy when you go into their classroom and provide a language lesson for all kids." She also stated that the collaboration needed to ensure an effective, smooth lesson requires time for general education teachers and speech–language pathologists to plan, something that seems to always be a problem.

## Use Storytelling and Process Writing

When children listen to and retell a story, they incorporate it into their oral language repertoire. McKamey (1991) has described a structure for allowing students to retell stories they had heard, to tell stories from their own experience, and to write down and illustrate their oral presentations. In process writing, students are instructed based on what they can already do. This and other whole language experiences often allow students who have had negative language experiences to begin to succeed, to link written and spoken language, and to grow as communicators.

## *LANGUAGE DIFFERENCES RELATED TO CULTURE*

**CONSIDER THIS**
What are some of the ways that culture can have an impact on a child's language, that in turn will affect the child's functioning in school?

Children's patterns of speech and use of language reflect their culture and may be different from that of some of their peers. It is important not to mistake a language *difference* for a language *disorder,* but also a disorder must not be overlooked in a student with language differences. Cultural variations in family structure, child-rearing practices, family perceptions and attitudes, and language and communication styles can all influence students' communication (Wayman, Lynch, & Hanson, 1990).

## Relationship between Communication Style and Culture

Culture has a strong influence on the *style* of communication. Many areas of communication style can be affected by factors including gender, status, and age roles; rules governing interruptions and turn taking; use of humor; and how to greet or leave someone (Erickson, 1992). Teachers must be aware of the many manifestations of culture in nonverbal communication, as well. Differences in rules governing eye contact, the physical space between speakers, use of gestures and facial expression, and use of silence can cause dissonance between teachers and students of differing cultures. Walker (1993) has described how differences such as directness of a conversation, volume of voices, and reliance on verbal (low-context) versus nonverbal (high-context) parts of communication affect attitudes toward the speaker. Teachers can respond to cultural differences in several ways. These suggestions are adapted from Walker (1993) and should be helpful for teachers who want to enhance both overall achievement and communication skills with students who are culturally or linguistically different:

▴ Try to involve community resources, including churches and neighborhood organizations, in school activities.
▴ Make home visits.
▴ Allow flexible hours for conferences.
▴ Question your own assumptions about human behavior, values, biases, personal limitations, and so on.
▴ Try to understand the world from the student's perspective.
▴ Ask yourself questions about an individual student's behavior in light of cultural values, motivation, and world views, and how these relate to his or her learning experiences.

# DIVERSITY FORUM   Considerations for Observing Linguistically Different Students

1. Identify exactly what is to be observed. Be specific and know what you are watching as a part of the ongoing behavior stream in classroom settings.
2. Record the time, date, and duration of your observation.
3. Number your observations of the same children across days. Important here is a systematic context and an easy, readily available reminder that this is, for example, the third observation of Juan, Tom, Hector, and Zoraida.
4. Make notes of what you are observing in a descriptive, specific form that tells exactly what

occurred. Also, jot down any unexpected events that happened during your observation. However, when taking notes of these occurrences, it is helpful to note that they were "unexpected."

5. Keep notes of your interpretations of what happened.

From *Assessment and Instruction of Culturally and Linguistically Diverse Students* (p. 105), by V. Gonzalez, R. Brusca-Vega, and T. Yawkey (1997), Boston: Allyn and Bacon. Used by permission.

## Considerations in Assessment

Assessment in the area of communication disorders is often complicated, just as it is for students with other disabilities. Because of the increasing numbers of students who are linguistically different and who require services in ESL (English as a second language) or who are limited English proficient (LEP), teachers should consult with personnel in special education, ESL, speech and language services, and bilingual education to obtain appropriate evaluation and programming services. Observation is an important form of assessment, particularly when assessing students who are linguistically different. The nearby Diversity Forum provides some suggestions for observing these children.

There are many considerations for assessment personnel who work with students having cultural and linguistic differences. The following suggestions have been adapted from Toliver-Weddington and Erickson (1992) and may be useful for classroom teachers who suspect that students may have communication disorders.

**TEACHING TIP**
Remember the basic tenets of nondiscriminatory assessment when evaluating students with diverse cultural backgrounds or when reviewing assessment data that has already been collected.

- When screening with tests, always select tests that have the most valid items for the skills to be assessed.
- Consider procedural modifications such as lengthening the time limit.
- Try to assess whether the minority child has had access to the information.
- Consider scoring the test in two ways, first as the manual indicates, then allowing credit for items that may be considered correct in the child's language system and/or experiences. (Record and report both ways and indicate the adjustments.)
- Focus on what the child does well rather than what he or she cannot do.

Because of the increasing number of students in public schools from cultural and/or linguistic minority groups, teachers are recognizing the need for information related to learning and communication styles as well as modifications to curriculum and instruction. Although many of these children will never be identified as having a communication disorder, teachers in general education must be aware that differences in language and culture may often impact a student's apparent proficiency in both oral and written communication.

The cultural background of a child will have a profound impact on the style of communication that is used.

# TECHNOLOGY TODAY

## Speech and Language Disorders and Types of Computer Applications

Computers and software are becoming increasingly more helpful for students with speech and language disorders.

| Disorder | Types of Applications |
| --- | --- |
| ARTICULATION | Phonologic analysis, intelligibility analysis, drill and practice, and games |
| VOICE | Biofeedback programs and client information |
| FLUENCY | Biofeedback and relaxation programs |
| SYNTACTIC | Language sample analysis, drill and practice, games, and tutorials |
| SEMANTIC | Language sample analysis and cognitive rehabilitation |
| PRAGMATIC | Problem solving and simulations |
| HEARING IMPAIRMENT | Visual feedback, sign language instruction with CAI, and telecommunication applications |

From "Computers and Individuals with Speech and Language Disorders" (p. 146), by P. S. Cochran and G L. Bull, in *Computers and Exceptional Individuals,* edited by J. D. Lindsey, 1993, Austin, TX: Pro-Ed. Used by permission.

# AUGMENTATIVE AND ALTERNATIVE COMMUNICATION

The term **augmentative communication** denotes techniques that supplement or enhance communication by complementing whatever vocal skills the individual already has (Harris & Vanderheiden, 1980). Other individuals (e.g., those who are severely neurologically impaired and cannot speak) must employ techniques that serve in place of speech—in other words, **alternative communication.** According to Shane and Sauer (1986), the term *alternative communication* applies when "the production of speech for communication purposes has been ruled out" (p. 2).

Communication techniques can be *aided* or *unaided.* Unaided techniques do not require any physical object or entity in order to express information (e.g., speech, manual signs or gestures, facial communication). Aided communication techniques require a physical object or device to enable the individual to communicate (e.g., communication boards, charts, and mechanical or electrical devices). Because substantial numbers of individuals lack speech because of mental retardation, traumatic brain injury, deafness, neurological disorders, or other causes, there has been increased demand for augmentative and alternative communication. The nearby Technology Today feature lists the types of computer applications suitable for students with speech and language disorders.

Students without spoken language may use a basic nonautomated *communication board* with no electronic parts. Typically, the board will contain common words, phrases, or numbers. The communication board can be arranged in either an alphabetic or nonalphabetic format (see Figure 10.5). Because they are easy to construct and can be modified to fit the student's vocabulary, nonautomated communication boards are very useful in communicating with teachers, family members, and peers. There are some commercially available sets of symbols, including *The Picture Communication Symbols* (Mayer-Johnson, 1986) and *The Oakland Picture Dictionary* (Kirsten, 1981).

Electronic communication aids encompass a wide variety of capabilities, from simple to complex. Often, a voice synthesizer is used to produce speech output, and written output is produced on printers or displays. Software, which is becoming increasingly sophisticated, can accommodate the many different needs of individuals who cannot produce spoken language. The following are some examples of communication aids and their key features (adapted from Shane & Sauer, 1986):

- ◢ AllTalk:
  - Human voice output communicator
  - Can store anyone's voice as a message for any given location
  - Completely user programmable
  - User can design overlays to correspond to messages
  - Voice programs can be stored on standard cassette player for later access
- ◢ Light Talker:
  - Microprocessor-based communication aid with synthesized speech output
  - Operates with either *Express* or *Minspeak* firmware
  - Fast, effective communication
- ◢ SpeechPAC/Epson:
  - Portable synthetic voice communicator
  - Includes full-sized keyboard, built-in printer, LCD screen, and built-in micro-cassette drive for saving and loading programs
  - User types messages on the keyboard
  - Messages may be spoken or directed to the printer
  - Can store up to 23,000 characters in memory, giving the user a completely customized voice output (adapted from Shane & Sauer, 1986)

**AUGMENTATIVE COMMUNICATION** involves techniques that are used to supplement and enhance communication by complementing existing vocal skills.

**ALTERNATIVE COMMUNICATION** involves techniques that are used to replace speech in communication.

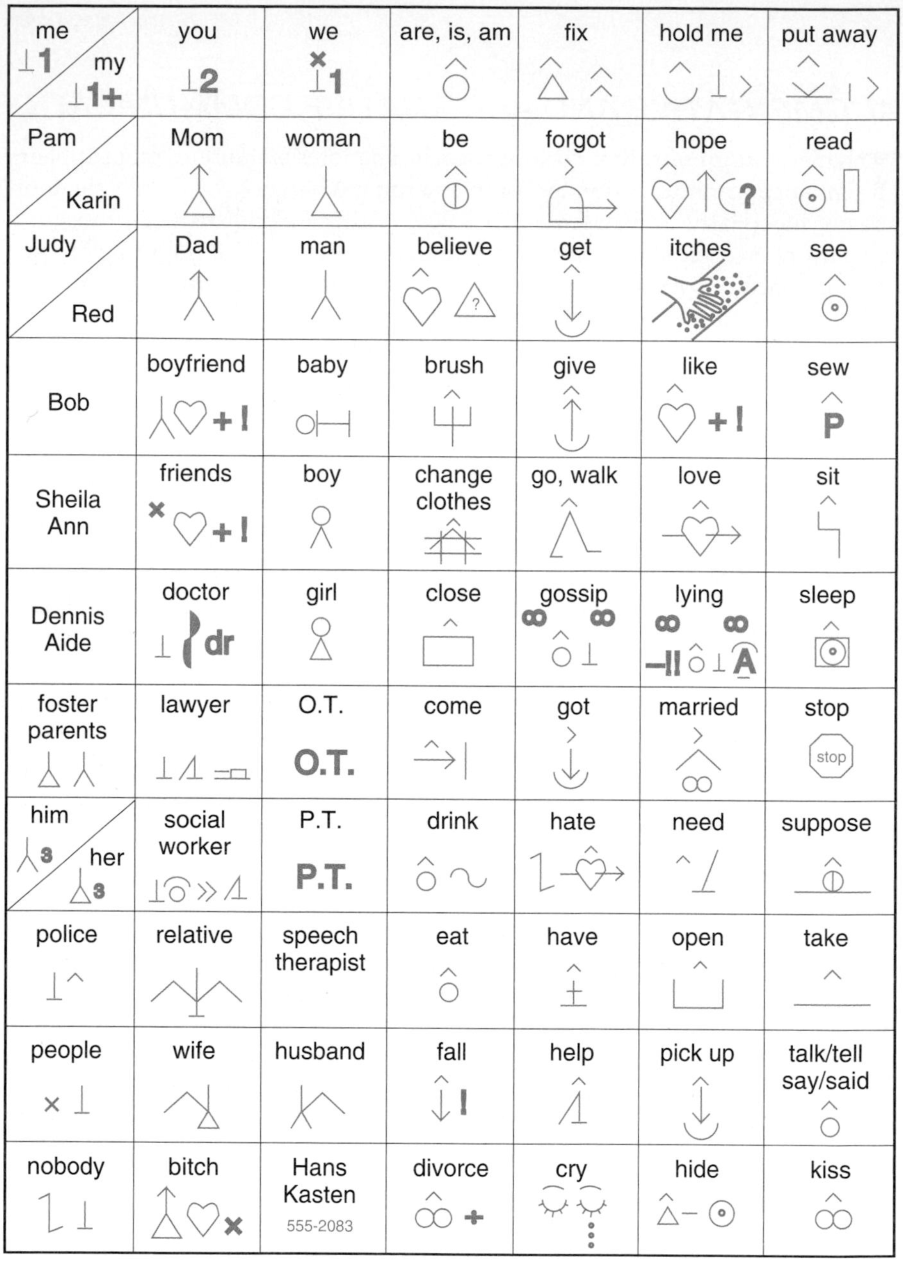

*FIGURE* **10.5**

Communication Board in Alphabetic and Nonalphabetic Formats

From *Augmentative and Alternative Communication* (p. 58), by H. C. Shane and M. Sauer, 1986, Austin, TX: Pro-Ed. Used by permission.

## Facilitated Communication

*Facilitated communication* is a process that has recently been used with individuals who have developmental disabilities, including autism. First introduced by Rosemary Crossley in Australia, facilitated communication usually involves having someone (a facilitator) support the arm or wrist of the person with autism, who then points to letters on a keyboard. The keyboard is often connected to a computer so that the individual's words can be displayed or printed (Kirk, Gallagher, & Anastasiow, 1993). Supposedly the support of the facilitator enables the individual to type out words and phrases.

Much of the work done in facilitated communication has been carried out by Biklen (1990), who has reported great success with the procedure. At this time, results of research on the effectiveness of facilitated communication are mixed; some individuals have shown great promise, and others have not done as well (see Chapter 9).

# ENHANCING INCLUSIVE CLASSROOMS FOR STUDENTS WITH COMMUNICATION DISORDERS

The traditional service delivery model for speech therapy used to include a twice weekly, 30 minutes per session, pull-out model in which speech–language pathologists worked with students in a separate setting. Even though this model may still be appropriate in clinical settings, there may be more effective approaches for public schools. Moreover, just as academic services to students with disabilities have become more and more integrated into general education programs, speech–language services are following a more inclusive model. This collaboration might involve bringing the speech–language pathologists into the classroom to work with individual students, the teacher and speech–language pathologists teaching alternate lessons, or professionals co-teaching the same lesson at the same time. The following delivery options have been recommended for the provision of speech and language services in the schools: direct instruction (pull-out), classroom-based, community-based, and consultation (ASHA, 1996). These service delivery options can be implemented independently or in any combination in order to best meet the individual needs of the student.

**CONSIDER THIS**
What are some of the advantages and disadvantages, to both the child and general classroom teacher, for pull-out speech therapy services?

◢ The traditional pull-out model is indicated for students who are in particular stages of the intervention process or for those who have very specific communication goals. Pull-out services are often provided within the classroom or in the therapy room and with individual students or in small groups.

◢ Classroom-based service delivery options usually involve a collaborative effort between teachers and speech–language pathologists. This model is particularly appropriate at the preschool and kindergarten grades and in classrooms with large numbers of students who have been identified as having communication disorders or as being at risk. This collaboration can involve the speech–language pathologist providing individual or small group instruction in the classroom or participating in team teaching or co-teaching lessons with the classroom teacher.

◢ The community-based service delivery model indicates that therapy services are being provided in more natural communication environments such as at home, on the playground, or in other age appropriate community settings. Providing speech and language therapy in a community-based setting is ideal for students who have pragmatic language disorders, those who need to generalize new skills to a variety of settings, and for students who are enrolled in vocational programs.

◢ Consultation is a model of service delivery in which the speech–language pathologist does not provide direct instruction to the student. Instead, the family, teacher, or other school staff are provided with assistance in the form of information, training, or resources to help the student reach specific communication goals. The provision of consultation services is indicated for those students who are working on generalization of communication skills or for those students who are receiving communication instruction from other instructional staff.

As schools try to maximize the positive impact of professional collaboration, it is important to recognize and overcome the barriers inherent in the process. According to Kerrin (1996), the barriers to greater collaboration among speech–language professionals and teachers can include the following:

◢ Territorial obstacles (*"This is my job; that is your job."*)
◢ Time concerns (*"When are general ed teachers supposed to find the time to meet, plan, and modify?"*)
◢ Terror (*"I'm afraid this new way won't work."*)

Fortunately, Kerrin has also offered some good ideas for overcoming these obstacles. She suggests that team members try the following tips:

◢ Try to be flexible and creative when scheduling conferences.
◢ Encourage everyone involved to ask questions.
◢ Invite speech–language professionals into the classroom.
◢ Ask for assistance in planning.
◢ Maintain open, regular communication.
◢ Keep an open mind, a cooperative spirit, and a sense of humor.

## FUTURE TRENDS

Several forces are changing the field of communication disorders. First, general education teachers are likely to see more students with moderate to severe disabilities in their classrooms. The movement toward more inclusive environments for students will require classroom teachers to provide more instruction for these students. The caseloads of speech–language pathologists are continuing to grow, and there is an ever-increasing demand for services, especially in the area of language disorders. Although "pull-out" speech–language remediation will still be offered, many of the services will be delivered in an increasingly collaborative framework, with teachers and pathologists cooperating and sharing resources.

Another area of change is the expected continuation of technological advances. Some of the improved technology has already been described here; however, it is virtually impossible to keep up with the rapid improvements in this area. With continued improvements in technology, students with more severe communication disorders will have opportunities to interact with family members, teachers, and peers, perhaps participating in activities that would have seemed impossible ten years ago.

*Authors' note:* The authors would like to express their appreciation to Janice Maxwell, B.A., M.S. (SLP), for her assistance in providing much of the practical information that was presented in this chapter. Janice is an exemplary speech pathologist and a wonderful friend to teachers in general education.

# Summary

## Basic Concepts about Communication Disorders

◢ Although most people take the ability to communicate for granted, communication problems can result in difficulties in even the most simple of interactions and lead to problems in socialization and emotional adjustment. Speech and language are the interrelated, rule-governed skills that we use to communicate.

◢ About 2% of the school-age population has been identified as having speech or language impairments.

◢ Because most students with speech and language impairments are served in a regular classroom or resource room placement, having students with speech and language disorders in the classroom is more the rule than the exception.

## Speech Disorders

◢ Speech disorders include impairments of articulation, voice, and fluency with articulation disorders being the most common.

◢ Speech disorders can be functional or organic in origin.

## Classroom Accommodations for Students with Speech Disorders

◢ Teachers can make numerous accommodations and modifications for students with speech disorders. For example, building a positive classroom environment is an important accommodation that can make inclusion easier for these students.

## Classroom Accommodations for Students with Language Disorders

◢ Language disorders can be expressive or receptive in nature and can affect the form, content, or use of language.

◢ Disorders of language can be classified into four basic categories: absence of verbal language, qualitatively different language, delayed language development, and interrupted language development.

◢ Significant language disorders directly impact a student's ability to interact with family, peers, and teachers.

◢ Specific, individualized intervention and instructional modifications (e.g., storytelling, facilitative play, classroom arrangement) are required.

## Language Differences Related to Culture

◢ Individual social and cultural experiences often affect the way in which we use speech and language as tools for communication.

◢ Teachers should be aware of the influence that culture has on the style and nonverbal aspects of communication.

◢ Special consideration should be given during assessment of students having diverse cultural and linguistic heritage. Some speech and language differences can be attributed to cultural diversity or environmental factors and are not considered disorders.

## Augmentative and Alternative Communication

◢ Augmentative and alternative communication options can facilitate the communicative abilities of persons with speech and language disorders.

◢ The level and type of technology needed to support augmentative and alternative communication methods varies widely.

◢ Research on the facilitated communication method has yielded mixed results.

## Enhancing Inclusive Classrooms for Students with Communication Disorders

◢ Speech–language pathologists employ a variety of service delivery models that can be used independently or in combination to meet the individual needs of each student. Most of these models involve some level of professional collaboration and consultation with the classroom teacher.

◢ Teachers and therapists need to work as a team to overcome common barriers to greater collaboration.

## Future Trends

◢ The movement toward more inclusive environments for students will require classroom teachers to serve greater numbers of students with moderate and severe communication disorders.

◢ Increasing caseloads will lead speech–language pathologists to provide many services using collaborative and consultative models rather than the more traditional "pull-out" approach.

◢ Technological advances will offer increased opportunities for students with severe communication disorders to interact with others and participate in a wider range of activities.

# *urther Readings*

American Speech-Language-Hearing Association. (1996, Spring). Inclusive practices for children and youth with communication disorders: Position statement and technical report. *ASHA, 38*(16), 35–44.

Fahey, K. B., & Reid, D. K. (2000). *Language development, differences, and disorders.* Austin, TX: Pro-Ed.

Fehling, R. H. (1993). *Weekday speech activities to promote carryover.* Austin, TX: Pro-Ed.

Kerrin, R. G. (1996). Collaboration: Working with the speech–language pathologist. *Intervention in School and Clinic, 21,* 56–59.

McNeill, J. H., & Fowler, S. A. (1996). Using story reading to encourage children's conversations. *Teaching Exceptional Children, 28,* 43–47.

Miller, R. (1996). *The developmentally appropriate inclusive classroom in early education.* Albany: NY: Delmar.

Parette, P., Hourcade, M., & Van-Biervliet, R. (1993, spring). "Selection of appropriate technology for children with disabilities." *Teaching Exceptional Children, 26,* 40–44.

Shames, G. H., Wiig, E. H., & Secord, W. A. (1994). *Human communication disorders: An introduction* (4th ed.). New York: Merrill.

# Chapter 11

# Teaching Students Who Are Gifted

*After reading this chapter, you should be able to:*

◢ Define giftedness
◢ Describe the characteristics of gifted students
◢ Describe ways to identify and evaluate gifted students
◢ Describe appropriate instructional methods for gifted students
◢ Discuss the curricular needs of gifted students
◢ Identify ways to enhance curriculum and instruction within the general education setting

Carmen is truly an exceptional child. She has been a student in classes for gifted/talented/creative students for six years, from the first to the sixth grade.

Learning came very easily for Carmen, and she excelled in all subjects. However, mathematics was her personal favorite. When she was in the fifth grade, she successfully completed pre-algebra, and, when she was a sixth grader, Carmen attended a seventh- and eighth-grade gifted mathematics class, where she received the highest grades in algebra. Carmen's writing skills were also well developed. Several of her essays and poems have already been published. When Carmen was a fourth grader, she presented testimony to a NASA board defending and encouraging the continuation of the junior astronaut program. After completing her first year of junior high school, Carmen was awarded two out of five academic awards given to seventh-grade students at her school for outstanding achievement in science and mathematics. The latest information on Carmen tops everything else: as a tenth-grader, she took the PSAT, and received a perfect score!

Carmen is also musically talented. When Carmen was in second grade, a music specialist who came to school on a weekly basis informed her teacher that Carmen should be encouraged to continue with piano lessons because she demonstrated concert pianist abilities. When Carmen entered junior high school, she took up playing the clarinet in the band. At the end-of-the-year banquet, she received the top honor after being in the band for only one year.

Carmen is also psychomotorically talented. She is an accomplished gymnast, dances both the hula and ballet, has been a competitive ice skater (an unusual sport for someone from Hawaii), played soccer for two years on champion soccer teams, and was a walk-on for her junior high's cross-country track team.

Carmen is also artistically talented, demonstrates leadership abilities, has good social skills, and, wouldn't you know it, is simply beautiful.

Carmen's career goals have remained consistent for a long time. She wants to be either a dentist or an astronaut; she can probably be both.

## QUESTIONS TO CONSIDER

1. What kinds of challenges can students like Carmen create for teachers and for themselves?
2. What are some activities and instructional strategies that teachers could employ that would be appropriate for Carmen?
3. Should children like Carmen be included in general education classrooms all of the time, separated for special instructional activities from time to time, or provided a completely different type of curriculum?

*C*hildren and youth such as Carmen, who perform or have the potential to perform at levels significantly above those of other students, have special needs as great as those of students whose disabilities demonstrably limit their performance. This is notable, as most of these students are likely to spend much of their school day in general education settings. As a result, teaching students who are gifted provides challenges to general education teachers that are equal to, if not greater than, those associated with meeting the needs of students with other special needs (McGrail, 1998). To feel confident to work with students who are gifted, classroom teachers should have basic information about giftedness and know some useful techniques for maximizing the educational experiences of these students.

Although there is no general agreement concerning the best way to educate students who are gifted, many professionals argue that such students benefit from a curricular focus different from that provided in general education. Yet, as noted, the vast majority spend a considerable amount of time in the general education classroom, offering teachers the challenges and rewards of working with them.

Although a set of exact competencies that general education teachers should have in working with students who are gifted remains elusive, certain ones are emerging as necessary. Nelson and Prindle (1992) surveyed teachers and principals and identified six competencies on which these groups tended to agree:

1. Promotion of thinking skills
2. Development of creative problem solving
3. Selection of appropriate methods and materials
4. Knowledge of affective needs
5. Facilitation of independent research
6. Awareness of the nature of gifted students

The purpose of the chapter is twofold: (1) to provide basic information about giftedness in children and youth and (2) to suggest practices for working with these students in inclusive settings. This chapter is a primer only; confidence and competence in teaching students who are gifted come with study and experience.

## BASIC CONCEPTS ABOUT STUDENTS WHO ARE GIFTED

**CONSIDER THIS**
Should there be federal mandates to provide appropriate educational programs for students who are gifted and talented?

*S*tudents with exceptional abilities continue to be an underidentified, underserved, and too often inappropriately served group. Unlike the situation for students with disabilities, no federal legislation *mandates* appropriate education for these students. Moreover, states and local school districts vary greatly in the type and quality of services provided—if indeed they are provided at all.

Students who could benefit from special programming are often not identified because of several factors. Teachers in general education may not be aware of the characteristics that suggest giftedness, particularly those associated with students who are culturally different. Historically, ineffective assessment practices have not identified gifted students coming from diverse backgrounds.

For students who are identified as gifted, a common problem is a mismatch between their academic, social, and emotional needs and the programming they receive. In many schools, a limited amount of instructional time is devoted to special activities. The point is reflected in the current focus on equity in education associated with the recent educational reform movement. As Gallagher (1997) notes, "It is this value that leads one to heterogeneous grouping, whereby no one gets any special programming or privileges, and thus all are 'equal'" (p. 17). Furthermore, some gifted programming that exists today favors students who are gifted in the linguistic and mathematical areas only. In too many instances, gifted students do not receive the education they need in the general education classroom.

Services to gifted students remain controversial, partly because the general public and many school personnel hold misconceptions about these students. Hallahan and Kauffman (1997) highlight some of these misguided beliefs:

▲ People who are gifted are physically weak, socially inept, narrow in interests, and prone to emotional instability or early decline. *Fact:* There are wide individual variations, and most gifted individuals are healthy, well adjusted, socially attractive, and morally responsible.

▲ Gifted children are usually bored with school and antagonistic toward those who are responsible for their education. *Fact:* Most gifted children like school and adjust well to their peers and teachers, although some do not like school and have social or emotional problems.

▲ Students who are truly gifted will excel without special education. They need only the incentives and instruction that are appropriate for all students. *Fact:* Some gifted children will perform at a remarkably high level without special education of any kind, and some will make outstanding contributions even in the face of great obstacles to their achievement. But most will not come close to achieving at a level commensurate with their potential unless their talents are deliberately fostered by instruction that is appropriate for their advanced abilities. (p. 453)

> **CONSIDER THIS**
> Why do you think misconceptions about children and adults who are gifted and talented have developed?

Many professionals in the field of gifted education find current services unacceptable and are frustrated by the lack of specialized programming for these students (Feldhusen, 1997). Undoubtedly, the programming provided in inclusive settings to students who are gifted should be improved. VanTassel-Baska (1997), highlighting key beliefs regarding curriculum theory, remarks that gifted students should be provided curriculum opportunities that allow them to attain optimum levels of learning. In addition, these curriculum experiences need to be carefully planned, implemented, and evaluated.

## "Gifted" Defined

Our understanding of giftedness has changed over time, and the terminology used to describe it has also varied. The term **gifted** is often used to refer to the heterogeneous spectrum of students with exceptional abilities, although some professionals restrict the use of this term only to certain individuals who display high levels of intelligence. Other terms such as *talented* and *creative* are used to differentiate subgroups of gifted people.

> **GIFTED** refers to a group of individuals who excel in some area.

The current definition of giftedness promoted by the U.S. Department of Education comes from the Jacob K. Javits Gifted and Talented Education Act. It contains many of the key concepts included in previous definitions.

**CROSS-REFERENCE**
Review the definitions of other categories of disabilities discussed in previous chapters to compare components of definitions.

Children and youth with outstanding talent perform or show the potential for performing at remarkably high levels of accomplishment when compared with others of their age, experience, or environment. These children and youth exhibit high performance capability in intellectual, creative, and/or artistic areas, possess an unusual leadership capacity, or excel in specific academic fields. They require services or activities not ordinarily provided by schools. Outstanding talents are present in children and youth from all cultural groups, across all economic strata, and in all areas of human endeavor. (U.S. Department of Education, 1993, p. 3)

A number of interesting observations can be made regarding this definition. First, attention is given to potential—students do not have to have already produced significant accomplishments to be considered gifted. Second, there is no mention of giftedness in athletics because this area is already addressed in existing school programs. Third, the need for special services or activities for these students is clearly stated, along with the observation that such intervention is not ordinarily provided. Finally, the fact that students who are gifted come from a range of diverse backgrounds is affirmed.

One way to conceptualize giftedness is to consider the interaction of three interlocking clusters of traits (Renzulli, 1979; Renzulli & Reis, 1991) as essential elements associated with outstanding accomplishments. The three clusters are as follows, their interacting nature is depicted in Figure 11.1.

1. High ability—including high intelligence
2. High creativity—the ability to formulate new ideas and apply them to the solution of problems
3. High task commitment—a high level of motivation and the ability to see a project through to its completion

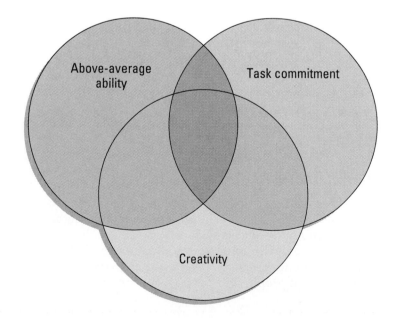

*FIGURE* **11.1**

Renzulli's Three-Ring Conception of Giftedness

From *What Makes Giftedness?* (Brief #6, p. 10), by J. Renzulli, 1979, Los Angeles: National/State Leadership Training Institute. Reprinted by permission.

These criteria are found in the two types of people who are truly gifted and noted in the U.S. Office of Education definition: those who produce and those who perform (Tannebaum, 1997).

A popular theory of intellectual giftedness has been developed by Sternberg (1991). His theory includes three types of abilities: analytic giftedness (i.e., ability to dissect a problem and understand its parts); synthetic giftedness (i.e., insightful, intuitive creative, or adept at coping with relatively novel situations); and practical giftedness (i.e., ability to apply aspects of analytical and synthetic strengths to everyday situations). All individuals demonstrate some blend of these three abilities. However, gifted individuals show high ability in one or more of these areas.

Another perspective, constituting a broad theory of intelligence, has important applications for conceptualizing giftedness and for programming. Gardner and his colleagues (Gardner, 1983; Gardner & Hatch, 1989) have developed a very popular model that proposes the idea of **multiple intelligences.** This model comprises eight areas of ability. Originally the model included only seven areas, but an eighth area (naturalistic) has been added in recent years. Table 11.1 describes the features of each type of intelligence and provides a possible role that might be characteristic of a person with a high degree of a given intelligence.

*MULTIPLE INTELLI-GENCES* refers to different areas in which individuals can excel.

| TABLE 11.1 | Multiple Intelligences | |
|---|---|---|
| **Intelligence** | **End States** | **Core Components** |
| LOGICAL–MATHEMATICAL | Scientist Mathematician | Sensitivity to, and capacity to discern, logical or numerical patterns; ability to handle long chains of reasoning |
| LINGUISTIC | Poet Journalist | Sensitivity to the sounds, rhythms, and meanings of words; sensitivity to the different functions of language |
| MUSICAL | Composer Violinist | Abilities to produce and appreciate rhythm, pitch, and timbre; appreciation of the forms of musical expressiveness |
| SPATIAL | Navigator Sculptor | Capacities to perceive the visual–spatial world accurately and to transform one's initial perceptions |
| BODILY–KINESTHETIC | Dancer Athlete | Abilities to control one's body movements and to handle objects skillfully |
| INTERPERSONAL | Therapist Salesperson | Capacities to discern and respond appropriately to the moods, temperaments, motivations, and desires of other people |
| INTRAPERSONAL | Person with detailed, accurate self-knowledge | Access to one's own feelings and the ability to discriminate among them and draw upon them to guide behavior; knowledge of one's own strengths, weaknesses, desires, and intelligences |
| NATURALISTIC | Naturalist Park Ranger | Affinity and appreciation for the wonders of nature |

Adapted from "Multiple Intelligences Go to School: Educational Implications of the Theory of Multiple Intelligences," by H. Gardner and T. Hatch, 1989, *Educational Researcher, 18*(8), p. 6. Copyright © 1989 by the American Educational Research Association. Reprinted by permission.

If Gardner's ideas were followed closely, students would be assessed in all areas of intelligence. If found to have strengths in an area, students would be provided opportunities to expand their interests, skills, and abilities accordingly. The attractiveness of this conceptualization is that (1) it acknowledges some ability areas that are frequently overlooked and (2) it recognizes the importance of different types of intelligences and gives them all equal footing.

## Prevalence and Origins of Giftedness

The number of students who display exceptional abilities is uncertain. It is, of course, influenced by how giftedness is defined and how it is measured. Figures of 3% to 5% are typically cited to reflect the extent of giftedness in the school population (National Center for Education Statistics, 1989).

**CONSIDER THIS**
How can the way in which "gifted" and "talented" are defined influence the prevalence of children classified?

The critical reader should also note the distinction between the number of students served and the number of students who might be gifted. Only certain types of gifted students may be served because of the methods used for identification. Another cautionary note is that such figures generally underestimate the number of gifted students who are ethnically or culturally different, disabled, or female. These subgroups are underrepresented in programs for students with exceptional abilities.

Much professional discussion has focused on what contributes to giftedness in a person. Most researchers suggest that giftedness results from the interaction between biology and environment. Research has shown that behavior is greatly affected by genetics. Although this notion is sometimes overemphasized, genetic factors do play a role in giftedness. Other biological factors, such as nutrition, also have an impact on an individual's development.

The environment in which a child is raised also affects later performance and intellectual abilities. Homes in which there is much stimulation and opportunity to explore and interact with the environment, accompanied by high expectations, tend to produce children more likely to be successful scholastically and socially.

## Characteristics of Students Who Are Gifted

Students who are gifted demonstrate a wide range of specific aptitudes, abilities, and skills. Though they should not be overgeneralized or considered stereotypical, certain characteristics distinguish students who are gifted or talented.

A comprehensive listing of characteristics of gifted children has been developed by Clark (1997); a summary is presented in Table 11.2. Her study also highlights the needs and possible problems that may surface in working with these individuals.

An interesting phenomenon is the paradoxical negative effect of certain positive behaviors displayed by gifted students. For instance, their sincere, excited curiosity about a topic being covered in class can sometimes be interpreted as annoying or disruptive by a teacher or fellow students. Their quick answers or certainty that they are right may be misconstrued as well. Such desirable behavior can be misperceived as problem behavior for students who are gifted.

A notable characteristic that has important classroom implications is the gifted student's expenditure of minimum effort while still earning high grades (Reis & Schack, 1993). Many gifted students are able to handle the general education curriculum with ease. But the long-term effect of being able to excel without working hard may be a lack of the work habits needed for challenging programs at a later point in time (i.e., high school or college).

| TABLE 11.2 | Differentiating Characteristics of the Gifted |
|---|---|
| **Domain** | **Characteristic** |
| THE COGNITIVE FUNCTION | ■ Extraordinary quantity of information; unusual retentiveness<br>■ Advanced comprehension<br>■ Unusual varied interests and curiosity<br>■ High level of language development<br>■ High level of verbal ability<br>■ Unusual capacity for processing information<br>■ Accelerated pace of thought processes<br>■ Flexible thought processes<br>■ Comprehensive synthesis<br>■ Early ability to delay closure<br>■ Heightened capacity for seeing unusual and diverse relationships, integration of ideas, and disciplines<br>■ Ability to generate original ideas and solutions<br>■ Early differential patterns for thought processing (e.g., thinking in alternatives; abstract terms; sensing consequences; making generalizations; visual thinking; use of metaphors and analogies)<br>■ Early ability to use and form conceptual frameworks<br>■ An evaluative approach toward oneself and others<br>■ Unusual intensity; persistent goal-directed behavior |
| THE AFFECTIVE FUNCTION | ■ Large accumulation of information about emotions that have not been brought to awareness<br>■ Unusual sensitivity to the expectations and feelings of others<br>■ Keen sense of humor—may be gentle or hostile<br>■ Heightened self-awareness, accompanied by feelings of being different<br>■ Idealism and a sense of justice, which appear at an early age<br>■ Earlier development of an inner locus of control and satisfaction<br>■ Unusual emotional depth and intensity<br>■ High expectations of self and others, often leading to high levels of frustration with self, others, and situations; perfectionism<br>■ Strong need for consistency between abstract values and personal actions<br>■ Advanced levels of moral judgment<br>■ Strongly motivated by self-actualization needs<br>■ Advanced cognitive and affective capacity for conceptualizing and solving societal problems<br>■ Leadership ability<br>■ Solutions to social and environmental problems<br>■ Involvement with the metaneeds of society (e.g., injustice, beauty, truth) |
| THE PHYSICAL/SENSING FUNCTION | ■ Unusual quantity of input from the environment through a heightened sensory awareness<br>■ Unusual discrepancy between physical and intellectual development<br>■ Low tolerance for the lag between their standards and their athletic skills<br>■ Cartesian split—can include neglect of physical well-being and avoidance of physical activity |
| THE INTUITIVE FUNCTION | ■ Early involvement and concern for intuitive knowing and metaphysical ideas and phenomena<br>■ Open to experiences in this area; will experiment with psychic and metaphysical phenomena<br>■ Creative approach in all areas of endeavor<br>■ Ability to predict; interest in future |

## Identification, Assessment, and Eligibility

General education teachers need to know about the assessment process used to confirm the existence of exceptional abilities. Teachers play a crucial role in the initial stages of the process, for they are likely to be the first to recognize that a student might be gifted. For this reason, teachers should provide opportunities across the range of ability areas (e.g., multiple intelligences) for students to explore their interests and abilities, particularly at the preschool and elementary levels. Ramos-Ford and Gardner (1997) suggest that this may help students discover certain abilities that might otherwise go unnoticed.

The assessment process includes a sequence of steps, beginning with an initial referral (i.e., nomination) and culminating with the validation of the decision. General education teachers are largely responsible for identifying gifted students. Although some children displaying exceptional abilities may be spotted very early (i.e., preschool years), many are not recognized until they are in school. For this reason, teachers need to be aware of classroom behaviors that gifted students typically display. A listing of such behaviors is provided in Table 11.3.

Teachers who recognize such behaviors should determine whether a student should be evaluated more comprehensively. This usually involves nominating the student for gifted services. Teachers can be involved in the next step in the assessment process as well. After a student has been nominated or referred, teachers can assemble information to help determine whether the student should receive special services. The following sources of information can contribute to understanding a student's demonstrated or potential ability: formal tests; informal assessments; interviews with teachers, parents, and peers; and actual student products. For example, a public elementary school may use various screening instruments to identify gifted students, including a standardized ability test, standardized creativity test, teacher observation form, student portfolio, and parent observation form.

A helpful technique used in many school systems to determine the performance capabilities of students is **portfolio assessment.** Portfolios contain a collection of student-generated products, reflecting the quality of a student's work. They may also contain permanent products such as artwork, poetry, or videotapes of student performance (e.g., theatrical production, music recital).

As VanTassel-Baska, Patton, and Prillaman (1989) point out, students who are culturally different and those who come from socially and economically disadvantaged backgrounds are typically overlooked in the process of identifying students for gifted programs. For the most part, this problem results from entry requirements that stress performance on standardized tests. When students obtain low test scores on standardized instruments that may be biased against them, exclusion results. VanTassel-Baska et al. provide these recommendations for improving the identification and assessment process:

▲ Use nontraditional measures for identification purposes.
▲ Recognize cultural attributes and factors in deciding on identification procedures.
▲ Focus on strengths in nonacademic areas, particularly in creativity and psychomotor domains. (p. 3)

It has also been difficult to identify and serve students who are twice exceptional—gifted and who also have disabilities. For instance, the problems that characterize a learning disability (e.g., problems in language-related areas) often mask high levels of accomplishment in other areas such as drama, art, or music. Special services or activities are warranted for these students, and are not yet ordinarily provided by schools.

*TEACHING TIP*
Classroom teachers need to be alert to students who may be gifted and talented and refer students to appropriate professionals for testing and services.

*PORTFOLIO ASSESSMENT* is a method of assessment that reviews a wide variety of student products and work.

**TABLE 11.3** **Observed Classroom Behaviors of Gifted Children**

**IN THE CLASSROOM, DOES THE CHILD:**
- Ask a lot of questions?
- Show a lot of interest in progress?
- Have lots of information on many things?
- Want to know why or how something is so?
- Become unusually upset at injustices?
- Seem interested and concerned about social or political problems?
- Often have a better reason than you do for not doing what you want done?
- Refuse to drill on spelling, math facts, flash cards, or handwriting?
- Criticize others for dumb ideas?
- Become impatient if work is not "perfect"?
- Seem to be a loner?
- Seem bored and often have nothing to do?
- Complete only part of an assignment or project and then take off in a new direction?
- Stick to a subject long after the class has gone on to other things?
- Seem restless, out of seat often?
- Daydream?
- Seem to understand easily?
- Like solving puzzles and problems?
- Have his or her own idea about how something should be done? And stay with it?
- Talk a lot?
- Love metaphors and abstract ideas?
- Love debating issues?

This child may be showing giftedness cognitively.

**DOES THE CHILD:**
- Show unusual ability in some area? Maybe reading or math?
- Show fascination with one field of interest? And manage to include this interest in all discussion topics?
- Enjoy meeting or talking with experts in this field?
- Get math answers correctly, but find it difficult to tell you how?

- Enjoy graphing everything? Seem obsessed with probabilities?
- Invent new obscure systems and codes?

This child may be showing giftedness academically.

**DOES THE CHILD:**
- Try to do things in different, unusual, imaginative ways?
- Have a really zany sense of humor?
- Enjoy new routines or spontaneous activities?
- Love variety and novelty?
- Create problems with no apparent solutions? And enjoy asking you to solve them?
- Love controversial and unusual questions?
- Have a vivid imagination?
- Seem never to proceed sequentially?

This child may be showing giftedness creatively.

**DOES THE CHILD:**
- Organize and lead group activities? Sometimes take over?
- Enjoy taking risks?
- Seem cocky, self-assured?
- Enjoy decision making? Stay with that decision?
- Synthesize ideas and information from a lot of different sources?

This child may be showing giftedness through leadership ability.

**DOES THE CHILD:**
- Seem to pick up skills in the arts—music, dance, drama, painting, etc.—without instruction?
- Invent new techniques? Experiment?
- See minute detail in products or performances?
- Have high sensory sensitivity?

This child may be showing giftedness through visual or performing arts ability.

From *Growing Up Gifted* (Fifth Edition) (p. 282), by Barbara Clark. Copyright 1997 by Merrill/Prentice-Hall. Reprinted by permission.

After the student has been identified as gifted and begins to participate in special programs or services, ongoing assessment should become part of the student's educational program. Practical and personal needs should be monitored regularly (Del Prete, 1996). Practical concerns, such as progress in academic areas and realization of potential, can be evaluated. On the other hand, the personal needs of students who are gifted (e.g., feeling accepted and developing confidence) need to be addressed as well.

*Too few students from minority cultural groups are identified as gifted and talented.*

Unlike those children classified as having a disability, gifted children are not eligible for special services under IDEA. The nearby Rights and Responsibilities feature summarizes some court cases dealing with this group of students.

## Multicultural Issues

As pointed out earlier, cultural diversity remains an area of concern in the education of gifted students. Too few students who are culturally different from mainstream students are identified and served through programs for gifted students. "Culturally

# RIGHTS & RESPONSIBILITIES

### Gifted Children

The Individuals with Disabilities Education Act (IDEA) does not include rights for gifted children. Some states, however, do provide programs for this group of students. Examples of state cases involving gifted students include:

1. In a court case in Pennsylvania, *Ellis* v. *Chester Upland School Dist.*, 651 A.2d 616 (Pa.Cmwlth. 1994), the court ruled that the school did not have to pay out-of-state tuition to a private school for a child who was classified as gifted because the state law did not entitle a gifted student to such services.

2. In the case *Broadley* v. *Bd. of Educ. of the City of Meriden*, 229 Conn. 1, 639 App.2d 502 (1994), the court ruled that the state of Connecticut did not have to provide special education to gifted children because, even though they were within the

broad definition of exceptional children, the law only required special education for children with disabilities.

3. In *Centennial School Dist.* v. *Commonwealth Dept. of Educ.*, 539 A.2d 785 (Pa.1988), the court ruled that the school district had to provide an IEP and special programs for gifted students because they were classified as *exceptional*. The court ruled, however, that this requirement did not entitle the student to specialized instruction beyond enrichment.

4. In *Student Roe* v. *Commonwealth,* 638 F.Supp. 929 (E.D.Pa.1986), the court ruled that while Pennsylvania law provides for children with an IQ of 130 and above to be admitted to its gifted programs, IDEA did not apply to children unless they had a disability as defined in the act. Therefore, while state law did require some programs for gifted children, this did not result in gifted students being eligible for IDEA protections.

From *Students with Disabilities and Special Education* (14th Edition), 1997, Burnsville, MN: Oakstone Publishing.

## DIVERSITY FORUM  Observational Checklist for Identifying Strengths of Culturally Diverse Children

1. Ability to express feeling and emotions
2. Ability to improvise with commonplace materials and objects
3. Articulateness in role-playing, sociodrama, and storytelling
4. Enjoyment of and ability in visual arts, such as drawing, painting, and sculpture
5. Enjoyment of and ability in creative movement, dance, drama, etc.
6. Enjoyment of and ability in music and rhythm
7. Use of expressive speech
8. Fluency and flexibility in figural media
9. Enjoyment of and skills in group or team activities
10. Responsiveness to the concrete

11. Responsiveness to the kinesthetic
12. Expressiveness of gestures, body language, etc., and ability to interpret body language
13. Humor
14. Richness of imagery in informal language
15. Originality of ideas in problem solving
16. Problem-centeredness or persistence in problem solving
17. Emotional responsiveness
18. Quickness of warmup

From "Identifying and Capitalizing on the Strengths of Culturally Different Children," by E. P. Torrance, in *The Handbook of School Psychology,* edited by C. R. Reynolds and J. B. Gulkin, 1982, pp. 451–500. New York: Wiley. Copyright 1982 by John Wiley & Sons. Reprinted by permission.

diverse children have much talent, creativity, and intelligence. Manifestations of these characteristics may be different and thus require not only different tools for measuring these strengths, but also different eyes from which to see them" (Plummer, 1995, p. 290). Teachers should look for certain behaviors associated with giftedness in children who are culturally different. An example of an observational checklist for accomplishing this task is presented in the nearby Diversity Forum.

Even when culturally diverse students have been identified as gifted, programming often has not been sensitive to their needs. As Plummer (1995) notes, few programs have the resources (i.e., personnel, materials) available to tap the interests and strengths of these students. Often the general education teacher needs such supports to address these students' educational needs in inclusive settings. The twofold challenge for teachers is (1) to respect racial, ethnic, and cultural differences of students from diverse backgrounds and (2) to integrate diverse cultural topics into the curriculum (Plummer, 1995).

**CONSIDER THIS**
How can teachers take into consideration multicultural issues when identifying children who are gifted and talented?

## STRATEGIES FOR CURRICULUM AND INSTRUCTION

The literature on providing effective services for students with exceptional abilities consistently stresses the need for **differentiated programming.** This means that learning opportunities provided to these students must differ according to a student's needs and abilities. Differentiation includes the content of what students learn, the processes used in learning situations, and the final products that students develop. Furthermore, as Lopez and MacKenzie (1993) note, "Difference lies in the depth, scope, pace, and self-directedness of the expectations" (p. 288).

**DIFFERENTIATED PROGRAMMING** refers to providing different learning opportunities for different students.

VanTassel-Baska (1989) notes some of the mistaken beliefs that some educators have about educating students with exceptional abilities:

**CROSS-REFERENCE**
Review chapters 4–10 and compare curriculum and instruction modifications suggested for students with other special needs.

▲ A "differentiated" curriculum for the gifted means "anything that is different from what is provided for all learners." *Fact:* A "differentiated" curriculum implies a coherently planned scope and sequence of instruction that matches the needs of students and that typically does differ from the regular education curriculum.
▲ All experiences provided for gifted learners must be creative and focused on process. *Fact:* Core content areas are important areas of instructional focus.
▲ One curriculum package will provide what is needed for the entire gifted population. *Fact:* Students need a variety of materials, resources, and courses.
▲ Acceleration, moving through the curriculum at a more rapid pace, can be harmful because it pushes children socially and leaves gaps in their knowledge. *Fact:* This approach to meeting the needs of students with exceptional abilities is the intervention technique best supported by research. (pp. 13–14)

Many professionals in the field of gifted education argue that the preferred setting for these students is not general education; they recommend differentiated programs delivered in separate classes for the greater part, if not all, of the school day. However, in reality gifted students are more likely to spend nearly all day in general education classrooms, possibly receiving some differentiated opportunities in a pull-out program. The nearby Inclusion Strategies feature lists curricular goals for gifted children.

## Realities of the General Education Classroom

In general education settings, students who are gifted or talented are sometimes subject to conditions that indeed hinder the possibility for having their individual needs met. The U.S. Department of Education (1993) has noted the following concerns related to educating gifted students in general education settings:

**CONSIDER THIS**
Should general classroom teachers be prepared to teach students who are gifted and talented in their classes?

▲ Elementary level
  • The general education curriculum does not challenge gifted students.
  • Most academically talented students have already mastered up to one half of the required curriculum offered to them in elementary school.
  • Classroom teachers do little to accommodate the different learning needs of gifted children.
  • Most specialized programs are available for only a few hours a week.
  • Students talented in the arts are offered few challenging opportunities.
▲ Secondary level
  • Appropriate opportunities in middle schools are scattered and uncoordinated.
  • High school schedules do not meet the needs of talented students (i.e., pacing or content of coverage).
  • The college preparatory curriculum in the United States generally does not require hard work from able students.
  • Small-town and rural schools often have limited resources and are unable to offer advanced classes and special learning opportunities.
  • Specialized schools, magnet schools, and intensive summer programs serve only a fraction of the secondary students who might benefit from them.
  • Dual enrollment in secondary school and college is uncommon.

## INCLUSION STRATEGIES

### Goals for Curricula of Gifted Children

▲ Include more elaborate, complex, and in-depth study of major ideas, problems, and themes—those that integrate knowledge with and across systems of thought.

▲ Allow for the development and application of productive thinking skills that enable students to reconceptualize existing knowledge or generate new knowledge.

▲ Enable students to explore constantly changing knowledge and information, and to develop the attitude that knowledge is worth pursuing in an open world.

▲ Encourage exposure to, selection of, and use of appropriate and specialized resources.

▲ Promote self-initiated and self-directed learning and growth.

▲ Provide for the development of self-understanding and the understanding of one's relationship to persons, societal institutions, nature, and culture.

▲ Evaluate students with stress placed on their ability to perform at a level of excellence that demonstrates creativity and higher-level thinking skills.

From *Diverse Populations of Gifted Children* (pp. 15–16), by S. Cline and D. Schwartz, 1999, Columbus, OH: Merrill.

Other more specific practices that can be problematic for gifted students include the following:

▲ When involved in group activities, (i.e., cooperative learning), gifted students may end up doing all of the work (Clinkenbeard, 1991).

▲ They are often subjected to more stringent grading criteria (Clinkenbeard, 1991).

▲ When they finish assignments early, they are given more of the same type of work or assigned more of the same types of tasks at the outset (Shaner, 1991).

▲ They are overused as co-teachers to help students who need more assistance.

▲ Vocabulary use in the average classroom is inappropriate for advanced learners (Clark, 1996).

▲ Advanced levels of critical thinking are not typically incorporated into lessons (Clark, 1996).

▲ Instructional materials in general education classrooms are frequently limited in range and complexity (Clark, 1996).

▲ Problem solving strategies not used in classrooms (Gallagher, 1997).

Unfortunately, most general education teachers are not provided with the necessary understanding, skills, and resources to deal appropriately with this population. This situation is exacerbated by the fact that teachers have to deal with a wide range of abilities and needs in their classrooms. The composition of the general education classroom in many of today's public schools requires a staggering array of accommodative knowledge and skills.

In addition, some teachers feel uncomfortable working with students who have exceptional abilities. Figure 11.2 highlights this situation by way of a personal experience. Shaner (1991) remarks that teachers who are working with gifted students can be "intimidated by him or her, paralyzed with a fear of not being able to keep up, or threatened by the student's challenges to authority" (pp. 14–15). Teachers are also concerned about being asked questions they are unprepared to answer or challenged on points they may not know well. These are reasonable fears; however, they can be minimized by using these opportunities as a way of increasing everyone's knowledge—a teacher's as well—and by understanding how to address gifted students' needs within the general classroom setting.

FIGURE **11.2**

A Personal Experience

From *Exceptional Children in Focus* (p. 216), by J. R. Patton, J. Blackbourn, and K. Fad, 1996, Columbus, OH: Merrill. Used by permission.

> Not long ago, I was invited to go on a "reef walk" with a class of gifted third- and fourth-graders. It was a very educational experience.
>
> While we were wading in shallow water, we came upon a familiar marine organism commonly called a feather duster (tube worm). Forgetting that these students had vocabularies well advanced of their nongifted age peers, I was ready to say something like, "Look how that thing hangs on the rock."
>
> Before I could get my highly descriptive statement out, Eddie, who always amazes us with his comments, offered the following: "Notice how securely anchored the organism is to the stationary coral?"
>
> All I could reply was "Yes. I did."

Differentiated programming for students with exceptional abilities, wherever it occurs, must address individual needs and interests in the context of preparing the students for a world characterized by change and complexity. Reis (1989) suggests that we reassess how we look at gifted education and move away from the content-based nature of most current curriculums to an orientation based on a realistic view of future education.

## Continuum-of-Placement Options

A variety of ways exist for providing educational programs to students who are gifted and talented. Some specific options include specialized grouping within the general education setting, various adjunct programs (e.g., mentorships, internships), special classes outside of general education, special schools, and special summer programs. The value of a particular option reflects the extent to which it meets an individual's needs. As Clark (1997) points out, all of the options have some merit; none address the needs of all students with exceptional abilities; however, the general education classroom as traditionally organized in terms of curriculum and instruction is inadequate for true gifted education. For this reason, school systems should provide a range of programmatic alternatives.

Gifted students who are in general education classrooms for the entire instructional day can have some of their needs met through a variety of special provisions such as enrichment, certain acceleration options, or special grouping. The challenge for teachers is to coordinate these provisions with those required for other students in the classroom.

In many schools, students who have been identified as gifted are pulled out for a specified period of time each day to attend a special class for gifted students. When they are in the general education setting, it may be possible for them to participate in an individualized program of study, apart from the regular curriculum.

Gifted students may also participate in various adjunct programs such as mentorships, internships, special tutorials, independent study, and resource rooms—many of which will occur outside the regular classroom. For students at the secondary level, spending time in special programming for part of the day, in addition to attending heterogeneous classes, is another possibility.

These programmatic options affect the role and responsibilities of the general education teacher. In some situations, the general education teacher will be the primary source of instruction for these students. In others, the general education teacher may serve as a manager, coordinating the services provided by others. However, it is probable that most teachers will be responsible for providing some level of instruction to gifted students.

## Approaches

Many approaches exist for designing programs for students who have exceptional abilities. Renzulli and Reis (1997) provide a comprehensive conceptualization for a "continuum of services for total talent development" that should be available within a school system. Many of the suggestions in their continuum involve options outside of a general education setting. The approaches most likely to be used by general education teachers are acceleration, enrichment, and special grouping.

**Acceleration** refers to practices that introduce content, concepts, and educational experiences to gifted students sooner than for other students. It presents gifted students with more advanced materials appropriate to their ability and interests. There are many types of accelerative practices, as reflected in the array of options provided by Southern and Jones (1991) in Table 11.4.

All of the accelerative options described by Southern and Jones (1991) have relevance for gifted students in general education classrooms. The techniques that have the most direct application in the general education classroom are **continuous progress, self-paced instruction, subject-matter acceleration,** combined classes, **curriculum compacting,** and **curriculum telescoping.** If these practices are to be used, teachers must plan and implement instructional activities.

Other accelerative practices have a more indirect impact on ongoing activities in the general education classroom. Nevertheless, teachers should be aware of them. They include early entrance to school, grade skipping, mentorships, extracurricular programs, concurrent enrollment, advanced placement, and credit by examination.

According to Gallagher and Gallagher (1994), the most common acceleration practices are (1) primary level—early admittance to school, ungraded primary, (2) upper elementary—ungraded classes, grade skipping, (3) middle school—three years in two, senior high classes for credit, and (4) high school—extra load (early graduation), advanced placement (AP). Interestingly, some professionals (Davis, 1996) advocate separate advanced placement classes for gifted students because their needs differ from those of nongifted students enrolled in AP classes.

**Enrichment** refers to techniques that provide topics, skill development, materials, or experiences that extend the depth of coverage beyond the typical curriculum. This practice is commonly used in general education classes to address the needs of students who move through content quickly. Many teachers' manuals and guides provide ideas on how to deliver enriching activities to students who finish their work quickly.

As Southern and Jones (1991) note, some enrichment activities ultimately involve acceleration. For instance, whenever topics of an advanced nature are introduced, a form of acceleration is actually being employed. There is, however, a distinction between materials or activities that are accelerated and involve a dimension of difficulty or conceptual complexity and materials or activities that provide variety but do not require advanced skills or understanding.

**Special grouping** refers to the practice whereby gifted students of similar ability levels or interests are grouped together for at least part of the instructional day. One commonly cited technique is the use of cluster grouping within the general education classroom. This practice allows for interaction with peers who share a similar enthusiasm, bring different perspectives to topics, and stimulate the cognitive and creative thinking of others in the group.

**ACCELERATION** refers to introducing content and concepts of educational material to gifted students before it is presented to other students.

**CONTINUOUS PROGRESS** means allowing students to progress at their own ability level.

**SELF-PACED INSTRUCTION** refers to students moving along the curriculum at their own pace.

**SUBJECT-MATTER ACCELERATION** allows students to move more rapidly in specific subjects than other areas of the curriculum.

**CURRICULUM COMPACTING** results in students having less introductory and review materials.

**CURRICULUM TELESCOPING** allows the student to move through a particular curriculum at an advanced pace.

**ENRICHMENT** refers to techniques that provide materials and skill development beyond the typical curriculum.

**SPECIAL GROUPING** is the practice of grouping together gifted students with similar interests and abilities for part of the school day.

| TABLE 11.4 | Range and Types of Accelerative Options |
|---|---|
| 1. Early entrance to kindergarten or first grade | The student is admitted to school prior to the age specified by the district for normal entry to kindergarten or first grade. |
| 2. Grade skipping | The student is moved ahead of normal grade placement. This may be done during an academic year (placing a third-grader directly into fourth grade), or at year end (promoting a third-grader to fifth grade). |
| 3. Continuous progress | The student is given material deemed appropriate for current achievement as the student becomes ready. |
| 4. Self-paced instruction | The student is presented with materials that allow him or her to proceed at a self-selected pace. Responsibility for selection of pacing is the student's. |
| 5. Subject matter acceleration | The student is placed for a part of a day with students at more advanced grade levels for one or more subjects without being assigned to a higher grade (e.g., a fifth-grader going to sixth grade for science instruction). |
| 6. Combined classes | The student is placed in classes where two or more grade levels are combined (e.g., third- and fourth-grade split rooms). The arrangement can be used to allow younger children to interact with older ones academically and socially. |
| 7. Curriculum compacting | The student is given reduced amounts of introductory activities, drill review, and so on. The time saved may be used to move faster through the curriculum. |
| 8. Telescoping curriculum | The student spends less time than normal in a course of study (e.g., completing a one-year course in one semester, or finishing junior high school in two years rather than three). |
| 9. Mentorships | The student is exposed to a mentor who provides advanced training and experiences in a content area. |
| 10. Extracurricular programs | The student is enrolled in course work or summer programs that confer advanced instruction and/or credit for study (e.g., fast-paced language or math courses offered by universities). |
| 11. Concurrent enrollment | The student is taking a course at one level and receiving credit for successful completion of a parallel course at a higher level (e.g., taking algebra at the junior high level and receiving credit for high school algebra as well as junior high math credits upon successful completion). |
| 12. Advanced placement | The student takes a course in high school that prepares him or her for taking an examination that can confer college credit for satisfactory performances. |
| 13. Credit by examination | The student receives credit (at high school or college level) upon successful completion of an examination. |
| 14. Correspondence courses | The student takes high school or college courses by mail (or, more recently, through video and audio presentations). |
| 15. Early entrance into junior high, high school, or college | The student is admitted with full standing to an advanced level of instruction (at least one year early). |

From *Academic Acceleration of Gifted Children* (Figure 1.1), by W. T. Southern and E. D. Jones, 1991, New York: Teachers College Press. Copyright © 1991 by Teachers College, Columbia University. All rights reserved. Used by permission.

*Teachers must create a psychological classroom climate that is conducive to a variety of ideas and viewpoints.*

# CLASSROOM ACCOMMODATIONS FOR STUDENTS WHO ARE GIFTED

This section highlights techniques for addressing the needs of students with exceptional abilities. Teachers who will be working closely with these students are encouraged to consult resources that thoroughly discuss teaching gifted students in general education settings—see Maker (1993), Parke (1989), Smutny, Walker, and Meckstroth (1997), or Winebrenner (1992).

First and foremost, teachers should strive to create classroom settings that foster conditions in which gifted students feel comfortable and are able to realize their potential. They need a comprehensive long-term plan of education and must enjoy learning experiences that reflect this plan (Kitano, 1993).

Although special opportunities for enrichment, acceleration, and the use of higher-level skills are particularly beneficial to gifted students, these opportunities can also be extended to other students when appropriate (Roberts, Ingram, & Harris, 1992). Many students in general education settings will find practices such as integrated programming (combining different subject matter) to be exciting, motivating, and meaningful.

**CONSIDER THIS**
How can special opportunities for gifted and talented children benefit other students, including those with other special needs?

## Management Considerations

It is essential to organize and systematically manage the classroom environment. Teachers must create a psychosocial climate that is open to a "variety of ideas, materials, problems, people, viewpoints, and resources" (Schiever, 1993, p. 209). The learning environment should be safe, accepting, and supportive.

Grouping gifted students is useful and can be done in a variety of ways. This might include cooperative cluster grouping on the basis of similar abilities or interests dyads, or seminar-type formats. Gifted students should be afforded an opportunity to spend time with other gifted students, just as competitive tennis players must play opponents with similar or more advanced ability in order to maintain their skills.

Even though the merits of cooperative learning in classroom settings have been established, heterogeneous cooperative learning arrangements involving gifted students

**TEACHING TIP**
Pairing gifted students with students who are not gifted can make an excellent cooperative learning situation for all students.

**Differentiated–Integrated Curriculum Report**

Student: _____
Teacher: _____
Semester/Year: _____

**CONTENT**

DISCIPLINES

| Area of Study | Broad-Based Theme | Language Arts Enrichment/Acceleration | | | | Math/Science Enrichment | | Social Science | Arts | Individual Extension Activities |
|---|---|---|---|---|---|---|---|---|---|---|
| | | Reading | Written Expression | Oral Expression | Spelling | Math | Science | Social Studies/ Social Issues | Music/ Visual Arts/ Performance Arts | |

**PROCESSES**

Basic Skills

Research Skills

- Reading for general information
- Creating hypothesis
- Taking notes
- Making an outline
- Reading for supportive evidence
- Writing the thesis
- Using various sources
- Writing bibliography
- Making appendices

- Brainstorm
- Observe
- Classify
- Interpret
- Analyze
- Evaluate
- Judge

Productive Thinking/Critical Thinking Skills

- Compare
- Categorize
- Synthesize
- Exhibit fluency
- Display flexibility
- Demonstrate originality
- Problem solve

- Elaborate
- Hypothesize
- Exhibit awareness
- Appreciate
- Create
- Redesign
- Prove

**PRODUCTS**

a variety of ways to communicate and express selves ▲ the opportunity to share information with an audience

☐ Proposed  } in-depth study of
☐ Completed } student's choice:

FIGURE *11.3*  Differentiated-Integrated Curriculum Report
Adapted from S. N. Kaplan by J. Kataoka, revised 1990. Copyright © ASSETS 1986.

340

must be managed carefully, as there are some potential pitfalls. Teachers must guarantee that most of the work does not always fall on gifted students in such arrangements. Cooperative learning arrangements can be used effectively but need to be continually monitored to ensure productiveness and fairness.

Teachers should develop comprehensive record-keeping systems that monitor the progress of all students, including gifted students who may be involved in a mix of enrichment and accelerated activities. A differentiated report card may be useful for conveying to parents more information about a gifted student's performance. An example of such a report is shown in Figure 11.3. Much qualitative information about student performance can be communicated through this document.

The following are some specific management-related suggestions on dealing with gifted students:

- Get to know gifted students early in the school year through interviews, portfolios of previous work, child-created portfolios, and dynamic assessment (test–teach–retest) (Smutny et al., 1997).
- Enlist parents as colleagues early in the school year by soliciting information and materials (Smutny et al., 1997).
- Require gifted students to follow classroom rules and procedures while allowing them to explore and pursue their curiosity when appropriate (Feldhusen, 1993a and b).
- Include gifted students in the development of class procedures that emerge during the course of a school year (e.g., introduction of animals in the room).
- Explain the logic and rationale for certain rules and procedures.
- Use cluster seating arrangements rather than strict rows (Feldhusen, 1993a).
- Identify a portion of the room where special events and activities take place and where stimulating materials are kept.
- Include instructional ideas for gifted students within all lesson plans.
- Let students who are working in independent arrangements plan their own learning activities (Feldhusen, 1993a).
- Use contracts with students who are involved in elaborate independent study projects to maximize communication between teacher and students (Rosselli, 1993).
- Involve students in their own record keeping, thus assisting the teacher and developing responsibility.
- Use periodic progress reports, daily logs, and teacher conferences to monitor and evaluate students who are in independent study arrangements (Conroy, 1993).

## Curricular and Instructional Considerations

General education teachers should develop instructional lessons that consider a range of abilities and interests. For gifted students, instructional activities may be qualitatively different from those assigned to the class in general—or completely different if certain accelerative options are being used.

When designing instructional activities for the entire class, teachers can use the following series of questions offered by Kitano (1993) to guide planning for gifted students:

- Do the activities include provisions for several ability levels?
- Do the activities include ways to accommodate a variety of interest areas?
- Does the design of activities encourage development of sophisticated products?
- Do the activities provide for the integration of thinking processes with concept development?
- Are the concepts consistent with the comprehensive curriculum plan? (p. 280)

**CONSIDER THIS**
How can differential programming be used effectively with students with a variety of different learning needs?

FIGURE 11.4

Curriculum
Compacting Form

From *The Revolving Door
Identification Model* (p.
79), by J. Renzulli, S.
Reis, and L. Smith,
1981, Mansfield Center,
CT: Creative Learning
Press. Reprinted with
permission from
Creative Learning Press,
copyright © 1981.

## Individual Educational Programming Guide
### The Compactor

Name _____  Age _____  Teacher(s) _____  Individual conference dates and persons participating in planning of IEP

School _____  Grade _____  Parent(s) _____

| *Curriculum areas to be considered for compacting.* Provide a brief description of basic material to be covered during this marking period and the assessment information or evidence that suggests the need for compacting. | *Procedures for compacting basic material.* Describe activities that will be used to guarantee proficiency in basic curricular areas. | *Acceleration and/or enrichment activities.* Describe activities that will be used to provide advanced-level learning experiences in each of the regular curricula. |
|---|---|---|
| | | |
| | | |
| | | |
| | | |
| | | |

# *T*ECHNOLOGY *T*ODAY

## Web Sites That Offer Curriculum, Strategies, and Interventions

◢ http://www.kn.pacbell.com/wired/bluewebn
(lesson plans and teaching resources)

◢ http://www.education-world.com
(curriculum ideas)

◢ http://www.capecod.net.schrockguide
(list of sites useful for enhancing curriculum and professional growth)

◢ http://www.yahooligans.com
(child-safe search engine, links, discussion groups)

◢ http://rtec.org
(links to 6 regional technology consortia to support improved teaching)

◢ http://www.nyu.edu/projects/mstep/menu/html
(lesson plans, activities, and information for math and science teachers)

◢ http://www.planemath.com/
(InfoUse with NASA provides student activities in math and aeronautics)

◢ http://forum.swarthmore.edu/index.js.html
(database of math lesson plans by topic and grade level)

◢ http://www.enc.org
(variety of math and science lessons for grades 4–12)

◢ http://theory.lcs.mit.edu:80/-emjordan/famMath.html
(K–6 math program; activities)

From *Quick Guide to the Internet for Special Education* (2000 Edition) by M. Male and D. Gotthoffer, 2000, Boston: Allyn and Bacon.

FIGURE 11.5   Adapting Curricular Content for Teaching *Romeo and Juliet*

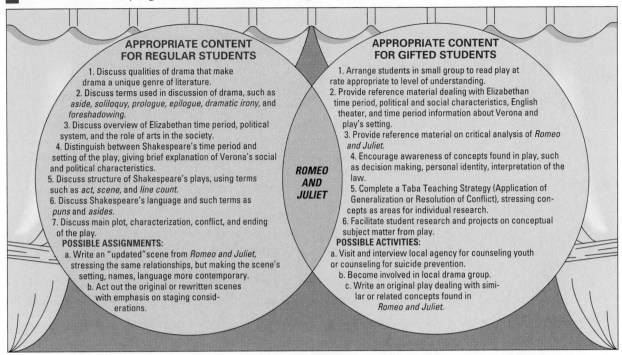

**APPROPRIATE CONTENT FOR REGULAR STUDENTS**

1. Discuss qualities of drama that make drama a unique genre of literature.
2. Discuss terms used in discussion of drama, such as *aside, soliloquy, prologue, epilogue, dramatic irony,* and *foreshadowing.*
3. Discuss overview of Elizabethan time period, political system, and the role of arts in the society.
4. Distinguish between Shakespeare's time period and setting of the play, giving brief explanation of Verona's social and political characteristics.
5. Discuss structure of Shakespeare's plays, using terms such as *act, scene,* and *line count.*
6. Discuss Shakespeare's language and such terms as *puns* and *asides.*
7. Discuss main plot, characterization, conflict, and ending of the play.

**POSSIBLE ASSIGNMENTS:**

a. Write an "updated" scene from *Romeo and Juliet,* stressing the same relationships, but making the scene's setting, names, language more contemporary.
b. Act out the original or rewritten scenes with emphasis on staging considerations.

**ROMEO AND JULIET**

**APPROPRIATE CONTENT FOR GIFTED STUDENTS**

1. Arrange students in small group to read play at rate appropriate to level of understanding.
2. Provide reference material dealing with Elizabethan time period, political and social characteristics, English theater, and time period information about Verona and play's setting.
3. Provide reference material on critical analysis of *Romeo and Juliet.*
4. Encourage awareness of concepts found in play, such as decision making, personal identity, interpretation of the law.
5. Complete a Taba Teaching Strategy (Application of Generalization or Resolution of Conflict), stressing concepts as areas for individual research.
6. Facilitate student research and projects on conceptual subject matter from play.

**POSSIBLE ACTIVITIES:**

a. Visit and interview local agency for counseling youth or counseling for suicide prevention.
b. Become involved in local drama group.
c. Write an original play dealing with similar or related concepts found in *Romeo and Juliet.*

From "Becoming Content with Content" (pp. 43–89), by R. Shanley, in *Critical Issues in Gifted Education: Vol. 1. Defensible Programs for the Gifted,* edited by C. J. Maker, 1993, Austin, TX: Pro-Ed. Used by permission.

Another technique that can be used effectively with gifted students in general education classes is curriculum compacting. This practice allows students to cover assigned material in ways that are faster or different. As Renzulli, Reis, and Smith (1981) point out, this process involves three phases: the assessment of what students know and the skills they possess, identification of ways of covering the curriculum, and suggestions for enrichment and accelerative options. Renzulli et al. have developed a form to assist teachers in compacting curriculum. This form is presented in Figure 11.4.

One of the recommended ways to address the needs of gifted students within the context of the general education classroom is to use enrichment techniques. Figure 11.5 provides an example of enrichment by showing how the play *Romeo and Juliet* can be taught, keeping in mind the needs of the regular and gifted students. This example developed by Shanley (1993) shows how the content of the play and the activities used by the teacher can be adapted for gifted students.

The following are more specific suggestions related to instructional strategies and product differentiation:

◢ Balance coverage of basic disciplines and the arts (Feldhusen, 1993a).
◢ Consult teacher/instructor guides of textbook series for ideas for enrichment activities.
◢ Use Internet resources (see nearby Technology Today feature).
◢ Acquire an array of different learning-related materials for use with gifted students—these can include textbooks, magazines, artifacts, software, CD-ROMs, Internet sources, and other media.
◢ Include time for independent study—use independent study contracts (Pugh, 1999).
◢ Teach research skills (data-gathering and investigative techniques) to gifted students to develop their independent study abilities (Reis & Schack, 1993).
◢ Use integrated themes for interrelating ideas within and across domains of inquiry (VanTassel-Baska, 1997). This type of curricular orientation can be used

for all students in the general education setting, with special activities designed for gifted students.

▲ Include higher-order thinking skills in lessons (Winocut & Mauer, 1997).

▲ Allocate time for students to have contact with adults who can provide special experiences and information to gifted students (e.g., mentors).

▲ Avoid assigning regular class work missed when gifted students spend time in special programs.

▲ Manage classroom discussions so that all students have an equal opportunity to contribute, feel comfortable doing so, and understand the nature of the discussion.

▲ Use standard textbooks and materials carefully, as gifted students will typically be able to move through them rapidly and may find them boring.

▲ Include questions that are open-ended and of varying conceptual levels in class discussions—see Table 11.5.

▲ Ensure that gifted students have access to technology—especially various types of applications (e.g., simulations, researching, presentation), various interactive/telecommunicative options (e-mail, mailing lists, discussion groups, bulletin boards), and the Internet.

▲ Provide a range of options for final product development—see Figure 11.6 for a list of examples.

---

**TABLE 11.5**    **Question Analysis Chart for a Class Discussion on George Washington Carver**

| Question Type | Explanation | Example |
|---|---|---|
| 1. **Data-recall questions** | Requires remembering | What was the name given to George Washington Carver's laboratory? |
| 2. **Naming questions** | Lacks insight | Name 10 peanut products developed by George Washington Carver. |
| 3. **Observation questions** | Requires minimal understanding | What obstacles did George Washington Carver overcome as a black scientist? |
| 4. **Control questions** | Modifies behavior | How will you remember George Washington Carver's scientific contribution to the farming community? |
| 5. **Pseudo-questions** | Conveys expected answer | Were George Washington Carver's accomplishments inspirational to black people? |
| 6. **Hypothesis-generating questions** | Involves speculation | Would George Washington Carver have been famous if he were white? |
| 7. **Reasoning questions** | Requires rationale | Why did George Washington Carver want to preserve the small family farm? |
| 8. **Personal response questions** | Invites personal opinions | What, in your opinion, was George Washington Carver's greatest accomplishment? |
| 9. **Discriminatory questions** | Requires weighing of pros and cons | Which of George Washington Carver's discoveries was the most significant, those evolving from the sweet potato or the peanut? |
| 10. **Problem-solving questions** | Demands finding ways to answer questions | If you were to design a memorial for George Washington Carver, what sources would you study for inspiration? |

From "Process Differentiation for Gifted Learners in the Regular Classroom: Teaching to Everyone's Needs" (pp. 139–155), by H. Rosselli, in *Critical Issues in Gifted Education: Vol. 3. Programs for the Gifted in Regular Classrooms,* edited by C. J. Maker, 1993, Austin, TX: Pro-Ed. Used by permission.

FIGURE 11.6 Outlet Vehicles for Differentiated Student Products

## LITERARY

Literary magazine (prose or poetry)
Newspaper for school or class
Class reporter for school newspaper
Collections of local folklore (*Foxfire*)
Book reviews of childrens' books for children,
  by children
Storytelling
Puppeteers
Student editorials on a
  series of topics
Kids' page in a city newspaper
Series of books or stories
Classbook or yearbook
Calendar book
Greeting cards (including original poetry)
Original play and production
Poetry readings
Study of foreign languages
Organizer of story hour in local or school library
Comic book or comic book series
Organization of debate society
Monologue, sound track, or script

## MATHEMATICAL

Contributor of math puzzles, quizzes, games for
  children's sections in newspapers, magazines
Editor/founder of computer magazine or newsletter
Math consultant for school
Editor of math magazine, newsletter
Organizer of metrics conversion
  movement
Original computer programming
Programming book
Graphics (original use of) films

## MEDIA

Children's television show
Children's radio show
Children's reviews (books, movie)
  on local news shows
Photo exhibit (talking)
Pictorial tour
Photo essay
Designing advertisement (literary magazine)
Slide/tape show on self-selected topic

## ARTISTIC

Displays, exhibits
Greeting cards
Sculpture
Illustrated books
Animation
Cartooning

## MUSICAL, DANCE

Books on life of famous composer
Original music, lyrics
Electronic music (original)
Musical instrument construction
Historical investigation of folk songs
Movement—history of dance, costumes

## HISTORICAL AND SOCIAL SCIENCES

Roving historian series in newspaper
"Remember when" column in newspaper
Establishment of historical society
Establishment of an oral history tape library
Published collection of local folklore and historical
  highlight stories
Published history (written, taped, pictorial)
Historical walking tour of a city
Film on historical topic
Historical monologue
Historical play based on theme
Historical board game
Presentation of historical research topic
  (World War II, etc.)
Slide/tape presentation of historical research
Starting your own business
Investigation of local elections
Electronic light board explaining historical battle, etc.
Talking time line of a decade (specific time period)
Tour of local historical homes
Investigate a vacant lot
Create a "hall" of local historical figures
Archaeological dig
Anthropological study  (comparison of/within groups)

## SCIENTIFIC

Science journal
Daily meteorologist posting weather conditions
Science column in newspaper
Science 'slot' in kids television show
Organizer at a natural museum
Science consultant for school
"Science Wizard" (experimenters)
Science fair
Establishment of a nature walk
Animal behavior study
Any prolonged experimentation involving
  manipulation of variables
Microscopic study involving slides
Classification guide to natural habitats
Acid rain study
Future study of natural conditions
Book on pond life
Aquarium study/study of different ecosystems
Science article submitted to national magazines
Plan a trip to national parks (travelogue)
Working model of a heart
Working model of a solar home
Working model of a windmill

From "Differentiating Products for the Gifted and Talented: The Encouragement of Independent Learning" (pp. 161–186), by S. M. Reis and G. D. Schack, in *Critical Issues in Gifted Education: Vol. 3. Programs for the Gifted in Regular Classrooms,* edited by C. J. Maker, 1993, Austin, TX: Pro-Ed. Used by permission.

Gifted and talented students need to learn about possible career choices that await them. They may need to do so at an earlier time than other students because they may participate in accelerated programs that necessitate early decisions about career direction. Students should learn about various career options, the dynamics of different disciplines, and the training required to work in a given discipline.

Teachers can select different ways to address the career needs of students. One way is to ensure that gifted students have access to mentor programs spending time with adults who are engaged in professional activities that interest them. Another method is to integrate the study of careers into the existing curriculum by discussing various careers when appropriate and by requiring students to engage in some activities associated with different careers. Students can become acquainted with a number of different careers while covering traditional subject areas.

Career counseling and guidance are also recommended. As Hardman, Drew, Egan, and Wolf (1993) point out, because of their multiple exceptional abilities and wide range of interests, some gifted students have a difficult time making career choices or narrowing down mentorship possibilities. These students should spend some time with counselors or teachers who can help them make these choices and other important postsecondary decisions.

**TEACHING TIP**
Arrange a career day for students and have community members discuss various careers with students.

## Social–Emotional Considerations

Gifted students have the same physiological and psychological needs as their peers. Yet, as Cross (1999) points out, "The lives of gifted students are both the same as and different from other students' lives" (p. 33). They may also be dealing with perplexing concepts that are well ahead of the concerns of their peers. For instance, a gifted fourth-grade girl asked her teacher questions related to abortion—a topic with which she was already dealing conceptually. In addition, gifted students may be dealing with some issues that are different from their nongifted peers, such as stress, hypersensitivity, control, perfectionism, underachievement/lack of motivation, coping mechanisms, introversion, peer relationships, need for empathy, self-understanding, and self-acceptance (Smutny et al., 1997).

Perhaps the most important recommendation is for teachers to develop relationships with students that make them feel comfortable discussing their concerns and questions. Teachers can become important resources to gifted students, not only for advice, but also for information. Regularly scheduled individual time with a teacher can have important paybacks for the student.

Teachers may also find it beneficial to schedule weekly room meetings (Feldhusen, 1993b) or class councils (Kataoka, 1987) to identify and address social, procedural, or learning-related problems that arise in the classroom. The group discussion includes articulation of a problem, brainstorming and discussion of possible solutions, selection of a plan of action, and implementation, evaluation, and reintroduction of the problem if the plan of action is not effective.

The nearby Personal Spotlight highlights one teacher's suggestions for adjusting the curriculum to meet the individual needs of all the students in the classroom. Following are some specific suggestions for dealing with the social–emotional needs of gifted students:

◢ Know when to refer students to professionals trained to deal with certain types of emotional problems.
◢ Create a classroom atmosphere that encourages students to take academic risks and allows them to make mistakes without fear of ridicule or harsh negative critique.

▲ Provide time on a weekly basis, if at all possible, for individual sessions with students so that they can share their interests, ongoing events in their lives, or concerns.

▲ Maintain regular, ongoing communication with the families of gifted students, notifying them of the goals, activities, products, and expectations you have for their children.

▲ Require, and teach if necessary, appropriate social skills (e.g., appropriate interactions) to students who display problems in these areas.

▲ Work with parents on the personal development of students.

▲ Use different types of activities (e.g., social issues) to develop self-understanding and decision-making and problem-solving skills. Rosselli (1993) recommends the use of bibliotherapy (literature that focuses on children with disabilities).

▲ Teach gifted students how to deal with their "uniqueness."

▲ Recognize that gifted students may experience higher levels of social pressure and anxiety—for example, peer pressure not to achieve at a high level or lofty expectations originating internally or from others (Del Prete, 1996).

## *personal* SPOTLIGHT

### Special Education Teacher

**JOY KATAOKA**
*Austin, Texas*

Joy Kataoka has taught students with special needs for ten years. While teaching students with many different types of disabilities, she believes that the most challenging teaching year she had was with students with learning disabilities, some of whom were also gifted. To meet the unique needs of these students, Joy had to develop an approach that met individual student needs while challenging their intellectual advancement. In order to do this, she selected a differentiated-integrated curriculum, which is a common approach for students classified as gifted. "I selected a broad-based theme that was implemented throughout the entire school year."

Using this model, learning activities and experiences were developed that related to the theme as well as to the basic skill needs of some of the students. For example, one year the theme "change" was chosen. Activities associated with this theme included the study of weather, seasons, the theory of continental drift, the theory of evo-

lution, the Civil Rights movement, and people who made significant contributions to the Civil Rights movement. Conflict resolution in literature and factors that influence change in people were topics that were also included. In addition, students were also engaged in taking a scientific phenomenon such as lightning, thunder, or rain, and researching how it was represented in mythology, examining the scientific explanation, and also looking at how different poets describe the scientific occurrence in poetry.

The implementation of the curriculum required some individualization. Basic concepts were presented to the entire class and all students participated in class discussions. However, products were individualized according to each student's ability and each student was evaluated based on what he or she could successfully accomplish. Gifted students were required to complete projects in much more detail and at a higher level of sophistication than students who were not gifted. However, all students had to meet certain basic or minimum requirements.

Joy noted that "although such a diverse group of learners in one classroom initially presented a challenge, this curricular approach turned out to be the most successful and productive teaching experience in my career." Inclusion often results in having to teach students with diverse needs and abilities. Teachers must analyze the situation and develop an approach that can meet the needs of all students.

*M*ethods that are effective with gifted students are also useful for nongifted students.

## PROMOTING A SENSE OF COMMUNITY AND SOCIAL ACCEPTANCE

**CROSS-REFERENCE**
Review Chapters 4–10 to determine if methods of enhancing an inclusive classroom for students with other special needs will be effective with students who are gifted and talented.

**TEACHING TIP**
Assigning students who are gifted and talented to be peer tutors can both enhance their acceptance as well as give them opportunities for leadership.

Addressing the needs of students with exceptional abilities in the context of the general education classroom is a monumental challenge. Current realities and probable trends in programming for gifted students suggest that general education will continue to be the typical setting in which they receive instruction. Thus it is important that we do all that we can to enrich the educational experiences of this population in these settings. To do so requires (1) creating classrooms where gifted students feel wanted and supported, in addition to having their instructional needs met by appropriate programming, and (2) providing the necessary supports to general education teachers to achieve desired outcomes for this group of students.

The climate of any classroom is determined by the interaction between the teacher and the students in the class; in particular, the teacher plays a leading role in establishing the parameters by which a classroom operates and the foundation for classroom dynamics. The degree to which a classroom becomes a community in which students care for one another and strive to improve the daily experience for everyone will depend on each class's unique dynamics. When a healthy and nurturing classroom context is established, students who are gifted can be important members of the classroom community. In such an environment, their abilities are recognized as assets to the class rather than something to be jealous of, envied, or despised.

To promote acceptance of gifted students, teachers should strive to dispel prevailing stereotypes. Discuss the uniqueness of these students in terms of the diversity of the classroom, implying that everyone is different. The notion that we all have strengths and weaknesses is also useful. It is particularly important to support gifted students who come from underserved groups, such as students with disabilities, those who are economically disadvantaged, and those from different racial or ethnic groups. Special attention should also be given to the needs of gifted females. Some suggestions for nurturing giftedness in females are listed in Figure 11.7.

- Believe in girls' logicomathematical abilities, and provide many opportunities for them to practice mathematical reasoning within other subject areas.
- Accelerate girls through the science and mathematics curriculum whenever possible.
- Have special clubs in mathematics for girls who are high-achieving.
- Design coeducational career development classes in which both girls and boys learn about career potentialities for women.
- Expose boys and girls to role models of women in various careers.
- Discuss nontraditional careers for women, including salaries for men and women and schooling requirements.
- Help girls set long-term goals.
- Discuss underachievement among females who are gifted, and ask how they can combat it in themselves and others.
- Have girls read biographies of famous women.
- Arrange opportunities for girls to "shadow" a female professional for a few days to see what her work entails.
- Discourage sexist remarks and attitudes in the classroom.
- Boycott sexist classroom materials, and write to the publishers for their immediate correction.
- Discuss sexist messages in the media.
- Advocate special classes and afterschool enrichment opportunities for students who are gifted.
- Form support groups for girls with similar interests.

*FIGURE* **11.7**

Suggestions for Teachers and Counselors in Fostering Giftedness in Girls

Adapted from "What Happens to the Gifted Girl?" (pp. 43–89), by L. K. Silverman, in *Critical Issues in Gifted Education: Vol. 1. Defensible Programs for the Gifted*, edited by C. J. Maker, 1986, Austin, TX: Pro-Ed. (Copyright owned by author.) Used by permission.

Instructionally, many of the strategies suggested for gifted students can also be used successfully with nongifted students (Del Prete, 1996). By doing this, teachers can accommodate the needs of gifted students without drawing undue attention to the special programming they are receiving.

To be a successful general education teacher of gifted students, a wide range of competencies are needed. Maker (1993) highlighted the following competencies as important in teaching gifted students: commitment, belief that people learn differently, high expectations, organization, enthusiasm, willingness to talk less—listen more, facilitative abilities, creativity, and the ability to juggle.

## Supports for the General Education Teacher

The responsibility to deliver a quality education to gifted students in general education settings rests on the shoulders of the instructional staff, especially general education teachers. Given the realities of the general education classroom, teachers face a mighty challenge in meeting the needs of gifted students. To maximize the chances of successfully addressing the needs of gifted students who are in these settings, Coleman (1998) recommends that schools:

◢ Group students in teachable clusters—groups of 6–10 students whose instructional needs are similar.

◢ Reduce class size.

◢ Provide additional instructional resources.

◢ Modify schedules so that there are greater amounts of time available to work with gifted students.

**CONSIDER THIS**

What kind of supports would be ideal for general classroom teachers to meet the needs of gifted and talented students in their classes?

◢   Provide additional support personnel.

◢   Require and/or provide training in working with gifted students.

School-based supports such as teacher assistance teams (Chalfant & Van Dusen Pysh, 1993) can also assist with addressing the needs of gifted students. When staffed properly, these teams become a rich resource of experience and ideas for dealing with a myriad of student needs. Parents also play an important, and often indirect role, in the school-based programs of their children. As Riley (1999) suggests, it is worthwhile to develop parents into good "dance partners" (i.e., to create and maintain positive relationships) in this process.

If the preceding issues are addressed correctly, we will do a great service to students with exceptional abilities. It is only when these conditions are met that teachers will be able to "stimulate the imagination, awaken the desire to learn, and imbue the students with a sense of curiosity and an urge to reach beyond themselves" (Mirman, 1991, p. 59).

# Summary

## Basic Concepts about Students Who Are Gifted

◢   Gifted students continue to be an underidentified, underserved, and often inappropriately served segment of the school population. A host of misconceptions exists in the minds of the general public about these individuals.

◢   Definitional perspectives of giftedness and intellectual abilities vary and contribute to some of the problems related to identification, eligibility, and service delivery. A key component of most definitions is the student's remarkable potential to achieve at levels above the level of peers, as well as high ability, high task commitment, and high creativity.

◢   The notion of multiple intelligences suggests that there are different areas where one can show high ability.

◢   The identification of gifted students is a complex and multifaceted process. Multiple sources of information are needed to determine whether a student is gifted.

◢   Gifted students with diverse cultural backgrounds are underrepresented in gifted programs often due to biased assessment practices. Special effort must be given to serving all students who show promise.

## Strategies for Curriculum and Instruction

◢   Most educators of gifted students prefer programs that are typically apart and different from those of nongifted students. The reality, however, is that most gifted students are in general education classes for most of their education.

◢   The major ways of addressing the needs of gifted students in general education are through the use of acceleration, enrichment, or special grouping.

## Classroom Accommodations for Students Who Are Gifted

◢   Many of the special methods used with gifted students are often effective with other students as well. The career development needs of gifted students were also highlighted.

## Promoting a Sense of Community and Social Acceptance

◢   Teachers can do a great deal to promote a sense of community and social acceptance of gifted students in their classrooms. It is difficult to address the needs of gifted students in the context of a large class with a great range of diverse needs.

◢   The probability of successfully helping gifted students reach their potential is contingent upon a number of key factors.

# *urther Readings*

Baum, S. M., Owen, S. V., & Dixon, J. (1991). *The gifted and learning disabled*. Mansfield Center, CT: Creative Learning Press.

Clark, B. (1997). *Growing up gifted* (5th ed.). Upper Saddle River, NJ: Merrill/Prentice-Hall.

Cline, S., & Schwartz, D. (1999). *Diverse populations of gifted children*. Boston: Allyn & Bacon.

Colangelo, N., & Davis, G. A. (Eds.), (1997). *Handbook of gifted education* (2nd ed.). Boston: Allyn and Bacon.

Csikszentmihalyi, M., Rathunde, K., & Whalen, S. (1997). *Talented teenagers. The roots of success and failure*. Cambridge, U.K.: Cambridge University Press.

Gardner, H. (1993). *Multiple intelligences: The theory in practice*. New York: Basic Books.

Heller, K., Monks, F., & Passow, A. H. (Eds.). (1993). *International handbook of research and development of giftedness and talent*. Oxford: Pergamon Press.

Jarwan, F. A., & Feldusen, J. F. (1993). *Residential schools of mathematics and science for academically talented youth: An analysis of admission programs*. Storrs, CT: The National Resource Center on the Gifted and Talented.

Maker, C. J. (Ed.). (1993). *Critical issues in gifted education: Vol. 3. Programs for the gifted in regular classrooms*. Austin, TX: Pro-Ed.

Passow, A. H., & Runitski, R. A. (1993). *State policies regarding education of the gifted as reflected in legislation and regulation*. Storrs, CT: National Research Center for the Gifted and Talented.

Smutny, J. F., Walker, S. Y., & Meckstroth, E. A. (1997). *Teaching young gifted children in the regular classroom: Identifying, nurturing, and challenging ages 4–9*. Minneapolis, MN: Free Spirit Publishing.

Subotnik, R. F., & Arnold, K. D. (Eds.). (1994). *Beyond Terman: Contemporary longitudinal studies of giftedness and talent*. Norwood, NJ: Ablex.

VanTassel-Baska, J. (1998). *Gifted and talented learners*. Denver: Love Publishing.

Winebrenner, S. (1992). *Teaching gifted kids in the regular classroom: Strategies and techniques every teacher can use to meet the academic needs of the gifted and talented*. Minneapolis, MN: Free Spirit Publishing.

# Chapter 12

# Teaching Students Who Are at Risk

*After reading this chapter, you should be able to:*

◢ Define students who are considered to be at risk

◢ Describe the different types of children who are considered at risk for developing learning and behavior problems

◢ Discuss general considerations for teaching at risk students

◢ Describe specific methods that are effective for teaching at risk students

Mary is a thin, 8-year-old girl with blonde hair and blue eyes. She is finishing first grade; she was kept back once in kindergarten. Ms. Skates, her teacher, does not know how to help her. She referred Mary for special education, but the assessment revealed that she was not eligible. Although her intelligence is in the low-average range, she does not have mental retardation or any other qualifying disability. Mary is shy and very insecure. She frequently cries if Ms. Skates leaves the classroom; she is very dependent on her teacher. Mary does not have any close friends, but a few of the other girls in the classroom will play with her from time to time. Mary is reading at the preprimer level and does not recognize all letters and sounds. She can count to 10, but does not understand any math facts.

Mary lives with her mother and three younger brothers in a three-room apartment. Her mother has been divorced twice and works as a waitress at a local coffee shop. Her mother's income barely covers rent and groceries plus day care for her brothers. Occasionally, when Mary's mother gets the chance to work extra hours at night, when tips are better, she leaves Mary in charge of her brothers. Although Mary's mother appears interested in Mary's schoolwork, she has been unable to get to a teacher's meeting with Ms. Skates, even though several have been scheduled. Ms. Skates is not sure if she should refer Mary for special education again, retain her in first grade, or promote her so that she does not fall farther behind her age peers.

One thing that can be done for Mary is prereferral interventions. These are actions that teachers can take that may improve the performance of students. If prereferral interventions are successful, further consideration for special education may not be necessary.

## QUESTIONS TO CONSIDER

1. Should Mary be provided special education services to prevent her from experiencing more failure? What services would you recommend?
2. What can teachers do with Mary and students like her to help prevent failure?

# BASIC CONCEPTS ABOUT STUDENTS WHO ARE AT RISK

The movement to include students with special needs in general education has made substantial progress over the past several years. One beneficial result has been the recognition that many students who are not officially eligible for special education services still need special supports. Although they do not manifest problems severe enough to result in a disability classification, these students are **at risk** for developing achievement and behavior problems that could limit their success in school and later as young adults.

Mary, the student in the vignette, is a good example of a child who is at risk for developing major academic and behavior problems. In the current system, children like Mary cannot be provided with special education and related services from federal programs. The result, too often, is that Mary and children like her drop out of school and experience major problems as adults.

*AT RISK* students are those who, because of various factors such as poverty or homelessness, are more likely to experience learning and behavior problems than other students.

## "At Risk" Defined

*CONSIDER THIS*
Should students at risk for failure be identified as disabled and served in special education programs? Why or why not?

The term *at risk* can be defined in many different ways. It is often used to describe children who have personal characteristics, or who live in families that display characteristics, that are associated with problems in school (Bowman, 1994). Students identified as being at risk generally have difficulty learning basic academic skills, exhibit unacceptable social behaviors, and cannot keep up with their peers (Pierce, 1994). They represent a very heterogeneous group (Davis, 1995).

Unlike students with disabilities, who have historically been segregated full-time or part-time from their age peers, students who are considered at risk have been fully included in educational programs. Unfortunately, rather than receiving appropriate interventions, they have been neglected in the classroom and consigned to failure. Although not eligible for special education and related services, students who are at risk need special interventions. Without them, many will be retained year after year, become behavior problems, develop drug and alcohol abuse problems, drop out of school, fail as adults, and possibly even commit suicide (Huff, 1999). School personnel need to recognize students who are at risk for failure and develop appropriate programs to facilitate their success in school and in society. Not doing so will result in losing many of these children, and "to lose today's at risk students implies [that] society is more than a little out of control itself" (Greer, 1991, p. 390).

## Prevalence and Causes of Being at Risk

Many factors place students at risk for developing school problems. These include poverty, homelessness, single-parent homes, abusive parents, substance abuse, and unrecognized disabilities. Although the presence of these factors often makes failure

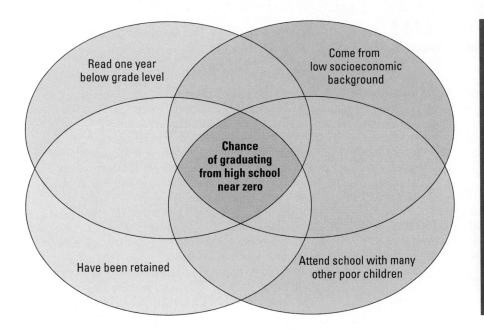

**FIGURE 12.1**

Research on Third-Grade Students

From *Policy Perspectives Increasing Achievement of At-Risk Students at Each Grade Level,* by J. M. McPartland and R. E. Slavin, 1990, Washington, D.C.: U.S. Department of Education. Cited in *Hope at Last for At-Risk Youth* (p. 10), by R. D. Barr and W. H. Parrett, 1995, Boston: Allyn and Bacon. Used by permission.

more likely for students, it is important not to label every child who is poor or who lives with a single parent as an at risk student.

Although overly simplistic conclusions should not be drawn concerning students at risk, research identifies certain factors as having a clear correlation with school problems. Using only a few factors, "schools can predict with better than 80% accuracy students in the third grade who will later drop out of school" (Barr & Parrett, 1995, p. 9). For example, in a government report, McPartland and Slavin (1990) reported that third-graders who (1) read one year below grade level, (2) have been retained in one grade, (3) come from low socioeconomic backgrounds, and (4) attend school with many other poor children have almost no chance of graduating from high school. Figure 12.1 depicts the relationship between these four factors that are such strong predictors of school failure.

Even when children are strongly indicated as being at risk, school personnel must be cautious about predicting their actual abilities and potential for achievement. Similarly, before teachers refer students who appear to be at risk and who represent culturally different backgrounds, they should consider the characteristics included in the nearby Diversity Forum. Addressing these issues will decrease the likelihood of referring students for special education programs when in-class interventions might be effective.

**STUDENTS WHO GROW UP IN POVERTY**     Poverty is a social condition associated with many different kinds of problems. Poverty has been related to crime, physical abuse, learning problems, behavior problems, and emotional problems. Professionals in the field of learning disabilities have even begun to realize that poverty can be a significant factor in the etiology of that particular disability (Young & Gerber, 1998). Davis (1993) notes that poverty is the number one factor that places children at risk for academic failure. Unfortunately, poverty is a fact of life for many children. In 1997, 19.9% of children 18 years old and younger lived in poverty in the United States.

***CROSS-REFERENCE***

For the impact of poverty on mental retardation and learning disabilities, review Chapters 4 and 7.

# DIVERSITY FORUM
## Issues to Consider before Referring Students from Culturally Diverse Backgrounds for Special Education Programs

▲ *Stage of language development:* At what stage of language proficiency, oral and written, is the student in L1 (student's first language) and L2 (student's second language)? What impact have past educational experiences had on language development? Will the environment facilitate further development?

▲ *Language skills:* What are the particular strengths and weaknesses of the student in oral and written L1 and L2 skills? What curriculum materials and instructional expertise are available to meet the student's needs? What skills are the parents able to work on at home?

▲ *Disability/at risk status:* What impact does the student's specific disability or at risk circumstances have on the acquisition of language skills in L1 and L2 and on other academic skills? Does the teacher have an adequate knowledge base to provide effective services? Does the school have access to community supports?

▲ *Age:* What impact does the student's age have on the ability to acquire L1 and L2 and to achieve in content areas? Is there a discrepancy between a child's age and emotional maturity? Is the curriculum developmentally appropriate?

▲ *Needs of the student:* What are the short-term and long-term needs of the student in academic, vocational, and community life? What are the needs of the student in relation to other students in the environment?

▲ *Amount of integration:* How much time will be spent in L1 and L2 environments? Will the student be able to interact with students who have various levels of ability?

▲ *Personal qualities:* How might the student's personality, learning style, and interests influence the acquisition of L1 and L2, achievement in content areas, and social–emotional growth? How might personal qualities of the student's peers and teacher influence learning?

From *Assessment and Instruction of Culturally and Linguistically Diverse Students with or at Risk of Learning Problems* (pp. 221–222), by V. Gonzalez, R. Brusca-Vega, and T. Yawkey, 1997, Boston: Allyn and Bacon. Used by permission.

---

**FIGURE 12.2**

Percentages of Children Less Than 18 Years Old Who Live in Families with Incomes below the Poverty Level: Selected Years, 1960–1997

From *Poverty in the United States*, 1998, Washington, D.C.: U.S. Census Bureau.

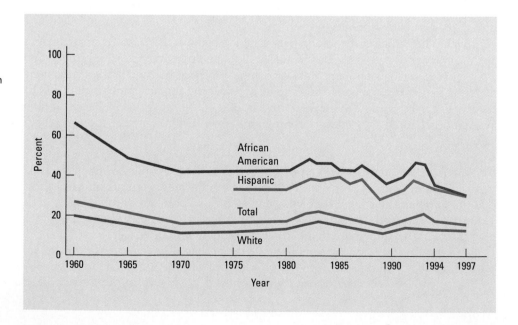

| Country | | Before Assistance | After Assistance | Percent of Children Lifted Out of Poverty by Government Assistance* |
|---|---|---|---|---|
| United States | 1991 | 26% | 22% | 17% |
| Australia | 1989 | 20% | 14% | 29% |
| Canada | 1991 | 23% | 14% | 40% |
| Ireland | 1987 | 30% | 12% | 60% |
| Israel | 1986 | 24% | 11% | 54% |
| United Kingdom | 1991 | 30% | 10% | 67% |
| Italy | 1991 | 12% | 10% | 17% |
| Germany | 1989 | 9% | 7% | 24% |
| France | 1984 | 25% | 7% | 74% |
| Netherlands | 1991 | 14% | 6% | 55% |
| Norway | 1991 | 13% | 5% | 64% |
| Luxembourg | 1985 | 12% | 4% | 65% |
| Belgium | 1992 | 16% | 4% | 77% |
| Denmark | 1992 | 10% | 3% | 79% |
| Switzerland | 1982 | 5% | 3% | 35% |
| Sweden | 1992 | 19% | 3% | 86% |
| Finland | 1991 | 12% | 3% | 78% |

\* Based on unrounded data

**FIGURE 12.3**

Child Poverty in 17 Developed Countries before and after Government Assistance

From "Doing Poorly: The Real Income of American Children in a Comparative Perspective," by Lee Rainwater and Timothy M. Smeeding, 1995, Working Paper No. 127, Luxembourg Income Study, Syracuse, NY: Maxwell School of Citizenship and Public Affairs, Syracuse University. Reprinted in *Kids Count Data Book 1996* (p. 17), Annie E. Casey Foundation, 1996, Baltimore, MD: Author. Used by permission.

While this number was down from 22% in 1992, it still represented more than 14 million children. The rate of poverty among children varies significantly from state to state and race to race. For example, while only 16.1% of white children lived in poverty in 1997, 36.8% of Hispanic children and 37.2% of African American children lived in such circumstances. And, during the same year, 59.1% of children in a household with a single female parent lived in poverty (*Poverty in the United States: 1997*). Figure 12.2 shows the greater incidence of poverty among Hispanic and African American children as compared to white children.

Although the overall numbers have not gotten worse, the disheartening fact is that they have not improved significantly during the past ten years. And the rate of poverty among children is higher in the United States than in any other developed country. Figure 12.3 compares the poverty rates of children in 17 industrialized countries and reflects the impact of government assistance on children and poverty. The figure reveals that government assistance provided by the United States has comparatively little impact on poverty (*Kids count data book,* 1998).

Poverty is associated with different kinds of disabilities (Smith & Luckasson, 1992), including mental retardation (Beirne-Smith, Patton, & Ittenbach, 1994), learning disabilities (Smith, Dowdy, Polloway, & Blalock, 1997; Young & Gerber, 1998), and various health problems. Poverty is also associated with poor prenatal care, poor parenting, hunger, limited health care, single-parent households, poor housing conditions, and even homelessness (Yamaguchi, Strawser, & Higgins, 1997).

**CROSS-REFERENCE**
Review Chapter 3 for due-process requirements of schools and consider the impact single-parent homes have on these requirements.

For children whose parents are divorced, schools must consider the involvement of the noncustodial parent. Unfortunately, many schools do not even include spaces for information on forms for students' noncustodial parents (Austin, 1992). In order to ensure that noncustodial parents are afforded their rights regarding their children, and to actively solicit the involvement of the noncustodial parent, school personnel should

1. establish policies that encourage the involvement of noncustodial parents.
2. maintain records of information about the noncustodial parent.
3. distribute information about school activities to noncustodial parents.
4. insist that noncustodial parents be involved in teacher conferences.
5. structure parent conferences to facilitate the development of a shared relationship between the custodial and noncustodial parent.
6. conduct surveys to determine the level of involvement desired by noncustodial parents. (Austin, 1992)

**TEACHING TIP**
Involve the school counselor and other support personnel when providing information on death and dying; invite these persons into the class when a student is confronted with this issue.

**STUDENTS WHO EXPERIENCE SIGNIFICANT LOSSES**   Although the continued absence of one or both parents through separation or divorce is considered a loss, the loss created by the death of a parent can result in significantly more problems for children. Unlike children living in the earlier centuries, when extended families often lived together and children actually observed death close at hand, often in the home environment with grandparents, children of today are generally insulated from death. Therefore, when death does occur, especially that of a significant person in a child's life, the result can be devastating, often resulting in major problems in school.

*Death of a Parent.*   When a child's parent dies, external events impinge on the child's personality in three main ways (Felner, Ginter, Boike, & Cowan, 1981; Moriarty, 1967; Tennant, Bebbington, & Hurry, 1980):

1. The child must deal with the reality of the death itself.
2. The child must adapt to the resulting changes in the family.
3. The child must contend with the perpetual absence of the lost parent.

Children respond in many different ways to a parent's death. Some responses are guilt, regression, denial, bodily distress, hostile reactions to the deceased, eating disorders, enuresis (incontinence), sleep disturbances, withdrawal, anxiety, panic, learning difficulties, and aggression (Anthony, 1972; Elizer & Kauffman, 1983; Van Eerdewegh, Bieri, Parrilla, & Clayton, 1982). It is also not unusual for sibling rivalry to become very intense and disruptive. Often, extreme family turmoil results from the death of a parent, especially when the parent who dies was the controlling person in the family (Van Eerdewegh et al., 1982).

*Death of a Sibling.*   A sibling plays an important and significant part in family dynamics, so the death of a sibling can initiate a psychological crisis for a child. Sometimes the grief of the parents renders them unable to maintain a healthy parental relationship with the remaining child or children, significantly changing a child's life situation.

When experiencing the death of a sibling, children frequently fear that they will die. When an older sibling dies, the younger child may revert to childish behaviors in hopes of not getting older, thereby averting dying. Older children often react with extreme fear and anxiety if they are ignored by parents during the grieving period. Often these children become preoccupied with the horrifying question about their own future: "Will it happen to me tomorrow, or next week, or next year?" (McKeever, 1983). Children can also develop severe depression when a sibling dies (McKeever, 1983).

STUDENTS WHO ARE ABUSED   Growing up in an abusive family places children at significant risk. Child abuse occurs in families from every socioeconomic level, race, religion, and ethnic background. Family members, acquaintances, or strangers may be the source of the abuse. Although there is no single cause, there are many factors that add to the likelihood of abuse. These include poverty, large family size, low maternal involvement with children, low maternal self-esteem, low father involvement, and a stepfather in the household (Brown, Cohen, Johnson, & Salzinger, 1998).

There are two major types of abuse (1) emotional abuse and (2) physical abuse, which includes sexual abuse. Emotional abuse, which accompanies all other forms of child abuse, involves unreasonable demands placed on children by parents, siblings, peers, or teachers, and the failure of parents to provide the emotional support necessary for children to grow and develop (Thompson & Kaplan, 1999). Research has revealed that verbal abuse, by itself, can result in lowered self-esteem and school achievement (Solomon & Serres, 1999). Although difficult to identify, several characteristics may be exhibited by children who are being emotionally abused. These include the following:

▲ Absence of a positive self-image
▲ Behavioral extremes
▲ Depression
▲ Psychosomatic complaints
▲ Attempted suicide
▲ Impulsive, defiant, and antisocial behavior
▲ Age-inappropriate behaviors
▲ Inappropriate habits and tics
▲ Enuresis
▲ Inhibited intellectual or emotional development
▲ Difficulty in establishing and maintaining peer relationships
▲ Extreme fear, vigilance
▲ Sleep and eating disorders
▲ Self-destructive tendencies
▲ Rigidly compulsive behaviors (Gargiulo, 1990, p. 22)

**CONSIDER THIS**
Think how being abused would affect you at this point in your life; then transfer those feelings into a young child's perspective. How they would affect the child's school activities.

**Physical abuse** is more easily identified than emotional abuse. Physical abuse includes beating, strangulation, burns to the body, and other forms of physical brutalization. It is defined as "any physical injury that has been caused by other than accidental means, including any injury which appears to be at variance with the explanation of the injury" (*At Risk Youth in Crisis,* 1991, p. 9). The rate of child abuse in this country is staggering. Prevent Child Abuse America (1998) reported that over 3 million children were referred for child protective service agencies in the United States in 1997. More than one million children were confirmed as victims of abuse. The number of child abuse cases has increased 41% between 1988 and 1997. Statistics indicate that the prevalence of child abuse is 1 out of every 1,000 U.S. children (Prevent Child Abuse America, 1998).

**PHYSICAL ABUSE**
includes any form of physical brutalization, including sexual abuse.

Children who are physically abused are two to three times more likely than nonabused children to experience failing grades and to become discipline problems. They have difficulty with peer relationships, show physically aggressive behaviors, and are frequent substance abusers (Emery, 1989). Studies also show that children who suffer from physical abuse are likely to exhibit social skill deficits, including shyness, inhibited social interactions, and limited problem-solving skills. Deficits in cognitive functioning are also found in greater numbers in students who are abused than in their nonabused peers (Weston, Ludolph, Misle, Ruffins, & Block, 1990).

Sexual abuse is another form of physical abuse that puts children at risk for school failure. The rate for sexual abuse of female children in the United States ranges from 15% to 32%, depending on the method of calculation used. Sexual abuse is more likely to occur in girls younger than the age of 15 (Vogeltanz et al., 1999). Children may be sexually abused by their own families as well as by strangers. Sexual abuse can include actual physical activities, such as touching a child's genital areas, attempted and completed sexual intercourse, and the use of children in pornography. Exposing children to sexual acts by adults with the intention of shocking or arousing them is another form of sexual abuse (Jones, 1982; Williamson, Borduin, & Howe, 1991). Children who are sexually abused are not only at risk for developing problems during their school years, but will typically manifest problems throughout their adulthood (Silverman, Reinherz, & Giaconia, 1996).

School personnel should be aware of typical physical and behavioral symptoms of sexual abuse:

*CROSS-REFERENCE*
Review Chapter 6 on emotional and behavioral disorders and consider the impact of child abuse on emotional and behavioral functioning.

- Physical injuries to the genital area
- Sexually transmitted diseases
- Difficulty in urinating
- Discharges from the penis or vagina
- Pregnancy
- Aggressive behavior toward adults, especially a child's own parents
- Sexual self-consciousness
- Sexual promiscuity and acting out
- Inability to establish appropriate relationships with peers
- Running away, stealing, and abusing substances
- Using the school as a sanctuary, coming early, and not wanting to go home

The first thing that school personnel should be prepared to do when dealing with children who might be abused is to report any incident to the appropriate agencies (Pearson, 1996). School personnel have a moral and legal obligation to report suspected child abuse. The Suspected Child Abuse Network **(SCAN)** provides a reporting network for referral purposes. School personnel need to understand their responsibility in reporting suspected abuse and know the specific procedures to follow when making such a report. In addition to reporting suspected cases of abuse, school personnel can also do the following.

*SCAN* is the agency that receives and investigates allegations of child abuse and neglect.

1. Work with local government officials to establish awareness of child abuse and neglect as a priority in the community.
2. Organize a telephone "hotline" service where parents or other caregivers can call for support when they believe a crisis is impending in their families.
3. Offer parent education programs that focus on parenting skills, behavior management techniques, child care suggestions, and communication strategies.
4. Establish a local chapter of **Parents Anonymous,** a volunteer group for individuals who have a history of abusing their children.
5. Develop workshops on child abuse for concerned individuals and disseminate literature on the topic.
6. Arrange visits by public health nurses to help families at risk for abuse after the birth of their first child.
7. Provide short-term respite day care through a Mother's Day Out program.
8. Encourage individuals to serve as foster parents in the community.

*PARENTS ANONYMOUS* is a support group for parents who have a tendency to engage in child abuse.

9. Institute a parent aide program in which parent volunteers assist single-parent homes by providing support.
10. Make structured group therapy available to abuse victims (Kruczek & Vitanza, 1999).

**STUDENTS WHO ABUSE SUBSTANCES**    **Substance abuse** among children and adolescents results in major problems and places students significantly at risk for school failure (Vaughn & Long, 1999). Students who are abusing substances have a much more difficult time succeeding in school than their peers.

Although there were indicators that substance abuse among children declined during the late 1980s and early 1990s, data indicate that substance abuse is on the rise again (*Teen drug use is on the rise again*, 1996; *The condition of education*, 1998). According to the National Center for Education Statistics, in 1997 74.8% of high school seniors reported using alcohol during the previous school year. Table 12.1 shows the percentage of seniors using drugs, by type of drug, between 1975 and 1997. While there was a definite decline in the use of some substances during this period, there appears to be an increase in other areas. The disturbing fact is that after years of drug abuse education, the use of alcohol and drugs has not been significantly influenced (*The condition of education*, 1998).

A disturbing fact about substance abuse is that while the level of use by high school seniors has remained virtually constant, the level of use by younger students has increased significantly. For example, in 1991 only 3.2% of eighth graders indicated that they had used marijuana or hashish during the previous 30 days. This number had increased to 10.2% in 1997 (*The condition of education*, 1998). Nagel et al. (1996) report that boys have a tendency to use illegal drugs slightly more than girls, but that girls actually use more over-the-counter drugs inappropriately than boys do.

While no factors are always associated with drug use in children, some appear to increase the likelihood of such use. Parental factors, such as (1) drug use by parents, (2) parents' attitudes about drug use, (3) family management styles, and (4) parent–child communication patterns have an impact on children's drug use (Young, Kersten, & Werch, 1996). Additional cross-pressures such as the perception of friends' approval or disapproval of drug use, peer pressure to use drugs, and the assessment of individual risk also play a role (Robin & Johnson, 1996).

Although a great deal of attention has been paid to the impact of marijuana, cocaine, and alcohol abuse on children and youth, only recently has attention been focused on **inhalants.** Inhalant use increased for every grade level from 1991 to 1995 (*The condition of education*, 1998). One of the problems with inhalants is the wide number that can be used by students, many of which are readily available. Examples include cleaning solvents, gasoline, room deodorizers, glue, perfume, wax, and spray paint.

School personnel must be alert to the symptoms of substance abuse, whether the substance is alcohol, marijuana, inhalants, or something else. The following characteristics might indicate possible substance abuse:

- Inability to concentrate
- Chronic absenteeism
- Poor grades or neglect of homework
- Poor scores on standardized tests not related to IQ or learning disabilities
- Uncooperative and quarrelsome behavior
- Sudden behavior changes
- Shy and withdrawn behavior
- Compulsive behaviors

*SUBSTANCE ABUSE* is the act of using illegal or inappropriate substances, such as alcohol or marijuana.

*CONSIDER THIS* Why do violence, drug abuse, and other problems seem to be affecting younger children than they did ten years ago?

*INHALANTS* are common substances and products that are abused; they include glue, cleaning solvents, and deodorants.

▲ Chronic health problems
▲ Low self-esteem
▲ Anger, anxiety, and depression
▲ Poor coping skills
▲ Unreasonable fears
▲ Difficulty adjusting to changes

Once a student is identified as having a substance abuse problem, a supportive classroom environment must be provided (Lisnov, Harding, Safer, & Kavenagh,

| TABLE 12.1 | Percentage of High School Seniors Who Reported Using Alcohol or Drugs Any Time during the Previous Year, by Type of Drug |

| Type of Drug | 1975 | 1976 | 1977 | 1978 | 1979 | 1980 | 1981 | 1982 | 1983 | 1984 | 1985 | 1986 |
|---|---|---|---|---|---|---|---|---|---|---|---|---|
| Alcohol | 84.8 | 85.7 | 87.0 | 87.7 | 88.1 | 87.9 | 87.0 | 86.8 | 87.3 | 86.0 | 85.6 | 84.5 |
| Marijuana | 40.0 | 44.5 | 47.6 | 50.2 | 50.8 | 48.8 | 46.1 | 44.3 | 42.3 | 40.0 | 40.6 | 38.8 |
| Any illicit drug other than marijuana | 26.2 | 25.4 | 26.0 | 27.1 | 28.2 | 30.4 | 34.0 | 30.1 | 28.4 | 28.0 | 27.4 | 25.9 |
| Stimulants | 16.2 | 15.8 | 16.3 | 17.1 | 18.3 | 20.8 | 26.0 | 20.3 | 17.9 | 17.7 | 15.8 | 13.4 |
| LSD | 7.2 | 6.4 | 5.5 | 6.3 | 6.6 | 6.5 | 6.5 | 6.1 | 5.4 | 4.7 | 4.4 | 4.5 |
| Cocaine | 5.6 | 6.0 | 7.2 | 9.0 | 12.0 | 12.3 | 12.4 | 11.5 | 11.4 | 11.6 | 13.1 | 12.7 |
| Sedatives | 11.7 | 10.7 | 10.8 | 9.9 | 9.9 | 10.3 | 10.5 | 9.1 | 7.9 | 6.6 | 5.8 | 5.2 |
| Tranquilizers | 10.6 | 10.3 | 10.8 | 9.9 | 9.6 | 8.7 | 8.0 | 7.0 | 6.9 | 6.1 | 6.1 | 5.8 |
| Inhalants | — | 3.0 | 3.7 | 4.1 | 5.4 | 4.6 | 4.1 | 4.5 | 4.3 | 5.1 | 5.7 | 6.1 |

| Type of Drug | 1987 | 1988 | 1989 | 1990 | 1991 | 1992 | 1993 | 1994 | 1995 | 1996 | 1997 |
|---|---|---|---|---|---|---|---|---|---|---|---|
| Alcohol | 85.7 | 85.3 | 82.7 | 80.6 | 77.7 | 76.8 | *72.7 | *73.0 | *73.7 | *72.5 | *74.8 |
| Marijuana | 36.3 | 33.1 | 29.6 | 27.0 | 23.9 | 21.9 | 26.0 | 30.7 | 34.7 | 35.8 | 38.5 |
| Any illicit drug other than marijuana | 24.1 | 21.1 | 20.0 | 17.9 | 16.2 | 14.9 | 17.1 | 18.0 | 19.4 | 19.8 | 20.7 |
| Stimulants | 12.2 | 10.9 | 10.8 | 9.1 | 8.2 | 7.1 | 8.4 | 9.4 | 9.3 | 9.5 | 10.2 |
| LSD | 5.2 | 4.8 | 4.9 | 5.4 | 5.2 | 5.6 | 6.8 | 6.9 | 8.4 | 8.8 | 8.4 |
| Cocaine | 10.3 | 7.9 | 6.5 | 5.3 | 3.5 | 3.1 | 3.3 | 3.6 | 4.0 | 4.9 | 5.5 |
| Sedatives | 4.1 | 3.7 | 3.7 | 3.6 | 3.6 | 2.9 | 3.4 | 4.2 | 4.9 | 5.3 | 5.4 |
| Tranquilizers | 5.5 | 4.8 | 3.8 | 3.5 | 3.6 | 2.8 | 3.5 | 3.7 | 4.4 | 4.6 | 4.7 |
| Inhalants | 6.9 | 6.5 | 5.9 | 6.9 | 6.6 | 6.2 | 7.0 | 7.7 | 8.0 | 7.6 | 6.7 |

—Not available

*In 1993, the questions regarding alcohol consumption changed; therefore, data for alcohol use from 1993 through 1997 may not be comparable to earlier years. For example, in 1993, the original wording produced an estimate of 76 percent for alcohol use. The new wording produced an estimate of 73 percent.

*Note:* Only drug use not under a doctor's orders is included.

From *The Condition of Education* (p. 277), by Office of Educational Research and Improvement, 1998, Washington, D.C.: U.S. Department of Education.

1998). This includes a structured program to build self-esteem and create opportunities for students to be successful. Research has shown that substance-abusing adolescents do not respond positively to lecturing. Rather, successes appear to be related to the development of self-esteem and interventions that are supportive. School personnel involved with students who are substance abusers should consider establishing connections with Alcoholics Anonymous and Narcotics Anonymous to help provide support (Vaughn & Long, 1999).

**STUDENTS WHO BECOME PREGNANT**    Teenage pregnancy in the United States continues at an extremely high rate. In fact, teenage pregnancy rates in the United States are the highest of any Western nation. While there are many unfortunate outcomes from teenage pregnancy, including an increased risk that the resulting child will have problems, one of the most prevalent is that the teenage mother will drop out of school (Trad, 1999). In an era of extensive sex education and fear of AIDS, the continued high levels of teenage pregnancy are surprising. Despite all of the information available for adolescents about sex and AIDS, it appears that many adolescents continue to engage in unprotected sexual activity (Weinbender & Rossignol, 1996).

School personnel should get involved in teenage pregnancy issues before pregnancy occurs. Sex education, information about AIDS, and the consequences of unprotected sex should be a curricular focus. Unfortunately, sex education and practices such as distributing free condoms are very controversial, and many schools refuse to get too involved in such emotion-laden issues.

> **TEACHING TIP**
> Work with school health personnel or state department of education personnel to obtain useful and appropriate teaching materials and suggestions for AIDS education.

In addition to having a pregnancy prevention program, school personnel can do the following to intervene in teenage pregnancy situations:

1. Provide counseling for girls who become pregnant.
2. Develop programs that encourage girls who are pregnant to remain in school.
3. Provide parenting classes for all students.
4. Do not discriminate against students who become pregnant, have children, or are married.
5. Consider establishing a school-based child care program for students who have babies and wish to remain in school.
6. Work with families of girls who are pregnant to ensure that family support is present.
7. Provide counseling support for boys who are fathers.

**STUDENTS WHO ARE DELINQUENTS**    Students who get into trouble with legal authorities are frequently labeled juvenile delinquents. Morrison (1997) defines *delinquency* as "behavior that violates the rules and regulations of the society" (p. 189). **Juvenile delinquency** often results in school failure; students who are involved in illegal activities often do not focus on school activities. Juvenile delinquency must be considered in light of other factors related to at risk students, though the relationship of these factors may be difficult to discern. Juvenile delinquency is highly correlated with substance abuse and may be found in higher rates among poor children than among children who are raised in adequate income environments. It is also more prevalent in single-parent homes (Morgan, 1994).

> *JUVENILE DELINQUENCY* is illegal and antisocial activity by youth.

Juvenile delinquency is frequently related to gang activity. Gangs currently represent a major problem for adolescents, especially in large urban areas. In 1997, there were approximately 30,500 gangs in the United States with 816,000 gang members (National Youth Gang Center, 1999). Morgan (1994) cites numerous studies showing that adolescents raised in single-parent homes or homes that sustain a great deal of conflict often join gangs and exhibit other delinquent behaviors. Again, although no single factor leads children to delinquent behaviors, certain factors can indicate high risk. Delinquent behaviors often disrupt school success. School personnel need to work with legal and social service agencies to reduce delinquency and academic failure. In addition, the educational needs of children with disabilities who are in the juvenile justice system must be met the same as for other children with disabilities (Robinson & Rapport, 1999).

## STRATEGIES FOR CURRICULUM AND INSTRUCTION FOR STUDENTS WHO ARE AT RISK

There are four primary approaches to dealing with students who are at risk for failure in schools: compensatory education, prevention programs, intervention programs, and transition programs. Figure 12.7 depicts these approaches. Compensatory education programs "are designed to compensate or make up for existing or past risk factors and their effects in students' lives" (Morrison, 1997, p. 192). Head Start and Chapter I reading programs are examples of efforts to reduce the impact of poverty on children (Morrison, 1997). Reading Recovery, a program that is gaining popularity, has been shown to effectively improve the reading skills of at risk students (Dorn & Allen, 1995; Ross, Smith, Casey, & Slavin, 1995).

Prevention programs focus on keeping certain negative factors from having an impact on students. Drug prevention programs, antismoking educational efforts, and sex education programs are examples of efforts designed to keep students from developing problem behaviors. Intervention programs focus on eliminating risk factors. They include teaching teenagers how to be good parents and early intervention programs that target at risk preschool children (Sexton et al., 1996). Finally, transition programs are designed to help students see the relationship between what they learn in school

**CONSIDER THIS**

How can programs like Head Start have an impact on students who are at risk? Should these programs be continuously emphasized? Why or why not?

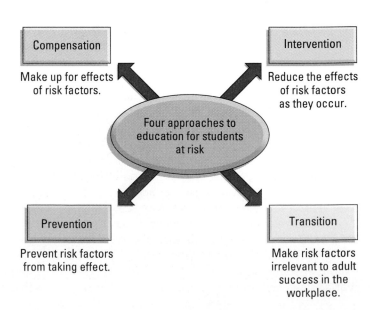

**FIGURE 12.7**

Four Approaches to Education for Students at Risk

From *Teaching in America* (p. 193), by G. S. Morrison, 1997, Boston: Allyn and Bacon. Used by permission.

Compensation — Make up for effects of risk factors.

Intervention — Reduce the effects of risk factors as they occur.

Four approaches to education for students at risk

Prevention — Prevent risk factors from taking effect.

Transition — Make risk factors irrelevant to adult success in the workplace.

and how it will be used in the real world. School-to-work programs, which help students move from school to work, are effective transition programs (Morrison, 1997).

After-school programs provide schools with an opportunity to implement many strategies that are effective with at risk students. Many students who are at risk for problems face extreme challenges in the afternoon hours following school. "School-age children and teens who are unsupervised during the hours after school are far more likely to use alcohol, drugs, and tobacco, engage in criminal and other high-risk behaviors, receive poor grades, and drop out of school than those children who have the opportunity to benefit from constructive activities supervised by responsible adults" (*Safe and smart*, 1998, p. 5). After-school programs combine prevention, intervention, and compensatory programs.

Schools must use a variety of programs to prevent problems from developing and to address problems that do develop. The use of technology often proves beneficial. The nearby Technology Today feature provides information about how computers can be used with multicultural and bilingual groups, two at risk populations.

Schools must ensure that they do not discriminate against at risk students because of their race or socioeconomic status. The use of nondiscriminatory

# *T*ECHNOLOGY *T*ODAY

## Using Technology with Multicultural and Bilingual Students Who May Be at Risk

### MICROCOMPUTERS

As computerized language translators begin to develop, there may be a significant impact for special education students with a primary language other than English. Imagine if the student could use a computer to write an assignment in his or her primary language, check the spelling and punctuation, then press a button to translate the work into English and transmit it to the teacher. Or perhaps the student wrote the assignment in a dialect, and then the computer was able to translate it into the standard form of that language. Such technology is possible.

One successful use of the microcomputer has been for the students to write their journals and for the teacher to respond via computer (Goldman and Rueda, 1988). Multicultural bilingual special education students were successful in developing their writing skills and their interaction skills with their teacher.

George Earl (1984) created a Spanish-to-English as well as an English-to-Spanish computerized version of the word game "hangman." Hangman is one of the many instructional games used by special education teachers to help improve language skills. Although the program had some difficulty (Zemke, 1985) with dialects (it translates standard Spanish), it demonstrates how technology can be applied to

*Technology applications can reduce the chance of failure for some at risk students.*

the learning needs of children who are multicultural and bilingual.

Computers have contributed to improved education for migrant children. A nationwide computerized transcript service, the Migrant Student Record Transfer System (MSRTS) in Little Rock, Arkansas, serves as a centralized location for transcripts and health records. A special education component contains information on the existence of a disability, assessment results, related services provided, and IEPs.

From *Introduction to Special Education* (3rd Edition) (p. 71), by D. D. Smith and R. Luckasson, 1998, Boston: Allyn and Bacon. Used by permission.

## At Risk Children's Right to Nondiscriminatory Assessment

Schools are required, under IDEA, to use nondiscriminatory practices when evaluating students since many at risk children experience poverty and come from single-parent homes and homes where English is not the primary language. The case law supporting this requirement came out of the *Larry P. v. Riles* case that was first filed in 1972. The court in this case

> held that schools no longer may use standardized IQ tests for the purpose of identifying and placing African American children into segregated special education classes for students classified as educable mentally retarded. . . .
>
> The district court found that the Stanford-Binet, Wechsler, and Leiter IQ tests discriminate against African Americans on several grounds.

1. They measure achievement, not ability.
2. They rest on the "plausible but unproven assumption that intelligence is distributed in the population in accordance with a normal statistical curve" and thus are "artificial tools to rank individuals according to certain skills, not to diagnose a medical condition (the presence of retardation)."
3. They "necessarily" lead to placement of more African Americans than Whites into classes for students with mild or moderate mental retardation."

On appeal, the Ninth Circuit Court of Appeals affirmed the lower court decision and rejected the state's argument that tests are good predictors of academic performance, even if they have a discriminatory impact; found that the state did not use any means of diagnosing disability other than IQ tests; and agreed that inappropriate placement of children can result in a profound negative impact on their education (Turnbull & Turnbull, 2000, pp. 153–154).

assessment is mandated by IDEA. The nearby Rights and Responsibilities feature focuses on this issue.

## Characteristics of Effective Programs

Several factors are associated with schools that provide effective programs for students who are at risk. The U.S. Department of Education has noted that some research-based school reform models have been very successful in improving the achievement scores of students who are at risk for school failure. While differing in many respects, successful programs appear to share several characteristics (*Tools for schools*, 1998, p. 2):

**CONSIDER THIS**
Why have research-based reform models been successful in improving the achievement scores of students who are at risk for failure?

◢ They provide a clear blueprint with specific instructions for the changes that are to be made by the school in order to improve its educational performance;

◢ They offer a system of guidance and technical assistance for schools, often by the developer, and, in order to have the widest application, offer instructions on how the model may be scaled up at a large number of sites;

◢ The changes that the models propose for implementation are comprehensive, involving school organization, social relations (parental involvement, relationships between school staff and student), curriculum and instruction, and educational standards and goals;

◢ The models are flexible, which allows them to be implemented on variable time scales and with adaptations to meet local circumstances; and

◢ The model designs are based on up-to-date research on curriculum and the learning environment.

Figure 12.8 summarizes characteristics associated with schools that are effective and those that are ineffective in working with students who are at risk.

The movement to include students with disabilities in general education classrooms provides an opportunity to meet the needs of at risk students as well. In an inclusive classroom, students should be educated based on their needs rather than on their clinical labels. In fact, inclusion, rather than separate programming, is supported by the lack of evidence that different teaching techniques are required by students in different disability groups. Techniques developed for a specific population often benefit everyone. When schools remove labels from students and provide programs

**FIGURE 12.8**    Effective and Ineffective Low Socioeconomic Status Schools

**EFFECTIVE LOW SOCIOECONOMIC STATUS SCHOOLS**

1. Although principals and teachers had modest long-term expectations for their students' achievement, particularly in regard to higher education, they held firm present academic expectations for their students.

2. Teachers reported spending more time on reading and math and assigning more homework rather than the other two low socioeconomic status groups [in the study].

3. Students perceived teachers as pushing them academically. They also reported receiving more teacher help than did students in less successful low socioeconomic status schools.

4. Students perceived their teachers as having high present expectations for them.

5. Teachers reported that principals visited their classrooms frequently.

6. The teachers in this group [effective low socioeconomic status schools] were the youngest and least experienced of the low socioeconomic status group.

7. The teachers in this group were the most likely of all the teachers to have teacher's aides.

8. Principals in these schools were the most likely to say that they had major input in hiring teachers. Twenty-three percent of the principals in the effective low socioeconomic status schools said that they hired their teachers. No other group of schools had more than 9% of its principals report this power.

**INEFFECTIVE LOW SOCIOECONOMIC STATUS SCHOOLS**

1. An overall negative academic climate in these schools appears to have contributed to the low student achievement. Of all the groups [studied], teachers had the lowest expectations for students and rated them the lowest academically; the teachers accepted little responsibility for and perceived having little influence on student outcomes; they also appeared less satisfied with teaching and perceived themselves as unsuccessful in helping students attain goals.

2. When compared with students in low socioeconomic status groups, students perceived their teachers as less praising, less caring, less helpful, and more critical. More than in the other groups, these students reported that their teachers did not consider learning important.

3. Principals, teachers, and pupils all perceived the lack of achievement within the schools.

4. Compared with the other groups [studied], a higher percentage (21%) of teachers in these schools would rather teach in another school. By contrast, only 2% of the teachers in the typical middle socioeconomic status schools wanted to teach elsewhere. Teachers in the low socioeconomic status, ineffective schools were absent an average of 3.51 days in the fall semester, whereas teachers in effective low socioeconomic status schools were absent only an average of 2.03 days. (Teddlie & Stringfield, 1993, pp. 34–35)

From *Hope at Last for At-Risk Youth* (p. 56), by R. D. Barr and W. H. Parrett, 1995, Boston: Allyn and Bacon. Used by permission.

| TABLE 12.2 | Strategies for Teaching Students at Risk |
|---|---|
| **Strategy** | **Description** |
| READING EMPHASIS | ■ Recognizes the importance of reading<br>■ Emphasizes teaching reading early to each child |
| ACCELERATED SCHOOLS | ■ Utilize the same approaches used with gifted and talented children<br>■ Use an extended school day with emphasis on language and problem solving<br>■ Stress acceleration rather than remediation |
| ALTERNATIVE SCHOOLS | ■ Have a separate focus that may meet the needs of at risk students better than regular schools<br>■ Example: Montessori schools, back-to-basics schools, nongraded schools, and open schools |
| ONE-ON-ONE TUTORING | ■ Provides concentrated time for direct instruction<br>■ Uses volunteers from the community, peers, or older students as tutors<br>■ Example: Reading Recovery, a one-on-one program (using a certified teacher) showing major success |
| EXTENDED SCHOOL DAY | ■ Provides after-school programs as an opportunity for extra tutoring time<br>■ Is staffed with regular teachers or volunteers |
| COOPERATIVE LEARNING | ■ Provides opportunities for learning from other students in small groups<br>■ Shown by research to be a very successful model for at risk students |
| MAGNET SCHOOLS | ■ Focus on specific areas, such as the arts or international studies<br>■ Give students an opportunity to focus on their strengths and interests |
| TEEN PARENT PROGRAMS | ■ Provide opportunities for students to learn parenting techniques<br>■ Help students with young children stay in school |
| VOCATIONAL–TECHNICAL<br>PROGRAMS | ■ Enable students to develop skills that are specific to jobs<br><br>■ Help with transition from school to postschool environments<br>■ Enable students who do poorly in academic areas to perform well in other areas |
| MENTORING | ■ Provides role models for students<br>■ Creates opportunities for tutoring and social skills development |
| SCHOOL-TO-WORK<br>PROGRAMS | ■ Give students the opportunity to begin work early<br>■ Provide training for students in real jobs |

Adapted from *Hope at Last for At-Risk Youth,* by R. D. Barr and W. H. Parrett, 1995, Boston: Allyn & Bacon.

based on individual needs, students who are at risk can benefit from the strategies and activities supplied for students with various disabilities (Wang, Reynolds, & Walberg, 1994/1995).

## Specific Strategies for Students at Risk

In addition to the general principles cited earlier, specific programs can prove effective with these students. These include an emphasis on teaching every child to read, **accelerated schools, alternative schools,** one-on-one tutoring, extended day programs, cooperative learning activities, **magnet schools,** teen parent programs, vocational–technical programs, mentoring, and school-to-work programs (Barr & Parrett, 1995). Table 12.2 provides a brief description of each of these approaches.

One program described in Table 12.2 has been used effectively in many schools: a **mentor program** (Slicker & Palmer, 1993). Elementary, middle, and high schools design such programs to provide students with a positive personal relationship with an adult—something that many children and youth lack (Barr & Parrett, 1995). A mentor can be any person of any background who is committed to serve as a support person for a child or youth.

Mentor programs range in scope from national programs such as Big Brothers/Big Sisters to programs developed by and for specific schools, such as a program wherein adults employed in the community have lunch with students (Friedman & Scaduto, 1995). Programs large and small proved effective for many children. It is important to ensure that a positive match is made between the mentor and the child. Other features of successful mentor programs are listed in the nearby Inclusion Strategies feature.

The population of at risk children is incredibly diverse. Many different professionals need to get involved in developing and implementing programs for this group of students. For more information on the topic, as well as a comprehensive list of available support services, see the book *Hope at Last for At-Risk Youth*, by R. D. Barr and W. H. Parrett, published in 1995 by Allyn & Bacon.

**ACCELERATED SCHOOLS** emphasize a fast-paced curriculum that focuses on acceleration rather than remediation to fully engage students.

**ALTERNATIVE SCHOOLS** include schools that strictly enroll students who are unsuccessful in regular schools.

**MAGNET SCHOOLS** emphasize a particular curricular area to attract students, such as an arts magnet or science magnet.

**MENTOR PROGRAMS** assign adult mentors to students to provide guidance and support.

**CROSS-REFERENCE** Review some of the strategies included in Chapters 4–8 and determine whether any of these methods would be effective with children at risk for school problems.

*School personnel should be proactive in efforts to prevent school drop-outs.*

## INCLUSION STRATEGIES

### Components of Effective Mentoring Programs for At Risk Students

◢ *Program compatibility:* The program should be compatible with the policies and goals of the organization. In a program for students in a community group, for example, program organizers should work closely with school personnel to ensure that the mentoring they provide complements the student's education.

◢ *Administrative commitment:* The program must be supported from the top as well as on a grass-roots level. In a school-based program, all school and district administrators, teachers, and staff must provide input and assistance. For a sponsoring business, the president or chief executive officer must view the program as important and worthy of the time and attention of the employees.

◢ *Proactive:* Ideally the programs should be proactive; that is, not a quick-fix reaction to a crisis. Successful mentoring programs for youth work because they are well thought out, they have specific goals and objectives, and they exist within a larger realm of programs and policies that function together.

◢ *Participant oriented:* The program should be based on the goals and needs of the participants. These goals will determine the program's focus, recruitment, and training. For example, if the primary aim of a mentoring program is career awareness, students should be matched with successful businesspeople in the youth's area of interest. Activities and workshops should be job related.

◢ *Pilot program:* The first step should be a pilot program of 6 to 12 months, with 10 to 40 participants, in order to work out any problems before expanding to a larger audience. Trying to start out with a large-scale plan that includes more than this number can prove unwieldy and disastrous. In the words of Oregon's guide to mentorship programs, "Think big but start small."

◢ *Orientation:* An orientation should be provided for prospective participants. It will help determine interest and enthusiasm, as well as give prospective mentors and students an idea of what to expect. In addition, it will provide them with opportunities to help design the program.

◢ *Selection and matching:* Mentors and their protégés should be carefully selected and matched. Questionnaires are helpful in determining needs, areas of interest, and strengths.

◢ *Training:* Training must be provided for all participants, including support people, throughout the program. Assuming that because a person is knowledgeable, caring, and enthusiastic he or she will make a good mentor is a mistake. Training must be geared to the specific problems experienced by at risk youth as well as different styles of communication.

◢ *Monitoring progress:* The program should be periodically monitored for progress and results to resolve emerging conflicts and problems.

◢ *Evaluation and revision:* The program should be evaluated with respect to how well goals and objectives are achieved. This can be done using questionnaires, interviews, etc.

From *Mentoring Programs for At-Risk Youth* (pp. 5–6) by National Dropout Prevention Center, 1990, Clemson, SC: Clemson University.

## Summary

### Basic Concepts about Students Who Are at Risk

◢ Students who are at risk may not be eligible for special education programs.

◢ At risk students include those who are in danger of developing significant learning and behavior problems.

◢ Poverty is a leading cause of academic failure.

◢ Poverty among children is increasing in this country.

◢ Poverty is associated with homelessness, poor health care, hunger, and single-parent households.

◢ Hunger is a major problem in our country.

◢ As many as 25% of all homeless people are children.

◢ Students in single-parent homes face major problems in school.

▲ About 25% of all children live in single-parent homes.

▲ Divorce is the leading cause of children living in single-parent homes.

▲ Children react in many different ways to divorce.

▲ Schools must take into consideration the rights of the noncustodial parent.

▲ The death of a parent, sibling, or friend can have a major impact on a child and school success.

▲ Child abuse is a major problem in this country and causes children to experience major emotional trauma.

▲ School personnel are required by law to report suspected child abuse.

▲ Drug use among students is on the increase after several years of decline.

▲ Teenage pregnancy continues to be a problem, despite the fear of AIDS and the presence of sex education programs.

## Strategies for Curriculum and Instruction for Students Who Are at Risk

▲ Numerous programs and interventions have proved effective in working with at risk students.

# *urther Readings*

Annie E. Casey Foundation. (1998). *1998 kids count data book: Overview*. Baltimore, MD: Author.

Barnes, K. E. (1982). *Preschool screening: The measurement and prediction of children at risk*. Springfield, IL: Thomas.

Barr, J. R., & Parrett, S. (1995). *Hope at last for at-risk youth*. Boston: Allyn & Bacon.

Carnegie Council on Adolescent Development. (1989). *Turning point: Preparing American youth for the 21st century*. New York: Author.

National Law Center on Homelessness and Poverty. (1990). *Shut out: Denial of education to homeless children*. Washington, DC: Author.

National Education Goals Panel. (1998). *Ready schools*. Washington, DC: Author.

Office of Education Research and Improvement. (1988). *Youth indicators, 1988: Trends in the well-being of American youth*. Washington, DC: U.S. Department of Education.

Office of Juvenile Justice and Delinquency Prevention. (1995). *Juvenile offenders and victims: A national report*. Pittsburgh, PA: National Center for Juvenile Justice.

Siccone, F. (1995). *Celebrating diversity: Building self-esteem in today's multi-cultural classrooms*. Boston: Allyn & Bacon.

U.S. Department of Education. (1998). *Tools for schools: From at-risk to excellence*. Washington, DC: Author.

U.S. Department of Education. (1998). *Safe and smart: Making the after-school hours work for kids*. Washington, DC: Author.

U.S. Department of Education. (1999). *The condition of education, 1998*. Washington, DC: Author.

Ysseldyke, J. E., Algozzine, B., & Thurlow, M. L. (2000). *Critical issues in special education* (3rd ed.). Boston: Houghton Mifflin.

# Chapter 13
# Classroom Organization and Management

*After reading this chapter, you should be able to:*

◢ Identify the components of classroom management

◢ Describe the roles of students, teachers, peers, and family members in promoting a positive classroom climate

◢ Describe ways to increase desirable and decrease undesirable classroom behaviors

◢ Identify self-management approaches and procedures

◢ Identify possible strategies to enhance classroom and personal organization

This year has been particularly challenging for Ray Chung. Ray has been teaching fifth grade for ten years but he cannot recall any year in which his students' needs were more diverse and his ability to manage the classroom and motivate his students have been more challenging tasks.

While many of his students present unique needs, 11-year-old Joey clearly stands out as the most disruptive student in the class. Joey is too frequently out of his seat and often yells out to other students across the room. He has difficulty staying on task during instructional periods and at times spreads a contagion of misbehavior in the classroom.

During lessons with his reading group, Joey is inattentive and frequently uncooperative. Ray is beginning to believe that his high level of disruptive behavior may make it virtually impossible for him to progress and achieve in the general education classroom, although, at the same time, he does not see him as a candidate for a special class or other pull-out program. Further, his disruptive behavior is gradually resulting in his falling far behind academically. Although it is only November, Ray seriously wonders whether this will be a productive year for Joey.

Joey currently receives no special education supports or services. However, Ray has referred Joey to the child study team, and they are pondering suggestions that may be effective within Ray's classroom as well as considering a request for a full assessment battery that may elucidate instructional and/or curricular alternatives.

## QUESTIONS TO CONSIDER

1. What recommendations would you have for Ray in focusing on the specific nature of Joey's behavior and its consequences?
2. What procedures can Ray implement that may significantly reduce the undesirable behaviors?
3. How can Joey's peers be involved in a comprehensive behavior management program?
4. How can a cooperative teaching arrangement facilitate successful intervention efforts in the inclusive classroom?

CLASSROOM MANAGEMENT calls for managing the classroom in order to facilitate instruction.

A teacher's ability to manage his or her classroom effectively and efficiently can greatly enhance the quality of the educational experience for all students. Well-organized and well-managed classrooms allow more time for productive instruction for all students, including those with special needs.

This chapter presents a model for thinking about the major dimensions of **classroom management**, a discussion of these dimensions, and specific suggested pedagogical practices. Sound organizational and management tactics promote the learning of all students and are particularly relevant to the successful inclusion of students with disabilities. When they are devised by general and special educators working collaboratively, the likelihood of success is further enhanced.

## FUNDAMENTALS OF CLASSROOM ORGANIZATION AND MANAGEMENT

CONSIDER THIS
Does the inclusion of students with special needs result in greater or less need for good classroom management? Why?

The importance of good classroom organization and management techniques has been affirmed numerous times by professionals in the field of education. Although much attention is given to curricular and instructional aspects of students' educational programs, organizational and management dimensions are typically underemphasized, despite their importance as prerequisites to instruction. It is the one area that first-year teachers consistently identify as most problematic. Further, classroom management often represents a challenge for teachers as classrooms become more diverse. Although reading about classroom management cannot take the place of practice and experience, this chapter offers a variety of management strategies to assist both new and experienced educators.

Most definitions describe *classroom management* as a systematic structuring of the classroom environment to create conditions in which effective teaching and learning can occur. This chapter broadly defines it as all teacher-directed activities that support the efficient operations of the classroom and that help establish optimal conditions for learning.

### Model of Classroom Management

Every classroom environment involves a number of elements that have a profound impact on the effectiveness of instruction and learning (Doyle, 1986). Six of these are described briefly here:

1. *Multidimensionality* refers to the wide variety of activities that occur in a classroom within the course of an instructional day.
2. *Simultaneity* refers to the fact that many different events occur at the same time.
3. *Immediacy* refers to the rapid pace at which events occur in classrooms.
4. *Unpredictability* refers to the reality that some events occur unexpectedly and cannot consistently be anticipated, but require attention nonetheless.

5. *Publicness* refers to the fact that classroom events are witnessed by a significant number of students who are very likely to take note of how teachers deal with these ongoing events.

6. *History* refers to the reality that, over the course of the school year, various events (experiences, routines, rules) will shape the evolving dynamics of classroom behavior.

Considering these elements reaffirms the complexity of teaching large numbers of students who have diverse learning needs. To address these classroom dynamics, teachers need to identify ways to organize and manage their classrooms to maximize the potential opportunities for learning. Figure 13.1 depicts the multifaceted dimensions of classroom organization and management. This model of organization and management evolved from one designed by Polloway, Patton, and Serna (2001). It reflects an adaptation of what they identify as "precursors to teaching."

The effective and efficient management of a classroom is based on numerous considerations. To create an environment conducive to learning, teachers must pay attention to psychosocial, procedural, physical, behavioral, instructional, and organizational variables that have a critical impact on learning and behavior. Teachers need to consider much of what is in the dimensional model (Figure 13.1), which is discussed in this chapter, before the beginning of the school year to prevent problems from developing. Prevention is frequently more effective than powerful behavior management strategies.

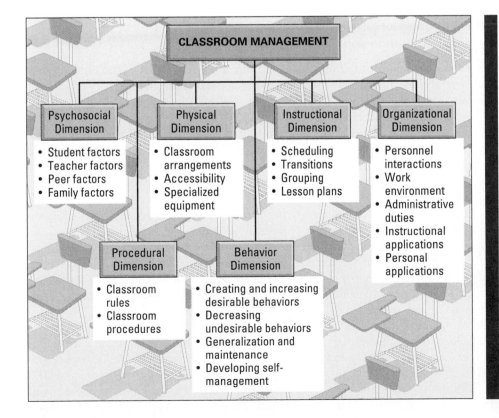

**FIGURE 13.1**

Dimensions of Classroom Organization and Management

## Guiding Principles

Five overarching principles guide the development and implementation of appropriate classroom organization and management procedures:

1. Good classroom organization and management must be planned.
2. Successful management derives from a positive classroom climate.
3. Proactive management is preferable to reactive approaches.
4. Consistency is the key to establishing an effective management program.
5. Two characteristics identified in classic classroom research enhance a teacher's ability to manage classrooms effectively (Kounin, 1970):
   ◢ *With-it-ness:* Overall awareness of what is happening in the classroom.
   ◢ *Overlap:* The ability to deal with more than one event simultaneously.

Although sound classroom management practices are useful in working with all students, the recommendations provided in this chapter are particularly helpful for students who have special needs and require individualized consideration. Often, these students struggle to learn in an environment that is not well organized and effectively managed.

## COMPONENTS OF EFFECTIVE CLASSROOM ORGANIZATION AND MANAGEMENT

This section of the chapter discusses the major elements and subcomponents of classroom management highlighted in the dimensional model in Figure 13.1.

### Psychosocial Dimension

This dimension refers to the psychological and social dynamics of the classroom. It focuses attention on **classroom climate,** the classroom atmosphere in which students must function.

The dynamics of classrooms are influenced by certain *student factors.* Their attitudes about school, authority figures, and other classmates can have a remarkable impact on how they behave and react to organizational and management demands. Other factors that shape student attitudes include the nature of previous educational experiences, how they feel about themselves, and their own expectations (i.e., potential for success or failure).

The psychological atmosphere of any classroom depends in great part on certain *teacher factors,* including disposition, competencies and skills, and actions. A teacher's attitudes toward students with special needs can dramatically affect the quality of education that a student will receive during the time he or she is in that teacher's classroom. Personal philosophies about education, discipline, and curriculum weigh heavily. The type of expectations a teacher holds for students can significantly influence learning outcomes.

*Peers* are also key players in forming the psychological and social atmosphere of a classroom, especially among older students. Teachers must understand peer values and pressures and use them to benefit students with special needs. Valuable cooperative learning opportunities can evolve based on successful peer involvement strategies.

The final component involves a variety of *family-generated factors.* Three major issues include family attitudes toward education, level of family support and involve-

*The dynamics of a classroom are determined by many different student factors.*

ment in the student's education, and amount of pressure placed on a child by the family. Extremes can be problematic—for example, a family that burdens a child with overwhelming pressure to succeed can cause as many difficulties as one that takes limited interest in a child's education.

These recommendations should help create a positive, nurturing environment that contributes to positive outcomes for all students:

◢ Let students know that you are sensitive to their needs and concerns.

◢ Convey enthusiasm about learning and the school experience.

◢ Create a supportive, safe environment in which students who are different can learn without fear of being ridiculed or threatened.

◢ Treat all students with fairness.

◢ Acknowledge all students in some personal way each day to affirm that they are valued within the room.

◢ Create a learning environment that is built on success and minimizes failure experiences common to the learning histories of students with disabilities.

◢ Understand the family and cultural contexts from which students come.

◢ Establish that each student in the classroom has rights (e.g., not to be interrupted when working or responding to a teacher inquiry) and that you expect everyone to respect those rights.

◢ Instill in students the understanding that they are responsible for their own behavior.

◢ Convey to students that every student's thoughts and ideas are important.

◢ Encourage risk taking and nurture all students (i.e., gifted, average, and disabled) to take on scholastic challenges.

## Procedural Dimension

As noted in Figure 13.1, this dimension refers to the rules and procedures that are part of the operating program of a classroom. The guidelines discussed here provide direction to school staff and students as to what is expected of all. The teacher must identify all rules, procedures, and regulations before the school year begins and should plan to teach them to students during the first days of the school year.

| TABLE 13.1 | Recommendations for Classroom Rules |
|---|---|

- Develop no more than seven rules for the classroom.

- Involve students in rule setting.

- Keep the rules brief, and state them clearly.

- Explain the rules thoroughly, and discuss the specific consequences if they are violated.

- State the rules in a positive way—avoid statements that are worded in a negative way, such as "not allowed."

- Post the rules in a location that all students can see.

- Discuss exceptions in advance so that students understand them.

- Teach the rules through modeling and practice and verify that all have been learned.

- Review the rules on a regular basis and when new students join in the class.

- Use reminders of rules as a preventive measure for times when possible disruptions are anticipated.

Equally important is preparation for dealing with violations of rules. Immediate and consistent consequences are needed. Various disciplinary techniques can be implemented to ensure that inappropriate behavior is handled effectively. (These will be covered in a subsequent section of the chapter.)

Students with exceptional needs will benefit from being taught systematically the administrative and social rules operative in a classroom. The suggestions provided in this section focus on classroom rules and in-class procedures.

**CONSIDER THIS**

Why are classroom rules such an important component of classroom management? Describe the likely climate of classrooms with effective rules and those without effective rules.

Most individuals respond best when they know what is expected of them. *Classroom rules* provide a general sense of what is expected of students. The rules that are chosen should be essential to classroom functioning and help create a positive learning environment (Christenson, Ysseldyke, & Thurlow, 1989; Smith & Rivera, 1995). Reasonable classroom rules, presented appropriately, will be particularly beneficial to students with special needs who are in general education settings because this process assists in clarifying expectations. Some specific suggestions are presented in Table 13.1.

An area of classroom management that may be overlooked is the development of logical *classroom procedures,* the specific way in which certain activities will be performed or the way certain situations will be handled. For example, depending on age, procedures may need to be established for using the pencil sharpener, using the rest room, and entering and leaving the classroom. Again, clear procedures are of particular importance especially for some students with special needs who may have difficulty attending to details or following instructions.

This area can cause distress for teachers if not attended to at the beginning of the school year. Teachers are often surprised by the complexity and detail associated with many seemingly trivial areas. The procedures for these areas combine to form the mosaic of one's management system. Here are some suggestions:

◢ Identify all situations for which a procedure will be needed. Develop the procedures collaboratively with the students.

◢ Explain each procedure thoroughly.

◢ Teach each procedure through modeling, guided practice, and independent practice, letting every student have an opportunity to demonstrate learning on an appropriate level.
◢ Introduce classroom procedures during the first week of school, scheduling priority procedures for the first day and covering other ones on subsequent days.
◢ Avoid introducing too many procedures at once.
◢ Incorporate any school regulation of importance and relevance into classroom procedures (e.g., hall passes).

## Physical Dimension

This dimension includes the aspects of the physical environment that teachers can manipulate to enhance the conditions for learning. For students with disabilities, some features of the physical setting may need to be especially arranged to ensure that individual needs are met.

**Classroom arrangements** refer to physical facets of the classroom, including layout, storage, wall space, and signage. Figure 13.2 recommends seating arrangement. Teachers are encouraged to consider carefully where to seat students who have problems with controlling their behaviors, those who experience attention deficit, and students with sensory impairments. The judicious use of seating arrangements can minimize problems as well as create better learning opportunities for students.

Other suggestions for classroom arrangement are listed here:

*CLASSROOM ARRANGEMENTS* involve the organization of the physical elements in the classroom (e.g., position of desks).

◢ Consider establishing areas of the classroom for certain types of activities (e.g., discovery or inquiry learning, independent reading).
◢ Clearly establish which areas of the classroom, such as the teacher's desk, are off limits.
◢ Begin the year with a structured environment, moving to more flexibility after rules and procedures have been established.
◢ Notify students with visual impairments of changes made to the physical environment.
◢ Arrange furniture so that the teachers and students can move easily around the classroom.
◢ Direct students' attention to the information to be learned from bulletin boards, if they are used for instructional purposes.
◢ Establish patterns that students can use in moving around the class that minimize disruption.
◢ Secure materials and equipment that are potentially harmful if used without proper supervision, such as certain art supplies, chemicals, and science equipment.
◢ Avoid creating open spaces that have no clear purpose, as they often can become staging areas for problem behaviors (Rosenberg et al., 1991).
◢ Provide labels and signs for areas of the room to assist younger or more delayed students in better understanding what and where things are.

The accessibility of the classroom warrants special attention because of legal mandates (e.g., Section 504 of the Rehabilitation Act of 1973). The concept of **accessibility,** of course, extends beyond physical accessibility, touching on overall program accessibility for students with special needs. Students with disabilities must

*ACCESSIBILITY* refers to the availability of educational programs for students with disabilities.

*FIGURE* **13.2**
Seating Arrangements

- Seat students with behavior problems first so that they are in close proximity to the teacher for as much of the time as possible.

- After more self-control is demonstrated, more distant seating arrangements are possible and desirable.

- Locate students for whom visual distractions can interfere with attention to tasks (e.g., learning and attentional problems, hearing impairments, behavior problems) so that these distractions are minimized.

- Establish clear lines of vision (a) for students so that they can attend to instruction and (b) for the teacher so that students can be monitored throughout the class period (Rosenberg et al., 1991).

- Ensure that students with sensory impairments are seated so that they can maximize their residual vision and hearing.

- Consider alternative arrangements of desks (e.g., table clusters) as options to traditional rows.

be able to utilize the classroom like other students and the room must be free of potential hazards. Specific suggestions for creating an accessible classroom include:

- Ensuring that the classroom is accessible to students who use wheelchairs, braces, crutches, or other forms of mobility assistance—this involves doorways, space to move within the classroom, floor coverings, learning centers, microcomputers, chalkboards or dry-erase boards, bookshelves, sinks, tables, desks, and any other areas or physical objects that students use.
- Guaranteeing that the classroom is free of hazards (e.g., low-hanging mobiles or plants) that could injure students who have a visual impairment.
- Labeling storage areas and other parts of the classroom for students with visual impairments by using raised lettering or braille.
- Paying special attention to signs identifying hazards by providing nonverbal cautions for nonreaders.

**CROSS-REFERENCE**
Review Chapter 9 on students with low-incidence disabilities and Chapter 8 on those with sensory impairments, and consider the implications of equipment needed by these groups of students.

Some students with disabilities require the use of *specialized equipment,* such as wheelchairs, hearing aids and other types of amplification systems, communication devices, adaptive desks and trays, prone standers (i.e., stand-up desks), and medical equipment. These types of assistive devices were introduced earlier in the book so that teachers may understand how the equipment works, how it should be used, and what adaptations will need to be made to the classroom environment to accommodate the student using it. The other students in the classroom should be introduced to the special equipment as well. Instructional lessons on specific pieces of equipment will not only be helpful in creating an inclusive environment, but may also provide a basis for curricular tie-ins in areas including health and science. Suggestions include the following:

- Identify what special equipment will be used in the classroom prior to the arrival of the student who needs it.
- Learn how special equipment and devices work and how to identify problems or malfunctions.
- Find out how long students need to use time-specified equipment or devices.
- Structure learning activities in which the student with a disability (perhaps paired with a peer) demonstrates appropriate usage of the specialized equipment.

## Behavioral Dimension

The ability to manage inappropriate behaviors that may disrupt the learning environment is an important component of classroom management. Yet, this ability is only a part of a comprehensive behavior management program. Such a plan should also include techniques for developing new behaviors or increasing desirable behaviors within the students' repertoire. Moreover, a sound program must ensure that behaviors learned or changed will be maintained over time and generalized (e.g., demonstrated in different contexts). It must also teach self-control mechanisms. The nearby Inclusion Strategies feature describes the basic components of a behavior management plan based on functional assessment procedures.

Given the importance of the behavioral dimension, most general educators will probably work with special educators on a regular basis to develop effective programs for students with disabilities as well as for other students with behavioral problems in the classroom. To provide a flavor of the areas for possible emphasis, Etscheidt and Bartlett (1999, p. 171) identified the following sample factors to consider:

▲ *Skill Training*: Could the student be involved in social skill instruction? Does the student need counseling?

▲ *Behavior Management Plan*: Does the student need a behavior management plan that describes a reinforcement system, supportive signals, and corrective options?

▲ *Self-Management*: Could the student use self-monitoring of target behaviors?

▲ *Peer Support*: Could peers help monitor and/or redirect behavior? Could peers take notes, help prepare for exams, etc.?

▲ *Class-Wide Systems*: Could the teacher implement an interdependent group contingency for the class? Could a "Circle of Friends" be initiated?

**CROSS-REFERENCE**
Review Chapter 2 where this concept was introduced.

All facets of behavior management cannot be covered in sufficient detail here. However, the following sections provide recommendations that should guide practice in increasing desirable behaviors, decreasing undesirable behaviors, promoting generalization and maintenance, and enhancing self-management. The final section discusses the mandated requirement in IDEA for behavioral intervention plans (BIPs).

---

# INCLUSION STRATEGIES

## Components of a Behavior Management Plan

**CONDUCT A FUNCTIONAL ASSESSMENT**
1. Collect information.
   ▲ Identify and define the target behavior.
   ▲ Identify events/circumstances associated with the problem behavior.
   ▲ Determine potential function(s) of the problem behavior.

2. Develop hypothesis statements about the behavior.
   ▲ Events/circumstances associated with the problem behavior.
   ▲ Function/purpose of the behavior.

**DEVELOP AN INTERVENTION**
**(Based on Hypothesis Statements)**
1. Teach alternative behavior.
2. Modify events/circumstances associated with the problem behavior.

From "Using Functional Assessment to Develop Effective, Individualized Interventions for Challenging Behaviors," by L. F. Johnson and G. Dunlap, 1993, *Teaching Exceptional Children, 25,* p. 46. Used by permission.

**TEACHING TIP**
Students should be involved in selecting positive reinforcers to make sure that they are indeed attractive to the student.

**REINFORCER** is something that follows a behavior and is linked to that behavior.

**POSITIVE REINFORCER** is something positive that follows a particular behavior.

**CONSIDER THIS**
Some people say that contracts, as well as other forms of positive reinforcement, amount to little more than bribery. Do you agree or disagree, and why?

**CONTINGENCY CONTRACTING** is a formal agreement between the student and teacher related to behavior and reinforcers.

Because research confirms the effectiveness of behavioral techniques for promoting learning in students with special needs (see Lloyd, Forness, & Kavale, 1998), such interventions should clearly be key components of a teacher's repertoire.

**CREATING AND INCREASING DESIRABLE BEHAVIORS** The acquisition of desired new behaviors, whether scholastic, personal, social, or vocational, is a classroom goal. A new desired behavior can be affirmed with a **reinforcer,** any event that rewards, and thus strengthens, the behavior it follows. *Positive reinforcement* presents a desirable consequence for performance of an appropriate behavior. **Positive reinforcers** can take different forms; what serves as reinforcement for one individual may not work for another. Reinforcers can consist of praise, physical contact, tangible items, activities, or privileges. The use of reinforcement is the most socially acceptable and instructionally sound tactic for increasing desired behaviors.

Three basic principles must be followed for positive reinforcement to be most effective. It must be meaningful to the student, contingent upon the proper performance of a desired behavior, and presented immediately. In other words, for positive reinforcement to work, students must find the reinforcement desirable in some fashion, understand that it is being given as a result of the behavior demonstrated, and receive it soon after they do what was asked. Principles for the use of positive reinforcement are presented in Figure 13.3. Generally, attention to the systematic nature of the reinforcement program should parallel the severity of a student's intellectual, learning, or behavioral problem.

The first illustrative application of the principle of positive reinforcement is **contingency contracting,** a concept first introduced by Homme (1969). With this method, the teacher develops contracts with students that state (1) what behaviors (e.g., academic work, social behaviors) students are to complete or perform and (2) what consequences (e.g., reinforcement) the instructor will provide. These contracts

**FIGURE 13.3**
Implementing Positive Reinforcement Techniques

- Determine what reinforcements will work for particular students:
    1. Ask the child by using direct formal or informal questioning or by administering an interest inventory or reinforcement survey.
    2. Ask those knowledgeable about the student (e.g., parents, friends, or past teachers).
    3. Observe the student in the natural environment as well as in a structured observation (e.g., arranging reinforcement alternatives from which the student may select).
- Select meaningful reinforcers that are easy and practical to deliver in classroom settings (Idol, 1993).
- "Catch" students behaving appropriately, and provide them with the subsequent appropriate reinforcement (referred to as the differential reinforcement of behavior *incompatible* with problem behavior). Begin this technique early so that students experience the effects of positive reinforcement.
- Use the Premack (1959) principle ("Grandma's law": "eat your vegetables and then you can have dessert") regularly.
- Use reinforcement techniques as the student makes gradual progress in developing a desired behavior that requires the mastery of numerous substeps (reinforce each successive approximation). This concept is called *shaping.*
- Demonstrate to a student that certain behaviors will result in positive outcomes by reinforcing nearby peers.

are presented as binding agreements between student and teacher. To be most effective, contracts should (1) initially reward imperfect approximations of the behavior, (2) provide frequent reinforcement, (3) reward accomplishment rather than obedience, and (4) be fair, clear, and positive. Figure 13.4 shows an example of a contract for a secondary school student.

*Group contingencies,* which are set up for groups of students rather than individuals, provide excellent alternatives for managing behavior and actively including students with special needs in the general education classroom. There are three types:

1. *Dependent contingencies:* All group members share in the reinforcement if one individual achieves a goal (i.e., the "hero" strategy).
2. *Interdependent contingencies:* All group members are reinforced if all collectively (or all individually) achieve the stated goal.
3. *Independent contingencies:* Individuals within the group are reinforced for individual achievement toward a goal.

Whereas independent contingencies are commonly used, the other two forms are less widely seen in the classroom. The dependent strategy is sometimes referred to as

**FIGURE *13.4***

Sample Contract between Student and Teacher

From *Behavior Management: Applications for Teachers and Parents* (p. 189), by T. Zirpoli and G. Melloy, 1993, Columbus, OH: Merrill. Used by permission.

---

**Contract**

_____ will demonstrate the following
(Student's name)
appropriate behaviors in the classroom:

1. Come to school on time.

2. Come to school with homework completed.

3. Complete all assigned work in school without prompting.

4. Ask for help when necessary by raising hand and getting teacher's attention.


_____ will provide the following reinforcement:
(Teacher's name)

1. Ten tokens for the completion of each of the above four objectives. Tokens for the first two objectives will be provided at the beginning of class after all homework assignments have been checked. Tokens for objectives 3 and 4 will be provided at the end of the school day.

2. Tokens may be exchanged for activities on the Classroom Reinforcement Menu at noon on Fridays.


_____          _____
Student's signature                   Teacher's signature

                                      _____
                                      Date

a "hero approach" because it singles out one student's performance for attention. Although it can be abused, such an approach may be particularly attractive for a student who responds well to peer attention. A student with special needs may feel more meaningfully included in class when his or her talents are recognized in this way.

Others may feel reinforced and accepted as part of a group when interdependent contingencies are employed. The most common use of an interdependent strategy is the "good behavior game." Because it is most often used as a behavioral reduction intervention, it is discussed later in the chapter.

The benefits of group-oriented contingencies (or peer-mediated strategies, as they are often called) include the involvement of peers, the ability of teachers to enhance motivation, and increased efficiency for the teacher. In some instances, students will raise questions of fairness concerning group contingency programs. Those who typically behave appropriately may feel that they are being penalized for the actions of others if reinforcement occurs only when the whole group evidences a desired behavior. You can assure them that, ultimately, they and everyone else will benefit from group success with particular guidelines or goals.

**DECREASING UNDESIRABLE BEHAVIORS** Every teacher will face situations involving undesirable behaviors that require behavior reduction techniques. Teachers can select from a range of techniques; however, it is usually best to begin with the least intrusive interventions (Smith & Rivera, 1995). A recommended sequence of reduction strategies is depicted in Figure 13.5. As teachers consider reductive strategies, they are cautioned to keep records, develop plans of action, and follow state and local guidelines.

The use of *natural* and *logical consequences* can help children and adolescents learn to be more responsible for their behaviors (West, 1986, 1994). These principles are particularly important for students with special needs who often have difficulty seeing the link between their behavior and the resulting consequences.

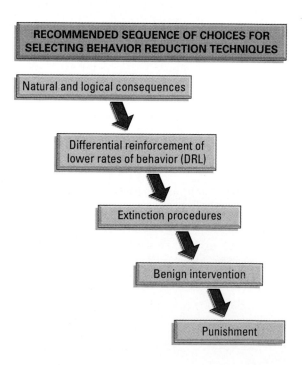

**FIGURE 13.5**

Recommended Sequence of Selected Behavior Reduction Techniques

With **natural consequences,** the situation itself provides the contingencies for a certain behavior. For example, if a student forgets to return a permission slip to attend an off-campus event, the natural consequence is that the student is not allowed to go and must remain at school. Thus, rather than intervening in a given situation, the teacher allows the situation to teach the students. Natural consequences are an effective means to teach common sense and responsibility (West, 1994).

In **logical consequences,** there is a logical connection between inappropriate behavior and the consequences that follow. If a student forgets lunch money, a logical consequence might be that money must be borrowed from someone else. The uncomfortable consequence is the hassle or embarrassment of requesting financial assistance. These tactics can help students recognize that their own behavior has created the discomfort and not something the teacher has done to them. When using this approach, teachers should clarify to students that they are responsible for their own behaviors. Logical consequences relate the disciplinary response directly to the inappropriate behavior.

**NATURAL CONSEQUENCES** are those consequences that typically follow a particular behavior.

**LOGICAL CONSEQUENCES** are the expected consequences that follow a behavior.

An important, recently developed approach to behavioral reduction is through the use of positive behavioral supports. As Horner (2000) notes, "positive behavior support involves the assessment and reengineering of environments so people with problem behaviors experience reductions in (these behaviors) and increased social [and] personal quality in their lives. . . . it is an approach that blends values about the rights of people with disabilities with the practical science about how learning and behavior change occur" (p. 181).

The essential element of positive behavior support is the emphasis on fixing environments rather than focusing just on changing the behavior of individuals. Thus, the key element is to design schools and curricula to prevent problem behaviors from occurring and thus make them "irrelevant, inefficient, and ineffective" (Horner, 2000, p. 182). As discussed in Chapter 6, the basis for effective positive behavior support programs is the use of functional behavior assessment which identifies classroom events that serve to predict the occurrence of problem behaviors and function to maintain these behaviors (Horner, 2000). Thus, the reader is encouraged to consider the remaining behavioral reduction strategies discussed within this chapter in light of the need to balance the focus on the individual with the more significant focus on designing a curriculum and operating a classroom in ways in which behavioral disturbances are minimized and students with special needs are more accepted members of the classroom.

The next option on the continuum is the use of *differential reinforcement of lower (DRL) rates of behavior.* This technique uses positive reinforcement strategies as a behavior reduction tool. A teacher using this procedure provides appropriate reinforcement to students for displaying lower rates of a certain behavior that has been targeted for reduction. It is important to remember that the goal should be to decrease the frequency or duration of the unwanted behavior.

**CONSIDER THIS**
What are some advantages of using a DRL approach when working on a complex behavior, rather than simply reinforcing the student only after a targeted behavior has completely disappeared?

An example of this technique used with groups of students is the "good behavior game" (originally developed by Barrish, Saunders, & Wolf, 1969), in which student teams receive reinforcement if the number of occurrences of inappropriate behaviors remains under a preset criterion. Tankersley (1995) provides a good overview of the use of the good behavior game:

> First, teachers should define target behaviors that they would like to see improved and determine when these behaviors are most problematic in their classrooms. Criteria for winning must be set and reinforcers established; the students should be taught the rules for playing. Next, the classroom is divided into teams and

team names are written on the chalkboard. If any student breaks a rule when the game is in effect, the teacher makes a mark by the name of the team of which the disruptive student is a member. At the end of the time in which the game is played, any team that has fewer marks than the preestablished criterion wins. Members of the winning team(s) receive reinforcers daily. In addition, teams that meet weekly criterion receive reinforcers at the end of the week. (p. 20)

Here are additional considerations:

◢ Understand that undesirable behaviors will still occur and must be tolerated until target levels are reached.
◢ Reduce the criterion level after students have demonstrated stability at the present level.
◢ Avoid making too great a jump between respective criterion levels to ensure that students are able to meet the new demands.

Tankersley (1995, p. 23) stresses the value of this strategy in noting that it "can be very effective in changing students' behaviors, can lead to improved levels of academic skills . . . , can reduce the teacher's burden of incorporating several individual contingency systems for managing behavior, . . . [makes] use of natural supports available in the classroom, [and] can help promote generalization" (p. 26).

**EXTINCTION** is the termination of an undesirable behavior.

The next reduction option involves **extinction** procedures. In this technique, the teacher withholds reinforcement for a behavior. Over time, such action, in combination with the positive reinforcement of related desirable behaviors, should extinguish the inappropriate behavior. One example is for the teacher to cease responding to student misbehavior. For some situations, it will be necessary to involve a student's peers in the extinction process to eliminate a behavior because the peers' actions are controlling the relevant reinforcers. The following are additional suggestions:

**TEACHING TIP**
When attempting to reduce an inappropriate behavior by ignoring it, teachers must remember to positively reinforce behaviors that are desired.

◢ Analyze what is reinforcing the undesirable behavior, and isolate the reinforcer(s) before initiating this procedure.
◢ Understand that the extinction technique is desirable because it does not involve punishment, but it will take time to be effective.
◢ Do not use this technique with behaviors that require immediate intervention (e.g., fighting).
◢ Recognize that the withholding of reinforcement (1) is likely to induce an increase ("spiking" effect) in the occurrence of the undesirable behavior, as students intensify their efforts to receive the reinforcement they are used to getting, and (2) may produce an initial aggressive response.
◢ Provide reinforcement to students who demonstrate appropriate incompatible behaviors (e.g., taking turns vs. interrupting).

The fourth option is the use of techniques that border on being punishment but are so unobtrusive that they can be considered *benign tactics*. These suggestions are consistent with a concept developed by Cummings (1983) called the "law of least intervention." Her idea is to eliminate disruptive behaviors quickly with a minimum of disruption to the classroom or instructional routine. The following suggestions can be organized into physical, gestural, visual, and verbal prompts:

**TEACHING TIP**
Being physically close to students who often display behavior problems is a powerful method of reducing inappropriate behaviors.

◢ Position yourself physically near students who are likely to create problems.
◢ Touch a student's shoulder gently to convey your awareness that the student is behaving in some inappropriate way.

*Positioning yourself by a student who is disruptive is often a powerful management technique.*

⊿ Use subtle and not-so-subtle gestures to stop undesirable behaviors (e.g., pointing, head-shaking).

⊿ Establish eye contact and maintain it for a while with a student who is behaving inappropriately. This results in no disruption to the instructional routine.

⊿ Stop talking for a noticeable length of time to redirect student attention.

⊿ Call on students who are not attending, but ask them questions that they can answer successfully.

⊿ Use humor to redirect inappropriate behavior.

⊿ Avoid sarcasm and confrontation.

The last option in this reduction hierarchy and the one that is most intrusive is the use of **punishment.** It is the least preferable option because it involves the presentation of something unpleasant or the removal of something pleasant as a consequence of the performance of an undesirable behavior. However, in situations in which punishment becomes necessary a more immediate cessation of undesirable behaviors is required. Because of their potency, punishment strategies should be weighed carefully; they can interfere with the learning process if not used sparingly and appropriately. Given that all teachers must use some punishment, the key is to ensure that it is used appropriately.

Three punishment techniques are commonly used in classrooms: **reprimands, time out,** and **response cost.** For these forms of punishment to work, it is critical that they be applied immediately after the occurrence of the undesirable behavior and that students understand why they are being applied. A useful overview of these techniques is provided in Table 13.2.

**PUNISHMENT** is applying something negative after an undesirable behavior.

**REPRIMANDS** are an unpleasant verbal response from a teacher to a behavior.

**TIME OUT** is the removal of the student from the classroom or specific activity.

**RESPONSE COST** is the loss of something valued by the student.

| TABLE 13.2 | Three Commonly Used Punishment Techniques | | |
|---|---|---|---|
| **Type** | **Definition** | **Advantages** | **Disadvantages** |
| **REPRIMAND** | A verbal statement or nonverbal gesture that expresses disapproval | Easily applied with little or no preparation required<br><br>No physical discomfort to students | Sometimes not effective<br><br>Can serve as positive reinforcement if this is a major source of attention. |
| **RESPONSE COST** | A formal system of penalties in which a reinforcer is removed contingent upon the occurrence of an inappropriate behavior | Easily applied with quick results<br><br>Does not disrupt class activities<br><br>No physical discomfort to students | Not effective once student has "lost" all reinforcers<br><br>Can initially result in some students being more disruptive |
| **TIME OUT** | Limited or complete loss of access to positive reinforcers for a set amount of time | Fast-acting and powerful<br><br>No physical discomfort to students | Difficult to find secluded areas where students would not be reinforced inadvertently<br><br>May require physical assistance to the time-out area<br><br>Overuse can interfere with educational and prosocial efforts |

From *Student Teacher to Master Teacher* by M. S. Rosenberg, L. O'Shea, and D. J. O'Shea, 1991, New York: Macmillan. Reprinted by permission.

A reprimand represents a type of punishment in which an unpleasant condition (verbal reprimand from the teacher) is presented to the student. The following are some specific suggestions:

**TEACHING TIP**
To ensure proper compliance, teachers must always be aware of state or local guidelines when using time out for reducing student behavior.

▲ Do not let this type of interchange dominate your interactions with students.
▲ Look at the student and talk in a composed way.
▲ Do not verbally reprimand a student from across the room. Get close to the student, maintain a degree of privacy, and minimize embarrassment.
▲ Let the student know exactly why you are concerned.
▲ Convey to the student that it is the behavior that is the problem and not him or her.

With time out a student is removed from a situation in which he or she typically receives positive reinforcement, thus being prevented from enjoying something pleasurable. There are different ways to remove a student from a reinforcing setting: (1) Students are allowed to observe the situation from which they have been removed (contingent observation); (2) students are excluded from the ongoing proceedings entirely (exclusion time out); and (3) students are secluded in a separate room (seclusion time out). The first two versions are most likely to be considered for use in general education classrooms. The following suggestions are extremely important if time out is to succeed.

◢ Confirm that the ongoing situation from which a student is going to be removed is indeed reinforcing; if not, this technique will not serve as a punisher and rather may be a form of positive reinforcement.

◢ Ensure that the time-out area is devoid of reinforcing elements. If it is not a neutral setting, this procedure will fail.

◢ Do not keep students in time out for long periods of time (i.e., more than ten minutes) or use it frequently (e.g., daily), as students will miss significant amounts of instructional time.

◢ As a rule of thumb with younger children, never allow time-out periods to extend beyond one minute for every year of the child's age (up to a maximum of ten minutes).

◢ Use a timer to ensure accuracy in the length of time out.

◢ Incorporate this procedure as one of the classroom procedures explained and taught at the beginning of the school year.

◢ Consider using a time-out system in which students are given one warning before being removed.

◢ Signal to the student when it is appropriate to return.

◢ Do not use this technique with certain sensitive students.

◢ Keep records on frequency, reason for using, and amount of time placed when using seclusion time out procedures.

Response cost involves the loss of something the student values, such as privileges or points. It is a system in which a penalty or fine is levied for occurrences of inappropriate behavior. The following are some specific suggestions:

◢ Explain clearly to students how the system works and how much one will be fined for a given offense.

◢ Make sure all penalties are presented in a nonpersonal manner.

◢ Confirm that privileges that are lost are indeed reinforcing to students.

◢ Make sure that all privileges are not lost quickly, resulting in a situation in which a student may have little or no incentive to behave appropriately.

◢ Tie this procedure in with positive reinforcement at all times.

**GENERALIZATION AND MAINTENANCE** After behaviors have been established at acceptable levels, the next stages involve transferring what has been learned to new contexts and maintaining established levels of performance. Teachers often succeed in teaching students certain behaviors but fail to help them apply the skills to new situations or to retain them over time. Teaching appropriate behaviors and then hoping that students will be able to use various skills at some later time is detrimental to many students with special needs because a core difficulty they experience is performing independently in the classroom.

Teachers need to program for generalization, the wider application of a behavior skill, by giving students opportunities to use new skills in different settings, with different people, and at different times. Students often need help in identifying the cues that should trigger the performance of an acquired behavior, action, or skill.

Students also need to practice what they have learned previously, in order to maintain their skills. Instructional planning should allow time for students to determine how well they have retained what they have learned. This usually can be done during seatwork activities or other arrangements.

Suggestions for generalization and maintenance include the following:

◢ Create opportunities for students to practice in different situations what they have learned.

◢ Work with other teachers to provide additional opportunities.

◢ Place students in situations that simulate those that they will encounter in the near and distant future, both within school and in other areas of life.

◢ Show students how these skills or behaviors will be useful to them in the future.

◢ Prompt students to use recently acquired skills in a variety of contexts.

◢ Maintain previously taught skills by providing ongoing practice or review.

As noted previously, the use of positive behavior supports has become more popular in working with students with special needs, particularly because of its effectiveness and its emphasis on the environment rather than the individual. A key to behavioral generalization and maintenance, therefore, is to focus beyond the child and ensure that the learning environment is designed in such a way that students can use their newly acquired skills effectively to become accepted and active members of the classroom while enhancing their learning opportunities. In addition, key elements of generalization and maintenance relate to self-management strategies, which become essential in work with adolescents.

**SELF-MANAGEMENT**  Ultimately, we want all students to be able to manage their own behaviors without external direction because this ability is a requirement of functioning independently in life. Special attention needs to be given to those who do not display independent behavioral control and thus must develop *student-regulated strategies*—interventions that, though initially taught by the teacher, are intended to be implemented independently by the student. The concept is an outgrowth of cognitive behavior modification, a type of educational intervention for students with disabilities in use since the 1980s, that stresses active thinking about behavior. Shapiro, DuPaul, and Bradley-Klug (1998) provide a good overview of self-management. They state:

> It is helpful to conceptualize self-management interventions as existing on a continuum. At one end, the intervention is completely controlled by the teacher. . . ; this individual provides feedback regarding whether the student's behavior met the desired criteria and administers the appropriate consequences for the behavior. At the other end, the student engages in evaluating his or her own behavior against the criteria for performance, without benefit of teacher. . . input. The student also self-administers the appropriate consequences. In working with students with behavior problems, the objective should be to move a student as far toward the self-management side of the continuum as possible. Although some of these students may not be capable of reaching levels of independent self-management, most are certainly capable of approximating this goal. (p. 545)

**CONSIDER THIS**

Why is it so important to teach students to manage their own behaviors without external guidance from teachers? How can self-management assist students with disabilities in their inclusion in the community?

Fiore, Becker, and Nerro (1993) state the rationale for such interventions: "Cognitive–behavioral [intervention] is . . . intuitively appealing because it combines behavioral techniques with cognitive strategies designed to directly address core problems of impulse control, higher order problem solving, and self-regulation" (p. 166). Whereas traditional behavioral interventions most often stress the importance of teacher-monitoring of student behavior, extrinsic reinforcement, and teacher-directed learning, cognitive interventions instead focus on teaching students to monitor their own behavior, to engage in self-reinforcement, and to direct their own learning in strategic fashion (Dowdy, Patton, Smith, & Polloway, 1997).

Such approaches have become particularly popular with students with learning and attentional difficulties because they offer the promise of

◢ increasing focus on selective attention.

◢ modifying impulsive responding.

◢ providing verbal mediators to assist in academic and social problem-solving situations.

▲ teaching effective self-instructional statements to enable students to "talk through" tasks and problems.

▲ providing strategies that may lead to improvement in peer relations. (Rooney, 1993)

While using self-management strategies with students with special needs in inclusive settings has been far more limited than studies of using them in pull-out programs, the moderate to strong positive outcomes reported in research are encouraging (McDougall, 1998).

Student-regulated strategies form the essence of self-management. Although variations exist in how these are defined and described, the components listed in Figure 13.6 represent the central aspects of self-management.

Two components with particular utility for general education teachers are self-monitoring and self-instruction. **Self-monitoring,** a technique in which students observe and record their own behavior, has been commonly employed with students with learning problems. Lloyd, Landrum, and Hallahan (1991) note that self-monitoring was initially seen as an assessment technique, but as individuals observed their own behavior, the process also resulted in a change in behavior. Self-monitoring of behavior, such as attention, is a relatively simple technique that has been validated with children who have learning disabilities, mental retardation, multiple disabilities, attention deficits, and behavior disorders; it has also been profitable for nondisabled students (McDougall, 1998; Lloyd et al., 1991; Prater, Joy, Chilman, Temple, & Miller, 1991). Increased attention, beneficial to academic achievement, has been reported as a result.

A common mechanism for self-monitoring was developed by Hallahan, Lloyd, and Stoller (1982). It involves using a tape-recorded tone, which sounds at random intervals (e.g., every 45 seconds), and a self-recording sheet. Each time the tone sounds, children ask themselves whether they are paying attention and then mark the *yes* or the *no* box on the tally sheet. While students are often *not* accurate in their recording, nevertheless positive changes in behavior have been observed in many research studies. While self-monitoring procedures may prove problematic for one

***SELF-MONITORING*** is a system where the student monitors his or her own progress.

**CONSIDER THIS**
Do you engage in any self-monitoring techniques? If so, how do you use them, and how effective are they?

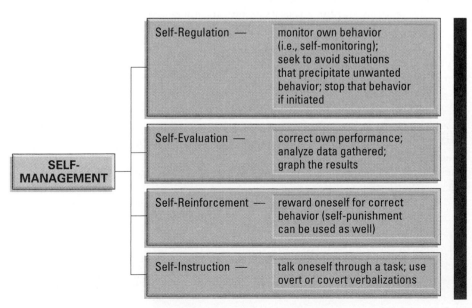

**FIGURE 13.6**
Components of Self-Management

From *Guide to Attention Deficits in the Classroom,* by C. A. Dowdy, J. R. Patton, E. A. Polloway, and T. E. C. Smith, 1998, Austin, TX: Pro-Ed. Used by permission.

teacher to implement alone, a collaborative approach within a cooperative teaching arrangement offers much promise.

Teachers should consider ways to creatively use self-monitoring in their classrooms as an adjunct to other ongoing management strategies. McDougall (1998) offered this unique suggestion:

> Practitioners. . . could train students to use tactile cues to mediate self-management in much the same manner that students use visually cued, audio-cued, or covert self-monitoring. Tactile cues such as those produced by vibrating pagers might be a functional option for (a) students who have difficulty responding to visual and auditory cues, (b) students with multiple, profound, or sensory disabilities, (c) situations in which audio or visual cues might distract other students, and (d) students who wish to maintain privacy when self-monitoring. (p. 317)

**SELF-INSTRUCTION** is the process where a student identifies what is to be learned and devises a learning procedure.

**Self-instruction** represents another useful intervention. Pfiffner and Barkley (1991) describe components of a self-instruction program as follows:

> Self-instructions include defining and understanding the task or problem, planning a general strategy to approach the problem, focusing attention on the task, selecting an answer or solution, and evaluating performance. In the case of successful performance, self-reinforcement (usually in the form of a positive self-statement, such as "I really did a good job") is provided. In the case of an unsuccessful performance, a coping statement is made (e.g., "Next time I'll do better if I slow down") and errors are corrected. At first, an adult trainer typically models the self-instructions while performing a task. The child then performs the same task while the trainer provides the self-instructions. Next, the child performs the task while self-instructing aloud. These overt verbalizations are then faded to covert self-instructions. (p. 525)

**CROSS-REFERENCE**
Review Chapter 4 on learning disabilities to see how self-monitoring and self-instructional techniques are used with students with learning disabilities.

Clear, simple self-instruction strategies form an appropriate beginning for interventions with students with learning or attentional difficulties in the general education classroom. Such approaches are likely to enhance success. Pfiffner and Barkley (1991, p. 529) recommend the STAR program, in which "children learn to *Stop, Think* ahead about what they have to do, *Act* or do the requested task while talking to themselves about the task, and *Review* their results."

Detailed and systematic procedures have been developed for implementing self-management strategies. Some basic recommendations follow:

▲ Allocate sufficient instructional time to teach self-management to students who need it.

▲ Establish a sequence of activities that move by degrees from teacher direction to student direction and self-control.

▲ Include objectives relevant to improved behavior and enhanced learning (e.g., increased attention yields reading achievement gains).

▲ Provide strategies and assistive materials (e.g., self-recording forms) for students to use.

▲ Model how effective self-managers operate. Point out actual applications of the elements of self-management (as highlighted in Figure 13.6), and give students opportunities to practice these techniques with your guidance.

▲ Provide for the maintenance of learned strategies and for generalization to other settings in and out of school.

| TABLE 13.3 | Considerations for Working with Adolescents |
|---|---|

Anticipate the likely consequences of any intervention strategy being considered.

Emphasize self-management strategies.

Stress the application of natural and logical consequences.

Use group-oriented contingencies to involve peers in a comprehensive plan for change.

Select only age-appropriate reinforcers.

Avoid response cost procedures that are likely to result in confrontations.

Collaborate with other professionals and parents in designing effective programs.

Select strategies that will not exacerbate problem situations.

This section has outlined management strategies to use with a variety of students. Table 13.3 highlights strategies especially helpful to older students.

**BEHAVIORAL INTERVENTION PLANS (BIPS)** The concept of BIPs was introduced earlier in the book for its particular relevance to students with emotional and behavioral problems. This planning process, mandated under IDEA for instances of serious behavioral concerns (e.g., guns at school, possession or sale of drugs), is built on the following principles and affords a proactive response to these significant problems. See the nearby Rights and Responsibilities feature.

# RIGHTS & RESPONSIBILITIES

## Disciplinary Issues and Federal Law

Under P.L. 94-142, relevant state statues, and IDEA, students with disabilities were protected from arbitrary suspension or expulsion in instances in which their behavioral difficulty is determined to be related to their disability. This provision was promoted as a major victory for the rights of students with disabilities because it decreased the likelihood that they could be denied a free, appropriate public education. The unforeseen side effect was that the protection of the rights of an individual came to be perceived as a potential threat to school discipline in general and to the safety and security of other students, teachers, and staff by creating a two-tiered system of discipline.

The extent of serious behavioral problems associated with students with disabilities has been a controversial issue. Nevertheless, a distinct minority of such students may present troublesome behaviors that challenge a school's ability to effectively educate all children and youth. As a result, it is not surprising that when possible amendments to the IDEA were discussed, concern was determining the balance between the rights of students with disabilities and the need for an orderly learning environment in the schools.

The legal resolution of this debate was the incorporation of a requirement for specific practices within the new regulations under P.L. 105-17 (1997 amendments to IDEA). Foremost among these were the establishment of clearer guidelines for the removal of students with disabilities from the regular school setting, the need for a functional behavioral assessment, and the establishment of a requirement for the development of a behavioral intervention plan for individual students who present challenging behaviors within the school setting. The final regulations issued in March 1999 reaffirmed the use of these procedures.

Adapted from *Behavioral Intervention Planning* (p. 27), by K. Fad, J. R. Patton, E. A. Polloway, 2000, Austin, TX: Pro-Ed. Used by permission.

## V. Behavioral Intervention Plan (BIP)

This plan provides strategies for improving the student's behavior.

| Specific Goal(s) | Proposed Intervention(s) | Person(s) Responsible | Methods | Evaluation | | | |
|---|---|---|---|---|---|---|---|
| | | | | Criterion | Schedule Date | Progress Codes: / = ongoing X = mastered D = discontinued | Code |
| 1. Casey will increase respectful language in class, including saying "yes, sir" or "yes, ma'am" when requested to do something. | 1. Contract for • positive comments • saying "yes, ma'am" or "yes, sir" • refrain from verbal threats | 1. Student Teachers Counselor | –Contract forms –Discipline referrals | 1. Respectful language 90% of time | 9/1/99 10/15/99 12/1/99 1/15/00 3/1/00 | | |
| 2. Casey will decrease verbal threats and teasing. | 2. Delay release from classroom to hallway by 5 minutes | 2. Teachers | | 2. Contract • positive comments: 5 per day • "yes" responses: 80% of time • verbal threats: fewer than 8 per 6 weeks | 4/15/00 6/1/00 | | |
| 3. Casey will decrease aggressive incidents toward peers (fighting, hitting, tripping). | 3. Continuum of responses to aggression: • Parent–Asst. Principal conference and suspension to AEP for 3 days • Go to 3 antiaggression classes • Notify probation officer | 3. Parents Assistant Principal Counselor | | 3. Aggression: No incidents in next 6 weeks | | | |

**These goals were developed with consideration of the following information:**

☐ Parent concerns regarding special circumstances: _____  ☐ Teacher/administrator concerns regarding special circumstances: _____

☑ Outside agency/professional concerns regarding special circumstances: Probation officer requires notification. _____

A detailed analysis of this federal requirement for BIPs and functional behavioral assessment is presented by Fad, Patton, and Polloway (1998/2000) and also is discussed by McConnell, Hivitz, and Cox (1998); Simpson (1998); and Zurkowski, Kelly, and Griswold (1998). The specific steps in the planning process typically include:

1. Conduct a functional behavioral assessment in which you analyze the relationship of the target behavior to environmental antecedents and consequences and you explore the purpose of the behavior.
2. Determine whether the behavior in question is directly related to the student's disability (i.e., whether the behavior is a manifestation of the disability).
3. Determine a specific goal that involves either increasing or decreasing the target behavior.
4. Develop the intervention strategy(ies) that will be used and the person(s) who will be responsible for implementation.
5. Implement the plan and evaluate its effectiveness.
6. Use information from the implementation of the intervention to revisit the assessment information as a basis for further intervention efforts.

A completed BIP is shown in Figure 13.7. Further information on the use of this BIP form is available from Fad et al. (2000).

## Instructional Dimension

All of the dimensions discussed in this chapter relate to broad concern for instructional outcomes. However, certain aspects of instruction are closely related to sound organizational and management practices, such as scheduling, transitions, grouping, and lesson planning, and can have a significant impact on quality of instruction.

*Scheduling* involves the general temporal arrangement of events for both (1) the entire day (i.e., master schedule) and (2) a specific class period. This section focuses on the latter. The importance of a carefully planned schedule cannot be overemphasized. This is particularly true in classrooms that include students with special needs.

The thoughtful scheduling of a class period can contribute greatly to the amount of time that students can spend actively engaged in learning. It can also add to the quality of what is learned. For instance, a science lesson might include the following components:

◢ Transitional activities
◢ Attention-getting and motivating techniques
◢ Data-gathering techniques
◢ Data-processing techniques
◢ Closure activities
◢ Transitional activities

*FIGURE 13.7* Behavioral Intervention Plan: Example
From *Behavioral Intervention Planning* (2nd Ed.) (p. 40), by K. Fad, J. R. Patton, & E. A. Polloway, 2000, Austin, TX: Pro-Ed.

*L*esson planning helps teachers prepare for instruction and aids in managing classrooms.

All components support the instructional goal for the day. Reminders or cues from the teacher can augment such a system. The following are some specific suggestions:

▲ Provide time reminders (visual and audible) for students during the class period so that they know how much time is available.
▲ Plan for transitions (see next section).
▲ Require students to complete one activity or task before moving on to the next.
▲ Vary the nature of class activities to keep students engaged and to create a stimulating instructional tempo and pace.
▲ Minimize noninstructional time when students are not academically engaged.

Scheduling involves planning for class period *transitions.* Efficient transitions can minimize disruptions, maximize the amount of time allocated to instructional tasks, and maintain desired conditions of learning. Structured approaches to transitions will be particularly helpful to students with special needs. Several ways to ease transitions follow:

▲ Model appropriate transitions between activities (Rosenberg et al., 1991).
▲ Let students practice appropriate transition skills.
▲ Use specific cues (e.g., blink lights, a buzzer, teacher signal) to signal students that it is time to change instructional routine.

Several other examples of strategies for transitions are listed in Table 13.4.

*Grouping* refers to how students are organized for instructional purposes. The need to place students into smaller group arrangements depends on the nature of the curricular area or the goal of a specific lesson. For students with special needs, the main concern within a group setting is attention to individual needs. Using innovative grouping arrangements and different cooperative learning opportunities allow

| TABLE 13.4 | Potential Transition Problems and Suggested Solutions |
|---|---|
| **Transition Problem** | **Suggested Solution** |
| Students talk loudly at the beginning of the day. The teacher is interrupted while checking attendance, and the start of content activities is delayed. | Establish a beginning-of-day routine, and clearly state your expectations for student behavior at the beginning of the day. |
| Students talk too much during transitions, especially after a seatwork assignment has been given but before they have begun working on it. Many students do not start their seatwork activity for several minutes. | Be sure students know what the assignment is; post it where they can easily see it. Work as a whole class on the first several seatwork exercises so that all students begin the lesson successfully and at the same time. Watch what students do during the transition, and urge them along when needed. |
| Students who go for supplemental instruction stop work early and leave the room noisily while rest of the class is working. When these students return to the room, they disturb others as they come in and take their seats. They interrupt others by asking for directions for assignments. | Have a designated signal that tells these students when they are to get ready to leave, such as a special time on the clock. Have them practice leaving and returning to the room quietly. Reward appropriate behavior. Leave special instructions for what they are to do, when they return, in a folder, on the chalkboard, or on a special sheet at their desks. Or for younger students, establish a special place and activity (e.g., the reading rug) for returning students to wait until you can give them personal attention. |
| During the last afternoon activity students quit working well before the end; they then begin playing around and leave the room in a mess. | Establish an end-of-day routine so that students continue their work until the teacher gives a signal to begin preparations to leave; then instruct students to help straighten up the room. |
| Whenever the teacher attempts to move the students from one activity into another, a number of students don't make the transition, but continue working on the preceding activity. This delays the start of the next activity or results in confusion. | Give students a few minutes' notice before an activity is scheduled to end. At the end of the activity students should put all the materials from it away and get out any needed materials for the next activity. Monitor the transition to make sure that all students complete it; do not start the next activity until students are ready. |

From *Classroom Management for Elementary Teachers* (2nd ed.) (pp. 127–128), by C. M. Evertson, E. T. Emmer, B. J. Clements, J. P. Sanford, and M. E. Worsham, 1989, Englewood Cliffs, NJ: Prentice-Hall. Used by permission.

for variety in the instructional routine for students with special needs. Some specific suggestions follow:

▲ Give careful consideration to the makeup of groups.
▲ Make sure that group composition is not constant. Vary membership as a function of having different reasons for grouping students.
▲ Use different grouping arrangements that are based on interest or for research purposes (Wood, 1996).
▲ Use cooperative learning arrangements on a regular basis, as this approach, if structured properly, facilitates successful learning and socialization.
▲ Determine the size of groups based on ability levels: the lower the ability, the smaller the size of the group (Rosenberg et al., 1991).
▲ Use mixed ability groups when cooperative learning strategies are implemented to promote the active involvement of all students.

**CROSS-REFERENCE**
See Chapter 14 for more information on using grouping strategies for students with disabilities.

*Lesson plans* help teachers prepare for instruction. Many teachers start out writing very detailed lesson plans and eventually move to less comprehensive formats. However, some teachers continue to use detailed plans throughout their teaching careers, as they find the detail helpful in providing effective instruction. Detailed planning is frequently needed for lessons that must be modified to be appropriate for gifted students or students with disabilities. Typical components include objectives, anticipatory set, materials, guided practice, independent practice, closure, options for early finishers, specific accommodations, and evaluation. Suggestions for developing lesson plans follow:

▲  Create interest in and clarify the purpose of lessons. This is particularly important for students with special needs.
▲  Consider the importance of direct instruction to help students acquire an initial grasp of new material.
▲  Assign independent practice, some of which can be accomplished in class and some of which should be done as homework.
▲  Plan activities for students who finish early. This might be particularly useful for gifted students.
▲  Anticipate problems that might arise during the course of the lesson, and identify techniques for dealing with them.

## *personal* SPOTLIGHT

### Third-Grade Teacher

Karen Weeks Canfield is a third-grade teacher. As such, she has to deal with a very heterogeneous group of children. Some children in Karen's room have identified disabilities and receive special education for part of the day, some appear to be at-risk for developing problems, and others seem to be your

**KAREN WEEKS CANFIELD**
*Lynchburg Public Schools, Lynchburg, Virginia*

"typical nine-year-old." Karen notes that "with so many types of teaching, and with parents involved in the classroom in various ways, attention to organization is critical."

Karen uses several methods to help herself stay organized. Without a certain level of organization, she believes that teaching would be an impossible task. Some of Karen's methods for staying organized include:

1. Completing forms as soon as she receives them so they do not get lost "in the shuffle"
2. Not taking part in conversations during the school day that do not benefit herself or her students in some way
3. Grading all papers the same day that they are turned in
4. Using a correspondence file for all students so she has a record of all of her communications with parents—both good communication and negative communication
5. Using a "to do" list for her planning periods

These organizational tips help Karen manage her classroom more efficiently. Without such strategies, she believes that she would have to spend a great deal of time at home doing schoolwork, which would take away time from her family.

Karen notes that "being a well-organized teacher affects not only my job performance, but the students' performance as well. The days that I am less organized are the days that the students seem to be 'crazy.' I don't think it's a coincidence. I am constantly looking for ways to make the most out of a priceless commodity—time."

## INCLUSION STRATEGIES

### Collaboration: Ways to Involve Other Personnel in Management

1. The school principal or administrator can
   - Supply any necessary equipment or materials
   - Provide flexibility in staffing patterns
   - Show support for the teacher's actions
2. The school guidance counselor can
   - Provide individual counseling sessions
   - Work with other students who may be reinforcing the inappropriate behavior of the disruptive student
   - Offer the teacher information about what may be upsetting to the student
3. The school nurse can
   - Review the student's medical history for possible causes of difficulties
   - Recommend the possibility and practicality of medical or dietary intervention
   - Explain the effects and side effects of any medication the student is taking or may take in the future

4. The school psychologist can
   - Review the teacher's behavior management plan and make recommendations for changes
   - Observe the student in the classroom and in other settings to collect behavioral data and note possible environmental instigators
   - Provide any useful data on the student that may have been recently collected, e.g., test scores, behavioral observations, etc.
5. The social worker can
   - Provide additional information about the home environment
   - Schedule regular visits to the home
   - Identify other public agencies that may be of assistance
6. Other teachers can
   - Provide curricular and behavior management suggestions that work for them
   - Offer material resources
   - Provide carryover and consistency for the tactics used

Adapted from *The Special Educator's Handbook* (p. 119), by D. L. Westling and M. A. Koorland, 1989, Boston: Allyn & Bacon. Used by permission.

## Organizational Dimension

The increased diversity in today's general education classrooms has created numerous new challenges for the teacher. Some have likened the current classroom to a "one-room schoolhouse," in which the classroom teacher must respond to the unique needs of many students. This section acknowledges how time management in the areas of personnel interactions, the work environment, administrative duties, instructional applications, and personal applications can promote success. The nearby Personal Spotlight offers one teacher's perspective.

In the typical education classroom, teachers regularly interact with special education teachers, other classroom teachers, professional support staff (e.g., speech–language pathologists, psychologists), paraeducators, teacher trainees, volunteers, and peer tutors. To enhance *personnel interactions,* teachers should consider these recommendations:

- Establish good initial working relationships with support personnel.
- Clarify the supports professional personnel are providing to students in your class. See the nearby Inclusion Strategies feature for more ideas.

**CONSIDER THIS**

How has the inclusion of students with disabilities and other special needs affected classroom management? Is teaching more difficult or about the same as a result of inclusion?

◢ Clarify the roles of these persons and the classroom teachers as collaborators for instructional and behavioral interventions.

◢ Establish the roles and responsibilities of aides, volunteers, and trainees.

◢ Determine the level of expertise of paraeducators and discuss with them specific activities that they can perform and supports they can provide to students.

◢ Delegate noninstructional (and, as appropriate, instructional) duties to classroom aides when these assistants are available.

◢ In cases in which a paraeducator accompanies a child with a disability in the general education classroom, develop a comprehensive plan with the special education teacher for involving this assistant appropriately.

The *work environment* refers to the immediate work area used by teachers—usually the desk and files. Teachers must consider how to utilize work areas and how to organize them. For instance, a teacher's desk may be designated as off-limits to all students or may be used for storage only or as a work area. Suggestions for establishing a work environment are listed here:

◢ Keep the teacher's desk organized and free of stacks of papers.

◢ Organize files so that documents and information can be retrieved easily and quickly. Use color-coded systems if possible.

Along with instructional duties, teaching includes numerous *administrative duties.* Two of the most time-demanding activities are participating in meetings and handling paperwork, including various forms of correspondence. The presence of students with special needs will increase such demands. The following are some strategies for handling paperwork:

◢ Prepare form letters for all necessary events (e.g., permissions, notifications, status reports, memo formats, reimbursement requests).

◢ Prepare master copies of various forms that are used regularly (e.g., certificates and awards, record sheets, phone conversation sheets).

◢ Keep notes of all school-related phone conversations with parents, teachers, support staff, administrators, or any other person.

◢ Handle most paperwork only once.

◢ Make the most of meetings—request an agenda and ask that meetings be time-limited and be scheduled at times that are convenient.

**TEACHING TIP**
Teachers must develop their own time management strategies; adopting strategies that are effective for other teachers may or may not be effective for you.

Some additional *instructional applications* of time-management techniques are provided here, focusing on materials and technology that can make the job of teaching easier. The most attractive piece of equipment available to teachers is the microcomputer. With the appropriate software, teachers can greatly reduce the amount of time spent on test generation, graphic organizers, IEP development, and so on. The following are some specific suggestions:

▲ Use self-correcting materials with students to reduce the amount of time required to correct student work.
▲ Use software programs for recording student scores and determining grades.
▲ Use computers to generate a variety of instructionally related materials (tests, graphic organizers, puzzles).
▲ Give students computer-generated calendars that include important dates.

Since it is impossible to completely divorce the management of one's personal time from management of professional time, it is worthwhile considering various time management tactics that have a more *personal application* but can affect one's efficiency and effectiveness in the classroom as well. Some basic recommendations are provided here:

▲ Use a daily to-do list.
▲ Break down major tasks into smaller pieces and work on them.
▲ Avoid getting overcommitted.
▲ Work during work time. This might mean avoiding situations at school in which long social conversations will cut into on-task time.
▲ Avoid dealing with trivial activities if important ones must be addressed.
▲ Use idle time (e.g., waiting in lines) well. Always be prepared for these situations by having reading material or other portable work available.

The efficient management of one's professional and personal time can pay off in making day-to-day demands less overwhelming. Thus, the efforts to become a better time manager are certainly worthwhile.

## Multicultural Considerations

Educators must always remember the multicultural issues related to classroom management. Different cultural groups expect different behaviors from their children. Methods used for disciplining children vary significantly from group to group. Expectations of the school, regarding discipline and management principles, also vary from culture to culture. The nearby Diversity Forum includes information regarding discipline and behaviors in families with Asian roots.

As schools become increasingly more diverse, teachers and other school personnel must take the time to learn about the different cultures represented in the school district. Having a better understanding of parents' expectations of the school, as well as of their children, can facilitate communication between parents and school personnel and lead to more effective behavior management programs.

# DIVERSITY FORUM  Behaviors and Punishments in Asian American Families

Observance of specific roles, relationships, and codes of conduct results in a persistent awareness of the effects of one's behavior on others. In contrast to the more egocentric individualistic orientation, Asian children are socialized to think and act in proper relation to others and must learn to transcend their personal concerns. They are obliged to be sensitive to the social environment. The parent thus effectively controls the child by modeling appropriate behaviors by appealing to the child's sense of duty or obligation. Parents may thus periodically evoke fear of personal ridicule or the prospect of family shame as a consequence of misbehavior.

Behaviors that are punished include disobedience, aggression (particularly sibling directed), and failure to fulfill one's primary responsibilities. Typical forms of discipline include the use of verbal reprimands such as scolding and shaming, which result in disgrace. The child is reminded that his or her negative behaviors reflect poorly on the entire family and family name. The child can absolve him- or herself of this "loss of face" by actively displaying changes in behavior. It is not sufficient for children to ask for forgiveness and verbally promise to do better. Actions speak louder than words. Parents may respond to more serious transgressions by either threatening or actually engaging in temporary removal of the child from the family household and/or isolating the child

from the family social life. On occasion, the use of physical punishment (e.g., spanking or paddling with a stick on the buttocks) is considered acceptable. While assuming primary responsibility for teaching the child to behave properly, the mother serves as the main disciplinarian for daily problems. The father assumes the role of implementing harsher punishment for more serious misbehavior.

In general, Asian parents who adhere to more traditional childrearing values and practices are relatively controlling, restrictive, and protective of their children. Children are taught to suppress aggressive behavior, overt expressions of negative emotions, and personal grievances; they must inhibit strong feelings and exercise self-control in order to maintain family harmony. There is a typical avoidance of frank discussion or highly verbal communication between parent and child—particularly in the area of sexuality, which is suppressed in cultures where physical contact between members of the opposite sex is minimized and public displays of affection are rare and embarrassing. The communication pattern is also one way: parent to child (the parent speaks, and the child listens).

From "Families with Asian Roots," (p. 219), by S. Chang, in *Developing Cross-Cultural Competence,* edited by E. W. Lynch and M. J. Hanson, 1992. Baltimore: Brookes. Used by permission.

# Summary

## Fundamentals of Classsroom Organization and Management

▲ Classroom management includes all teacher-directed activities that support the efficient operations of the classroom and establish optimal conditions for learning.

▲ The key elements of the classroom environment that have a significant effect on instruction and learning include multidimensionality, simultaneity, immediacy, unpredictability, publicness, and history, while the key principles of successful manage-

ment are careful planning, proactive strategies, consistency, awareness, and overlapping.

## Components of Effective Classroom Organization and Management

▲ Classroom rules provide a general sense of what is expected of students.

▲ Rules chosen should be essential for classroom functioning and for the development of a positive learning environment.

◢ Classroom procedures should include the specific ways in which certain activities or situations will be performed.

◢ Effective physical management includes classroom arrangement, accessibility, seating, and the use of specialized equipment.

◢ Desirable behaviors are increased through the use of positive reinforcement.

◢ On the other hand, undesirable behaviors can be reduced through a variety of reduction strategies.

◢ Hierarchy of options would include (from least to most restrictive) natural and logical consequences, differential reinforcement, extinction, benign tactics, reprimands, response costs, and time out.

◢ Successful educational programs help students develop self-management strategies.

◢ Instructional management includes careful attention to scheduling, transitions, grouping, and lesson plans.

◢ Successful teachers are organized and engage in the careful management of time. Technology can assist teachers in time management.

◢ Teachers need to take the student's culture into consideration when dealing with management issues.

# ◢urther Readings

Christian, B. T. (1999). *Outrageous behavior modification*. Austin, TX: Pro-Ed.

Everston, C., Emmer, E. T., & Worsham, M. E. (2000). *Classroom management for elementary teachers* (5th ed.). Boston: Allyn & Bacon.

Everston, C., Emmer, E. T., & Worsham, M. E. (2000). *Classroom management for secondary teachers* (5th ed.). Boston: Allyn & Bacon.

Fad, K. M., Patton, J. R., & Polloway, E. A. (1999). *Behavioral intervention planning*. Austin, TX: Pro-Ed.

Hammill, D. D., & Bartel, N. R. (1995). *Teaching students with learning and behavior problems*. Austin, TX: Pro-Ed.

Jones, V. F., & Jones, L. S. (1995). *Comprehensive classroom management: Creating positive learning environments for all students* (4th ed.). Boston: Allyn & Bacon.

Kaplan, J. S., & Carter, J. (1999). *Beyond behavior modification: A cognitive-behavioral approach to behavior management in the school* (3rd ed.). Austin, TX: Pro-Ed.

Koegel, L. K., Koegel, R. L., & Dunlap, G. (Eds.). (1996). *Positive behavioral support*. Baltimore: Brookes.

Lavelle, L. (1998). *Practical charts for managing behavior*. Ausitn, TX: Pro-Ed.

Levin, J., & Nolan, J. F. (2000). *Principles of classroom management* (3rd ed.). Boston: Allyn & Bacon.

Scotti, J. R., & Meyer, L. H. (Eds.). (1999). *Behavioral intervention: Principles, models, and practices*. Baltimore: Brookes.

# Chapter 14

# Teaching Students with Special Needs in Elementary Schools

*After reading this chapter, you should be able to:*

◢ Describe the impact of the inclusion movement on elementary students with disabilities

◢ Define the concept of comprehensive curriculum for students at the elementary level

◢ Identify curricular content considerations for academic, social skills, and transitional instruction

◢ Describe ways that cooperative teaching can enhance inclusion in elementary schools

◢ Identify appropriate instructional adaptations

Julie Bennington was told by one of her college professors that the elementary classrooms of the new millennium were becoming increasingly similar to the "one-room school houses of the turn of the century," encompassing a diversity of learning needs that had never been greater. Julie was excited by this challenge and, in her first year of teaching, often reflected on this comment.

Julie is teaching a class of second-graders in a self-contained arrangement. She has full responsibility for 22 eager students for all subjects except art, music, and health and physical education. She has found their diversity to be both exciting and somewhat overwhelming.

Naturally, one of her greatest concerns has been in the area of language arts. After doing some informal evaluation and after reading the records of her students, she realized during the second week of the academic year that the ability levels of her students ranged greatly; two students were virtual nonreaders, whereas five pupils were significantly above grade level.

It has become apparent to Julie that these students do not all learn in the same way, but she continues to struggle to find approaches that will meet the needs of this diverse classroom. She is fortunate to be working two hours a day during her language arts block with Alisa Ramirez, a special education teacher who is certified in learning disabilities.

## QUESTIONS TO CONSIDER

1. How can Julie and Alisa develop effective cooperative teaching strategies that will take advantage of their own talents and meet the needs of their students?

2. How can they resolve the ongoing questions about the effectiveness of holistic versus decoding approaches for beginning reading instruction for young children in general and for those with learning difficulties in particular.

3. What adaptations in the curriculum can be made to more effectively meet the needs of students with special needs in this classroom?

$A$s the opening vignette illustrates, elementary school presents both unique challenges and unique opportunities for young students with disabilities and other special needs to be included in general education. Although the learning needs of the students are frequently quite diverse and challenging, the degree of curricular differentiation (i.e., the need for alternative curricular focuses) tends to be more limited than it is at the secondary level. In elementary school, the necessity for the relative similarity of educational content for all students is at its greatest. Thus, in terms of curricular content there is an excellent opportunity for students with special needs to prosper in general education with the support of special education professionals.

Elementary school also offers an important beginning point for students with disabilities to profit from positive interactions with their nondisabled peers. Preparation for successful lives beyond the school setting requires the ability to learn, live, and work with a diversity of individuals. Thus, inclusion offers benefits both to students who are disabled and their peers. There is clearly no better time for school interaction to commence than in early childhood and throughout the primary and elementary grades.

**CONSIDER THIS**

Inclusive classrooms are more common at the elementary than secondary level. Why do you think this is true?

The advent of the inclusion movement has increased the likelihood that many students with disabilities will receive a significant portion, or all, of their instruction in the general education classroom. According to the *20th Annual Report to Congress,* 79.14% of all students with disabilities (ages 6–11) were served in general education–based programs (i.e., general education classes and/or resource rooms) during 1995–1996. As Table 14.1 indicates, this reflects a clear trend (U.S. Department of Education, 1998). Thus, beginning at the elementary level, careful attention must be given to these students' educational needs.

This chapter provides an overview of curricular and instructional accommodations for elementary-age students with special needs in inclusive settings. The initial section outlines core curriculum considerations. The discussion that follows emphasizes instructional accommodations and modifications that provide the means for achieving curricular goals.

| TABLE 14.1 | Placement Trends for Students with Disabilities (Ages 6–11) | | | |
| --- | --- | --- | --- | --- |
| | Regular Classroom (%) | Resource Room (%) | Special Class (%) | Other Settings (%) |
| 1988–1989 | 41.02 | 34.17 | 20.48 | 4.33 |
| 1989–1990 | 41.98 | 33.51 | 20.74 | 3.77 |
| 1991–1992 | 45.91 | 30.98 | 19.79 | 3.32 |
| 1992–1993 | 49.76 | 26.38 | 20.45 | 3.41 |
| 1994–1995 | 54.40 | 24.27 | 18.96 | 2.38 |
| 1995–1996 | 55.03 | 24.11 | 18.48 | 2.36 |

From U.S. Department of Education, 1991, 1994, 1995, 1997, Washington, D.C.: Author.

## GENERAL CURRICULAR CONSIDERATIONS

**C**urriculum has been defined in varied ways. Hoover (1988) describes it as the planned learning experiences that have intended educational outcomes. Armstrong (1990) refers to it as a "master plan for selecting content and organizing learning experiences for the purpose of changing and developing learners' behaviors and insights" (p. 4). For all students, any consideration of curriculum should include an outcomes orientation; our working definition of curriculum thus embraces the preparation of students for life after the completion of K–12 schooling.

Although curriculum design often is preordained in some general education programs, it is nevertheless important to consider the concept of *comprehensive curriculum*. It takes into account the reality that students are enrolled in school on a time-limited basis. Educators must consider what will happen to their students in the future and take into account the environments that students will need to adapt to in order to function successfully. Thus, curriculum design should be predicated on a focus on these **subsequent environments** (e.g., high school, college, community) (Polloway, Patton, Smith, & Roderique, 1992). The degree to which this subsequent environments attitude permeates general education will significantly affect the ultimate success of students with disabilities taught in such settings.

An elementary-level comprehensive curriculum reflects the following qualities:

- ◢ Responsive to the needs of the individual at the current time
- ◢ Reflective of the need to balance maximum interaction with peers against critical curricular needs
- ◢ Derived from a realistic appraisal of potential long-term outcomes for individual students
- ◢ Consistent with relevant forthcoming transitional needs (e.g., transition from elementary to middle school) (adapted from Polloway, Patton, Epstein, & Smith, 1989)

As mentioned before, the curricular needs of the vast majority of students at the elementary level, both those with and without special needs, are quite consistent. Thus, with appropriate modification in instruction and with collaborative arrangements, most students' needs can be met to a significant extent in the general education classroom.

IDEA, as noted earlier, requires schools to provide students with disabilities with a free, appropriate public education. Schools are not required to provide the *best* education for students, only an education that is *appropriate*. Modifications in instruction and curriculum necessary to provide a student with an appropriate education, therefore, would be required by IDEA. (See the nearby Rights and Responsibilities feature.)

## CURRICULAR CONTENT

### Academic Instruction

Elementary students in general, and certainly most students with disabilities, primarily need sound instruction in reading, writing, and mathematics to maximize their academic achievement. These needs can typically be met by a developmental approach to instruction, supplemented as needed by a remedial focus. In the sections that follow, an overview of principles and practices is provided.

**CURRICULUM** is the planned learning experience with intended educational outcomes.

**SUBSEQUENT ENVIRONMENTS** are the environments students will encounter after they complete school.

**CONSIDER THIS**
Although general educators can rarely offer a truly "comprehensive curriculum," collaborative efforts with special educators can effect a more broad-based program. How can this work?

editing, and sharing their own writing; and finally reading and writing activities that involve a content area theme such as science or social studies. (p. 241)

Whole language programs rely on authentic reading sources (e.g., literature) as the main source of content for reading opportunities. Literature (e.g., novels, stories, magazine articles) has the following advantages: it is varied; it is current, since it reaches the market quickly; it provides a basis for meeting diverse student needs and interests; and it offers alternative views on topics and issues as well as opportunities to study them in depth. In addition, with the broad spectrum of choices in literature, students can be given more opportunity to select their own reading material (Mandlebaum, Lightbourne, & VardenBrock, 1994).

While holistic programs remain popular, questions have arisen in the late 1990s about their use, particularly with students who are at risk or have identified disabilities. Mastropieri and Scruggs (1997) point to the issue of validation:

> Although position statements advocating for whole language instruction for students with learning disabilities have been available for many years. . . , experimental or quasi-experimental research directly comparing whole language with more skill-based approaches is apparently unavailable. . . . In part, experimental research is lacking because of the position taken by many advocates of whole language that traditional, quantitative research, including quantitative measures of reading achievement, is not valid. However, qualitative research to date has failed to demonstrate the superiority of whole language methods in facilitating reading comprehension of students with learning disabilities over direct, skill-based teaching. . . .
>
> Until more empirical evidence validating whole language practices with students with learning disabilities becomes available, however, teachers should be advised to proceed with caution. Nevertheless, some aspects of whole language, such as students making choices about their reading, having time for private reading, and taking ownership for their own learning, appear positive. Future research combining the positive aspects of whole language with effective instructional procedures when appropriate might help determine the ultimate benefits of whole language. (pp. 208–209)

The emphasis on meaning which is inherent in holistic approaches takes on greater emphasis as students move through the elementary grades. Comprehension thus becomes "arguably, the most important academic skill learned in school" (Mastropieri & Scruggs, 1997, p. 197).

**READING PERSPECTIVES**    These three methods can each enhance the inclusion of students with disabilities in general academic programs. However, teachers must review progress on a regular basis and make modifications as needed, because it is unlikely that a single program can meet all of a student's needs. Mather (1992) presents an excellent review of issues surrounding both whole language and the decoding emphasis of direct instruction programs. Her review of the literature argues persuasively that students who are not good readers need specific skill instruction to achieve satisfactory progress. The challenge for classroom teachers is to balance the needs of able readers (for whom explicit instruction in phonics may prove unnecessary and for whom meaning-based instruction is clearly most appropriate) with the needs of students who require more systematic instruction to unlock the alphabetic relationships within our written language.

The arguments parried between these two general approaches reflect the concerns revised by Durden (1995) about the absence of a "middle ground" in education. As he notes,

> Dualistic, mutually exclusive thinking permeates education in this country. A pervasive set of educational either/ors (e.g., ability grouping vs. cooperative learning, phonics vs. whole language, "exclusion" vs. full inclusion, and homogeneous grouping vs. heterogeneous grouping) is involved, and the potential harm both to educators and students is immense.
>
> Teachers are asked daily by theoreticians and their supporters in professional associations and the public at large to make choices between polar opposites. They are deprived of a reflective professionalism. Each pole of their choice range is championed as a solution for an astonishing and dissimilar array of education problems. (p. 47)

Inclusion presents a complex challenge in the area of curriculum design. Teachers who rigidly adhere to one position in the controversy concerning reading instruction may inadvertently neglect the learning needs of individual children who experience difficulties in school. Outstanding teachers draw eclectically from a variety of approaches to design reading programs (Pressley & Rankin, 1994).

One program for elementary reading instruction developed by Englert, Mariage, Garmon, and Tarrant (1998) illustrates how an approach that blends holistic and skills-based reading can be established within the context of effective instructional principles. Their Early Literacy Project has been used effectively with students with special needs in inclusive classrooms and involves a combination of instructional activities. Table 14.2 summarizes these elements.

**MATHEMATICS**   Mathematics represents another challenging area for students with disabilities. Development of both computational skills and problem-solving abilities forms the foundation of successful math instruction and learning.

*Computation.*   In the area of computation, teachers should focus first on the students' conceptual understanding of a particular skill and then on the achievement of automaticity with the skill. Cawley's (1984) interactive unit and Miller, Mercer, and Dillon's (1992) concrete/semiconcrete/abstract systems afford excellent options to the teacher (see Figure 14.1 on page 420). The interactive unit gives teachers 16 options for teaching math skills, based on four teacher input variables and four student output variables. The resulting $4 \times 4$ matrix provides a variety of instructional approaches that can be customized to assist learners who experience difficulties. The interactive unit also reflects a logical process that begins with the important emphasis on the concrete (do/do) to build concepts, moves to a semiconcrete focus (see/see) to enhance concept development, and at last arrives at the abstract (say/say, write/write), leading to automaticity (automatic responses to math facts). These emphases offer two proven benefits in the general education classroom: they have been used successfully with students with disabilities, and they offer alternative teaching strategies for nondisabled learners—a particularly significant advantage, given that math is the most common area of failure in schools.

**CONSIDER THIS**
The emphasis on meaning and the integration of the language arts make whole language approaches particularly attractive for use with students with special needs. Why do you think this is effective?

| TABLE 14.2 | Early Literacy Project | |
|---|---|---|
| **Activity** | **Description** | **Purpose** |
| THEMATIC UNIT | ■ Teacher and students brainstorm, organize, write drafts, read texts, or interview people to get additional information about a topic or theme from multiple sources<br>■ Students use reading/writing strategies flexibly to develop and communicate their knowledge<br>■ Theme is used as basis for selecting expository and narrative texts, and to organize and relate all activities<br>■ Reading and writing are continuously connected as students participate in discussions and read for information as a basis for writing, comprehending and responding to texts | Model learning-to-learn strategies; introduce language, genres, and strategies; model reading/writing processes and connections; provide interrelated and meaningful contexts for acquisition and application of literacy knowledge; conventionalize and develop shared knowledge about the purpose, meaning, and self-regulation of literacy acts |
| CHORAL READING | ■ Teachers and students chorally read poems, predictable books, class stories, literature, student-authored texts<br>■ Teachers model and teach a number of reading strategies, including predicting, organizing, summarizing, asking questions, rereading, locating information, and clarifying meaning | Develop word recognition, phonic skills, context clues, and voice-print match<br><br>Provide experience reading whole texts and talking about literature<br><br>Develop literacy success immediately<br><br>Develop comprehension and personal response to texts |
| UNDISTURBED SILENT READING | Students engage in reading under several conditions:<br>■ Reading alone<br>■ Reading to an adult or peer<br>■ Listening to new story at listening center | Develop fluency; provide practice in preparation for author's chair; provide experience with varied genres; read texts related to thematic unit<br><br>Students ask and answer questions; prepare to make comments about or interpretations of the stories |
| PARTNER READING/WRITING | ■ Students read books or poems; or write stories with partner or small group<br>■ Students listen to taped stories with partner<br>■ Students make personal responses to texts, complete story maps, or construct maps with partners that will be shared with whole class | Work on fluency for author's chair; provide opportunities for students to fluently read and write connected texts; provide opportunities for students to use literacy language and knowledge; develop reading/writing vocabulary and enjoyment of reading |
| SHARING CHAIR | ■ Students share books, poems, or their own personal writing<br>■ Students control discourse and support each other<br>■ Students ask questions, answer questions and act as informants to peers and teacher | Promote reading/writing connection; empower students as members of the community; allow students to make public their literacy knowledge and performance and develop shared knowledge; develop students' notions of 'community' |

From "Accelerating Reading Progress in Early Literacy Project Classrooms: Three Exploratory Studies," by C. S. Englert, T. B. Mariage, M. A. Garman, and K. L. Tarrant, 1998, *Remedial and Special Education, 19,* pp. 144–145. Used by permission.

| Activity | Description | Purpose |
|---|---|---|
| **MORNING NEWS** | ■ Students dictate personal-experience stories for newspaper publication—group composition of story <br> ■ Teacher acts as a scribe in recording ideas and as a coach in modeling, guiding, and prompting literacy strategies in text composition and comprehension <br> ■ Students interact with authors to ask questions which elicit information from that author in order to shape and edit the language and content of the news story | Model and conventionalize writing and self-monitoring strategies; demonstrate writing conventions and skills; provide additional reading and comprehension experiences; make connections between oral and written texts; promote sense of community; empower students; provide meaningful and purposeful contexts for literacy strategies |
| **STORY RESPONSE/ DISCUSSION** | ■ Students read narrative stories and respond to them in various ways (e.g., sequence or illustrate story events, map story events or information, summarize story, make personal response, etc.) <br> ■ Students work with partners or small groups to develop response | Promote students' application of literacy strategies; present varied genres to students; promote students' ownership of the discourse about texts; further students' enjoyment of texts; make text structures visible to students |
| **JOURNAL WRITING** | ■ Students write entries in a journal <br> ■ Teachers may assign topic related to thematic unit which requires students to write, or they may ask students to write freely about any self-selected topic <br> ■ Teacher reads and responds to journal, or asks students to share journal entry in sharing chair | Promote writing fluency; provide opportunities for students to write varied genres and about personal topics; provide an opportunity for students to write stories that they can share with other members of the classroom during sharing chair; provide specific occasions for students to experience and develop specific writing strategies (e.g., generate written retellings about a narrative or expository text) |
| **AUTHOR'S CENTER** | ■ Process writing approach (students plan, organize, gather information from sources, draft, edit, and publish texts) <br> ■ Students write and work collaboratively to brainstorm ideas, gather additional information from texts, write drafts, share drafts, receive questions, and write final draft <br> ■ Students use literacy and learning-to-learn strategies modeled in thematic center | Develop sense of community; develop shared knowledge; provide opportunities for students to rehearse literacy strategies; empower students in the appropriation and transformation of strategies |
| **PROJECT READ** | ■ Sound–symbol correspondences are emphasized <br> ■ Students are taught how to perform phonemic segmentation and sound blending in order to read and spell words <br> ■ Students learn "red words" which represent sight words that are not phonetically regular | Develop basic skills for recognizing and spelling printed words |

**FIGURE 14.1** Interactive Unit Model

| Group A: Geometry (8 students) | Group B: Fractions (10 students) | Group C: Addition (5 students) |
|---|---|---|
| **15 minutes** | | |
| Manipulate/Manipulate* | Display/Write | Write/Write |
| *Input:* | *Input:* | *Input:* |
| Teacher walks the perimeter of a geometric shape. | Write the fraction that names the shaded part. | $\begin{array}{r} 3 \\ +2 \\ \hline \end{array}$ |
| | | Write the answer. |
| *Output:* | *Output:* | *Output:* |
| Learner does the same. | Learner writes | Learner writes |
| | $\frac{1}{2}$ | 5 |
| **15 minutes** | | |
| Display/Identify | Manipulate/Say* | Display/Write |
| *Input:* | *Input:* | *Input:* |
| From the choices, mark the shape that is the same as the first shape. | Teacher removes portion of shape and asks learner to name the part. | Write the number there is in all. |
| *Output:* | *Output:* | *Output:* |
| Learner marks | Learner says, | Learner writes |
| | "One fourth" | 5 |
| **15 minutes** | | |
| Write/Identify | Write/Write | Say/Say* |
| *Input:* | *Input:* | *Input:* |
| Circle [shapes] Mark the shape that shows the word. | one half — Write this word statement as a numeral. | Teacher says, "I am going to say some addition items. Six plus six. Tell me the answer." |
| *Output:* | *Output:* | *Output:* |
| Learner marks | Learner writes | Learner says, |
| Circle [shapes] | $\frac{1}{2}$ | "Twelve" |

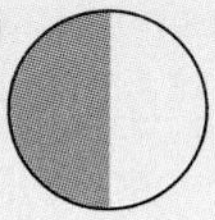

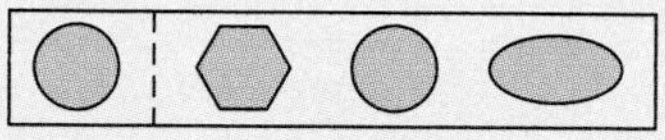

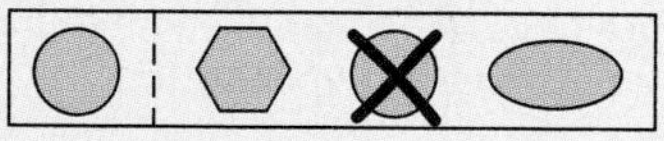

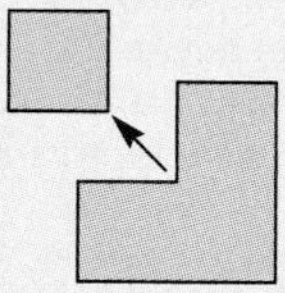

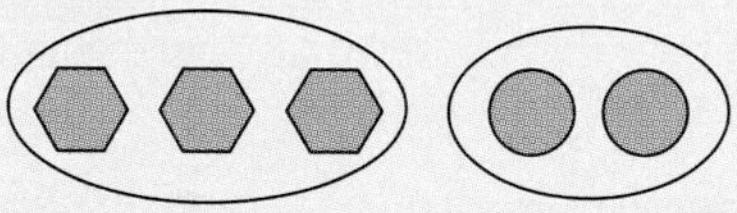

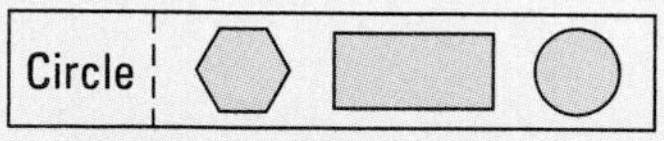

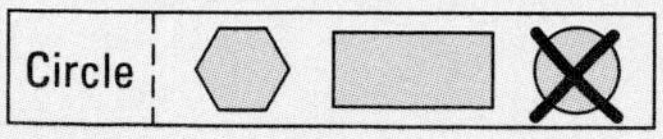

*Teacher present in group

From *Developmental Teaching of Mathematics for the Learning Disabled* (p. 246), by J. F. Cawley (Ed.), 1984, Austin, TX: Pro-Ed. Copyright 1984 by Pro-Ed, Inc. Used by permission.

| S | **SAY** | the problem to yourself (repeat). |
|---|---------|-----------------------------------|
| O | **OMIT** | any unnecessary information from the problem. |
| L | **LISTEN** | for key vocabulary indicators. |
| V | **VOCABULARY** | Change vocabulary to math concepts. |
| E | **EQUATION** | Translate problem into a math equation. |
| I | **INDICATE** | the answer. |
| T | **TRANSLATE** | the answer back into the context of the word problem. |

**FIGURE 14.2**
Problem-Solving Strategy for Mathematics

From *Strategies for Teaching Learners with Special Needs* (7th ed.) (p. 328), by E. A. Polloway, J. R. Patton, and L. Serna, 2001, Columbus, OH: Merrill. Used by permission.

*Problem Solving.*    Problem solving can be particularly difficult for students with disabilities and thus warrants special attention. For learners with special needs, and for many other students as well, instruction in specific problem-solving strategies can greatly enhance math understanding. After a strategy has been selected or designed, the strategy's steps should be taught and followed systematically so that students learn to reason through problems and understand problem-solving processes. One such example is the SOLVE-IT strategy (see Figure 14.2). The use of learning strategies in general and their value for students with and without disabilities are discussed further in Chapter 15.

The potential benefits of including students with special needs in general education classrooms to study core academic areas also extend to other academic areas. Subjects such as science, social studies, health and family life, and the arts offer excellent opportunities for social integration, while effective instructional strategies can lead to academic achievement. These subjects also lend themselves well to integrated curricular approaches (discussed later in the chapter). **Cooperative teaching** (discussed later in the chapter) presents an excellent instructional alternative in these areas because it combines the expertise and resources of the classroom teacher with the special talents of the special education teacher, rather than requiring them each to develop separate curricula in these areas.

*COOPERATIVE TEACHING* is the collaborative teaching efforts of general classroom teachers and special education teachers.

## Social Skills Instruction

Virtually all students identified with mental retardation or emotional and behavioral disorders, and many with learning disabilities, need instruction in the area of **social skills** (Cullinan & Epstein, 1985). The challenge for classroom teachers is to find ways to incorporate this focus in their classes. Seeking assistance from a special education teacher or a counselor is a good idea. Because performance in the social domain is often predictive of success or failure in inclusive settings, the development of social skills should not be neglected. Gresham (1984) notes that students with disabilities interact infrequently and, to a large extent, negatively with their peers because many lack the social skills that would enable them to gain acceptance by their peers.

*SOCIAL SKILLS* are the skills necessary to interact with other individuals in order to be successful in one's environment.

Polloway et al. (2001) identify four approaches to educating students about appropriate social behavior: (1) direct social skills training, (2) behavioral change, (3) affective education, and (4) cognitive interventions. *Direct social skills training* focuses on attaining skills that help students overcome situations in classrooms and elsewhere that prevent assimilation. A *behavioral change* strategy typically targets a behavior that needs modification and creates a reinforcement system that will lead to a behavior change. Steps in such programs typically include selecting the target behavior, collecting baseline data, identifying reinforcers, implementing a procedure for reinforcing appropriate behaviors, and evaluating the intervention (see Chapter 13). *Affective education* typically emphasizes the relationship between self and others in the environment. The emotional, rather than only the behavioral, aspects of social adjustment figure prominently in this approach. Finally, *cognitive interventions* (see Chapter 13) have proved fruitful in effecting behavioral change and social skills acquisition; they involve teaching students to monitor their own behavior, engage in self-instruction, and design and implement their own reinforcement programs. All four programs offer significant promise for social adjustment programming in the future.

Korinek and Polloway (1993) note several key considerations related to social skills instruction for students who have difficulties in this area. First, priority should be given to skills most needed for immediate interactions in the classroom, thus enhancing the likelihood of a student's successful inclusion. Teachers can begin by teaching behaviors that will "naturally elicit desired responses from peers and adults" (Nelson, 1988, p. 21), such as sharing, smiling, asking for help, attending, taking turns, following directions, and solving problems (McConnell, 1987). These skills will promote social acceptance and can be applied across many settings.

A second consideration involves selecting a social adjustment program that promotes both social skills and *social competence*. Whereas social skills facilitate individual interpersonal interactions, social competence involves the broader ability to use skills

---

**TABLE 14.3** **Sample Social Skills Curriculum Sequence**

**SESSION I**

Listening
Meeting people—introducing self, introducing others
Beginning a conversation
Listening during a conversation
Ending a conversation
Joining an ongoing activity

**SESSION II**

Asking questions appropriately
Asking favors appropriately
Seeking help from peers and adults
Following directions

**SESSION III**

Sharing
Interpreting body language
Playing a game successfully

**SESSION IV**

Suggesting an activity to others
Working cooperatively
Offering help

**SESSION V**

Saying thank you
Giving and accepting a compliment
Rewarding self

**SESSION VI**

Apologizing
Understanding the impact your behavior has on others
Understanding others' behavior

From *Managing Attention Disorders in Children: A Guide for Practitioners* (pp. 342–343), by S. Goldstein and M. Goldstein, 1990, New York: John Wiley. Used by permission.

at the right times and places, showing social perception, cognition, and judgment of how to act in different situations (Sargent, 1991). A focus limited to specific skill training may make it difficult for the child to maintain the specific social skills or transfer them to various settings. Table 14.3 outlines a typical sequence within a social skills curriculum.

Third, a decision must be made as to who will teach social skills. Often initial instruction occurs in pull-out programs (e.g., resource rooms) with generalization plans developed for transfer to the general education classroom. However, in full inclusion classrooms, a useful strategy is the use of the complementary instructional model of cooperative teaching (see p. 427).

Finally, there is a need to consider those who have significant learning needs, as the placement of students with severe disabilities in inclusive classes has clear implications for the social environment. Research provides little assurance that the social skills of these students will develop simply because they are physically integrated into such classes. McEnvoy, Shores, Wehby, Johnson, and Fox's (1990) review of the literature reveals that the more that teachers provide specific instruction, physical props, modeling, and praise directed to the acquisition and maintenance of social skills, the more these students succeed in learning appropriate patterns of interaction.

## Transitional Needs

In addition to the academic and social components of the curriculum, career education and transition form an important emphasis even for younger children. For all elementary students, career awareness and a focus on facilitating movement between levels of schooling (i.e., vertical transitions) are curricular essentials. Figure 14.3 outlines key vertical transitions and also illustrates the concept of horizontal transitions (i.e., from more to less restrictive settings).

**TRANSITION FROM PRESCHOOL TO PRIMARY SCHOOL**  Research on students moving from preschool programs into school settings has identified variables that predict success in school. Four such variables include early academic (i.e., readiness) skills, social skills, responsiveness to instructional styles, and responsiveness to the structure of the school environment (Polloway et al., 1991). Analyzing the new school environment can help a teacher determine the skills a student will need to make this crucial adjustment.

Academic readiness skills have traditionally been cited as good predictors of success at the primary school level. Examples include the ability to recognize numbers and letters, grasp a writing utensil, count to ten, and write letters and numbers. Yet a clear delineation between academic readiness and academic skills is not warranted. Rather, to use reading as an example, it is much more productive to consider readiness as inclusive of examples of early reading skills, or what has been termed emergent literacy. Programming in this area should focus on academic activities that advance the processes of learning to read, write, or calculate.

Social skills consistent with the developmental attributes of other 5- and 6-year-olds are clearly important to success in the elementary school. It is particularly critical that students be able to function in a group. Thus, introducing small group instructional activities in preschool programs prepares students to function in future school situations.

Developing responsiveness to new instructional styles is another challenge for the young child. Since the instructional arrangement in the preschool program may

*TEACHING TIP*
Teachers should accept responsibility to prepare students for their next school-life challenge or transition (e.g., preschool to elementary school, middle school to secondary school).

*FIGURE* **14.3**

Vertical and Horizontal
Transitions

From *Transition from School to
Young Adulthood: Basic Concepts
and Recommended Practices*
(p. 2), by J. R. Patton and
C. Dunn, 1998, Austin, TX:
Pro-Ed. Used by permission.

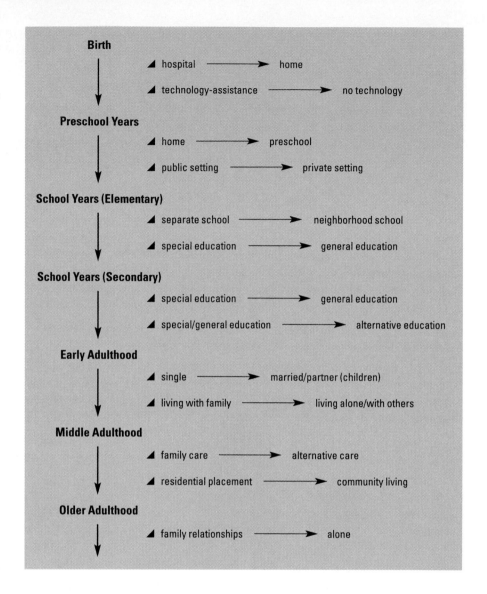

vary significantly from that of the school program, providing instructional experiences that the student can generalize to the new school setting will be helpful; some learning activities in the preschool class should approximate those of kindergarten to provide the preparation.

Responsiveness to the environment is a fourth concern. Changes may include new transportation arrangements, extended instructional time, increased expectations of individual independence, and increased class size resulting in a reduction in individual attention. Teachers may set up opportunities for the preschoolers to visit kindergarten classes to familiarize them with the future environment.

Increasingly, public schools have provided pre-kindergarten programs for young children, particularly those deemed at risk for later school difficulties. In addition, federal law requires that young children with disabilities be provided special educa-

tion programs, with the actual years of eligibility and the nature of the service delivery program determined by individual state guidelines. The discussion, herein, does not focus on the needs of preschoolers with disabilities or those at risk, but the particular discussions on areas such as listening, following directions, and cooperative learning are equally applicable for young children as they are for those at the elementary school level. For a specific focus on preschoolers with special needs, the reader is encouraged to review the discussion in Patton, Blackbourn, and Fad (1996).

**TRANSITION CURRICULAR CONSIDERATIONS**   **Career education** in general, and **life skills** education in particular, have become major emphases among secondary school teachers, especially those who work with students who have disabilities. Yet life skills concepts should also be incorporated into elementary and middle school programs (Cronin, 1988; Patton & Cronin, 1993). Table 14.4 provides a matrix of topics that may be incorporated into an elementary-level life skills curriculum. Even programs for young children should be designed to encourage positive long-term outcomes for all students.

Concepts and topics related to life skills can be integrated into existing subject areas, thus broadening the curriculum without the necessity of creating a "new subject." This can be done in three ways. The first approach, *augmentation*, uses career education–oriented materials to supplement the existing curriculum. The second approach *infuses* relevant career education topics into the lessons laid out in the existing curriculum. A third approach employs an *integrated curriculum*, similar to the unit approach traditionally used in many education programs. An integrated curriculum addresses a topic by drawing together content related to it from various academic areas, enabling students to apply academic skills across these areas. Life skills related to the broad topic can be woven into the curriculum. Using a matrix format (see Table 14.5 on pp. 428–429), reading, math, and language skills, as well as career topics and life skills, can be tied together. This curriculum can also help primary- and elementary-age students understand that different academic subjects have important interrelationships.

**CAREER EDUCATION** is an orientation that is incorporated at all levels of school that emphasizes skills and knowledge needed to be successful as an adult.

**LIFE SKILLS** are the specific skills necessary to be successful in the community as an independent person.

**TEACHING TIP**
Integrated curricular approaches also can enable gifted students to extend their learning beyond the curriculum.

**TABLE 14.4** Life Skills in the Elementary School Curriculum

| | Consumer Economics | Occupational Knowledge | Health | Community Resources | Government and Law |
|---|---|---|---|---|---|
| **READING** | Look for ads in the newspaper for toys. | Read books from library on various occupations. | Read the school lunch menu. | Find television listing in the *TV Guide*. | Read road signs and understand what they mean. |
| **WRITING** | Write prices of items to be purchased. | Write the specific tasks involved in performing one of the classroom jobs. | Keep a diary of food you eat in each food group each day. | Complete an application to play on a Little League team. | Write a letter to the mayor inviting him/her to visit your school. |
| **SPEAKING, WRITING, VIEWING** | Listen to bank official talk about savings accounts. | Call newspaper in town to inquire about delivering papers in your neighborhood. | View a film on brushing teeth. | Practice the use of the 911 emergency number. | Discuss park playground improvements with the mayor. |
| **PROBLEM SOLVING** | Decide if you have enough coins to make a purchase from a vending machine. | Decide which job in the classroom you do best. | Role-play what you should do if you have a stomachache. | Role-play the times you would use the 911 emergency number. | Find the city hall on the map. Decide whether you will walk or drive to it. |
| **INTERPERSONAL RELATIONS** | Ask for help finding items in a grocery store. | Ask a student in the class to assist you with a classroom job. | Ask the school nurse how to take care of mosquito bites. | Call the movie theater and ask the show times of a movie. | Role-play being lost and asking a police officer for help. |
| **COMPUTATION** | Compute the cost of a box of cereal with a discount coupon. | Calculate how much you would make on a paper route at $3 per hour for 5 hours per week. | Compute the price of one tube of toothpaste if they are on sale at 3 for $1. | Compute the complete cost of going to the movie (admission, food, transportation). | Compute tax on a candy bar. |

From "Curricular Considerations: A Life Skills Orientation" (p. 31), by J. R. Patton, M. E. Cronin, E. A. Polloway, D. R. Hutchison, and G. A. Robinson, in *Best Practices in Mild Mental Retardation*, edited by G. A. Robinson, J. R. Patton, E. A. Polloway, and L. Sargent, 1989. Reston, VA: CEC-MR. Used by permission.

**TRANSITION TO MIDDLE SCHOOL** Elementary students with disabilities need to be prepared for movement to middle school or junior high school. To make this vertical transition successfully, students need an organized approach to their work, time management and study skills, note-taking strategies, homework strategies, and the ability to use lockers. Robinson, Braxdale, and Colson (1988) observe that the new behavior demands faced by students in junior high school fall into three categories: academic skills, self-management and study skills, and social–adaptive skills. Problems in any of these three areas may cause significant difficulties for students.

Wenz-Gross and Siperstein (1998) focused on transitional issues relative to students' success at the middle school level. They concluded that interventions for students in middle school should emphasize developing coping skills for academic demands, peer stress, and relationships with teachers. Helping students develop time management and organizational skills should also be a focus. To do this, teachers and parents should help these students prioritize multiple tasks and integrate and master the information needed at the middle school level.

Students need to strengthen interpersonal skills so that they can build more positive peer relationships. To assist students in these areas, schools should start before middle school and add emphasis in this area in middle school, when peer relationships become so important. Students also need to be empowered to better deal with the problems experienced by adolescence.

Consistent with this research, Alber, Heward, and Hippler (1999) stress that one key concern, particularly at the middle school level, is for students to learn how to recruit positive attention from teachers by learning how and when to, for example, ask for help and solicit feedback.

A variety of instructional strategies may assist in the transition process: having middle school faculty visit elementary classes to discuss programs and expectations, viewing videotaped middle school classes, and taking field trips to the middle school to get a sense of the physical layout, the changing of classes, and environmental and pedagogical factors (Jaquish & Stella, 1986). Cooperative planning and follow-up between both general and special education teachers at the two school levels will smooth the transition.

**COMMUNITY-BASED INSTRUCTION** In developing life skills and facilitating transition, community-based instruction can benefit all students but is particularly effective for students with disabilities, as it addresses common problems in applying academic learning to life outside the classroom. Field trips to stores to make purchases, to observe work patterns, and to learn about advertising and marketing techniques can be supplemented by bringing community members into the classroom to speak about careers or demonstrate life skills. Community-based instruction affords teachers ways to enhance the relevance and meaningfulness of the curriculum while providing excellent opportunities for generalization training.

## COOPERATIVE TEACHING

Cooperative, or collaborative, teaching can be defined as

> a restructuring of teaching procedures in which two or more educators possessing distinct sets of skills work in a coactive and coordinated fashion to jointly teach academically and behaviorally heterogeneous groups of students in educationally integrated settings, that is, in general [education] classrooms. (Bauwens & Hourcade, 1995, p. 46)

| TABLE 14.5 | Integrated Curriculum | | |

| SCIENCE SUBTOPICS | Science Activities | Math | Social Studies |
|---|---|---|---|
| INTRODUCTORY LESSON | ■ Attraction of ants<br>■ Collection<br>■ Observation<br>■ Research ant anatomy | ■ Measurement of distance traveled as a function of time | ■ Relationship of population demographics for ants and humans |
| ANT FARMS | ■ Individual set-ups<br>■ Daily observation<br>■ Development of collection procedures | ■ Linear measurement<br>■ Frequency counts | ■ Roles in the community<br>■ Relationship to human situations |
| FOOD PREFERENCES CHART | ■ Research and predict<br>■ Construct apparatus for determining preference<br>■ Design data collection procedures<br>■ Collect/record data<br>■ Experiment with food substance positions | ■ Frequency counts<br>■ Graphs of daily results | ■ Discussion of human food preferences<br>■ Cultural differences |
| ANT RACES | ■ Conduct races with and without food<br>■ Data collection<br>■ Predictive activities | ■ Temporal measurement<br>■ Averages | ■ History of racing<br>■ Sports and competition |
| CLOSING | ■ Analyze information | ■ Tabulate data | |

From "Integrated Curriculum," by J. C. Kataoka and J. R. Patton, *Science and Children, 16,* pp. 52–58. Reprinted with permission from NSTA Publications, copyright 1989 from *Science and Children,* National Science Teachers Association, 1840 Wilson Boulevard, Arlington, VA 22201-3000.

Cooperative teaching is a logical outgrowth of collaborative efforts between teachers that include consultative arrangements, additional help given by special education teachers to children not identified as eligible for special services, and the sharing of teaching assistants, especially to accompany students who are disabled in the general education classroom. It has particular relevance at the primary and elementary school levels because, as noted earlier, curricular needs for students with and without disabilities tend to be most congruent at these levels.

Cooperative teaching involves a team approach to supporting students within the general classroom, combining the content expertise of the classroom teacher with the pedagogical skills of the special education teacher.

Cooperative teaching also is essential to implementing the prereferral interventions discussed in Chapter 2; it can prevent or correct the learning problems of all stu-

**RELATED SUBJECT/SKILL AREAS**

| Arts | Computer Application | Life Skills | Language Arts |
|---|---|---|---|
| ■ Drawings of ant anatomy<br>■ Ant mobiles<br>■ Creative exploration | ■ Graphic drawings of ants | ■ Picnic planning<br>■ Food storage and protection | ■ Oral sharing of observations |
| ■ Diagram of farm<br>■ Diorama<br>■ Ant models<br>■ Role-playing of ant behavior | ■ Spreadsheets for calculations<br>■ Graphing<br>■ Database storing observations | ■ Relate to engineers, architects, sociologists, geographers | ■ Library skills<br>■ Creative writing<br>■ Spelling<br>■ Research involving note taking, outlining, and reading<br>■ Vocabulary development<br>■ Oral reports |
| ■ Design data collection forms<br>■ Role-play ant eating behavior | | ■ Graphic designer<br>■ Food services<br>■ Researchers | |
| ■ Film making<br>■ Rewrite lyrics to "The Ants Go Marching In" based on activities | ■ Graphic animation | ■ Athletics<br>■ Coaches | |
| ■ Finalize visual aids | ■ Printout | ■ Guest speakers | ■ Presentation |

dents while effecting the remediation of identified deficits for students with disabilities. Perhaps the best vehicle for attaining successful inclusion, it truly provides **supported education,** the school-based equivalent of supported work in which students are placed in the least restrictive environment and provided the necessary support (e.g., by the special educator) to be successful.

*SUPPORTED EDUCATION* is the provision of educational services for students that meet their specific learning needs.

## Cooperative Teaching Arrangements

Although cooperative teaching can be implemented in many ways, it basically involves collaboration between special and general education teachers in the environment of the general education classroom, typically for several periods per day. Bauwens, Hourcade, and Friend (1989) discuss three distinct yet related forms of cooperative teaching: complementary instruction, team teaching, and supportive learning activities. These options and the work of Vaughn, Schumm, and Arguelles (1997) outline a mosaic for designing effective programs. Further, they foster strategies that are more effective than simply engaging in what Vaughn et al. (1997) refer to as "grazing" (unstructured roaming around to monitor work) or "tag team teaching" (taking turns being active/passive instructors).

## *personal* SPOTLIGHT

### Teacher Educator

Over the past 23 years, Val Sharpe has taught in many educational settings. She notes: "It is the ongoing process of change in order to meet the needs of students with disabilities that has afforded me the opportunity for diversification as an educator." Val is a teacher educator and, with Dr. Roberta Strosnider, at Hood College has developed a "hands-on" approach to teaching special education methods courses in a professional development school setting (PDS).

**VAL SHARPE**
*Hood College,*
*Frederick, MD*

During the teacher training process, the future special educator is exposed to a variety of learning theories, adaptations, and modifications designed to facilitate instruction and enhance concept mastery. Within the confines of the professional development school, the student is provided with multiple opportunities to practice these theories, adaptations, and modifications with children in the classroom setting. Initially, Val and Roberta teach a concept through modeling and incorporating the necessary adaptations and strategies that facilitate learning. The next step is for the student to practice teach this concept to other future educators. Once the student acquires mastery of the concept, the student teaches this concept to children. This is the stage when the future educator is introduced to the collaborative process.

In teaching the collaborative process, Val feels it necessary for future educators to be afforded the opportunity to become acquainted with this process through the implementation of various reality-based activities. After teaching the prerequisite skills and successful ingredients involved in the collaborative process, Val has her students actively participate in this process using the following vehicles:

1. Students become knowlegeable about a variety of learning theories, adaptations, and modifications and their implementation.
2. These students complete a collaborative worksheet.
3. Students are given an assignment to teach a science lesson to a group of children within an inclusive classroom setting. Using the collaboration process, decisions are made regarding appropriate topics for the lesson, as well as the necessary adaptations and modifications needed to facilitate the learning process. Via the collaborative process, the students then decide upon the lesson topic and develop a lesson plan. The lesson is then taught to the children. The implemented lesson is evaluated by the children, the students, the PDS teachers, and Val.
4. Students then reflect upon this venture by referring back to their collaborative worksheet as well as discussing this experience with their classmates.

Throughout their student teaching practicum, Val and Roberta enable their students to utilize the collaborative process. These future educators are required to collaborate with parents in the form of a conference; collaborate with general education and special education teachers with regard to lesson development and implementation; collaborate with administrators in terms of scheduling and school policy; and collaborate with the multidisciplinary team in developing an IEP.

This hands-on approach to the collaborative process enables the future teacher to practice this process in a variety of settings. It is beneficial because it helps them make connections about the collaborative process. This approach to teaching about collaboration incorporates the elements of good instructional practices through the use of modeling, repetition, guided practice, independent practice, and reflection. Future special educators become familiar with the collaborative process and become comfortable using this process.

*Complementary instruction* involves teaching students the skills related to success in learning. Bauwens and Hourcade (1995) define these as thinking skills (i.e., processing information cognitively), learning skills (e.g., study skills, learning strategies), and acting skills (i.e., social behaviors related to school success). One teacher, typically the special education teacher, can provide instruction on these skills to complement the content instruction taught by the partner teacher. In this example, the two teachers can work collaboratively to ensure that information is presented clearly and that learning is facilitated. For example, in social studies, the general education teacher might be teaching a lesson on the Kennedy Administration while the special education teacher may be providing specific examples of personal perspectives on "Camelot" and the spirit of the early 1960s. The nearby Personal Spotlight feature describes how to help new teachers learn how to collaborate with other professionals.

In *team teaching,* the general and special education teachers plan one lesson jointly and teach it to all students, both with and without disabilities. Each teacher may take responsibility for one aspect of the teaching. Vaughn et al. (1997) refer to this as "teaching on purpose" in which one teacher has responsibility for the larger group while the other teacher provides short (e.g., two-minute or five-minute lessons) to a small group, student pairs, or individual students such as to provide a follow-up to previous instruction or checks for understanding by the students.

Another option is one described by Vaughn et al. (1997) in which the two teachers teach the same content to two smaller groups. The intent of this arrangement is to provide further opportunities for students to be actively involved in the instruction, to respond to the teacher and peers, and to have their responses monitored by the teacher. It can serve as a wrap-up session for the larger group instruction.

In *supportive learning activities*, the general and special educators plan and teach the lesson to the whole class. The general educator typically delivers the main content; the special educator then plans and implements activities that reinforce the learning of the content material (e.g., cooperative learning groups, tutoring, reciprocal teaching, simulations).

Figure 14.4 shows how the different types of cooperative teaching can be combined in an instructional lesson at the upper elementary level.

Wiedemeyer and Lehman (1991) have outlined key features of a collaborative instructional model, including cooperative teaching. The specific functions that can be shared by general and special education teachers are outlined in the nearby Inclusion Strategies feature.

## Special Considerations and Challenges

Cooperative teaching and supported education (a school-based equivalent of "supported employment"), have also been recommended for students with more severe disabilities as a component of a program of inclusion. Hamre-Nietupski, McDonald, and Nietupski (1992) provide a detailed discussion of how to modify programs to respond to four key challenges: providing a functional curriculum in the general education classroom, providing community-based learning opportunities, scheduling staff coverage, and promoting social integration. In particular, emphasis must be placed on developing friendships between peers with and without disabilities. Teachers can pair different students for different activities, modeling and encouraging socialization. Formal lessons can be developed that encourage students to talk about their similarities and differences.

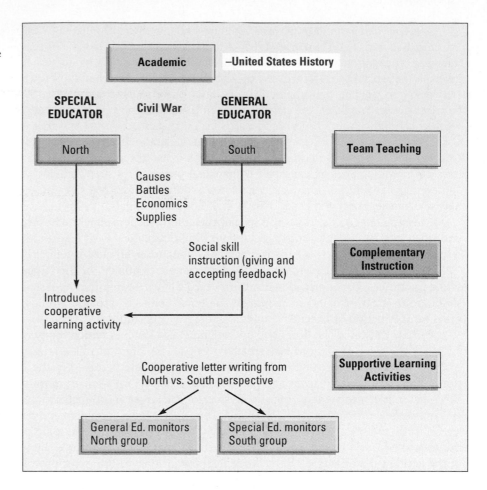

**FIGURE 14.4**

Variations of Cooperative
Teaching: U.S. History

From *Cooperative Teaching*
(p. 64), by J. Bauwens and
J. Hourcade, 1995, Austin,
TX: Pro-Ed. Used by
permission.

# INCLUSION STRATEGIES

## Collaborative Teaching Functions

1. Collaborative teaching
   A. Sharing in planning, presenting, and check-
      ing assignments
   B. Adapting curriculum to meet needs of
      those with unique learning requirements
   C. Incorporating joint input into IEPs for
      shared students
   D. Participating in parent conferences
2. Monitoring of students
   A. Checking for attending behaviors
   B. Checking for note taking and writing
      down of assignments
   C. In-class individual or small-group tutoring

   D. Supplementary note taking
   E. Checking for appropriate use of in-class
      study time
3. Developing units in social, problem-solving, or
   study skills, especially as required by students
   experiencing difficulty
4. Sharing materials and expertise in programming
5. Developing materials at a lower level
6. Providing generalization opportunities and
   activities
7. Sharing special instructional techniques and
   strategies

Adapted from "House Plan: Approach to Collaborative
Teaching and Consultation," by D. Wiedemeyer and J.
Lehman, 1991, *Teaching Exceptional Children, 23*(3), pp. 7–8.

*Team teaching involving a general classroom teacher and special education teacher works well in inclusive settings.*

Cooperative teaching is not a simple panacea for the many challenges of accommodating a broad range of students with disabilities. Bauwens et al. (1989) and Harris (1998) have identified obstacles that must be successfully overcome—time, cooperation with others, and workload—to include these students. *Time* problems can be alleviated through careful planning, regularly scheduled discussions on teaching, and support for planning periods from administrators. The issue of *cooperation* is best addressed through training in the use of cooperative teaching, experience with the process, development of guidelines specific to the program, and attention to effective communication accompanied, as needed, by conflict resolution. The concern for workload should be addressed as the team relationship develops, delegating tasks in a way that allows each individual to focus on areas of expertise and interests. Evaluation should be a component of the workload as well.

A final critical issue regarding cooperative teaching is *voluntary involvement*. Setting up cooperative teaching arrangements by decree, without regard to input from the teachers themselves, will not set the stage for success for teachers or ultimately for the students. Teachers should be given some choice and flexibility—for example, allowing general and special education teachers to select partners with whom to collaborate has worked well.

Cooperative teaching is but one structural change in the traditional elementary classroom that can facilitate the successful inclusion of students with disabilities. The following practices have been identified by the National Center on Educational Restructuring and Inclusion as enhancing inclusive education:

▲ *Multilevel instruction* allows for different kinds of learning within the same curriculum. Here the focus is on key concepts to be taught, alternatives in presentation methods, acceptance of varying types of student activities and multiple outcomes, different ways in which students can express their learning, and diverse evaluation procedures.

◢ *Cooperative learning* involves heterogeneous groupings of students, allowing for students with a wide variety of skills and traits to work together. Models of cooperative learning differ in the amount of emphasis given to the process of the group's work and to assessing outcomes for individual members as well as for the team as a whole.

◢ *Activity-based learning* emphasizes learning in natural settings, the production of actual work products, and performance assessment. It moves learning from being solely classroom-based to preparing students to learn in community settings.

◢ *Mastery learning* specifies what a student needs to learn and then provides sufficient practice opportunities to gain mastery.

◢ *Technology* is often mentioned as being a support for students and teachers. Uses include record keeping, assistive devices such as reading machines and braille-to-print typewriters, and drill and instructional programs.

◢ *Peer support and tutoring programs* have multiple advantages. Placing students in instructional roles enhances the teaching resources of the school. It recognizes that some students learn by teaching others.

Several of these examples are discussed later in the chapter.

## INSTRUCTIONAL ADAPTATIONS

Adaptations made to instructional programs in the general education classroom form the keys to successful inclusion. As the traditional adage goes, special education is not necessarily special, it is just *good teaching*. "Good teaching" often means making appropriate modifications and accommodations. Assuming the curricular content is appropriate for individual students who have disabilities, the challenge is to adapt it to facilitate learning.

It is useful to have a common set of definitions to build upon in discussing classroom adaptations. Polloway, Bursuck, and Epstein (1999) provide the following guidance:

> *Accommodations* refer to changes in input and output processes in teaching and assessment such as: the format of instructional presentations, and test practice and/or preparation activities . . . (Adams, 1997). The concept of *modifications* refers to changes in content and/or standards. In curricular areas, modifications could involve changes in content and/or skill expectations for different groups of students. . . . As a general pattern, we have found that teachers report a greater willingness to consider accommodations . . . while they express more reluctance to consider modifications . . . (p. 31).

In inclusive programs, instruction must be adapted to ensure that all students learn successfully. As Fuchs, Fuchs, Hamlett, Phillips, and Karns (1995) note:

> General education's capacity to incorporate meaningful adaptation has become a critical issue during the past decade, as the rhetoric of the . . . inclusive schools movement has increased pressure to provide educational programs to students with disabilities in general education classrooms. (p. 440)

Thus, a key component of successful inclusion is the treatment acceptability of specific interventions to accommodate the needs of students with disabilities. The term *treatment acceptability* has been used in a variety of ways. Polloway, Bursuck, Jayanthi, Epstein, and Nelson (1996) use the term in a broad sense to refer to the likelihood that certain specific classroom interventions will be acceptable to the general education teacher. Thus it may include, for example, the helpfulness, desirability, feasibility, and fairness of the intervention, as well as how other students will perceive it in a particular setting. As Witt and Elliott (1985) note, the "attractiveness" of an intervention is important: if the treatment is not deemed acceptable, it is unlikely to be implemented.

In a review of the literature on adaptations, Scott, Vitale, and Masten (1998) summarized the types of adaptations that have been researched for their effectiveness. They use the qualifier *typical* to refer to specific examples that are routine, minor, or applicable to an entire class, and *substantial* to refer to those that are tailored to the needs of individual students. Their categories (as adapted) are:

▲ *Adapting instruction:* typical (concrete classroom demonstrations, monitoring classroom understanding); substantial (adjusting the pace to individual learners, giving immediate individual feedback, using multiple modalities)
▲ *Adapting assignments:* typical (providing models); substantial (breaking tasks into small steps, shortening assignments, lowering difficulty levels)
▲ *Teaching learning skills:* typical (study skills, note-taking techniques); substantial (learning strategies, test-taking skills)
▲ *Altering instructional materials:* substantial (using alternative materials, taping textbooks, using supplementary aids)
▲ *Modifying curriculum:* substantial (lowering difficulty of course content)
▲ *Varying instructional grouping:* substantial (using peer tutoring, using cooperative groups)
▲ *Enhancing behavior:* typical (praise, offering encouragement); substantial (using behavioral contracts, using token economies, frequent parental contact)
▲ *Facilitating progress monitoring:* typical (read tests orally; give extended test-taking time; give frequent, short quizzes; provide study guides); substantial (retaking tests, obtaining direct daily measures of academic progress, modifying grading criteria) (p. 107).

In Table 14.6, the findings of Scott et al. (1998) relative to research on specific accommodations and modifications are presented.

Technology also can assist teachers in modifying the curriculum, providing additional supports for the student, and increasing instructional effectiveness. The nearby Technology Today feature (on p. 438) provides specific examples.

The specific modifications and accommodations for students with disabilities in elementary classes discussed next vary in nature and in terms of treatment acceptability. The authors do not intend to suggest that all suggestions will be appropriate or desirable in a given situation. Many of the suggested adaptations will prove beneficial to all students, not only to those with special needs.

## Enhancing Content Learning through Listening

Children will not listen simply because they are told to do so. Rather, they often need oral presentations provided in ways that promote successful listening. Students who struggle with *selective attention* (i.e., focus) or *sustained attention* (i.e., maintained over a

**TEACHING TIP**
For many students with disabilities, the skill of listening must be directly targeted if academic success is to occur in inclusive settings.

## TABLE 14.6  Representative Examples of Instructional Adaptations

| | |
|---|---|
| Munson, 1986–1987 (elementary) | 1. Simplify/supplement the curriculum<br>2. Provide concrete materials<br>3. Change papers, worksheets<br>4. Shorten assignments<br>5. Provide peers for individual instruction |
| Johnson & Pugach, 1990 (elementary) | 1. Adjust performance expectations in the student's problem area to increase the likelihood that the student will succeed<br>2. Use peer tutors, volunteers, or aides to work with student physically<br>3. Use alternative textbook or materials<br>4. Talk with school psychologist, special education teachers, counselor, or other special education personnel about ways to work on the student's academic problem<br>5. Give additional explicit oral or written instructions to the student |
| Ysseldyke, Thurlow, Wotruba, & Nania, 1990 (K–12) | 1. Alter instruction so student can experience success<br>2. Use different materials to instruct failing student<br>3. Adjust lesson pace to meet student's rate of mastery<br>4. Inform student frequently of his/her instructional needs<br>5. Use alternative methods to instruct failing student |
| Bacon & Schulz, 1991 (K–12) | 1. Use lower-level workbooks or worksheets<br>2. Provide volunteer tutor (adult)<br>3. Provide note takers<br>4. Use taped lectures<br>5. Provide hands-on activities, manipulatives |
| Schumm & Vaughn, 1991 (K–12) | 1. Establish personal relationship with mainstreamed student<br>2. Adapt daily plans<br>3. Use alternative materials<br>4. Pair with classmate<br>5. Modify long-term curriculum goals |
| Whinnery, Fuchs, & Fuchs, 1991 (1–6) | 1. Regroup students for language arts across grades into homogeneous groups<br>2. Regroup students for language arts within grades into homogeneous groups<br>3. Use resource staff in classroom for the lowest language arts groups<br>4. Establish mixed-ability student partners with low- and high-ability pairs<br>5. Cover the same basic instructional activities each day with the lowest language arts group |
| Fuchs, Fuchs, & Bishop, 1992 (elementary) | 1. Vary goals<br>2. Use alternative materials<br>3. Alter teaching activities<br>4. Vary groupings<br>5. Adjust schedule |
| Schumm & Vaugh, 1992 (K–12) | 1. Plan or make adaptations in the curriculum<br>2. Plan or make adaptations to tests<br>3. Make adaptations while the student is working |

From "Implementing Instructional Adaptations for Students with Disabilities in Inclusive Classrooms: A Literature Review," by B. J. Scott, M. R. Vitale, and W. G. Masten, 1998, *Remedial and Special Education, 19,* pp. 111–112. Used by permission.

period of time) respond more easily to speaking that supports the listener. Wallace, Cohen, and Polloway (1987, p. 75) note that listeners attend more when

- ▲ the salience of content is increased through repetition, vocal emphasis, and cuing.
- ▲ the message is meaningful, logical, and well organized.
- ▲ messages are given in short units.
- ▲ the speaker allows for listener participation in the form of clarification, feedback, or responding.

| Blanton, Blanton, & Cross, 1994 (elementary) | 1. Provide extra time for the student's reading instruction<br>2. Provide instruction for the student in smaller steps<br>3. Use computer-assisted instruction<br>4. Make use of teacher-directed reading instruction<br>5. Use peer tutors, volunteers, or aides to work with student physically |
|---|---|
| Schumm, Vaughn, & Saumell, 1994 (K–12) | 1. Preview textbook with students<br>2. Read textbook aloud to students<br>3. Write abridged versions of textbooks<br>4. Provide questions to guide reading<br>5. Model effective reading strategies |
| Polloway, Epstein, Bursuck, Jayanthi, & Cumblad, 1994 (K–12) | 1. Adjust length of assignment<br>2. Evaluate on the basis of effort, not performance<br>3. Provide extra credit opportunities<br>4. Check more frequently with student about assignments and expectations<br>5. Allow alternative response formats |
| Schumm, Vaughn, Gordon, & Rothlein, 1994 (K–12) | 1. Vary group composition (e.g., small group, large group, whole class) for mainstreamed students<br>2. Adapt daily planning for mainstreamed students<br>3. Use frequent checks with individual students to monitor the progress of mainstreamed students |
| Bender, Vail, & Scott, 1995 (elementary-middle) | 1. Suggest particular methods of remembering<br>2. Provide peer tutoring to assist slow learners<br>3. Use reading materials that highlight the topic sentence and main idea for slow learners<br>4. Use several test administration options, such as oral tests or extended-time tests<br>5. Use advance organizers to assist students in comprehension of difficult concepts |
| Schumm, Vaughn, Haager, McDowell, Rothlein, & Saumell, 1995 (K–12) | 1. Preplan lesson(s) experiences for students with LD<br>2. Monitor a lesson and make adaptations in response to the progress of students with LD<br>3. Postplan for later lessons (e.g., reteach a lesson) |
| Jayanthi, Epstein, Polloway, & Bursuck, 1996 (K–12) | 1. Prepare tests that are typewritten rather than handwritten<br>2. Give shorter, more frequent tests rather than fewer, more comprehensive tests<br>3. Change the setting in which the student takes the test<br>4. Allow students to dictate their responses<br>5. Limit the number of matching items to 10 |
| Bursuck, Polloway, Plante, Epstein, Jayanthi, & McConeghy, 1996 (K–12) | 1. Base grades on amount of improvement an individual makes<br>2. Award separate grades for process (e.g., effort) and product (e.g., tests)<br>3. Adjust grades according to student's ability<br>4. Base grades on less content than for the rest of the class<br>5. Base grades on a modified grading scale (e.g., from 93–100 = A to 90–100 = A) |

▰ the speaker has focused attention by stating how aspects of content should be of importance to the listener.

▰ reinforcement for attending is given in the form of participation, praise, or increased ability to perform.

▰ oral presentations are accompanied by visual aids that emphasize important points.

▰ the listener knows there will be an opportunity to reflect upon and integrate the message before having to formulate a response.

# TECHNOLOGY TODAY

### Computer Applications Facilitating Teacher's Productivity

*Technology can greatly facilitate successful inclusion in elementary grades.*

| Stage | Description | Related Topics and Strategies |
|---|---|---|
| **PLANNING** | Assist in the outlining of instructional interventions and strategies. | Assess student abilities and difficulties; indentify software that enhances instructional objectives; use computer lesson plans. |
| **PREPARING** | Facilitate the production of print and electronic instructional materials. | Use utilities that create worksheets, certificates, flash cards; use authoring systems to create online lessons. |
| **MANAGING** | Conduct and manage instruction; facilitate and manage student behavior and interests during computer-based learning activities. | Implement time management of classroom-based and lab-based computers; monitor students' computer performance. |
| **EXTENDING** | Use existing technology creatively and effectively for additional instructional impact. | Review and maintain skills; remain current with teaching/practice-oriented literature on technology. |

Adapted from "Teaching Applications with Exceptional Individuals" (p. 247), by J. E. Gardner and D. L. Edyburn, in *Computers and Exceptional Individuals,* edited by J. D. Lindsey, 1993, Austin, TX: Pro-Ed. Used by permission.

To complement this approach, strategies to build listening skills can also be taught. A variety of techniques can enhance listening. Mandlebaum and Wilson (1989, pp. 451–452) suggest that teachers select from the following techniques:

1. Provide students with direct instruction in listening strategies.
2. Establish a goal for the lesson so that students will know what is expected.
3. Plan listening lessons so that students are actively involved with the information they have learned.
4. Plan purposeful listening activities that relate to other curriculum areas.
5. Make messages logical and well organized, repeating important information.
6. Give information in short segments.
7. Ask questions that require more than simply recalling facts following a listening activity.
8. Act as a model of listening behavior, use peer models, and have students self-monitor their listening behavior.
9. Involve students in rehearsing, summarizing, and taking notes of the information to be learned.
10. Use verbal, pictorial, or written advance organizers to cue students concerning important information before a lesson begins.

11. Prompt students that the information about to be presented is important to remember or to write down.
12. Review the rules for good listening behavior (e.g., sitting quietly, not getting up and moving around, paying close attention), before beginning a listening activity.
13. Involve students in a wide variety of listening activities that relate to the skills that they will need outside the school environment.
14. Use teacher questions and prompts to cue students to respond (e.g., "Tell me more").
15. Teach students to use a self-questioning technique while listening.

## Adapting Oral Presentations

To facilitate learning, teachers must consider vehicles for the effective presentation of content. Adaptations in this area typically prove beneficial to all students. Some specific considerations follow:

- Use concrete concepts before teaching abstractions (e.g., teach the concept of freedom by discussing specific rights to which students are entitled) when mastery of prior content is uncertain.
- Relate information to students' prior experiences.
- Provide students with an overview before beginning.
- Reduce the number of concepts introduced at a given time.
- Encourage children to detect errors in messages and report what they could not understand.
- Monitor and adapt presentation language to make sure that students understand you. Adjust vocabulary level and complexity of sentence structures accordingly.
- Review lessons before additional content is introduced.
- Reduce distractions within the environment (e.g., visual, auditory).
- Keep oral directions short and direct, and supplement them with written directions as needed.
- Provide repetition, review, and additional examples.
- Provide further guided practice by requiring more responses, lengthening practice sessions, or scheduling extra sessions.
- Clarify directions for follow-up activities so that tasks can be completed successfully. (Adapted from Chalmers, 1991; Cheney, 1989; Dowdy, 1990; McDevitt, 1990.)

**TEACHING TIP**
Few students at the elementary level, disabled or not, can attend to a lengthy lecture. Although learning to focus for 20 minutes is a useful skill to acquire for upper elementary students, teachers should plan for variety within a given instructional period.

**FACILITATING NOTE TAKING**   Learning from classroom presentations is obviously critical to academic achievement. For students in the primary grades, instruction is generally not delivered through lengthy oral presentation. However, as lecturing becomes more common in the upper elementary grades and in middle school, students will need to develop note-taking skills. The teaching of note taking may be undertaken by special education teachers; how content is presented by the teacher is an important factor to focus on. The following pointers are derived from Beirne-Smith (1989); they overlap somewhat with ideas for listening and adapting presentations discussed earlier.

1. Organize your lecture.
2. Use key words and phrases, such as "first," or "the main theme."
3. Summarize ideas.
4. Repeat important statements to emphasize the importance of the statement.
5. Pause occasionally to allow students time to fill in blank spaces or catch up to the previous statement.
6. Provide advance organizers (e.g., topic outlines, partially completed notes) to assist the student.

   7. Write important points on the board.
   8. Simplify overhead transparencies. Too much information is confusing and less likely to be recorded.
   9. Encourage students to record all visually presented material exactly as displayed and to leave space between main sections for questions about the material.
   10. Use humor or anecdotes to illustrate important points.
   11. Model note-taking skills (e.g., with the overhead projector).

## Adapting Reading Tasks

In many instances, instructional tasks, assignments, or materials may be relevant and appropriate for students with disabilities, but may present problematic reading demands. Teachers should consider options for adapting the task or the textual materials. The following suggestions address problems that may arise in processing reading content:

▲ Establish a given assignment's purpose and importance.

▲ Highlight key words and phrases (e.g., color coding of text) and concepts (e.g., providing outlines, study guides).

▲ Encourage periodic feedback from students to check their understanding.

▲ Preview reading material with students to assist them in establishing purpose, activating prior knowledge, budgeting time, and focusing attention.

▲ Preteach vocabulary words to ensure that students can use them rather than simply recognize them.

▲ Provide page numbers where specific answers can be found in a reading comprehension or content assignment.

**CROSS-REFERENCE**
Ultimately, students will need to learn to adapt reading tasks themselves, through the use of learning strategies, in order to become independent learners. See Chapter 15 for how this plays out at the secondary level.

▲ Use brief individual conferences with students to verify their comprehension.

▲ Locate lower-level content material on the same topic to adapt tasks for students with reading difficulties.

▲ Tape text, or have it read orally to a student. Consider using peers, volunteers, and paraprofessionals in this process.

▲ Rewrite material (or solicit volunteers to do so) to simplify its reading level, or provide chapter outlines or summaries.

▲ Utilize advance organizers and visual aids (e.g., charts, graphs) to provide an orientation to, or supplement, reading tasks.

▲ Demonstrate how new content relates to content previously learned.

▲ Encourage students to facilitate their comprehension by raising questions about a text's content.

▲ Teach students to consider K-W-L as a technique to focus attention. "K" represents prior knowledge, "W" what the student wants to know, and "L" what has been learned as a result.

▲ Teach the use of active comprehension strategies in which students periodically pause to ask themselves questions about what they have read.

▲ Use reciprocal teaching. Have students take turns leading discussions that raise questions about the content read, summarize the most important information, clarify concepts that are unclear, and predict what will occur next. (Adapted from CEC Today, 1997; Chalmers, 1991; Cheney, 1989; Gartland, 1994; Hoover, 1990; Reynolds & Salend, 1990; Schumm & Strickler, 1991.)

## Enhancing Written Responses

The adaptations noted here may assist students who may have difficulty with responding in written form. These adaptations relate not to the presentation of material but rather to the responses implicit in the task or assignment.

◢ Avoid assigning excessive amounts of written classwork and homework.
◢ When appropriate, allow children to select the most comfortable method of writing (i.e., cursive or manuscript).
◢ Change the response mode to oral when appropriate.
◢ Set realistic, mutually agreed upon expectations for neatness.
◢ Allow children to circle or underline responses.
◢ Let students type or tape-record answers instead of giving them in writing.
◢ Fasten materials to the desk to alleviate coordination problems.
◢ Provide the student with a copy of lecture notes produced by the teacher or a peer.
◢ Reduce amounts of board copying or text copying; provide the written information itself or an outline of the main content.
◢ Allow sufficient space for answering problems.
◢ Allow group-written responses (via projects or reports) (Adapted from Chalmers, 1991; Cheney, 1989; Dowdy, 1990).

In addition to enhancing written responses, teachers should work to improve students' writing ability. Provide sufficient opportunities to write relative to meaningful tasks (e.g., for an authentic audience, or a topic important or interesting to the student). Graham (1992, p. 137) suggests the following ideas for providing frequent and meaningful writing opportunities:

◢ Assist students in thinking about what they will write.
◢ Ask students to establish goals for what they hope to achieve.
◢ Arrange the writing environment so that the teacher is not the sole audience for students' writing.
◢ Provide opportunities for students to work on the same project across days or even weeks.
◢ Incorporate writing into broad-based curricular activities (e.g., integrated curriculum).

Portfolios also represent a positive approach to enhancing writing development. Portfolios involve the student in the evaluation of their own writing samples by selecting samples to be kept and by comparing changes in their writing over time.

## Promoting Following Instructions and Completing Assignments

Another key area is enhancing students' ability to follow instruction and complete work assignments. The following suggestions are adapted from CEC Today (1997, p. 15).

◢ Get the student's attention before giving directions.
◢ Use alerting cues.
◢ Give oral and written directions.
◢ Give one direction at a time.
◢ Quietly repeat the directions to the student after they have been given to the entire class.
◢ Check for understanding by having the student repeat the directions.
◢ Break up tasks into workable and obtainable steps and include due dates.
◢ Provide examples and specific steps to accomplish the task.
◢ List and/or post requirements necessary to complete each assignment.
◢ Check assignments frequently.
◢ Arrange for the student to have a "study buddy" in each subject area.
◢ Define all requirements of a completed activity (e.g., your math is complete when all five problems are complete and corrected).

## Involving Peers

**COOPERATIVE LEARNING**   Cooperative learning has been promoted as a key means of facilitating the successful inclusion of students with disabilities in general education classrooms. It is categorized by classroom techniques that involve students in group learning activities, in which recognition and reinforcement are based on group, rather than individual, performance. Heterogeneous small groups work together to achieve a group goal, and an individual student's success directly affects the success of other students (Slavin, 1987).

A variety of formats can be used to implement cooperative learning. These include peer tutoring, group projects, the jigsaw technique, and student-team achievement division.

*Peer Tutoring.*   Peer teaching, or peer tutoring, is a relatively easy-to-manage system of cooperative learning. It can benefit both the student being tutored and the tutor. Specific activities that lend themselves to peer tutoring include reviewing task directions, drill and practice, recording material dictated by a peer, modeling of acceptable or appropriate responses, and providing pretest practice (such as in spelling). Cooke, Heron, and Heward (1983) summarize the advantages of peer tutoring:

> First, [students] can be highly effective tutors. Research clearly indicates that children can effectively teach each other skills. These gains are optimized when the peer tutoring program is highly structured, when there is an emphasis on repetition, when learning reaches mastery levels before the tutee advances, when a review system is incorporated, and when tutors are trained. Second, tutors benefit academically from teaching skills to a peer. Third, with a peer tutoring program, both the content and pairs can be individualized to meet each student's needs. Fourth, peer tutoring allows for intensive one-to-one instruction without requiring the rest of the class to work on "independent seat work." Fifth, one-to-one instruction can substantially increase the number of opportunities a child has to give correct responses and receive immediate feedback on those responses. Sixth, peer tutoring is an excellent tool for successfully [including] students [with special needs] into the regular classroom for academic instruction. Finally, . . . students can be taught valuable social skills through a structured and positive peer tutoring program. (p. 2)

One effective tutoring program is *classwide peer tutoring* (CWPT). As summarized by Seeley (1995), this system involves the following arrangements:

◢ Classes are divided into two teams, which engage in competitions of 1–2 weeks' duration.
◢ Students work in pairs, both tutoring and being tutored on the same material in a given instructional session.
◢ Partners reverse roles after 15 minutes.
◢ Typical subjects tutored include math, spelling, vocabulary, science, and social studies.
◢ Teachers break down the curriculum into manageable sub-units.
◢ Students accumulate points for their team by giving correct answers and by using correct procedures, and they receive partial credit for corrected answers.
◢ Individual scores on master tests are added to the team's total.

CWPT is a promising approach to use in inclusive settings. It has been positively evaluated in terms of enhancing content learning, promoting diversity and integration, and freeing teachers to prepare for other instructional activities (King-Sears & Bradley, 1995; Simmons, Fuchs, Hodge, & Mathes, 1994).

Another example of a successful peer tutoring approach is the Peer Assisted Learning Strategies (PALS) program described by Mathes and Torgesen (1998). In this program, beginning readers are assisted in learning through paired instruction in which each member of the pair takes turns serving as a coach and a reader. The first coach is the reader who is at a higher achievement level who listens to, comments, and reinforces the other student before the roles are reversed. These researchers found that the use of this approach enhanced students' reading by promoting careful attention to saying and hearing sounds, sounding out words, and reading stories. They recommended using the approach three times a week for approximately sixteen weeks with each session lasting 35 minutes. The PALS program complements general education instruction by enhancing the academic engaged time of each student.

*Group Projects.*  *Group projects* allow students to pool their knowledge and skills to complete an assignment. The task is assigned to the entire group, and the goal is to develop a single product reflecting the contributions of all members. For example, in art, creating a collage is a good example of a group project. In social studies, a report on one of the 50 states might involve making individual students responsible for particular tasks: drawing a map, sketching an outline of state history, collecting photos of scenic attractions, and developing a display of products from that state. The benefits of groups are enhanced when they include high, average, and low achievers.

*The Jigsaw Technique.*  The *jigsaw format* involves giving all group members individual tasks to be completed before the group can reach its goal. Each individual studies a portion of the material and then shares it with other members of the team. For example, Salend (1990) discussed an assignment related to the life of Dr. Martin Luther King, Jr., in which each student was given a segment of his life to research. The students then had to teach others in their group the information from the segment they had mastered.

*Student-Team Achievement Divisions.*  The concept of student-team achievement divisions (STAD) involves assigning students to diversely constituted teams (typically four to a group), which then meet together to review specific teacher-generated lessons. This technique typically focuses on learning objectives that relate to one correct answer (e.g., facts). The teams work together toward content mastery, comparing answers, discussing differences, and questioning one another. Subsequently all students take individual quizzes, without assisting one another. The combined scores of the group determine how well the team succeeds. As Slavin (1987) notes, STAD embraces three concepts central to successful team learning methods: team rewards, individual accountability, and equal opportunities for success. Team rewards derive from content learning by members, who are then assessed by team scores produced by pooled individual scores. Individual accountability is essential because all must learn the content for the team to be successful. Equal opportunities for success come by focusing on degree of individual improvement.

Cooperative learning strategies offer much promise as inclusive practices. The various approaches can be used successfully with low, average, and high achievers to promote academic and social skills and to enhance independence. Cooperative learning also can enhance the social adjustment of students with special needs and help create natural support networks involving nondisabled peers. Peer involvement in supports (such as a "circle of friends" approach discussed in Chapter 7) can help effect successful school and community inclusion.

## Adapting the Temporal Environment

Time is a critical element in classroom assignments and can be associated with special challenges for students with disabilities. Thus, adapting deadlines and other requirements can help promote success. When handled properly, these adaptations need not impinge on the integrity of the assignments nor place undue burdens on the classroom teacher. Some suggestions follow:

▲ Develop schedules that balance routines (to establish predictability) with novelty (to sustain excitement).
▲ Review class schedules with students to reinforce routines.
▲ Provide each student with a copy of the schedule.
▲ Increase the amount of time allowed to complete assignments or tests.
▲ Contract with students concerning time allotment, and tie reinforcement to a reasonable schedule of completion.
▲ Allow extra practice time for students who understand content but need additional time to achieve mastery.
▲ Teach time-management skills (use of time lines, checklists, and prioritizing time and assignments).
▲ Space short work periods with breaks or changes of task (thus using the Premack principle for scheduling: making desirable events contingent on completion of less desirable events). (Adapted from Chalmers, 1991; Guernsey, 1989; Polloway et al., 2001.)

## Adapting the Classroom Arrangement

Changes in the classroom arrangement can also help in accommodating students with special needs. Some specific examples are listed here:

▲ Establish a climate that fosters positive social interactions between students.
▲ Balance structure, organization, and regimentation with opportunities for freedom and exploration.
▲ Use study carrels.

**CROSS-REFERENCE**
See also the discussion on classroom arrangement in Chapter 13.

▲ Locate student seats and learning activities in areas free from distractions.
▲ Allow students to decide where it is best for them to work and study.
▲ Help students keep their work spaces free of unnecessary materials.
▲ Arrange materials in the class based on frequency of use.
▲ Provide opportunities for approved movement within the class.
▲ Establish high- and low-frequency areas for class work (thus using the Premack principle—allow students to move to "fun" areas contingent on work completion in more academically rigorous areas).
▲ Set aside space for group work, individual seatwork, and free-time activities. (Adapted from Cheney, 1989; Guernsey, 1989; Hoover, 1990; Minner & Prater, 1989; Polloway et al., 2001.)

## Enhancing Motivation

Given the failure often experienced by students with disabilities, as well as the boredom experienced by gifted students, motivational problems can seriously undermine the learning process. Although this typically becomes more problematic at the secondary level, young students must be taught in a way that prevents subsequent motivational problems. Attention to both the motivational qualities of the material and the characteristics of the student can develop and sustain a positive attitude toward learning. The following suggestions, which are particularly apt for students with special needs, can help spark motivation:

◢ Have students set personal goals and graph their progress.
◢ Use contingency contracts in which a certain amount of work at a specified degree of accuracy earns the student a desired activity or privilege.
◢ Allow students to choose where to work, what tools to use, and what to do first, as long as their work is being completed.
◢ Make drill-and-practice exercises into game-like activities.
◢ Provide immediate feedback (e.g., through teacher monitoring or self-correcting materials) on the correctness of work.
◢ Give extra credit for bonus work.
◢ For certain students with special needs, camouflage instructional materials at a lower instructional level (using folders, covers).
◢ Use high-status materials for instructional activities (magazines, catalogs, newspapers, checkbooks, drivers' manuals).
◢ Allow students to earn points or tokens to exchange for a valued activity or privilege.
◢ Provide experiences that ensure success, and offer positive feedback when students are successful. (Adapted from Cheney, 1989, p. 29.)

## Developing Effective Homework Programs

Homework has always been an essential element of education, but recent educational reforms have led to its increased use by elementary general education teachers. In a national survey, teachers reported that they most commonly assigned homework from two to four times per week (Polloway et al., 1994). Research on the effectiveness of homework as an instructional tool suggests that it leads to increased school achievement for students in general, with particular benefits in the area of habit formation for elementary students (Cooper, 1989; Walberg, 1991). However, students with disabilities experience significant problems in this area because of difficulties in attention, independence, organization, and motivation (Epstein, Polloway, Foley, & Patton, 1993; Gajria & Salend, 1995).

Homework for students with disabilities presents several dilemmas for general education teachers. In a recent study, Epstein et al. (1996) recognized that communication concerning homework is often negatively affected by the inadequate knowledge base of general education teachers. Figure 14.5 presents typical problems (ordered from most to least serious by teachers) in this area.

Epstein et al. (1993) suggest the following homework interventions:

◢ Assess possible problem areas as a basis for designing individualized programming.
◢ Provide assistance in study and organizational skills.
◢ Increase the relevance of the assignment by relating it to student interests and life skills.
◢ Assign homework that can be completed on an independent basis.
◢ Provide sufficient initial guidance when assignments are made.
◢ Control the time that assignments may take so that successful completion is realistic.
◢ Provide feedback to students on specific assignments.

Finally, Polloway, Epstein, Bursuck, Jayanthi, and Cumblad (1994) asked teachers to rate specific strategies that were most helpful to students with disabilities.

**CONSIDER THIS**
The importance of homework adaptations to the successful inclusion of students with special needs has been confirmed in numerous research studies. How important do you think it is? Why?

**CROSS-REFERENCE**
Parental involvement in homework is discussed at length in Chapter 16.

**FIGURE 14.5**

Homework Communication Problems Noted by Elementary Teachers

*Note:* Items were ranked by general education teachers from *most* to *least* serious.

From "Homework Communication Problems: Perspectives of General Education Teachers," by M. H. Epstein, E. A. Polloway, G. H. Buck, W. D. Bursuck, L. M. Wissinger, F. White-hause, and M. Jayanthi, 1997. In *Learning Disabilities Research and Practice 12,* pp. 221–227. Used by permission.

1. Do not know enough about the abilities of students with disabilities who are mainstreamed in their classes.

2. Do not know how to use special education support services or teachers to assist students with disabilities about homework.

3. Lack knowledge about the adaptations that can be made to homework.

4. Are not clear about their responsibility to communicate with special education teachers about the homework of students with disabilities.

5. Are not aware of their responsibility to communicate with parents of students with disabilities about homework.

Table 14.7 summarizes these responses; each column reflects teachers' ratings from most to least helpful.

## Developing Responsive Grading Practices

The assignment of grades is an integral aspect of education. As Hess, Miller, Reese, and Robinson (1987) indicate, "Grading is an important aspect of documenting the educational experience of students, [and thus] assignment of grades has created and will continue to create debate within the educational community" (p. 1). Thus, grading practices have been subject to frequent evaluation and review, generating a number of problematic issues.

Grading received little attention prior to the increased inclusion of students with disabilities. In the 1990s, a series of research papers has addressed various aspects of grading. In a study of school district policies, Polloway, Epstein, Bursuck, Roderique, McConeghy, and Jayanthi (1994) reported that over 60% of districts with grading policies had one related to students with disabilities; most common was the inclusion of stated accommodations within the IEP. Bursuck, Polloway, Plante, Epstein, Jayanthi, and McConeghy (1996) found that approximately 40% of general educators shared responsibilities for grading with special education teachers. Thus, there is some evidence that the trend toward collaboration has had an impact on this important area.

CROSS-REFERENCE

Grading issues become more problematic at the secondary level; see Chapter 15 for more information.

This collaboration is timely because existing grading systems make success challenging for students who are disabled. Studies on grading patterns have documented generally poor grades for students with disabilities in general education (e.g., Donahue & Zigmond, 1990; Valdes, Williamson, & Wagner, 1990). Further, although general education teachers reported that written comments and checklists are most helpful with these individuals, the most common systems in use at the elementary level are letter grades (Bursuck et al., 1996).

In a study by Bursuck et al. (1996), elementary teachers evaluated adaptations and indicated that adaptations allowing for separate grades for process and product and grades indexed against student improvement were particularly helpful, whereas passing students "no matter what" or basing grades on effort alone was not. Figure 14.6 presents their ranking of grading adaptations.

A related issue is the feasibility of specific adaptations in general education. Bursuck et al. (1996) assessed this question by determining whether teachers actually use

| TABLE 14.7 | Teachers' Ratings of Helpfulness of Homework Adaptations and Practices | | | |
|---|---|---|---|---|
| | CONSEQUENCES | | CONSEQUENCES | |
| Types of Homework | Teacher-Directed Activities | Failure to Complete | Complete Assignments | Adaptations |
| **PRACTICE OF SKILLS ALREADY TAUGHT** | Communicate clear consequences about successfully completing homework. | Assist students in completing the assignment. | Give praise for completion. | Provide additional teacher assistance. |
| **PREPARATION FOR TESTS** | Begin assignment in class, and check for understanding. | Make adaptations in assignment. | Provide corrective feedback in class. | Check more frequently with student about assignments and expectations. |
| **UNFINISHED CLASS WORK** | Communicate clear expectations about the quality of homework completion. | Talk to them about why the assignment was not completed. | Give rewards for completion. | Allow alternative response formats (e.g., oral or other than written). |
| **MAKEUP WORK DUE TO ABSENCES** | Use a homework assignment sheet or notebook. | Require corrections and resubmission. | Monitor students by charting performance. | Adjust length of assignment. |
| **ENRICHMENT ACTIVITIES** | Communicate clear consequences about failure to complete homework. | Call students' parents. | Record performance in grade book. | Provide a peer tutor for assistance. |
| **PREPARATION FOR FUTURE CLASS WORK** | Give assignments that are completed entirely at school. | Keep students in at recess to complete the assignment. | Call students' parents. | Provide auxiliary learning aids (e.g., calculator, computer). |
| | Begin assignment in class without checking for understanding. | Keep students after school to complete the assignment. | | Assign work that student can do independently. |
| | | Lower their grade. | | Provide a study group. |
| | | Put students' names on board. | | Provide extra credit opportunities. |
| | | | | Adjust (i.e., lower) evaluation standards. |
| | | | | Adjust due dates. |
| | | | | Give fewer assignments. |

*Note:* Arranged from most helpful to least helpful.

From "A National Survey of Homework Practices of General Education Teachers" by E. A. Polloway, M. H. Epstein, W. Bursuck, M. Jayanthi, and C.Cumblad, *Journal of Learning Disabilities, 27,* p. 504. Used by permission.

**FIGURE 14.6**

Elementary Teachers' Ratings of Helpfulness of Grading Adaptations for Students with Disabilities

*Note:* Items ranked from most helpful to least helpful by general education teachers. Numbers in parentheses refer to general education rankings of adaptations from most likely to least likely to be used with nondisabled students.

Adapted from "Report Card Grading Practices and Adaptations," by W. Bursuck, E. A. Polloway, L. Plante, M. H. Epstein, M. Jayanthi, and J. McConeghy, 1996, *Exceptional Children, 62,* pp. 301–318. Used by permission.

1. Grades are based on the amount of improvement an individual makes. (#1)
2. Separate grades are given for process (e.g., effort) and product (e.g., tests). (#3)
3. Grades are based on meeting IEP objectives. (#9)
4. Grades are adjusted according to student ability. (#2)
5. Grading weights are adjusted (e.g., efforts on projects count more than tests). (#4)
6. Grades are based on meeting the requirements of academic or behavioral contracts. (#5)
7. Grades are based on less content than the rest of the class. (#7)
8. Students are passed if they make an effort to pass. (#6)
9. Grades are based on a modified grading scale (e.g., from 93 – 100 = A, 90 – 100 = A). (#8)
10. Students are passed no matter what. (#10)

these same adaptations with students without disabilities. As can be seen in Figure 14.6, three of the four adaptations deemed most helpful for students with disabilities (i.e., grading on improvement, adjusting grades, giving separate grades for process and product) were also feasible because they were used by 50% or more of the teachers (regardless of grade level) with nondisabled students. On the other hand, basing grades on less content and passing students no matter what are frowned upon.

Questions of fairness also influence the discussion on grading—that is—are adaptations in grading made only for students with disabilities really fair to other students? Bursuck et al. (1996) report that only 25% of general education teachers thought such adaptations were fair. Those who believed they were fair noted that students should "not be punished" for an inherent problem such as a disability, that adaptations for effort are appropriate because the students are "fighting uphill battles," and that adaptations allow students to "be successful like other kids."

Those teachers who thought adaptations unfair indicated that other students experience significant learning problems even though they have not been formally identified, that some students have extenuating circumstances (e.g., divorce, illness) that necessitate adaptations, and that all students are unique and deserve individual consideration (i.e., both students with and without disabilities may need specific adaptations). Finally, a significant minority of general educators believe that because classes have standards to uphold, all students need to meet those standards without adaptations (Bursuck et al., 1996).

One last perspective on fairness is provided by students. Bursuck, Munk, and Olsen (1999) reported that a majority of all students without disabilities felt that no adaptations were fair; while some were perceived by more students as relatively more fair, the researchers concluded that equity was the greatest concern of these students.

It is clear that collaborative work is essential to appropriate grading practices for students with special needs. Christiansen and Vogel (1998) developed a decision model to illustrate how a collaborative process can be implemented. The use of their system involves following four steps (see Figure 14.7).

To provide an analysis of specific procedures to follow in the grading process, Munk and Bursuck (in press, p. 23) offered the following practical guidelines.

1. Clarify teacher purposes for grades (information grade should convey).
2. Clarify parent and student purposes for grades (information they want to receive).
3. Arrive at mutually agreed upon purpose(s) of grades.
4. Review current class requirements and grading system.
5. Examine student learning characteristics (achievement level, impact of disability, areas of strength, limitations).
6. Identify potential grading problems (learner characteristics interacting with class requirements and grading system).
7. Identify instructional or curricular adaptations that have been or should be made prior to or in addition to grading adaptations.
8. Determine whether a grading adaptation is needed.
9. Select an adaptation that meets agreed upon purposes and addresses grading problems identified previously.
10. Document adaptation in the IEP and begin implementation.
11. Monitor effectiveness of adaptation.

Polloway et al. (2001) suggest these summative considerations about grading:

◢ Plan for special and general education teachers to meet regularly to discuss student progress.

◢ Emphasize the acquisition of new skills as a basis for grades assigned, thus providing a perspective on the student's relative gains.

◢ Investigate alternatives for evaluating content that has been learned (e.g., oral examinations for poor readers in a science class).

◢ Engage in cooperative grading agreements (e.g., grades for language arts might reflect performance both in the classroom and the resource room).

◢ Use narrative reports as a key portion of, or adjunct to, the report card. These reports can include comments on specific objectives within the student's IEP.

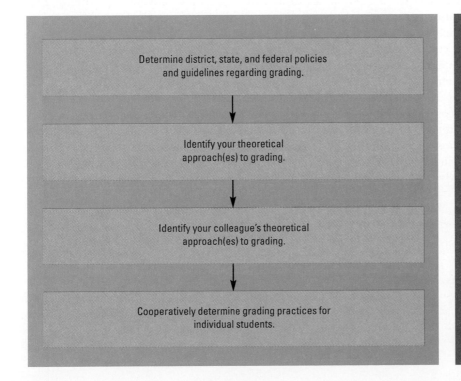

*FIGURE* **14.7**

Decision Model for Grading Students with Disabilities

From "A Decision Model for Grading Students with Disabilities," by J. Christiansen and J. R. Vogel, 1998, *Teaching Exceptional Children, 31*(2), pp. 30–35. Used by permission.

## *DIVERSITY FORUM* Strategies for Working with Students with Different Language

1. Avoid negative statements about the child's language or dialect, exercising particular caution in front of large groups. Rather than say, "I don't understand you" or "You're not saying that right," offer a statement such as, "Could you say that in a different way to help me understand?"

2. Reinforce oral and written language production as it occurs naturally throughout the day. A first goal in working with language-different pupils is to maintain and subsequently increase their language output. Reinforcing desired productions will help ensure that this goal is reached.

3. During any formal language instruction period, work with five or fewer pupils so each has several chances to make an oral response. Working with a small group allows group members to see each other and permits the teacher to physically prompt and reinforce each student.

4. Set specific goals and objectives for language development just as you would for other instructional areas.

5. Reduce tension during language instruction by moving to a less formal part of the room. Arrange as relaxed an environment as possible so that pupils feel free to make oral and written contributions in the new language they are learning.

6. Encourage the learners to produce longer and more complex utterances. Develop and maintain systematic records showing each pupil's growth in language.

7. During language instruction, encourage standard and nonstandard English speakers to talk about language differences and to compare different language forms.

8. Involve people from the linguistically different community in the total school program as much as possible so these persons can share language experiences.

From *Language Instruction for Students with Disabilities* (p. 83), by E. A. Polloway and T. E. C. Smith, 2000, Denver: Love. Used by permission.

### Multicultural Issues in Elementary Curriculum and Instruction

Educators need to consider issues related to cultural diversity when working with elementary-age students with special needs. Students who come from different language backgrounds and whose families adopt values that differ from those of the majority culture must be treated with sensitivity and respect. The nearby Diversity Forum feature offers guidelines for working with students from language-different backgrounds.

Considerations of linguistic and cultural diversity must inform all aspects of curriculum design and should be reflected in instructional practices. The continued over-representation of minority children in high-incidence special education categories underscores the importance of this focus. Because students with special needs benefit from direct, hands-on approaches to such topics, teachers should introduce a variety of activities to develop students' appreciation of diversity at the elementary level.

## Summary

### General Curricular Considerations

▲ The curriculum for elementary students with disabilities should meet their current and long-term needs, facilitate their interactions with nondisabled peers, and facilitate their transition into middle school.

### Curricular Content

▲ Reading instruction should reflect emphases on both decoding and whole language to provide a comprehensive, balanced program.

- Math instruction should provide students with concrete and abstract learning opportunities and should stress the development of problem-solving skills.
- Teachers should select programs and strategies that focus on the social skills most needed by students in their classrooms.
- Life skills instruction should be a part of the elementary curriculum through the use of augmentation, infusion, or an integrated curriculum.

## Cooperative Teaching

- Cooperative teaching involves a team approach in which teachers share their talents in providing class instruction to all students. This requires a commitment to planning, time, and administrative support to reach its potential for success.
- Instructional adaptations should be evaluated against their "treatment acceptability"—that is, their helpfulness, feasibility, desirability, and fairness.

## Instructional Adaptations

- Listening is a skill that requires conscious effort on the part of students and planned intervention strategies on the part of teachers.
- Reading tasks can be adapted through a variety of instructional strategies such as clarifying intent, highlighting content, modifying difficulty level, and using visual aids.
- Written responses can be facilitated through modification of the response requirement.
- Cooperative learning affords teachers a unique opportunity to involve students with disabilities in classroom activities.
- Adaptations in class schedules or classroom arrangements should be considered in order to enhance the learning of students with disabilities.
- Educational programs should be designed to reflect the importance of motivation.
- Homework creates significant challenges for students with special needs; these should be addressed by using intervention strategies.
- Classroom grading practices should be flexible enough to facilitate inclusion.

# urther Readings

Bashan, A., Appleton, V. E., & Dykeman, C. (2000). *Team building in education: A how-to guidebook.* Denver: Love.

Bauwens, J., & Hourcade, J. (1995). *Cooperative teaching.* Austin, TX: Pro-Ed.

Bereiter, C., & Englemann, S. (1966). *Teaching disadvantaged children in the preschool.* Upper Saddle River, NJ: Prentice-Hall.

Coutinho, M. J., & Repp, A. C. (1999). *Inclusion: The integration of students with disabilities.* Belmont, CA: Wadsworth.

Hoover, J. J. (1990). Curriculum adaptation: A five-step process for classroom implementation, *Academic Therapy, 25,* 407–416.

Mastropieri, M. A., & Scruggs, T. E. (2000). *The inclusive classroom: Strategies for effective instruction.* Columbus, OH: Merrill

Patton, J. R., & Cronin, M. E. (1993). *Life skills instruction for all students with disabilities.* Austin, TX: Pro-Ed.

Polloway, E. A., & Patton, J. R. (2001). *Strategies for teaching learners with special needs,* 7th ed. Columbus, OH: Merrill.

Sargent, L. R. (1991). *Social skills for school and community.* Reston, VA: CEC-MR.

Shell, M., & Drake, G. P. (1994). Replacing cascade with supported education, *Journal of Special Education, 27,* 393–409.

Slavin, R. E. (1987). *What research says to the teacher on cooperative learning: Student teams* (2nd ed.). National Education Association.

Issues of
*Teaching Exceptional Children*
*Remedial and Special Education*
*Intervention in School and Clinic*
*Education and Training in Mental Retardation and Developmental Disabilities*
*Journal of Special Education*

# Chapter 15

# Teaching Students with Special Needs in Secondary Schools

*After reading this chapter, you should be able to:*

▲ Define the concept of a comprehensive curriculum and discuss curricular alternatives for students with disabilities

▲ Discuss the ways to determine the curricular needs of secondary school students

▲ Identify and describe the key elements of effective instruction

▲ Discuss the role of general education and special education teachers in ensuring successful secondary school programs for students with special needs

▲ Identify accommodations and adaptations that can facilitate learning for secondary school students

▲ Identify and give examples of study skills and learning strategies that can enhance school performance for adolescent learners

▲ Define transition and describe how school personnel should implement transition planning and services

**M**ike Boyer has just turned 16 years old. While extremely happy about reaching this milestone in his life, he has begun to feel very frustrated in school. Mike was identified as having a learning disability in the third grade. Since then, he has spent time in resource room programs every year, ranging from one hour daily in the elementary grades to three hours last year as a ninth grader in middle school. Now, as a sophomore in high school, Mike is embarrassed when he has to go to the resource room. His classmates have begun to call him "dummy" and "retard." While he knows that a learning disability has nothing to do with intelligence, he wants to stop going to the resource room so his friends will stop calling him names. He has told his parents about these feelings. They are meeting this afternoon with the high school counselor, special education teacher, and assistant principal. As the high school special education resource room teacher, you have been asked by the principal to conduct the meeting and be prepared to make some specific recommendations about Mike's program. You are weighing the benefits of the resource room versus the negatives associated with peer rejection.

## QUESTIONS TO CONSIDER

1. What are the benefits of continuing to serve Mike in the resource room?
2. How can Mike be provided with support services without experiencing peer ridicule and rejection?
3. What is your final recommendation for Mike? What is this recommendation based on?

*I*mportant differences exist between elementary and secondary settings in terms of organizational structure, curricula, and learner variables. These differences create special challenges for successful inclusion. Certainly one concern is the gap found between the demands of the classroom setting and the ability of many students with disabilities. Academically, this gap widens; many students with disabilities exhibit limited basic skills and therefore experience difficulty in performing higher-level cognitive tasks. These basic skills include gaining information from textbooks, memorizing large amounts of information, paraphrasing, discriminating important information from the less important, taking notes, writing themes, proofreading papers, and taking tests successfully (Schumaker & Deshler, 1988).

A second concern is that teachers are often trained primarily as content specialists, yet are expected to present complex material in such a way that a diverse group of students can master the information (Masters, Mori, & Mori, 1999). Secondary teachers are more likely to focus on teaching the content than on individualizing instruction to meet the unique needs of each student. Further, because there may be reluctance to change grading systems or make other accommodations, it may become difficult for students with disabilities to experience success in general education settings.

A third challenge is the general nature of adolescence. Adolescence is a difficult and trying time for all young people. For students with disabilities, the developmental period is even more challenging. Problems associated with adolescence are exacerbated by the presence of a disability (Masters et al., 1999). A fourth problem in including students with disabilities at the secondary level is the current movement to reform schools. For example, these changes may mean that all students will have to take more math and science courses or achieve a passing grade on a minimum competency test; such requirements may prove difficult to meet for many students who experience learning and behavior problems.

Perhaps, given these concerns, it is not surprising to find that secondary teachers have been less positive overall toward efforts at inclusion (Scruggs & Mastropieri, 1996). However, regardless of the difficulties associated with placing adolescents with special needs in general education programs, more students with disabilities are going to depend on classroom teachers to provide appropriate educational programs. Therefore, classroom teachers in secondary schools must be prepared to deal with students who require specialized instruction or modified curricula.

## SECONDARY SCHOOL CURRICULA

**M**ore curricular differentiation has been advocated at the secondary level to accommodate the individual needs and interests of the wide variety of students attending America's comprehensive high schools. At the same time, most high schools have a general curriculum that all students must complete. This curriculum, generally prescribed by the state education agency, includes science, math, social studies, and English. Often, state and local education agencies add to the required general curriculum areas such as education on sexuality, drug education, and foreign languages.

Students have opportunities to choose curricular alternatives, which are usually related to postschool goals. For example, students planning to go to college choose a college preparatory focus, which builds on the general curriculum with higher-level academic courses. This college preparatory option helps prepare students for the rigorous courses found at college. Other students choose a vocational program, which is designed to help prepare them for specific job opportunities after high school. Still other students choose a general curriculum, with some course choices for students who do not plan to go to college and who are not interested in a specific vocational choice (Smith, 1990).

Although the specific curricula offered in different secondary schools vary, they generally follow state guidelines. Individual schools, however, do offer unique curricular options that appeal to particular students. The curricular focus that students choose should be an important consideration because the decision could have long-term implications after the student exits school.

The educational reform movements of the 1980s and 1990s have had a direct impact on the secondary curriculum. Schools have begun to offer, and in some cases require, more science and math courses. Also, in many states and districts, students must successfully complete high school competency examinations before they are eligible for graduation. More stringent rules related to the number of electives students can take mean that many students cannot take the courses they want. One result of this could be more school dropouts (Smith, Price, & Marsh, 1986).

## Special Education Curriculum in Secondary Schools

The curriculum for students with disabilities is the most critical programming consideration in secondary schools. Even if students have excellent teachers, if the curriculum is inappropriate to meet their needs, then the teaching may be ineffective. The high school curriculum for students with disabilities must be comprehensive; that is, it must

- ◢ be responsive to the needs of individual students.
- ◢ facilitate maximum integration with nondisabled peers.
- ◢ facilitate socialization.
- ◢ focus on the students' transition to postsecondary settings.

Masters and colleagues (1999) identified seven different curricular approaches that can be used in a variety of educational settings for students with special needs. These include (1) modified course content, (2) learning strategies, (3) remediation, (4) life skills, (5) parallel alternative, (6) vocational, and (7) cross-curricula. Table 15.1 describes each of these curricular options.

## Determining Curricular Needs of Students

The curriculum for any student should be based on an appraisal of desired long-term outcomes and an assessment of current needs and selected to meet the individual needs of students. The *20th Annual Report to Congress on the Implementation of IDEA* (U.S. Department of Education, 1999) reported that only 32.8% of all students with disabilities, aged 14 and above, who left special education during the 1995–1996 year, graduated with a diploma or certificate. The drop-out rate for these students was 17%. Figure 15.1 shows other avenues of exit for these students.

**CONSIDER THIS**

Describe some of the reforms made in secondary schools and their impact on providing services to students with special needs. For example, how does increasing graduation requirements affect students with special needs?

**TEACHING TIP**

Teachers must remember that students with disabilities can be successful in an academic curriculum. The curricular needs of each student should be assessed before any conclusions are drawn about the student's program of study.

| TABLE 15.1 | Special Curricula for Secondary Students |
|---|---|
| **MODIFIED COURSE CONTENT** | ▪ Offers a simplified version of the content available in general classrooms<br>▪ Instructional goals, objectives, and competencies are written at levels lower than for nondisabled students |
| **LEARNING STRATEGIES** | ▪ Focus on various instructional strategies that help students to acquire, organize, store, and retrieve information needed in the general curricula<br>▪ Primarily used to supplement the general classroom curricula |
| **REMEDIATION** | ▪ Purpose is to change the way students approach reading, decoding and comprehension, writing, speaking, and problem solving<br>▪ Remediation may be focused on the process of learning and target how students use perception, language, thinking, and reasoning skills |
| **LIFE SKILLS** | ▪ Focus on students acquiring basic functional and survival skills in reading, writing, and mathematics<br>▪ Include a vocational focus |
| **PARALLEL ALTERNATIVE** | ▪ Instructional modification rather than stand-alone curriculum<br>▪ Enables students with limited reading, spelling, writing, and listening skills to use other means for communication |
| **VOCATIONAL** | ▪ Designed to guide students to gain knowledge and skills in a particular vocational area<br>▪ Goals and objectives focus on competencies needed for successful employment |
| **CROSS-CURRICULA MODEL** | ▪ A combination of other curricular approaches that attempts to meet the needs of students<br>▪ Can be accomplished by targeting communication, assertiveness, self-responsibility, training, and problem solving |

From *Teaching Secondary Students with Mild Learning and Behavior Problems* (3rd Edition) (p. 216), by L. F. Master, B. A. Mori, and A. A. Mori, 1999, Austin, TX: Pro-Ed. Used by permission.

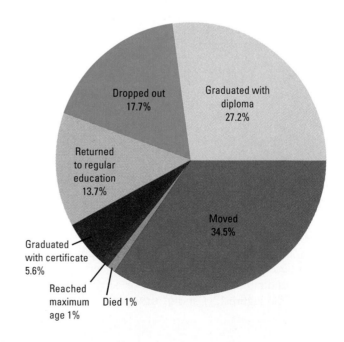

*FIGURE* **15.1**

Basis of Exit for Students with Disabilities, Age 14 and Older: School Year 1996–1997

From *20th Annual Report to Congress on the Implementation of IDEA* (p. A–181), by U.S. Department of Education, 1999, Washington, D.C.: Author.

Dropped out 17.7%
Graduated with diploma 27.2%
Returned to regular education 13.7%
Moved 34.5%
Graduated with certificate 5.6%
Reached maximum age 1%
Died 1%

In addition, several follow-up studies have shown that adults with disabilities are likely to be employed part-time, underemployed, or unemployed to a significantly greater degree than their nondisabled peers (Edgar, 1988; Edgar & Polloway, 1994). Therefore, regardless of the efforts made in secondary schools to meet the individual needs of students with disabilities, many of these students seem unprepared to achieve success as young adults.

Students themselves are aware that they are not being adequately prepared for post–high school demands. In comparing the transitional needs of high school students with learning disabilities to those of their nondisabled peers, Dowdy, Carter, and Smith (1990) found that, although both groups expressed an interest in help with career decisions, significant differences were noted in their thoughts about the future. For example, students with learning disabilities were far more concerned with learning how to find a job, how to keep a job, and how to live independently. As a group, students with disabilities expressed greater insecurity about their futures than did students without disabilities.

To ensure that students have the optimum chance at success after schooling concludes, transition planning is an essential responsibility and legal requirement (see Rights and Responsibility feature). Transitions represent ongoing challenges that can be identified as horizontal (from a more segregated to a more integrated setting) and

**CONSIDER THIS**
What are some things that schools could do to increase the number of students with disabilities who stay in school and graduate? Should schools do these things?

# RIGHTS & RESPONSIBILITIES

## Legal Requirements Related to Transition

The 1997 Reauthorization of IDEA states the following regarding transition:

1. Beginning at age 14, and updated annually, a statement of the transition service needs of the child under the applicable components of the child's IEP that focuses on the child's course of study (such as participation in advanced placement courses or a vocational education program);

2. Beginning at age 16 (or younger, if determined appropriate by the IEP team), a statement of needed transition services for the child, including, when appropriate, a statement of the interagency responsibilities or any needed linkages.

Regarding transfer of parental rights to the child:

1. When a child with a disability reaches the age of majority under state law (except for a child with a disability who has been determined to be incompetent under state law)—

a. The public agency shall provide any notice required by this section to both the individual and the parents;

b. All other rights accorded to parents under this part transfer to the child;

c. The agency shall notify the individual and the parents of the transfer of rights; and

d. All rights accorded to parents under this part transfer to children who are incarcerated in adult or juvenile federal, state, or local correctional institutions.

2. SPECIAL RULE   If, under state law, a child with a disability who has reached the age of majority under state law, who has not been determined to be incompetent, but who is determined not to have the ability to provide informed consent with respect to the education program of the child, the state shall establish procedures for appointing the parent of the child, or if the parent is not available another appropriate individual, to represent the educational interests of the child throughout the period of eligibility of the child under this part.

From *Final Regulation, IDEA* by U.S. Department of Education, 1999, Washington, D.C.: Author.

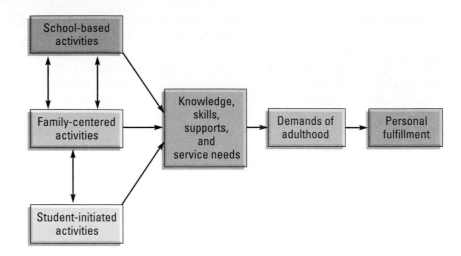

**FIGURE 15.2**

Elements of the Transition Process

From *Transition from School to Adult Life for Students with Special Needs: Basic Concepts and Recommended Practices* (p. 10), by J. R. Patton, 1995, Austin, TX: Pro-Ed. Copyright 1995 by Pro-Ed. Used by permission.

**TEACHING TIP**

Teachers and other school personnel must include students with disabilities and their family members in planning for the future.

vertical (across the lifespan). Of primary concern here is the transition to adulthood from school, which is in itself a multifaceted process (see Figure 15.2 for a model).

One method of facilitating the transition planning for students is to use a person-centered approach, which is based on the premise that the student is the central part of the planning process. Using this model, school personnel acknowledge that all students, regardless of their disability, have certain strengths and capacities and interweave these with formal and informal community supports. Table 15.2 compares the use of a personal futures planning model to the more traditional transition planning model that many schools use. As you can see, the futures planning approach is based on a circle of support that is available for the student (Everson, 1998).

Everson (1998) notes that mapping can be used as one approach in transition planning. This approach requires the development of a personal profile of the student, which consists of the following maps:

▲ background map
▲ relationship map
▲ setting map
▲ choice map
▲ preference map

These maps can then be used to develop a transition plan. Table 15.3 (on p. 460) shows how transition mapping information can be translated into transition goals and objectives. For students with disabilities, these goals should be delineated in the IEP and also reflected in individual transition plans (ITPs), according to IDEA, for students over the age of 14. But such planning should commence even earlier (Battle, Dickens-Wright, & Murphy, 1998).

Although students with disabilities have IEPs that detail specific goals, objectives, and services, the programs must be related to a particular curricular model. As previously noted, without an appropriate curriculum, educational programs necessarily become unfocused. Several factors should be considered when determining an appropriate curriculum for students with disabilities including (1) student factors, (2) family factors, (3) general educational factors, and (4) special education factors (Polloway et al., 1989).

| TABLE 15.2 | Comparison of Personal Futures Planning and Traditional Transition Planning Concepts |
|---|---|
| **Traditional Transition Planning** | **Personal Futures Planning** |
| A team of service providers meets annually with parents to develop a plan for educational and related services. | A circle of support made up of the focus person with a disability, parents, and other family members meets with service providers and other community members monthly or as frequently as needed to develop and implement a future vision for the focus individual. |
| A transdisciplinary team conducts and interprets assessment data using standardized and nonstandardized assessment mechanisms. | A circle of support gathers, organizes, and manages assessment information into a personal profile and future vision using highly visual and graphic maps. |
| The student with a disability is invited to participate in the team meeting as appropriate. | The circle defines a role for every focus person and assists the person in assuming the role in a respected and competent manner. |
| Parents are invited to participate in the development of the individualized service plan. | Parents, other family members, friends, and general community members define the personal profile and future vision and look to service providers for support. |
| An IEP with a statement of needed transition services is mandated to guide services. | A future vision and action plan guide the circle's activities and should be used to drive IEP/transition plan content. |
| Implementation of the plan is ensured through provision of entitlement services, due process, and professional services. | Implementation of the plan depends upon the commitment and energy of the circle of support and their connections with the focus person and family. |

From *Transition Services for Youths Who Are Deaf–Blind: A "Best Practices" Guide for Educators* (p. 27), edited by J. M. Everson, 1995, Sands Point, NY: Helen Keller National Center–Technical Assistance Center. Used by permission.

## PROGRAMS FOR STUDENTS IN SECONDARY SCHOOLS

Most secondary students with disabilities are currently included in general education classrooms for at least a portion of each school day. *The 20th Annual Report to Congress* indicated that 70% of students with disabilities, aged 12–17, were served in either resource rooms or regular classrooms (U.S. Department of Education, 1998). Therefore, the responsibility for these students becomes a joint effort between general education classroom teachers and special education personnel (Walther-Thomas et al., 2000). Unfortunately, many of these students do not experience success in the general classroom setting. They frequently fail classes, become frustrated and act out, and may even drop out of school because they are not prepared to meet the demands placed on them by secondary teachers. There are numerous reasons why many students with disabilities fail in secondary classes:

▲ Lack of communication between special education personnel and classroom teachers
▲ Discrepancies between the expectations of classroom teachers and the abilities of students
▲ Students' lack of understanding about the demands of the classroom
▲ Classroom teachers' lack of understanding about students with disabilities
▲ Special education personnel's lack of knowledge about working with classroom teachers
▲ School policies that are inflexible

| TABLE 15.3 | Translating Mapping "Data" into Transition Planning Goals and Objectives |
|---|---|

**STEP #1:** Create personal profile and future vision maps for all transition-age youth. These maps may be created as part of personal futures planning team activities, as units in high school self-advocacy or career exploration activities, as youth group or church activities, or as family activities.

**STEP #2:** Bring maps to IEP/transition planning meetings. Use them to open the meeting and establish a more person-centered environment for discussion. Post the original copies on the wall during the meetings. Staple reduced-sized copies of the maps to the youth's educational file. Ask the youth and his or her family members to summarize the maps.

**STEP #3:** Discuss themes, things that work, and things that don't work in the personal profile maps. Think about people, places, materials, activities, schedules, and communication patterns. Discuss the implications of these findings for the youth's current educational programming. Discuss the implications of these findings for the youth's future educational program.

**STEP #4:** Discuss the future vision map. What services and supports currently exist to support the youth's future dreams? What gaps exist? What opportunities, experiences, and environments does the youth need to fulfill his or her future dreams? If a local community or regional transition planning team exist, share both future vision and service gap information with them. If the youth has a personal future planning team, ensure that some members serve as members of both teams.

**STEP #5:** Discuss each transition planning area along with associated mapping data. For example, employment goals can be clarified by reviewing the future vision map, preferences map, and setting map. The optional communication and health maps may also yield important employment planning information.

**STEP #6:** Select educational environments and activities for instruction based upon mapping information, other assessment information, demographics of community, and school logistics. For example, if the relationship map indicates that the youth has little opportunity to interact with typical peers and non-paid adults, look for environments and activities that will expand the number and type of people in the youth's life.

**STEP #7:** Develop IEP/transition planning goals. Use the future vision map as a checkpoint. Will the articulated goals move the focus individual toward his or her desired future? Will mastery of these goals assist the individual in leading a more community-inclusive adult life? If the answer is no or if there is uncertainty, the team should discuss and possibly reconsider the goals.

**STEP #8:** For each goal, determine necessary IEP/transition planning components. Create an "obstacles and opportunities" map to identify existing services as well as service gaps needed to achieve the individual's future vision. Identify interagency linkages and responsibilities. When service gaps exist, brainstorm potential solutions—are some team members willing to engage in personal futures planning activities? Is there a local community or regional team willing to assist in the necessary systems change?

**STEP #9:** Repeat this process each year, refining the future vision and obstacles and opportunities map each year. Celebrate small and large successes.

From *Transition Services for Youths Who Are Deaf–Blind: A "Best-Practices" Guide for Educators* (p. 31), edited by J. M. Everson, 1995, Sands Point, NY: Helen Keller National Center–Technical Assistance Center. Used by permission.

Regardless of the reasons why some students with disabilities do not achieve success in general education settings, the fact remains that the majority will be taught in inclusive settings. Therefore, classroom teachers and special education personnel must work together to increase the chances that these students will be successful.

## Roles of Personnel

As noted, the responsibility for educating students with disabilities in public schools is shared by general classroom teachers and special education personnel. Therefore, educators must improve their skills at working together to help students with various learning and behavior problems.

GENERAL EDUCATION TEACHERS   The primary role of general classroom teachers is to assume the responsibility for students with disabilities in particular classes or subject areas. Most classroom teachers present information using one general technique, but they will probably have to expand their instructional activities when dealing with students with disabilities. Various accommodations and modifications in instructional techniques and materials will be discussed later in the chapter.

Classroom teachers have general responsibilities that apply to students with and without disabilities. These include managing the classroom environment; providing instruction at an appropriate level and pace; using an appropriate curriculum; and evaluating student success and modifying instruction as appropriate. For students with disabilities, general classroom teachers have the added responsibility of participating on an interdisciplinary team (Masters et al., 1999).

In addition, teachers should ensure that all students have an opportunity to answer questions and a good chance at achieving at least moderate success in classroom activities. This is not a call for teachers to "give" students with disabilities passing grades, only a requirement that students with disabilities receive an equal chance at being successful.

**CONSIDER THIS**
The roles of general educators and special educators must change for effective inclusion to occur. What are some potential barriers to these changes and how can they be overcome?

*General education teachers are primarily responsible for students with special needs in their classrooms.*

# DIVERSITY FORUM

## Teachers's Expectations of Students from Diverse Backgrounds

Diversity in secondary schools continues to present challenges for general and special education teachers. In an article on the impact of teacher expectations of minority students with disabilities, Obiakor (1999) presented a series of implications for practice for teachers as well as some teacher beliefs that could benefit educators who work with diverse backgrounds.

Questions that teachers need to be able to answer:

1. Does my student's language affect my expectations of him or her?
2. What characteristics do I bring to my classroom and how do they create problems for my students?
3. Do I perpetuate stereotypes that hamper my students' development?
4. Do my stereotypes create inappropriate expectations for minority members (i.e., students, parents, and colleagues) in school programs?
5. Do I misjudge appropriate behaviors because of my cultural values?
6. Do I interpret individual differences on the basis of my cultural values?
7. Do my interpretations affect my intervention/ instruction? In other words, do I have "real pedagogical power" to reach all my students, including those who come from different cultural and linguistic backgrounds?

Teacher beliefs that can benefit general and special education teachers:

1. There is no perfect human being.
2. Human beings differ intraindividually and interindividually.
3. A person's environment contributes to his or her growth and development, and this environment can be positively manipulated.
4. Because of human differences, our assessment and intervention techniques must be multidimensional.

5. Behavior problems do not occur in isolation— they are based on our personal idiosyncrasies.
6. A problem behavior is not always a disordered behavior.
7. What is a disordered behavior to one teacher/ professional might not be a disordered behavior to another teacher/professional.
8. A behavior is a disordered behavior when (a) it departs from acceptable standards considering age, culture, situation, circumstance, and time; (b) its frequency is well-documented; and (c) its duration is well-documented.
9. Even when a behavior is disordered, the person exhibiting that behavior is not disordered or disturbed.
10. Assessment/intervention techniques that work for one student might not work for another student.
11. Two testers/assessors/diagnosticians might test one student and get different results.
12. The ways tests are conducted and interpreted can have far-reaching effects on learners.
13. We create problem behaviors when we try to solve problems that do not exist (i.e., iatrogenic intervention).
14. Collaboration, consultation, and cooperation can make behavioral and academic assessment more meaningful to students, parents, and educators.
15. It takes a whole village to raise a child—this comprehensive support model (CSM) incorporates the student, family, school, community, and government. No part of the village should be excluded in behavioral and academic assessment/ intervention.

From "Teacher Expectations of Minority Exceptional Learners: Impact on 'Accuracy' of Self-Concepts," by F. E. Obiakor, 1999, *Exceptional Children, 66,* p. 49. Used by permission.

learning problems know how to use these kinds of strategies, they will have a better chance of achieving success in general classrooms.

When working with students with disabilities in general education classrooms, the role of the special educator expands to include informing the general educator as to the unique abilities and challenges presented by each student, providing ongoing support and collaboration for the student and teacher, and frequent monitoring to ensure that the arrangement is satisfactory for both the student and the teacher.

**PREPARING FOR THE HIGH SCHOOL GRADUATION EXAM**   Passing a high school graduation exam as a requirement for receiving a regular diploma began in many states in the 1980s as part of the national reform movements in education. Students with disabilities may or may not be required to take the exam, depending on state regulations and local school district policies. In some states, students with disabilities are granted a regular high school diploma without having to complete the examination; in others, students with disabilities who do not pass the graduation exam are given a certification of attendance.

Special education teachers, in conjunction with classroom teachers, have two roles regarding the high school graduation exam. On one hand, they are obligated to help the student prepare for the exam if it is the decision of the IEP team that the student should be prepared to take the exam. On the other hand, the special education teacher and classroom teachers may choose to focus on convincing the student and parents that time could more appropriately be spent on developing functional skills rather than on preparing for the graduation exam. Information on testing is discussed later in the chapter.

**PREPARING FOR POSTSECONDARY TRAINING**   Students with disabilities absolutely should aim for postsecondary education if they have the ability and motivation. Postsecondary education does not have to mean attending a four-year institution. A community college, vocational–technical school, trade school, or some other form of postsecondary education and training are other possibilities. Teachers, both general and special education, need to inform students about future employment trends and help them select a realistic career with employment potential. A variety of reports regarding the importance of education in the future for students with and without disabilities have concluded the following:

1. Higher levels of academic achievement will be required, and very few jobs will be appropriate for individuals deficient in reading, writing, and math.
2. There will be an increase in service industry jobs and a decrease in manufacturing jobs.
3. More than half of the new jobs created in the 1990s require education beyond high school, and more than a third are filled by college graduates.
4. Technology will play an increasing role for all individuals.

**PREPARING FOR INDEPENDENT LIVING**   Independent living is a realistic goal for the vast majority of individuals with disabilities; however, to live successfully in today's complex, automated world, direct instruction in certain independent living skills may be required. This is also important in a student's transition program. The following areas may be problematic for persons with disabilities:

- Sexuality
- Managing personal finances
- Developing and maintaining social networks
- Maintaining a home
- Managing food
- Employment
- Transportation
- Self-confidence and self-esteem
- Organization
- Time management

# *T*ECHNOLOGY *T*ODAY

## Journals: Marriage and Relationship Issues

Most of the journal listings contain contact and subscription information and a table of contents for recent issues. A few of the links contain abstracts or full text for selected articles.

▲ *American Journal of Family Therapy*
<http://www.tandfdc.com/JNLS/AFT.htm>
Contact and subscription information, table of contents.

▲ *Child Abuse & Neglect*
<http://www.elsevier.nl:80/inca/publications/store/5/8/6>
Contact and subscription information.

▲ *Child and Family Social Work*
<http://www.uea.ac.uk/swk/publicat/cfsw.htm>
Contact and subscription information, table of contents.

▲ *Community, Work & Family*
<http://www.carfax.co.uk/cwf-ad.htm>
Contact and subscription information, table of contents.

▲ *Contemporary Family Therapy*
<http://www.plenum.com/title.cgi?1010>
Contact and subscription information, table of contents.

▲ *The Family Journal: Counseling and Therapy for Couples and Families*
<http://www.familycounselors.org/pubs.html>
Contact and subscription information.

▲ *Family Process* <http://www.familyprocess.org>
Contact and subscription information.

▲ *Family Relations*
<http://www.iog.wayne.edu/FR/homepage.html>
Contact and subscription information.

▲ *Journal of Child and Family Studies*
<http://www.plenum.com/title.cgi?1042>
Contact and subscription information, table of contents.

▲ *Journal of Child Sexual Abuse*
<http://www.haworthpressinc.com>
Contact and subscription information, table of contents.

▲ *Journal of Couples Therapy*
<http://www.haworthpressinc.com>
Contact and subscription information, table of contents.

▲ *Journal of Divorce & Remarriage*
<http://www.haworthpressinc.com>
Contact and subscription information, table of contents.

▲ *Journal of Family Issues*
<http://www.sagepub.co.uk/journals/details/j0179.html>
Contact and subscription information.

▲ *Journal of Family Psychology*
<http://www.apa.org:80/journals/fam.html>
Contact and subscription information, table of contents, abstracts.

▲ *Journal of Family Violence*
<http://www.plenum.com/title.cgi?2044>
Contact and subscription information, table of contents.

▲ *Journal of Feminist Family Therapy*
<http://www.haworthpressinc.com>
Contact and subscription information, table of contents.

▲ *Journal of Interpersonal Violence*
<http://www.sagepub.co.uk/journals/details/j0015.html>
Contact and subscription information.

▲ *Journal of Marital and Family Therapy*
<http://www.aamft.org/resources/jmft_menu.htm>
Contact and subscription information, table of contents, abstracts, full text for selected articles.

▲ *Journal of Marriage and the Family*
<http://www.ncfr.com/jour_intro.html>
Contact and subscription information.

▲ *Journal of Sex and Marital Therapy*
<http://www.tandfdc.com/JNLS/smt.htm>
Contact and subscription information, table of contents.

From *The Mayfield Quick Guide to the Internet* (pp. 44–45), by P. M. Galupo et al., 1999, Mountain View, CA: Mayfield Publishing. Used by permission.

Special education teachers must help students with disabilities achieve competence in these areas. Several curricular guides are available to structure intervention in these areas. Two excellent resources are the Life-Centered Career Education Program (Brolin, 1989) and Cronin and Patton's (1993) life skills program. The former presents a comprehensive curriculum for teaching life skills, whereas the latter is a resource guide for program development. Cronin and Patton (1993) present particularly useful models and strategies for infusing life skills into the regular curriculum. In addition, creative teachers can use community resources, gathering real materials from banks, restaurants, the local court house, and so forth, for developing their own program. Web materials are also available. See the Technology Today feature.

**PREPARING FOR EMPLOYMENT**    The ultimate goal of all education is the employment of graduates at their maximum vocational potential. The passage of the Americans with Disabilities Act (ADA) in 1990 has made that dream a reality for millions of people with disabilities. Encompassing areas of employment, transportation, public accommodations, and telecommunications, the law prohibits discrimination against individuals with disabilities. ADA requires employers to make "reasonable accommodations" to assist persons with disabilities in performing their jobs. Supported employment initiatives (i.e., providing job coaches to support workers on the job) have emerged as particularly powerful tools. Teachers need to help students prepare for employment by teaching them the necessary skills for vocational success.

Inclusive vocational and technical programs present a unique opportunity to offer students both a functional curriculum as well as integration with nondisabled peers. These programs can provide appropriate entry into work–study programs, business apprenticeships, and technical and trade school programs.

Teachers must be sure that students with disabilities can communicate their strengths and limitations to persons in postsecondary and future employment settings. These self-advocacy skills will empower individuals to seek employment and independent living opportunities on their own. Field, Hoffman, and Spezia (1998) suggest the following to assist students with disabilities in developing self-determination skills:

▲ Encourage students to take risks through participating in an approved Adventure Challenge Program. Higher level challenges include scaling a 40-foot wall, traveling across a high ropes course, and using a map and compass to find your way back to a campsite. Students should always be asked, "What do you have to lose?" and "What can you gain from this experience?" A key component of Adventure Challenge Education is the firm commitment that all group members act in a manner that keeps themselves and their classmates safe. This encourages trust and emphasizes responsibility.

▲ While watching a tape with the sound turned off, instruct students to analyze the nonverbal communication of characters through their facial expressions, hand gestures, and body language. Discuss what the class believes the characters are communicating. Replay the tape with the sound on and evaluate how accurate they were in the translation. This is especially effective with tapes of the daily soap operas. Students enjoy the opportunity to view their favorite soap while analyzing the nonverbal communication signals.

**CONSIDER THIS**
In what ways can self-advocacy and self-determination affect young adults with disabilities? Should schools teach self-advocacy skills to adolescents with disabilities? Why or why not?

◢ Use small groups to identify characteristics of the ideal or "dream" mentor. Give each group a large piece of paper and marking pens. Ask them to draw a person or an outline of one and fill in the characteristics of their ideal mentor on the drawing. To make the outline of a person, one student can lie on the paper and another can draw an outline around him or her.

◢ Demonstrate to students the concept of active listening by role-playing how to actively listen and how not to actively listen. Review the following steps of active listening with students:
  • Listen carefully.
  • Ask clarifying questions.
  • State back to the speaker what you heard.
  • Accept what the speaker says; do not challenge.

◢ Have students practice verbal communication skills through memorizing and reciting poetry. This process takes time and practice. Students quickly learn the value of "practice makes perfect." Record the students' recitations on individual cassette tapes. Encourage students to analyze their tapes for the quality of tone, volume, and pitch. Save the tapes and record often to measure progress.

◢ Emphasize the importance of not giving in or giving up! Identify support resources early and assist students as they plan how and when they will access support.

◢ Provide students with opportunities to interact with individuals who have personally experienced goal setting and self-determination. Design a single-page interview form. Select a sample group and instruct students to complete the interview with a representative of the sample group. Examples of sample groups include parents, grandparents, individuals with disabilities or illnesses, businesspeople or entrepreneurs, athletes, and teachers. Students should be encouraged to openly share the results of their interview and to look for common elements of self-determination among all of the interviews. Another variation of this activity includes using books or magazines to research famous people such as politicians, actors and actresses, television personalities, authors, and musicians. Create a collection of these reports organized by topic. Encourage students to write personally to their favorite celebrity. It is likely many will receive personal responses.

***TEACHING TIP***
Use role-playing situations to help students understand how to utilize conflict management strategies. When situations occur where such strategies are not used, initiate a class discussion to talk about how things could have been handled better.

◢ Provide the entire class with the opportunity to be trained in Conflict Management and Peer Mediation. These courses not only provide individuals with important survival skills but equip all students with the skills necessary to resolve conflicts with their peers. Often, students who experience the most difficulty in resolving personal conflicts do very well at helping others resolve theirs.

◢ Provide a variety of games for the class. Select games that simulate life experiences. Many of these games are available through teacher supply catalogs and stores, but many are also available at local toy stores. Purchase four or five copies of each game and set up for tournaments. Suggest that students rate the games they play to determine their effectiveness. Value student opinions as they rate the games. Play games with the students to get a feel for the level of difficulty.

◢ Find an appropriate simulation kit at a teacher supply store or in an education catalog. Simulations can last for as little as one hour or as long as a full semester. Students work their way through the simulation and evaluate themselves on their effectiveness. Simulations provide an opportunity for students to practice skills prior to real life application. Examples of simulations that seem most effective include job search, independent living, interviewing, and entrepreneurship.

◢ Explore computer software stores and catalogs for materials that provide practice and simulation in the skills of negotiation and conflict resolution. Groups of students can be assigned a computer task for resolution. Numerous software programs are also available to support the development of all the self-determination skills, including self-esteem, job skills, problem solving, and goal setting.

◢ Create "Self-Determination Portfolios." Have students maintain their own portfolios, providing examples of their efforts in self-determination. Review the portfolios with the individual students often. This strategy encourages ongoing review of the action plan and discourages the tendency to give up.

◢ Help students learn about the effectiveness of various communication styles by asking them to describe the type of communication they used in different situations during the week (i.e., passive, assertive, or aggressive). Then have them tell what the outcome of that communication was.

◢ Have students generate a list of the pros and cons of avoiding conflict and of confronting conflict. Then discuss the pros and cons and when they might want to avoid conflict and when they would want to confront it. (p. 29–31)

The nearby Personal Spotlight highlights a secondary special education teacher who wants schools to focus more on preparing students for life after high school.

## *personal* SPOTLIGHT

### High School Special Education Teacher

**IRIS KIRBIS PUCCINI**
*Niles High School*
*Chicago, Illinois*

Iris Kirbis Puccini teaches special education at the high school level in Chicago, Illinois. While not an opponent of inclusion and generic services, she strongly favors placing secondary students with disabilities in the setting where their educational and future needs can best be met. The following is her statement regarding how she views special education for secondary students with disabilities.

I have been teaching in secondary grades for a long time, and I can assure you that teaching these students is different than teaching in elementary grades. For one, students with disabilities in secondary grades do not have a great deal of time before they are placed in the big, bad world. While many of these students [receive] substantial supports during their public school years, many [do] not receive services as adults. Therefore, they must be ready to take care of themselves, get a job, live alone, and a variety of other things that most of us take for granted.

Inclusion has been shown to be very effective for many students, especially for students who are younger. However, I have some real concerns about including older students in classes that will not help them become independent later in life. Now, for students with learning disabilities and other disabilities that will not preclude their going to college or some other postsecondary training opportunity, inclusion may work and it may be the best approach. However, for the many secondary students who, because of their disability, cannot go to college or even a vocational–technical school, the high school years are critical in preparing them for life after high school. For many of these students, I do not feel like their inclusion in some high school courses [is] appropriate. Rather than being in a classroom where they have a hard time just understanding what is going on, much less the relevancy of the course to their future, I think many of these students need to be focusing on learning real-life skills that will help them survive as young adults. If these courses need to be taught in separate classes, then I am for separate classes. I am not opposed to the concept of inclusion at all, just the appropriateness of including some students when their needs could better be met in other settings.

If students need to be in separate classes for these "specialized" learning opportunities, I do think that they should be given opportunities to interact with their nondisabled peers, as much as possible. However, their need to have opportunities for interaction cannot overcome their need to learn skills that will help them be independent adults.

## METHODS TO FACILITATE STUDENTS' SUCCESS IN GENERAL EDUCATION CLASSES

Students with disabilities traditionally have been placed in general education classrooms for instruction when they were determined to have the requisite academic ability necessary for success. With the advent of the inclusion movement, however, students with disabilities are often placed in such classes for other reasons. For most of these students, there is no need to dilute the curriculum; however, teachers will probably need to make accommodations, and students will need to use special learning strategies in order to achieve success.

### Accommodations and Adaptations

In most instances, general education teachers are responsible for making accommodations or adaptations to help students with disabilities achieve in the secondary school. This process is hampered by the fact that typically only one fourth to one half of secondary teachers have either taken a class or participated in in-service training in this area (e.g., Bursuck et al., 1996; Struyk et al., 1996; Struyk et al.,1995). Unfortunately, even though most general education teachers view accommodations as desirable and reasonable, they often do not implement them. After reviewing numerous studies on this topic, Scott, Vitale, and Masten (1998) reported that the main reasons given by teachers for not implementing accommodations were a lack of training and school support.

Accommodations, or instructional adaptations, can either be typical/routine or substantial/specialized. "Typical/routine adaptations are either strategies directed toward the class as a whole or relatively minor adaptations that a teacher might make for any student. In contrast, substantial/specialized adaptations refer to individually tailored adjustments intended to address the needs of individual students with disabilities" (Scott, Vitale, & Masten, 1998, p. 107).

The following are examples of major categories of teacher adaptations (previously cited in Chapter 14 for elementary students) that have been modified for application with secondary students (Scott et al., 1998):

▲ Modify instruction by using different instructional approaches, focusing on different learning styles, and relating instruction to activities' engaged in by adolescents.
▲ Modify assignments in ways to facilitate success for adolescents with disabilities, and basic skill deficits.
▲ Teach study skills such as note taking, test taking, reading for content, and memory strategies that can be applied in content classes.
▲ Use alternative instructional materials that are interesting to adolescents and that can be accessed easily by adolescents with basic skill deficits.
▲ Alter curricula by providing adolescents with life skills, study skills, and prevocational opportunities.
▲ Vary instructional grouping to take advantage of cooperative learning and peer support systems.
▲ Enhance behavior by using age-appropriate reinforcement for adolescents.
▲ Facilitate progress monitoring by using a wide variety of methods to evaluate progress that meets the individual needs of students.

Accommodations should be designed to offer the *least* amount of alteration of the regular programming that will still allow the student to benefit from instruction. This approach is fair to nondisabled students and provides the students with disabilities with a realistic sense of their abilities and limitations. If too many accommodations are made, some students may be set up for failure in a college or other academically demanding environments. Students with too many accommodations may also begin to feel that they bring very little to the class; this can further damage an already fragile self-concept. Modifications used in settings or classes designed to prepare an individual for a future job or postsecondary training program should reflect real conditions present in these future environments.

**CROSS-REFERENCE**
Review Chapters 4–10 to determine specific accommodations suggested for children with different disabilities.

Many different accommodations can be used effectively with students with disabilities. These include altering the way information is presented, the materials used, and the physical environment. Table 15.4 describes sample accommodative strategies.

Teachers can take other actions to accommodate a student's learning difficulties, such as using vocabulary guides, cued text, advance organizers, and a structured overview (Leverett & Diefendorf, 1992). Often, a great deal of a student's grade may be determined by the quality of work on assignments; yet sometimes students with disabilities may not understand an assignment or may lack the ability or time to

**TABLE 15.4**  Sample Accommodative Strategies

| Strategy | Description |
| --- | --- |
| **OUTLINES** | Simple course outlines assist pupils in organizing notes and information. |
| **STORY GUIDES** | Expanded outlines provide specific information such as assignments and evaluation criteria. |
| **ADVANCE ORGANIZERS** | A set of questions or other guides indicate the most important parts of reading assignments. |
| **AUDIOVISUAL AIDS** | Overhead projectors, films, film strips, and chalkboard are examples, which can reinforce auditory information and enable students with auditory deficits to access information. |
| **VARYING INSTRUCTIONAL STRATEGIES** | Alternative teaching strategies enable students to utilize their most efficient learning style. |
| **SEATING ARRANGEMENT** | Place students in locations that minimize problems. Examples: close to front of class for children with auditory and visual problems; away from other children for students with behavior problems; away from windows and doors for those with distractibility problems. |
| **TAPE RECORDERS** | Using tape recorders can greatly benefit children with visual problems, memory problems, reading problems, etc. Taped textbooks, tests, and lectures can facilitate learning. |

From *Language Instruction for Students with Disabilities* (p. 440), by E. A. Polloway and T. E. C. Smith, 2000, Denver: Love. Used by permission.

**CONSIDER THIS**
Should teachers who refuse to make accommodations for students in their classes with different learning needs be required to make such efforts? What are the consequences for students included in classrooms where teachers refuse to make accommodations?

complete it. Therefore, teachers may need to make some accommodations in the area of assignments. Chalmers (1991) suggests the following:

1. *Preteach vocabulary and preview major concepts:* Students must have the vocabulary necessary to complete an assignment. If they do not know a particular word, they may not know how to find its definition, causing them to possibly fail the assignment. Similarly, students need to understand the major concepts required to complete the assignment.
2. *State a purpose for reading:* Students need to know *why* they have to do things. Helping them understand the context of the assignment may aid in motivating them.
3. *Provide repetition of instruction:* Choral responding, group work, and hands-on activities are examples of providing students with disabilities with the opportunities necessary for learning. One instance of instruction may simply not be sufficient to ensure learning.
4. *Provide clear directions and examples:* "I didn't understand" is a common response from students when they fail. For many students, this response may simply be an effort to evade negative consequences. For many students with disabilities, however, the statement may reflect a true misunderstanding of the assignment. Therefore, teachers need to make every effort to explain all assignments in such a way that they are understandable to all students.
5. *Make time adjustments:* Teachers should individualize the time requirements associated with assignments. Some students may be capable of performing the work successfully, only to become frustrated with time restraints. Teachers should make adjustments for students who simply need more time or who may become overwhelmed by the volume of work required in a particular time period.
6. *Provide feedback:* All individuals need feedback; they need to know how they are doing. For students with disabilities and a history of failure, the feedback, especially positive feedback, is even more critical. Teachers should provide feedback for every assignment as soon as possible after the assignment is completed.
7. *Have students keep an assignment notebook:* Often, students with disabilities are disorganized; they may need some organization imposed upon them externally. Requiring students to keep an assignment notebook is an example. The assignment notebook not only negates the excuse "I did not have my assignment" or "I lost my assignment," but it also helps some students maintain a semblance of order in their assignments and facilitates their completion of all required work.
8. *Provide an alternate assignment:* Provide opportunities for students to complete an assignment differently. For example, if a student has difficulty with oral language, the teacher could accept a written book report rather than an oral one. Videotaped, tape-recorded, and oral presentations can be used in conjunction with written presentations.
9. *Allow manipulatives:* Cue cards, charts, and number lines are examples of manipulatives that can help some students comprehend information. Some students prefer to learn visually, whereas others prefer the auditory mode. Manipulatives can facilitate the learning of all students.
10. *Highlight textbooks:* Highlight the important facts in textbooks. These books can be passed on to other students with similar reading problems next year. Highlighting material enables students to focus on the important content.

**TEACHING TIP**
These accommodations are helpful for all students, including those without disabilities who do not need specialized instruction.

Another important accommodation that teachers can make is the alteration of materials. Deshler, Ellis, and Lenz (1996) describe a way to reduce the content in textbooks. Often, some students, while capable of reading and understanding, take significantly longer to read than their peers. Therefore, teachers may wish to reduce the amount of content without altering the nature of the content. When selecting materials, teachers should consider cultural diversity issues.

In addition to significant curricular modifications, teachers can make numerous simple adjustments to teach specific information to students:

- ◢ Repeat important information several times.
- ◢ Write important facts on the board.
- ◢ Repeat the same information about a particular topic over several days.
- ◢ Distribute handouts that contain only the most important information about a particular topic.

## Homework, Grading, and Testing

Homework, grading, and testing stand out as important considerations in students' success within secondary school classrooms. They have become more significant in light of trends toward an increase in academic standards and accountability in general education classrooms (Hocutt, Martin, & McKinney, 1990; Schumaker & Deshler, 1988). For example, the National Assessment of Education Progress Report found that by 1988 students in general education classrooms were being assigned more homework than they had been four years before (U.S. Department of Education, 1990). Higher expectations for student performance in general education classes affect testing and grading; further reforms such as a national achievement test, higher graduation standards, performance-based testing, and the essay rather than multiple-choice formats in tests are being discussed (Harrington-Lueker, 1991; Ysseldyke et al., 1992). This section explores these problem areas, focusing on adaptations to facilitate student success.

**CONSIDER THIS**
Should standardized tests play such an important role in public schools? How does the expansion of these tests affect students with disabilities?

**HOMEWORK** Problems in homework often become more pronounced at the secondary level. The trend has been to require more homework of students, which has become an issue in raising the standards of public education (Bryan & Sullivan-Burstein, 1998). Roderique et al. (1994) report that for school districts with a homework policy, the average amount of homework assigned at the high school level was over 1 hour and 40 minutes per daily assignment, and the frequency was 4.28 nights per week. Struyk et al. (1995) report that 70% of the teachers assigned homework two to four times per week; 11% assigned it five times per week. The time period needed to complete the homework varied from less than 30 minutes to 1.5 hours per day; 43% of the teachers assigned at least 30 minutes of homework per night. Given that students typically have 4–6 teachers, assignments represent a significant hurdle for middle and high school students with disabilities. While the amount of homework assigned provides a challenge, the unique difficulties of students with disabilities are underscored by the types of problems they are likely to have. Figure 15.3 lists the highest-rated homework problems of adolescents. Yet each problem carries implicit potential remedies.

Given that students with special needs experience problems with homework, a number of strategies can be pursued. For example, Struyk et al. (1995) found that, with regard to the helpfulness of specific *types of homework*, teachers rated preparation for tests and practice of skills already taught as moderately helpful, whereas enrichment activities and preparation for future class work were seen as least helpful. They rated in-class structures such as checking the level of the students' understanding when beginning an in-class assignment and using a homework assignment sheet or notebook as the most helpful *procedures*. Finally, teachers also rated the helpfulness of

*FIGURE* **15.3**

Homework Problems of Adolescents with Behavior Disorders

*Note:* These are the highest rated problems noted by special educators.

From "A Comparison of Homework Problems of Secondary School Students with Behavior Disorders and Nondisabled Peers," by J. Soderlund, W. Bursuck, E. A. Polloway, and R. A. Foley, 1995, *Journal of Emotional and Behavioral Disorders, 3,* p. 152. Used by permission.

1. Easily distracted by noises or activities of others.
2. Responds poorly when told by parent to correct homework.
3. Procrastinates, puts off doing homework.
4. Fails to complete homework.
5. Whines or complains about homework.
6. Easily frustrated by homework assignment.
7. Must be reminded to sit down and start homework.
8. Fails to bring home assignment and necessary materials.
9. Daydreams or plays with objects during homework session.
10. Refuses to do homework assignment.
11. Takes unusually long time to do homework.
12. Produces messy or sloppy homework.
13. Hurries through homework and makes careless mistakes.

specific *adaptations* for students with disabilities. Their responses are summarized in Figure 15.4.

Collaboration among general and special education teachers and parents will encourage successful completion of homework. Teachers should attend to communication problems that can evolve regarding homework. Struyk et al. (1996) cite communication problems as experienced by parents, special education teachers, and general education teachers. Parents' highest-ranked problems were frequency of communication, early initiation of communication, and follow-through. Similar concerns were voiced by special education teachers (i.e., early initiation, frequency, follow-through). Finally, general education teachers cited the following challenges to regular communication: the competing demands of record keeping and paperwork, difficulty in coordinating schedules to set up time to talk with parents, and the large number of students with disabilities in their classes.

**CONSIDER THIS**

Should school policies regarding homework be altered to increase the likelihood of success for students with disabilities, or should these students be required to follow a rigid policy designed for all students? Why or why not?

*FIGURE* **15.4**

Homework Adaptations for Adolescents with Disabilities

*Note:* Items are ranked from most helpful to least helpful.

From "Homework, Grading, and Testing Practices Used by Teachers with Students with and without Disabilities," by L. R. Struyk, M. H. Epstein, W. Bursuck, E. A. Polloway, J. McConeghy, and K. B. Cole, 1995, *The Clearing House, 69,* p. 52. Used by permission.

1. Provide additional teacher assistance.
2. Check more frequently with student about assignments and expectations.
3. Provide a peer tutor for assistance.
4. Allow alternative response formats (e.g., oral or other than written).
5. Provide auxiliary learning aids (e.g., calculator, computer).
6. Adjust length of assignment.
7. Assign work that student can do independently.
8. Provide a study group.
9. Provide extra credit opportunities.
10. Evaluate based on effort, not on performance.
11. Adjust (i.e., lower) evaluation standards.
12. Adjust due dates.
13. Give fewer assignments.

Certain policies and procedures can increase students' success with homework. The following ideas have proved effective for general education teachers:

◢ Schedule after-school sessions at which students can get extra help on their homework.
◢ Provide peer tutoring programs that concentrate on homework.
◢ Provide sufficient study hall time during school hours for students to complete their homework.
◢ Use community volunteers to assist students in completing homework. (Epstein et al., 1996)

Students can also get help with their homework through the Internet. Secondary teachers need to become familiar with this new source of support and make this information available to students.

**GRADING** The challenges of inclusion of adolescents with disabilities are perhaps most clearly reflected in the area of grading. The extant research in this area has not shown positive results. For example, Zigmond and her associates (Donahue & Zigmond, 1990; Zigmond, Levin, & Laurie, 1985) report that approximately 60% to 75% of high school students with learning disabilities received passing grades in their general education classes, but they consistently received below-average grade-point averages (GPAs) (i.e., an overall GPA of 0.99 on a 4.0 scale, or D work). These patterns seem to reflect a persistent lack of academic success, particularly as compared to students without disabilities (e.g., Wood, Bennett, Wood, & Bennett, 1990). Similarly, Valdes, Williamson, and Wagner (1990) report that 60.2% of high school students with disabilities had averages of C+ or lower, with a subset of 35.4% receiving averages below the C– level. Furthermore, these researchers note that more than one third of students enrolled in graded general education classes had at least one failing grade.

In researching classroom report card practices, Struyk et al. (1995) found that, in determining grades, teachers weighed tests and quizzes highest, and in-class work and homework second highest. Teachers reported that checklists indicating level of competence and skills, supplemented by written comments, were the most helpful apparatus for reporting grades for students with disabilities.

Teachers' responses for grading adaptations for students with disabilities are summarized in Figure 15.5. This list provides a basis for designing grading practices that

**CONSIDER THIS**

If alternative grading requirements are used with students with disabilities, should these students be eligible for honor roll, honors programs, and so forth? Why or why not?

---

1. Separate grades are given for process (e.g., effort) and product (e.g., tests).
2. Grades are based on the amount of improvement an individual makes.
3. Grading weights are adjusted (e.g., effort or projects count more than tests).
4. Grades are based on meeting the requirements of academic or behavioral contracts.
5. Grades are based on meeting IEP objectives.
6. Grades are adjusted according to student ability.
7. Grades are based on a modified grading scale (e.g., change 93 – 100 = A to 90 – 100 = A).
8. Grades are based on less content than required for the rest of the class.
9. Students are passed if they make an effort to pass.
10. Students are passed no matter what.

*FIGURE* **15.5**

Grading Adaptations for Adolescents with Disabilities

*Note:* Items are ranked from most to least helpful.

From "Homework, Grading, and Testing Practices Used by Teachers with Students with and without Disabilities," by L. R. Struyk, M. H. Epstein, W. Bursuck, E. A. Polloway, J. McConeghy, and K. B. Cole, 1995, *The Clearing House, 69,* p. 53. Used by permission.

| TABLE 15.5 | Fairness of Grading Adaptations: With versus Without Disability | | | | | |
|---|---|---|---|---|---|---|
| | **FREQUENCY CLASSIFICATION** | | | | | |
| | **Learning Disability** | | **No Disability** | | **Significance** | |
| **QUESTION** | **Fair** | **Not Fair** | **Fair** | **Not Fair** | $\chi^2$ | $\rho$ |
| Do I think it is fair for teachers to . . . | | | | | | |
| 1. Give some students a higher report card grade because they show improvement. | 9 | 5 | 91 | 164 | 4.648 | .031 |
| 2. Give some students two grades for each subject (one for how hard they tried, and one for how well they did). | 7 | 7 | 117 | 139 | 0.099 | .753 |
| 3. Change how much certain things count toward the report card grades of some students (for example, make assignments worth more than tests). | 5 | 8 | 36 | 220 | 5.701 | .017 |
| 4. Give some students a higher report card grade when they do the best they can. | 7 | 7 | 113 | 143 | 0.185 | .667 |
| 5. Give some students a report card grade based on having to learn less material. | 4 | 10 | 47 | 206 | 0.858 | .354 |
| 6. Grade some students using a different grading scale (for example, 90–100 = A rather than 93–100 = A). | 9 | 5 | 34 | 222 | 25.790 | .001 |
| 7. Give some students a passing report card grade no matter what. | 2 | 13 | 13 | 242 | 1.831 | .176 |
| 8. Pass some students no matter how poorly they do (as long as they try hard). | 6 | 8 | 88 | 167 | 0.407 | .524 |
| 9. Grade some students on a pass–fail basis (without using number or letter grades). | 5 | 8 | 62 | 193 | 1.320 | .251 |

From "The Fairness of Report Card Grading Adaptations," by W. D. Bursuck, D. D. Munk, and M. M. Olson, 1999, *Remedial and Special Education, 20*, p. 84. Used by permission.

help adolescents with disabilities succeed in school. In addition, teachers should carefully evaluate the fairness of their grading patterns for students with special needs.

Bursuck, Munk, and Olson (1999) asked students with and without disabilities their opinions about report card and grading accommodations. The majority of students, both those with and those without disabilities, considered most of the accommodations to be unfair. Table 15.5 shows the number of individuals who considered specific accommodations as fair and unfair.

**TESTING** The inclusion movement has raised concerns regarding how students with special needs will be assessed. Although some adaptations are being made in standardized instruments, most adaptations for students with disabilities are made at the classroom level (Thurlow, Ysseldyke, & Silverstein, 1993).

Simple adaptations can make the difference between taking a test successfully or poorly. For example, reading a test to a student who is a very poor reader gives the student a chance to display knowledge or skills. If such students have to read the questions themselves, test results will reflect students' poor reading skills and fail to assess knowledge of a particular content area. Teachers can address this situation in the following ways:

- ◢ Have another student read the test to the student.
- ◢ Have the special education teacher or aide read the test to the student.
- ◢ Give the student additional time to complete the test.
- ◢ Reword the test to include only words that are within the student's reading vocabulary.

A full consideration of adaptations in testing, however, extends beyond the consideration of reading ability. Smith et al. (1993) list ways in which teachers can make tests more accessible to students: generous spacing between items on the pages, adequate space allowed for responses, generous margins, readability of text, appropriate test length, logical organization, and clear instructions. The following examples are techniques to adapt measurement instruments:

**CROSS-REFERENCE**
Review Chapters 4–10 and determine specific testing adaptations that might be necessary with students with different types of disabilities.

- ◢ Using information about performance outside of school in making evaluations
- ◢ Administering frequent short tests, rather than a few long tests
- ◢ Dividing tests or tasks into smaller, simpler sections or steps
- ◢ Developing practice items or pretest trials using the same response format as the test
- ◢ Considering the appropriateness of the instrument or procedure in terms of age or maturity
- ◢ Giving open-book tests
- ◢ Reducing the number of test items or removing items that require more abstract reasoning or have high levels of difficulty
- ◢ Using different levels of questions for different students
- ◢ Having a student develop a product or packet of materials that show knowledge and understanding of the content of a unit (portfolio assessment)
- ◢ Providing alternative projects or assignments
- ◢ Having peers administer tests
- ◢ Allowing students to make up tests
- ◢ Videotaping a student performing a task and then playing it back to him or her to show skills learned and areas needing improvement
- ◢ Using a panel of students to evaluate one another on task performance
- ◢ Allowing students to type answers
- ◢ Allowing students to use a computer during testing
- ◢ Allowing small groups to work together on a task to be evaluated (such as a project or test)
- ◢ Using short written or verbal measures on a daily or weekly basis to provide more feedback on student progress
- ◢ Increasing the amount of time allowed to complete the test
- ◢ Altering the presentation (written, oral, visual) of tests
- ◢ Altering the types of responses to match a student's strengths (written, oral, short answer, or simple marking)
- ◢ Having a student review the course or unit content verbally so that he or she is not limited to test item recall
- ◢ Limiting the number of formal tests by using checklists to observe and record learning
- ◢ Assessing participation in discussions
- ◢ Giving extra credit for correction of mistakes

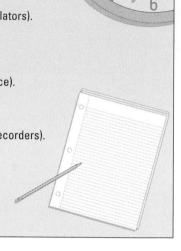

**FIGURE 15.6**

Testing Adaptations for Adolescents with Disabilities

*Note:* Items are ranked from most to least helpful.

From "Homework, Grading, and Testing Practices Used by Teachers with Students with and without Disabilities," by L. R. Struyk, M. H. Epstein, W. Bursuck, E. A. Polloway, J. McConeghy, and K. B. Cole, 1995, *The Clearing House, 69*, p. 54. Used by permission.

1. Give extended time to finish tests.
2. Give extra help preparing for tests.
3. Simplify wording of test questions.
4. Give individual help with directions during tests.
5. Give practice questions as a study guide.
6. Use black and white copies (rather than ditto).
7. Read test questions to students.
8. Allow use of learning aids during tests (e.g., calculators).
9. Highlight key words in questions.
10. Use tests with enlarged print.
11. Give the actual test as a study guide.
12. Give feedback to individual students during test.
13. Change question type (e.g., essay to multiple choice).
14. Give open-book/note tests.
15. Allow students to answer fewer questions.
16. Teach students test-taking skills.
17. Allow oral instead of written answers (e.g., tape recorders).
18. Test on less content than rest of the class.
19. Provide extra space on tests for answering.
20. Allow word processors.
21. Allow answers in outline format.
22. Give tests to small groups.
23. Give take-home tests.

**CROSS-REFERENCE**

Refer to Chapter 14 for information regarding treatment acceptability.

Testing adaptations raise questions of treatment acceptability. Relative to this concern, Struyk et al. (1995) report that adaptations commonly used for students *without* disabilities include extending the time students have for completing the test (92%), giving feedback to individual students during the test (94%), and allowing students to take open-book or open-notes tests (96%). Since these techniques already are commonly in use, they should be considered as the initial adaptation options for students with disabilities. General education teachers' preferences in testing adaptations for adolescent students with disabilities are summarized in Figure 15.6.

*Effective teachers use a master plan for lessons, including specific teaching goals.*

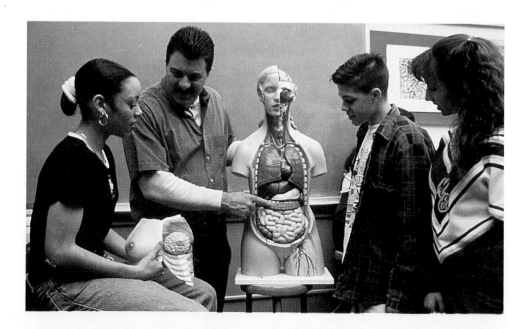

For students to perform successfully on tests, they will need to learn individual test-taking and organizational strategies, which are often difficult for students with disabilities (Scruggs & Mastropieri, 1988). Such strategies are typically subsumed within the area of study skills, discussed in the next section.

## Study Skills and Learning Strategies

Teachers' accommodations are insufficient to guarantee that students with special needs will be successful. Students must develop their own skills and strategies to help them overcome, or compensate for, a disability. Understanding how to use study skills will greatly enhance their chances for being successful in future academic, vocational, or social activities. Classroom teachers can help students acquire a repertoire of study skills. Study skills are tools that students can use to assist them with their learning. They include listening, note taking, reading rate, test taking, remembering information, managing time, managing behavior, motivation, and goal setting (Hoover, & Patton, 1995).

Many students have an innate ability in these areas. For example, some students are good readers, adept at comprehension and able to read quickly; other students find it easy to memorize facts. These students may not need instruction in study skills. For other students, however, study skills represent an "invisible curriculum" that must be taught directly if they are to be successful. For example, the study skill of listening is critical in most educational settings because teachers provide so much information verbally. If students are not able to attend to auditory information, they will miss a great deal of content. Table 15.6 summarizes key study skills and their significance for learning.

| **TABLE 15.6** | **Study Skills and Their Significance for Learning** |
|---|---|
| **Study Skill** | **Significance for Learning** |
| READING RATE | Rates vary with type and length of reading materials; students need to adjust rate to content. |
| LISTENING | Ability to listen is critical in most educational tasks and throughout life. |
| NOTE TAKING/OUTLINING | Ability to take notes and develop outlines is critical in content courses and essential for future study. |
| REPORT WRITING | Written reports are frequently required in content courses. |
| ORAL PRESENTATIONS | Some teachers require extensive oral reporting. |
| GRAPHIC AIDS | Visual aids can help students who have reading deficits understand complex material. |
| TEST TAKING | Students must be able to do well on tests if they are to succeed in content courses. |
| REFERENCE MATERIAL/ DICTIONARY USAGE | Using reference materials makes learners more independent. |
| TIME MANAGEMENT | Ability to manage and allocate time is critical for success in secondary settings. |
| SELF-MANAGEMENT OF BEHAVIOR | Self-management assists students in assuming responsibility and leads to independence. |

Adapted from *Teaching Students with Learning Problems to Use Study Skills: A Teacher's Guide* (p. 7), by J. J. Hoover and J. R. Patton, 1995, Austin, TX: Pro-Ed.

# INCLUSION STRATEGIES

## Learning Strategies

### ACQUISITION STRATEGIES

**Word identification strategy:** teaches students a problem-solving procedure for quickly attacking and decoding unknown words in reading materials allowing them to move on quickly for the purpose of comprehending the passage.

**Paraphrasing strategy:** directs students to read a limited section of material, ask themselves the main idea and the details of the section, and put that information in their own words. This strategy is designed to improve comprehension by focusing attention on the important information of a passage and by stimulating active involvement with the passage.

**Self-questioning strategy:** aids reading comprehension by having students actively ask questions about key pieces of information in a passage and then read to find the answers for these questions.

**Visual imagery strategy:** improves students' acquisition, storage, and recall of prose material. Students improve reading comprehension by reading short passages and visualizing the scene which is described, incorporating actors, action, and details.

**Interpreting visuals strategy:** aids students in the use and interpretation of visuals such as maps, graphs, pictures, and tables to increase their ability to extract needed information from written materials.

**Multipass strategy:** involves making three passes through a passage for the purpose of focusing attention on key details and main ideas. Students survey a chapter or passage to get an overview, size up sections of the chapter by systematically scanning to locate relevant information which they note, and sort out important information in the chapter by locating answers to specific questions.

### STORAGE STRATEGIES

**FIRST–Letter mnemonic strategy:** aids students in memorizing lists of information by teaching them to design mnemonics or memorization aids, and in finding and making lists of crucial information. (Published by Edge Enterprises)

**Paired associates strategy:** aids students in memorizing pairs of small groups of information by using visual imagery, matching pertinent information with familiar objects, coding important dates, and a first-syllable technique.

**Listening and note-taking strategy:** teaches students to develop skills that enhance their abil-

▼

Closely related to study skills are *learning strategies*—ways to use active learning to acquire and use new information and solve problems ("learning to learn") (see the nearby Inclusion Strategies feature). Teachers should be alert to ways to teach not only content but also ways to learn and use the content. This is particularly important in areas such as reading comprehension, error monitoring in writing, problem solving in math, and test preparation. A comprehensive source on numerous strategies for learning (and their use) is provided by Masters et al. (1999). Teachers may have to instruct students how to use a given learning strategy. Alley and Deshler (1979) described an eight-step procedure for teaching strategies to students. While this model has been modified from time to time, the general approach

▼ ity to learn from listening experiences by identifying the speaker's verbal cues or mannerisms which signal that important information is about to be given, noting key words, and organizing their notes into an outline for future reference or study.

## EXPRESSION AND DEMONSTRATION OF COMPETENCE STRATEGIES

**Sentence writing strategy:** teaches students how to recognize and generate four types of sentences: simple, compound, complex, and compound-complex.

**Paragraph writing strategy:** teaches students how to write well-organized, complete paragraphs by outlining ideas, selecting a point-of-view and tense for the paragraph, sequencing ideas, and checking their work.

**Error monitoring strategy:** teaches students a process for detecting and correcting errors in their writing and for producing a neater written product. Students are taught to locate errors in paragraph organization, sentence structure, capitalization, overall editing and appearance, punctuation, and spelling by asking themselves a series of questions. Students correct their errors and rewrite the passage before submitting it to their teacher.

**Theme writing strategy:** teaches students to write a five-paragraph theme. They learn how to generate ideas for themes and how to organize these ideas into a logical sequence. Then the student learns how to write the paragraphs, monitor errors, and rewrite the theme.

**Assignment completion strategy:** teaches students to monitor their assignments from the time an assignment is given until it is completed and submitted to the teacher. Students write down assignments; analyze the assignments; schedule various subtasks; complete the subtasks, and ultimately, the entire task; and submit the completed assignment.

**Test taking strategy:** aids students during test taking. Students are taught to allocate time and read instructions and questions carefully. A question is either answered or abandoned for later consideration. The obviously wrong answers are eliminated from the abandoned questions and a reasonable guess is made. The last step is to survey the entire test for unanswered questions.

From "The Strategic Intervention Model," by R. Tralli, B. Colombo, D. D. Deshler, and J. B. Schumaker, 1996, *Remedial and Special Education, 17,* p. 206. Used by permission.

still remains effective. The following steps are included in the approach (Masters et al., 1999):

1. Testing the student's current level of functioning
2. Describing the steps of the strategy and providing a rationale for each step
3. Modeling the strategy so the student can observe all of the processes involved
4. Verbally rehearsing the steps of the strategy to criterion
5. Practicing controlled materials written at the student's reading ability level
6. Practicing content materials from the student's grade placement level
7. Giving positive and corrective feedback
8. Giving the post test (p. 119)

The following are examples of learning strategies.

◢ SCROL (Grant, 1993) is a strategy that helps students learn how to use textbook headings to improve comprehension. There are five steps in the strategy (Scholes, 1998, p. 111):

1. **S**urvey the heading. Read each heading and subheading and answer the following questions: What do I already know about this topic? What do I expect the author to include in this section?
2. **C**onnect. How are the headings related to each other? Write down words from the headings that provide connections between them.
3. **R**ead the text. As you read, look for words or phrases that provide important information about the headings. Stop and make sure you understand the major ideas and supporting details at the end of each section. Reread if you don't understand.
4. **O**utline. Outline the major ideas and supporting details in the section. Try to do this without looking back.
5. **L**ook back. Look back at the text to check the accuracy of your outline. Correct your outline as needed.

◢ The **COPS** strategy (Schumaker et al., 1981) is an error-monitoring strategy for writing. The acronym stands for four tasks:

1. **C**apitalization,
2. **O**verall appearance (e.g., neatness, appropriate margins),
3. **P**unctuation, and
4. **S**pelling.

These strategies have proved effective for use with students with learning problems at the upper elementary, middle, and secondary school levels (Shannon & Polloway, 1993).

Efforts to validate the use of specific strategies within inclusive classrooms continue. An exciting aspect of instruction in strategies is its potential to benefit students with and without disabilities (Fisher, Schumaker, & Deshler, 1995).

 **ummary**

## Secondary School Curricula

◢ Important differences exist between elementary and secondary settings in terms of organizational structure, curriculum, and learner characteristics.

◢ From a curricular perspective, integrating students with disabilities into general classes is more challenging at the secondary level than at the elementary level.

◢ The period of adolescence adds to the problems experienced by students with disabilities.

## Programs for Students in Secondary Schools

◢ Curricular options for students at the secondary level with particular relevance for students with disabilities include basic skills, social skills, tutoring, learning strategies, vocational skills, and life skills.

◢ Future-based assessment offers one method for developing programs for adolescents with disabilities.

◢ Classroom teachers and special education teachers must collaborate to ensure effective secondary school programs.

◢ Special education teachers must help prepare students for academic content classes.

◢ Transition to the secondary level is a major endeavor for students with disabilities.

## Methods to Facilitate Students' Success in General Education Classes

◢ Accommodations are changes that teachers can make to facilitate the success of students with disabilities.

◢ Specific challenges for successful inclusion occur in the areas of homework, grading, and testing.

◢ Study skills are skills that students with disabilities can use to help them achieve success in general and special education classes.

◢ Learning strategies enable students to achieve independence as they "learn how to learn."

# urther Readings

Baker, B. L., Brightman, A. J., Blacher, J. B., Heifetz, L. J., Hinshaw, S. P., & Murphy, D. M. (1997). *Steps to independence: Teaching everyday skills to children with special needs.* Baltimore: Brookes.

Bley, N. S., & Thornton, C. A. (1995). *Teaching mathematics to students with learning disabilities.* Austin, TX: Pro-Ed.

Hoover, J. J., & Patton, J. R. (1995). *Teaching students with learning problems to use study skills.* Austin, TX: Pro-Ed.

Hoover, J. J., & Patton, J. R. (1997). *Curriculum adaptations for students with learning and behavior problems* (2nd ed.) Austin, TX: Pro-Ed.

Hughes, C., Carter, E. W. (1999). *The transition handbook: Strategies high school teachers use that work.* Baltimore: Brookes.

Lovitt, T. C. (1991). *Preventing school dropouts.* Austin, TX: Pro-Ed.

Lyndsey, J. D. (Ed.) (1999). *Technology and exceptional individuals* (3rd ed.). Austin, TX: Pro-Ed.

Masters, L. F., Mori, B. A., & Mori, A. A. (1999). *Teaching secondary students with mild learning and behavior problems.* Austin, TX: Pro-Ed.

Mastropieri, M. A., & Scruggs, T. E. (1993). *A practical guide for teaching science to students with special needs in inclusive settings.* Austin, TX: Pro-Ed.

Wehman, P. (1996). *Life beyond the classroom: Transition strategies for young people with disabilities* (2nd ed.). Baltimore: Brookes.

Wehman, P. (Ed.) (1997). *Exceptional individuals in school, community, and work.* Austin, TX: Pro-Ed.

Wehman, P., & Kregel, J. (Eds.) (1998). *More than a job: Securing satisfying careers for people with disabilities.* Baltimore: Brookes.

# Working with Families of Students with Disabilities

*After reading this chapter, you should be able to:*

◢ Identify changes in the American family structure that have implications for the public schools of the 1990s

◢ Discuss the particular challenges experienced by parents of individuals with disabilities

◢ Discuss effective ways to involve the family in education programs

◢ List principles of effective communication with parents

◢ Delineate support roles that parents and family members can play

◢ Understand the perspectives of parents of children with special needs

As advocates for all children, teachers are frequently confronted with difficult family situations in which their assistance is requested and needed. Place yourself in the position of Jody Alvarez, a primary school educator, who was approached by Josh and Sally Williams with the following concern.

"One month ago, Josh and I were told by our family doctor that our 4-year-old daughter, Susie, is developmentally delayed. Her language is deficient and her learning is slow. The doctor indicated that the problem is probably related to an accident in which she was involved. Further, he suggested that the prognosis indicates that she may eventually be identified as having mental retardation. Needless to say, this information came to us as a total shock. During that time, we have gone over and over how this could have happened, why this happened, and what we should do about it.

We still really haven't adjusted to the news that our doctor gave us, and I guess we both would admit that our concerns as well as our disappointments have been a real problem for us. Our biggest worry now is, what lies ahead?

Some of my friends have said that in the past, a child like our Susie might have been sent away for residential care. Certainly, we would never consider that but still we don't know what there is that we can do. Naturally, we would be very grateful for any assistance or information that can help us personally deal with our concerns and, most important, can help Susie. Thank you very much."

## QUESTIONS TO CONSIDER

1. Analyze Josh and Sally's current and potential feelings and discuss their possible reactions upon learning that their child has a disability.
2. What advice, recommendations, and assistance would you provide for these two concerned parents?
3. What would you convey to them about the advantages and challenges of inclusive school programs for their daughter?

**CONSIDER THIS**
The advent of federal laws mandating special education ended a laissez-faire period of home–school relation-ships. What do you think the situation would be like today without these federal laws mandating parental involvement?

A significant change in special education in the past two decades has been the increased involvement of parents and family. Prior to Public Law 94-142 (later IDEA), schools frequently did not encourage parents to actively participate in the education of their children. However, given the numerous concerns that parents may have (such as those mentioned in the opening vignette) and given the value of family input into educational programs, certainly parental involvement is a welcome trend. In this chapter, the challenges facing parents, examples of perspectives provided by parents, and strategies for collaboration with parents are highlighted.

Although the important role of families in all aspects of child growth and devel-opment has been acknowledged for many years, federal law formally established the importance of their role relative to students with special needs. As referenced earlier in the text, IDEA requires schools to:

◢ Involve parents in all decision-making activities regarding the education of their child.
◢ Inform parents of impending actions regarding their child.
◢ Provide information to parents in a form that can be easily understood.
◢ Make available due-process rights for parents and their child.
◢ Enable parents to request a due-process hearing if the disagreement with school personnel cannot be resolved.

Clearly, legislation and parental advocacy have established a current high level of family involvement in the education of students with disabilities. School personnel acknowledge the merit of having parents actively participate in the educational pro-cess, including identification, referral, assessment, program planning, and implemen-tation. Comprehensive programs of family involvement begin when children with disabilities are young and continue through the transition process out of school and into adulthood.

The challenge for educators is to consider diverse, effective ways to involve fam-ilies in the education of children with disabilities. As an overview, look at the six con-siderations of Dunst, Johanson, Trivette, and Hamby (1991) involving families:

**CROSS-REFERENCE**
See Chapter 7 to review how supports have been provided to families of students with mental retardation.

**FAMILY SUPPORT** is the intervention model that provides services to the entire family who has a child with a disability.

1. Enhancing a sense of community among the families
2. Mobilizing resources and supports
3. Sharing responsibility and collaboration
4. Protecting family integrity
5. Strengthening family functioning
6. Implementing proactive human service practices

Table 16.1 describes each of these six categories and gives examples of **family support** principles associated with each.

| TABLE 16.1 | Major Categories and Examples of Family Support Principles |
| --- | --- |
| **Category/Characteristic** | **Examples of Principles** |
| **1. ENHANCING A SENSE OF COMMUNITY**<br>Promoting the coming together of people around shared values and common needs in ways that create mutually beneficial interdependencies | ■ Interventions should focus on the building of inter-dependencies between members of the community and the family unit.<br>■ Interventions should emphasize the common needs and supports of all people and base intervention actions on those commonalities. |
| **2. MOBILIZING RESOURCES AND SUPPORTS**<br>Building support systems that enhance the flow of resources in ways that assist families with parenting responsibilities | ■ Interventions should focus on building and strengthening informal support networks for families rather than depending solely on professionals' support systems.<br>■ Resources and supports should be made available to families in ways that are flexible, individualized, and responsive to the needs of the entire family unit. |
| **3. SHARED RESPONSIBILITY AND COLLABORATION**<br>Sharing of ideas and skills by parents and professionals in ways that build and strengthen collaborative arrangements | ■ Interventions should employ partnerships between parents and professionals as a primary mechanism for supporting and strengthening family functioning.<br>■ Resources and support mobilization interactions between families and service providers should be based on mutual respect and sharing of unbiased information. |
| **4. PROTECTING FAMILY INTEGRITY**<br>Respecting the family's beliefs and values and protecting the family from intrusion upon its beliefs by outsiders | ■ Resources and supports should be provided to families in ways that encourage, develop, and maintain healthy, stable relationships among all family members.<br>■ Interventions should be conducted in ways that accept, value, and protect a family's personal and cultural values and beliefs. |
| **5. STRENGTHENING FAMILY FUNCTIONING**<br>Promoting the capabilities and competencies of families necessary to mobilize resources and perform parenting responsibilities in ways that have empowering consequences | ■ Interventions should build on family strengths rather than correct weaknesses or deficits as a primary way of supporting and strengthening family functioning.<br>■ Resources and supports should be made available to families in ways that maximize the family's control over and decision-making power regarding services they receive. |
| **6. PROACTIVE HUMAN SERVICE PRACTICES**<br>Adoption of consumer-driven human service-delivery models and practices that support and strengthen family functioning | ■ Service-delivery programs should employ promotion rather than treatment approaches as the framework for strengthening family functioning.<br>■ Resource and support mobilization should be consumer-driven rather than service provider-driven or professionally prescribed. |

From "Family-Oriented Early Intervention Policies and Practices: Family-Centered or Not?" by C. J. Dunst, C. Johanson, C. M. Trivette, and D. Hamby, 1991, *Exceptional Children, 58,* p. 117. Copyright 1991 by the Council for Exceptional Children. Used by permission.

Some families will become more involved with the education of their child than others. For example, Haring, Lovett, and Saren (1991) reported that 23% of their survey respondents said they had no involvement in the education of their children in public school special education programs, 43% said they were somewhat involved, and only 34% said they were actively involved in their child's special education programs. School personnel need to encourage those parents who are active in their child's education to maintain their commitment while developing strategies to increase the involvement of other parents.

**CONSIDER THIS**
Not unexpectedly, the degree of parental participation in the IEP process is correlated with socioeconomic level. Why do you think this is the case?

Family participation can and should occur in many areas. These include involvement with the student's assessment and IEP development, involvement with parent groups, observation of the student in the school setting, and communication with educators. Of these areas, participation in developing the IEP process occurs the most frequently. In a study of 99 families with children with disabilities, 85 families reported that their level of participation in their child's IEP development was either very high or somewhat high. Only 10 families indicated little participation. Sixty-seven of the families said they had some level or high levels of participation in the assessment process, and 52 families indicated they participated in parent groups at some or at high levels (Meyers & Blacher, 1987).

Thus, some families are very involved in their child's special education program, while others have limited involvement. Professionals can meet the letter of the law by simply inviting parental participation; however, school personnel should develop strategies to facilitate family involvement. Although some parents create challenges

# TECHNOLOGY TODAY

## Technology Resources for Families

Technology vastly expands families' access to information. The National Rehabilitation Information Center (NARIC) and ABLEDATA Data Base of Assistive Technology (800-346-2742) will conduct computer searches for families concerning products and devices, disability organizations, and funding opportunities. NARIC has more than 20,000 products on its service list, and users can call the electronic bulletin boards to search the database, get messages, and download fact sheets. (At this time, the computer dial is 301-589-3563.) Another option for accessing the database is through CD-ROM. NARIC has a directory of national information sources on disabilities, including 42 databases, 700 organizations, and more than 100 resource directories.

Computer list servers provide new and immediate access to information for families. All list servers have unique characteristics. For example, a recent check of the autism list server revealed 30 to 40 daily messages on topics such as teenagers, toilet training, the use of aversive intervention, inclusive education, research possibilities, sign language, and siblings.

Another technology resource is operated by the U.S. Department of Education, Office of Educational

*Technology has greatly expanded the information available to families with children with disabilities.*

Research and Innovation (OERI). Its National Library of Education maintains an electronic repository of education information and provides public access through electronic networks. You can call 202-219-1547 or access the library through e-mail at gopher adm@inet.ed.gov.

From *Families, Professionals, and Exceptionality* (pp. 186–187), by A. P. Turnbull and H. R. Turnbull, 1997, Columbus, OH: Merrill. Used by permission.

for the school because of their intense level of involvement, for the most part educational programs are greatly strengthened by parental support.

Families are getting more and more involved in special programs for their children. Some families are learning more about special education programs and particular types of disabilities through technology. The Internet offers a wide variety of information about disabilities, educational programs, and how to provide supports for individuals at home. The nearby Technology Today feature provides information regarding families and technology access.

## THE FAMILY

The viewpoint of what constitutes a family has changed dramatically in recent decades. Traditionally, a *family* has been described as a group of individuals who live together that includes a mother, a father, and one or more children. However, this stereotypical picture has been challenged. "The idealized *nuclear family* of yesteryear with the stay-at-home, take-care-of-the-children mother and the outside-the-home breadwinner father no longer represents the typical American family" (Allen, 1992, p. 319). This traditional view has been changed by the reality that many, perhaps most, families do not resemble this model. Thus, the "Leave It to Beaver" or "Ozzie and Harriet" family of the 1950s has given way to the diversity of the twenty-first century family (Hanson & Carta, 1996), which can best be defined as a group of individuals who live together and care for each others' needs.

Numerous family constellations exist. For example, a large number of families are single-parent families, most frequently with father absent. Fully 90% of families that receive Aid to Families with Dependent Children are headed by a single mother (Allen, 1992). Some single-parent families are headed by a father, and, in some cases, children live with one or more of their grandparents, without either mother or father present. And, although not as common as they once were, some families constitute extended family units, with grandmother or grandfather living with the parents and child. Some children also live in foster homes, in which the foster parents fill all legal roles as birth parents would. Finally, regardless of one's individual opinions, school personnel must also be able to interact with families composed of parents living in gay or lesbian relationships.

The realities of the early twenty-first century pose further challenges to the family: the increase in both younger and older parents, the increase in the number of families living below the poverty line, the realities of substance abuse, the permeation of violence throughout society, and the move away from state residential care for children with serious support needs (see Agosta & Melda, 1996; Hanson & Carta, 1996; Lesar, Gerber, & Semmel, 1996; Simpson, 1996). There may never have been a time when family changes and challenges have more clearly called for understanding and support.

Although undergoing major changes in structure, the family remains the basic unit of our society. It is a dynamic, evolving social force. Although there is debate about the current role of families and their composition, the family remains the key ingredient in a child's life. Teachers must be sensitive to the background of the family to ensure that cultural differences do not interfere with school–family relationships. In addition, it is critical that school personnel remember that students' parents, or others when they are in the role of parents, should be involved in educational programs regardless of the specific composition of the family. School personnel must put aside any personal feelings they may have about various lifestyles and work with students' families to develop and implement the most effective programs for the students.

## Families and Children with Disabilities

The arrival of any child results in changes in family structure and dynamics. Obviously, children change the lives of the mother and father, and each child alters the dynamics of the family unit, including finances, amount and quality of time parents can devote to specific children, relationship between the husband and wife, and future family goals. The arrival of a child with a disability exacerbates the challenges that such changes bring. For example, the almost immediate financial and emotional impact can create major problems for all family members, including siblings.

**CONSIDER THIS**

What are some problems faced by families following the birth of a child with a disability or the identification of a child with a disability?

When a child with a disability becomes a member of the family, whether through birth, adoption, or later onset of the disability, the entire family must make adjustments. The Rights and Responsibilities feature provides an illustration of the types of challenges that parents may experience on a regular basis when attempting to ensure an appropriate education for their child with a disability.

While all children present challenges to parents, a number of critical problems may face families of children with special needs, particularly when the child has a serious disability. For example, consider the following challenges that parents of a child with a severe difficulty may experience:

◢ Expensive medical treatment or hospitalization that may occur repeatedly and for extended periods
◢ Heavy expenses for needs such as special foods and equipment
◢ Frightening, energy-draining, often recurring crises
◢ Transportation problems
◢ Time away from jobs to get the child to consultation and treatment appointments
◢ Lack of affordable child care
◢ Continuous day-and-night demands on parents to provide routine but difficult caregiving tasks
◢ Constant fatigue, lack of sleep, and limited time to meet the needs of other family members
◢ Limited opportunity for recreational or leisure activities
◢ Difficulty of locating and additional expense for babysitters qualified to care for a child with a disability
◢ Babysitting needs for the other children
◢ Lack of respite care facilities
◢ Jealousy or feelings of rejection among brothers and sisters, who may feel their sibling with a disability gets *all* the family's attention and resources
◢ Marital problems arising from finances, fatigue, differences about management of the child's disability, or feelings of rejection by husband or wife that he or she is being passed over in favor of the child (adapted from Allen, 1992, p. 321)

In addition to these problems, a primary difficulty is accepting and understanding the child and the disability, which is critical to a family's acceptance of the child. Parents with a limited understanding of a diagnosis will probably have difficulty in developing realistic expectations of the child, possibly creating major problems between the child and other family members. For example, parents might not understand the nature of a learning disability and therefore accuse the child of being lazy and not trying. Parents who may overlook the potential of students with mental retardation might develop low expectations that will limit the child's success. For example, parents of adolescents might not support a school work program for their son or daughter because they believe that adults with mental retardation are not capable of holding a job.

## Schools Must Provide Continuous Care

The challenges of parents, individuals with disabilities, and local schools are well-illustrated by the case of *Cedar Rapids Community School District* v. *Garret F.*

WASHINGTON (AP)—Federal law requires public school districts to pay for one-on-one nursing services for some disabled students throughout the school day, the Supreme Court said (3/3/99) in a ruling that may strain educational budgets across the nation. The court, by a 7–2 vote in the case of an Iowa teenager, said such continuous care is not medical treatment, and therefore must be publicly funded under [IDEA]. The case, closely watched by school administrators and special education advocates nationwide, means the Cedar Rapids Community School District must pay thousands of dollars a year to provide nursing care for Garret Frey, a ventilator-dependent quadriplegic who is now a high school sophomore. The justices had been told by the National School Boards Association that "school district budgets cannot shoulder the additional financial strain. In light of congressional failure to provide the state and local education agencies with adequate financial assistance to pay for the costs of special education, any judicial interpretations of the IDEA which inflicts additional obligations . . . fall inordinately on already overburdened local public education budgets," the association had contended in a friend-of-the-court brief.

But Charlene Frey, Garret's mother, praised the ruling. "It's going to mean more for other kids than it means for Garret," she said when reached at her home. "I'm glad it will mean everything for other kids."

Garret, described by Justice John Paul Stevens today as a "friendly, creative and intelligent young man," was paralyzed from the neck down in a motorcycle accident when he was 4 years old. His daily health care includes urinary catheterization, suctioning of his tracheotomy, providing food and drink, repositioning in his wheelchair, monitoring his blood pressure and someone familiar with the various alarms on his ventilator.

School officials in Cedar Rapids said the special help Garret requires so he can attend his local high school is so involved and so expensive it should be considered medical treatment. A federal appeals court disagreed, and today the Supreme Court said the appeals court was right. "This case is about whether meaningful access to the public schools will be assured, not the level of education that a school must finance once access is attained," Stevens wrote for the court. "Under the statute, our precedent and the purposes of the IDEA, the district must fund such related services to help guarantee that students like Garret are integrated into the public schools."

Stevens acknowledged that the school district "may have legitimate financial concerns" in providing continuous, one-on-one nursing care, but said the court's only role was to interpret what the federal law requires. "Congress intended to open the door of public education to all qualified children and required participating states to educate handicapped children with non-handicapped children whenever possible," he added.

Through most of his schooling, Garret has been assisted by a licensed practical nurse, paid through an insurance policy and funds from the $1.3 million settlement with the motorcycle company involved in the accident that paralyzed him. This decision could subject the school district to more than $285,000 in legal fees and nursing costs, although there had been little agreement between the school district's lawyers and attorneys for Garret's mother over the cost of providing one-on-one nursing care for him. The school district's lawyers have estimated that [it will] cost as [much as] $30,000 to $50,000 per year in addition to the $10,000 to $12,000 now spent to provide Garret with a teacher associate. The Freys' lawyer has said the estimates are inflated, and that a registered nurse could take over the duties of the teacher associate and cost the school district about $18,000 a year.

Families who discover that their child has a disability may have a variety of reactions. These responses may include the following manifestations (adapted from Smith, 1997, pp. 2–3):

- *denial:* "This cannot be happening to me, to my child, to our family."
- *anger:* an emotion that may be directed toward the medical personnel who are involved in providing the information about the child's problem or at a husband or wife because of the need to assign blame.
- *grief:* an inexplicable loss that one does not know how to explain or deal with.
- *fear:* people often fear the unknown more than they fear the known. Having the complete diagnosis and some knowledge of the child's future prospects can be easier than uncertainty.
- *guilt:* concern about whether the parents themselves have caused the problem.
- *confusion:* as a result of not fully understanding what is happening and what will happen, confusion [may reveal] itself in sleeplessness, inability to make decisions, and mental overload.
- *powerlessness:* [the feeling may relate to the parents' inability to] change the fact that their child has a disability, yet parents want to feel competent and capable of handling their own life situations.
- *disappointment:* [the fact that] a child is not perfect may pose a threat to many parents' egos and a challenge to their value system.
- *rejection:* [this feeling] can be directed toward the child, toward the medical personnel, or toward other family members.
- *eventual acceptance:* the child has needs to be met and has value as a member of the family.

**CROSS-REFERENCE**
Review Chapters 4–10, which discuss specific disabilities that can affect children. Then reflect on how different types of problems can cause different reactions in parents.

Although it cannot be assumed that all or even most parents experience these particular reactions, many must deal with complicated emotions, often experienced as a "bombardment of feelings" that may recur over many years (Hilton, 1990). Sileo, Sileo, and Prater (1996) refer to the "shattering of dreams" that underlies many of the feelings. School personnel, including teachers, school social workers, counselors, and administrators, need to be aware of these dynamics and be prepared to deal with

*Many parents of students with special needs require assistance in their acceptance of their child's problems.*

family members who are experiencing various feelings. For example, when parents say that they feel guilt after learning that their child has a disability, school personnel should listen with acceptance to the parents and help them understand the nature of the disability and the fact that they are not responsible for it.

Many models of potential parental reactions reflect a "stage theory" approach to understanding these responses. However, it is important to realize that parental responses rarely follow any formal stage process (e.g., shock-denial-anger-rejection-acceptance). Rather, the reactions that were discussed above more often reflect responses that individual parents *may* experience in their ability to adjust to the knowledge that they have a child with a disability and that they need to meet that child's needs as well as their own.

School personnel need to be aware of family members' acceptance level of children with disabilities and make appropriate efforts to support this acceptance. This effort begins with assisting parents in understanding the needs of their child; at the same time, the educator should listen to the parents in order to better understand the child from their perspective. Summarizing previous research on this issue, Wilson (1995) lists the following things that parents want (and need) from professionals:

◢ Parents want professionals to communicate without jargon. When technical terms are necessary, they would like to have them explained.
◢ When possible, they want conferences to be held so both parents can attend.
◢ They want to receive written materials that provide information to assist them in understanding their child's problem.
◢ They want to receive a copy of a written report about their child.
◢ Parents want specific advice on how to manage the specific behavior problems of their children or how to teach them needed skills.
◢ Parents want information on their child's social as well as academic behavior. (p. 31)

Finally, parents may struggle with the issue of inclusion itself. Educators remain divided on this issue, as do parents and parents' groups. For example, some parents of students with learning disabilities (such as members of Learning Disabilities of America) have remained cautious about inclusion; on the other hand, the Arc (1995) (formerly the Association for Retarded Citizens) has actively favored it, to the extent of publishing a grading system for states relative to their commitment to inclusionary practices. Fisher, Pumpian, and Sax (1998) noted "the success and enhancement of any educational program depends on the attitude and involvement of many stakeholders, including parents, in its design and renewal" (p. 179). Teachers should be sensitive to the fact that individual parents and groups of parents may have quite different views of the benefits of inclusionary educational practice, and teachers should involve these parents in discussions related to the development of the most effective programs for their children.

## Involvement of Fathers

Frequently when people say that families should be involved in a child's education, the assumption is that the "family" is really the child's mother. This is unfortunate because the involvement of the entire family should be the preeminent goal. Often the individual who is left out of the planning process is the father. For example, governmental research indicates that fathers are only half as likely to be highly involved in their child's special education program (U.S. Department of Education, 1997). This same federal report highlighted the importance of the father's role in education indicating

**CONSIDER THIS**

As a teacher, how could you deal with families experiencing various reactions to a child with a disability? What role, if any, should a teacher play in helping parents work through their reactions?

**TEACHING TIP**

Teachers need to be aware of the different reactions that parents may experience and know some specific strategies for dealing with these reactions.

*A father's direct involvement with his child with disabilities increases the child's chance for success in school and in the community.*

that having both parents involved strengthened the child's chance for academic success. The report concluded (U.S. Department of Education, 1997, p. 3):

- ▲ Children are more likely to get (good grades) and less likely to repeat a grade if their fathers are involved in their schools.
- ▲ Children do better in school when their fathers are involved, regardless of whether their fathers live with them and whether their mothers are also involved.
- ▲ Many fathers in two-parent families, as well as fathers not living with their children, have low involvement.
- ▲ The relationship between fathers' involvement and children's success in school is important, regardless of income, race/ethnicity, or the parent's education.

Hietsch (1986) describes a program that aims at encouraging fathers to get involved in the educational program of their child. The program focuses on Father's Day, when the fathers of children in the class are invited to participate in a specific activity. Its goal is to encourage fathers to become more involved in all aspects of the child's educational program. However, a note of caution to teachers—be sensitive to single-parent (i.e., mother) homes in arranging such an event. The inclusion of a grandfather or an uncle would be a good option. The following list outlines the Father's Day outing:

1. Make sure that fathers are given sufficient notice to arrange to have the day off from work. (If a day off is not an option, alternative plans should be investigated.)
2. Send a reminder letter home a week to 10 days before Father's Day to develop enthusiasm and ensure attendance.
3. Know the first names of the fathers so that introductions are easier.
4. Have children show their fathers special items (e.g., papers, puppets) in the classroom.

5. Make trophies or awards ahead of time for categories related to scheduled activities.
6. On the next day, give individual help to the children in writing and illustrating experience stories to help make Father's Day a learning experience. (adapted from Hietsch, 1986, p. 259)

## Involvement of Siblings

Like adults, siblings in a family are important in developing and implementing appropriate educational programs. Because approximately 10% of the school population is identified as disabled, the number of children with siblings who are disabled must be significant: a working estimate of 20% or more seems realistic. Although not all nondisabled siblings experience adjustment problems, many will have significant difficulties responding to the disability (Gargiulo, O'Sullivan, Stephens, & Goldman, 1989–1990). The mere presence of a child with a disability can have "a profound impact on family structure and dynamics" (Gargiulo et al., 1989–1990, p. 21). On the other hand, these siblings also have a unique opportunity to learn about the diversity of individual needs.

A child with a disability may have an impact on siblings in two primary ways: economic and emotional. As a result of the financial impact, siblings may feel that they are being deprived of having certain things. They may feel resentment if they think that the sibling with a disability is draining important economic resources from the family.

Siblings may also feel emotionally deprived because their parents may spend a great deal more time with the child with the disability than with them. Although this may be a necessity, the nondisabled brother or sister may not be mature enough to understand this reality. Parents must convey to them that they are loved just as much as the child with the disability (Creekmore, 1988).

There are a number of ways that parents and school personnel can help siblings:

1. *Inform siblings of the nature and cause of the disability.* Often, siblings are concerned that they might become disabled like their brother or sister and may fear possible genetic influences. In most situations, these occurrences are far from likely.
2. *Allow siblings to attend conferences with school personnel.* When they are mature enough to understand, siblings will be in a better position to help the child with special needs if they are aware of the educational program and their role in it. Siblings may also have useful suggestions.
3. *Openly discuss the disability with all family members.* Trying to be secretive about a family member's disability can only encourage inaccurate conclusions and unwarranted fears.

One way some schools are involving siblings of children with disabilities is through **sibling support groups** (Summers, Bridge, & Summers, 1991). In addition to disseminating basic information about disabilities, sibling support groups can also provide a forum in which children share experiences and support with other children who have siblings with disabilities. Like parent support groups, sibling support groups can help children cope with having a brother or sister with a disability. Understanding that similar problems exist in other families and learning new ways to deal with them can be very helpful.

An innovative program for connecting the schools with the talents and needs of siblings is reported by Cramer et al. (1997). The article describing the program provides extensive information related to identifying the concerns of siblings, the linking

**CONSIDER THIS**
The recent emphasis on family (rather than parental) involvement reflects the importance of siblings and others in supporting the child. Is it a good idea to include siblings in the education of a brother or sister with a disability? Why or why not?

**SIBLING SUPPORT GROUP** is a support group developed for siblings of students with disabilities.

of the concerns to existing resources, the stimulation of the development of new opportunities for siblings, parents, and professionals, and the importance of motivation to ensure successful programs.

## HOME–SCHOOL COLLABORATION

**TEACHING TIP**
Teachers and other school personnel must keep in mind that parents are not only partners in the education of their children, but are the senior partners and should be involved in all major decisions.

**P**arents of children with disabilities and educators must be partners in ensuring that appropriate education is available to children. In reality, parents should be seen as the "senior partners" because they are responsible for the child every day until he or she reaches adulthood. In order to best meet the child's needs, classroom teachers, special education teachers, administrators, and support personnel need to be actively involved with families. Figure 16.1 outlines a comprehensive model of parent and family involvement.

**FIGURE 16.1**    Model of Family Involvement

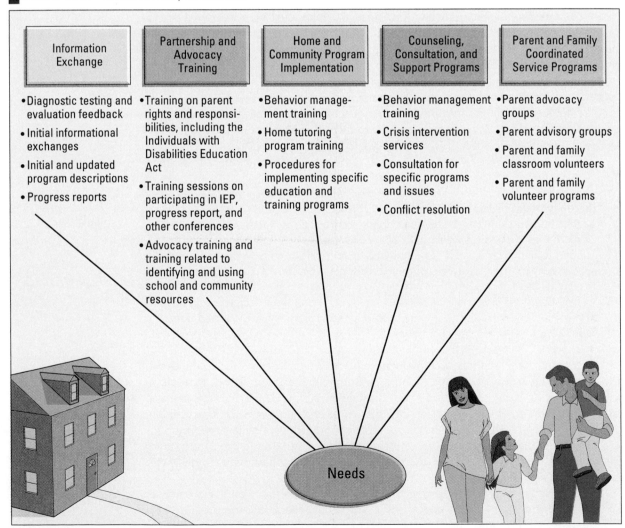

From *Working with Parents and Families of Exceptional Children and Youth* (p. 32), by R. L. Simpson, 1996, Austin, TX: Pro-Ed. Used by permission.

| TABLE 16.2 | Parent-to-Parent Suggestions |
|---|---|

- Seek the assistance of another parent of a child with a disability
- Communicate feelings with spouse, family members, and significant others.
- Rely on positive sources in your life (e.g., minister, priest rabbi, counselor).
- Take one day at a time.
- Learn the key terminology.
- Seek accurate information.
- Do not be intimidated by medical or educational professionals.
- Do not be afraid to show emotion.
- Learn how to deal with natural feelings of bitterness and anger.
- Maintain a positive outlook.
- Keep in touch with reality (e.g., there are some things that can be changed and others that cannot be changed).
- Find effective programs for your child.
- Take care of yourself.
- Avoid pity.
- Keep daily routines as normal as possible.
- Remember that this is your child.
- Recognize that you are not alone.

Adapted from "You Are Not Alone: For Parents When They Learn that Their Child Has a Disability," by P. M. Smith, 1997, *NICHY News Digest, 2,* pp. 3–5.

In working with parents of students with special needs, educators will soon realize that there is a tremendous variance in the knowledge and expertise of parents relative to education. For example, some parents may be well-versed in special education laws and practices and have informed opinions which must be considered in effective instructional planning. At the same time, it is important to acknowledge that many other parents are very limited in their awareness of disabilities and their understanding of special education law. In this case, the important responsibility of professional educators is to inform parents so that they can become knowledgeable, effective advocates for their child and thorough partners in educational programming.

Although effective collaboration cannot be based on professionals' presumptions that they understand the way a parent feels, nevertheless it is useful to consider the advice that parents give other parents in learning how to respond effectively to the needs of their child and also of themselves. Table 16.2 provides a summary of some parent-to-parent suggestions.

## Communicating with Parents

Many parents feel that too little communication flows between themselves and the school. Perhaps this is to be expected—approximately 50% of both general and special education teachers indicate that they have received no training in this area and consequently rate themselves as only moderately skilled (e.g., Buck et al., 1996; Epstein et al., 1996). This is particularly unfortunate since problems between parents and school personnel often can be avoided with proper communication by school professionals.

**TEACHING TIP**
When communicating with parents, avoid using educational jargon, including acronyms, that might be meaningless to parents.

*Teachers must communicate regularly with parents to keep them informed about their child's progress and needs.*

Wilson (1995, pp. 31–32) outlined the following principles of effective communication with the parents of students with disabilities:

- ◢ *Accept:* Show respect for the parents' knowledge and understanding, and convey a language of acceptance.
- ◢ *Listen:* Actively listen and make an effort to confirm the perceptions of the speaker's intent and meaning.
- ◢ *Question:* Probe to solicit parents' perspectives. Often questions will generate helpful illustrations.
- ◢ *Encourage:* Stress students' strengths along with weaknesses. Find positive aspects to share and end meetings or conversations on an encouraging note.
- ◢ *Stay directed:* Keep the discussions focused on the issues being discussed, and direct the parents to resources regarding concerns that lie beyond the teacher's scope.
- ◢ *Develop an alliance:* Stress that the parents and teachers share a common goal: to help the child.

Effective communication must be regular and useful. Communicating with parents only once or twice per year, or communicating with parents regularly but with information that is not useful, will not facilitate meeting educational goals.

Communication between school personnel and parents can take many forms. It does not have to be formal written communication. Effective communication can be informal, including telephone calls, written notes, or newsletters. When communicating with parents, school personnel should be aware of how they convey messages. For example, they should never "talk down" to parents. They should also choose their words thoughtfully. Some words convey very negative meanings, while other words are just as useful in transmitting the message, and are more positive. Table 16.3 lists words that should be avoided along with preferred alternatives. When communicating with parents, school personnel should also be aware of cultural and language differences. The nearby Diversity Forum (on p. 500) offers some interesting cross-cultural perspectives that may assist teachers in putting the question

| TABLE 16.3 | Making Positive Word Choices |
|---|---|
| **Avoid** | **Use Instead** |
| Must | Should |
| Lazy | Can do more with effort |
| Culturally deprived | Culturally different, diverse |
| Troublemaker | Disturbs class |
| Uncooperative | Should learn to work with others |
| Below average | Works at his (her) own level |
| Truant | Absent without permission |
| Impertinent | Discourteous |
| Steals | Takes things without permission |
| Dirty | Has poor grooming habits |
| Disinterested | Complacent, not challenged |
| Stubborn | Insists on having his (her) own way |
| Wastes time | Could make better use of time |
| Sloppy | Could be neater |
| Mean | Has difficulty getting along with others |
| Time and time again | Usually, repeatedly |
| Poor grade or work | Works below his (her) usual standard |

Adapted from *Parents and Teachers of Children with Exceptionalities: A Handbook for Collaboration* (2nd ed.) (p. 82), by T. M. Shea and A. M. Bauer, 1991, Boston: Allyn and Bacon. Used by permission.

of a disability in an appropriate cross-cultural perspective. Taking these factors into consideration enhances the quality of communication with family members.

## Informal Exchanges

Informal exchanges can take place without preparation. Teachers may see a parent in the community and stop and talk momentarily about the parent's child. Teachers should always be prepared to talk briefly to parents about their children, but should avoid talking about confidential information, particularly in the presence of individuals who do not need to know about it. If the conversation becomes too involved, the teacher should request that it be continued later, in a more appropriate setting.

## Parent Observations

Parents should be encouraged to visit the school to observe their child in the educational setting. Although the parents' presence could cause some disruption in the daily routine, school personnel need to keep in mind that parents have a critical stake in the success of the educational efforts. Therefore, parents should always feel welcome to observe the student in the educational setting. If the teacher feels that one time would be better than another, this information should be conveyed to the parent. Both teacher

**TEACHING TIP**
When talking with parents outside the school in an informal manner, avoid discussing items that are related to due-process requirements—they require that several individuals be present, and formal documents must validate the meeting.

# DIVERSITY FORUM
## Cross-Cultural Perspectives: A Disability or a Gift?

Imagine a world in which a 52-year-old woman with severe kyphosis (hunchback) had never been referred to as disabled. Instead, she was known as her community's best breadmaker. Her kyphosis, if anything, was thought of as a gift, for it made her the right height to work the ovens. As a result, she was the fastest breadmaker in the village, and she was revered for her skill.

Sound like a fairy tale that could never come true in real life? The woman's name is Effie, and she is a member of the Navajo tribe in Arizona.

In fact, many indigenous peoples throughout the world have a very different perception of disability than those of Anglo-American descent. In some cultures, there is no word for—and no concept of—disability. Rather, individuals with disabilities are accepted as they are, they have their place in the community, and family or community members see no need to "fix" them. As with Effie, a "disability" may even be thought of as a gift because it helps an individual develop other talents.

Other cultures believe the spirit, which guides the body and its experiences in the world, comes here for certain purposes—the spirit may need to experience the disability for its own enlightenment. Thus, the disability is a gift that allows the spirit to learn a particular lesson.

In some cultures, those who are disabled are thought to be touched by God. Other cultures believe that a disability is someone's fate, as determined by God. In such cultures, no stigma or shame is attached to an individual with a disability. A person with special needs is seen as an integral part of the community who has his or her own talents to contribute. Because of this total acceptance, there is no need to try to improve the individual.

**HONORING DIFFERENT CULTURAL BELIEFS**
It can be a challenge for educators to honor traditional beliefs and also provide educational services that will help a child with special needs overcome or deal with his or her disabilities. Some suggestions for accomplishing these goals are:

◢ Avoid words that have a negative implication such as deficit or disability. When educators speak with parents, they should ask the parent to tell them about the child, thus inviting parents to share their perceptions of the child. Then the teachers could explain that they are trying to help expand the child's abilities, rather than trying to make him or her "better."

◢ Educators should learn what the parents want for their child. One way to open the discussion is for the educator to explain what the child is doing in the classroom, as well as what the educator wants the child to be able to do. In this way, the teacher can find out if these things are important for the family and what the family perceives as a problem. Often, teachers and parents want the same things for the child. Then the teacher can explain that the child might do better if he or she had a special teacher to show him or her how to do a particular task.

◢ The teacher should learn about the child's likes and abilities. In this way, educators can capitalize on the child's strengths and help him or her acquire additional talents and skills.

Adapted from "A Disability or a Gift?" by The Council for Exceptional Children, 1997, *CEC Today,* 4(3), p. 7.

and parents should realize that children tend to behave differently when being observed by parents.

## Telephone Calls

Many teachers use telephone calls a great deal and very effectively to communicate with parents. Parents feel that teachers are interested in their child if the teacher takes the time to call and discuss the child's progress with the parent. When using the telephone for communication purposes, teachers should remember to call when there is good news about the child as well as to report problems the child is experiencing. It makes parents feel very good to get a call from a teacher who says that the child is doing well and having no problems. Again, understanding the language and culture of the home is important when making telephone calls. Giving parents your home telephone number is an option that may prove reassuring to parents. Used appropriately, voice mail may enhance ongoing communication, especially when contact times are not mutually convenient.

## Written Notes

Written communication to parents is also an effective method of communicating about a child's progress. When using written communication, teachers should consider the literacy level of the parents and use words and phrases that will be readily understandable. They should also be aware of the primary language of the home. Written communications that are not understood can be very intimidating for parents. When using written communication, teachers should provide an opportunity for parents to respond, either in writing or through a telephone call. Increasingly, e-mail offers opportunities for ongoing communication with the families of individual students.

**CONSIDER THIS**
Some teachers think that daily written communication with parents is too much for them to do. When might this form of communication be necessary, and is it a legitimate responsibility for teachers?

## Home Visits

There is no better way to get an understanding of the family than making a home visit. When possible, school personnel should consider making the extra effort required to arrange and make home visits. When visiting homes, school personnel need to follow certain procedures, including the following:

- ◢ Have specific information to deliver or obtain.
- ◢ If you desire to meet with parents alone, find out if it is possible to have the child elsewhere during the scheduled visit.
- ◢ Do not stay more than an hour.
- ◢ Arrive at the scheduled time.
- ◢ Dress as a professional.
- ◢ Make visits with another school system resource person, such as the school social worker.
- ◢ Be sure to do as much listening as talking.
- ◢ Leave on a positive note. (Westling & Koorland, 1988)

Although we list home visits as an option, we are also cognizant of the low "treatment acceptability" (see Chapter 14) of this practice. General education teachers report that they consider home visits the least effective (and perhaps least desirable) alternative available to them in terms of home–school collaborations (Polloway et al., 1996). Among other possible concerns, home visits for a potentially large number of children simply may be unrealistic. They tend to be more common, and perhaps more effective, at the preschool level.

## Other Forms of Communication

Numerous other vehicles exist for educators to covey helpful information to parents. Among these are newsletters, family support groups, and open houses. School personnel should use every available means to communicate with parents. This is a responsibility of both general and special education teachers. Teachers should never assume that other school personnel will take care of communicating with parents.

**TEACHING TIP**
School personnel might support a parent newsletter that could go out to all school patrons, or at least a column or section in the school newsletter could be contributed by a parent.

**FIGURE 16.2** Questions Asked by Parents and Teachers

| QUESTIONS PARENTS MAY ASK TEACHERS | QUESTIONS TEACHERS SHOULD ASK PARENTS |
|---|---|
| What is normal for a child this age? | What activities at home could you provide as a reward? |
| What is the most important subject or area for my child to learn? | What particular skill areas concern you most for inclusion on the IEP? |
| What can I work on at home? | What behavior at home do you feel needs to improve? |
| How can I manage her behavior? | Would you be interested in coming to a parent group with other parents of my students? |
| Should I spank? | When is a good time to call at home? |
| When will my child be ready for community living? | May I call you at work? What is the best time? |
| Should I plan on her learning to drive? | Is there someone at home who can pick the child up during the day if necessary? |
| Will you just listen to what my child did the other day and tell me what you think? | Would you be interested in volunteering in our school? |
| What is a learning disability? | What is the most difficult problem you face in rearing your child? |
| My child has emotional problems; is it my fault? | What are your expectations for your child? |
| The doctor said my child will grow out of this. What do you think? | How can I help you the most? |
| Will physical therapy make a big difference in my child's control of his hands and arms? | What is your home routine in the evenings? Is there a quiet place for your child to study? |
| Have you become harder on our child? Her behavior has changed at home. | Can you or your spouse do some special activity with your child if he or she earns it at school? |
| Can I call you at home if I have a question? | Can you spend some time tutoring your child in the evening? |
| What is the difference between delayed, retarded, and learning disabled? | Would you like to have a conference with your child participating? |
| What kind of after-school activities can I get my child involved in? | When is the best time to meet? |
| Can my child live on his own? | |
| What should I do about sexual activity? | |
| What's he going to be like in five years? | |
| Will she have a job? | |
| Who takes care of him when I can no longer care for him? | |
| What happens if she doesn't make her IEP goals? | |

Adapted from *The Special Educator's Handbook* (pp. 208–209), by D. L. Westling and M. A. Koorland, 1988, Boston: Allyn and Bacon. Used by permission.

## Parent–Teacher Formal Meetings

Parent–teacher formal meetings are required components of special education and represent additional excellent methods of fostering strong communication. Under federal law, these formal meetings include conferences to develop the individualized educational program (IEP), the **individualized family service plan (IFSP),** the individualized transitional plan (ITP), and, as applicable, behavioral intervention plans (BIPs) (see Chapter 13). Regardless of the purpose of the meeting, school personnel should focus attention on the topics at hand. They should send advance information home (e.g., a week before the meeting) to parents and make the parents feel at ease about their participation in the meeting. Directing their attention to academic, social, and transitional goals before such meetings enhances their participation.

*INDIVIDUALIZED FAMILY SERVICE PLAN (IFSP)* is the equivalent of an IEP for infants and toddlers.

When preparing to meet with parents to discuss children who are experiencing problems, school personnel need to anticipate the components of the discussion. This includes gathering information about the questions that parents may ask, as well as knowing what questions they should address to the parents. Figure 16.2 provides typical questions raised at such conferences. By anticipating the questions in advance, school personnel will be in a better position to have a successful meeting. To increase parental participation in formal conferences, school personnel may wish to consider whether parents should have an advocate present at formal conferences. The advocate could be a member of the school staff or, in some cases, will be privately contracted by the parents. An advocate can facilitate parental participation by enhancing communication, encouraging parental participation, and providing them a summary of the discussions and decisions at the end of the conference. State regulations govern this practice; teachers should consult with administrative colleagues concerning this practice.

**IEP MEETINGS**  Parents should be involved in the development of students' IEPs for two reasons. First, the law requires parental participation. IDEA requires that parents be invited to participate in the development of the child's IEP and must "sign off" on the completed IEP (see Chapter 2).

The more important reason for involvement, however, is to gain the input of parents. In most regards, parents know more about their children than school personnel do. They have been involved with the child longer, and beyond the hours of a school

*S*chool personnel must take steps to ensure parental involvement in their children's education program.

day. Schools need to take advantage of this knowledge about the child in the development of the IEP.

An example of how parents should be involved in the development of IEPs is described in the future-based assessment and intervention model (Smith & Dowdy, 1992) discussed in Chapter 15. In this model, school personnel, parents, and the student discuss likely "futures" for the student and the necessary interventions that will help the student achieve them. These agreed-upon goals then guide the development and implementation of educational programs for the student. Such a focus is critical to the joint development of individual transition plans, which are required for all students with disabilities by at least age 16.

To obtain increased parental involvement in IEP conferences, school personnel need to be proactive in soliciting parental input. Simply inviting parents to attend is not sufficient. In facilitating exchanges between school personnel and parents, de Bettencourt (1987) suggests the following:

**CROSS-REFERENCE**
For more information on the IDEA requirements for family involvement, read Chapter 2.

1. Hold conferences in a small location that is free from external distractions; hold phone calls and other interruptions so that parents feel you are truly interested in them and their child.
2. Hold conferences on time and maintain the schedule; do not let conferences start late or run late because many parents may be taking time off from work to attend.
3. Arrange the room so that parents and school personnel are comfortable and can look at one another without barriers, such as desks and tables, between them.
4. Present information clearly, concisely, and in a way that parents can understand; do not "talk down" to the parents.

**IFSP MEETINGS** Public Law 99-457 significantly altered the relationship between families and agencies serving young children with disabilities. The law requires that agencies serving preschool children develop an IFSP for each child in his/her family. The IFSP requirement is based on the assumption that families cannot be as effective in a child's intervention program if their own needs are not being met. Thus the IFSP takes family needs (e.g., respite care, transportation) into consideration and provides strategies that can help solve some of the family's problems while delivering services to children with disabilities.

Like the IEP, the IFSP must contain specific information concerning the child and family. The first meeting to develop the IFSP must be held within 45 days of the date when the child was referred for an evaluation (Colarusso & Kana, 1991). The IFSP must minimally contain the following:

◢ A statement of the child's present functioning level in the following areas: physical development, cognitive development, language and speech development, psychosocial development, and self-help skills
◢ A statement of the family's strengths and needs
◢ Specific goals or outcomes for the family and child
◢ Means to evaluate goals
◢ Services required to facilitate goal achievement
◢ The family's case manager (Krauss, 1990)

Family involvement in the development of the IFSP is a primary consideration. Public Law 99-457, which implemented the IFSP requirement, was the first federal legislation that truly focused services for individuals with disabilities on the entire family, not only on the child with the disability. Family input is both legally mandated and essential to the development of successful programs.

## Mediation

The legal requirements that are in place concerning parental involvement in their child's education provide a foundation for appropriate practices in home–school collaboration. Nevertheless, even when careful efforts at compliance are made by school personnel and when educators attempt to fulfill both the letter and spirit of the law, some conflicts are inevitable in such an emotionally charged area as the determination of an appropriate education for a student with a disability. A helpful procedure that many state and local education agencies use to resolve ensuing disagreements between parents and school personnel is **mediation**. In mediation, the parties both share their concerns and then work to develop a solution that is mutually acceptable, typically through the facilitation of a third party.

Mediation can be a common-sense method of working through conflicts. It creates an environment in which both parents and educators develop a consensus regarding a child's education program (Dobbs, Primm, & Primm, 1991). If effective, a mediation process can also result in the avoidance of the active involvement of legal representation, the subsequent cost of attorney fees, and the potential for an adversarial relationship occurring through due-process hearings.

**MEDIATION** is an informal effort to resolve differences between parents and school personnel.

**COMMON CONCERNS**  The preceding discussion highlighted vehicles for effective communication between teachers and other school personnel and parents and other family members. We conclude this section by noting the value for teachers in anticipating possible concerns that parents may express about their child's education. Table 16.4 identifies domains of possible concerns of parents. It addresses three areas: parental expectations for their child, expectations of schools, and parental expectations of teachers. These examples provide a rich picture of ways in which teachers can anticipate and respond to parents effectively.

## HOME-BASED INTERVENTION

Families can become involved with the education of a family member with a disability through home-based intervention. For preschool children, home-based services are fairly common; however, parents less frequently provide instruction at home for older students. Still, many reports have noted that such instruction can be very beneficial to students with disabilities (e.g., Brown & Moore, 1992; Ehlers & Ruffin, 1990). Parents can be helpful in numerous ways.

Parents and other family members at home can get involved in the student's educational program by providing reinforcement, and direct instructional support and facilitating homework efforts. At the same time, teachers should be sensitive to the numerous other roles parents must play in addition to supporting their child with special needs.

### Providing Reinforcement

Most students with disabilities experience lots of failure and frustration. Frequently, the more they attend school, the more they fail. This failure cycle becomes difficult to break, especially after it becomes established over several years. Reinforcing success can help break this cycle. Parents need to work with school personnel to provide positive reinforcement for all levels of success. If students are not capable of achieving full

**CROSS-REFERENCE**
A full description of the principles of reinforcement is presented in Chapter 13.

| **TABLE 16.4** | **What Do Parents Want?** | |
|---|---|---|
| **What Do Parents Want for Their Children?** | **What Do Parents Expect of Teachers?** | **What Do Parents Expect of Schools?** |
| **PERSONAL AND SOCIAL ADJUSTMENT**<br>"To belong to more groups."<br>"More socialization."<br>"To open up a little bit so he can learn to mix and mingle more."<br><br>**ACCOMMODATION AND ADAPTATION**<br>"One-to-one learning environment for academics."<br>"More hands-on learning."<br>"Sometimes the test should be given verbally."<br><br>**RESPONSIBILITY AND INDEPENDENCE**<br>"To buckle down and study [to get better grades]."<br>"To learn to finish his tasks."<br>"To be able to set limits with people she goes out with [when she is on her own]."<br><br>**ACADEMIC AND FUNCTIONAL LITERACY**<br>"To read better."<br>"To get every opportunity to learn what he should know . . . and continue to progress every year."<br><br>**SUPPORTIVE ENVIRONMENT**<br>"A sense of accomplishment, success."<br>"A positive environment."<br>"Constant encouragement to stick to the tasks he is [working] on." | **PERSONAL CHARACTERISTICS**<br>"Enjoy what they are teaching."<br>"Love what they are doing."<br>"Be enthusiastic."<br>"Be open-minded, friendly, and down-to-earth."<br>"Be caring and patient."<br><br>**ACCOUNTABILITY AND INSTRUCTIONAL SKILLS**<br>"Evaluate themselves instead of turning to outside sources to evaluate what they are doing."<br>"Direct the students toward resources and information that can further their studies."<br><br>**MANAGEMENT SKILLS**<br>"Make [students] follow through with assignments."<br>"Be very well-organized."<br>"Be fair in remediating disputes between students."<br><br>**COMMUNICATION**<br>"Consider parents as part of a team for learning."<br>"Keep in touch with parents at times other than IEP meetings." | **RESPONSIBILITY AND INDEPENDENCE**<br>"Help them make decisions."<br>"Train them to be self-sufficient."<br>"[Help] them handle a checking and savings account."<br><br>**ACADEMIC AND FUNCTIONAL LITERACY**<br>"[Help them] meet certain proficiency requirements to get their high school degree or whatever."<br>"Prepare him to go on to [further education]."<br><br>**SUPPORTIVE ENVIRONMENT**<br>"Keep kids interested [in learning]."<br>"Provide an atmosphere for learning."<br>"[Provide an environment] where they feel safe and respected. . . . Warmth is important." |

Adapted from "Parents' Perspectives on School Choice," by C. M. Lange, J. E. Ysseldyke, and C. A. Lehr, 1997, *Teaching Exceptional Children, 30*(1), pp. 17–19.

success in an area, they need to be rewarded for their positive efforts in the appropriate direction.

Parents are in an excellent position to provide reinforcement. They are with the child more than school personnel and are involved in all aspects of the child's life. As a result, parents can provide reinforcement in areas where a child most desires rewards, such as time with friends, money, toys, or trips. For many students, simply allowing them to have a friend over or stay up late at night on a weekend may prove reinforcing. School personnel do not have this range of reinforcers available to them; therefore, parents should take advantage of their repertoire of rewards to reinforce the positive efforts of students.

Brown and Moore (1992) describe a method to motivate poor elementary readers at home. It requires that parents listen to their children read four nights each week for a month. Stickers, later redeemable for pizzas, T-shirts, and a pizza party, are used as reinforcers.

Parents should also help motivate their older children's efforts in school. Using a reinforcement system can provide incentives for adolescents who need a little extra "push" to get started. School personnel can assist parents in motivating adolescents by discussing potentially desirable reinforcers and by suggesting some home activities.

A special example of reinforcement in the home are *home-school contingencies*. Home-school contingencies can be highly effective and also cost efficient (Pfiffner & Barkley, 1990). They typically involve providing reinforcement contingencies in the home, based on the documentation of learning or behavioral reports from school.

**TEACHING TIP**
Regardless of the format, the key element in home-school contingencies is ongoing, effective communication between school personnel and parents.

The basic mechanism for home-school contingencies are written reports that highlight a student's behavior relative to particular targets or objectives. Two popular forms are daily report cards and passports. *Daily report cards* give feedback on schoolwork, homework, and behavior. They range in complexity from forms calling for responses to simple rating scales to more precisely designed behavioral instruments with direct, daily behavioral measures of target behaviors. *Passports* typically take the form of notebooks, which students bring to each class and then take home daily. Individual teachers (or all of a student's teachers) and parents can make regular notations. Reinforcement is based both on carrying the passport and on meeting the specific target behaviors that are indicated on it (Walker & Shea, 1988).

## Providing Direct Instructional Support

Parents and other family members may become directly involved with instructional programs at home, which can be critical to success. Unfortunately, many family members provide less direct instruction as the child gets older, assuming that the student is capable of doing the work alone. Too often, the reverse is true; students may need more assistance at home as they progress through the grades. Since parents are generally with the child more than school personnel, it seems logical to involve them in direct instruction; with methods such as coincidental teaching, in which parents teach their children various skills in real-life situations, parental involvement in teaching skills is not burdensome and can be truly effective (Schulz, Rule, & Innocenti, 1989).

**CONSIDER THIS**
Parents generally know more about their children than school personnel. In what ways can this knowledge be used to develop programs that meet the needs of children?

Advocates for expanding the role of parents in educating their children adhere to the following assumptions:

◢ Parents are the first and most important teachers of their children.
◢ The home is the child's first schoolhouse.
◢ Children will learn more during the early years than at any other time in life.
◢ All parents want to be good parents and care about their child's development. (Ehlers & Ruffin, 1990, p. 1)

**CROSS-REFERENCE**
School-based aspects of homework are discussed in Chapters 14 and 15.

One effective intervention is a systematic home tutoring program. Thurston (1989) describes an effective program that includes four steps. In step 1, the parents and teachers discuss the area in which home tutoring would be most helpful. Many parents will feel more comfortable with helping their children "practice" skills than with teaching them new skills. Therefore, teachers should help identify topics in which practice would benefit the student.

In step 2, family members implement home tutoring procedures: selecting the location for the tutoring, deciding on a time for tutoring, and so on. In step 3, the family member who provides the tutoring uses techniques for encouragement, reinforcement, and error correction. In step 4, family members complete the tutoring session and make a record of the student's accomplishments. Tutoring periods should be short, probably no more than 15 minutes, and should end with a record of the day's activities. A visual chart, on which the student can actually see progress, is often very reinforcing to the student (Thurston, 1989).

### Providing Homework Support

In many ways, finishing this chapter with the topic of homework concludes this book with the area that may be most problematic for successful home–school collaboration. The problems of students with disabilities in this area are well documented (e.g., Epstein et al., 1993; Gajria & Salend, 1995) and outline the challenges faced by teachers and parents working together (Patton, 1994). For example, Jayanthi, Nelson, Sawyer, Bursuck, and Epstein's (1995) report on communication problems within the homework process reveals significant misunderstandings among general and special

---

## INCLUSION STRATEGIES

### Facilitating Family Involvement

When she was a child, Mary Russo knew that going to school was her job. The time used to complete homework assignments was considered sacred. "There was always a place in our home for homework," Russo recalls. "My grandmother— who spoke only Italian—would bring me and my brother sandwiches and milk while we studied." And, says Russo, although her grandmother couldn't *tell* them, her actions "*showed* us the value of what we were doing."

Russo is now the principal at Samuel Mason Elementary School in Roxbury, Massachusetts, and regularly stresses the importance of homework to parents. "Children have to understand that their work—school work—is important," she asserts, and they get that message when families make homework a priority. What's more, says Russo, making homework a priority gives children more opportunities to learn. "We want children to continue learning beyond the school day," she explains. "Homework is a powerful way to extend learning."

What [too often] isn't taught [to teachers] says Russo, is the power homework has to engage parents in school life. "Teachers need to consider how parents can contribute to a child's development," she contends. The homework policy at Samuel Mason Elementary School requires teachers to create homework assignments that are "interactive" and to include activities children can do with their parents or older siblings.

"We call our homework Homelinks because it's the link between home and school," says Peg Sands, a kindergarten teacher at Samuel Mason. "Throughout Homelinks, parents have an opportunity to reinforce learning, to become involved in their child's education."

The Homelinks program asks parents to guide students through the 30 minutes of homework assigned each night, except Friday. Each night's homework focuses on a different content area: On Monday, students take a book home, read it with a family member, and then do a short book report. On Tuesday, the homework focuses on math. Wednesday's homework is connected to themes, such as bus safety or holidays. On Thursday, the homework involves practicing a writing skill—letter, word, or sentence recognition, or differentiating between uppercase and lowercase letters, for example. Parents then sign the completed homework.

The Homelinks program also features parenting workshops that teach parents how to best help their children complete homework assignments. When the homework requires parents and children to read together, for example, Sands and her colleagues share with parents "the kinds of questions to ask to help develop early literacy skills." When parents ask children questions such as, "What is the title of this book? Who is the author?" children learn to "examine books and understand a book's parts."

Adapted from "Homework: A New Look at an Age-Old Practice," by ASCD, 1997, *Education Update, 39*(7), pp. 1, 5.

education teachers and parents regarding the development, implementation, and coordination of homework practices for students with disabilities in inclusive settings. Teachers and parents indicated concerns about failures to initiate communication (in terms of informing the other of a student's learning and behavior characteristics as well as the delineation of roles and responsibilities) and to provide follow-up communications, especially early on, when problems first become evident. In addition, respondents identified several variables that they believed influence the severity of these problems (e.g., lack of time, student-to-teacher ratio, student interference, not knowing whom to contact).

While the problems experienced by students with special needs have been well-documented and the challenges in this area are clear, nevertheless there is evidence that effective practices can be implemented to significantly enhance the homework performance, and thus the academic achievement, of students who experience school difficulties. For example, Callahan, Redemacher, and Hildreth (1998) developed an intensive program that included parent training sessions, student training, systematic homework procedures, and self-management strategies followed by home- and school-based positive reinforcement programs. They reported that homework completion as well as the quality of homework significantly increased for children of those parents who were able to follow the homework program and that significant increases in achievement in mathematics also were the result. The nearby Inclusion Strategies feature provides a further strategy of how parents and educators can work together to solve the homework dilemma.

As Epstein et al. (1996) further reviewed these problem areas, they found that general education teachers reported the following key communication problems: lack of followthrough by parents, lateness of communication, the relative lack of importance placed on homework, parental defensiveness, and denial of problems. These concerns were generally consistent with the reports of special education teachers in a parallel study (Buck et al., in press). However, these data are open to interpretation—they are survey responses by teachers *about* parents.

Despite the numerous problems associated with homework, solutions can be found. Based on their study, Bursuck et al. (in press) found that special education teachers indicated the following general recommendations:

◢ General educators and parents need to take an active and daily role in monitoring and communicating with students about homework.
◢ Schools should find ways to provide teachers with the time to engage in regular communication with parents and should provide students with increased opportunities to complete homework after school.
◢ Teachers need assistance in taking advantage of technological innovations (e.g., homework hotlines, computerized student progress records).
◢ Students need to be held responsible for keeping up with their homework.
◢ Special educators need to share with general educators more information about the needs of students with disabilities and appropriate instructional accommodations.

Examples of strategies that general education teachers ranked most effective in resolving homework dilemmas are provided in Figure 16.3. Note that many of these strategies have validity for all students, not only those with special needs.

Because of the challenges associated with homework, a number of new innovations are being developed on the local level. Refer back to the Inclusion Strategies feature, which describes one such program that was developed in an elementary school and can be considered for use with students both with and without disabilities.

**FIGURE 16.3**    Effective Strategies Relative to Homework

**Parents' Efforts to Communicate**
**Parents should**
• check with their child about homework daily.
• regularly attend parent–teacher conferences.
• sign their child's assignment book daily.

**Adopting Policies to Facilitate Communication**
**Schools should**
• provide release time for teachers to communicate with parents on a regular basis.
• require frequent written communication from teachers to parents about homework (e.g., monthly progress reports).
• schedule conferences in the evenings for working parents.

**General Education Teachers' Roles**
**Teachers should**
• require that students keep a daily assignment book.
• provide parents at the start of school with a list of suggestions on how parents can assist with homework.
• remind students of due dates on a regular basis.

**Technologies to Enhance Communication**
**Schools should**
• establish telephone hotlines so that parents can call when questions or problems arise.
• regularly provide computerized student progress reports for parents.
• establish systems that enable teachers to place homework assignments on audiotapes so that parents can gain access by telephone or voice mail.

From "Strategies for Improving Home–School Communication Problems about Homework for Students with Disabilities," by M. H. Epstein, D. D. Munk, W. D. Bursuck, E. A. Polloway, and M. M. Jayanthi, 1999, *Journal of Special Education, 33,* pp. 166–176.

Finally, based on their review of the literature on home and school collaboration relative to homework, Jayanthi, Bursuck, Epstein, and Polloway (1997) identified the following strategies that had been found effective:

▲ Provide periodic progress reports on homework performance to parents. These reports should include descriptive comments about performance.

▲ Communicate using written modes of communication (e.g., progress reports, notes, letters, forms). Use brightly colored paper to grab attention and prevent misplacement.

▲ At the beginning of the year/semester, give parents information regarding assignments, homework adaptations available in the classroom, and policies related to missed assignments and extra credit homework.

▲ Communicate with other teachers to avoid overloading the student with homework and to prevent homework completion problems at home.

▲ Have face-to-face communication with other teachers and parents.

▲ Help students to complete and submit homework on time (e.g., remind students of assignment due dates periodically, assign homework in small units, write assignments on the board).

Homework is a challenge to students with special needs and their parents. Without question, home-school partnerships can foster success in this area. At the same time, teachers should be sensitive to the demands that are placed on parents in general and particularly in this area. Thus, teachers should reflect an understanding in communication with parents that homework may be a lower priority for families when compared with other issues (e.g., school attendance, family illness) and respond accordingly by helping to address these other issues first.

## FINAL THOUGHTS

Establishing good working relationships with parents and families enhances the school experience of their children. Thus an important objective for the schools should be to achieve and maintain such relationships. Most professionals acknowledge the importance of parent and family involvement in the schooling of their children, and this importance can be especially critical for students with disabilities. However, programs that promote home-school collaboration must aim for more than students' classroom success. Often, parental involvement has been focused on their children's goals (i.e., student progress), with less attention given to parental

### *personal* SPOTLIGHT

#### Fourth-Grade Teacher

Jo Matthews has a unique perspective on educating students with disabilities and on school inclusion. Jo began teaching in special education in the areas of mental retardation and learning disabilities. After teaching for 12 years in special education programs (e.g., self-contained classes, resource room), she

**JO MATTHEWS**
*Campbell County Public
Schools, Campbell
County, Virginia*

moved to a general education classroom where she has taught for 10 years. From Jo's professional perspective, the influence of IDEA in encouraging movement toward regular class placement has been significant because it has provided the necessary incentive for inclusion to occur. At the elementary level, inclusion is "good for both groups of kids . . . they both adapt to the inclusive setting and it promotes a good learning environment. In my school, inclusion works because of the philosophy we have adopted and because of the supports that are available. Paraeducators are a significant advantage and having a 'gem of an LD teacher' has been critical. Our regular education faculty have a high degree of willingness to cooperate and the attitude that is prevalent in our school is 'How will it work?' vs. 'Will it work?' Our LD teacher is realistically positive and presents no overly rosy pictures but works closely with us to ensure that students receive the education they need. Our administrative support is also critical and enhances the teachers' attitudes."

In addition to her school experiences, Jo also is the mother of Patrick, a 9-year-old with special needs. Patrick has Down syndrome and has been the beneficiary of an intensive early intervention program. He is currently in second grade in an inclusion class. There is a full-time aide in the classroom who provides special education supports for Patrick and a young girl with cerebral palsy. The special education teacher spends approximately $1\frac{1}{2}$ hours a day in the class. The class is heterogeneously grouped with the two children with special needs taught separately when they have special need for instruction. The school uses pull-out services for OT, PT, and speech therapy. From her perspective as a parent, Jo feels that inclusion is "wonderful." "I cannot say enough about the progress that Patrick has made since his placement in an inclusive environment. I attribute his advancement to his opportunity to observe others and model both academic and social skills. Two particular accomplishments of note are that he is learning to read and that he has developed the ability to sit quietly and attentively for ten minutes at a time. His self-stimulatory behaviors have decreased and his social appropriateness has increased; of course, modeling other students occasionally has both positive and not so positive effects on behavioral patterns." The children in Patrick's class were fully informed about his learning needs and have responded well. One second grader recently reported that when he grows up he wants to become a scientist so that he can cure all problems related to disabilities. Patrick still experiences some degree of social isolation in the classroom. Jo would prefer that there be more attention in his IEP to social interaction and more of a focus on social skills development to decrease his isolation. When she asks Patrick, he says that he loves his classroom but that it is hard work! Interestingly, one of his favorite things is homework.

outcomes (i.e., their particular needs). Teachers, parents, and other family members all should gain from cooperative relationships that truly flow in both directions and are concerned with success in both home and school settings. Both general and special education teachers need to help family members understand the importance of their involvement, give them suggestions for how to get involved, and empower them with the skills and confidence they will need. Students with disabilities, and those at risk for developing problems, require assistance from all parties in order to maximize success. Family members are critical components of the educational team. The preceding Personal Spotlight feature (on p. 511) reflects a situation when families are heavily involved in their child's special education program.

# Summary

### The Family

◢ A major change in the past two decades in provision of educational services to students with special needs is the active involvement of families.

◢ Historically, getting parents to participate in school decisions has proven difficult but is nevertheless essential.

◢ Schools should take proactive steps to ensure the involvement of families of students with disabilities. Regardless of their own values, school personnel must involve all family members of a student with special needs, regardless of the type of family.

◢ All family members must make adjustments when a child with a disability becomes a family member.

◢ Siblings of students with disabilities in particular may also experience special problems and challenges.

### Home–School Collaboration

◢ Families and schools must collaborate to ensure appropriate educational programs for students with disabilities and IDEA requires that schools involve families in educational decisions for students with disabilities.

◢ A critical component in any collaboration between school personnel and family members is effective communication. All types of communication, formal and informal, between school and families are important.

### Home-Based Intervention

◢ Family members should be encouraged and taught how to become involved in the educational programs implemented in the school. A variety of strategies are available to facilitate successful home intervention programs.

# Further Readings

Darling, R. B., & Baxter, C. (1996). *Families in focus: Sociological methods in early intervention.* Austin, TX: Pro-Ed.

Gallagher, J. J. (Ed.) (1980). *New directions for exceptional children: Parents and families of handicapped children.* San Francisco: Jossey-Bass.

Hallahan, D., & Kauffman, J. (1995). *The illusion of full inclusion.* Austin, TX: Pro-Ed.

Hanson, M. J., & Carter, J. J. (1996). Addressing the challenges of families with multiple risks. *Exceptional Children 62,* 201–211.

Mastropieri, M. A., & Scruggs, T. E. (2000). *The inclusive classroom: Strategies for effective instruction.* Columbus, OH: Merrill.

Rosenkoetter, S. E., Hains, A. H., & Fowler, S. A. (1994). *Bridging early services for children with special needs and their families.* Baltimore: Brookes.

Summers, M., Bridge, J., & Summers, C. R. (1991). Sibling support groups. *Teaching Exceptional Children 23,* 83-86.

Turnbull, A. P., & Turnbull, H. R. (1997). *Families, professionals, and exceptionality: A special partnership.* Columbus, OH: Merrill.

Turnbull, H. R., & Turnbull, A. P. (2000). *Free appropriate public education,* (6th ed.). Denver: Love.

Welch, M., & Sheridan, S. M. (1995). *Educational partnerships: Serving students at risk.* Ft. Worth, TX: Harcourt Brace.

# References

Abikoff, H. (1991). Cognitive training in ADHD children: Less to it than meets the eye. *Journal of Learning Disabilities, 24,* 205–209.

Ackerman, P. T., Dykman, R. A., & Gardner, M. Y. (1990). Counting rate, naming rate, phonological sensitivity, and memory span: Major factors in dyslexia. *Journal of Learning Disabilities, 23,* 325–327.

Affleck, J. Q., Edgar, E., Levine, P., & Kortering, L. (1990). Postschool status of students classified as mildly mentally retarded, learning disabled, or non-handicapped: Does it get better with time? *Education and Training in Mental Retardation, 25,* 315–324.

Agnew, C. M., Nystul, B., & Conner, L. A. (1998). Seizure disorders: An alternative explanation for students' inattention. *Professional School Counselor, 2,* 54–59.

Agosta, J., & Melda, K. (1996). Supporting families who provide care at home for children with disabilities. *Exceptional Children, 62,* 271–282.

Alber, S. R., Heward, W. L., & Hippler, B. J. (1999). Teaching middle school students with learning disabilities to recruit positive teacher attention. *Exceptional Children, 65,* 253–270.

Alberto, P. A., & Troutman, A. C. (1995). *Applied behavior analysis for teachers* (4th ed.). Englewood Cliffs, NJ: Merrill.

Allen, K. E. (1992). *The exceptional child: Mainstreaming in early childhood education* (2nd ed.). Albany, NY: Delmar.

Alley, G. R., & Deshler, D. D. (1979). *Teaching the learning disabled adolescent: Strategies and methods.* Denver: Love.

American Academy of Allergy and Immunology. (1991). *Asthma and the school child (Tip #19).* Milwaukee, WI: Author.

American Academy of Ophthalmology. (1984). Policy statement. *Learning disabilities, dyslexia, and vision.* San Francisco: Author.

American Academy of Pediatrics. (1988). *Learning disabilities and children: What parents need to know.* Elk Grove Village, IL: Author.

American Association on Mental Retardation. (1992). *Mental retardation: Definition, classification, and systems of supports* (9th ed.). Washington, D.C.: Author.

American Foundation for the Blind. (1998). *AFB directory of services for blind and visually impaired persons in the United States and Canada* (27th ed.). New York: Author.

American Psychiatric Association. (1994). *Diagnostic and statistical manual of mental disorders (DSM-IV)* (5th ed.). Washington, D.C.: Author.

American Speech-Language-Hearing Association. (1982). Definitions: Communicative disorders and variations, *ASHA, 24,* 949–950.

Amerson, M. J. (1999). Helping children with visual and motor impairments make the most of their visual abilities. *Review, 31,* 17–20.

Annie E. Casey Foundation. (1998). *1998 kids count data book: Overview.* Baltimore: Author.

Anthony, S. (1972). *The discovery of death in childhood and after.* New York: Basic Books.

Arc (1993, November/December). Second national status report on inclusion reveals slow progress. *ARC Newsletter,* p. 5.

Arc (1995). Report finds nation's schools still failing at inclusion. *The Arc Today, 44*(4), 1, 4.

Armstrong, D. G. (1990). *Developing and documenting the curriculum.* Boston: Allyn & Bacon.

Arnos, K. S., Israel, J., Devlin, L., & Wilson, M. P. (1996). Genetic aspects of hearing loss in childhood. In F. N. Martin & J. G. Clark (Eds.), *Hearing care for children* (pp. 20–44). Boston: Allyn & Bacon.

ASHA (1999). *Terminology pertinent to fluency and fluency disorders: Guidelines, 41,* 29–36.

Association for Supervision and Curriculum Development (1997, November). Homework: A new look at an age-old practice. *Education Update, 39*(7), 1, 5, 8.

*At-risk youth in crisis: A handbook for collaboration between schools and social services.* (1991). Albany, OR: Linn-Benton Education Service Digest.

Atkins, M. S., & Pelham, W. E. (1991). School-based assessment of attention deficit–hyperactivity disorder. *Journal of Learning Disabilities, 24*(4), 197–204.

Austin, J. F. (1992). Involving noncustodial parents in their student's education. *NASSP Bulletin, 76,* 49–54.

Baker, B. L., Brightman, A. J., Blacher, J. B., Heifetz, L. J., Hinshaw, S. P., & Murphy, D. M. (1997). *Steps to independence: Teaching everyday skills to children with special needs.* Baltimore: Brookes.

Baker, S. B., & Rogosky-Grassi, M. A. (1993). Access to school. In F. L. Rowlley-Kelly & D. H. Reigel (Eds.), *Teaching the students with spina bifida* (pp. 31–70). Baltimore: Brookes.

Banks, J. (1992). A comment on "Teacher perceptions of the Regular Education Initiative." *Exceptional Children, 58,* 564.

Banks, J. A. (1989). Multicultural education: Characteristics and goals. In J. Banks & C. M. Banks (Eds.), *Multicultural education: Issues and perspectives* (pp. 2–26). Boston: Allyn & Bacon.

Barkley, R. A. (1990). *Attention deficit hyperactivity disorder: A handbook for diagnosis and treatment.* New York: Guilford Press.

Barkley, R. A. (1991). *Attention deficit hyperactivity disorder: A clinical workbook.* New York: Guilford Press.

Barnes, K. E. (1982). *Preschool screening: The measurement and prediction of children at risk.* Springfield, IL: Thomas.

Barr, R. D., & Parrett, W. H. (1995). *Hope at last for at-risk youth.* Boston: Allyn & Bacon.

Barraga, N. C., & Erin, J. N. (1992). *Visual handicaps and learning* (3rd ed.). Austin, TX: Pro-Ed.

Barrish, H. H., Saunders, M., & Wolf, M. M. (1969). Good-behavior game: Effects of individual contingencies for group consequences on disruptive behavior in a classroom. *Journal of Applied Behavior Analysis, 2,* 119–124.

Batshaw, M. L., & Parret, Y. M. (1986). *Children with handicaps: A medical primer.* Baltimore: Brookes.

Battle, D. A., Dickens-Wright, L., & Murphy, S. C. (1998). How to employ adolescents. *Teaching Exceptional Children, 30,* 28–33.

Bau, A. M. (1999). Providing culturally competent services to visually impaired persons. *Journal of Visual Impairment & Blindness, 93,* 291–297.

Bauer, E. J., Lurie, N., Yeh, C., & Grant, E. N. (1999). Screening for asthma in an inner city elementary school in Minneapolis, MN. *Journal of School Health, 69,* 12–16.

Baum, S. M., Owen, S. V., & Dixon, J. (1991). *The gifted and learning disabled.* Mansfield Center, CT: Creative Learning Press.

Bauwens, J., & Hourcade, J. J. (1995). *Cooperative teaching: Rebuilding the schoolhouse for all students.* Austin, TX: Pro-Ed.

Bauwens, J., Hourcade, J., & Friend, M. (1989). Cooperative teaching: A model for general and special education integration. *Remedial and Special Education, 10*(2), 17–22.

Beale, I. L., & Tippett, L. J. (1992). Remediation of psychological process deficits in learning disabilities. In N. N. Singh & I. L. Beale (Eds.), *Learning disabilities: Nature, theory, & treatment* (pp. 526–568). New York: Springer-Verlag.

Beirne-Smith, M. (1989a). A systematic approach for teaching notetaking skills to students with mild learning handicaps. *Academic Therapy, 24,* 425–437.

Beirne-Smith, M. (1989b). Teaching note-taking skills. *Academic Therapy, 24,* 452–458.

Beirne-Smith, M., Ittenbach, R. F., & Patton, J. R. (1998). *Mental retardation* (5th ed.). Upper Saddle River, NJ: Prentice-Hall/Merrill.

Bender, W. N. (1995). *Learning disabilities: Characteristics, identification, and teaching strategies* (2nd ed.). Boston: Allyn & Bacon.

Bender, W. N., Rosenkrans, C. B., & Crane, M. K. (1999). Stress, depression and suicide among students with learning disabilities: Assessing the risk. *Learning Disability Quarterly, 42*(2), 143–156.

Bennett, T., Rowe, V., & DeLuca, D. (1996). Getting to know Abby. *Focus on Autism and Developmental Disabilities, 11,* 183–188.

Bergland, M., & Hoffbauer, D. (1996). New opportunities for students with traumatic brain injury: Transition to postsecondary education. *Teaching Exceptional Children, 28,* 54–57.

Berres, M. S., & Knoblock, P. (1987). Introduction and perspective. In M. S. Berres & P. Knoblock (Eds.), *Program models for mainstreaming* (pp. 1–18). Austin, TX: Pro-Ed.

Berry, V. S. (1995). Communication strategies for fully inclusive classrooms. In B. Rittenhouse & J. Dancer (Eds.), *The full inclusion of persons with disabilities in American society* (pp. 57–65). Levin, New Zealand: National Training Resource Centre.

Beukelman, D. R., & Mirenda, P. (1998). *Augmentative and alternative communication* (2nd ed.). Baltimore: Brookes.

Bigge, J. L. (1991). *Teaching individuals with physical and multiple disabilities* (3rd ed.). New York: Macmillan.

Biklen, D. (1990). Communication unbound: Autism and praxis. *Harvard Educational Review, 60*(3), 291–314.

Biklen, D., Morton, M. W., Gold, D., Berrigan, C., & Swaminathan, S. (1992). Facilitated communication: Implications for individuals with autism. *Topics in Language Disorders, 2,* 23.

Blackman, H. P. (1989). Special education placement: Is it what you know or where you live? *Exceptional Children, 55,* 459–462.

Blackman, J. A. (1990). *Medical aspects of developmental disabilities in children birth to three* (2nd ed.). Rockville, MD: Aspen.

Blackman, J. A. (Ed.). (1984). *Medical aspects of developmental disabilities in children birth to three.* Rockville, MD: Aspen.

Blalock, G., & Patton, J. R. (1996). Transition in students with learning disabilities: Creating sound futures. In J. R. Patton & G. Blalock (Eds.), *Transition in students with learning disabilities: Facilitating the movement from school to adult life* (pp. 1–18). Austin, TX: Pro-Ed.

Blasi, M. J., & Priestly, L. (1998). A child with severe hearing loss joins our learning community. *Young Children, 22,* 44–49.

Blatt, B. (1987). *The conquest of mental retardation.* Austin, TX: Pro-Ed.

Blenk, K. (1995). *Making school inclusion work: A guide to everyday practices.* Cambridge, MA: Brookline Books.

Bley, N. S., & Thornton, C. A. (1995). *Teaching mathematics to students with learning disabilities.* Austin, TX: Pro-Ed.

Bloom, T. (1996). Assistive listening devices. *The Hearing Journal, 49,* 20–23.

Bowman, B. T. (1994). The challenge of diversity. *Phi Delta Kappa, 76,* 218–224.

Brackett, D. (1990). Communication management of the mainstreamed hearing-impaired student. In M. Ross (Ed.), *Hearing-impaired children in the mainstream* (pp. 119–130). Parkton, MD: York Press.

Brackett, D. (1997). Intervention for children with hearing impairment in general education settings. *Language, Speech, and Hearing Services in Schools, 28,* 355–361.

Brandenburg, N. A., Friedman, R. M., & Silver, S. E. (1990). The epidemiology of childhood psychiatric disorders: Prevalence findings from recent studies. *Journal of the American Association of Child and Adolescent Psychiatry, 29,* 76–83.

Breeding, M., Stone, C., & Riley, K. (n.d.) *LINC: Language in the classroom.* Unpublished manuscript. Abilene, TX: Abilene Independent School District.

Brody, J., & Good, T. (1986). Teacher behavior and student achievement. In M.C. Wittrock (Ed.), *Handbook of research on teaching* (pp. 328–375). New York: Macmillan.

Brolin, D. E. (1989). *Life-centered career education.* Reston, VA: CEC.

Broome, S. A., & White, R. B. (1995). The many uses of videotape in classrooms serving youth with behavior disorders. *Teaching Exceptional Children, 27,* 10–13.

Browder, D., & Snell, M. E. (1988). Assessment of individuals with severe disabilities. In M. E. Snell (Ed.), *Severe disabilities.* Columbus, OH: Merrill.

Brown, D. L., & Moore, L. (1992). The Bama bookworm program: Motivating remedial readers to read at home with their parents. *Teaching Exceptional Children, 24,* 17–20.

Brown, J., Cohen, P., Johnson, J. G., & Salzinger, S. (1998). A longitudinal analysis of risk factors for child maltreatment: Findings of a 17-year prospective study of officially recorded and self-reported child abuse and neglect. *Child Abuse & Neglect, 22,* 1065–1078.

Brown, J., Gable, R. A., Hendrickson, J. M., & Algozzine, B. (1991). Prereferral intervention practices of regular classroom teachers: Implications for regular and special education preparation. *Teacher Education and Special Education, 14,* 192–197.

Bryan, T. (1999). Reflections on a research career: It ain't over til it's over. *Exceptional Children, 65*(4), 438–447.

Bryan, T., Bay, M., & Donahue, M. (1988). Implications of the learning disabilities definition for the regular education initiative. *Journal of Learning Disabilities, 21*(1), 23–27.

Bryan, T., Bay, M., Lopez-Reyna, N., & Donahue, M. (1991). Characteristics of students with learning disabilities: A summary of the extent data base and its implications for educational programs. In J. W. Lloyd, N. N. Singh, & A. C. Repp (Eds.), *The regular education initiative: Alternative perspectives* (pp. 121–131). Sycamore, IL: Sycamore.

Bryan, T. A., & Sullivan-Burstein, K. (1998). Teacher selected strategies for improving homework completion. *Remedial and Special Education, 19,* 263–273.

Buck, G., & Smith, T. E. C. (in press). *Children and adults with mental retardation.* Ft. Worth: Harcourt Brace.

Buck, G. H., Bursuck, W. D., Polloway, E. A., Nelson, J., Jayanthi, M., & Whitehouse, F. A. (1996). Homework-related communication problems: Perspectives of special educators. *Journal of Emotional and Behavioral Disorders, 4,* 105–113.

Buck, G. H., Polloway, E. A., Kirkpatrick, M. A., Patton, J. R., & Fad, K. (1999). *Developing behavioral intervention plans: A sequential approach.* Unpublished manuscript.

Bullock, L. (1992). *Exceptionalities in children and youth.* Boston: Allyn & Bacon.

Bullock, L. M., Zagar, E. L., Donahue, C. A., & Pelton, G. B. (1985). Teachers' perceptions of behaviorally disordered students in a variety of settings. *Exceptional Children, 52,* 123–130.

Burchum, B. G., & DeMers, St. T. (1995). Comprehensive assessment of children and youth with ADHD. *Intervention in School and Clinic, 30*(4), 211–219.

Burnley, G. D. (1993). A team approach for identification for an attention deficit hyperactivity disorder child. *The School Counselor, 40,* 228–230.

Burns, B. J., Hoagwood, K., & Maultsby, L. T. (1999). Improving outcomes for children and adolescents with serious emotional and behavioral disorders: Current and future directions. In M. H. Epstein, K. Kutash, & A. Duchnowski (Eds.), *Outcomes for children and youth with behavioral and emotional disorders in their families: Programs and evaluation of best practices* (pp. 685–707). Austin, TX: Pro-Ed.

Bursuck, W., Harniss, M. K., Epstein, M. H., Polloway, E. A., Jayanthi, M., & Wissinger, L. M. (in press). Solving communication problems about homework: Recommendations of special education teachers. *Learning Disabilities Research & Practice.*

Bursuck, W., Munk, D., & Olson, M. (1999). The fairness of report card grading adaptations: What do students with and without disabilities think? *Remedial and Special Education, 20,* 84–92, 105.

Bursuck, W., Polloway, E., Epstein, M., & Jayanthi, M. (n.d.). Recommendations of general education teachers regarding communication problems about homework and students with disabilities. Manuscript in preparation.

Bursuck, W. D., Polloway, E. A., Plante, L., Epstein, M. H., Jayanthi, M., & McConeghy, J. (1996). Report card grading and adaptations: A national survey of classroom practices. *Exceptional Children, 62,* 301–318.

Bussing, R., Zima, B., Perwien, A. R., Belin, T. R., & Widawski, M. (1998). Children in special education programs: Attention deficit hyperactivity disorder, use of services, and unmet needs. *American Journal of Public Health 88*(6), 880–886.

Butera, G., Klein, H., McMullen, L., & Wilson, B. (1998). A statewide study of FAPE and school discipline policies. *The Journal of Special Education, 32,* 108–114.

Butler-Hall, B. (1987). *Hall's articulation remediation training sheets (HARTS).* Henderson, TX: Creations Publications.

Callahan, K., Redemacher, R., & Hildreth, T. A. (1998). The effectiveness of parent participation in strategies to improve homework performance of students at risk. *Remedial and Special Education, 19,* 131–141.

Calloway, C. (1999). Promote friendship in the inclusive classroom. *Intervention in School and Clinic, 34*(3), 176–177.

Candler, A. C., & Hildreth, B. L. (1990). Characteristics of language disorders in learning disabled students. *Academic Therapy, 25*(3), 333–343.

Cantrell, M. L. (1992). Guest editorial. *Journal of Emotional and Behavioral Problems, 1,* 4.

Cantu, N. (1993). OCR clarifies evaluation requirements for ADD. *The Special Educator, 9*(1), 11–12.

Carnegie Council on Adolescent Development. (1989). *Turning point: Preparing American youth for the 21st century.* New York: Carnegie.

Carnine, D., Silbert J., & Kameenui, E. J. (1990). *Direct instruction reading* (2nd ed.). Columbus, OH: Merrill.

Carpenter, S. L., & McKee-Higgins, E. (1996). Behavior management in inclusive classrooms. *Remedial and Special Education, 17,* 195–203.

Cassidy, V. M., & Stanton, J. E. (1959). An investigation of factors involved in the education placement of mentally retarded children: A study of differences between children in regular and special classes in Ohio. Columbus, OH: Ohio State University. (ERIC Document Reproduction Service No. ED 002752).

Caton, H. (Ed.). (1997). *Tools for selecting appropriate learning media.* Louisville, KY: American Printing House for the Blind.

Cawley, J. (1984). *Developmental teaching of mathematics for the learning disabled.* Austin, TX: Pro-Ed.

Center, D. B. (1985). PL 94-142 as applied to *DSM-III* diagnosis: A book review. *Behavioral Disorders, 10,* 305–306.

Center, D. B., & Eden, A. (1989–1990). A search for variables affecting under-identification of students with behavior disorders: II. *National Forum of Special Education Journal, 1,* 12–18.

Center, D. B., & Obringer, J. (1987). A search for variables affecting underidentification of behaviorally disordered students. *Behavioral Disorders, 12,* 169–174.

Center for Future of Teaching and Learning. (1996). Overview of reading research. Washington D.C.: Author.

Center for Teaching and Learning. (1986). Thirty years of NICHD research: What we now know about how children learn to read. *Effective School Practices, 15*(3), 33–46.

Centers for Disease Control. (1988). *AIDS surveillance report.* Atlanta, GA: Author.

Centers for Disease Control. (1997). AIDS among children—United States, 1996. *Journal of School Health, 67,* 175–177.

Chalfant, J. C., & Pysh, M. V. (1989). Teacher assistance teams: Five descriptive studies on 96 teams. *Remedial and Special Education, 10*(6), 49–58.

Chalfant, J. C., Pysh, M. V., & Moultrie, R. (1979). Teacher assistance teams: A model for within-building problem solving. *Learning Disability Quarterly, 2*(3), 85–96.

Chalfant, J. C., & Van Dusen Pysh, R. L. (1993). Teacher assistance teams: Implications for the gifted. In C. J. Maker (Ed.), *Critical issues in gifted education: Vol 3. Programs for the gifted in regular classrooms* (pp. 32–48). Austin, TX: Pro-Ed.

Chalmers, L. (1991). Classroom modifications for the mainstreamed student with mild handicaps. *Intervention in School and Clinic, 27*(1), 40–42, 51.

Chase, P. A., Hall, J. W., & Werkhaven, J. A. (1996). Sensorineural hearing loss in children: Etiology and pathology. In F. N. Martin & J. G. Clark (Eds.), *Hearing care for children* (pp. 73–88). Boston: Allyn & Bacon.

Cheney, C. O. (1989). The systematic adaptation of instructional materials and techniques for problem learners. *Academic Therapy, 25,* 25–30.

Chiriboga, D. A., & Catron, L. S. (1991). *Divorce.* New York: University Press.

Christenson, S. L., Ysseldyke, J. E., & Thurlow, M. L. (1989). Critical instructional factors for students with mild handicaps: An integrative review. *Remedial and Special Education, 10*(5), 21–31.

Christian, B. T. (1999). *Outrageous behavior model.* Austin, TX: Pro-Ed.

Christiansen, J., & Vogel, J. R. (1998). A decision model for grading students with disabilities. *Teaching Exceptional Children, 31*(2), 30–35.

Cipani, E. C. (1995). Be aware of negative reinforcement. *Teaching Exceptional Children, 27,* 37–40.

Clark, B. (1996). The need for a range of program options for gifted and talented students. In W. Stainback & S. Stainback (Eds.), *Controversial issues confronting special education: Divergent perspectives* (2nd ed., pp. 57–68). Boston: Allyn & Bacon.

Clark, B. (1997). *Growing up gifted: Developing the potential of children at home and at school* (5th ed.). Upper Saddle River, NJ: Merrill/Prentice-Hall.

Clark, G. M., Field, S., Patton, J. R., Brolin, D. E., & Sitlington, P. L. (1994). Life skills and instruction: A necessary component for all students with disabilities: A position statement of the Division on Career Development and Transition. *Career Development for Exceptional Individuals, 17,* 125–134.

Clark, J. G., & Jaindl, M. (1996). Conductive hearing loss in children: Etiology and pathology. In F. N. Martin & J. G. Clark (Eds.), *Hearing care for children* (pp. 45–72). Boston: Allyn & Bacon.

Clary, D. L., & Edwards, S. (1992). Spoken language. In E. A. Polloway, J. R. Patton, J. S. Payne, & R. A. Payne (Eds.), *Strategies for teaching learners with special needs* (4th ed., pp. 185–285). Columbus, OH: Merrill.

Clay, J. W. (1991, March). Respecting and supporting gay and lesbian parents. *Young Children,* March, 51–57.

Cline, S., & Schwartz, D. (1999). *Diverse populations of gifted children.* Boston: Allyn & Bacon.

Clinkenbeard, P. R. (1991). Unfair expectations: A pilot study of middle school students' comparisons of gifted and regular classes. *Journal for the Education of the Gifted, 15,* 56–63.

Cochran, P. S., & Bull, G. L. (1993). Computers and individuals with speech and language disorders. In J. D. Kindsey (Ed.), *Computers and exceptional individuals* (pp. 211–242). Austin, TX: Pro-Ed.

Colangelo, N., & Davis, G. A. (Eds.). (1997). *Handbook of gifted education* (2nd ed.). Boston: Allyn & Bacon.

Colarusso, R. P., & Kana, T. G. (1991). Public Law 99-457, Part H, infant and toddler programs: Status and implications. *Focus on Exceptional Children, 23,* 1–12.

Coleman, E. B. (1998). Using explanatory knowledge during problem solving in science. *Journal of Learning Science, 1,* 387–427.

Conderman, G., & Katsiyannis, A. (1995). *Intervention in School and Clinic, 31*(1), 44.

*Condition of Education.* (1990). Washington, D.C.: Office of Educational Research and Improvement.

Connolly, A. J. (1988). *Keymath—Revised: A diagnostic inventory of essential mathematics.* Circle Pines, MN: American Guidance Service.

Conoley, J. C., & Kramer, J. J. (1989). *Tenth mental measurements yearbook.* Lincoln, NE: Buros Institute.

Conte, R. (1991). Attention disorders. In B. Y. L. Wong (Ed.), *Learning about learning disabilities* (pp. 55–101). New York: Academic Press.

Cook, R. E., Tessier, A., & Klein, M. D. (1992). *Adapting early childhood curricula for children with special needs.* New York: Merrill.

Cooke, N. L., Heron, T. E., & Heward, W. L. (1983). *Peer tutoring: Implementing classroom-wide programs.* Columbus, OH: Special Press.

Cooper, H. (1989). *Homework.* White Plains, NY: Longman.

Corn, A. L., Hatlen, P., Huebner, K. M., Ryan, F., & Siller, M. A. (1995). *The national agenda for the education of children and youths with visual impairments, including those with multiple disabilities.* New York: American Foundation for the Blind.

Corn, A. L., & Koening, A. J. (Eds.). *Foundations of low vision: Clinical and functional perspectives.* New York: American Foundation for the Blind.

Cosden, M. A. (1990). Expanding the role of special education. *Teaching Exceptional Children, 22,* 4–6.

Cotler, S. (1986). Epidemiology and outcome. In J. M. Reisman (Ed.), *Behavior disorders in infants, children, and adolescents* (pp. 196–211). New York: Random House.

Council for Exceptional Children. (1992). *Children with ADD: A shared responsibility.* Reston, VA: Author.

Council for Exceptional Children. (1997a). A disability or a gift? *CEC Today, 4*(3), 7.

Council for Exceptional Children. (1997b). Effective accommodations for students with exceptionalities. *CEC Today, 4*(3), 1, 9, 15.

Council for Exceptional Children. (1999). The hidden problem among students with exceptionalities—depression. *CEC Today, 5*(5), 1, 5, 15.

Council of Administrators in Special Education. (1992). *Student access: Section 504 of the rehabilitation act of 1973.* Reston, VA: Author.

Coutinho, M. J., & Repp, A. C. (1999). *Inclusion: The integration of students with disabilities.* Belmont, CA: Wadsworth.

Cozzins, G., Dowdy, C. A., & Smith, T. E. C. (1999). *Adult Agencies.* Austin: TX: Pro-Ed.

Cramer, S. (1998). *Collaboration: A successful strategy for special education.* Boston: Allyn & Bacon.

Cramer, S., Erzkus, A., Mayweather, K., Pope, K., Roeder, J., & Tone, T. (1997). Connecting with siblings. *Teaching Exceptional Children, 30*(1), 46–51.

Crawford, H. (1998). Classroom acoustics: Creating favorable environments for learning. *ADVANCE for Speech-Language Pathologists & Audiologists, 36,* 25–27.

Creekmore, W. N. (1988). Family–classroom: A critical balance. *Academic Therapy, 24,* 207–220.

Crews, W. D., Bonaventura, S., Hay, C. L., Steele, W. K., & Rowe, F. B. (1993). Gilles de la Tourette disorder among individuals with severe or profound mental retardation. *Mental Retardation, 31,* 25–28.

Cronin, J. F. (1993). Four misconceptions about authentic learning. *Educational Leadership, 50* (7), 78–80.

Cronin, M. E. (1988). Adult performance outcomes/life skills. In G. Robinson, J. R. Patton, E. A. Polloway, & L. Sargent (Eds.), *Best practices in mental disabilities* (Vol. 2, pp. 39–52). Des Moines: Iowa State Department of Education.

Cronin, M. E., & Patton, J. R. (1993). *Life skills instruction for all students with special needs.* Austin, TX: Pro-Ed.

Cross, T. L. (1999). Psychological and sociological aspects of educating gifted students. *Peabody Journal of Education, 72,* 180–200.

Csikszentmihalyi, M., Rathunde, K., & Whalen, S. (1997). *Talented teenagers. The roots of success and failure.* Cambridge, England: Cambridge University Press.

Cullinan, D., & Epstein, M. (1985). Teacher related adjustment problems. *Remedial and Special Education, 6,* 5–11.

Cummings, C. (1983). *Managing to teach*. Edmonds, WA: Teaching Inc.

Dagenais, P. A., Critz-Crosby, P., Fletcher, S. G., & McCutcheon, M. J. (1994). Comparing abilities of children with profound hearing impairments to learn consonants using electropalatography or traditional aural–oral techniques. *Journal of Speech and Hearing Research, 37,* 687–699.

Daly, D. A. (1991, April). *Multi-modal therapy for fluency clients: Strategies that work.* Paper presented at the Spring Convention of the Texas Speech-Language-Hearing Association, Houston, TX.

Darling, R. B., & Baxter, C. (1996). *Families in focus: Sociological methods in early intervention.* Austin, TX: Pro-Ed.

Davies, P. W. S., & Joughin, C. (1993). Using stable isotopes to assess reduced physical activity of individuals with Prader-Willi syndrome. *American Journal on Mental Retardation, 98,* 349–353.

Davis, J. (1996). Two different flight plans: Advanced placement and gifted programs—different and necessary. *Gifted Child Today, 19*(2), 32–36, 50.

Davis, W. E. (1993). *At-risk children and educational reform: Implications for educators and schools in the year 2000 and beyond.* Orono, ME: College of Education, University of Maine.

Davis, W. E. (1995). Students at risk: Common myths and misconceptions. *The Journal of At-Risk Issues, 2,* 5–10.

deBettencourt, L. U. (1987). How to develop parent relationships. *Teaching Exceptional Children, 19,* 26–27.

Deiner, P. L. (1993). *Resources for teaching children with diverse abilities: Birth through eight.* Ft. Worth, TX: Harcourt Brace Jovanovich.

Del Prete, T. (1996). Asset or albatross? The education and socialization of gifted students. *Gifted Child Today, 19*(2), 24–25, 44–49.

DeLong, R. (1995). Medical and pharmacological treatment of learning disabilities. *Journal of Child Neurology, 10*(suppl. 1), 92–95.

Denning, C. B., Chamberlain, J. A., & Polloway, E. A. (2000). An evaluation of state guidelines for mental retardation: Focus on definition and classification practices. *Education and Training in Mental Retardation and Developmental Disabilities, 35,* 135–144.

Deno, E. (1970). Special education as development capital. *Exceptional Children, 55,* 440–447.

Deno, S. L., Foegen, A., Robinson, S., & Espin, C. (1996). Commentary: Facing the realities of inclusion for students with mild disabilities. *Journal of Special Education, 30,* 345–357.

Deno, S. L., & Fuchs, L. S. (1987). Developing curriculum-based measurement systems for data-based special education problem-solving. *Focus on Exceptional Children, 19*(8), 1–16.

Deshler, D. D., Ellis, E. S., & Lenz, B. K. (1996). *Teaching adolescents with learning disabilities: Strategies and methods* (2nd ed.). Denver: Love.

Deshler, D. D., & Lenz, B. K. (1989). The strategies instructional approach. *International Journal of Disability, Development and Education, 36*(3), 203–224.

Deshler, D., & Schumaker, J. B. (1988). Learning strategies: An instructional alternative for low-achieving adolescents. *Exceptional Children, 52,* 83–89.

Desrochers, J. (1999). Vision problems—How teachers can help. *Young Children, 54,* 36–38.

*Diana* v. *State Board of Education*, C-70-37 R.F.P. (N.D., California, Jan. 7, 1970, and June 18, 1972).

Diefendorf, A. O. (1996). Hearing loss and its effects. In F. N. Martin & J. G. Clark (Eds.), *Hearing care for children* (pp. 3–18). Boston: Allyn & Bacon.

Dobbs, R. F., Primm, E. B., & Primm, B. (1991). Mediation: A common sense approach for resolving conflicts in education. *Focus on Exceptional Children, 24,* 1–12.

Donahue, K., & Zigmond, N. (1990). Academic grades of ninth-grade urban learning disabled students and low-achieving peers. *Exceptionality, 1,* 17–27.

Dorn, L., & Allen, A. (1995). Helping low-achieving first-grade readers: A program combining reading recovery tutoring and small-group instruction. *Journal of School Research and Information, 13,* 16–24.

Dowdy, C. A. (1998). Strengths and limitations inventory: School version. In C. A. Dowdy, J. R. Patton, T. E. C. Smith, & E. A. Polloway. *Attention deficit/hyperactivity disorder in the classroom: A practical guide for teachers.* Austin, TX: Pro-Ed.

Dowdy, C. A., Carter, J., & Smith, T. E. C. (1990). Differences in transitional needs of high school students with and without learning disabilities. *Journal of Learning Disabilities, 23*(6), 343–348.

Dowdy, C. A., Patton, J. R., Smith, T. E. C., & Polloway, E. A. (1998). *Attention deficit/hyperactivity disorders in the classroom.* Austin, TX: Pro-Ed.

Dowdy, C. A., & Smith, T. E. C. (1991). Future-based assessment and intervention. *Intervention in School and Clinic, 27*(2), 101–106.

Doyle, W. (1986). Classroom organization and management. In M. C. Wittrock (Ed.), *Handbook of research and teaching* (3rd ed., pp. 392–431). New York: Macmillan.

Drug use increasing. (1992). *Youth Today, 1,* 27–29.

Duane, D. D., & Gray, D. B. (Eds.) (1991). *The reading brain: The biological basis of dyslexia.* Parkton, MD: York.

Dunlap, L. K., Dunlap, G., Koegel, L., & Koegel, R. L. (1991). Using self-monitoring to increase independence. *Teaching Exceptional Children, 23*(3), 17–26.

Dunn, L. M. (1973). *Exceptional children in the schools: Special education in transition.* New York: Holt, Rinehart & Winston.

Dunst, C. J., Johanson, C., Trivette, C. M., & Hamby, D. (1991). Family-oriented early intervention policies and practices: Family-centered or not? *Exceptional Children, 58,* 115–126.

DuPaul, G. J., & Eckert, T. L. (1998). Academic interventions for students with attention-deficit/hyperactivity disorder: A review of the literature. *Reading and Writing Quarterly, 14*(1), 59–83.

Durden, W. G. (1995, October 4). Where is the middle ground? *Education Week,* pp. 47–48.

Dyches, T. (1998). The effectiveness of switch training on communication of children with autism and severe disabilities. *Focus on Autism and Other Developmental Disabilities, 13,* 151–162.

Easterbrooks, S. R. (1999). *Adapting regular classrooms for children who are deaf/hard of hearing.* Paper presented to the Council for Exceptional Children convention, Minneapolis, MN.

Eaves, R. C. (1992). Autism. In P. J. McLaughlin and P. Wehman (Eds.), *Developmental disabilities* (pp. 68–80). Boston: Andover Medical Publishers.

Edgar, E. (1987). Secondary programs in special education: Are many of them justifiable? *Exceptional Children, 53,* 555–561.

Edgar, E. (1988). Employment as an outcome for mildly handicapped students: Current status and future directions. *Focus on Exceptional Children, 21*(1), 1–8.

Gartland, D. (1994). Content area reading: Lessons from the specialists. *LD Forum, 19*(3), 19–22.

Gearheart, B. R., Weishahn, M. W., & Gearheart, C. J. (1996). *The exceptional student in the regular classroom* (6th ed.). Columbus, OH: Merrill.

Geisthardt, C., & Munsch, J. (1996). Coping with school stress: A comparison of adolescents with and without learning disabilities. *Journal of Learning Disabilities, 29*(3), 287–296.

Gerber, P. J., & Reiff, H. B. (1998). Reframing the learning disabilities experience. *Journal of Learning Disabilities, 29*(1), 98–102.

Gersh, E. S. (1991). What is cerebral palsy? In E. Geralis (Ed.), *Children with cerebral palsy: A parents' guide.* New York: Woodbine House.

Gerstein, R., Brengleman, S., & Jimenez, R. (1994). Effective instruction for culturally and linguistically diverse students: A reconceptualization. *Focus on Exceptional Children, 27*(1), 1–6.

Gerstein, R., & Woodward, J. (1994). The language-minority student and special education: Issues, trends, and paradoxes. *Exceptional Children, 60*(4), 310–322.

Getch, Y. Q., Neuhart-Pritchett, S. (1999). Children with asthma: Strategies for educators. *Teaching Exceptional Children, 31,* 30–36.

Giangreco, M. F., Dennis, R., Cloninger, C., Edelman, S., & Schattman, R. (1993). I've counted Jon: Transformational experiences of teachers educating students with disabilities. *Exceptional Children, 59,* 359–372.

Gillberg, C. (Ed.). (1989). *Diagnosis and treatment of autism.* New York: Plenum Press.

Ginsberg, R., Gerber, P. J., & Reiff, H. B. (1994). Employment success for adults with learning disabilities. In P. Gerber & H. Reiff (Eds.), *Learning disabilities in adulthood* (pp. 204–213). Stoneham, MA: Andover Medical Publishers.

Ginsburg, H. P. (1989). *Children's arithmetic: How they learn it and how you teach it* (2nd ed.). Austin, TX: Pro-Ed.

Glazer, S. M. (1998). At risk students: No instant solutions. *Teaching Pre-K–8, 28*(7), 84–86.

Goldstein, S., & Goldstein, M. (1990). *Managing attention disorder in children: A guide for practitioners.* New York: John Wiley & Sons.

Goldstein, S., & Turnbull, A. P. (1981). Strategies to increase parent participation in IEP conferences. *Exceptional Children, 48,* 360–361.

Gorman, J. C. (1999, January/February). Understanding children's hearts and minds. *Teaching Exceptional Children, 31,* 72–77.

Graden, J. L., Casey, A., & Christenson, S. L. (1985). Implementing a prereferral intervention system: Part I, the model. *Exceptional Children, 51,* 377–384.

Graham, S. (1992). Helping students with LD progress as writers. *Intervention in School and Clinic, 27,* 134–144.

Graham, S., & Harris, K. R. (1997). Whole language and process writing: Does one approach fit all? In I. W. Lloyd, E. J. Kameenui, & D. Chard (Eds.), *Issues in educating students with disabilities* (pp. 239–258). Mahwan, NJ: Erlbaum.

Grant, R. (1993). Strategic training for using text headings to improve students' processing of content. *Journal of Reading, 36,* 482–488.

Greenbaum, P. E., Dedrick, R. F., Friedman, R. M., Kutash, K., Brown, E. C., Lardieri, S. P., & Pugh, A. M. (1998). National adolescent and child treatment study (NACTS): Outcomes for children with serious emotional behavioral disturbance. In M. H. Epstein, K. Kutash, & A. Duchnowski (Eds.), *Outcomes for children and youth with emotional and behavioral disor-ders and their families: Programs and evaluation best practices* (pp. 21–54). Austin, TX: Pro-Ed.

Greenspan, S. (1996, October 11). *Everyday intelligence and a new definition of mental retardation.* Fifth Annual MRDD Conference, Austin, TX.

Greenspan, S., & Driscoll, J. (in press). The role of intelligence in a broad model of personal competence. In D. Flanagan, J. Genshaft, & P. Harrison (Eds.), *Contemporary intellectual assessment.* New York: Guilford.

Greer, J. V. (1991). At-risk students in the fast lanes: Let them through. *Exceptional Children, 57,* 390–391.

Gregory, C., & Katsiyannis, A. (1995). Section 504 accommodation plans. *Intervention in School and Clinic, 31*(1), 42–45.

Gresham, F. M. (1982). Misguided mainstreaming: The case for social skills training with handicapped children. *Exceptional Children, 48*(5), 422–431.

Gresham, F. M. (1984). Social skills and self-efficacy for exceptional children. *Exceptional Children, 51,* 253–261.

Grosenick, J. K., George, N. L., George, M. P., & Lewis, T. J. (1991). Public school services for behaviorally disordered students: Program practices in the 1980s. *Behavioral Disorders, 16,* 87–96.

Grossman, H. J. (1983). *Classification in mental retardation.* Washington, D.C.: American Association on Mental Deficiency.

Guernsey, M. A. (1989). Classroom organization: A key to successful management. *Academic Therapy, 25,* 55–58.

Guetzloe, E. (1988). Suicide and depression: Special education's responsibility. *Teaching Exceptional Children, 20,* 25–28.

Guterman, B. R. (1995). The validity of categorical learning disabilities services: The consumer's view. *Exceptional Children, 62,* 111–124.

Hadden, S., & Fowler, S. A. (1997). Preschool: A new beginning for children and parents. *Teaching Exceptional Children, 30*(1), 36–39.

Hallahan, D. P., & Kauffman, J. M. (1995). *The illusion of full inclusion.* Austin, TX: Pro-Ed.

Hallahan, D. P., & Kauffman, J. M. (1997). *Exceptional learners: Introduction to special education* (7th ed.). Boston: Allyn & Bacon.

Hallahan, D. P., & Kauffman, J. M. (1999). *Exceptional children: Introduction to special education* (8th ed.). Boston: Allyn & Bacon.

Hallahan, D. P., Kauffman, J. M., & Lloyd, J. W. (1996). *Introduction to learning disabilities.* Boston: Allyn & Bacon.

Hallahan, D. P., Kauffman, J. M., & Lloyd, J. W. (1999). *Introduction to learning disabilities* (2nd ed.). Boston: Allyn & Bacon.

Hallahan, D. P., Lloyd, J. W., & Stoller, L. (1982). *Improving attention with self-monitoring: A manual for teachers.* Charlottesville, VA: University of Virginia Press.

Hammill, D. D., & Bartel, N. R. (1995). *Teaching students with learning and behavior problems.* Austin, TX: Pro-Ed.

Hammill, D. D., & Larsen, S. C. (1974). The effectiveness of psycholinguistic training. *Exceptional Children, 41,* 5–14.

Hammill, D. D., Leigh, J. E., McNutt, G., & Larsen, S. C. (1981). A new definition of learning disabilities. *Learning Disability Quarterly, 7,* 429–436.

Hamre-Nietupski, S., Ayres, B., Nietupski, J., Savage, M., Mitchell, B., & Bramman, H. (1989). Enhancing integration of students with severe disabilities through curricular infusion: A general/special educator partnership. *Education and Training in Mental Retardation, 24,* 78–88.

Hamre-Nietupski, S., McDonald, J., & Nietupski, J. (1992). Integrating elementary students with multiple disabilities into supported regular classes: Challenges and solutions. *Teaching Exceptional Children, 24,* 6–9.

Hansen, C. R. (1992). What is Tourette syndrome? In T. Haerle (Ed.), *Children with Tourette syndrome: A parents' guide* (pp. 1–25). Rockville, MD: Woodbine House.

Hanson, M. J., & Carta, J. J. (1996). Addressing the challenges of families with multiple risks. *Exceptional Children, 62,* 201–212.

Hardman, M. L., Drew, C. J., Egan, M. W., & Wolf, B. (1993). *Human exceptionality: Society, school, and family* (4th ed.). Boston: Allyn & Bacon.

Haring, K. A., Lovett, D. L., & Saren, D. (1991). Parent perceptions of their adult offspring with disabilities. *Teaching Exceptional Children, 23,* 6–10.

Harrington-Lueker, D. (1991). Beyond multiple choice: The push to assess performance. *The Executive Educator, 13*(4), 20–22.

Harris, D., & Vanderheiden, G. C. (1980). Augmentative communication techniques. In R. L. Schiefelbusch (Ed.), *Nonspeech language and communication: Analysis and intervention* (pp. 259–302). Austin, TX: Pro-Ed.

Harris, K. C. (1998). *Collaborative elementary teaching: A casebook for elementary special and general educators.* Austin, TX: Pro-Ed.

Harry, B. (1992). *Cultural diversity, families, and the special education system: Communication and empowerment.* New York: Teachers College Press.

Harwell, J. M. (1989). *Learning disabilities handbook.* West Nyack, NY: Center for Applied Research in Education.

Hasbrouck, J. E., & Tindal G. (1992). Curriculum-based oral reading fluency norms for students in grades 2 through 5. *Teaching Exceptional Children, 24*(3), 41–44.

Hasselbring, T., & Goin, L. (1993). Integrated media and technology. In E. A. Polloway & J. R. Patton (Eds.), *Strategies for teaching learners with special needs* (5th ed., pp. 145–162). Columbus, OH: Macmillan.

Hazel, J. S., Schumaker, J. B., Shelon, J., & Sherman, J. A. (1982). Application of a group training program in social skills to learning disabled and non-learning disabled youth. *Learning Disability Quarterly, 5,* 398–408.

*Healthy People 2000.* (1992). Washington, D.C.: U.S. Government Printing Office.

Heaton, S., & O'Shea, D. J. (1995). Using mnemonics to make mnemonics. *Teaching Exceptional Children, 28*(1), 34–36.

Heflin, L. J., & Simpson, R. (1998). The interventions for children and youth with autism: Prudent choices in a world of extraordinary claims and promises: Part II. *Focus on Autism and Other Developmental Disabilities, 13,* 212–220.

Heller, K., Monks, F., & Passow, A. H. (Eds.). (1993). *International handbook of research and development of giftedness and talent.* Oxford: Pergamon Press.

Heller, K. W., Alberto, P. A., Forney, P. E., & Schwartzman, M. N. (1996). *Understanding physical, sensory, and health impairments.* Pacific Grove, CA: Brooks/Cole.

Helmsetter, E., Curry, C. A., Brennan, M., & Sampson-Saul, M. (1998). Comparison of general and special education classrooms of students with severe disabilities. *Education and Training in Mental Retardation and Developmental Disabilities, 33,* 216–226.

Henry, N. A., & Flynt, E. S. (1990). Rethinking special education referral: A procedural model. *Intervention in School and Clinic, 26,* 22–24.

Herer, G., & Reilly, M. (1999). Pediatric audiology: Poised for the future. *ASHA, 13,* 24–30.

Herskowitz, J., & Rosman, N. P. (1982). *Pediatric, neurology, and psychiatry—Common ground.* New York: Macmillan.

Hess, R., Miller, A., Reese, J., & Robinson, G. (1987). *Grading-credit-diploma: Accommodation practices.* Des Moines, IA: Department of Education.

Hetfield, P. (1994). Using a student newspaper to motivate students with behavior disorders. *Teaching Exceptional Children, 26,* 6–9.

Heward, W. L. (1995). *Exceptional children: An introductory survey of special education* (4th ed.). New York: Macmillan.

Heward, W. L. (2000). *Exceptional children: An introduction to special education* (7th ed.). Englewood Cliffs, NJ: Prentice-Hall.

Heward, W. L., & Orlansky, M. D. (1992). *Exceptional children: An introductory survey of special education* (4th ed.). New York: Merrill.

Hietsch, D. G. (1986). Father involvement: No moms allowed. *Teaching Exceptional Children, 18,* 258–260.

Hill, D. (1991). Tasting failure: Thoughts of an at-risk learner. *Phi Delta Kappan, 73,* 308–310.

Hill, M., Szefler, S. J., & Larsen, G. L. (1998). Asthma pathogenesis and the implications for therapy in children. *Pediatric Clinics of North America, 39,* 1205–1222.

Hiller, J. F. (1990). Setting up a classroom-based language instruction program: One clinician's experience. *Texas Journal of Audiology and Speech Pathology, 16*(2), 12–13.

Hilton, A. (1990). *Parental reactions to having a disabled child.* Paper presented at annual International Conference of the Council for Exceptional Children.

Hobbs, T., & Westling, D. L. (1998). Promoting successful inclusion. *Teaching Exceptional Children, 34,* 10–14.

*Hobson* v. *Hansen,* 269 F. Supp. 401 (D.D.C.), 1967.

Hocutt, A., Martin, E., & McKinney, J. (1990). Historical and legal context of mainstreaming. In J. W. Lloyd, N. N. Singh, & A. C. Repp (Eds.), *The Regular Education Initiative: Alternative perspectives on concepts, issues, and models* (pp. 17–28). Sycamore, IL: Sycamore.

Hoeffer, T. D. (1981). *Alternative family styles.* St. Louis: Mosby.

Hoida, J. A., & McDougal, S. E. (1998). Fostering a positive school environment for students with cancer. *NASSP Bulletin, 82,* 59–72.

Holcomb, D., Lira, J., Kingery, P. M., Smith, D. W., Lane, D., & Goodway, J. (1998). Evaluation of *jump into action:* A program to reduce the risk of non–insulin-dependent diabetes mellitus in school children on the Texas–Mexico border. *Journal of School Health, 68,* 282–287.

Homme, L. (1969). *How to use contingency contracting in the classroom.* Champaign, IL: Research Press.

Hoover, J. J. (1988a). *Curriculum adaptation for students with learning and behavior problems: Principles and practices.* Lindale, TX: Hamilton Publications.

Hoover, J. J. (1988b). Implementing a study skills program in the classroom. *Academic Therapy, 24,* 471–476.

Hoover, J. J. (1990). Curriculum adaptations: A five-step process for classroom implementation. *Academic Therapy, 25,* 407–416.

Hoover, J. J., & Patton, J. R. (1995). *Teaching students with learning problems to use study skills: A teacher's guide.* Austin: TX: Pro-Ed.

Hoover, J. J., & Patton, J. R. (1997). *Curriculum adaptations for students with learning and behavior problems* (2nd ed.). Austin, TX: Pro-Ed.

Horner, R. H. (2000). Positive behavior supports. In M. L. Wehmeyer & J. R. Patton (Eds.), *Mental retardation in the 21st century* (pp. 181–196). Austin, TX: Pro-Ed.

Hoy, C., & Gregg, N. (1994). *Assessment: The special educator's role.* Pacific Grove, CA: Brooks/Cole.

Huff, C. R. (1999). Comparison of criminal behaviors of youth gangs and at-risk youth. Washington, D.C.: Department of Justice National Institute of Justice.

Hughes, C., & Carter, E. W. (1999). *The transition handbook: Strategies high school teachers use that work.* Baltimore: Brookes.

Huntze, S. L. (1985). A position paper of the Council for Children with Behavior Disorders. *Behavior Disorders, 10,* 167–174.

Huure, T. M., Komulainen, E. J., & Aro, H. M. (1999). Social support and self-esteem among adolescents with visual impairments. *Journal of Visual Impairment & Blindness, 93,* 326–337.

Hux, K., & Hackley, C. (1996). Mild traumatic brain injury. *Intervention in School and Clinic, 31,* 158–165.

Hynd, G. W., Marshall, R., & Gonzalez, J. (1991). Learning disabilities and presumed central nervous system dysfunction. *Learning Disability Quarterly, 14,* 283–295.

*ICD-10: International statistical classification of diseases and related health problems* (10th rev. ed.). (1992). Geneva, Switzerland: World Health Organization.

Idol, L. (1983). *Special educator's consultation handbook.* Austin, TX: Pro-Ed.

Idol, L., & West, F. (1991). Educational collaboration: A catalyst for effective schooling. *Intervention in School and Clinic, 27,* 70–78.

Individuals with Disabilities Education Act. (1997). Washington, D.C.: U.S. Government Printing Office.

Infusini, M. (1994). From the patient's point of view. *The Journal of Cognitive Rehabilitation, 12,* 4–5.

Inge, K. J. (1992). Cerebral palsy. In P. J. McLaughlin & P. Wehman (Eds.), *Developmental disabilities* (pp. 30–53). Boston: Andover Press.

Iskowitz, M. (1998). Psychosocial issues. *ADVANCE for Speech-Language Pathologists and Audiologists, 36,* 14–15.

Jahoda, G. (1993). *How can I do this if I can't see what I'm doing?* Washington, D.C.: National Library Service for the Blind and Physically Handicapped.

Jaquish, C., & Stella, M. A. (1986). Helping special students move from elementary to secondary school. *Counterpoint, 7*(1), 1.

Jarwan, F. A., & Feldusen, J. F. (1993). *Residential schools of mathematics and science for academically talented youth: An analysis of admission programs.* Storrs, CT: The National Resource Center on the Gifted and Talented.

Jastak, S. R., & Wilkinson, G. S. (1984). *The wide range achievement test—Revised.* Wilmington, DE: Jastak Associates.

Jayanthi, M., Bursuck, W., Epstein, M. H., & Polloway, E. A. (1997). Strategies for successful homework. *Teaching Exceptional Children, 30*(1), 4–7.

Jayanthi, M., Bursuck, W. D., Polloway, E., & Epstein, M. (1996). Testing adaptations for students with disabilities: A national survey of classroom practices. *Journal of Special Education, 30,* 99–115.

Jayanthi, M., Nelson, J. S., Sawyer, V., Bursuck, W. D., & Epstein, M. H. (1994). Homework-communication problems among parents, general education, and special education teachers: An exploratory study. *Remedial and Special Education, 16*(2), 102–116.

Jenkins, J. R., & Heinen, A. (1989). Students' preferences for service delivery: Pull-out, in-class, or integrated models. *Exceptional Children, 55,* 516–523.

Johnson, D. J. (1999). The language of instruction. *Learning Disabilities: A Multidisciplinary Journal 9*(2), 1–7.

Johnson, L. J., Pugach, M. C., & Devlin, S. (1990). Professional collaboration. *Teaching Exceptional Children, 22,* 9–11.

Johnson, L. R., & Johnson, C. E. (1999, March/April). Teaching students to regulate their own behavior. *Teaching Exceptional Children,* 6–10.

Jones, V. F., & Jones, L. S. (1995). *Comprehensive classroom management* (4th ed.). Boston: Allyn & Bacon.

Jordan, A., Lindsay, L., & Stanovich, P. J. (1997). Classroom teachers' instructional interactions with students who are exceptional, at risk, and typically achieving. *Remedial and Special Education, 18,* 82–93.

Kamps, D. B., Leonard, B. R., Vernon, S., Dugan, E. P., Delquadri, J. C., Gershon, B., Wade, L., & Folk, L. (1992). Teaching social skills to students with autism to increase peer interactions in an integrated first-grade classroom. *Journal of Applied Behavior Analysis, 25,* 281–288.

Kaplan, J. S., & Carter, J. (1999). *Beyond behavior modification: A cognitive-behavioral approach to behavior management in the school* (3rd ed.). Austin, TX: Pro-Ed.

Kaplan, P. S. (1996). *Pathways for exceptional children: School, home, and culture.* St. Paul, MN: West Publishing.

Kataoka, J. C. (1987). *An example of integrating literature.* Unpublished manuscript.

Kataoka, J. C., & Patton, J. R. (1989). Integrated curriculum. *Science and Children, 16,* 52–58.

Katisyannis, A., Landrum, T. J., & Vinton, L. (1997). Practical guidelines for monitoring treatment of Attention-Deficit/Hyperactivity Disorder. *Prevention of School Failure, 41*(3) 132–136.

Kauffman, J. M. (1993). *Characteristics of emotional and behavioral disorders of children and youth.* Columbus, OH: Merrill.

Kauffman, J. M., Lloyd, J. W., Baker, J., & Riedel, T. M. (1995). Inclusion of all students with emotional or behavioral disorders? Let's think again. *Phi Delta Kappan,* 542–546.

Kauffman, J. M., & Wong, K. L. H. (1991). Effective teachers of students with behavioral disorders: Are generic teaching skills enough? *Behavioral Disorders, 16,* 225–237.

Kavale, K. A., & Forness, S. R. (1996). Efficacy of special education and related services. Washington, D.C.: American Association on Mental Retardation.

Kavale, K. A., & Forness, S. R. (1996). Treating social skill deficits in children with learning disabilities: A meta-analysis of the research. *Learning Disability Quarterly, 19*(1), 2–13.

Kerrin, R. G. (1996). Collaboration: Working with the speech-language pathologist. *Intervention in School and Clinic, 32*(1), 56–59.

King-Sears, M. E., & Bradley, D. (1995). Classwide peer tutoring: Heterogeneous instruction in general education classrooms. *Preventing School Failure, 40,* 29–36.

King-Sears, M. E., & Cummings, C. S. (1996). Inclusive practices of classroom teachers. *Remedial and Special Education, 17,* 217–225.

Kirchner, C., Peterson, R., & Suhr, C. (1985). Trends in school enrollment and reading methods among legally blind school children, 1963–1978. In C. Kirchner (Ed.), *Data on blindness and visual impairment in the U.S.: A resource manual on characteristics, education, employment, and service delivery* (pp. 126–131). New York: American Foundation for the Blind.

Kirk, S. A. (1962). *Educating exceptional children.* Boston: Houghton Mifflin.

Kirk, S. A., & Gallagher, J. J. (1989). *Educating exceptional children* (5th ed.). Boston: Houghton Mifflin.

Kirk, S. A., Gallagher, J. J., & Anastasiow, A. (2000). *Educating exceptional children* (8th ed.). Boston: Houghton Mifflin.

Kirk, S. A., Gallagher, J. J., & Anastasiow, N. J. (1993). *Educating exceptional children* (7th ed.). Boston: Houghton Mifflin.

Kirsten, I. (1981). *The Oakland picture dictionary.* Wauconda, IL: Don Johnston.

Kitano, M. K. (1993). Critique of Feldhusen's "individualized teaching of the gifted in regular classrooms." In C. J. Maker (Ed.), *Critical issues in gifted education: Vol. 3. Programs for the gifted in regular classrooms* (pp. 274–281). Austin, TX: Pro-Ed.

Kluwin, T. N. (1996). Getting hearing and deaf students to write to each other through dialogue journals. *Teaching Exceptional Children, 28,* 50–53.

Kluwin, T. N., Moores, D. F., & Gaustad, M. G. (Eds.). (1998). *Toward effective public school programs for deaf students: Context, process, and outcomes.* New York: Teachers College Press.

Knitzer, J., Steinberg, Z., & Fleisch, B. (1990). *At the schoolhouse door.* New York: Bank Street College of Education.

Knoblock, P. (1982). *Teaching and mainstreaming autistic children.* Denver: Love.

Knowles, M. (1984). *The adult learner: A neglected species* (3rd ed.). Houston: Gulf Publishing.

Koegel, L. K., Koegel, R. L., & Dunlap, G. (Eds.). (1996). *Positive behavioral support.* Baltimore: Brookes.

Koegel, L. K., Koegel, R. L., Hurley, C., & Frea, W. D. (1992). Improving social skills and disruptive behavior in children with autism through self-management. *Journal of Applied Behavior Analysis, 25,* 341–353.

Koegel, R. L., & Koegel, L. K. (1995). *Teaching children with autism.* Baltimore: Brookes.

Koenig, A. J., & Holbrook, M. C. (1995). *Learning media assessment of students with visual impairments: A resource guide for teachers* (2nd ed.). Austin, TX: Pro-Ed.

Korinek, L., & Polloway, E. A. (1993). Social skills: Review and implications for instruction for students with mild mental retardation. In R. A. Gable & S. F. Warren (Eds.), *Advances in mental retardation and developmental disabilities* (Vol. 5, pp. 71–97). London: Jessica Kingsley.

Kounin, J. (1970). *Discipline and group management in classrooms.* New York: Holt, Rinehart & Winston.

Krauss, M. W. (1990). New precedent in family policy: Individualized family service plan. *Exceptional Children, 56,* 388–395.

Kruczek, T., & Vitanza, S. (1999). Treatment effects with an adolescent abuse survivor's group. *Child Abuse & Neglect, 23,* 477–485.

Kuster, J. M. (1993). Experiencing a day of conductive hearing loss. *Journal of School Health, 63,* 235–237.

Lahey, M. (1988). *Language disorders and language development.* New York: Macmillan.

Lambros, K. M., Ward, S. L., Bocian, K. M., MacMillan, D. L., & Gresham, F. M. (1998). Behavioral profiles of children at-risk for emotional and behavioral disorders: Implications for assessment and classification. *Focus on Exceptional Children, 30*(5), 1–16.

Landau, S., Milich, R., & Diener, M. B. (1998). Peer relations of children with attention-deficit hyperactivity disorders. *Reading and Writing Quarterly, 14*(1) 83–106.

Lang, G., & Berberich, C. (1995). *All children are special: Creating an inclusive classroom.* York, ME: Stenhouse Publishers.

Lang, L. (1998). Allergy linked to common ear infection. *ADVANCE for Speech-Language Pathologists and Audiologists, 36,* 8–9.

Lange, C. M., Ysseldyke, J. E., & Lehr, C. A. (1997). Parents' perspectives on school choice. *Teaching Exceptional Children, 30*(1), 14–19.

Lapadat, J. C. (1991). Pragmatic language skills of students with language and/or learning disabilities: A quantitative synthesis. *Journal of Learning Disabilities, 24*(3), 147–158.

*Larry P.* v. *Riles,* C-71-2270 (RFP, District Court for Northern California), 1972.

Lavelle, L. (1998). *Practical charts for managing behavior.* Austin, TX: Pro-Ed.

LDA Newsbriefs. (1996). Toll free access to adult services. *LDA Newsbriefs, 31*(3), 22 and 24.

Lerner, J. W. (1993). *Learning disabilities: Theories, diagnosis, and teaching strategies.* Boston: Houghton Mifflin.

Lesar, S., Gerber, M. M., & Semmel, M. (1996). HIV infection in children: Family stress, social support, and adaptations. *Exceptional Children, 62,* 224–236.

Leverett, R. G., & Diefendorf, A. O. (1992). Suggestions for frustrated teachers. *Teaching Exceptional Children, 24,* 30–35.

Levin, J., & Nolan, J. F. (2000). *Principles of classroom management* (3rd ed.). Boston: Allyn & Bacon.

Lewis, T. J., & Sugai, G. (1999). Effective behavior support: A systems approach to proactive school-wide management. *Focus on Exceptional Children, 31*(6), 1–24.

Lipsky, D. K., & Gartner, A. (1996). The evaluation of inclusive programs. *NCERI Bulletin, 2,* 1–7.

Lisnov, L., Harding, C. G., Safer, L. A., & Kavanagh, J. (1998). Adolescents' perceptions of substance abuse prevention strategies. *Adolescence, 33,* 301–312.

Lloyd, J. (1988). Academic instruction and cognitive techniques: The need for attack strategy training. *Exceptional Education Quarterly, 1,* 53–63.

Lloyd, J. W., Forness, S. R., & Kavale, K. A. (1998). Some methods are more effective than others. *Intervention in School and Clinic, 33,* 195–200.

Lloyd, J. W., Kauffman, J. M., Landrum, T. J., & Roe, D. L. (1991). Why do teachers refer pupils for special education? An analysis of referral records. *Exceptionality, 2,* 115–126.

Lloyd, J. W., Landrum, T., & Hallahan, D. P. (1991). Self-monitoring applications for classroom intervention. In G. Stoner, M. R. Shinn, & H. M. Walker (Eds.), *Interventions for achievement and behavior problems* (pp. 201–213). Washington, D.C.: NASP.

Locke, M. N., Banken, L. L., & Mahone, T. E. (1994). *Adapting early childhood curriculum for children with special needs.* New York: Merrill.

Lopez, R., & MacKenzie, J. (1993). A learning center approach to individualized instruction for gifted students. In C. J. Maker (Ed.), *Critical issues in gifted education: Vol. 3. Programs for the gifted in regular classrooms* (pp. 282–295). Austin, TX: Pro-Ed.

Lovitt, T. C. (1991). *Preventing school dropouts.* Austin, TX: Pro-Ed.

Lovitt, T. C., Cushing, S. S., & Stump, C. S. (1994). High school students rate their IEPs: Low opinions and lack of ownership. *Intervention in School and Clinic, 30*(1), 34–37.

Lucas, C. (Ed.). (1990). *Sign language research.* Washington, D.C.: Gallaudet University Press.

Luckasson, R., Coulter, D., Polloway, E. A., Reiss, S., Schalock, R., Snell, M., Spitalnik, D., & Stark, J. (1992). *Mental retardation: Definition, classification and systems of supports.* Washington, D.C.: American Association on Mental Retardation.

Luckasson, R., Schalock, R., Snell, M., & Spitalnik, D. (1996). The 1992 AAMR definition and preschool children:

Response from the committee on terminology and classification. *Mental Retardation, 34,* 247–253.

Luckner, J. (1994). Developing independent and responsible behaviors in students who are deaf or hard of hearing. *Teaching Exceptional Children, 26,* 13–17.

Luckner, J. (1999). An example of two coteaching classrooms. *American Annals of the Deaf, 44,* 24–34.

Lueck, A. H. (1999). Setting curricular priorities for students with visual impairments. *Review, 31,* 54–63.

Lynch, E. C., & Beare, P. L. (1990). The quality of IEP objectives and their relevance to instruction for students with mental retardation and behavioral disorders. *Remedial and Special Education, 11*(2), 48–55.

Lynch, E. W., & Hansen, M. J. (1992). *Developing cross-cultural competence.* Baltimore: Brookes.

Lyndsey, J. D. (Ed.). (1999). *Technology and exceptional individuals* (3rd ed.). Austin, TX: Pro-Ed.

Lyon, G. R. (1991). Research in learning disabilities (technical report). Bethesda, MD: National Institutes of Child Health and Human Development.

Lyon, G. R. (1995). Research initiatives in learning disabilities: Contributions from scientists supported by the National Institutes of Child Health and Human Development. *Journal of Child Neurology, 10*(1), 5120–5126.

Maag, J. W., & Katsiyannis, A. (1998). Challenges facing successful transition for youths with E/BD. *Behavioral Disorders, 23,* 209–221.

MacArthur, C. A. (1998, July/August). From illegible to understandable. *Teaching Exceptional Children,* 66–71.

MacMillan, D. L. (1989). Mild mental retardation: Emerging issues. In G. Robinson, J. R. Patton, E. A. Polloway, & L. R. Sargent (Eds.), *Best practices in mild mental retardation* (pp. 1–20). Reston, VA: CEC-MR.

MacMillan, D. L., & Borthwick, S. (1980). The new educable mentally retarded population: Can they be mainstreamed? *Mental Retardation, 18,* 155–158.

Macmillan, D. L., & Forness, S. R. (1998). The role of IQ in special education placement decisions: Primary and determinative or peripheral and inconsequential? *Remedial and Special Education, 19,* 239–253.

MacMillan, D. L., Gresham, F. M., & Siperstein, G. N. (1993). Conceptual and psychometric concerns about the 1992 AAMR definition of mental retardation. *American Journal of Mental Retardation, 98,* 325–335.

Maker, C. J. (1993). Gifted students in the regular education classroom: What practices are defensible and feasible? In C. J. Maker (Ed.), *Critical issues in gifted education: Vol. 3. Programs for the gifted in regular classrooms* (pp. 413–436). Austin, TX: Pro-Ed.

Malott, R. W., Whaley, D. L., & Malott, M. E. (1997). *Elementary principles of behavior* (3rd ed.). Upper Saddle River, NJ: Prentice-Hall.

Mandlebaum, L. H. (1989). Reading. In J. R. Patton, E. A. Polloway, & L. R. Sargent (Eds.), *Best practices in mild retardation.* Reston, VA: CEC-MR.

Mandlebaum, L. H., Lightbourne, L., & VardenBrock, J. (1994). Teaching with literature. *Intervention in School and Clinic, 29,* 134–150.

Mandlebaum, L. H., & Wilson, R. (1989). Teaching listening skills in the special education classroom. *Academic Therapy, 24,* 449–459.

Mangold, S. S., & Roessing, L. J. (1982). Instructional needs of students with low vision. In S. S. Mangold (Ed.), *A teacher's guide to the special educational needs of blind and visually handicapped children.* New York: American Foundation for the Blind.

Manzo, A. V. (1975). Expansion modules for the ReQuest, CAT, GRP, and REAP reading study procedures. *Journal of Reading, 42,* 498–502.

Marchant, J. M. (1992). Deaf-blind handicapping conditions. In P. J. McLaughlin & P. Wehman (Eds.), *Developmental disabilities* (pp. 113–123). Boston: Andover Press.

Markwardt, F. C. (1989). *Peabody individual achievement test—Revised.* Circle Pines, MN: American Guidance Service.

Marston, D., & Magnusson, D. (1985). Implementing curriculum-based measurement in special and regular education settings. *Exceptional Children, 52,* 266–276.

Martin, D. S. (1991). *Advances in cognition, education, and deafness.* Washington, D.C.: Gallaudet University Press.

Mascari, B. G. & Forgnone, C. (1982). A follow-up study of EMR students four years after dismissal from the program. *Education and Training of the Mentally Retarded, 17,* 288–292.

Masi, G., Mucci, M., & Favilla, L. (1999). Depressive symptoms in adolescents with mild mental retardation. *Education and Training in Mental Retardation and Developmental Disabilities, 34,* 223–226.

Masters, L. F., Mori, B. A., & Mori, A. A. (1999). *Teaching secondary students with mild learning and behavior problems.* Austin, TX: Pro-Ed.

Mastropieri, M. A., & Scruggs, T. E. (1993). *A practical guide for teaching science to students with special needs in inclusive settings.* Austin, TX: Pro-Ed.

Mastropieri, M. A., & Scruggs, T. E. (1994). *Effective instruction for special education* (2nd ed.). Austin, TX: Pro-Ed.

Mastropieri, M. A., & Scruggs, T. E. (1997). Best practices in promoting reading comprehension in students with learning disabilities: 1976 to 1996. *Remedial and Special Education, 18,* 197–218.

Mastropieri, M. A., & Scruggs, T. E. (2000). *The inclusive classroom: Strategies for effective instruction.* Columbus, OH: Merrill.

Mather, N. (1992). Whole language reading instruction for students with learning disabilities: Caught in the crossfire. *Learning Disabilities Research and Practice, 7,* 87–95.

Mathes, P., & Torgesen, J. (1998, November). *Early reading basics: Strategies for teaching reading to primary-grade students who are at risk for reading and learning disabilities.* Paper presented at the Annual Council for Learning Disabilities Conference, Albuquerque, NM.

Mathinos, D. A. (1991). Conversational engagement of children with learning disabilities. *Journal of Learning Disabilities, 24*(7), 439–446.

Mayer-Johnson, R. (1986). *The picture communications symbols* (Book 1). Solana Beach, CA: Mayer-Johnson.

McAnally, P. L., Rose, S., & Quigley, S. P. (1999). *Reading practices with deaf learners.* Austin, TX: Pro-Ed.

McBurnett, K., Lahey, B., & Pfiffner, L. (1993). Diagnosis of attention deficit disorders in *DSM-IV:* Scientific basis and implications for education. *Exceptional Children, 60*(2), 108–117.

McCarney, S. B., & Wunderlich, K. K. (1988). *The pre-referral intervention manual.* Columbia, MO: Hawthorne Educational Services.

McConnell, J. (1987). Entrapment effects and generalization. *Teaching Exceptional Children, 17,* 267–273.

McConnell, M. E., Hilvitz, P. B., & Cox, C. J. (1998). Functional assessment: A systematic process for assessment and intervention in general and special education classrooms. *Intervention in School and Clinic, 34,* 10–20.

McDevitt, T. M. (1990). Encouraging young children's listening. *Academic Therapy, 25,* 569–577.

McDonnell, J. J., Hardman, M. L., McDonnell, A. P., & Kiefer-O'Donnell, R. (1995). *An introduction to persons with severe disabilities.* Boston: Allyn & Bacon.

McDougall, D. (1998). Research on self-management techniques used by students with disabilities in general education settings: A descriptive review. *Remedial and Special Education, 19,* 310–320.

McEachlin, J. J., Smith, T., & Lovaas, O. I. (1993). Long-term outcome for children with autism who received early intensive behavioral treatment. *American Journal on Mental Retardation, 97,* 359–372.

McEnvoy, M. A., Shores, R. E., Wehby, J. H., Johnson, S. M., & Fox, J. J. (1990). Special education teachers' implementation of procedures to promote social interaction among children in integrated settings. *Education and Training in Mental Retardation, 25,* 267–276.

McEwen, M., Johnson, P., Neatherlin, J., Millard, M. W., & Lawrence, G. (1998). School based management of chronic asthma among inner city African American school children in Dallas, Texas. *Journal of School Health, 68,* 196–201.

McGrail, L. (1998). Modifying regular classroom curricula for high ability students. *Gifted Child Today, 21,* 36–39.

McKamey, E. S. (1991). Storytelling for children with learning disabilities: A first-hand account. *Teaching Exceptional Children, 23,* 46–48.

McKeever, P. (1983). Siblings of chronically ill children: A literature review with implications for research and practice. *American Journal of Orthopsychiatry, 53,* 209–217.

McLaughlin-Cheng, E., (1998). The Asperger syndrome and autism: A literature review and meta-analysis. *Focus on Autism and Other Developmental Disabilities, 13,* 234–245.

McLesky, J. (1992). Students with learning disabilities at primary, intermediate, and secondary grade levels: Identification and characteristics. *Learning Disability Quarterly, 15*(1), 13–19.

McLesky, J., Henry, D., & Hedges, D. (1999). Inclusion: What progress is being made across disability categories? *Teaching Exceptional Children, 31,* 60–64.

McLoughlin, J. A., & Lewis, R. B. (1990). *Assessing special students* (3rd ed.). Columbus, OH: Merrill.

McNeill, J. H., & Fowler, S. A. (1996). Using story reading to encourage children's conversations. *Teaching Exceptional Children, 28*(2), 43–47.

McPartland, J. M., & Slavin, R. E. (1990). *Policy perspectives increasing achievement of at-risk students at each grade level.* Washington, D.C.: U.S. Department of Education.

McReynolds, L. (1990). Functional articulation disorders. In G. H. Shames & E. H. Wiig (Eds.), *Human communication disorders: An introduction* (2nd ed., pp. 139–182). Columbus, OH: Merrill.

Meltzer, L., Roditi, B., Haynes, D. P., Biddle, K. R., Paster, M., & Taber, S. (1996). *Strategies for success: Classroom teaching techniques for students with learning problems.* Austin, TX: Pro-Ed.

Mercer, C. D. (1997). *Students with learning disabilities.* (5th ed.). New York: Merrill.

Mercer, C. D., Jordan, L., & Miller, S. P. (1994). Implications of constructivism for teaching math students with moderate to mild disabilities. *Journal of Special Education, 28,* 290–306.

Miller, R. J. (1995). Preparing for adult life: Teaching students their rights and responsibilities. *CEC Today, 1*(7), 12.

Miller, S. P., Mercer, C. D., & Dillon, A. S. (1992). CSA: Acquiring and retaining math skills. *Intervention in School and Clinic, 28,* 105–110.

Minner, S., & Prater, G. (1989). Arranging the physical environment of special education classrooms. *Academic Therapy, 25,* 91–96.

Mira, M. P., Tucker, B. F., & Tyler, J. S. (1992). *Traumatic brain injury in children and adolescents: A sourcebook for teachers and other school personnel.* Austin, TX: Pro-Ed.

Mirman, N. J. (1991). Reflections on educating the gifted child. *G/C/T, 14,* 57–60.

Moats, L. C., & Lyon, G. R. (1993). Learning disabilities in the United States: Advocacy, science, and the future of the field. *Journal of Learning Disabilities, 26*(5), 282–294.

Moecker, D. L. (1992, November). Special education decision process: For Anglo and Hispanic students. Paper presented at the *Council for Exceptional Children* Topical Conference on Culturally and Linguistically Diverse Exceptional Children, Minneapolis.

Montague, M., McKinney, J. D., & Hocutt, L. (1994). Assessing students for attention deficit disorder. *Intervention in School and Clinic, 29*(4), 212–218.

Moores, D. (1999). *Educating the deaf: Psychology, principles, and practices* (5th ed.). Columbus, OH: Merrill.

Moores, G. (1993). *Educating the deaf* (4th ed.). Boston: Houghton Mifflin.

Morgan, S. R. (1994a). *At-risk youth in crises: A team approach in the schools* (2nd ed.). Austin, TX: Pro-Ed.

Morgan, S. (1994b). *Children in crisis: A team approach in the schools* (2nd ed.). Austin, TX: Pro-Ed.

Moriarty, D. (1967). *The loss of loved ones.* Springfield, IL: Charles C Thomas.

Morrison, G. S. (1997). *Teaching in America.* Boston: Allyn & Bacon.

Mundschenk, N. A., & Foley, R. M. (1997). Collaborative activities and competencies of secondary schools special educators: A national survey. *Teacher Education in Special Education, 20,* 47–60.

Munger, R., & Morse, W. C. (1992). When divorce rocks a child's world. *The Educational Forum, 43,* 100–103.

Munk, D. D., & Bursuck, W. D. (in press). Grading students in inclusive educational settings: A systematic approach. In L. Dente & P. Cousins (Eds.), *Looking at learning disabilities in new ways: Connections to classroom practice.* Denver: Love.

Musselwhite, C. R. (1987). Augmentative communication. In E. T. McDonald (Ed.), *Treating cerebral palsy: For clinicians by clinicians* (pp. 209–238). Austin, TX: Pro-Ed.

Myles, B. S., & Simpson, R. L. (1998). Aggression and violence by school-age children and youth: Under the aggression cycle and prevention/intervention strategies. *Intervention in School and Clinic, 33,* 259–264.

Nagel, L., McDougall, D., & Granby, C. (1996). Students' self-reported substance use by grade level and gender. *Journal of Drug Education, 26,* 49–56.

Naremore, R. C. (1980). Language disorders in children. In T. J. Hixon, L. D. Shriberg, & J. H. Saxman (Eds.), *Introduction to communication disorders* (pp. 111–132). Englewood Cliffs, NJ: Prentice-Hall.

National Cancer Foundation. (1997). Cancer risk report. Washington, D.C.: Author.

National Center for Education Statistics. (1989). *Digest of educational statistics, 1989.* Washington, D.C.: U.S. Department of Education, Office of Research and Improvement.

National Center for Education Statistics. (1991). *The condition of education, 1991 edition.* Washington, D.C.: Author.

National Center on Child Abuse and Neglect. (1986). *Status of child abuse in the United States.* Washington, D.C.: Author.

National Education Goals Panel. (1998). *Ready schools.* Washington, D.C.: Author.

National Head Injury Foundation. (1988). *An educator's manual: What educators need to know about students with traumatic brain injury.* Southborough, MA: Author.

National Heart, Lung, and Blood Institute. (1998). How asthma friendly is your school? *Journal of School Health, 68,* 167–168.

National Information Center for Children and Youth with Handicaps. (1990). *Children with autism.* Washington, D.C.: Author.

National Information Center for Children and Youth with Handicaps. (1991). *The education of children and youth with special needs: What do the laws say?* Washington, D.C.: Author.

National Joint Committee on Learning Disabilities. (1988). Letter to NJCLD member organizations.

National Law Center on Homelessness and Poverty. (1990). *Shut out: Denial of education to homeless children.* Washington, D.C.: Author.

National study on inclusion: Overview and summary report. *National Center on Educational Restructuring Inclusion, 2,* 1–8.

Neito, S. (1996). *Affirming diversity* (2nd ed.). White Plains, NY: Longman.

Nelson, K. C., & Prindle, N. (1992). Gifted teacher competencies: Ratings by rural principals and teachers. *Journal of the Education of the Gifted, 15,* 357–369.

Nelson, N. W. (1988). Curriculum-based language assessment and intervention. *Language, Speech and Hearing Services in School, 20,* 170–183.

Ness, J., & Price, L. A. (1990). Meeting the psychosocial needs of adolescents and adults with LD. *Intervention, 26,* 16–21.

Nolan, E. E., Volpe, R. J., Gadow, K. D., & Sprafkin, J. (1999). Developmental, gender, and co-morbidity differences in clinically referred children with ADHD. *Journal of Emotional & Behavioral Disorders, 7*(1), 11–21.

Nowacek, E. J., & McShane, E. (1993). Spoken language. In E. A. Polloway & J. R. Patton (Eds.), *Strategies for teaching learners with special needs* (5th ed., pp. 183–205). Columbus, OH: Merrill.

Office of Education Research and Improvement. (1988). *Youth indicators, 1988: Trends in the well-being of American youth.* Washington, D.C.: U.S. Department of Education.

Office of Educational Research. (1998). *Tools for schools: From at-risk to excellence.* Washington, D.C.: Office of Educational Research.

Office of Juvenile Justice and Delinquency Prevention. (1995). *Juvenile offenders and victims: A national report.* Pittsburgh, PA: National Center for Juvenile Justice.

Olson, J. L., & Platt, J. M. (1996). *Teaching children and adolescents with special needs* (2nd ed). Englewood Cliffs, NJ: Merrill.

Orr, T. J., Myles, B. S., & Carlson, J. R. (1998). The impact of rhythmic entertainment on a person with autism. *Focus on Autism and Other Developmental Disabilities, 13,* 163–166.

Oswald, D. P., Coutinho, M. J., Best, A. M., & Singh, N. N. (1999). Ethnic representation in special education: The influence of school-related economic and demographic values. *The Journal of Special Education, 32,* 194–206.

Owens, R. E., Jr. (1984). *Language development: An introduction.* Columbus, OH: Merrill.

Oyer, H. J., Crowe, B., & Haas, W. H. (1987). *Speech, language, and hearing disorders: A guide for the teacher.* Boston: Little, Brown.

Palinscar, A., & Klenk, L. (1992). Fostering literacy learning in supportive contexts. *Journal of Learning Disabilities, 25,* 211–225.

Pancheri, C., & Prater, M. A. (1999, March/April). What teachers and parents should know about Ritalin. *Teaching Exceptional Children,* 20–26.

Parke, B. N. (1989). *Gifted students in regular classrooms.* Boston: Allyn & Bacon.

Parker, H. G. (1992). *The ADD hyperactivity handbook for schools.* Santa Barbara, CA: Special Needs Project.

Passow, A. H., & Runitski, R. A. (1993). *State policies regarding education of the gifted as reflected in legislation and regulation.* Storrs, CT: National Research Center for the Gifted and Talented.

Patton, J. R. (1994). Practical recommendations for using homework with students with learning disabilities. *Journal of Learning Disabilities, 27,* 570–578.

Patton, J. R., Blackburn, J., & Fad, K. (1996). *Focus on exceptional children.* Columbus, OH: Merrill.

Patton, J. R., & Cronin, M. E. (1993). *Life skills instruction for all students with disabilities.* Austin, TX: Pro-Ed.

Patton, J. R., & Dunn, C. R. (1998). *Transition from school to adult life for students with special needs: Basic concepts and recommended practices.* Austin, TX: Pro-Ed.

Patton, J. R., Polloway, E. A., & Smith, T. E. C. (2000). Educating students with mild mental retardation. In M. L. Wehmeyer & J. R. Patton (Eds.), *Mental retardation in the 21st century.* Austin, TX: Pro-Ed.

Patton, J. R., Polloway, E. A., Smith, T. E. C., Edgar, E., Clark, G. M., & Lee, S. (1996). Individuals with mild mental retardation: Postsecondary outcomes and implications for educational policy. *Education and Training in Mental Retardation and Developmental Disabilities, 31,* 77–85.

Paul, P. V. (1998). *Literacy and deafness: The development of reading, writing, and literate thought.* Boston: Allyn & Bacon.

Pearpoint, J., Forest, M., & O'Brien, J. (1996). MAPs, circles of friends, and PATH. In S. Stainback & W. Stainback (Eds.), *Inclusion: A guide for educators* (pp. 67–86). Baltimore: Brookes.

Pearson, S. (1996). Child abuse among children with disabilities. *Teaching Exceptional Children, 29,* 34–38.

Peck, G. (1989). Facilitating cooperative learning: A forgotten tool gets it started. *Academic Therapy, 25,* 145–150.

Pennington, B. F. (1995). Genetics of learning disabilities. *Journal of Child Neurology, 10*(1), 69–77.

Pfiffner, L., & Barkley, R. (1991). Educational placement and classroom management. In R. Barkley (Ed.), *Attention deficit hyperactivity disorder: A handbook for diagnosis and treatment* (pp. 498–539). New York: Guilford.

*Physician's Desk Reference* (1994). Oravell, NJ: Medical Economics Company.

*Physician's Desk Reference* (1999). Oravell, NJ: Medical Economics Company.

Pickett, A. L., & Gerlach, K. (1997). *Paraeducators.* Austin, TX: Pro-Ed.

Pierce, C. (1994). Importance of classroom climate for at-risk learners. *Journal of Educational Research, 88,* 37–44.

Pless, I. B. (Ed.) (1997). *The epidemiology of childhood disorders.* New York: Oxford Press.

Plummer, D. L. (1995). Serving the needs of gifted children from a multicultural perspective. In J. L. Genshaft, M. Bireley, & C. L. Hollinger (Eds.), *Serving gifted and talented students: A resource for school personnel* (pp. 285–300). Austin, TX: Pro-Ed.

Podemski, R. S., Marsh, G. E., Smith, T. E. C., & Price, B. J. (1995). *Comprehensive administration of special education.* Columbus, OH: Merrill.

Polloway, E. A. (1984). The integration of mildly retarded students in the schools: A historical review. *Remedial and Special Education, 5*(4), 18–28.

Polloway, E. A. (1997). Developmental principles of the Luckasson et al. AAMR definition: A retrospective. *Education and Training in Mental Retardation and Developmental Disabilities, 32,* 174–178.

Polloway, E. A., Bursuck, W., & Epstein, M. H. (1999). Testing adaptations in the general education classroom. *Reading and Writing Quarterly.*

Polloway, E. A., Bursuck, W., Jayanthi, M., Epstein, M., & Nelson, J. (1996). Treatment acceptability: Determining appropriate interventions within inclusive classrooms. *Intervention in School and Clinic, 31,* 133–144.

Polloway, E. A., Epstein, M. H., Bursuck, W. D., Jayanthi, M., & Cumblad, C. (1994). Homework practices of general education teachers. *Journal of Learning Disabilities, 27,* 500–509.

Polloway, E. A., Epstein, M. H., Bursuck, W. D., Roderique, T. W., McConeghy, J., & Jayanthi, M. (1994). Classroom grading: A national survey of policies. *Remedial and Special Education, 15*(2), 162–170.

Polloway, E. A., & Jones-Wilson, L. (1992). Principles of assessment and instruction. In E. A. Polloway & T. E. C. Smith (Eds.), *Language instruction for students with disabilities* (pp. 87–120). Denver: Love.

Polloway, E. A., Patton, J. R., Epstein, M. H., & Smith, T. E. C. (1989). Comprehensive curriculum: Program design for students with mild handicaps. *Focus on Exceptional Children, 21*(8), 1–12.

Polloway, E. A., Patton, J. R., Payne, J. S., & Payne, R. A. (1989). *Strategies for teaching learners with special needs* (5th ed). Columbus, OH: Merrill.

Polloway, E. A., Patton, J. R., & Serna, L. (2001). *Strategies for teaching learners with special needs* (7th ed.). Columbus, OH: Merrill.

Polloway, E. A., Patton, J. R., Smith, J. D., & Roderique, T. W. (1992). Issues in program design for elementary students with mild retardation: Emphasis on curriculum development. *Education and Training in Mental Retardation, 27,* 142–150.

Polloway, E. A., Patton, J. R., Smith, T. E. C., & Buck, G. H. (1997). Mental retardation and learning disabilities: Conceptual issues. *Journal of Learning Disabilities, 30,* 219–231.

Polloway, E. A., & Smith, J. D. (1988). Current status of the mild mental retardation construct: Identification, placement, and programs. In M. C. Wang, M. C. Reynolds, & H. J. Walberg (Eds.), *The handbook of special education: Research and practice* (Vol. II, pp. 1–22). Oxford, UK: Pergamon Press.

Polloway, E. A., Smith, J. D., Chamberlain, J., Denning, C., & Smith, T. E. C. (1999). Levels of deficit vs. levels of support in mental retardation classification. *Education and Training in Mental Retardation and Development Disabilities, 34,* 48–59.

Polloway, E. A., Smith, J. D., Patton, J. R., & Smith, T. E. C. (1996). Historic changes in mental retardation and developmental disabilities. *Education and Training in Mental Retardation and Developmental Disabilities, 31,* 3–12.

Polloway, E. A., & Smith, J. E. (1982). *Teaching language skills to exceptional learners.* Denver: Love.

Polloway, E. A., & Smith, T. E. C. (2000). *Language instruction for students with disabilities.* Denver: Love.

Popp, R. A. (1983, Winter). Learning about disabilities. *Teaching Exceptional Children,* 78–81.

Powers, M. D. (1989). *Children with autism: A parent's guide.* New York: Woodbine House.

Pracek, E. (1996). Software for survival. In J. L. Olson & J. M. Platt (Eds.), *Teaching children and adolescents with special needs* (2nd ed.). Englewood Cliffs, NJ: Prentice-Hall.

Prasse, D. P. (1986). Litigation and special education: An introduction. *Exceptional Children, 52,* 311–312.

Prater, M. A. (1992). Increasing time-on-task in the classroom. *Intervention in School and Clinic, 28*(1), 22–27.

Prater, M. A., Joy, R., Chilman, B., Temple, J., & Miller, S. R. (1991). Self-monitoring of on-task behavior by adolescents with learning disabilities. *Learning Disability Quarterly, 14,* 164–177.

Premack, D. (1959). Toward empirical behavior laws: 1. Positive reinforcement. *Psychological Review, 66,* 219–233.

Pressley, M., & Rankin, J. (1994). More about whole language methods of reading instruction for students at risk for early reading failure. *Learning Disabilities Research & Practice, 9,* 157–168.

Public Law 94-142 (1975). *Federal Register, 42,* 42474–42518.

Public Law 101-476 (1990). *Federal Register, 54,* 35210–35271.

Pugh, S. (1999). Working with families of individual students. *Gifted Children Today, 22,* 26–31.

Quay, H., & Peterson, D. (1987). *Revised behavior problem checklist.* Coral Gables, FL: University of Miami.

Quinn, M. M., Kavale, K. A., Mathur, S. R., Rutherford, R. B., Jr., & Forness, S. R. (1999). A meta-analysis of social skill interventions for students with emotional and behavioral disorders. *Journal of Emotional and Behavioral Disorders, 7,* 54–64.

Ramos-Ford, V., & Gardner, H. (1997). Giftedness from a multiple intelligences perspective. In N. Colangelo & G. A. Davis (Eds.), *Handbook of gifted education* (2nd ed., pp. 54–66). Boston: Allyn & Bacon.

Raza, S. Y. (1997). Enhance your chances for success with students with ADHD. *Intervention in School and Clinics, 33*(1), 56–58.

Reeve, R. E. (1990). ADHD: Facts and fallacies. *Intervention in School and Clinic, 26,* 71–78.

Reid, E. R. (1986). Practicing effective instruction: The exemplary center for reading. *Exceptional Children, 52,* 510–519.

Reid, R., Maag, J. W., Vasa, S. F., & Wright, C. (1994). Who are the children with attention-deficit-hyperactivity disorder? A school-based study. *The Journal of Special Education, 28,* 117–137.

Reif, S. F. (1993). *How to reach and teach ADD/ADHD children.* Boston: Allyn & Bacon.

Reis, S. M. (1989). Reflections on policy affecting the education of gifted and talented students. *American Psychologist, 44,* 399–408.

Reis, S. M., & Schack, G. D. (1993). Differentiating products for the gifted and talented: The encouragement of independent learning. In C. J. Maker (Ed.), *Critical issues in gifted education: Vol. 3. Programs for the gifted in regular classrooms* (pp. 161–186). Austin, TX: Pro-Ed.

Renzulli, J. S. (1979). *What makes giftedness: A reexamination of the definition of the gifted and talented.* Ventura, CA: Ventura County Superintendent of Schools Office.

Renzulli, J. S., & Reis, S. M. (1991). *The schoolwide enrichment model: A comprehensive plan for educational excellence.* Mansfield Center, CT: Creative Learning Press.

Renzulli, J. S., & Reis, S. M. (1997). The schoolwide enrichment model: new directions for developing high-end learning. In N. Colangelo & G. A. Davis (Eds.), *Handbook of gifted education* (2nd ed.). Boston: Allyn & Bacon.

Renzulli, J. S., Reis, S. M., & Smith, L. M. (1981). *The revolving door identification model.* Wethersfield, CT: Creative Learning Press.

Repp, A. C., & Horner, R. H. (Eds.). (1999). *Functional analysis of problem behavior: From effective assessment to effective support.* Pacific Grove, CA: Brooks/Cole.

Reschly, D. (1988). Incorporating adaptive behavior deficits into instructional programs. In G. A. Robinson, J. R. Patton, E. A. Polloway, & L. R. Sargent (Eds.), *Best practices in mental disabilities* (Vol. 2, pp. 53–80). Des Moines, IA: Iowa State Department of Education.

Reynolds, C. T., & Salend, S. J. (1990). Teacher-directed and student-mediated textbook comprehension strategies. *Academic Therapy, 25,* 417–427.

Riccio, C. A., Hynd, G. W., Cohen, M., & Gonzales, T. (1994). Attention deficit hyperactivity disorder (ADHD) and learning disabilities. *Learning Disabilities Quarterly, 17,* 113–122.

Rich, H. L., & Ross, S. M. (1989). Students' time on learning tasks in special education. *Exceptional Children, 55,* 508–515.

Rich, H. L., & Ross, S. M. (1991). Regular class or resource room for students with disabilities? A direct response to "Rich and Ross, A Mixed Message." *Exceptional Children, 57,* 476–477.

Riley, T. (1999). The role of advocacy: Creating change for gifted children throughout the world. *Gifted Child Today, 22,* 44–47.

Riley, T. L., & Brown, M. E. (1998). The magic of multimedia: Creating leaders of yesterday, today, and tomorrow. *Gifted Children Today, 21,* 20–22.

Roach, V. (1995). Supporting inclusion: Beyond the rhetoric. *Phi Delta Kappan, 77,* 295–299.

Roberts, C., Ingram, C., & Harris, C. (1992). The effect of special versus regular classroom programming on higher cognitive processes of intermediate aged elementary gifted and average ability students. *Journal of the Education of the Gifted, 15,* 332–343.

Robertson, J., Alper, S., Schloss, P. J., & Wisniewski, L. (1992). Teaching self-catheterization skills to a child with myelomeningocele in a preschool setting. *Journal of Early Intervention, 16,* 20–30.

Robin, S. S., & Johnson, E. O. (1996). Attitude and peer cross pressure: Adolescent drug and alcohol use. *Journal of Drug Education, 26,* 69–99.

Robinson, S. M., Braxdale, C. T., & Colson, S. E. (1988). Preparing dysfunctional learners to enter junior high school: A transitional curriculum. *Focus on Exceptional Children, 18*(4), 1–12.

Rock, E. E., Rosenberg, M. S., & Carran, D. T. (1995). Variables affecting the reintegration rate of students with serious emotional disturbance. *Exceptional Children, 6,* 254–268.

Rockwell, S., & Guetzloe, E. (1996). Group development for students with emotional/behavioral disorders. *Teaching Exceptional Children, 29,* 38–42.

Roderique, T. W., Polloway, E. A., Cumblad, C., Epstein, M. H., & Bursuck, W. (1994). Homework: A study of policies in the United States. *Journal of Learning Disabilities, 22,* 417–427.

Rogers, J. (1993). The inclusion revolution. *Research Bulletin.* Washington, D.C.: Phi Delta Kappa Center for Evaluation, Development, and Research.

Roller, C. (1996). *Variability not disability: Struggling readers in a workshop class.* Newark, DE: International Reading Association.

Rooney, K. (1989). Independent strategies for efficient study: A care approach. *Academic Therapy, 24,* 389–390.

Rooney, K. (1993). *Attention deficit hyperactivity disorder: A videotape program.* Richmond, VA: State Department of Education.

Rooney, K. J. (1991). Controversial therapies: A review and critique. *Intervention in School and Clinic, 26*(3), 134–142.

Rooney, K. J. (1995). Dyslexia revisited: History, educational philosophy, and clinical assessment applications. *Intervention in School and Clinic, 31*(1), 6–15.

Rosenberg, M. S., O'Shea, L., & O'Shea, D. J. (1991). *Student teacher to master teacher: A handbook for preservice and beginning teachers of students with mild and moderate handicaps.* New York: Macmillan.

Rosenberg, M. S., Wilson, R., Maheady, L., & Sindelar, P. (1992). *Educating students with behavior disorders.* Boston: Allyn & Bacon.

Rosenkoetter, S. E., Hains, A. H., & Fowler, S. A. (1994). *Bridging early services for children with special needs and their families.* Baltimore: Brookes.

Ross, S. M., Smith, L. J., Casey, J., & Slavin, R. E. (1995). Increasing the academic success of disadvantaged children: An examination of alternative early intervention programs. *American Educational Research Journal, 32,* 773–800.

Rosselli, H. (1993). Process differentiation for gifted learners in the regular classroom: Teaching to everyone's needs. In C. J. Maker (Ed.), *Critical issues in gifted education: Vol. 3. Programs for the gifted in regular classrooms* (pp. 139–155). Austin, TX: Pro-Ed.

Rylance, B. J. (1998). Predictors of post-high school employment for youth identified as severely emotionally disturbed. *The Journal of Special Education, 32,* 184–192.

Sabatino, D. A. (1987). Preventive discipline as a practice in special education. *Teaching Exceptional Children, 19,* 8–11.

Sacks, S., Wolffe, B. A., & Tierney, F. (1998). Lifestyles of students with visual impairments: Preliminary studies of social networks. *Exceptional Children, 64,* 63–78.

Sacks, S. Z., & Silberman, R. K. (1998). *Educating students who have visual impairments with other disabilities.* Baltimore: Brookes.

Safer, D. J., & Krager, J. M. (1988). A survey of medication treatment for hyperactive/inattentive students. *Journal of the American Medical Association, 260,* 2256–2258.

Safran, S. P., & Safran, J. S. (1996). Intervention assessment programs and pre-referrential teams: Directions for the twenty-first century. *Remedial and Special Education, 17,* 363–369.

Saintonge, S., Achille, P. A., & Lachance, L. (1998). The influence of big brothers on the separation-individuation of adolescents from single-parent families. *Adolescence, 33,* 343–352.

Salend, S. J. (1994). *Effective mainstreaming: Creating inclusive classrooms* (2nd ed.). Columbus, OH: Merrill/Prentice-Hall.

Salend, S. J. (1998). Using an activity based approach to teach science to students with disabilities. *Intervention in School and Clinic, 34,* 67–72.

Salvia, J., & Ysseldyke, J. E. (1998). *Assessment.* Boston: Houghton Mifflin.

Samuels, S. J. (1986). Why children fail to learn and what to do about it. *Exceptional Children, 53,* 7–16.

Sander, E. K. (1972). When are speech sounds learned? *Journal of Speech and Hearing Disorders, 37,* 62.

Sanders, R., Colton, M., & Roberts, S. (1999). Child abuse fatalities and cases of extreme concern: Lessons from reviews. *Child Abuse and Neglect, 23,* 257–273.

Sandieson, R. (1998). A survey on terminology that refers to people with mental retardation/developmental disabilities. *Education and Training in Mental Retardation and Developmental Disabilities, 33,* 290–295.

Santrock, J. W., & Warshak, R. A. (1979). Father custody and social development in boys and girls. *Journal of Social Issues, 35,* 112–125.

Sargent, L. R. (1991). *Social skills for school and community.* Reston, VA: CEC-MR.

Savage, R. C. (1988). Introduction to educational issues for students who have suffered traumatic brain injury. In R. C. Savage & G. F. Wolcott (Eds.), *An educator's manual: What educators need to know about students with traumatic brain injury.* Southborough, MA: National Head Injury Foundation.

Savage, R. C. (1997). Integrating the rehabilitation and education services for school–age children. *Journal of Head Trauma Rehabilitation, 12,* 11–20.

Savage, R. C., & Wolcott, G. F. (Eds.) (1994). *Educational dimensions of acquired brain injury.* Austin, TX: Pro-Ed.

Schaffner, C. B., & Buswell, B. E. (1996). Ten critical elements for creating inclusive and effective school communities. In S. Stainback & W. Stainback (Eds.), *Inclusion: A guide for educators* (pp. 49–65). Baltimore: Brookes.

Schalock, R. L., Stark, J. A., Snell, M. E., Coulter, D. L., Polloway, E. A., Luckasson, R., Reiss, S., & Spitalnik, D. M. (1994). Changing conceptualizations of and definition of mental retardation: Implications for the field. *Mental Retardation, 32,* 181–193.

Schaughency, E. A., & Rothlind, J. (1991). Assessment and classification of attention deficit hyperactivity disorders. *School Psychology Review, 20*(2), 197–202.

Scheuerman, B., Jacobs, W. R., McCall, C., & Knies, W. (1994). The personal spelling dictionary: An adoptive approach to reducing the spelling hurdle in written language. *Intervention in School and Clinic, 29*(5), 292–299.

Schiever, S. W. (1993). Differentiating the learning environment for gifted students. In C. J. Maker (Ed.), *Critical issues in gifted education: Vol. 3. Programs for the gifted in regular classrooms* (pp. 201–214). Austin, TX: Pro-Ed.

Schleichkorn, J. (1993). *Coping with cerebral palsy: Answers to questions parents often ask* (2nd ed.). Austin, TX: Pro-Ed.

Schnailberg, L. (1994, October 19). E.D. report documents "full inclusion" trend. *Education Week,* p. 8.

Schniedewind, N., & Saland, S. (1987). Cooperative learning works. *Teaching Exceptional Children, 19,* 22–25.

Schopler, E., & Mesibov, G. B. (Eds.). *Learning and cognition in autism.* New York: Plenum Press.

Schulz, E. (1994, October 5). Beyond behaviorism. *Education Week, 14*(5), 19–21, 24.

Schulz, J. B., & Carpenter, C. D. (1995). *Mainstreaming exceptional students: A guide for classroom teachers.* Boston: Allyn & Bacon.

Schulze, K. A., Rule, S., & Innocenti, M. S. (1989). Coincidental teaching: Parents promoting social skills at home. *Teaching Exceptional Children, 21,* 24–27.

Schumaker, J. B., & Deshler, D. D. (1988). Implementing the regular education initiative in secondary schools: A different ball game. *Journal of Learning Disabilities, 21*(1), 36–42.

Schumaker, J. B., Deshler, D. D., Alley, G. R., & Denton, D. H. (1982). Multipass: A learning strategy for improving comprehension. *Learning Disability Quarterly, 5,* 295–304.

Schumaker, J. B., Deshler, D. D., Nolan, S., Clark, F. L., Alley, G. R., & Warren, M. M. (1981). *Error monitoring strategy: A learning strategy for improving academic performance of LD adolescents.* (Research Report No. 32). Lawrence, KS: University of Kansas IRLD.

Schumm, J. S., & Strickler, K. (1991). Guidelines for adapting content area textbooks: Keeping teachers and students content. *Intervention in School and Clinic, 27,* 79–84.

Schwartz, S. E., & Karge, B. D. (1996). *Human diversity: A guide for understanding* (2nd ed.). New York: McGraw-Hill.

Scott, A. (1998). Education and acceptance. *ADVANCE for Speech-Language Pathologists and Audiologists, 36,* 10–12.

Scott, B. J., Vitale, M. R., & Masten, W. G. (1998). Implementing instructional adaptations for students with disabilities in inclusive classrooms: A literature review. *Remedial and Special Education, 19,* 106–119.

Scott, T. M., & Nelson, M. C. (1998). Confusion and failure in facilitating generalized social responding in the school setting: Sometimes 2+2=5. *Behavioral Disorders, 23,* 264–275.

Scotti, J. R., & Meyer, L. H. (Eds.). (1999). *Behavioral intervention: Principles, models, and practices.* Baltimore: Brookes.

Scruggs, T. E., & Mastropieri, M. A. (1994). Successful mainstreaming in elementary science classes: A qualitative study of three reputational cases. *American Educational Research Journal, 31,* 785–811.

Scruggs, T. E., & Mastropieri, M. A. (1996). Teacher perceptions of mainstreaming/inclusion, 1958–1995: A research synthesis. *Exceptional Children, 63,* 59–74.

Searcy, S., & Meadows, N. B. (1994). The impact of social structures on friendship development for children with behavior disorders. *Education and Treatment of Children, 17,* 255–268.

Seeley, K. (1995). Classwide peer tutoring. Unpublished manuscript, Lynchburg College (VA).

Sexton, D., Snyder, P., Wolfe, B., Lobman, M., Stricklin, S., & Akers, P. (1996). Early intervention inservice training strategies: Perceptions and suggestions from the field. *Exceptional Children, 62,* 485–496.

Shane, H. C., & Sauer, M. (1986). *Augmentative and alternative communication.* Austin, TX: Pro-Ed.

Shaner, M. Y. (1991). Talented teachers for talented students. *G/C/T, 22,* 14–15.

Shanker, A. (1994–1995). Educating students in special programs. *Educational Leadership, 52,* 43–47.

Shannon, T., & Polloway, E. A. (1993). Promoting error monitoring in middle school students with learning disabilities. *Intervention in School and Clinic, 28,* 160–164.

Shapiro, E. S., DuPaul, G. J., & Bradley-Klug, K. L. (1998). Self-management as a strategy to improve the classroom behavior of adolescents with ADHD. *Journal of Learning Disabilities, 31,* 545–555.

Shaywitz, S., & Shaywitz, B. (1997, November). *The science of reading: Implications for children and adults with learning disabilities.* Paper presented at the 13th Annual Harvard University Institute on Learning Disorders, Cambridge, MA.

Shields, J. M., & Heron, T. E. (1989). Teaching organizational skills to students with learning disabilities. *Teaching Exceptional Children, 20,* 8–13.

Shimon, D. A. (1992). *Coping with hearing loss and hearing aids.* San Diego: Singular Publishing.

Siccone, F. (1995). *Celebrating diversity: Building self-esteem in today's multicultural classrooms.* Boston: Allyn & Bacon.

Sileo, T. W., Sileo, A. P., & Prater, M. A. (1996). Parent and professional partnerships in special education: Multicultural considerations. *Intervention in School & Clinic, 31,* 145–153.

Silver, L. B. (1995). Controversial therapies. *Journal of Child Neurology, 10*(1), 96–100.

Silverman, A. B., Reinherz, H. Z., & Giaconia, R. M. (1996). The long-term sequelae of child and adolescent abuse: A longitudinal community study. *Child Abuse and Neglect, 20,* 709–723.

Silverthorn, K. H., & Hornak, J. E. (1993). Beneficial effects of exercise on aerobic capacity and body composition in adults with Prader-Willi syndrome. *American Journal on Mental Retardation, 97,* 654–658.

Simmons, D., Fuchs, D., Hodge, J., & Mathes, P. (1994). Importance of instructional complexity and role reciprocity to classwide peer tutoring. *Learning Disabilities Research and Practice, 9,* 203–212.

Simpson, R. (1996). *Working with parents and families of exceptional children and youth* (3rd ed.). Austin, TX: Pro-Ed.

Simpson, R. (1998). Behavior modification for children and adolescents with exceptionalities. *Intervention in School and Clinic, 33,* 219–226.

Skiba, R., Grizzle, K., & Minke, K. M. (1994). Opening the floodgates? The social maladjustment exclusion and state SED prevalence rates. *Journal of School Psychology, 32,* 267–283.

Slavin, R. E. (1987). *What research says to the teacher on cooperative learning: Student teams* (2nd ed.). Washington, D.C.: National Education Association.

Slicker, E. K., & Palmer, D. J. (1993). Mentoring at-risk high school students: Evaluation of a school-based program. *The School Counselor, 40,* 327–334.

Smith, A., & Cote, K. S. (1983). *Look at me. A resource manual for the development of residual vision in multiple impaired children.* Philadelphia, PA: College of Optometry Press.

Smith, C. R. (1994). *Learning disabilities: The interaction of learner, task, and setting* (3rd ed.). Boston: Allyn & Bacon.

Smith, C. R. (1998). From gibberish to phoneme awareness: Effective decoding instruction. *Teaching Exceptional Children, 30,* 20–25.

Smith, D. D., & Luckasson, R. (1998). *Introduction to special education: Teaching in an age of challenge.* Boston: Allyn & Bacon.

Smith, D. D., & Rivera, D. (1993). *Effective discipline* (2nd ed.). Austin, TX: Pro-Ed.

Smith, D. D., & Rivera, D. P. (1995). Discipline in special and regular education. *Focus on Exceptional Children, 27*(5), 1–14.

Smith, J. D. (1994). The revised AAMR definition of mental retardation: The MRDD position. *Education and Training in Mental Retardation and Developmental Disabilities, 29,* 179–183.

Smith, J. D. (1995). Inclusive school environments and students with disabilities in South Carolina: The issues, the status, the needs. *Occasional Papers, 1,* 1–5.

Smith, M. D., Belcher, R. G., & Juhrs, P. D. (1995). *A guide to successful employment for individuals with autism.* Baltimore: Brookes.

Smith, P. M. (1997). You are not alone: For parents when they learn that their child has a disability. *NICHY News Digest, 2,* 2–5.

Smith, S. W. (1990a). A comparison of individualized education programs (IEPs) of students with behavioral disorders and learning disabilities. *Journal of Special Education, 24,* 85–100.

Smith, S. W. (1990b). Individualized education programs (IEPs) in special education: From intent to acquiescence. *Exceptional Children, 57,* 6–14.

Smith, S. W., & Simpson, R. L. (1989). An analysis of individualized education programs (IEPs) for students with behavior disorders. *Behavioral Disorders, 14,* 107–116.

Smith, T. E. C. (1990). *Introduction to education* (2nd ed.). St. Paul, MN: West Publishing.

Smith, T. E. C., & Dowdy, C. A. (1992). Future-based assessment and intervention and mental retardation. *Education and Training in Mental Retardation, 27,* 23–31.

Smith, T. E. C., Dowdy, C. A., Polloway, E. A., & Blalock, G. (1997). *Children and adults with learning disabilities.* Boston: Allyn & Bacon.

Smith, T. E. C., Finn, D. M., & Dowdy, C. A. (1993). *Teaching students with mild disabilities.* Ft. Worth, TX: Harcourt Brace Jovanovich.

Smith, T. E. C., & Hendricks, M. D. (1995). *Prader-Willi syndrome: Practical considerations for educators.* Little Rock, AR: Ozark Learning.

Smith, T. E. C., & Hilton, A. (1994). Program design for students with mental retardation. *Education and Training in Mental Retardation and Developmental Disabilities, 29,* 3–8.

Smith, T. E. C., Price, B. J., & Marsh, G. E. (1986). *Mildly handicapped children and adults.* St. Paul, MN: West Publishing.

Smutny, J. F., Walker, S. Y., & Meckstroth, E. A. (1997). *Teaching young gifted children in the regular classroom: Identifying, nurturing, and challenging ages 4–9.* Minneapolis, MN: Free Spirit Publishing.

Snell, M., & Drake, G. P. (1994). Replacing cascades with supported education. *Journal of Special Education, 27,* 393–409.

Solomon, C. R., & Serres, F. (1999). Effects of parental verbal aggression on children's self-esteem and school marks. *Child Abuse & Neglect, 23,* 339–351.

Southern, W. T., & Jones, E. D. (1991). Academic acceleration: Background and issues. In W. T. Southern & E. D. Jones (Eds.), *Academic acceleration of gifted children* (pp. 1–17). New York: Teachers College Press.

Sparks, S., & Caster, J. A. (1989). Sex education. In G. Robinson, J. Patton, E. Polloway, & L. Sargent (Eds.), *Best practices in mild mental retardation* (pp. 299–302). Reston, VA: Division on Mental Retardation, CEC.

Spencer, T., Biederman, J., Wilens, T., Harding, M., O'Donnell, D., & Griffin, S. (1996). Pharmacotherapy of attention-deficit hyperactivity disorder across the life cycle. *Journal of American Academy Child Adolescent Psychiatry, 35*(4), 409–432.

Spirito, A., Hart, K. I., Overholser, J., & Halverson, J. (1990). Social skills and depression in adolescent suicide attempters. *Adolescence, 25,* 543–552.

Squires, E. C., & Reetz, L. J. (1989). Vocabulary acquisition activities. *Academic Therapy, 14,* 589–592.

Stainback, S., Stainback, W., East, K., & Sapon-Shevin, M. (1994). A commentary on inclusion and the development of a positive self-identity by people with disabilities. *Exceptional Children, 60,* 486–490.

Stainback, W., & Stainback, S. (1984). A rationale for the merger of special and regular education. *Exceptional Children, 51,* 102–111.

Stainback, W. C., Stainback, S., & Wehman, P. (1997). Toward full inclusion into general education. In P. Wehman (Ed.),

*Exceptional individuals in school, community, and work* (pp. 531–557). Austin, TX: Pro-Ed.

Staub, D., & Peck, C. A. (1994–1995). What are the outcomes for nondisabled students? *Educational Leadership, 52,* 36–41.

Stephien, S., & Gallagher, S. (1993). Problem-based learning: As authentic as it gets. *Educational Leadership, 50*(7), pp. 25–28.

Sternberg, R. J. (1991). Giftedness according to the triarchic theory of human intelligence. In N. Colangelo & G. A. Davis (Eds.), *Handbook of gifted education* (pp. 45–54). Boston: Allyn & Bacon.

Storey, K. (1993). A proposal for assessing integration. *Education and Training in Mental Retardation and Developmental Disabilities, 28,* 279–286.

Stover, D. (1992, May). The at-risk students schools continue to ignore. *The Education Digest,* 37–40.

Streeter, C. E., & Grant, C. A. (1993). *Making choices for multicultural education.* New York: Macmillan.

Streett, S., & Smith, T. E. C. (1996). *Section 504 and public schools: A practical guide.* Little Rock, AR: The Learning Group.

Struyk, L. R., Cole, K. B., Epstein, M. H., Bursuck, W. D., & Polloway, E. A. (1996). Homework communication: Problems involving high school teachers and parents of students with disabilities. Manuscript submitted for publication.

Struyk, L. R., Epstein, M. H., Bursuck, W., Polloway, E. A., McConeghy, J., & Cole, K. B. (1995). Homework, grading, and testing practices used by teachers with students with and without disabilities. *The Clearing House, 69,* 50–55.

Subotnik, R. F., & Arnold, K. D. (Eds.). (1994). *Beyond Terman: Contemporary longitudinal studies of giftedness and talent.* Norwood, NJ: Ablex.

Sugai, G., & Maheady, L. (1988). Cultural diversity and individual assessment for behavior disorders. *Teaching Exceptional Children, 21,* 28–31.

Summers, M., Bridge, J., & Summers, C. R. (1991). Sibling support groups. *Teaching Exceptional Children, 23,* 20–25.

Tankersley, M. (1995). A group-oriented management program: A review of research on the good behavior game and implications for teachers. *Preventing School Failure, 40,* 19–28.

Tavzel, C. S., & Staff of LinguiSystems. (1987). *Blooming recipes.* East Moline, IL: LinguiSystems.

Teen drug use is on the rise again. (1996). *Executive Educator, 18,* 7–8.

Templeton, R. A. (1995). ADHD: A teacher's guide. *The Oregon Conference Monograph, 7,* 2–11.

Tennant, C., Bebbington, P. R., & Hurry, J. (1980). Parental death in childhood and risk of adult depressive disorders: A review. *Psychological Medicine, 10,* 289–299.

*Tests in Print.* (1989). Austin, TX: Pro-Ed.

Thomas, P. J., & Carmack, F. F. (1993). Language: The foundation of learning. In J. S. Choate (Ed.), *Successful mainstreaming: Proven ways to detect and correct special needs* (pp. 148–173). Boston: Allyn & Bacon.

Thompson, A. E., & Kaplan, C. A. (1999). Emotionally abused children presenting to child psychiatry clinics. *Child Abuse & Neglect, 23,* 191–196.

Thousand, J. S., & Villa, R. A. (1990). Strategies for educating learners with severe disabilities within their local home schools and communities. *Focus on Exceptional Children, 23,* 1–24.

Thurston, L. P. (1989). Helping parents tutor their children: A success story. *Academic Therapy, 24,* 579–587.

Tirosh, E., & Canby, J. (1993). Autism with hyperlexia: A distinct syndrome? *American Journal on Mental Retardation, 98,* 84–92.

Toliver-Weddington, G., & Erickson, J. G. (1992). Suggestions for using standardized tests with minority children. In J. G. Erickson (Ed.), *Communication disorders in multicultural populations* (1992, April). Paper presented at Texas Speech-Language-Hearing Association Annual Convention, San Antonio, TX.

Torres, I., & Corn, A. L. (1990). *When you have a visually handicapped child in your classroom: Suggestions for teachers.* New York: American Foundation for the Blind.

Tovey, R. (1995). Awareness programs help change students' attitudes towards their disabled peers. *Harvard Educational Letter, 11*(6), 7–8.

Trad, P. V. (1999). Assessing the patterns that prevent teenage pregnancy. *Adolescence, 34,* 221–238.

Turnbull, A. P., Strickland, B., & Hammer, S. E. (1978). IEPs: Presenting guidelines for development and implementation. *Journal of Learning Disabilities, 11,* 40–46.

Turnbull, A. P., & Turnbull, H. R. (1997). *Families, professionals, and exceptionality: A special partnership.* Columbus, OH: Merrill.

Turnbull, H. R. (1993). *Free appropriate public education: The law and children with disabilities.* (4th ed.). Denver: Love.

Turnbull, H. R. (1998). *Free appropriate public education: The law and children with disabilities* (5th ed.). Denver: Love.

Turnbull, H. R., & Turnbull, A. P. (2000). *Free appropriate public education* (6th ed.). Denver: Love.

U.S. Department of Commerce. (1993). *Poverty in the United States: 1992.* Washington, D.C.: Author.

U.S. Department of Commerce. (1995). *Population Profile of the United States, 1995.* Washington, D.C.: Author.

U.S. Department of Education. (1989). *11th annual report to Congress on the implementation of IDEA.* Washington, D.C.: Author.

U.S. Department of Education. (1990). *12th annual report to Congress on the implementation of the Education of the Handicapped Act.* Washington, D.C.: Author.

U.S. Department of Education. (1990, January 9). Reading and writing proficiency remains low. *Daily Education News,* pp. 1–7.

U.S. Department of Education. (1991, September 16). Memorandum: Clarification of policy to address the needs of children with attention deficit disorders within general and/or special education. Washington, D.C.: Author.

U.S. Department of Education. (1993). *15th annual report to Congress on the implementation of IDEA.* Washington, D.C.: Author.

U.S. Department of Education. (1994). *16th annual report to Congress on the Implementation of the Individuals with Disabilities Education Act.* Washington, D.C.: U.S. Government Printing Office.

U.S. Department of Education. (1996). *18th annual report to Congress on the implementation of IDEA.* Washington, D.C.: Author.

U.S. Department of Education. (1997). New report links fathers' involvement with children's success. *Community Update, 52,* 3.

U. S. Department of Education. (1998). *Safe and smart: Making the after-school hours work for kids.* Washington, D.C.: Author.

U.S. Department of Education. (1998). *20th annual report to Congress on the implementation of the Individuals with Disabilities Education Act.* Washington, D.C.: Author.

U. S. Department of Education. (1999). *The condition of education, 1998.* Washington, D.C.: Author.

U.S. Office of Education (USOE). (1977). Assistance to states for education of handicapped children: Procedures for evaluating specific learning disabilities. *Federal Register, 42,* 65082–65085.

U.S. Office of Education (USOE). (1999, March 12). Assistance to the states for the education of children with disabilities and the early intervention program for infants and toddlers with disabilities; final regulations. *Federal Register, 64*(48) 12406–12458. Washington, D.C.: U.S. Government Printing Office.

Valdes, K. A., Williamson, C. L., & Wagner, M. M. (1990). *The national longitudinal transition study of special education students* (Vol. 1). Menlo Park, CA: SRI International.

Van Eerdewegh, M. M., Bieri, M. D., Parrilla, R. H., & Clayton, P. J. (1982). The bereaved child. *British Journal of Psychiatry, 140,* 23–29.

Van Laarhoven, T., Coutinho, M., Van Laarhoven-Myers, T., & Repp, A. C. (1999). Assessment of the student instructional setting, and curriculum to support successful integration. In M. J. Coutinho & A. C. Repp (Eds.), *Inclusion: The integration of students with disabilities.* Belmont, CA: Wadsworth Publishing.

Van Riper, C., & Emerick, L. (1984). *Speech correction: An introduction to speech pathology and audiology* (7th ed.). Englewood Cliffs, NJ: Prentice-Hall.

VanTassel-Baska, J. (1989). Appropriate curriculum for gifted learners. *Educational Leadership, 47,* 13–15.

VanTassel-Baska, J. (1998). *Gifted and talented learners.* Denver: Love.

VanTassel-Baska, J., Patton, J., & Prillaman, D. (1989). Disadvantaged gifted learners at-risk for educational attention. *Focus on Exceptional Children, 22*(3), 1–16.

Vaughn, C., & Long, W. (1999). Surrender to win: How adolescent drug and alcohol users change their lives. *Adolescence, 34,* 9–22.

Vaughn, S., Boss, C. S., & Schumm, J. S. (2000). *Teaching exceptional, diverse, and at-risk students in the general education classroom* (2nd ed.). Boston: Allyn & Bacon.

Vaughn, S., Schumm, J. S., & Arguelles, M. E. (1997). The ABCDEs of co-teaching. *Teaching Exceptional Children, 30*(2), 4–10.

Victory in landmark "full inclusion" case. (1994). *Disability Rights Education and Defense Fund News, 1,* 6.

Vogeltanz, N. D., Wilsnack, S. C., Harris, T. R., Wilsnack, R. W., Wonderlich, S. A., & Kristjanson, A. F. (1999). Prevalence and risk factors for childhood sexual abuse in women: National survey findings. *Child Abuse & Neglect, 23,* 579–592.

Wadsworth, D. E., & Knight, D. (1999). Preparing the classroom for students with speech, physical, and health needs. *Intervention in School and Clinic, 34,* 170–175.

Walberg, H. J. (1991). Does homework help? *School Community Journal, 1*(1), 13–15.

Waldon, N. L., & McLusky, J. (1998). The effects of an inclusive school program on students with mild and severe learning disabilities. *Exceptional Children, 64,* 395–405.

Walker, B. (1993, January). *Multicultural issues in education: An introduction.* Paper presented at Cypress–Fairbanks Independent School District In-Service, Cypress, TX.

Walker, J. E., & Shea, T. M. (1988). *Behavior management: A practical approach for educators* (4th ed.). New York: Merrill/Macmillan.

Walker, J. E., & Shea, T. M. (1995). *Behavior management: A practical approach for educators* (6th ed.). Columbus, OH: Merrill.

Wallace, G., Cohen, S., & Polloway, E. A. (1987). *Language arts: Teaching exceptional children.* Austin, TX: Pro-Ed.

Wallace, G., Larsen, S. C., & Elksnin, L. K. (1992). *Educational assessment of learning problems.* Boston: Allyn & Bacon.

Walther-Thomas, C., Korinek, L., McLaughlin, V. L., & Williams, B. T. (2000). *Collaboration for inclusive education.* Boston: Allyn & Bacon.

Wanat, C. L. (1992). Meeting the needs of single-parent children: School and parent views differ. *NASSP Bulletin, 76,* 43–48.

Wang, M. C., Reynolds, M. C., & Walberg, H. J. (1994–1995). Serving students at the margins. *Educational Leadership, 52,* 12–17.

Warren, D. (1994). *Blindness in children.* Cambridge, MA: Cambridge University Press.

Waterman, B. B. (1994). Assessing children for the presence of a disability. *NICHY News Digest, 4*(1), Washington, D.C.: U.S. Government Printing Office.

Wayman, K., Lynch, E., & Hanson, M. (1990). Home-based early childhood services: Cultural sensitivity in a family systems approach. *Topics in Early Childhood Special Education, 10*(4), 65–66.

Webber, J. (1997). Responsible inclusion: Key components for success. In P. Zionts (Ed.), *Effective inclusion of students with behavior and learning problems.* Austin, TX: Pro-Ed.

Webber, J., & Scheuermann, B. (1991). Accentuate the positive . . . Eliminate the negative! *Teaching Exceptional Children, 24,* 14–17.

Wehby, J. H., Symons, F. J., Canale, J. A., & Go, F. J. (1998). Teaching practices in classrooms for students with emotional and behavioral disorders: Discrepancies between recommendations and observations. *Behavioral Disorders, 24,* 51–56.

Wehman, P. (1996). *Life beyond the classroom: Transition strategies for young people with disabilities* (2nd ed.). Baltimore: Brookes.

Wehman, P. (Ed.). (1997). *Exceptional individuals in school, community, and work.* Austin, TX: Pro-Ed.

Wehman, P., & Kregel, J. (Eds.). (1998). *More than a job: Securing satisfying careers for people with disabilities.* Baltimore: Brookes.

Wehmeyer, M. (1993). Self-determination as an educational outcome. *Impact, 6*(4), 16–17, 26.

Wehmeyer, M. (1994). Perceptions of self-determination and psychological empowerment of adolescents with mental retardation. *Education and Training in Mental Retardation and Developmental Disabilities, 29,* 9–21.

Wehmeyer, M. L., & Patton, J. R. (2000). *Mental retardation in the 21st century.* Austin, TX: Pro-Ed.

Weinbender, M. L. M., & Rossignol, A. M. (1996). Lifestyle and risk of premature sexual activity in a high school population of Seventh-Day Adventists: Valuegenesis 1989. *Adolescence, 31,* 265–275.

Weiner, Z., Reich, W., Herjanic, B., Jung, K. G., & Amado, H. (1987). Reliability, validity, and parent–child agreement studies of the Diagnostic Interview for Children and Adolescents (DICA). *Journal of the American Academy of Child and Adolescent Psychiatry, 26,* 649–653.

Welch, M., & Link, D. P. (1991). The instructional priority system: A method for assessing the educational environment. *Intervention in the School and Clinic, 27*(2), 91–96.

Welch, M., & Sheridan, S. M. (1995). *Educational partnerships: Serving students at risk.* Ft. Worth, TX: Harcourt Brace.

Wenz-Gross, M., & Siperstein, G. N. (1998). Students with learning problems at risk in middle school: Stress, social support, and adjustment. *Exceptional Children, 65,* 91–100.

Wesson, C. L., & Deno, S. L. (1989). An analysis of long-term instructional plans in reading for elementary resource room students. *Remedial and Special Education, 10*(1), 21–28.

West, G. K. (1986). *Parenting without guilt.* Springfield, IL: Thomas.

West, G. K. (1994, Nov. 10). Discipline that works: Part 1. *The News and Daily Advance.*

Westling, D. L., & Koorland, M. A. (1988). *The special educator's handbook.* Boston: Allyn & Bacon.

Weston, D., Ludolph, P., Misle, B., Ruffins, S., & Block, J. (1990). Physical and sexual abuse in adolescent girls with borderline personality disorder. *American Journal of Orthopsychiatry, 60,* 55–66.

Wetherby, A. M., & Prizant, B. M. (Eds.). (2000). *Autism spectrum disorders: A transactional developmental perspective.* Baltimore: Brookes.

White, C. C., Lakin, K. C., Bruininks, R. H., & Li, X. (1991). *Persons with mental retardation and related conditions in state-operated residential facilities: Year ending June 30, 1989, with longitudinal trends from 1950 to 1989.* Minneapolis, MN: University of Minnesota, Institute on Community Integration.

Wicks-Nelson, R., & Israel, A. C. (1991). *Behavior disorders of childhood.* Englewood Cliffs, NJ: Prentice-Hall.

Wiedemeyer, D., & Lehman, J. (1991). House plan: Approach to collaborative teaching and consultation. *Teaching Exceptional Children, 23*(3), 6–10.

Wiederholt, J. L., & Bryant, B. (1986). *Gray oral reading test—Revised.* Austin, TX: Pro-Ed.

Wiig, E. H. (1986). Language disabilities in school-age children and youth. In G. H. Shames & E. H. Wiig (Eds.), *Human communication disorders* (2nd ed., pp. 331–383). Columbus, OH: Merrill.

Wiig, E. H., & Semel, E. (1984). *Language assessment and intervention for the learning disabled* (2nd ed.). Columbus, OH: Merrill.

Will, M. C. (1984). Educating children with learning problems: A shared responsibility. *Exceptional Children, 52,* 411–415.

Williamson, J. M., Borduin, C. M., & Howe, B. A. (1991). The ecology of adolescent maltreatment: A multilevel examination of adolescent physical abuse, sexual abuse, and neglect. *Journal of Consulting and Clinical Psychology, 59,* 449–457.

Wilson, C. L. (1995). Parents and teachers: Can we talk? *LD Forum, 20*(2), 31–33.

Winebrenner, S. (1992). Teaching gifted kids in the regular classroom: Strategies and techniques every teacher can use to meet the academic needs of the gifted and talented. Minneapolis, MN: Free Spirit Publishing.

*Winners all: A call for inclusive schools.* (1992). Alexandria, VA: The National Association of State Boards of Education.

Winocur, S. L., & Mauerer, P. A. (1997). Critical thinking and gifted students: Using IMPACT to improve teaching and learning. In N. Colangelo and G. A. Davis (Eds.), *Handbook of gifted education* (2nd ed., pp. 308–317). Boston: Allyn & Bacon.

Winton, P. (1986). Effective strategies for involving families in intervention efforts. *Focus on Exceptional Children, 19*(2), 1–10.

Witt, J. C., & Elliott, S. N. (1985). Acceptability of classroom management strategies. In T. R. Kratochwill (Ed.), *Advances in school psychology* (Vol. 4, pp. 251–288). Hillsdale, NJ: Erlbaum.

Wolery, M., Werts, M. G., & Holcombe, A. (1994). Current practices with young children who have disabilities: Placement, assessment, and instruction issues. *Focus on Exceptional Children, 26*(6), 2–12.

Wolfe, P. S. (1997). Deaf-blindness. In P. Wehman (Ed.), *Exceptional individuals* (pp. 357–381). Austin, TX: Pro-Ed.

Wong, B. Y. L. (1991). The relevance of metacognition to learning disabilities. In B. Y. L. Wong (Ed.), *Learning about learning disabilities* (pp. 231–258). New York: Academic Press.

Wood, J. W. (1984). *Adapting instruction for the mainstream.* Columbus, OH: Merrill.

Wood, J. W. (1991). *Adapting instruction for mainstreamed and at-risk students* (2nd ed.). New York: Merrill.

Wood, J. W. (1996). *Adapting instruction for mainstreamed and at-risk students* (3rd ed.). New York: Merrill.

Wood, M. (1998). Whose job is it anyway? Educational roles in inclusion. *Exceptional Children, 64,* 181–196.

Wood, P. H., Bennett, T., Wood, J., & Bennett, C. (1990). *Grading and evaluation practices and policies of school teachers.* (ERIC Document Reproduction Service No. ED 319 782)

Woodrich, D. L. (1994). *What every parent wants to know: Attention deficit hyperactivity disorder.* Baltimore: Brookes.

Woodrich, D. L. (1998). Managing AD/HD in the classroom minus medication. *Education Digest, 63,* 50–56.

Woronov, T. (1996). Assistive technology for literacy produces impressive results for the disabled. In E. Miller & R. Tovey (Eds.), *Inclusion and special education* (pp. 9–11). Cambridge, MA: Harvard Educational Letter.

Worthington, L. A., Patterson, D., Elliott, E., & Linkous, L. (1993). *Assessment of children with ADHD: An inservice education program for educator and parents.* Unpublished manuscript. University of Alabama, Department of Special Education, Tuscaloosa.

Wright, J. V. (1995). Multicultural issues and attention deficit disorders. *Learning Disabilities Research and Practice, 10*(3), 153–159.

Wright-Strawderman, C., & Watson, B. L. (1992). The prevalence of depressive symptoms in children with learning disabilities. *Journal of Learning Disabilities, 25,* 258–264.

Yamaguchi, B. J., Strawser, S., & Higgins, K. (1997). Children who are homeless: Implications for educators. *Intervention in School and Clinic, 33,* 90–98.

Yehle, A. K., & Wambold, C. (1998, July/August). An ADHD success story: Strategies for teachers and students. *Teaching Exceptional Children,* 8–13.

Yell, M. L., & Shriner, J. G. (1997). The IDEA amendments of 1997: Implications for special and general education teachers, administrators, and teacher trainers. *Focus on Exceptional Children, 30,* 1–12.

Ylvisaker, M., Hartwick, P., & Stevens, M. (1991). School reentry following head injury. *Journal of Head Trauma Rehabilitation, 6,* 10–22.

Ylvisaker, T., Szekeres, N., Hartwick, R., & Tworek, L. L. (1994). Collaboration in preparation for personal injury suits after TBI. *Topics in Language Disorders, 15,* 1–20.

York, J., & Vandercook, T. (1991). Designing an integrated program for learners with severe disabilities. *Teaching Exceptional Children, 23,* 22–28.

York, J., Vandercook, T., MacDonald, C., Heise-Neff, C., & Caughey, E. (1992). Feedback about integrating middle-school students with severe disabilities in general education classes. *Exceptional Children, 58,* 244–258.

Young, G., & Gerber, P. J. (1998). Learning disabilities and poverty: Moving towards a new understanding of learning disabilities as a public health and economic-risk issue. *Learning Disabilities, 9,* 1–6.

Young, M. E., Kersten, L., & Werch, T. (1996). Evaluation of patient-child drug education program. *Journal of Drug Education, 26,* 57–68.

Ysseldyke, J. E., & Olsen, K. (1999). Putting alternative assessments into practice: What to measure and possible sources of data. *Exceptional Children, 65,* 175–185.

Ysseldyke, J. E., Algozzine, B., & Thurlow, M. L. (2000). *Critical issues in special education* (3rd ed.). Boston: Houghton Mifflin.

Zabel, R. H., & Zabel, M. K. (1996). *Classroom management in context.* Boston: Houghton Mifflin.

Zargoza, N., Vaughn, S., & McIntosh, R. (1991). Social skills instruction and children with behavior problems: A review. *Behavior Disorders, 16,* 260–275.

Zigmond, N., Levin, E., & Laurie, T. (1985). Managing the mainstream: An analysis for teacher attitudes and student performance in mainstream high school programs. *Journal of Learning Disabilities, 18,* 535–541.

Zionts, P. (1997). *Inclusion strategies for students with learning and behavior problems.* Austin, TX: Pro-Ed.

Zirpoli, T., & Melloy, G. (1993). *Behavior management: Applications for teachers and parents.* Columbus, OH: Merrill.

Zucker, S. H., & Polloway, E. A. (1987). Issues in identification and assessment in mental retardation. *Education and Training in Mental Retardation, 22,* 69–76.

Zurkowski, J. K., Kelly, P. S., & Griswold, D. E. (1998). Discipline and IDEA 1997: Instituting a new balance. *Intervention in School and Clinic, 34,* 3–9.

# Name Index

# ◢◤ Subject Index

*Note:* Page numbers followed by *f* indicate figures; page numbers followed by *t* indicate tables.